INDEPENDENT

INDEPENDENT
A Biography of Lewis W. Douglas

Robert Paul Browder
and
Thomas G. Smith

Alfred A. Knopf  New York 1986

THIS IS A BORZOI BOOK
PUBLISHED BY ALFRED A. KNOPF, INC.

Copyright © 1986 by Robert Paul Browder and Thomas G. Smith

All rights reserved under International and Pan-American Copyright Conventions. Published in the United States by Alfred A. Knopf, Inc., New York, and simultaneously in Canada by Random House of Canada Limited, Toronto. Distributed by Random House, Inc., New York.

Library of Congress Cataloging-in-Publication Data

Browder, Robert Paul.
Independent: a biography of Lewis W. Douglas.

Bibliography: p.
Includes index.
1. Douglas, Lewis W. (Lewis Williams), 1894–1974.
2. Legislators—United States—Biography.   I. Smith, Thomas G. (Thomas Gary).   II. Title.
E748.D679B76   1986   328.73′092′4 [B]   85-23697
ISBN 0-394-49878-X

Manufactured in the United States of America
FIRST EDITION

For Joanne and Sandra and for our children

Contents

	Preface	xi
	PART ONE Prologue to Service	1
1	*The Family and the Frontier*	3
2	*Education, War, and Marriage*	17
	PART TWO Legislator	29
3	*State Representative*	31
4	*The Road to Washington*	40
5	*Congress and the Colorado River*	49
6	*A Remedy for Hard Times*	59
	PART THREE Budget Director	71
7	*Toward the New Deal*	73
8	*Working with Roosevelt*	84
9	*Resistance and Resignation*	99
	PART FOUR Against the Current	117
10	*Private Man and Public Critic*	119
11	*An American in Canada*	131
12	*Preparing for War*	145
	PART FIVE The Second World War	161
13	*On Board: The War Shipping Administration*	163
14	*The Struggle with the Military*	175
15	*From Casablanca to First Quebec*	191
16	*Cairo and Resignation*	204
17	*Recalled to Duty*	216

	PART SIX Ambassador	239
18	*To the Court of St. James's*	241
19	*Launching the Marshall Plan*	252
20	*Marshall Plan Missionary*	266
21	*The London Conference*	278
22	*The Berlin Blockade*	291
23	*Palestine and Presidential Politics*	303
24	*Personal Misfortune and Diplomatic Tensions*	318
25	*The End of the Mission*	334
26	*Farewells*	346
	PART SEVEN The Later Years	357
27	*Home*	359
28	*Monitoring Eisenhower*	374
29	*Sunset*	392
	Notes	407
	Bibliography	463
	Index	475

List of Illustrations

FOLLOWING PAGE 272

Grandfather Douglas (Special Collections, University of Arizona)

Josephine Leah Williams shortly before her marriage (Arizona Historical Society)

Bisbee, Arizona Territory, viewed from the west, 1895 (Arizona Historical Society)

Lewis with his grandfather (Arizona Historical Society)

Lewis and his horse in Nacozari (Arizona Historical Society)

Douglas at eighteen as a freshman at Amherst College (Arizona Historical Society)

Lieutenant Douglas in 1917 (Laurmer, Tacoma/Special Collections, University of Arizona)

James S. Douglas at midlife (Special Collections, University of Arizona)

Congressman Douglas (Harris & Ewing, Washington, D.C./Special Collections, University of Arizona)

James S. Douglas mansion at Jerome, Arizona, with mine in foreground (Arizona Historical Society)

At the Isabella Greenway ranch with Franklin D. Roosevelt, 1932 (Arizona Historical Society)

Cartoon: "Shot Full of Holes," January 7, 1934 (Providence *Journal-Bulletin*)

Cartoon: "There's a Time and a Place for Everything," September 7, 1934 (New York *Post*)

The Cairo Conference, 1943 (U.S. Army Signal Corps/Special Collections, University of Arizona)

Peggy Douglas as a wartime fund-raiser for the Red Cross (G. Maillard Kesslere, BP/Special Collections, University of Arizona)

Briefing the new ambassador to Great Britain (Special Collections, University of Arizona)

Sharman, Douglas, Peggy, and Lewis, Jr. at a garden party at the Residence (Special Collections, University of Arizona)

Douglas, Marshall, and Bevin at the Residence, 1947 (*New York Times*/Special Collections, University of Arizona)

Luncheon at the Residence, October, 1948 (Associated Press/Special Collections, University of Arizona)

Douglas and Churchill on their way to the House of Commons, September, 1949 (Associated Press/Arizona Historical Society)

Peggy and Douglas arriving in New York on the *Queen Elizabeth*, November, 1950 (Cunard Line/Special Collections, University of Arizona)

John J. McCloy and Douglas at the dedication of the Marshall Library, May, 1964 (George C. Marshall Research Library/Andre Studio/Special Collections, University of Arizona)

Douglas and Frank Brophy (Bale Wilcox Studio/Special Collections, University of Arizona)

Preface

IN THE FALL OF 1974, I received a letter from Alfred A. Knopf, suggesting that I write a life of Lewis W. Douglas, who had died in Tucson in March. I found the idea very attractive. Douglas had begun the transfer of his papers to the University of Arizona in 1969, the year I arrived as history department head. I had been acquainted with him in his last years, had enjoyed his company and admired his accomplishments. After further correspondence with Knopf and senior editor Ashbel Green, I began work in the spring of 1975. Until his death in 1984, Alfred's support and enthusiasm for the project in conversation and correspondence were constant. I owe him an immense debt of gratitude for the invitation, for his confidence, and for the privilege of his friendship.

This is an authorized biography in only a very limited sense. The Douglas family approved of my (and later Thomas G. Smith's) selection. Peggy Douglas arranged to have her husband's papers placed under my control for ten years. She graciously gave me a great deal of time for a series of intensive interviews and encouraged many of Douglas's friends and associates in this country and abroad to share their experiences of him. But neither she nor her family exercised any substantive or editorial control over the manuscript. It would be difficult to exaggerate our obligation to Peggy for her cooperation, her candor, her kindness—and her patience, for the work took much longer than any of us had anticipated.

In 1978, I received from Professor Thomas G. Smith a copy of his dissertation on Douglas, submitted to the University of Connecticut the previous year. I was aware that he had used the incomplete Douglas collection earlier, but did not realize he had continued with his research and writing. I was impressed with the quality of his coverage, especially on the early years of Douglas's career. By that time, I was also more fully conscious of the scope of the task I had undertaken. A large and unexpected infusion of Douglas papers had just been received to be catalogued, many U.S. and British sources were yet to be consulted, and administrative duties had slowed my progress. Above all, I was convinced that Smith should be associated in the endeavor on the basis of his commendable work. In

1979, with the approval of Knopf and Green, I asked him to join me. He has taken primary responsibility for the years to 1942 and I for the war and postwar period. It has been a remarkably fruitful and friendly collaboration. Our views on Douglas have almost always coincided and our few differences have been quickly and cordially resolved.

Time limitations on access to certain materials caused delays. In particular, the thirty-year rule of the British Public Records Office held up use of the Foreign Office and Prime Minister's files for the years 1947 to 1950. The useful Bevin Papers were still not available when I worked at the PRO in 1981. But Bevin's biographer, Lord Bullock (who had access to them by exceptions granted under the old fifty-year rule), assured me that I would find little on Douglas there that was not duplicated in the large and undifferentiated files then open. The recent publication of his *Ernest Bevin: Foreign Secretary* has confirmed his advice. I am grateful to Lord Bullock for his counsel.

A number of other scholars have been helpful and supportive. Professor Smith would like to acknowledge especially his debts to Thomas G. Paterson, Dennis R. Sexton, James L. Conrad, Roger Clark, and all his colleagues at Nichols College. It is a particular pleasure for me to express my appreciation for the encouragement and assistance of my friends the late Sir John Wheeler-Bennett, Frank Freidel, Forrest C. Pogue, Boyd C. Shafer, and J. Robert Vignery. I must claim personal privilege to thank also a physician-scholar, Dr. Jerry Goldstone, of the University of Arizona College of Medicine, whose timely and skillful surgery, in 1983, delayed the book but probably ensured my presence for its completion.

Our reception by librarians and archivists was unfailingly courteous, their assistance extraordinary. Our own institutional libraries and their staffs deserve a special word of appreciation. But one name stands above the rest. Phyllis Ball at the Special Collections of the University of Arizona Library transformed an amorphous mass of material, received over a period of years, into the elegantly catalogued Douglas Papers (514 document boxes). Her accomplishment and her continued help in locating and checking elusive items made our work possible. Our debt to her is incalculable.

We are most grateful to those listed in the bibliography who granted us interviews or corresponded about Lewis Douglas. All of them were generous with their time and recollections. Many of them gave us hospitality as well as information. I would like to mention especially Lady Wheeler-Bennett, Joan Bright Astley, and Lord Muirshiel. During my two trips to Britain, in 1976 and 1981, they provided delightful social interludes in my daily rounds of interviewing and research. Other hosts in England to whom I am particularly indebted are Sir William Hawthorne, Master, and Jack R. Pole, Vice-Master, of Churchill College, Cambridge. Dr. Pole kindly arranged for my residence in the college during my work in its archives.

Professor Smith was fortunate to have had three formal interviews with Lewis Douglas in late 1972 and early 1973. We were both privileged to interview or correspond with several valuable witnesses who have since died.

In the course of our work, we both received financial assistance. Professor Smith was awarded a grant from the Nichols College Faculty Development fund and from the Harry S. Truman Library and Institute. I received a very generous grant from the Rockefeller Foundation and support from the University of Arizona Foundation and the university's College of Arts and Sciences. University President John Shaefer, Vice-President for Research Richard Kassander, and Dean Paul Rosenblatt were particularly helpful to me. Both of us were awarded grants from the Eleanor Roosevelt Institute and received sabbatical leaves. We are deeply grateful for these evidences of confidence in our project.

For typing, photocopying, support, and encouragement, all with good humor, Professor Smith expresses his appreciation to Kathy Piniarski. With equal enthusiasm, I record my appreciation to Dawn Polter for her efficient and accommodating supervision of the departmental office and to Dorothy Donnelly, Marilyn Bradian, and Nikki Matz for their cheerful and accurate transcribing of interview and note tapes and the typing of several drafts of my contribution to the manuscript.

Some of the material in this book appeared previously in *Arizona and the West* and the *Journal of Arizona History*.

Crown copyright materials in the Public Records Office, Kew, England, appear by permission of H.M. Stationery Office.

The pictures in the photographic insert are from the holdings of the Special Collections of the University of Arizona Library, the Arizona Historical Society, and the Douglas family.

We were extremely fortunate to have as our editor Ashbel Green, whose experience, keen eye, taste, and intelligence greatly benefited this volume.

Throughout our work, we have been immeasurably sustained by my dear friend Joanne Farmer Suppes, by Tom's wife, Sandra, and by our children of all ages.

Tucson, Arizona　　　　　　　　　　　　　　　　　　　　ROBERT PAUL BROWDER
July, 1985

PART ONE

Prologue to Service

1

The Family and the Frontier

DURING A CONVERSATION ONE EVENING IN LONDON, Ambassador Lewis Douglas, Winston Churchill, and Field Marshal Montgomery discussed their personal heroes. Churchill wavered between his illustrious ancestor the Duke of Marlborough and his idolized father, Lord Randolph, and Montgomery considered a pantheon of military figures of valor or genius. Without hesitation Douglas named Jesús García.

Douglas told his friends the story of the young railway engineer, an older companion of his boyhood, who gave his life to save a town. García drove the train between Nacozari, Mexico, and the Phelps Dodge mine six miles away. On November 7, 1907, the cars, loaded with explosives, caught fire as they left the yard. Instead of abandoning the locomotive, García piloted the train away from the town to his inevitable destruction. Douglas never forgot "this example of a person with a very high and deep-seated sense of responsibility so great he was prepared to face death." After the disaster, Douglas accompanied his father, the superintendent of the mine, to Mexico City, where, in the castle of Chapultepec, he listened as President Porfirio Díaz was told the circumstances of García's bravery. Díaz "ordered that it be recorded in every primer throughout the land of Mexico." A handsome monument was dedicated to García in Nacozari, with Douglas's grandfather, president of Phelps Dodge, officiating, and memorials to his deed were erected elsewhere in the country.[1]

Actually, Douglas had other heroes, including Clemenceau, George Marshall, and Churchill himself. But none surpassed those of his early impressionable years in the Mexican-American borderlands—his inspiring grandfather and strong-willed father, both copper magnates of the last frontier, and the courageous García. Although his remarkable career would take him to Washington, New York, Montreal, and London Douglas always considered himself a westerner, and Arizona his home.

. . .

Bisbee, Arizona Territory, where Lewis Douglas was born in 1894, was a thriving mining community of six thousand people. Located in the rugged, mineral-rich Mule Mountains, the mile-high city clung to the steep slopes of Mule Pass Gulch. From the flourishing business district on the canyon floor, narrow streets and crooked dirt trails wound their way to weather-beaten wood and adobe dwellings, which hugged the treeless mountainsides.[2]

In 1905 a newspaper writer depicted the town as "the bustling hamlet on the hillsides, the city of foul odors and sickening smells, the busiest burg in the Territory." Describing Brewery Gulch, the city's most notorious street of debauchery, the same journalist commented: "You could not forget it if you wanted to. The street is somewhat frightful from a sanitary standpoint. It is covered with a slime several inches deep and about four feet wide." Like its sister towns of Tombstone and Charleston, Bisbee had saloons, gambling houses, and dancehalls, which provided plenty of excitement. Street brawls, shootouts, lynchings, and rowdyism, however, were uncommon—especially after a concerned group of residents formed a vigilante party in 1891 to rid the town of undesirables.[3]

Founded in 1880, three years after the discovery of copper ore at Mule Pass, Bisbee quickly became one of the largest copper producers in the country. Its vast ore body was owned by the Copper Queen Consolidated Mining Company, a subsidiary of the eastern metal firm of Phelps Dodge. A result of the merger of the camp's principal mining concerns in 1885, the Copper Queen was the town's only mining company until 1899. As owner of the mines, smelters, hotel, company store, newspaper, and much of the land, and as the community's major employer, the Copper Queen enjoyed supreme dominion in Bisbee.

Despite its hegemony, the company in its early years was a responsible employer and alert to the needs of the community. Unlike other western mining camps, labor-management relations in Bisbee were relatively harmonious until the First World War. Industrial peace resulted from the labor policies established by the Copper Queen president, James Douglas, who tried to treat employees with fairness and respect. Douglas, one Bisbee resident recalled, "radiated an influence like a country squire." Alarmed at the ever-increasing number of mining accidents, he installed new safety devices and urged miners to heed safety rules. He considered unions unnecessary if workers and employers dealt fairly with one another, and he paid at least prevailing union wages to discourage labor from organizing. He encouraged laborers to read, attend cultural events and religious services, spend their money wisely, and participate in town government. And, under his leadership, the Copper Queen established a hospital, dispensary, meeting house, school, library, church, gymnasium, and Young Men's Christian Association for the town's benefit.[4]

In early July, 1894, the residents of Bisbee were preparing for Independence Day. Civic leaders planned speeches and a parade, home owners decorated their houses in patriotic bunting, and employees of the Copper Queen readied dynamite and other noisemakers for the celebration. Two of the town's most respected residents, Lewis and Harriet Williams, were anticipating another event: the birth of a grandchild. The Williamses lived in a comfortable mountainside home overlooking Main Street. From their house they could watch eighteen- and twenty-mule teams hauling wooden ore wagons from the mines to the smelter. They could also see burros laden with water, wood, and groceries struggling up the paths to their hillside destinations. On July 2, inside the Williams home, Josephine Leah Williams Douglas and James S. Douglas—son of the Copper Queen president—became the parents of a boy, and named him Lewis Williams Douglas after Josephine's father.[5]

Lewis's maternal grandfather was a small, wiry man who supervised the Copper Queen smelter. Known as Don Luís to his friends, Lewis Williams had immigrated to the United States from Wales with his parents and brother Ben. His father, John, had tried prospecting in New Hampshire, Michigan, and several western states before settling in San Francisco in 1870. There, in partnership with Judge Dewitt Bisbee, John Williams established a brokerage office. Early in 1880, Edward Reilly, who held an option on the Copper Queen mining claims at Mule Pass in Arizona, asked the firm of Williams and Bisbee to find a buyer for the holdings. After closely inspecting the property, Williams and Bisbee persuaded William Martin and John Ballard of San Francisco to purchase a seven-tenths share. In June of that year, Martin, Ballard, and Reilly formed a company to work the claims.

The town that grew up around the mining property took the name Bisbee in honor of John Williams's partner. The new mining company asked Williams's son Lewis to head the smelting operations and his other son, Ben, to manage the mines. In 1880, Lewis and Ben Williams moved to Mule Pass and helped organize the town of Bisbee. Lewis Williams became a stockholder in the Copper Queen Consolidated Mining Company and served as superintendent of the smelter until 1901, when he retired and moved to Los Angeles.[6]

The Williamses left Bisbee when their grandson, Lewis, was only seven years old. The boy was much closer to his paternal grandparents. Indeed, Lewis's personality and outlook were shaped mainly by his grandfather, James Douglas, and his father, James Stuart Douglas. The father probably exaggerated only slightly when he bluntly told his son that he had inherited all his "advantageous characteristics" from the Douglas line: "You get nothing from your mother's side of the family."[7]

The first of Lewis Douglas's Scottish forebears to reside in the United States was Dr. James Douglas, his great-grandfather. Born in 1800 near Aberdeen, Scotland, Douglas was a physician's apprentice for five years before entering Edinburgh University to study surgery. After certification, in 1818, he served as a ship's surgeon on an Arctic whaler, fought cholera near Calcutta, and attended the colonists of the Poyais settlement in Honduras in 1822. Nearly dying from typhus with scores of other colonists at Poyais, Douglas left Central America and settled in Utica, New York, in 1824. There he taught anatomy and practiced surgery until a bizarre incident forced him to leave the area.

At that time, it was not unusual, although it was unlawful, for physicians to exhume the bodies of slaves, paupers, and transients to perform post-mortems. Indeed, Douglas converted the attic of his home into a dissecting office. In the autumn of 1825, he visited a local graveyard to disinter the body of a recently buried transient. By mistake he unearthed the corpse of a prominent citizen instead, and a few days later someone discovered the cadaver in the doctor's unattended office. Fearing reprisals from the authorities, in large part because he had been caught (though not punished) once before for body-snatching, Douglas went with his wife to Canada.

They settled in the city of Quebec, and he became one of the most famous surgeons and psychiatrists in the province. In 1845, he was the first physician to contract with the province for the care of the mentally ill. Three years later, he abandoned his lucrative surgical practice and, for the next two decades, devoted his full attention to providing these heretofore neglected people with humane and proper care. Leaving medicine in 1865, Douglas spent the next ten years traveling abroad and speculating in Canadian mining projects. Unwise investments dissipated his fortune, and in 1875 he was forced to sell his property. He moved with his middle-aged son, also James, to Phoenixville, Pennsylvania. He died eleven years later in Tarrytown, New York, at the age of eighty-six.[8]

Although Dr. Douglas was the first of his family to reach America, his son James, Lewis's grandfather, was the first to make the United States his permanent home. Born on November 4, 1837, in the city of Quebec, James Douglas, Jr., was educated in private schools, the University of Halle in Germany, Edinburgh University in Scotland, and Queens University in Ontario. After graduating from Queens in 1858, he returned to Edinburgh to study for the Presbyterian ministry. In 1860, he married Naomi Douglas, daughter of Commodore Walter Douglas of the Cunard Trans-Atlantic Steamship Line, and a year later passed his examinations for admission to the clergy. He was not ordained, however, because he refused to sign the Confession of Faith.

Having sacrificed a career in the ministry, Douglas and his wife returned to Quebec, where he assisted his father at the Beauport Insane Asylum. He also studied medicine and surgery at Laval University to enable him someday to manage the asylum. In 1865, however, the province awarded the contract for the care of the insane to another bidder, and young Douglas was compelled to seek a different occupation. For the next decade, he tried unsuccessfully to transform one of his father's mining ventures into a profitable enterprise. Hoping a familiarity with chemistry, geology, and mineralogy would enhance his chances for mining success, Douglas studied under his friend T. Sterry Hunt, a chemist and geologist, and together they developed a novel leaching method for refining copper ore.

Word of the new copper treatment spread rapidly. Soon Douglas was demonstrating the process throughout the United States and in Latin America. In 1874, Charles M. Wheatley and the celebrated mineralogist Dr. Benjamin Silliman, Jr., organized the Chemical Copper Company to use the process at the Jones Mine in Phoenixville, Pennsylvania. Hunt and Douglas were given shares of stock in the company, and a year later Douglas resigned his teaching position at Morrin College in Quebec to become superintendent of the company's copper works. He worked at Phoenixville until 1881, when fires forced the plant to suspend operations. Two years later, the company dissolved, and Douglas moved to Tarrytown, New York.

At Phoenixville, Douglas had gained practical mining experience and enhanced his reputation as a metallurgist and mineralogist. Always experimenting, he devised a marketable method of refining copper electrolytically. This discovery increased the demands for his services as a mining consultant. He traveled to several western states and territories, giving mining advice and searching for new sources of copper ore. In 1880, Edward Reilly, co-owner of the Copper Queen Mine at Bisbee sent Douglas some copper ore to be refined. Impressed with the quality of the ore, Douglas visited Arizona in December to examine the mining potential of the Bisbee district and to locate additional sources of ore. Two months later, at the request of Silliman, who had an option on the Copper Queen Mine, Douglas returned to Bisbee to make a closer inspection of the mining property. He urged Silliman to buy the property, but the doctor was unable to raise enough money.

Early the next year, William E. Dodge and D. Willis James of the Phelps Dodge Company asked Douglas for advice on the building of a copper smelter on Long Island. Douglas told them that such a project would be unwise because in the future smelters would be erected at western ore locations. Impressed by his breadth of knowledge and logic, Dodge and James asked him to appraise the mining properties of the Detroit Copper Company at Morenci, Arizona. After Douglas had inspected and reported favorably on the Morenci properties, the company made the investment.[9]

From Morenci, Douglas traveled to Bisbee, where he again assessed the Copper Queen Mine and claims adjacent to it. He was particularly taken with the potential of the Atlanta Mining claims, which bordered the Copper Queen, and, after another inspection of the property, he advised Phelps Dodge to purchase the claims for $40,000. For his consulting services, Douglas's employers offered him the alternatives of a flat fee or a 10 percent interest in the mining property. He chose the latter and, "on that sudden impulse and hasty decision," he wrote, "depended my whole subsequent career—successful beyond anything I had ever dreamed of."[10]

In the summer of 1881, the Atlanta Mining Company was formed, and Douglas journeyed to Bisbee to supervise company operations. After three years, however, Phelps Dodge had spent $80,000 on the property without discovering ore. Understandably, the directors of the company were reluctant to make additional investments. But Douglas persuaded them to risk another $15,000, and in July a large bed of ore was discovered two hundred feet below the surface. Almost concurrently, the Copper Queen Company—whose profitable ore body had played out—burrowed into the same ore nest from another direction. To avoid a protracted and bitter legal battle over ownership rights, the two companies merged in August, 1885. James Douglas became president of the new Copper Queen Consolidated Mining Company and served in this capacity until 1908. During his presidency, the Copper Queen Mines yielded over 730 million pounds of copper and provided its stockholders with over $30 million in dividends.

The parent Phelps Dodge Company began to expand into a full-fledged copper empire. Throughout the southwestern United States and in Mexico, the company developed new claims, bought out rival firms, built towns, erected smelters and company stores, and constructed hundreds of miles of railroad lines. In 1897, James Douglas persuaded Phelps Dodge to purchase the Nacozari mines in Sonora, Mexico, and three years later, to build an enormous smelter midway between

Nacozari and Bisbee. The border town that grew up around the smelter was named Douglas in honor of the Copper Queen president. To ship copper from smelter to markets, Phelps Dodge completed a railroad line from Douglas to El Paso, and Douglas was appointed president of this newly formed El Paso and Southwestern Railroad. In 1909, he became president of Phelps Dodge and served in this capacity until his resignation to become chairman of the board of directors in 1916. Shortly before his death two years later, he retired from the company.[11]

After the turn of the century, labor conditions in Bisbee began to change. Between 1900 and 1906, three new companies—the Calumet and Arizona, the Shattuck Arizona, and the Denn Arizona—were formed to compete with the Copper Queen. Owing to this increased mining activity, thousands of unskilled laborers from Eastern Europe streamed into Bisbee. The enlarged work force and keen competition among the copper companies gradually broke down the amicable relationship between labor and management. Meantime James Douglas had begun to relinquish control over the Arizona mining operation to his son Walter. In 1901, Walter became general manager of the Copper Queen and, in 1909, assumed its presidency. Seven years later, he succeeded his father as president of the parent company, Phelps Dodge.[12]

In 1907, the Western Federation of Miners established a small local in Bisbee. In retaliation, the copper companies, including the Copper Queen, discharged 160 workers and blacklisted hundreds of others who were regarded as union sympathizers. This strong action broke the union, but left laborers resentful. In January, 1917, the Industrial Workers of the World, a socialist brotherhood, established Metal Mine Workers No. 800. This organization campaigned for "shorter hours, more wages, and better conditions *today*, while tomorrow we will be satisfied with no less than the complete ownership of the mills, mines, and smelters." After the United States entered the European war in April, 1917, commodity prices soared. In order to combat wartime inflation, the IWW sought higher wages. On June 24 the union presented to the copper companies a list of demands, which included higher wages, improved safety precautions, an end to job discrimination, and recognition of labor's right to organize and bargain collectively. The operators refused to consider the demands, and the workers went on strike on June 26.[13]

The copper companies and town merchants denounced the walkout as a treasonable act. Some believed that the strike was ordered and financed from Berlin. Most branded the strikers as saboteurs, foreign agents, and traitors who were bent on violence and destruction of the copper industry. Walter Douglas decreed that "there will be no compromise with a rattlesnake." He contended that there was "German influence" behind the walkout and recommended ridding the camp of all agitators.[14]

Following Douglas's proposal, members of the Citizens Protective League and the Workers Loyalty League voted to expel the strikers from the town—to protect women and children, they said, from possible violence. In the early-morning hours of July 12, Cochise County Sheriff Harry Wheeler and a posse of 2,000 rounded up 1,386 strikers, placed them in cattle cars of the El Paso and Southwestern Railroad, and shipped them to the New Mexican desert, where they were abandoned without adequate provisions of food and water. Federal troops rescued the men and transported them to Columbus, New Mexico. Walter Douglas and other instigators of this carefully planned action were indicted for kidnapping by a federal grand jury, but were never convicted. James Douglas, who had worked for more than two decades to achieve industrial harmony in Bisbee, apparently did not participate in the deportation decision. In poor health (he would die the following year), he left the day-to-day operations of the company to Walter.[15]

During his later years, James Douglas devoted his energies mainly to philanthropy. Having lost a daughter to cancer in 1910, he became intensely interested in the search for an effective treatment and cure for the disease. In 1914 he gave $600,000 to establish General Memorial Hospital in New York City as a research and treatment center. As one of the world's few holders of radium, he donated his supply of this rare element to the hospital for use in therapy.

Moreover, he supported World War I by purchasing nearly $1 million worth of war bonds. Blessed with an inquisitive mind, friendly personality, strong convictions, and a sense of humor, he was widely respected by his business and mining colleagues. He died at his Hudson River home in Spuyten Duyvil, in Manhattan, on June 25, 1918, leaving an estate of more than $18 million.[16]

For Lewis Douglas, nearly twenty-four years old at the time, the death was a profound loss. His grandfather had been more than a loving relative; he had been a friend, teacher, advisor, model of success and proper conduct, and a hero. Lewis had frequently visited, traveled, and fished with his grandfather and considered it "a very rare privilege" to have come under the guidance of such a distinguished, cultivated, and decent man.[17]

At his grandfather's insistence, young Lewis was raised to become a gentleman. He received an eastern liberal-arts education, and was exposed to travel, music, and good literature. He was taught proper manners: discourtesy was never excusable. Douglas made sure, also, that his grandson was acquainted with the pleasures of the outdoors. He introduced Lewis at an early age to fly fishing and initiated his development into an accomplished, lifelong devotee of the sport.[18]

Besides accepting the grandfather's code of conduct, Lewis absorbed the "essential goodness" of his mentor's philosophy. It affirmed the value of Christian ideals, the intrinsic benevolence of human nature, and the steady ascent of material and social progress. Both deplored violent protest, yet they tolerated opposing beliefs, encouraged constructive criticism, and welcomed peaceful change. They cherished the industrial pioneer, business competition, and the capitalist economic system, but condemned the idle rich, monopolists, the irresponsible, and the selfish.

Both Douglases held private property to be sacred so long as its owners were responsive to the needs and desires of the community. Both insisted that individual rights were sacrosanct unless they interfered with the rights of others. Both believed that one of society's most difficult yet pressing tasks was to protect the weak from the strong and the minority from the majority. They inveighed against the concentration of power in the hands of a few and attacked trade unions, trusts, and government agencies for assuming excessive powers. They decried the denigration and exploitation of workers, but opposed socialism, collectivism, and the closed shop. They felt that clashes between labor and capital could be resolved if employers shared their profits more equitably with workers and if both parties dealt honestly and fairly with one another. Their actions, it is true, did not always conform to their avowed ideals.[19]

If Lewis's grandfather was the "greatest man" he ever met, his father, James Stuart Douglas, was the "strongest." "My father," Lewis recalled, "was a very, very strong man, I think the strongest man I've ever known, and I've known Clemenceau and Wilson, Marshall and all of the great military leaders of the last half century, but I don't know of anyone who had the sheer power of personality that my father had." J.S., Jim, or Rawhide Jimmy, as the father was frequently called, gained notoriety and fabulous wealth from the copper-mining industry. But success was not handed to him by his celebrated father.[20]

Born in 1868 at the Harvey Hill Mine, Megantic Township, Quebec, James Stuart Douglas was educated at public schools in Phoenixville, Pennsylvania, and New York City. Headstrong, intemperate, and fiercely independent, James left the family home at the age of seventeen to homestead in Manitoba, Canada. Hoping to find relief from asthma, he moved to Arizona in 1890, and raised strawberries in the Sulphur Springs Valley. He settled in Bisbee in 1891, at his father's request, to work as an assayer at the Copper Queen Mine. On November 11 of that year he married Josephine Leah Williams. The marriage produced three sons: James, who died in childhood; Lewis; and another James, born in 1903.

James S. Douglas worked at the Copper Queen until 1892. In that year he moved to Prescott, Arizona, to work at the Senator Mine, which was operated by the Commercial Mining Company, an affiliate of Phelps Dodge. For the next eight years he was an assayer, timekeeper, bookkeeper, and mine superintendent. In 1900, he was transferred to Nacozari, where he became superintendent of the Picacho Mine and the Moctezuma Copper Company, two subsidiaries of Phelps Dodge. During this tenure, he supervised the building of the Nacozari Railroad, which stretched from the Douglas smelter to the Mexican copper mines. In 1909, he moved to Douglas, where he became one of the town fathers. As early as 1902, he and William Brophy had organized the Bank of Bisbee and a year later the Bank of Douglas. In 1903 he had joined Brophy in organizing the Douglas Investment Company, which owned most of the town's public utilities and much of its real estate. Within a decade, Douglas estimated his worth at approximately $600,000.[21]

Douglas's most daring and remunerative undertaking began in 1912, when he and George Tener reorganized the United Verde Extension Company. As president of the new company, Douglas secured enough capital to buy up the lands neighboring the rich United Verde Mine in Jerome, Arizona. In September, 1914, after several months of searching and more than $300,000 in expenditures, the company discovered ore. After a year's operation, J.S. predicted that the mine would be "a producer of great wealth."[22]

His forecast proved accurate. He wrote Lewis, in November, 1916, that the mine was "a wonder" because it was producing $700,000 worth of copper per month. By the end of the year, the mine's value was estimated to be $60 million. As president and major stockholder in the company, James S. Douglas became one of the richest men in the state. Under his leadership, the UVX yielded about $150 million worth of ore and $50 million in dividends.[23]

Douglas's fortune was boosted by high copper prices brought by the First World War. Like many other successful business leaders who profited from the war, Douglas volunteered his management talents when the United States entered the conflict in April, 1917. Sent to France, he served as head of the stores division of the American Red Cross. Almost immediately, he developed a love for that country. He became a friend of Premier Georges Clemenceau (in whose honor he later named a mining company and smelting town), embarked upon a study of French culture, and became an ardent Francophile. For his services during the war, he received from the French government the Order of the Chevalier Légion d'Honneur. After the Armistice, he returned to Arizona to preside over the UVX. He died in Montreal on January 1, 1949.[24]

James S. Douglas's stocky build, sharp features, and determined gaze made him seem larger than his five-foot-eight frame. Contemporaries claimed that he emanated "magnetic waves" and that "when he entered a room the entire atmosphere would change." An individual of intelligence and conviction, driven to excellence, he was also domineering and irascible. One acquaintance declared that he was "at war with all mankind, with himself, and with conditions over which no man may expect to exercise much control." Another friend, who knew him intimately, observed that Douglas had a "Dr. Jekyll and Mr. Hyde" personality. He "could be the kindest, most considerate and charming of men; then, suddenly, he would change into the most caustic, abrasive individual I have ever known." He was "adamant in his convictions and frequently his opinions were *law*."[25]

He was difficult for adversaries and associates alike. Once, at a board of directors meeting of a Phoenix bank, Douglas, in a fit of anger, called a fellow director a "goddamned fool," picked up a heavy oak chair, shouted, "This is what someone ought to do to you," and threw the chair against the wall. Old and dried out, it exploded, leaving everyone present in a state of shock. Douglas rarely forgave a slight. Frank Brophy, Lewis's oldest friend, recalled that after one business disagreement, Rawhide Jimmy refused to speak to him for seven years. According to Brophy, Douglas had alienated virtually every friend he had by the time he left Arizona for Canada in the 1930s.[26]

Douglas deplored publicity, shunned social gatherings, and rarely entertained. He seldom mixed with the wealthy, because he considered them pretentious and himself a democrat and an egalitarian. He championed compulsory military service because it would narrow the "gap which has been opening for years between the classes." He nurtured a man-of-the-people image by dressing in workclothes, complete with red suspenders, traveling by coach, and giving workmen money-making tips. A Phoenix newspaper once described him as a man who was "as plain and unassuming as an old shoe."

Douglas's lifestyle was not, however, always "plain and unassuming." In 1917, he built a home near the UVX mine on a mesa overlooking the Verde valley—a huge, two-story Spanish-style adobe mansion which cost about $125,000. Describing the edifice to his son, he wrote that the house was a "gigantic success," especially the cost, which was "the most gigantic thing about it." He added: "The two servants are fair. The cook is not good." Douglas also departed from the working-class image by educating his sons at private schools, purchasing French artworks, commissioning a sculptor to craft a bust of Clemenceau, and frequently traveling abroad, principally to France. When he traveled, he abandoned his slovenly dress in favor of elegance, including a frock coat.[27]

Douglas worked diligently to eliminate waste and extravagance in his various business enterprises. Frank Brophy told a story of Douglas inspecting the railroad bed between Nacozari and Douglas and finding an unused railroad spike beside the track. Carrying it to the section camp, "he waved it before the genial Irish foreman and spoke with some heat and feeling on the subject of waste and carelessness." When the foreman found an opportunity to reply, he said: " 'Shure you're absolutely right, Mr. Douglas, and I'm glad you found that spike. Would you believe it? I've had three men out for two whole days looking for it.' " Though the story may be apocryphal, there is little doubt about Douglas's penchant for economy. Indeed, many of his letters to Lew were written on the backs of used envelopes.[28]

And yet, despite his frugality, Douglas was a generous benefactor, giving much of his fortune to schools, hospitals, universities, and museums. Moreover, when Clemenceau could no longer afford to live at 8 Rue Franklin in Paris, Douglas purchased the house anonymously and rented it to his friend for a nominal fee. After the premier's death, Douglas donated the home to France as the Clemenceau Museum.[29]

As a parent Rawhide Jimmy was strict and demanding. He insisted that his sons adhere rigidly to a moral code that stressed hard work, fair play, humility, responsibility, and discipline. Once, to punish Lewis, Douglas sent him to a demolished schoolhouse and instructed him to "take every last nail out of every last board." Determined not to pamper his eldest son, the father insisted that Lewis begin in the mines as a mucker—a backbreaking laborer's job—so he would understand the meaning of hard work. Possessive as well as demanding, throughout his life he often berated Lewis for the inadequacy or infrequency of his letters. "I have just read your note of the 23rd of March for the third time and it is disappointing. Short, uninteresting & obviously written in a hurry with no endeavor to think of subjects that you might easily know I would like to hear about. Alors."[30]

Despite his forbidding nature, Douglas did not intimidate Lewis. Lewis loved and respected his father. For his part, James S. Douglas was "passionately crazy" about Lewis and admired the boy's ability to stand up to him. Lewis, one observer noted, was the only person J.S. ever truly loved. "Lewis was his life." Lewis's younger brother, James, was less resolute and was dominated by the father. In temperament, Lewis was closer to his grandfather. One family friend remarked that like the grandfather Lewis was gracious, charming, kind, even-tempered, and "the most hospitable man I ever knew." Yet he acquired Rawhide Jimmy's independence, grit, penchant for economy, and strength of conviction. Like the father, the son clung so rigidly to his principles that he sometimes appeared self-righteous and inflexible.[31]

Lewis, too, acquired many of his father's political views. James S. Douglas was an "Andrew Jackson Democrat," who firmly embraced individual liberty, minimal government regulations, equal economic opportunity, states' rights, strict economy, and low tariffs. Although he was a Democrat, he often crossed party lines. In the presidential election of 1916, for example, he voted for the Republican Charles Evans Hughes because President Wilson had thus far kept the United States neutral in World War I, and had failed to prepare the country militarily. After 1932, he was an implacable enemy of Franklin D. Roosevelt's domestic policies. The Democratic son also proved a political maverick.[32]

Lewis shared his father's admiration for Clemenceau. He met the former premier in 1929, and the memory remained with him a lifetime. According to Douglas, the Frenchman taught him that "only two things in life really mattered. The first is to love and be loved. The second is to be intellectually honest." Lewis tried to adhere to that advice. Although he admired French culture as well as Clemenceau, Lewis did not inherit his father's Francophilism. Instead, like his grandfather, he became an Anglophile.[33]

Josephine (Josalee) Williams Douglas was a gentle, sympathetic, indulgent parent, who often praised and seldom reprimanded her older son. She listened attentively and patiently to his problems, fears, and doubts, reassured him with kind words of encouragement, and urged him to be independent, considerate, and faithful to his convictions. She also tried to protect him from the demands of his father. A woman of refinement, Josalee cheered and delighted young Lewis with her stories, singing, and piano playing.

The relationship between the parents, by contrast, was strained, and the marriage fragile. Intellectually and emotionally, Josalee was no match for her forceful husband. She was frail, sensitive, at times, willful, and wished to be pampered. James was domineering, insensitive, harsh, inattentive, and seemingly unloving. He made all the family decisions, rarely consulted or confided in her, seldom indulged her, scolded her for spoiling the children, especially the younger son, James, and was frequently away from home. It is noteworthy that he named Samuel Applewhite, his private secretary, as the person to be first notified in the event of his injury or death. Despite their differences, Josalee was devoted to Jim, and yet she often irritated him. For example, she knew that he detested dining with candles, but she repeatedly adorned the table with them. He would remove them and rebuke her, leaving her in tears. More often than not, Frank Brophy recalled, family meals at the Douglas household were interrupted by sharp words and Josalee's weeping departure.[34]

Although parental fights were common, it is difficult to assess their effect on Lewis. He remembered his childhood with fondness, but seemed to cherish most the times spent with his grandparents, who adored one another. Lewis resented his father's harsh treatment of his mother and younger brother, but he never lost his love for him. Nevertheless, the frequent quarrels between James and Josalee may have helped shape Lewis's talents as a conciliator and negotiator. From early adulthood, he served as the family peacemaker, who calmed tempers and mediated rifts.

On one occasion, Lewis refused to see his father again until he promised to change his attitude toward Josalee. He wrote: "The following are the facts—1—you have been so critical of and have so criticized mother that her life has been almost unbearable—2—You have been so domineering and egotistical toward her that you have instilled in her a horrendous fear of you—3—You have used physical strength on Mother even to the extent of pulling her hair and striking her." Ending on a conciliatory note, Lewis asked his father to remember the happy times with Josalee. That "sporadic happiness," he wrote, was due to mutual respect and the ability to overlook one another's faults. To repair his strained relationship with Lewis, James agreed to work at being more patient and considerate. His promise was soon forgotten.[35]

Distressed by his father's intemperate remarks and cruel actions, Lewis took pains to avoid such behavior in his own life. He sidestepped heated confrontations, seldom spoke in anger, rarely lost his patience, and went out of his way to be kind and considerate. Lewis, said Frank Brophy, had a "facility with people," impeccable taste, and a sense of "fitness for things." He felt comfortable in any company and had a knack for putting people at ease. Perhaps as a reaction to his father's demeaning treatment of Josalee, Lewis was especially gallant toward women. One friend remembered that he "was absolutely sweet always to women. . . . He was very attractive to women because he would make them feel that they were terribly important. That at that moment they were the most important thing . . . in his life. And he was always very chivalrous." Although Douglas enjoyed the friendships of many women, one, Peggy Zinsser, whom he married in 1921, was the love of his life. Unlike his parents, Lew had a happy marriage. He was a thoughtful, indulgent, loving husband. Although he did not always confide in her, the two rarely quarreled and were seldom separated. The marriage lasted for fifty-three years.[36]

As a youngster, Lewis heard much about the colorful and courageous exploits of Arizona's mining pioneers and about the decidedly less heroic deeds of territorial desperadoes like Doc Holliday, the Earp brothers, John Heath, the Apache Kid, Black Jack Ketchum, Little Irish Mag, and Crazy Horse Lil. He learned, too, of the skillful opposition of the Apache Indians to white encroachment on Indian lands. Although the Apaches never attacked Bisbee, rumors of invasion had sent the townspeople to the mines for protection. By the time Lewis was born, however, Geronimo and his meager band of warriors had surrendered, and Indian outbreaks in the American Southwest were rare. Nevertheless, he remembered Apache and Yaqui Indians chasing him as a youth in Arizona and Mexico.[37]

The Douglas family lived in the frontier town of Nacozari from 1900 to 1909. Located ninety miles south of Bisbee in the Sierra Madre Mountains, the town was built by Phelps Dodge for miners working ore deposits on Pilares Mountain. Lewis's father supervised the operations. The company erected a hotel, store, hospital, public library, houses for employees, and schools for both Spanish- and English-speaking children. There, Lewis mingled with cattlemen, miners, and farmers of American, Mexican, and Indian origins.

During those years Lewis frequently visited his grandparents in the East. He seemed to enjoy these trips, but they were hard on his mother. After Lewis, at the age of eight, left alone by train for an extensive visit with his Grandfather Douglas in New York, his mother wrote: "By this time Lewis must be halfway to Deming [New Mexico]. Dear Little Boy! I can scarcely realize that he is gone to stay for such a long visit. But I must not think of it—but of the lovely time he will have with you all. I wish I had a picture of him as he looked starting off this morning. Jim was delighted to think he could send him with a strictly Mexican 'Sombrero.' I hope he will be a dear good boy and very obedient!"[38]

Lewis spent most of his time after 1906 in the East attending school. However, he returned to Mexico each summer to hunt, fish, hike, ride horseback, swim, frolic with his brother, James, and entertain visitors from Arizona, like Frank Brophy. During one summer Brophy learned to swim by taking morning baths in Cottonwood Pond. Lewis also introduced him to the practice of smoking hay leaves. At the age of ten, Lewis had organized and managed the first baseball team in Sonora—Los Muchachos of Nacozari—which played rival clubs from Douglas to Bisbee. He later speculated that these contests were the first ever international baseball games. Even after starting school in the East, he reorganized the Nacozari Muchachos upon his return for the summer.[39]

More boisterous than Bisbee, Nacozari was the scene of riots, banditry, insurrections, murders, and executions. According to Lewis, there were many threats against his father's life, and on one occasion an angry group of miners nearly killed him. Fortunately, the family moved to Douglas a year before the outbreak of the Mexican Revolution. But even that border town was not immune from the fury of the rebellion. On April 17, 1911, for example, the local mayor, S. F. McGuire, wired President Taft: "Battle still raging. Worse yet to come. Bullets falling all over city. Cannot something be done for our protection?" During most of the revolution, Lewis was in the eastern United States attending school. Yet his father kept him well informed about border developments before he returned to the Southwest for the summer. In the spring of 1913 he heard that his father had been seized by Mexican bandits at the Cananea Consolidated Copper Company in Sonora and held for a $500,000 ransom, but the reports proved untrue.[40]

Douglas, then, was part of the frontier and remembered his experiences with fondness. He recalled that "The frontier itself, I think because of the simplicity of life, the complete lack of any stratification of society and the lack of any sense of discrimination, was the general aura, social aura within which I grew up." Settlements were sparse and transportation inadequate; yet neighbors were helpful and hospitable. "We knew everybody and everybody knew us," he reminisced. "We were all companions together. I lived for a part of this period far beyond the end of a railroad, in Northern Sonora. The natives of the State of my age were my friends. . . . The communities were relatively small. . . . Indeed, I was wholly unconscious of any distinction of race or creed or color until later [when] I came eastward to sit in the House of Representatives."[41]

Actually, Douglas was aware of racial prejudice and class conflict long before he reached Washington. For decades Bisbee miners had kept Mexicans from working in the mines and the townspeople had prohibited Chinese from spending the night within the town limits; and there was strong prejudice as well against Indians and Eastern Europeans. Douglas grew up amidst outbreaks of extreme violence and vicious anti-union activity. While he mingled with miners, Indians, and Mexicans, he resided in the "White House," which took "a Sabbath Day's Journey" to walk across, when his playmates lived in poverty. Nonetheless, he downplayed class differences and the extent of racism, and was himself certainly free from prejudice. Today, Mexicans who remember Lewis Douglas describe him as "a friend of us."[42]

Less influential than family instruction, Douglas's frontier experience did help to foster his faith in the virtues of hard work, self-reliance, charity, and perseverance. Perhaps, too, it promoted his belief in economic laissez faire and weak government. And doubtless his proximity to the frontier brought about his love of nature, his devotion to conservation, his interest in American western history, and his passion for outdoor activities. He was proud of his western heritage and always considered himself an Arizonan.[43]

2

Education, War, and Marriage

WHEN LEWIS DOUGLAS REACHED THE AGE OF ELEVEN, he was sent East for his formal education. In the spring of 1906, he boarded a train in Arizona with his friend Frank Brophy, also bound for a preparatory school, and the boys set off alone. En route the train encountered a snowstorm in Kansas and was frozen to the tracks. After a delay of two days, it was freed and the boys eventually arrived in New York City, where they were met by Lewis's Grandfather Douglas.[1]

That fall Lewis joined sixteen others in entering the Hackley School at Tarrytown, New York. A preparatory school for boys, Hackley was established in 1899 on a seventy-eight-acre hilltop estate overlooking the Hudson River. Besides academic training, the school offered close supervision, religious instruction in the "simple and universal truths of Christian living," and comfortable quarters. "The social life of the boy is well provided for, and the good manners of a gentleman are expected," the catalog noted. The student population was kept small to avoid outgrowing "the familiar oversight of the Headmaster." A lower school was created for grades 5 through 7 and an upper school served grades 8 through 12. Lewis spent one year in each school, completing the equivalent of grades 7 and 8.[2]

Although his first year's progress gave his father "great satisfaction," the following year proved somewhat disappointing. He was intelligent, but did not excel academically, his marks ranging from a low of 70 in science to a high of 85 in Latin. Still, he impressed his teachers and classmates with his warm personality. A former Hackley instructor remembered that Lewis's "personality stood out from the others. Even as a boy he had about everything: emotional balance, ability to get along with boys and faculty, and a sense of humor that was hard to match." Moreover, a former classmate recalled that "Lewis was afraid of nobody and liked almost everybody. He showed no signs of peeve toward those who disagreed with him."[3]

As a Hackley scholar Lewis was expected to behave like a gentleman, but sometimes he fell short of the mark. On one occasion, he wanted to witness the twenty-four-hour Briarcliff Club Automobile Race. Prohibited from attending, Douglas recalled that he "clambered down a water spout from the second floor where my bedroom was, in the early hours of the morning when it was still dark, made my way to the road . . . and I managed to come back to the school just a little bit too late." On another occasion, Douglas remembered that he hurled "some snowballs into a teacher's bedroom, and with real serious intent hit him on top of his bald head. A number of escapades of this sort led the headmaster to think that I was an evil influence and so I was invited, not too courteously, to refrain from returning for the fall session."[4]

Actually, Lewis was not asked to leave Hackley. Disturbed by the apparent collapse of discipline at the institution, James S. Douglas, against the wishes of Headmaster Walter B. Gage, decided to withdraw his son in order to enroll him in a school that stressed discipline and character-building. In the autumn of 1908, Lewis entered Montclair Academy in New Jersey, where he soon fell under the influence of John G. MacVicar.[5]

Headmaster at Montclair since 1887, MacVicar presented an imposing figure with his white hair, luxuriant snowy sideburns, gold-rimmed spectacles, and dour expression. Though formidable in appearance, he had a sense of fairness and humor and got along well with his boys. In 1936 Lewis wrote his former headmaster that "as I look back upon the personalities who have come into my life that to you, to my grandfather, to a few at Amherst, to a Mexican locomotive engineer by the name of Jesus Garcia, and to my father must be given the credit for whatever small amount of good there is in me."[6]

MacVicar and his assistants stressed discipline. To the parents of each incoming student Montclair Academy sent a list of regulations which permitted boys to return home or to visit friends only on weekends and only if "their scholastic work and deportment for the current week are satisfactory." Requests to leave the academy had to be made in writing to the headmaster. Scholars were prohibited from receiving "boxes of good things to eat without the previous consent of the Headmaster."

MacVicar, too, frequently sent progress reports to the parents. After Lewis's first year, the headmaster wrote James S. Douglas that his son "shows the right spirit, is receptive to suggestions, and is doing consistent work." Indeed, except for occasional critical comments on the boy's tardiness, absences, and frequent "talking in class," reports on his progress were consistently laudatory.[7]

Lewis also kept his father abreast of his activities at Montclair. Each month he was required to send itemized accounts of his expenditures. If his account sheets did not balance, he was compelled to make a satisfactory explanation. Even when Lewis entered college, his father kept a tight rein on his finances. For example, James wrote him at Amherst: "I again regret to have to call your attention to the fact you are not religiously safeguarding your credit. There is absolutely no reason why a tailor at Amherst should send me a bill for $41.50. Write to me and tell me how this happened, and what is the detail of this business."[8]

With his financial reports, Lewis included news of social, academic, and sports events at Montclair. After giving an address on the founding of Rome, for instance, he wrote that he "rather liked the sensation of talking before a crowd." Only rarely did the boy's letters reveal evidence of homesickness, perhaps because he realized that his father would not tolerate such an emotion. Josalee Douglas, depressed by her son's long absences, unsuccessfully pressured her husband to withdraw Lewis from Montclair and enroll him in a school in the West.[9]

Although Lewis had little difficulty scholastically, he fretted a great deal to his father over his achievements on the baseball diamond. In April, 1910, he wrote: "Base-Ball started here about two or three weeks ago and I have been playing on the 1st team, which was a great surprise to me. I played in the first game which we won, but in the second game, I went up in the air and couldn't catch anything. Since then I have had a seat on the bench during the games, but if I keep on working hard I may get into the High School game (Montclair High School) and win my M." Almost as an afterthought he added: "Scholastically everything is going al right [sic]." Actually, Douglas rarely received grades below B. In June, 1911, MacVicar reported that "Lewis passed A in all of his examinations excepting Latin. . . . He won the scholastic prize in science and has received very flattering comments from all of his Masters. We are pleased with him."[10]

Graduating in 1912, Lewis won a prize for making the most progress during the school year. He also earned an honorable mention in English, first prize in history, and third place in the Lucia Pratt Ames Prize Debate. He captured the faculty gold medal "awarded to that boy in the upper school who reached the highest attainment in character, scholarship, deportment, and manliness."[11]

The "Arizona Knight" or "Duggie," as Lewis was called, also had an impressive extracurricular record. Besides playing baseball, he lettered in basketball and swimming. He was business manager of the school yearbook, captain of the rifle team, class treasurer, president of the debating team, and a member of the dance committee and photography club. The yearbook for 1912 described him as an "orator" who was the "politician of the class."[12]

Eighteen years old at graduation, Lewis was of medium height with a sturdy frame, unruly brown hair, dark brown eyes, a ready grin, and an infectious personality. He emerged from Montclair bursting with confidence and fully prepared to enter college. His father and grandfather both wanted him to have a good liberal-arts education, and sought advice about specific colleges from Cleveland H. Dodge and Arthur Curtiss James, executive officers with the Phelps Dodge corporation. They urged Lewis to attend their alma maters, Princeton and Amherst, respectively. After visiting the two schools and discussing the matter with his father and grandfather, Lewis selected Amherst.[13]

Located in the rolling hills of western Massachusetts about thirty-five miles north of Springfield, Amherst was a school for gentlemen. With over a hundred other "gentlemen," Douglas entered Amherst in September, 1912. He lived in Pratt Dormitory with Seeyle Bixler, who later became president of Colby College, and Bill Avirett, who would write for the New York *Herald Tribune.* Bixler recalled Douglas as not an eager or brilliant student, but as independent, friendly, a person of integrity and principle and unafraid to take an unpopular stand if he thought he was right. Lewis would not "truckle to anyone," Bixler remembered, and the entire class "looked to Lew for leadership in matters that required courage."

Occasionally Lewis revealed a mood that bordered on self-righteousness. He and Bixler once loaned a classmate enough money to remain in school. When the recipient of the loan appeared to be mishandling his funds, Lewis "lit" into him about his poor attitude toward budgeting money. Another classmate, John J. McCloy, also detected this characteristic in Lewis. He was extremely self-exacting, McCloy recalled, and tended to carry on agonizing moral debates with himself over issues and decisions. This dedication to principle, which some interpreted as a holier-than-thou attitude, remained with Lewis for a lifetime.[14]

From the beginning, Douglas immersed himself in extracurricular activities. He joined Alpha Delta Phi, the leading campus fraternity, despite his father's concern that such an organization might subvert his originality and individualism. James S. need not have worried. As a pledge, Lewis demonstrated his independence by leading a successful rebellion against severe hazing by older fraternity members. His stand impressed a classmate because "freshmen don't often stand up against their betters this way."[15]

Douglas was also active outside the fraternity. He served as class treasurer, played tennis and freshman baseball, swam on the class team, and tried out unsuccessfully for varsity baseball. Knee problems, the first of many physical ailments that would plague him during his lifetime, hampered his performance as a would-be infielder. A New York specialist found only that the boy had weak knees and ordered him to avoid rigorous exercise.[16]

Douglas often joined his grandfather on salmon- and trout-fishing excursions to Quebec and upstate New York. He also made frequent trips to New York City to visit his grandparents, tour museums, watch major-league baseball games, and attend plays such as *Peg o' My Heart* and *Potash and Perlmutter*. During the summer of 1913, he accompanied his grandparents on a tour of Europe. Leaving New York in late June aboard the *Carmania*, they sailed to England and then visited the major cities on the Continent, traveling as far east as Budapest. Lewis enjoyed the sights, but seemed to relish most his grandfather's companionship. "The trip was something like traveling with a living and talking history," he wrote a few years afterward. "The fascination of accompanying a man of such breadth of interest and such unity of understanding was almost indescribable." The following spring, Lewis visited Washington, D.C., where he met President Woodrow Wilson and Secretary of the Navy Josephus Daniels. The meeting with the President did not make much of an impression. He wrote his father: "I have been having a fine time here in Washington. I met President Wilson and the Secretary of the Navy."[17]

Inside the classroom Lewis was initially less energetic. During his freshman year he rarely took his studies seriously. In Professor John F. Genung's Biblical Literature course, he played poker with classmates. As a result, he failed the course and had to repeat it. He also did poorly in biology, receiving grades of D. As a sophomore, however, Lewis took a course in logic with the college president Alexander Meiklejohn, who, Douglas recollected, "fired my interest." Owing largely to Meiklejohn's influence, Lewis settled down and applied himself; he transformed mediocre grades into superior ones. By his senior year, his average had climbed to 90.[18]

A former dean at Brown University, Meiklejohn was installed as Amherst's eighth president during Lewis's freshman year. He was a progressive educator, who was determined to make learning instead of character building, sports contests, religious instruction, and narrow specialization the college's primary function. Stressing the importance of liberal arts, Meiklejohn altered the curriculum to permit students to take more elective courses. Although his educational reforms often provoked the ire of faculty and trustee members, they were enthusiastically welcomed by the students.[19]

Meiklejohn's liberal approach to education remained with Douglas for a lifetime. He recalled that the president "made Amherst the finest, most complete liberal college of the twentieth century." When the board of trustees, in 1923, forced the headstrong Meiklejohn to resign, Douglas stoutly defended him. He recalled that he was "devoted" to Meiklejohn "because I was deeply attracted by the quality of his mind, by his high sense of what he considered to be the truth, of his unwillingness to depart from the truth, of the intellectual heights I think he reached, and finally his capacity to find young men of quality to become much better men than they would have been had they not fallen under the aurora of his influence." Their friendship was to last until Meiklejohn's death.[20]

Of Lewis's professors, Meiklejohn seems to have been the only one who made a lasting impression. As an economics major, he took six semesters of work with Professors Walter H. Hamilton, James W. Crook, and John Maurice Clark, but was not won over to their philosophy, which stressed increased federal regulation and intervention in the economy. Douglas was influenced by progressivism, but preferred the variety advocated by Louis Brandeis and Woodrow Wilson, which emphasized the restoration of business competition, decentralization, and small government. Schooled in economic orthodoxy by his father and grandfather, Lewis did not depart from it as a student at Amherst.

In 1916, Douglas graduated *cum laude* in liberal arts with a major in economics, and he shared with two other students the Woods Prize for improved scholarship and leadership. As a senior, he also worked as a board member on the college yearbook *Olio* and chaired a committee that investigated the need for revamping and tightening the college honor system.[21]

At Amherst, Douglas learned that he was not a bold, imaginative thinker. Yet he also discovered that his mind was quick, retentive, and able to synthesize with ease. He proved a "regular devil at hanging on to his views," and his charm and ability to simplify usually enabled him to convince people of the correctness of his beliefs. His affability and concern for others won him popularity, yet a part of him always remained somewhat aloof. The *Olio* of 1916 referred to him as "a man of mystery, who makes the enigmas of the Sphinx and Brother Cobb's calculus look like a parade of the Swiss Navy." Indeed, throughout his lifetime, Lewis seldom completely opened up to anyone. He had many acquaintances, but few if any intimate friends. Those who knew him best say that when they tried to get too close to him a curtain would fall. Despite this reserve, Douglas emerged from Amherst self-assured and well-liked, aware of his powers of persuasion and leadership. He also graduated from college without any definite career plans.[22]

By 1916 most of Europe was deadlocked in war. Wilson's efforts to mediate a peace had failed. The British blockade of Germany and Germany's submarine warfare had entangled American shipping in the conflict and endangered American neutrality. At the front, soldiers awaited their fates in the muddy trenches that gouged the once-picturesque European countryside.

Douglas, like millions of other Americans, sympathized with the Allies. Yet he fervently hoped that the United States could avoid involvement in the European war. He also believed, however, that Americans must prepare themselves for the conflict. Like other gentlemen of wealth who regarded military duty as a patriotic responsibility, Douglas joined a YMCA army camp at Plattsburg, New York, in the summer of 1916. There he excelled in military training and was particularly impressive on the rifle range, earning the highest score in his class and barely missing the training-camp record. For the westerner the training was easy, and he was surprised by the number of men who were unfit, unfamiliar with guns, and barely able "to fend for themselves."[23]

Graduating from the camp in August, after a month's training, Lewis prepared for advanced university work. In September, he enrolled as a "listener" at the Massachusetts Institute of Technology. With a vague notion of pursuing a mining career, he took courses in economic geology and metallurgy, but struggled academically and was generally unhappy with technical studies.

When the United States declared war on the Central Powers in April, 1917, Douglas immediately volunteered for service. Before the Selective Service Act was passed, in May, he tried to join Teddy Roosevelt's volunteer division. But the Roosevelt Division failed to materialize, owing to the opposition of President Wilson, and Douglas entered the American Expeditionary Force.[24]

Lewis spent the summer of 1917 at the first Officers Training Camp at the Presidio in San Francisco. There he was trained by "one of the orneriest men I have ever met." The officer pushed the men hard, cursed them, and even struck their horses. His actions made Lewis "pretty hot sometimes," but he endured and was commissioned a second lieutenant of field artillery in July, 1917. After a brief furlough in Jerome, he reported to Camp Lewis, Tacoma, Washington, and was assigned to the 347th Field Artillery Regiment of the 91st Division.[25]

Shortly after his arrival in Washington, he was assigned to the staff of Brigadier General Edward Burr of the 166th Field Artillery Brigade. After serving Burr briefly, Douglas was awarded the prestigious position of aide-de-camp to Major General H. A. Greene, the commander of the 91st Division. While he welcomed the opportunity to become the commander's aide, he had doubts about leaving the field artillery. He wrote his grandfather that his post "might lead to better things." However, "if I don't make good and am sent back to the Field Artillery in which arm I hold my commission I will have lost a good deal of practical experience." Since life was "nothing more than a chance anyway," Lewis decided to gamble. "Whether or not I have decided well, time will tell. At any rate it is quite an honor to be appointed Aide."[26]

Douglas proved a successful aide and made first lieutenant in the spring of 1918. He was reassigned to Brigadier General Frederick S. Foltz of the 182nd Infantry Brigade, 91st Division. Lewis had reservations about his new commander's leadership qualities. After serving the general for only a few weeks, he confided to his father that Foltz "seems to have absolutely fallen down in his ability to take hold. In fact he is afraid to tell his subordinates where to head in."

Lewis was particularly disturbed by the lack of respect that career soldiers showed civilian officers like himself. Career officers, he wrote his father, "have formed a sort of union worse than the I.W.W. and the attitude of some of them towards some of the civilian officers is not one which will tend to make the latter good officers. The regular army fails to appreciate the fact that some from civilian life are beyond the age limit and have given up larger jobs than these army officers can ever handle. You know this war is going to be won by the much spurned at civilian officers because that same civilian officer is supplying the army with more brains than it ever had before." Douglas concluded his diatribe by declaring that the 91st Division "will succeed in spite of our leaders."

Douglas's misgivings about his commanding officer were not eased when he reached the training area near Chaumont, France, in early August, 1918. He described his superior as "a weak man with no grasp of the situation, even more ignorant of factual conditions and use of the various arms than I am which is an awful thing to say of anybody." Since he could not serve Foltz "with absolute loyalty," Douglas asked to be transferred.

He was reassigned to division headquarters as an assistant G-3 in the operations branch of the general staff. His duties consisted of heading the message center and directing communications from the front line to division headquarters. He sometimes worked sixteen hours a day. "It is hard work but very interesting and if I can deliver the goods I think that perhaps I can be of more service than any other place."[27]

Douglas headed the message center from September to the Armistice in November, 1918. He experienced battlefield action at St. Mihiel, the Meuse-Argonne and Ypres-Lys. In seventeen days of fighting in the Meuse-Argonne, the 91st Division suffered nearly 25 percent casualties. Douglas barely escaped injury when the message center at division headquarters in Epinonville was shelled on the evening of October 2. He remembered that "German 77s twice made direct hits through open windows, wounding many and scattering confusion and such furniture as there was." He also recalled German planes rushing "over us so low and so close that we could have drawn portraits of the pilots as they dropped bombs and hand grenades on us." Despite the confusion and destruction, the message center continued to function. At Epinonville, Lewis volunteered to carry a message to the front lines. Riding in a sidecar driven by "a magnificent operator," he embarked on "a hair-raising trip," with "machinegun fire and shells bursting all around," to warn of a German thrust to the left. His daring performance won him a decoration from General John J. Pershing for "exceptionally meritorious and conspicuous services at Epinonville, France."

Lieutenant Douglas also distinguished himself during the Belgian offensive in mid-October, 1918. At Lys-Escault, he successfully escorted a shell-shocked major from the front to safety. "How we happened to get through the shower of high explosives and hail of machinegun fire only Divine Providence will be able to tell," he recalled. For this act of heroism Lewis was awarded the Croix de Guerre by the Belgian government.

After the Armistice, Douglas remained in France until February, 1919, serving as an aide-de-camp to Brigadier General L. C. Andrews, Provost Marshal General of the AEF. He also had an opportunity to spend several days with his father, who was in Paris doing work with the Red Cross. In late February, he was discharged and returned to Arizona.[28]

Douglas's wartime experience left a lasting impression. He resented those Americans who had opposed intervention in the war. He held German leaders accountable for disrupting nearly a century of peace. And he became a lifelong devotee of military preparedness. He wrote his mother shortly after the conflict: "I notice that American Publishers have given the Kaiser one million dollars for his memoirs. It is disgraceful and worse! I also notice the Democrats are going to renominate Vardaman of Mississippi for the Senate. Vardaman was one of the '12 unreconcilables' who voted against the declaration of war against Germany. . . . Is it possible that we can forgive and forget the Hun and his army so soon?"[29]

Lewis also blamed Germany for hastening the death of his Grandfather Douglas. Before the outbreak of the Great War, James Douglas, the grandson wrote, believed that man is essentially good and that Christian ethics guide human behavior. "But when the bolt struck and Germany—the Germany which he had admired and almost loved—the Germany in which he and my grandmother had made their mutual pledge and in which together they had had so many pleasant associations—threw the world backward into a reign of barbaric savagry [sic] the whole structure of personal experience on which his faith was builded crashed into bits at his feet. From that moment health failed and life slowly ebbed away with each succeeding shock of brutality." James Douglas had died in June, 1918, five months before the Armistice, "a time when there seemed but little chance that the barbarism of the Teuton might be successfully defeated." During World War I Lewis also developed a healthy suspicion of the military mind, which was enhanced by his later experiences as director of the budget, deputy director of the War Shipping Administration, and ambassador.

Despite his resentment toward Germany, Douglas opposed the Versailles decision to impose harsh economic reprisals against the Central Powers. A punitive peace, he reasoned, would cause bitterness among the vanquished nations and possibly lead to another war. He supported Woodrow Wilson's proposed League of Nations, but believed with his father that an American alliance with France would prove a better check against future German expansion.[30]

After his separation from the AEF, Lewis divided his summer between Jerome, where he visited his father, and La Jolla, California, where his mother vacationed to escape the Arizona heat. Meiklejohn offered him a teaching position in history at Amherst for the spring 1920 semester, and Douglas accepted. Specifically, he was to serve as a teaching assistant to Ernest Barker and Richard Henry Tawney, visiting professors from Oxford University.

Douglas enjoyed his brief stint at Amherst. Teaching history was rewarding because it enabled him to obtain a better understanding of the present. Besides its "element of usefulness," history was an important discipline, Douglas believed, because it "enriches a person's life." At Amherst he met two colleagues who would be lifelong associates, John M. Gaus, who taught political science, and Walter Stewart, who lectured in economics. Other young colleagues included Robert Frost, Seeyle Bixler, and Walter R. Agard.[31]

After teaching at Amherst, Douglas took a position at Hackley School. He moved to Hackley to be near Margaret "Peggy" Zinsser, who lived in nearby Hastings-on-Hudson. Lewis had first met Peggy at a Smith-Amherst dance, but, as he recalled, "didn't actually fall violently in love with her until after the war."[32]

Daughter of Emma Sharmann Zinsser and Frederick G. Zinsser, Peggy was dark-haired, dark-eyed, refined, cheerful, intelligent, and attractive. Both sets of her grandparents, the Sharmanns and Zinssers, had immigrated to the United States from Germany in the mid-nineteenth century. Her father, a chemist, had established a factory that produced poison gas during World War I. An uncle, Hans Zinsser, was a noted virologist, epidemiologist, and author, later widely known for his *Rats, Lice and History*. Peggy's mother was a social leader and woman of culture, who played the piano, sang, appreciated the arts, assisted with the Girl Scouts, and founded a woman's club.

Like Lewis, Peggy was born to privilege. She lived in Locust Wood, a comfortable house surrounded by large trees, manicured shrubs, and spacious grounds. Unlike Lewis, however, Peggy, her older sister, Ellen, and her older brother, Jack, were raised in a peaceful, happy, loving household. Her parents were warm and kind, and Peggy's childhood, she remembers, was "the happiest you can have." Her parents were disciplinarians, but they were compassionate and fair and "made it all fun." They also instilled in Peggy a strong sense of family, which was something her father-in-law, James Douglas, never understood.[33]

Following her older sister, Peggy entered Smith College at Northampton, Massachusetts, in 1915. She was a good student, popular socially, and active in extracurricular functions. She was a member of the Current Events Club, Glee Club, baseball and basketball teams, and the Alpha Society, an organization that sponsored plays, musical performances, oral recitations, and a magazine. She was also drawn to the theatre, a lifelong passion along with music, appearing as a Serbian soldier in the production *The King and the Cook*.[34]

Peggy first met Lewis in 1915, when she was a freshman and he a senior. She later recalled that he was not especially handsome but he was fun-loving and mischievous, and always distinctive by virtue of his cowboy hat. "You never missed him in a room," Peggy recalled. "He had a great power about him in some way even as a young man." She frequently saw him go by the house in which she lived. Often, he was with some glamorous "older girl," and she remembers saying to a friend that "if Lew Douglas should ever ask me to dinner, I would just die of happiness." Later in the year, Lew's roommate, Stuart Rider, took Peggy to a social function where she had the opportunity to dance with Lewis. Dancing with him was the "pinnacle of happiness."

When Lewis went to MIT in Cambridge, Peggy occasionally dated him. More often, however, she saw him in the company of her brother, Jack, who had become a close friend of Lewis's, and of her sister, Ellen, who frequently drew his attention. Then in April, 1917, the United States entered World War I, and Peggy did not see Lewis again for two years.

In the fall of 1919, Lewis gave a somewhat belated "end of the war" party for some friends at his parents' home in Jerome. His friend Captain Jack Zinsser was the featured guest, and Ellen and Peggy were also invited. Peggy at first declined because she had plans to attend a football game "with a man I was very intrigued with." Her mother intervened, however, declaring that "this is probably the last holiday your brother will ever have and I not only beg of you I order you to go to Jerome." Peggy went to Jerome.

When she reached her destination she was appalled. Jerome was a city on stilts. Houses were perched on the steep hillside, with their overhanging fronts supported by slender posts. The mining camp was desolate and barren, parched by the fiery desert sky. Fortunately, Peggy found the party more appealing than the town. She met an Englishman who fascinated her. She also awakened Lewis's interest and learned later that her attention to the Englishman made her host jealous. Although Peggy enjoyed herself, her stay in Jerome was cut short: she had gone camping and developed pleurisy. Feeling miserable, she decided to terminate "an awful trip."

After boarding the train for Phoenix on the first leg toward New York, Peggy immediately went to bed. About fifteen minutes after departure, Lewis stopped by her berth to express his sympathy, and declared that he was going to care for her until she reached home. That gesture, Peggy reminisced, was "more or less where it began with him."

After their arrival in the East, the couple dated frequently until Lewis left to teach at Amherst. The romance continued when he transferred to Hackley in the fall of 1920. They attended the theatre, dinner parties, the opera, and baseball games. In September, Lewis proposed marriage but Peggy put him off. Although she was deeply in love, she hesitated to marry before her older sister. So she made Lewis wait.[35]

Meantime, Lewis informed his father of the proposal and sought his blessing. James Douglas initially disapproved because he was passionately anti-German and considered the Zinsser family "Boche." Irritated by his father's prejudice, Lewis wrote him in January, 1921: "As you undoubtedly know I have been going to Hastings frequently to call on the Zinissers [sic]. I know equally as well that you do not like the family for reasons which seem to me to be groundless. Nevertheless, sometime ago I made up my mind that the fates and the younger of the two girls willing, I would marry one of them. Some six months have been spent in waiting for an answer; I don't know how much more time will be spent in the same way or am I in any way able to anticipate the nature of the answer."

He urged his Francophile father to put aside his anti-German prejudice. He also assured him that Josalee had not in any way acted as matchmaker. "Mother knows nothing through any word of mine, nor has she influenced me in any way." He concluded: "Don't allow this to be the 'blow that killed father.'"[36]

Realizing that he could not dissuade his determined son, Douglas gave his blessing to the proposed match. Assuming that Peggy would accept his son, he offered his Jerome mansion to the young couple. He would leave the premises and move in with George Kingdon, his mine supervisor. Presumably, Josalee would live with Lewis and Peggy or stay in their home in Douglas. James ended his letter by berating Lewis for his unaffectionate letters.

Pleased that J.S. had "approved" Peggy, Lewis wrote his appreciation on February 4, 1921. He assured his father: "That I love Peggy Zinsser [sic] is beyond all question and I know that you too will love her for her own sake. It will be a great disappointment if you don't."

As for his father's offer of the house, Lewis considered it premature to discuss living arrangements until Peggy consented to marriage. If she did agree "and if we should live in your house the idea of your staying with Mr. Kingdon when your own son and daughter-in-law are living in your house at the very collar of your shaft is preposterous." Turning next to his "cold unsentimental letter," Lewis explained that "for some unknown reason I don't like to even attempt to express my feelings. But that does not mean that my feelings are any less true." Finally, Lewis notified his father that he did not plan to tell Josalee of his plans to marry Peggy until she had accepted him. "Perhaps in a couple of months or so there may be something worth telling."[37]

Actually, the very next day Lewis received news "worth telling." On February 5, Peggy agreed to become his wife. On February 6, Lewis wired his parents from Hastings-on-Hudson: "Peggie and I are engaged to be married. Very very happy. We send much love to you both and are writing long letters tonite. We are telling only the family." The prospective bride also sent a dutiful letter to her future father-in-law. Addressed to "Dear Father Douglas," the letter read: "I realize, I think, the ideals and ambitions you have always had for Lou [sic]—and my own hope is that I shall not fail him or you at any point. I want our lives to be far above the average and because our love is so great I think they will be." Won over, J.S. wrote his friend John Greenway: "Lewis wants to show you his prize. She is fine and he is a lucky boy and his mother and I are very happy."[38]

After a four-month engagement, Lew and Peggy were married on June 18, 1921. The ceremony took place under a huge tree on the grounds of Peggy's home. Bishop Atwood of Arizona and the Reverend Wadsworth, Jack Zinsser's father-in-law, performed the service. Both the bride and groom asked six friends to stand with them.

Following the wedding, the couple drove directly to Little Moose Lake in the Adirondacks, where they honeymooned in a cottage owned by Lewis's Grandmother Douglas. In his youth Lewis had spent many happy moments in that cottage with his grandfather. For three weeks the newlyweds swam, boated, fished, and hiked. Lew also worked sporadically on a biography of his grandfather. Discouraged with his efforts, he asked his friend John Gaus to read the manuscript and offer suggestions. Gaus made some criticisms, offered encouragement, and advised Lew to send his work to the famed historian Frederick Jackson Turner for an evaluation. Douglas demurred and the biography remained unfinished and unpublished.[39]

Growing weary of lake life, the couple drove to Canada to visit Quebec, a province where each had vacationed in earlier years. After spending a week in Canada, they returned to the Adirondacks for a week and then departed for Hastings-on-Hudson to spend some time with Peg's parents. In mid-August they ended their honeymoon of nearly two months by leaving the East for their home in Jerome, a locale Lew liked to call "the heart of the American desert."[40]

PART TWO
Legislator

3

State Representative

IN 1921 JEROME WAS AN ESTABLISHED MINING TOWN of four thousand people. Two-thirds of the townspeople were male, most earning their livelihood with one of two mining concerns: the United Verde Mining Company, controlled by Senator William A. Clark of Montana, and James S. Douglas's UVX Company. Principally because of wartime demand, the copper industry boomed during the second decade of the twentieth century. Following World War I, however, declining prices prompted mines and smelters to slow production or shut down. After a four-year recession lasting from 1919 through 1923, the industry recovered and Jerome flourished for the remainder of the decade.

Like most mining camps, Jerome was starkly unglamorous. Its steep, bleak hillsides were covered by ramshackle wooden buildings. It was afflicted with dust, reeking gases, and a scorching climate. Only Main Street was paved, and there were few cultural events. The town was not particularly boisterous, but it did have temptations. In 1919 "Two Desperate Wives" had written to ask the deputy sheriff why he did not "put a stop to the poker playing in private rooms? If you would take a walk down Main Street you would find several games running. Will you please try, or will the women have to do it?" Like other mining camps, Jerome had a history of racial and political intolerance. Blacks, Hispanics, and Orientals were discriminated against, and the Ku Klux Klan was active throughout the county. In 1917 the town fathers had exiled to the desert more than 100 IWW members who were considered disloyal and subversive. Two years later the town's daily newspaper, the Jerome *News*, endorsed the drive for a new library with the heading: "Wanted—A Library. Provide Good Books. Prevent Wobblies and Bolsheviks."[1]

Arriving by train at nearby Clarkdale on August 20, 1921, Lewis Douglas and his bride were driven up Cleopatra Mountain to the Douglas mansion, which overlooked the Verde valley more than five thousand feet below. To Peggy, the sprawling adobe mansion resembled a "pink battleship." That evening they were

31

greeted by nearly 150 townspeople, who cheered and rattled cowbells, pots, pans, and a large locomotive bell. The high school band provided music and miners set off dynamite and sounded the company's fire whistle. Peggy proved a good sport by honoring a request from the crowd to fire a six-shooter in the air. When the hullabaloo subsided, James S. Douglas invited the guests inside for refreshments. It was, as the Jerome *News* reported, "a grand and glorious occasion." Peggy Douglas was not so sure. Her genteel upbringing and cosmopolitan background had not prepared her for life in a mining town. When she went to bed that night she said to herself: "Maybe I've married the wrong man."[2]

Unlike Peggy, Lewis was in comfortable surroundings. Jerome, after all, was not unlike the mining towns of Bisbee and Douglas where he had grown up. Moreover, he had visited the town often, and made numerous friendships. Years later he remembered that it was a "fun" town, but not "any more rowdy than any other town around here at that time."

His father was unwilling to start him in a supervisory position in the mines, so Lewis worked underground. On one occasion, a piece of metal flew into his eye and nearly blinded him. Despite that accident, Douglas had fond memories of mining days. "It was great fun," he recalled years afterward. "I made a great many friends and learned how many fine people there are in the world. . . . I wanted the experience of working underground and going through the gamut of jobs."[3]

While her husband worked in the mines, Peggy lived virtually alone in the big house. Having no servants, she was responsible for the household and had to work "like a slave," doing the cooking and cleaning. Although she had once taken a cooking course in school, she had little practical experience. At Locust Wood, where she had been raised, the household chores were performed by servants.

James Douglas made the inexperienced housewife's task more difficult. He would sometimes telephone and announce that he was bringing twelve to lunch. Hastily, she would have to prepare a meal and then do the dishes afterward. Young, inexperienced, and eager to be accepted, Peggy initially tolerated her father-in-law's demands.

A difficult pregnancy gave Peggy a reprieve from household duties. Because there was some danger of her losing the baby, she had to stay in bed a good deal of the time, and her mother sent a servant to do the housework. Peggy's spirits were lifted further when she and Lewis moved into their own home. This "honeymoon cottage"—which had eight tons of copper, including a solid metal roof, in its construction—was a wedding gift from Lewis's parents.[4]

The couple remained in their new home only a few months. In April, 1922, Peggy, at her doctor's suggestion, left Jerome for Hastings-on-Hudson, where she spent the last two months of her pregnancy. Lew was originally due to join her in June, but arrived a month early after quarreling with his father and quitting his job. The feud was prompted by James's treatment of Josalee. Lew intervened by admonishing his father to be more considerate. "For some twenty years I have been observing certain features of our family life," he wrote his father in early May. "Until just recently I have never been able to make a definite decision as to the rights or wrongs of the case. I now, however, have information which obliges the conclusion that you have been guilty of mistreatment of my Mother. Under such conditions I can no longer remain loyal to you and am therefor [sic] leaving Jerome and the employ of the United Verde Extension Co." He informed his father that he would be willing to see him "only at such times as you can humbly apologize [to] my Mother for your past actions and give definite and concrete assurances to her and to me that your past attitudes will be materially and substantially changed."[5]

Apparently J.S. gave satisfactory assurances, because the rift was healed by mid-June. During that month Lew wrote both parents warm, chatty letters about Peg's health, the imminent birth, and family matters. "Peggy is very well—but nothing has happened yet." The suspense ended on June 20, when Peggy gave birth to an eight-pound nine-ounce boy and named him James Stuart Douglas II.[6]

Having spent an eventful summer in the East, Lew returned to Jerome with his family in mid-August. He expected to resume his job with the UVX Company, but when he reported to work he was given "quite a jolt" by George Kingdon, the general manager, who proposed to place him in charge of house rents and claims. Lew refused to accept the post. "If there is ever anything ahead of me here it can't be in house rents and claims," he protested to his father. "In addition, the old man said that so long as he had anything to do here no college graduate would ever hold a position of responsibility." He did not seek his father's intervention; instead, he again separated himself from the company. Fortunately, he had other prospects.[7]

That summer, while he was in the East, Douglas had permitted friends in Jerome to enter him in nomination for the state House of Representatives from the fourth precinct (Jerome) of Yavapai County.

Despite his youth, Douglas possessed impressive political potential. He had a readily recognizable name, a college education, and a creditable war record. Moreover, he was captain of the town baseball team, active in the American Legion, the son of one of the town's largest employers, and a Democrat in a Democratic state.[8]

To overcome his lack of experience, Douglas campaigned hard in the Democratic primary, seeking to meet as many voters as possible. As election day approached he told his father: "So far as I am concerned my friends tell me that it will be a landslide and my enemies tell me the opposite. I believe neither [and] so far I have committed myself [to] nothing and have used every justifiable means to get my name before the voters." In his initial bid for public office, Douglas handily defeated his opponent, Richard Lessley, by a vote of 317 to 249.[9]

Having won the primary, Douglas was confident that he could beat the one-term Republican incumbent, Elbert A. Stewart, in the general election. Still, he took "no chances." He wrote his father in early October: "I have been busy day and night and ready to fall into bed when the day has ended. Trying to be in politics is interesting, but a hard job and in many ways disagreeable."[10]

Douglas had reason to expect political success. Mired in a postwar recession, Arizonans in 1922 were generally dissatisfied with state Republican leaders. Democrats, usually torn between conservative and progressive factions, had united behind ex-Governor George W. P. Hunt, who had returned from his diplomatic post in Siam to capture the gubernatorial primary. Led by Hunt, Democrats pledged economy in government and lower taxes to restore prosperity. Lewis Douglas wholeheartedly supported those pledges.

Douglas also backed Hunt, but grudgingly. The former governor and James S. Douglas had long been political enemies. A progressive, George Hunt generally favored labor causes and blasted the mining companies for possessing too much power and inequitable tax advantages. Hunt charged James Douglas in particular with trying to use his wealth and influence to dominate the state politically.

Fearful that strong unions would push for higher corporate taxes and government regulations that would cripple the state's mining industry, conservatives, led by James Douglas, generally opposed pro-labor legislation and progressive politicians. Douglas considered Hunt a radical and had actively opposed his candidacy during the gubernatorial primary. Hunt accused Douglas of trying to thwart the primary system by handpicking the party's candidate behind closed doors. He also implied that Douglas had offered him a bribe to stay out of the primary and support the conservative Democratic candidate, Charles Ward. James Douglas hotly denied Hunt's charge, labeling it a "damnable lie."[11]

Despite the animosity, Lewis put aside these differences to work for a Democratic victory in the general election. Running with Hunt, he informed his father, "puts me in an embarrassing position, but that can't be helped." The father tried to ease his son's embarrassment by issuing a terse statement to the press: "I am for Hunt and the whole Democratic ticket."[12]

During the campaign, both Hunt and Lewis Douglas stressed party solidarity. Hunt even traveled to Jerome with Congressman Carl Hayden and United States Senator Henry Ashurst to stump for Douglas. On November 7, Arizona voted overwhelmingly Democratic, and Lewis Douglas won a seat in the state legislature by a vote of 686 to 396. Hunt, Ashurst, and Hayden were likewise victorious.[13]

Shortly after the election, Lewis and Peggy moved into a small house on Holly Street in Phoenix, which James Douglas purchased for them, so as to be near the state capitol. Yet the departure was also prompted by Peggy's desire to escape Jerome and her father-in-law. Although less eager than his wife, Lew also wanted to get away from James. Already a peacemaker between his father and mother, Lew did not want to play the same role between his father and his wife. Leaving Jerome would give Lew and Peggy more independence, privacy, and peace of mind. They never returned to the "honeymoon cottage" in Jerome.[14]

Even so, the couple had no intention of severing their relations with the head of the family. James Douglas often stopped to visit them in Phoenix, though he rarely spent the night. When he dined with them, Peggy Douglas recalled, he dined with Lew; she might as well not have been present. After dinner she would go about her work and he would never notice her absence. She was hurt by her father-in-law's indifference but endured it. She refused, however, to tolerate his surliness. One night at dinner he became so sarcastic that Peggy left the table and announced that she would not see him again or come down from her room until he left the house. He departed, but remained in Phoenix for three days. One day he sought her out in the garden at their home and apologized for his behavior. As Peggy put it, "you had to show your teeth" to make any impression upon him. Increasingly, Peggy was willing to show her teeth.[15]

Although Peggy gained her father-in-law's respect, she apparently never won his love—probably because he considered her a rival for his son's affection. In his letters to his son, he always referred to her as "your wife," never as Peggy. His letters to Lew often complained about his son's inattentiveness and lack of intimacy. On one occasion in the early 1920s he asked Lew to explain his indifference. "I think the greatest obstacle in the way of a real intimacy between us is that you are very intolerant toward my wife," Lew explained. "With the affection which I have for you both I naturally would like you and her to get along better. I know that she is very fond of you, that she has a great respect for you, and it hurts a little to see it unreturned." He reminded his father that he would be happier if he would allow his loved ones to get close to him.[16]

The Sixth State Legislature met in Phoenix from January 8 to March 11, 1923. Douglas backed Governor Hunt's attempts to curtail spending and eliminate waste. He successfully introduced a bill to investigate the state highway department. Appointed chairman of the three-man house committee, Douglas scrutinized the books of the state engineer's office and the highway department, and found evidence of shoddy record keeping and fiscal improprieties. He recommended an appropriation of $150,000, to pay off the department's debts, and the imposition of a gasoline tax of three cents per gallon to finance ongoing road projects. The legislature approved both measures. Economy-conscious, Douglas fought against a tax-relief bill for distressed farmers. The measure would have nullified penalties for tax delinquencies in 1921 and 1922 and given taxpayers one year to meet their debts. Characterizing the bill as "vicious in principle," he helped to defeat it. He also denounced a move to increase veterans' benefits.[17]

On other legislative issues, Douglas voted with the Democratic majority. He supported a bill that prohibited employers from interfering in the political activities of their employees, but opposed acts to enforce prohibition and allow women to sit on juries. He sponsored an anti–Ku Klux Klan bill, which passed both chambers, making it a felony for any individual to wear a mask or disguise "with intent to disturb, annoy, alarm, or intimidate any person" in Arizona.[18]

Reflecting his background, Douglas opposed most labor legislation. Although he supported a bill raising the minimum wage for women and another requesting that Congress restrict immigration, both of which were adopted, he vigorously opposed measures to prohibit mining companies from operating stores and making deductions from employees' paychecks to cover debts. Company stores and paycheck deductions were genuine conveniences for the workingman, he asserted. Both bills were tabled.

Douglas helped defeat a bill to exclude non-English-speaking employees from hazardous mining work. He argued that the measure would deprive aliens of jobs, not ensure worker safety. Foreign laborers were as skilled, safety-conscious, and responsible as workers who understood the language. As he undoubtedly knew also, alien workers were not prone to join unions and would work for lower wages.[19]

The most combustible issue that Lewis Douglas debated in the assembly was the Colorado River Compact. The decision to approve or reject the compact, the Jerome *News* maintained, was "the very greatest, the most vital business that has ever come before the legislative authorities of the state and . . . the future prosperity of every interest in Arizona depends upon its correct solution." Although only a freshman legislator, Douglas played a major role in shaping Arizona's position on this important document for nearly a decade.[20]

Originating high in the Rockies of Wyoming, the Colorado River flows south more than 1,400 miles before spilling into the Gulf of California. It drains 244,000 square miles in the states of Colorado, Wyoming, Utah, Nevada, New Mexico, Arizona, and California, and is one of the arid West's most valuable resources. From the early days, the river had been a menace during flood season. Each year from 1905 to 1907 it inundated thousands of acres of rich, irrigated farmland in the Imperial Valley of Southern California. And every year thereafter local farmers feared the rambunctious river would again drown their crops and destroy their homes.

Imperial Valley settlers also were troubled over the location of the irrigation channel that brought water to their fields. The Alamo Canal, as the aqueduct was called, started from the Colorado River just north of the border and stretched for sixty miles across Mexican soil before recrossing the international boundary into California. With Mexican governments so unstable, California farmers feared that an unfriendly regime or insurgent group might seize the canal and halt the flow of water to their farms. Consequently, they clamored for the construction of a canal located entirely within the United States.

In April, 1922, Representative Phil Swing and Senator Hiram Johnson of California introduced sister bills providing for federal construction of an All-American Canal and a flood-control dam and hydroelectric power station in the vicinity of Boulder Canyon. The sale of electricity produced by the power plant would finance the enterprise. Their proposals alarmed Arizonans. Claiming control over the portion of the river that flowed within the state's borders, many Arizonans, including Lewis Douglas, saw the Swing-Johnson bill as a devious and selfish attempt by California to acquire without compensation cheap electricity manufactured in Arizona.

The Swing-Johnson bill also disturbed the other basin states. Under western water law, the party that first put water to beneficial use had a prior and perpetual right to it. Less populous and economically developed than California, the other basin states feared that the construction of a large storage dam on the lower stretch of the river would permit California to utilize most of the stream's annual flow, leaving them an insufficient amount when it might be needed. Consequently, they sought an agreement that would guarantee each basin state a specific amount of water each year. Such an arrangement would ensure orderly economic development and prevent lengthy and costly legal squabbles. After months of negotiations, appointed delegates from the basin states concluded a water agreement at Santa Fe, New Mexico, on November 24, 1922.[21]

The Colorado River Compact divided the water supply between the upper and lower basins. The upper basin included Colorado, New Mexico, Utah, and Wyoming, while Arizona, California, and Nevada constituted the lower. With the annual river flow estimated at slightly less than 18 million acre-feet of water (an acre-foot equals 325,850 gallons), each basin would receive 7.5 million acre-feet annually, with an extra million acre-feet reserved yearly for the lower basin. At a later date, the individual states within each basin could apportion their share of the water. The compact also approved the impoundment of water for flood control, irrigation, and power production. To become effective, it had to be ratified by Congress and by the legislatures of the seven basin states. Six states quickly approved, but Arizona balked.[22]

From the first, there was little accord on the compact in Arizona. Republicans generally pushed adoption for economic reasons. By providing flood control, irrigation, and hydroelectricity, an all-purpose dam would boost land values, increase crop yields, and attract industries. Democrats were more skeptical, suspecting that river development would benefit California customers at Arizona's expense. Consequently, they sought to amend the compact to protect Arizona's economic interests.[23]

Lewis Douglas early became the legislature's most forceful and articulate advocate of an amendment. He believed that the pact jeopardized Arizona's right to collect taxes from private or federal power stations located within the state. Refusing to concede exclusive federal ownership over the interstate waterway, he insisted that the Colorado was a natural resource like copper, oil, and timber and therefore subject to state regulation and control. Arizona had a right to impose a tax on the production of power because the state controlled the portion of the Colorado that flowed inside its boundaries. He recommended that a power-tax amendment be attached to the compact.

Douglas painted a gloomy picture. Arizona would never become a major agricultural or industrial center, he declared, and its mineral wealth would eventually be exhausted. Therefore, future state prosperity must depend largely upon revenues from the production of cheap electricity on the Colorado. Arizona, he contended, should build plants on the river and sell the power directly, or allow private interests to develop the power and place a royalty on each unit of energy produced. California would be an insatiable consumer and provide Arizona with an everlasting source of revenue. Douglas blasted the compact as a subtle attempt by southwestern utility companies, particularly in California, to nationalize the river and deprive Arizona of the right to tax power produced inside its borders.[24]

During the House deliberations, Douglas pounded the power-tax issue. He advised John C. Greenway, manager of the Calumet and Arizona mines, that a levy would lessen the burden of the mines. Douglas estimated the tax would be approximately $30 million, a sum that would finance "all the running expenses" of the state government.[25]

The power tax met rigorous opposition in the legislature. Representative William Wisener branded the idea of a tax-free state as visionary. Why not place a one-cent-per-pound tax on the manufacture of copper? he asked. Taxes on copper and power would provide Arizona with so much money that "there would be nothing for the rest of us to do but hitch up the old flivver and drive to the beach and watch the mermaids disport themselves."[26]

Other legislators saw the royalty proposal as a simple device to lower rates on Arizona's mines. Douglas, the son of a prominent copper magnate representing a mining county, knew that the mines sought persistently to lighten their tax burden. In 1921 the United Verde and UVX companies paid $600,000 in Yavapai County taxes, which represented 60 percent of the county's total revenue. And mining companies shouldered about 50 percent of the entire state tax burden.

Mine operators claimed these taxes were excessive. In January, 1923, James S. Douglas brought suit in the United States district court against the "false, fraudulent, arbitrary, whimsical, capricious, fundamentally wrong and without warrant in law tax assessments" against his UVX company. The United Verde brought similar court action in February.[27]

Copper concerns did not actively endorse the power tax. The Jerome *News*, which usually reflected the views of the United Verde Company, branded the power tax as "bolshevism, pure and simple," and warned that it would prevent new industries from moving into the state.[28]

Some of Douglas's colleagues also criticized the royalty reservation because it would prevent ratification of the pact and delay the river's development. Some legislators contended that the state could impose a tax on power after the pact was approved and the power stations were constructed. Others said the tax would cause the plants and switchboards to be built outside the state. Only a few, however, challenged the state's right to impose a tax.[29]

Douglas stubbornly defended the power levy. He admitted that the royalty might be passed on to the consumer, but maintained that power revenues would permit the state to lower the general tax to such an extent that the royalty would not be burdensome. He brushed aside other criticisms. To those who contended the duty would kill the pact, he replied: "If others are unwilling to allow us to protect by compact that which is ours then let us not enter into [the] compact." To those who feared the levy would drive away power plants and industries, he stated that the grade of the river dictated the erection of the hydroelectric dam wholly or partially in Arizona. Finally, Douglas pointed out that if the royalty was attached to the pact and approved by Congress, it would be permanent.[30]

On February 15, 1923, the Arizona House approved ratification of the compact with three amendments—the power tax, a limit on Mexico's use of Colorado water, and the exclusion of the Gila from the Colorado River system. The Senate, however, refused to endorse the amended document. In the closing days of the session, Wisener tried again to secure approval of the compact without reservations, but failed when the House vote ended in a tie.[31]

Lewis Douglas had played a critical role in the debate over the compact in demanding that his colleagues amend the interstate treaty. It would be irresponsible, he believed, for the house to ratify a document that so inadequately protected Arizona's interests in the river. The future welfare of the state depended on its right to regulate and control the river within its boundaries. The state would lose nothing through delaying ratification until certain guarantees were written into the instrument. In short, had it not been for Douglas's pointed objections, the house would probably have approved the pact without reservations. Douglas stated later: "I suppose that I more than any other person am responsible for the defeat of the Colorado River Compact in the legislature."[32]

After the legislature adjourned in March, 1923, Douglas continued to shape Arizona's position on the compact. In May Governor Hunt asked him to chair a nine-man committee to work out an Arizona plan for Colorado River development. After a summer of study, including meetings with Secretary of Commerce Herbert Hoover in Washington, the Douglas committee agreed upon a plan and presented it to the Federal Power Commission in September.

Boldly Arizona announced that it intended to develop the Colorado River before the compact had been ratified. The state would construct a flood-control and water-storage dam at Glen Canyon, while private capital would erect a power facility at Diamond Creek, a tributary of the Colorado. The power plant would be controlled by a state board of commissioners and eventually be purchased by the state. Arizona and the other basin states could work out an agreement apportioning the waters of the Colorado and fixing a power tax while the dams were under construction. Douglas asked the FPC for a license to proceed, but the request was eventually denied. For the time being, neither Arizona nor any other state or agency could develop the river until the compact had been approved.[33]

4

The Road to Washington

LEWIS DOUGLAS'S RESPECTABLE RECORD IN THE LEGISLATURE, especially his strong states' rights position on Colorado River development, led some newspapers to predict that he would seek election to the state senate. To the surprise of many, Douglas shunned politics in 1924. When he again sought elective office two years later, he ran for Arizona's lone seat in the United States House of Representatives.[1]

Although Douglas never provided an explanation, several factors seem to have contributed to his decision to stay out of politics in 1924. Having moved from Jerome, he could not have legitimately run for office as a representative from that district. And he had not resided long enough in Phoenix to run effectively as a candidate there. Moreover, family responsibilities may have helped dissuade him. In 1924 Peggy was pregnant with their second child, and in the spring she and Lew went to New York to await the birth. On June 13, Peggy bore a son and named him Peter. (Later, the couple legally changed the boy's name to Lewis Williams Douglas, Jr., but he was always called Peter.)[2]

Lewis Douglas, too, began to have doubts about his dogged opposition to the Colorado River Compact. In October, 1923, he informed State Senator Harold A. Elliott that he was "seriously considering" coming out for ratification. He believed that Arizona would be granted a sufficient amount of water and doubted whether another state could build a power plant in Arizona without its consent. He questioned "whether our continued opposition now can be due to the subconscious influence of party politics."[3]

Renewed hostilities between Governor Hunt and James S. Douglas also may have influenced Lewis's decision not to seek office. In June, 1923, Hunt had threatened to call a special session of the legislature "to consider the taxation of state mines." The governor was outraged by suits filed in federal courts by the UVX and other mining companies protesting what they called unreasonable tax rates. Large rate payers such as J. S. Douglas, Hunt declared, must not be allowed to dictate to the state of Arizona the amount of taxes they would be assessed. For his part, James Douglas openly criticized the Hunt administration for inefficiency, mishandling public funds, and high taxes.[4]

Business activities also may have caused Lewis Douglas temporarily to forsake politics. Between 1923 and 1926 he joined his friend Frank Brophy in several ventures. Brophy inherited a fortune when his father, William, drowned in a fishing accident in 1922. With an assist from James Douglas, Lewis and Frank Brophy in late 1923 bought an abandoned thirty-acre orange grove along Seventh Street and Grand Canal in Phoenix. The following year they purchased an adjoining olive grove of twenty acres. Lew used three acres of the grove for a house, which he owned until the late 1940s.

The Douglas-Brophy ranch, as the enterprise was called, was managed by Brophy, who owned and operated other citrus property. Under his direction, the orange grove was revived and made productive. At the other grove, the olive trees were dynamited and replaced with grapefruit. Within two years the citrus ranch was yielding profits. Douglas and Brophy operated the ranch until the 1950s, when it was sold to real-estate developers for "a substantial profit."

Brophy and Douglas also cooperated in two mining ventures. In 1924 they purchased a dormant mining dump on the San Pedro River at Fairbank, a few miles from Tombstone. Called the Grand Central Mining and Milling Company, the enterprise was managed by Harry Hendrickson, an experienced mining man. Employing a process developed by Hendrickson, the company treated old tailings and managed to recover gold, silver, copper, and lead. After one year, the company made a profit of approximately $30,000. The concern remained in operation until 1936.

In 1925 the partners used the profits from the Grand Central to invest in a more ambitious undertaking. They formed the Aravaipa Mining Company to work old claims along the Aravaipa River near Klondyke in Graham County. As president of the company, Douglas decided to oversee the operation on a daily basis. He built a small house at Aravaipa and left Peg Monday mornings and returned Friday nights. Despite his hard work and dedication, the company was unsuccessful. All told, the shareholders, who consisted mainly of friends and relatives, lost about $250,000.[5]

Douglas's mixed business success may have helped turn him to politics in 1926. Rumors that Carl Hayden planned to leave his seat in the House of Representatives to challenge the incumbent, Ralph Cameron, for the United States Senate, also enticed him. In February, Governor Hunt announced to the press that Douglas planned to run for Congress. Hunt's revelation was premature and may have been calculated to stymie an effort, headed by State Senator A. T. Kilcrease, to persuade Douglas to seek the governorship. Douglas eventually decided against the governorship because a "better man," E. E. Ellinwood, a family friend and corporate attorney, planned to challenge Hunt.

Douglas declared his candidacy for the House on April 7, 1926, shortly after Hayden had announced for the Senate. Although a Democrat, Douglas disassociated himself from Hunt, who was seeking his sixth two-year term. Never fond of the corpulent, totally bald, mustached governor, whom he dismissed as that "damned old walrus," Douglas had become more disenchanted with him during his own absence from politics. He was disturbed by Hunt's perpetual occupancy of the governorship, and he blamed him for high taxes. Most important, he criticized Hunt for failing to bargain in good faith with the basin states in order to reach a suitable compromise on the Colorado River Compact. He assured anti-Hunt Democrats: "Neither in the Primary race nor in anything connected with the Primary race nor in policy do I intend, or will I agree, to be associated with the present incumbent."[6]

Douglas was one of six candidates to enter the Democratic primary. Only thirty-two years old, he had several advantages over his five rivals. He had a readily recognizable name, which his father kept in the news with business ventures, political disagreements, and philanthropies. In the midst of the primary, his father gained further statewide publicity by a gift of $1,000 to the University of Arizona polo team so it could travel to the East to compete. Money was another advantage. The candidate himself was not rich, but his father was a millionaire several times over, and his mother was also wealthy. Together they contributed more than $15,000 to their son's campaign.[7]

Douglas also had able advisors. Arthur Curlee, a boyhood friend and former legislative colleague, skillfully directed the campaign. He organized Douglas-for-Congress clubs throughout the state and managed publicity. Fred W. Lowery, an aide to James S. Douglas, and William Stuart, editor of the Prescott *Courier*, were shrewd students of politics who offered advice periodically. Moreover, J. S. Douglas served as counselor and contact man. Throughout the contest, he provided Lew with the names of both influential and ordinary citizens who should be contacted for support.[8]

Another advantage was Douglas's war record, which enabled him to attract widespread support among ex-servicemen. To the tune of "Where Do We Go from Here?" his veteran supporters backed his candidacy with this ditty:

> *Over the top with Douglas, over the top with Lew;*
> *It's up to all of us who served, to help and put him through;*
> *Go home and get your friends to vote, and all your buddies, too,*
> *So—over the top with Douglas, over the top with Lew!*[9]

The candidate possessed personal and intellectual qualities that gave him an edge. He was charming, modest, and an engaging speaker. Moreover, he had won statewide acclaim for his cautious approach to the Colorado River Compact.

Douglas also enjoyed strong press support. The state's largest Democratic paper, the Tucson *Arizona Daily Star*, warmly endorsed his candidacy. The *Star* was edited by Ralph Ellinwood, a college classmate and close friend. The editor acquired a 49-percent interest in the paper as a gift from his father, E. E. Ellinwood, who was running for the gubernatorial nomination with James S. Douglas's financial backing. William Mathews, an experienced newspaper hand from California, also purchased a 49-percent interest in the *Star* and served as business manager. Lewis Douglas had acquired the remaining 2 percent of the paper so that he could exercise a "judicial" influence on policy. The Prescott *Courier*, which owed Rawhide Jimmy $22,000, supported the Douglas candidacy, as did the Phoenix *Messenger*, Bisbee *Daily Review*, and several smaller papers.[10]

Finally, Douglas benefited from his wife's presence. Attractive and energetic, Peggy Douglas accompanied her husband on the campaign trail. Together they endured scalding temperatures, long hours, incessant travel by automobile over miserable roads, and frequent absences from their children. "We are on the last lap of this trip," Peggy wrote in July, "and I am very anxious to see my babies." They also tolerated rundown tourist courts, which were sometimes so dirty and bedbug-ridden that Peggy sat up all night rather than sleep in the beds.[11]

Of Douglas's primary opponents, Amos Betts had served ten years as chairman of the state corporation commission and was popular and able, but he lacked Douglas's energy, wealth, and speaking ability. Thomas Walton, a fiery Phoenix attorney, was deficient in political experience. Frank J. Duffy was a kindly and capable superior court judge from Santa Cruz County, who lacked statewide exposure and dynamism. H. A. Davis was a three-term state senator from populous Maricopa County, but he could not match Douglas's name, wealth, and political organization. Mulford Windsor from Yuma County was a state senator who favored the compact, but he eventually withdrew owing to a lack of funds.

The announcement of Ellinwood's candidacy in June brought the expected criticisms. Hunt declared that the gubernatorial race "will be notable because of the fact that a multi-millionaire operator of Yavapai and Cochise counties . . . has injected himself into it and is trying to obtain domination and control of the executive and legislative branches of the state of Arizona." He concluded by saying: "Previous experiences have demonstrated that this man does not always interest himself in an enterprise for philanthropic reasons."[12]

Lewis Douglas ignored the governor's barb. Yet being identified with the state's copper interests proved his chief handicap throughout the primary. Amos Betts was quick to portray Douglas as the "young man with the copper collar." On one occasion Betts was traveling by train to make a speech in Bisbee. Peggy Douglas happened to be a fellow passenger, and she overheard Betts telling the brakeman that he was running for Congress against a young man named Douglas who represented the mining interests. Betts went on to say that his rival "was spending millions to get the nomination . . . and would not be a suitable candidate for the ordinary common people."

Angered, Peggy decided to take Betts to task. She walked over to him and said: "I understand that you are a candidate for Congress, that you are Mr. Amos Betts." "Oh yes, my little lady, and I hope that I may have your vote." Peggy: "Well, Mr. Betts, I want you to know that I am Mrs. Lewis Douglas and you are a damn liar."[13]

Douglas worked hard to explode the notion that he was copper-collared. He expressed pride in his family's mining accomplishments, but denied seeking election to obtain special privileges for his father and the mining interests. He predictably pledged, if elected to Congress, to represent all Arizonans, not a particular class. He also distributed a doggerel poem written by a miner identified as "W.S.S." which read:

> It is truthfully said, he is a rich man's son,
> But if that is a handicap, we'd all like to have one,

*He comes from a stock that has made dreams come true
And if he once starts a thing, he will sure see it through.*

The connection with copper doubtless cost him some votes, but the family fortune and intense campaigning offset the loss.[14]

Throughout the campaign the Douglas camp portrayed their candidate as an honest, independent-minded individual with firm convictions. Opening his campaign in Kingman on June 12, he stated: "I am no political trimmer. I am strong for my beliefs and I am going to be frank about them. If you don't like frankness I hope you vote for my opponents."[15]

Douglas was usually forthright, but not always; on certain matters he kept silent for reasons of political expediency. He opposed Prohibition, for example, but dared not speak out against it. When the Women's Christian Temperance Union asked him to explain his "personal position on the question of total abstinence," he ignored the request. He detested the Hunt administration, but in public hid his feelings because, as one supporter reminded him, "there are several Terriers who are stuck on Hunt," and it would be foolhardy to "rail against" him. In one speech Douglas advocated canceling the Allies' World War I debts, but his father cautioned him to cease talking about such a controversial issue. "I think it would be very unwise to mention it to anybody just now . . . and from now until November I am laying off any activity along those lines."[16]

Although he accepted the support of ex-servicemen, Douglas failed to declare himself on veterans' issues. He opposed the soldiers' bonus—a monetary payment to veterans who served in World War I—because of the expense and because, in his view, one should be willing to serve one's country without inducements. He was also cool toward existing plans to increase veterans' benefits. Too many ablebodied men, he reasoned, would obtain payments. Avowing these views publicly would have cost him dearly at the polls.[17]

While Douglas was sometimes cautious on the issues, he was always industrious. At a time when highway transportation was in its infancy, Lew and Peggy traveled in an open flivver across desert and mountain roads, carrying the campaign to virtually every community in the state. Douglas estimated that he drove 21,000 miles and made 278 speeches and to Peggy it seemed that "there wasn't a hamlet of five people that we did not visit." Douglas generally sent an aide ahead to boost his candidacy and to schedule speaking engagements. A few days later the candidate would arrive to make a speech. Peggy's job was to go to the local telephone operator to find out which women in the town were influential. She then called upon them to try to enlist their support. Lew, meanwhile, contacted the principal men in town.[18]

Douglas made Colorado River development the primary issue in the campaign. Forsaking a momentary flirtation with ratification, he boldly stated his views on the compact. The staunchly Republican Jerome *News* commended him for "his courage in stating his stand on the Colorado issues in terms so plain that there can be no possible mistake as to his attitude." The candidate reiterated points he had made as a legislator three years before. Arizona's financial future, he insisted, depended heavily upon the state's right to collect revenue from Colorado River power. He urged Glen Canyon as the best site for a facility to provide power, flood control, and water for irrigation. Hydroelectric dams could also be erected farther down the canyon closer to California markets. All dams should be state or privately owned and pay power taxes. If the right to tax was not secured, he predicted, "those who are now engaged in permanent industry in Arizona will eventually be forced to carry a very large part, if not all, of the burden of taxation in this state."[19]

To prevent the construction of a federal power plant on the river, Douglas called for speedy negotiation of a river-development agreement with the other basin states. Taking a jab at Governor Hunt, he called for "action, not stalling." To harness the river, he declared, "we must quit the dog-in-the-manger attitude. We must remember that Arizona is a part of the United States and not a separate principality." Of course, one of the chief stumbling blocks to an interstate settlement was Douglas's insistence on levying a power royalty. Yet throughout his political career he never surrendered the belief that Arizona was entitled to collect such a tax as a matter of states' rights.[20]

Douglas also worked the stump to boost the senatorial candidacy of Carl Hayden. He expressed to Hayden a dislike for campaigning because an office seeker was required to "enlarge upon his own qualifications." Rather than do that Douglas wrote that he was "talking about you and urging my friends to be active in your behalf." He emphasized, however, that he took that action "not for the purpose of obtaining your support, but because I feel that you must be sent to the Senate rather than Ralph Cameron." Whether intentional or not, that tactic served to identify the campaigns of the two men and doubtless won Douglas votes among Hayden backers.[21]

On the night of the primary, it initially appeared that Douglas supporters had exaggerated the effectiveness of their candidate. When the results of the primary were first reported, it looked as though Douglas would be narrowly defeated. On September 8, newspapers showed Amos Betts in the lead by more than 350 votes. By September 10, however, it was clear that Douglas had won by about 2,000 votes out of approximately 35,000. Hunt outpolled Ellinwood for the gubernatorial nomination.[22]

Victorious in the primary, Douglas was confident of defeating his Republican opponent, Judge Otis J. Baughn, in November. Yet he did not take the election for granted. Baughn was an able campaigner, who supported the policies of the Coolidge administration. He favored Prohibition, prompt payment of war debts by the Allies, high tariffs, noninvolvement in European military and political affairs, and closing "the door of immigration to Europe's undesirables." Baughn's organization characterized Douglas as a young upstart who was unqualified to replace the experienced Hayden.[23]

Douglas made a whirlwind campaign across the state. In several towns Carl Hayden accompanied him, always assuring voters that Douglas was a worthy candidate for the House of Representatives. Douglas aides capitalized on their candidate's youth with the slogan "Elect a Young Man to Congress."[24]

Since most Arizonans were Democrats, Douglas emphasized his allegiance to that party's platform and principles. "I believe in the historical tenets of the Democratic party as enunciated by Thomas Jefferson," he told voters in Phoenix. For Douglas those tenets included equal justice and opportunity, individual freedom, special privileges for none, states' rights, government economy, and laissez faire. Like his father and grandfather, he believed that governmental powers should be used to enforce competition, but should not be employed to foster economic privilege, limit the free flow of goods, or hinder individual initiative. The system of unfettered competition was primarily responsible for making the United States a land of opportunity, liberty, and prosperity. And he repeatedly reminded voters that it was the Democratic party, not the Republican, which championed such a system.[25]

During the campaign Douglas spent sparingly to play down his wealth. A federal law, passed in 1925, limited expenditures to $2,500 and required candidates for Congress to file itemized reports of contributions received and money spent by himself "or by any person for him with his knowledge or consent." Otis Baughn was "making the point that rich men ought not to be sent to Congress," a Douglas advisor noted. "A great point will be made of any appearance of excessive expenditure." He recommended that Douglas restrict his father's spending. "I was not afraid of the expenditures made in your behalf in the primary campaign," he noted, "but in the general election campaign I am deathly afraid of anything which at all approaches a showing of large expense in your behalf." Wisely, as it turned out, Douglas followed the advice.[26]

As the campaign progressed, the tariff question surfaced as the key issue, rather than Colorado River development. Republican congressional hopefuls advocated a high tariff to protect Arizona copper producers. Hayden and Douglas believed the foreign threat was exaggerated and opposed the levy. James S. Douglas also deplored the tariff, claiming that experienced mining men were better able "than any meddling politicians" to know the needs of the industry.[27]

Senator Ralph Cameron hurled spectacular charges against anti-tariff Democratic candidates. Resurrecting a claim first made by George Hunt during the Democratic primary, Cameron described his opponents as servants of a cabal formed to dominate Arizona's state government and congressional delegation. Three groups composed the cabal: Americans owning lands along the Colorado River delta, who opposed any plan to reduce the water flowing to their fields south of the border; California power interests and Arizona businessmen who resisted state efforts to erect power projects on the Colorado; and owners of foreign mines who intended to shut down their expensive American properties and ship in cheaper foreign copper. These three groups, Cameron asserted, had combined to finance the election of those Arizona state and national officials who would support their schemes. The conspirators had supported the unsuccessful candidacy of E. E. Ellinwood for governor in the September primary, and were now using their vast financial resources to secure victories for Douglas and Hayden in the general election.[28]

Douglas vigorously denied the charges. "Must a man of character and integrity, when he runs for public office, be held up as a target for slanderous tongues?" he asked a Wickenburg audience. "I have no use for liars. I have not lied to obtain your votes. If you have not sufficient confidence in me and my character, my ability and my honesty, then vote for someone else."[29]

On October 27 Cameron telegraphed James A. Reed, chairman of the Senate committee investigating expenditures in senatorial primary and general elections.

In his telegram he claimed to have reliable information that eastern copper companies and California power interests had sent $100,000 to Arizona to elect Hayden and Douglas. Those two groups supposedly earlier had donated more than $300,000 to Ellinwood's primary campaign. Cameron demanded that "the special senatorial slush fund committee" immediately convene in Phoenix to correct the situation, so that an honest ballot might be cast in the general election in Arizona. He specifically requested a probe into the campaign funds of Ellinwood, Hayden, and Douglas. Although Democrats branded Cameron's contention as ridiculous, Senator Reed decided to appoint Democratic Senator William H. King of Utah to lead an investigation.[30]

Hearings began in Phoenix on October 30, 1926, and continued in Los Angeles a week later. Hunt, Cameron, Ellinwood, Hayden, Douglas, and scores of other individuals were required to testify. The most colorful witness, however, was James S. Douglas.

Interviewed by a Cameron attorney on October 31, Rawhide Jimmy dismissed the senator's accusations as "bunk":

Q.: Was your contribution to this election bunk?
A.: The work done is bunk. I lost out [in the gubernatorial primary election].
Q.: And your contribution to further the candidacy of Carl Hayden and your son is because of the fear that Ralph Cameron will be elected to the United States Senate?
A.: Because I hate Ralph for a crook.
Q.: And you hate him for his stand on the copper tariff, too?
A.: Sure I do.

Hearing the reference to a "crook," Senator Cameron leaped to his feet protesting: "I resent that word, Mr. Chairman." Douglas: "Take it and stew over it then." Lifting a chair Cameron threatened: "I will take this to you." Shaking his fist toward the senator, Douglas yelled: "You will, like hell." "Gentlemen!" admonished Chairman King, "please restrain yourselves with some dignity."[31]

After this spirited exchange, James Douglas dismissed as "a joke" the existence of a massive fund to elect anti-protectionist candidates. He denied owning copper properties abroad and conferring with copper magnates and utility officials on the Arizona election. He opposed the copper tariff, he testified, because he was a free-trade Democrat and adhered to the state Democratic platform. He concluded: "If Ralph Cameron was a gentleman I would be glad to see him go back to the Senate."

Although James Douglas hotly denied belonging to a conspiracy, he was extremely reluctant to list his contributions to the Democratic candidates. He also initially refused to answer questions about the gubernatorial and House campaigns, contending that they were outside the jurisdiction of the Senate investigation. When asked how much he had donated to candidates in the Democratic primary election, he responded: "I don't know. I've tried to forget." Pressed by Senator King, he guessed that he had contributed about $50,000 to the Ellinwood campaign, probably $15,000 to his son Lewis, and $2,000 to Hayden.[32]

Lewis Douglas and other individuals who possessed specific information on the size and disposition of James Douglas's contributions refused to answer questions that did not bear directly on the senatorial primary and general elections. Senator King threatened to have Lewis Douglas and other reticent witnesses cited for contempt, but with little effect. Lewis Douglas volunteered only information that was a matter of public record. He stated that he spent approximately $1,500 on the general election. He also denied any knowledge of a sizable slush fund designed to influence the primary or general election in Arizona. When pressed for details about expenditures during the primary, specifically those made by the Douglas-for-Congress Club, he refused to answer, claiming that such information was beyond the scope of the inquiry.[33]

Before the hearings ended, Arizona voters had swept Hayden and Douglas into Congress. Hayden defeated Cameron by a vote of 44,591 to 31,845, while Douglas won every county in trouncing Baughn 43,725 to 24,502. The election results indicated that many Arizonans apparently agreed with two Republican newspapers that described Cameron's allegations as a "dud," and the "richest farce Phoenix has enjoyed in many a blue moon." If voters were troubled by the evasiveness of the Douglases during the Senate hearings, they did not show it at the polls.[34]

On November 8 the special Senate committee completed its investigation. After analyzing the testimony of more than sixty witnesses, it found no evidence to support any of Cameron's charges. The hearings did reveal, however, that James Douglas's generous financial donations were critical in launching his son's political career. More than $15,000 was contributed and expended on Lewis's primary campaign, while the nearest competitor, Amos Betts, spent only a little more than $4,000. After he was victorious in the primary contest, the outcome of the general election was assured. Lewis Douglas would now have to prove that he was worthy of the office. The continuing controversy over Colorado River development would soon test his skill in the national Congress as it had in the state legislature.[35]

5

Congress and the Colorado River

THE SEVENTIETH CONGRESS DID NOT CONVENE until December, 1927, more than a year after the election. Lewis Douglas established an office in the Congressional Building, selected clerks to work in his Washington and Phoenix offices, and submitted to House leaders a list of preferred committees. He was assigned to the Committee on Irrigation and Reclamation and the Committee on Public Lands, two of his choices. Douglas also studied the activities of the outgoing Congress, especially in regard to the Swing-Johnson bill. He and Peggy leased for three years a house at 1805 Nineteenth Street, N.W., which she remembered as being "perfectly awful, dark and depressing." Having prepared himself for the task ahead, Douglas returned to Arizona.[1]

Shortly after his arrival, he surprised his constituents by publicly denouncing Governor Hunt. In a newspaper interview on September 12, 1927, he branded Hunt's administration the "most inefficient and deplorable in the history of Arizona." The state government, he asserted, was controlled "by a group of political tricksters seeking to further their own personal aims. . . . I feel ashamed when I look about me and see how this state is controlled." The tax rate, which was higher than in any western commonwealth except Nevada, was being used to perpetuate "the corrupt power" of Hunt's political machine. Finally, he predicted that Hunt's inability to effect a compromise on the Colorado River would lead to the passage of the Swing-Johnson bill in the next session of Congress.[2]

Douglas's interview caused a sensation. The Tucson *Arizona Daily Star*, edited by Ralph Ellinwood, praised him for his "courage and wisdom," but Hunt's followers denounced Douglas as a youthful ingrate. The Phoenix *Arizona Gazette* claimed that he was either "trying to commit political suicide or . . . his election to the post of representative in congress has bewildered him and in trying to get back into the spotlight, to bask in the sunlight of popular acclaim he attempted a dramatic scene." Arizona voters, the paper continued, were holding their noses and saying, "what a bloomer."[3]

As for the governor himself, he confided to his diary: "The outburst of young

Douglas has started something." On September 16 he issued an angry denial of the charges. With the exception of mining, the flow of capital into Arizona's industries had not been impeded, and the problem of mining investments could be attributed "a good deal to the management." How could Douglas accurately appraise the condition of state government when he was frequently absent from Arizona? Denying that his administration was corrupt, Hunt reminded Arizonans of the recent Senate investigation of Douglas's campaign expenditures and suggested that financial improprieties had not been uncovered because important witnesses were not forced to testify. Finally, Hunt censured Douglas for conceding defeat on the Swing-Johnson bill. In the past, Arizona's congressman had been able to ward off passage of the measure, and the newly elected representative should meet with equal success unless he lacked ability.[4]

Although he had disdained Hunt for years, Douglas's denunciation was apparently triggered by the governor's unwillingness to compromise on Colorado River development. Basin states' conferences had failed in January and again in September, 1927. Douglas blamed the lack of success on Hunt's stubbornness. Stories of corruption and misuse of funds in the state highway department, the resignation of four members of the university board of regents due to conflicts with Hunt, and incessant complaints by copper kings against state property assessments also contributed to his decision. Although Douglas asserted that the state's tax policies stunted economic growth, he cited no examples of lost economic opportunities. He charged the administration with inefficiency and corruption, but offered no evidence. When pressed for details, he replied that "the guilty know to whom I refer, and the innocent have nothing to fear. When the time is ripe, then I will be specific." That time never came.[5]

Douglas loathed machine politics and party bossism. Hunt was serving his sixth term as governor and had established a large personal organization, which was powerful, sometimes self-serving, and often contemptuous of opposing viewpoints. Douglas considered the machine inimical to the best interests of the state and clamored for reorganization of the party. His remarks had little effect on party leaders, but they did reveal basic tenets of his political credo: When he felt strongly about an issue or principle, he generally spoke out even if doing so meant damaging his party or his career. True, he waited until after his election to denounce Hunt, but he did not always play it so safe politically. Also, he believed that party allegiance should be subordinated to the welfare of the state and nation. Finally, political freedom and honest government were endangered when one party or set of officeholders remained in power for too long.

A family crisis also drew Lewis Douglas's attention before he departed for Washington. His brother James's unexpected marriage in the summer of 1927 incensed Jimmy and Josalee Douglas. Unable to prevent the union, they tried to have it dissolved. Their actions threatened to cause a permanent estrangement from their younger son, which Lew, acting as conciliator and mediator, tried to prevent.

Blond, blue-eyed, and slim, James Douglas was ten years younger than Lewis. As the baby of the family, he had been pampered and spoiled by Josalee. Unlike Lewis, he was overwhelmed by his domineering father and unable to stand up to his importunities. J.S. called him "the scrub." As an adult he was charming, likable and handsome, but also extravagant and self-indulgent. His carefree lifestyle and lack of application brought constant reproaches from his father. Over the years, Lew also talked to his brother on the necessity of finding steady employment and living within one's means, but the advice usually went unheeded. Periodically, he came to James's financial rescue—even, years later, after his brother dissipated his equal share in their father's estate.

When James did apply himself, he seemed unable to measure up to Lew. He followed his brother to Montclair and Amherst, but his record was undistinguished. After college he drifted until his father sent him to Paris to study French. Provided with a handsome allowance, James lived the life of a playboy. Eventually he entered into a relationship with an English cabaret singer, and when she became pregnant, he married her against the wishes of his parents.

Rawhide Jimmy and Josalee were horrified by their son's actions and rebuked him for disgracing the family. They asked James to terminate the union and return alone to Arizona. If he agreed, "the flapper," as J.S. called her, would be provided with a munificent monetary settlement. James balked, but sought his brother's counsel. Lew advised him to continue the marriage and not allow himself and his wife to be bought off. Any other course of action would be dishonorable.[6]

By refusing to leave his wife and unborn child, James alienated his parents and ended any chance of returning to Arizona to work for his father. Eager to avoid scandal, the father strongly urged James to seek employment abroad. Against Josalee's wishes, he offered to secure his son a mining position in Southern Rhodesia. The job would provide income and "test" the marriage, though privately he expected that the move to Africa would undo the union and bring James home alone. Josalee disagreed, fearing the arrangement would solidify rather than dissolve the marriage.

To Josalee's dismay, Lew advised James to accept his father's proposal and offered to help his brother financially. It would, Lew explained, enable James to maintain his dignity and make a life for himself, his wife, and the unborn child.[7]

Throughout the ordeal, Lew served as his brother's advocate, explaining to his father that James needed sound advice and emotional support. He also reasoned that, for the family to be reconciled, "there must be someone in James's immediate family who will be in a position to act as one who has not been unfriendly. I am the only one who can fit that position. It is the only protection you and Mother can have against the possible permanent estrangement."[8]

The African "test" lasted only three years. Josalee missed her son and pleaded with her husband to allow him to come home. At last J.S. relented. Although James was successful in Rhodesia, he yielded to his mother's wishes and returned to Arizona with his wife and son. The marriage soon ended in divorce. His wife disliked Arizona and resented her mother-in-law's meddling. Two more marriages followed, but they also ended in failure. A fourth marriage endured until James's death in 1980.[9]

Stinging sleet and bone-chilling winds pounded Washington when the Seventieth Congress convened on December 5, 1927. Inside the House chamber the climate was also tempestuous. During the swearing-in ceremony, a prestigious but usually humdrum event, Finis J. Garrett, Democratic floor leader from Tennessee, protested the seating of James N. Beck, a Republican representative from Pennsylvania, on the grounds that Beck had not been a resident of the state at the time he ran for office. The Republican majority, however, argued that an elected representative should not be prohibited from taking the oath of office until evidence of wrongdoing had been presented. That concern for due process prompted Victor Berger, the Wisconsin Socialist who had twice been denied his seat in earlier Congresses, to whisper to Douglas: "The birds have come home to roost." The House decided to seat Beck, pending an investigation. Douglas voted with the majority. The squabble, however, dampened his enthusiasm for the opening session.[10]

Douglas was also unimpressed with many of his colleagues. He surmised that most of them had achieved office by "hand shaking ability." Although his opinion would later change, he initially considered Speaker of the House Nicholas Longworth unfriendly. John Nance Garner of Texas had a poor command of English and struck him as "cryptic—sharp—insolent and rather contemptuous of others when on the floor." Another Texas Democrat, Claude B. Hudspeth, he regarded as "virulent." He was also disillusioned with President Calvin Coolidge. After meeting the Chief Executive and First Lady at a diplomatic reception, he confided to his diary that "Mrs. Coolidge has as much charm as any one I have ever met, but the President is much like a wooden indian [sic] except more tired looking."[11]

Despite his blunt private opinions, Douglas got along well. He pitched on the House baseball team and was a frequent dinner guest. Congenial and unpretentious, he made friends easily on both sides of the aisle, Joseph Martin and A. Piatt "Pine" Andrew of Massachusetts being two Republican associates. Douglas also soon developed a very high regard for Speaker Longworth who was an excellent parliamentarian, and an able and colorful legislator. Douglas recalled that at the close of each session Longworth, an accomplished musician, would serenade colleagues with his violin.[12]

The speaker, like his renowned wife, Alice Roosevelt Longworth, was a person of wit. Douglas remembered that on one occasion Longworth was seated in his chair in the House chamber. "Nick was as bald as a billiard ball. One of his friends came up to speak to him, happened to place his hand upon Nick's head, rubbed it and then made the remark: 'You know that feels just like my wife's bottom.' Nick then put his hand on top of his head, rubbed it caressingly, looked at his friend, and replied: 'By God, you're right.' "[13]

Douglas grew close to several Democrats, including Clifton Woodrum and Henry St. George Tucker of Virginia, John McDuffie of Alabama, and Cordell Hull of Tennessee. He especially admired Hull for his integrity, dignity, and free-trade philosophy. Hull, he recalled later, was "my father confessor and guide." Occasionally, also, Douglas socialized with the other members of Arizona's congressional delegation, Senators Ashurst and Hayden. He liked Ashurst, but had a low opinion of Hayden, viewing him as lacking in convictions and intellectual integrity.

Although Douglas's associates were generally conservative, he was also fond of ideological foes such as the acerbic Fiorello La Guardia of East Harlem. He and La Guardia often clashed on the House floor (the New Yorker once referred to the Arizonan as "an illegitimate son of an immoral alma mater"), but they respected and liked one another. Throughout his lifetime Douglas tried not to allow ideological and political differences to curdle personal relationships.[14]

Although a Democrat, Douglas often voted with the Republicans. Early in his first term he wrote his father: "I find that my sympathies are more Republican than Democratic which is disturbing from the point of view of being a Democrat." Party leaders like Garner found his waywardness disturbing and sometimes reproached him. Despite the reproofs, Douglas generally voted his conscience and won respect as an independent thinker and a man of principle. Indeed, one constituent recalled that Douglas had the "kind of guts the American people just go for." Congressional colleagues also commented on his industry, articulateness, and debating skill. Douglas, Representative Joseph Martin once remarked to journalist Frank McNaughton, was a "very hard-hitting debator; a man had to be to tangle with Cactus Jack Garner and come out unskinned."[15]

Naturally gregarious, the Douglases developed close relationships in the Washington community. In early February, 1928, Douglas wrote his father: "We have met a great many pleasant and interesting people and no longer feel isolated." Lew and Peggy formed a lifelong friendship with F. Trubee and Dorothy Peabody Davison, daughter of a famous headmaster of Groton. Trubee Davison, whose father was a partner in the J. P. Morgan Company, served as assistant secretary of war under Coolidge and Hoover. Dorothy Davison recalled that they first met Douglas at a dinner party they gave soon after his arrival in Washington. She remembered that they were "completely charmed" by the western congressman. During conversation over cocktails he asked them if they had ever tasted tequila. They had never heard of the drink, so the next morning he came by the house with a bottle he had managed to purchase. Like so many of his fellow citizens, Douglas flouted the Prohibition amendment.

The Davisons and Douglases, one newspaper columnist noted, "are seen at most of the smart dinner tables and even more frequently in each other's company." Fond of fun and practical jokes, Douglas and Davison sometimes carried their antics to excess. On one occasion, Davison persuaded Douglas to put him inside a large mail bag and deliver him to the home of his neighbor, the secretary of the British embassy. Once inside the home Davison tried to burst out in surprise, but found the bag locked. He "floundered all over the room, upset chairs, knocked down the fire screen trying to extract himself. Finally, red-faced, and almost suffocated, [he] had to [be extracted by Douglas]." To the embarrassment of the two pranksters, syndicated columnist Drew Pearson reported the escapade to readers nationwide.[16]

Peggy's departure from Washington in early 1928 caused Douglas to curb his social activities. Peg was pregnant with their third child, and extremely ill. As with her previous pregnancies, she went to Hastings to receive rest and medical attention, and remained until October, when she gave birth to a daughter. One of Lewis's friends pressed him to name the child Alberta or Alfreida in honor of Al Smith, the Democratic nominee for President. Lew and Peggy, however, decided to name their daughter Sharman, derived from the maiden surname of Peggy's mother.[17]

. . .

The most controversial issue Douglas tackled during his three terms in Congress was the Colorado River question. In the preceding Congress both House and Senate committees on irrigation and reclamation had reported favorably on the Swing-Johnson bill. Only the filibusters of Arizona Senators Ashurst and Cameron and the testimony of Representative Hayden before the House Rules Committee prevented the measure from coming to a vote before Congress adjourned.

When Congress convened in December, 1927, the Swing-Johnson bill was again introduced. This version called for an appropriation of $125 million—$41.5 million for a flood-control and water-storage dam, 550 feet high, at Black or Boulder Canyon on the Arizona-Nevada border; $31.5 million to establish a power facility; $31 million for an All-American Canal to California; and $21 million for interest charges. The government would regain its investment through the sale of electricity and water to states, municipalities, and private enterprises. Finally, six states, including California, had to ratify the Colorado River Compact before the enterprise could be started.[18]

Douglas believed that preventing passage of the Swing-Johnson bill would require a formidable effort. His task, he felt, might have been easier had his predecessor, Carl Hayden, worked harder to defeat the measure in previous sessions. Hayden was too disposed to compromise, Douglas lamented to his father. "The result is that I have to do in one year what Carl might have been doing during the last five." Douglas also criticized Senator Ashurst, saying he "jumps at his own shadow." Ashurst was more charitable toward Douglas, describing him as a person of "superb intellect" who "superbly led" the opposition forces in the House.[19]

Serving on the Committee on Irrigation and Reclamation, Douglas did his utmost to block the Swing-Johnson bill. In committee hearings he denounced the bill as economically defective and predicted huge cost overruns that would leave the government "with a white elephant on its hands." Despite this gloomy forecast, the committee approved the bill in early February, 1928. Douglas confessed to his father that the fight against the measure was "rather hard work," but "lots of fun."[20]

Douglas next tried to alter the bill. He filed a minority report detailing the measure's economic shortcomings, then introduced a substitute bill, recommending that a smaller flood-control dam be constructed at a site on the Colorado selected by a board of engineers appointed by the President. His efforts failed.[21]

On May 22 the floor discussion of the Swing-Johnson bill began in both houses. Douglas and two representatives from Utah, Elmer O. Leatherwood and Don B. Colton, led the opposition in the House. On the 23rd, Douglas delivered an impassioned blast at the measure, which the *New York Times* reported as having "riveted the attention of the House and held an unusually large number of members on the floor." Speaking for nearly two hours, Douglas based his opposition on five points: the project put the federal government into the power business; it was economically faulty; its engineering design and cost had been inadequately studied; it was unconstitutional; and it granted Mexico too much water.[22]

The main reason for building a high dam with a large storage capacity, Douglas believed, was to generate power for the cities and industries of Southern

California. Such an undertaking should not be a federal responsibility. California interests should develop it. And, if Californians decided to build a power facility on Arizona soil, they should be willing to compensate the state for the privilege.

Giving the Secretary of Interior "complete control" over power and water distribution, he said, would create "a great tyrannical, socialistic bureaucracy. Democracy will be in the throes of death." Predicting the project would run $100 to $200 million more than the estimated $125 million, Douglas believed that the southwestern power market would never be large enough to repay the costs. He also called for additional study of the engineering plans for the dam. The proposed sites were in earthquake zones, and only a few months before a poorly constructed dam in Southern California had crumbled and drowned hundreds of people. He urged the government to employ an independent group of engineers to investigate the project's cost estimates, location, and engineering plans before approving it.

Douglas insisted that the Swing-Johnson bill was unconstitutional. With the exception of Congress's right to improve navigation under the commerce clause of the Constitution, the states held exclusive sovereignty over the waters within their borders. As it was "perfectly ridiculous" to consider the Colorado River navigable, the federal government had no authority to utilize Arizona's water resources without state consent. Furthermore, it was illegal to make the compact effective without Arizona's approval, since that state was included in the Colorado River Basin. If the Swing-Johnson bill was passed, he warned, Arizona would "immediately bring suit to enjoin the construction" of the project.

Douglas concluded his lengthy attack on the bill by claiming that the lower-basin states could immediately use only half of their water allotment. To prevent Mexico from claiming the remainder, he advised House members to delay approval of the bill until the United States concluded a water treaty with Mexico.[23]

Douglas's speech impressed colleagues. John J. O'Connor of New York declared: "Of all the members of this House the gentleman from Arizona knows as much, if not more, about this bill than any man here." And Fiorello La Guardia considered it "as able a presentation" of the Arizona position "as could have been made." La Guardia, who supported the measure, went on to say "that every Member of the House admires the splendid presentation and the thorough study" Douglas gave to the subject. "He has demonstrated without doubt his ability, and, in fact, his keenness, readiness, and ability reminds one of the younger Pitt and he has the added charm and personal attraction of Disraeli."[24]

Sponsors of Swing-Johnson partially met some of Douglas's objections. They agreed to an amendment by Louis C. Cramton of Michigan that called for the Secretary of Interior, with the President's approval, to select five prominent engineers to examine and report on the proposed dam sites, engineering plans, and cost estimates by December 1, 1928.[25]

Douglas was not satisfied. On May 25, the last day of debate, he labeled Swing-Johnson "rotten to the core" and urged that it be recommitted to the Committee on Irrigation and Reclamation. His motion failed by a vote of 219 to 139. A few minutes later, the much-debated measure passed the House by a voice vote.[26]

Douglas was convinced that California's victory was "a pyrrhic one." An independent board of engineers, he predicted, would surely condemn the project, if there was "any honor among thieves." He also was encouraged by the fact that Ashurst and Hayden in the Senate had again carried out a successful filibuster against the measure, which buried it for the session. With the Senate's failure to pass the bill, Douglas believed that it was "very probable that even should it come to a vote in the next session, it will not pass."[27]

Spurning requests to run for governor, Douglas announced for reelection and returned to Arizona during the summer of 1928 to meet with constituents. Although unopposed in the primaries, he nevertheless canvassed the state, explaining his opposition to the Swing-Johnson bill. He rehashed his arguments, expressed confidence that the engineering board would reject plans for Boulder Dam, and asked voters to return him to Washington so he could continue to fight for their interests.[28]

In the fall election Douglas was opposed by Guy Axline, an assistant district attorney from Phoenix. One newspaper, noting Douglas's popularity, characterized Axline's task of unseating the incumbent as "thankless and hopeless." Indeed, Douglas outpolled Axline by nearly 20,000 ballots, winning every county. Other Democrats fared less well. In the presidential contest in Arizona, Herbert Hoover trounced Al Smith by almost 14,000 votes. In the Republican landslide, Governor Hunt was upset by John C. Phillips, and Senator Ashurst, running against Ralph Cameron, won by only 7,000 votes.[29]

In early December, 1928, the engineering board, headed by Major General William L. Sibert, filed its report on the Boulder Canyon project. Construction of a large storage dam at Black Canyon and the All-American Canal was approved. The project would cost $165 million, rather than $125 million, and an additional $11 million would be needed for aqueducts to reclaim lands in the Coachella valley. To restrict Mexico's use of stored water, the board recommended that the United States enter a water-limitation treaty with that country before starting the project. In conclusion, the board expressed doubts that stored water and power sales would pay off the project in fifty years.[30]

Douglas was encouraged by the Sibert report. After reviewing an advance copy, he exclaimed with exaggeration that it sustained "every argument raised against the project." He also momentarily entertained hopes that the odious bill might be shelved when President Coolidge, addressing Congress on December 5, urged legislators to consider favorably a measure to erect a flood-control, irrigation, and water-storage dam on the Colorado, but to leave power development there to private enterprise.[31]

Douglas's hopes were dashed. On December 14 the Senate approved the Swing-Johnson bill by a vote of 64 to 11. The Senate version, however, contained several significant amendments. It appropriated $165 million to construct the works at Black Canyon (Boulder Dam was actually located in Black Canyon). It made the entire sum reimbursable, with energy consumers paying for the dam and power plant and water users in the Imperial and Coachella valleys financing the All-American Canal. It recommended the division of the Colorado's water as follows: 300,000 acre-feet to Nevada; 4.4 million acre-feet to California, plus half of any excess; and 2.8 million acre-feet to Arizona, plus half of any excess. Gila River waters were reserved for Arizona's sole use. The bill also partially satisfied Arizona's demand for a power tax. Arizona and Nevada would each receive $18\frac{3}{4}$

percent of the surplus power revenues, after the government had received its yearly payments during the fifty-year amortization period.

The Senate version of Swing-Johnson carried several conditions before it could go into effect. First, California had to accept the 4.4-million-acre-feet water allocation. Second, the Colorado River Compact had to be ratified. If unanimous approval could not be obtained within six months after the bill became law, then the consent of six states, including California, would make the pact operative. Finally, before work started, the Interior Secretary had to obtain power and water contracts that would finance the project within fifty years.[32]

Despite the Senate amendments, Douglas continued to attack Swing-Johnson. He feared that there would be no surplus profits from the sale of electricity, and sought for Arizona a guaranteed revenue through the taxation of power. On December 18 he rose in the House, branded the proposed legislation a "box of lemons," and declared it violated the principle of states' rights. He vowed never to vote to inject the federal government, "directly or indirectly, into the power business." "No right of the State is more precious than its right to tax," he argued, "and this act is a blow at state sovereignty."[33]

He denounced a similar installation on the Tennessee River at Muscle Shoals, Alabama. Boulder Dam and Muscle Shoals, he argued, were "driving us one step farther toward a complete destruction of the States, toward pushing them into oblivion, toward depriving them of all the rights which should properly be vested in them, and more than this, toward destroying the principle of private initiative . . . which has made this country great among the nations of the world."[34]

Douglas's objections were in vain. The House accepted the Senate bill by a vote of 167 to 122, and the President approved it on December 21, 1928. But Douglas would not give up. Since the votes of six states were required for ratification of the compact, he urged prominent Utahans to reject the pact. If Utah and Arizona both resisted ratification, California would be forced to accept private or state taxable power development. Douglas also asked Arizona's newly elected Governor Phillips to sue the federal government to prevent the project's construction. Such a suit might force California to accept Arizona's demands for guaranteed power royalties. The governor and state attorney general agreed.[35]

Acting on Douglas's request, Arizona filed suit in the United States Supreme Court. Clifton B. Mathews, a prominent attorney from Globe, Arizona, and John Pinkham Gray from Coeur d'Alene, Idaho, were hired to assist State Attorney General K. Berry Peterson in presenting the case. When Gray became ill, the state retained Dean Acheson, of the Washington law firm of Covington, Burling, and Rublee, as his successor. Douglas had met Acheson in the fall of 1926. The Supreme Court case would initiate a friendship between Acheson and Douglas that would endure until the 1950s.[36]

While Arizona's attorneys prepared their case, lower-basin-states commissioners met to hammer out an agreement on the compact. In each case the meetings ended in deadlock over Arizona's demands for a power tax. On March 6, 1929, Utah became the sixth state to ratify the compact. A year later the secretary of interior announced that the power and water contracts had been made, and he asked Congress to appropriate $10.6 million to begin construction. Douglas fought the appropriation on the House floor. The Los Angeles *Times* called him "one of the strongest men in debate in the house and he has every bit of information from the Arizona standpoint at the tip of his tongue. He is the only one in Congress who stands out as a really serious threat against the Boulder Dam appropriation." Douglas's arguments, however, proved fruitless. By June 26, 1930, both houses had approved the appropriation, and work on the project was ready to begin.[37]

When the United States Supreme Court convened in early October, Arizona's attorneys entered a bill of complaint. The complaint, which Douglas described as a "peach," claimed that the Swing-Johnson act was unconstitutional because it deprived Arizona "of its sovereign jurisdiction and control of the water and other natural resources of the state, particularly the Colorado river and its tributaries." In March, 1931, Acheson and Mathews delivered arguments to support the suit. On May 18, however, the Supreme Court dismissed Arizona's bill. The Colorado River was a navigable stream and the federal government had the right to develop the project to improve navigation.[38]

The Supreme Court decision ended Douglas's long and scrappy campaign to block federal power development on the Colorado River. Fundamental to his opposition was his belief that Arizona had a right to benefit economically from the production of power within its borders. Swing-Johnson offered the possibility of revenue but only after amortization payments had been made. Douglas insisted upon private, taxable power development because it would have provided a bountiful and everlasting source of revenue and would have reduced taxes on the state's mining and agricultural enterprises. Although he failed to defeat the bill, his objections improved it. He had exaggerated the engineering hazards and underestimated the demand for hydroelectric power, but his plea for an independent board of engineers to review cost estimates, engineering designs, and economic feasibility of the project proved wise. The editor of the Bisbee *Review* summed up Douglas's role in the Colorado River deliberations: "Representative Douglas put up one of the most stubborn and brainy fights conducted in the lower house in many years in his unsuccessful efforts to block passage of the Swing-Johnson bill. That he lost does not detract in the least from the glory and credit due him." In defeat, Lewis Douglas had established himself as a respected and tough-minded politician.[39]

6

A Remedy for Hard Times

ALTHOUGH LEGISLATIVE AND JUDICIAL BATTLES OVER Boulder Dam continued to consume Douglas's time after his election to a second term in 1928, economic issues springing from the onset of the Great Depression also demanded his attention. In combatting hard times from 1929 to 1933, he displayed an unwillingness to depart from orthodox economic principles, sometimes to the frustration of his party and constituents. And, as had been the case with the Boulder Dam controversy, Douglas proved adept at mastering detail and articulating his position.

Fulfilling a campaign promise, Hoover called the Seventy-first Congress into emergency session in April, 1929, to consider remedies for the decade-long slump in farm prices. He recommended tariff revision and federal financial aid to buy up surpluses. As a result of the President's initiative, Congress passed the Agricultural Marketing Act, which sought to bolster prices by temporarily withholding farm surpluses from the market. It established a Federal Farm Board to make loans to agricultural associations for the purchase of excess commodities. Although he was skeptical about raising prices artificially, Douglas joined a majority of his colleagues to approve the measure.

He resisted, however, Hoover's proposal to reevaluate the tariff. The President hoped that Congress would raise duties on farm imports, thereby giving added protection against foreign competition. Willis C. Hawley of Oregon led the fight for increased tariffs in the House, while Reed Smoot of Utah championed the cause in the Senate. The Hawley-Smoot proposal hiked rates on agricultural products from 38 to 49 percent and increased them on other goods by an average of 3 percent.

Douglas believed the plan would stifle world trade. Foreign governments would respond by raising their tariffs and reducing their consumption of American products. The economy would be severely injured because prosperity depended upon the exportation of surpluses. He reminded colleagues that the United States was a creditor nation and the world's principal gold holder. Customers abroad could not obtain enough dollars to pay off World War I debts and purchase American goods unless they could readily sell their products in the United States. The high duties of the Hawley-Smoot bill, he held, constituted an "embargo" on imports and foreign customers would retaliate. The outcome of "superprotection," he warned, would be a glutted home market and "a general industrial depression."[1]

Despite such predictions of economic calamity, the Hawley-Smoot bill passed the House in late May, 1929. Disgusted by that decision, Douglas attributed the outcome to "political log rolling" and a disregard for "sound reasoning" based upon the facts. In June, 1930, more than a year after the House acted, the Senate passed the bill and Hoover signed it into law against the advice of more than one thousand economists. For the rest of his life, Douglas blamed the Hawley-Smoot tariff as the main cause for the hard times of the 1930s.[2]

In September of 1929 Douglas visited France with his father for a memorable two weeks (Peg was not invited by her crotchety father-in-law). They toured the country in a rented Citroën. At the Château de Condé they hunted rabbits and pheasants with French nobility, using more than fifty beaters to flush the prey. After that excursion, the Douglases drove to Sables d'Olonne in western France to visit Georges Clemenceau at his summer cottage on the Bay of Biscay. The former premier was then eighty-eight years old and in the last year of his life. For more than a decade he and James S. Douglas had been friends.

Lewis Douglas also admired Clemenceau. Late in life he contributed a flattering essay on the premier to a collection of biographies of prominent twentieth-century statesmen. He also began his unpublished memoirs with an account of his meeting with Clemenceau nearly fifty years before. In 1929 Douglas recorded his impressions in a notebook. On the morning the Americans arrived at Sables d'Olonne, "Old man met us. 'How do you like my kingdom' his first remark. Talked for an hour before lunch. . . . He in good spirits. Marvelous eyes. Great sense of humor." At luncheon they reminisced, discussed European politics, and sampled some of Clemenceau's best wines. Afterward the visitors strolled around the grounds with their host, stopping for a beer in a "quiet vine covered court." Clemenceau offered some advice. He counseled Lewis to remain true to his convictions and to keep a sense of humor. Then, turning to the elder Douglas, he remarked: "Be kind to your other boy—let him come home."

For his part, Clemenceau would later write a friend: "The Douglases father and son spent the day yesterday. . . . (The son comes from as fine a mold as the father.) I really took great pleasure in chatting with them."[3]

From the serenity of the French countryside, the Douglases returned to the tumult of New York. Many New Yorkers were uneasy over the stock market, and their concern turned to panic when prices plunged drastically in late October. The resulting crash precipitated the Great Depression which endured for more than a decade. Factories were shut down, banks were closed, farms were abandoned, and millions of workers were dismissed. Hunger, poverty, and fear engulfed the land. Soup kitchens, breadlines, fruit vendors, and looks of despair were common sights. As Lewis Douglas remembered it: "The human suffering was intense, the atmosphere, charged with tremendous tension, cannot be described by words."[4]

From a financial standpoint, Douglas himself was not seriously affected by the depression. His father continued to supplement his congressional salary of $10,000 with an annual allowance of $25,000. He added Robert Stroud, a young University of Arizona Law School graduate, to his congressional staff. He retained his stock in the Grand Central Mining Company and the Bank of Bisbee. He kept his homes in Phoenix and Jerome and maintained his interest in the citrus ranch operated by Frank Brophy. Moreover, in February, 1930, his father gave him $40,000 to buy a new four-story brick home in Georgetown.

Compared to most Americans, the Douglases lived splendidly. In the fall of 1930 Peg traveled to Europe with her mother. Lew took occasional fishing trips with friends, dressed in imported British clothes, and purchased only the best sporting equipment. The Douglases employed a cook and a nanny in their Georgetown home and hired men to care for their homes in Arizona. Peggy tried to persuade Lew to take on a valet, but he laughed off the suggestion. He also rejected the idea of a chauffeur and traded in his large Chevrolet sedan for a more economical and less ostentatious open Ford. He pedaled a bicycle to work, but that was more for exercise than economy. Basically, Lew and Peggy lived in accordance with their station—traveling, entertaining, seldom scrimping. They could not keep up with wealthier friends like the Trubee Davisons, but did not lag far behind.[5]

When the regular session of the Seventy-first Congress convened in early December, 1929, the legislature embarked upon a modest recovery program. To stimulate investment and consumer purchases, it supported Hoover's call for a 1 percent reduction in income taxes. Douglas sided with the majority. He also welcomed the President's call for the conservation of natural resources. Specifically, Hoover sought congressional approval to appoint an independent commission to study ways of conserving water, forests, grazing lands, oil, coal, and other minerals on more than 190 million acres of public domain. The majority of Democrats, following the lead of floor leader John Nance Garner, opposed such an undertaking as too vast and time-consuming.

Douglas defended the proposal, but Garner scolded him for being unfaithful to the party. Stung by the rebuke and still smarting over the floor leader's support for Boulder Dam, Douglas accused Garner of playing politics with an important issue. He told the Texan that he would never blindly follow his party. Asserting his independence, he declared that as a legislator his first priority would always be the nation, then Arizona, and then his party. He concluded by saying, "If by following such a course I am in conflict with my party, then I reserve to myself the right to hold that my party is wrong." His remarks won applause, but the conservation proposal was rejected.[6]

Of more concern to Douglas in 1930 was the potential destruction of one of Arizona's leading farm products, long-staple cotton. Valuable lands in the Salt River Valley and on the Pima Indian Reservation were being ravaged by the pink bollworm. Unless the worm could be stopped from spreading, experts predicted the loss of the entire cotton crop. To eradicate the pest, specialists asked farmers to establish non-cotton zones. Farmers, however, were reluctant to cease planting without compensation. Douglas sought federal relief. Citing several precedents, he requested a compensation fund of $2.5 million, half of which would be repaid by Arizona cotton growers. Congress agreed, and the crop was saved.[7]

Arizonans also felt troubled by Mexican immigrants who competed with them for jobs, especially in mining. Labor organizations asked Douglas to support legislation introduced by Representative John C. Box of Texas, calling for sharp reductions in the number of aliens entering the United States from the western hemisphere. The bill was directed primarily against Mexicans.

Although Douglas sympathized with efforts to safeguard America "against an influx of low class immigrants," he opposed the bill, arguing it would hurt southwestern farm owners and mine operators who employed Mexican labor. He also pointed out that drastic restrictions would damage diplomatic relations with Mexico. More to the point, he opposed the bill as a subtle attempt to abolish the open shop because Mexican workers were less inclined to join labor unions than English-speaking workers. The Box bill failed to pass.[8]

Some Arizonans considered Prohibition a major cause of hard times and urged Douglas to come out against it. Repeal, they reasoned, would increase tax revenues and create jobs. Douglas sympathized with their views, but was reluctant to broadcast his opinion publicly because "it would be borrowing trouble." Privately, however, he maintained that the "noble experiment" was unenforceable, economically injurious, and potentially dangerous to the public's health. Intimidated by the Anti-Saloon League, Congress, he claimed, was "operating under the terms of an entente cordiale with the purveyors not only of illicit but also deadly intoxicants." He also criticized Hoover for refusing "to exercise any leadership" on the issue. Lacking in "Intestinal Stamina" and "qualities of character," the President, he complained, neither urged repeal nor demanded additional legislation to enforce the Prohibition amendment.

But if Hoover failed to provide leadership, so did Douglas. He wanted to avoid being tagged either a wet or a dry, and when pressed he adopted a "moist" position. The abolition of the saloon, he maintained, was a positive result of Prohibition. But the "use of intoxicants is a habit which bears no relationship to the governmental functions of federal authority." For Douglas the fundamental issue of states' rights was at stake. The Eighteenth Amendment should be revised, he argued, to permit each state to determine its own policy on the sale of alcoholic beverages. Interestingly, he did not extend the argument to say that the consumption of alcohol was a matter of personal conscience. When he came out publicly for legalized beer in 1932, he did so on the grounds that jobs would be created and tax revenues would be gained to help balance the budget. Reviving the beer industry would also "give us the injection required to lift us out of our present industrial lethargy."[9]

The death of Douglas's friend Ralph Ellinwood, the thirty-seven-year-old editor of the Tucson *Arizona Daily Star*, forced him to cut short his reelection campaign a few days before the primary. Douglas's 2 percent interest in the paper compelled him to make a decision about the *Star*'s future editor. After Ellinwood's death two individuals vied for the editorship: the widow, Claire Ellinwood, who inherited

49 percent of the stock, and William Mathews, the business manager, who held the remaining 49 percent. To the lasting disappointment of Claire Ellinwood, Douglas selected Mathews to lead the paper because he was more experienced and held conservative views. He and Mathews became friends and rarely disagreed on policy. Mathews served as editor of the *Star* for nearly thirty years. Affection for Lew and Peggy outweighed Mrs. Ellinwood's chagrin over the decision, and they too remained close friends.[10]

Having won the uncontested primary, Douglas expected a strong challenge from the Republicans in the general election, but it did not materialize. Unopposed, the incumbent nevertheless campaigned vigorously. Called by the Coolidge *News* "perhaps the most popular man that Arizona has ever sent to Congress," Douglas received 52,343 votes in the general election. Only two office seekers, the state attorney general and state auditor, obtained more votes. George Hunt, benefiting from the unpopularity of Republicans due to the depression, won his seventh term by narrowly defeating the incumbent governor, John Phillips.[11]

Democrats nationwide were swept into office in 1930. When the first session of the Seventy-second Congress convened in December, 1931, Democrats constituted a majority in the House of Representatives for the first time since 1919. Douglas expressed confidence that his party would "lead the nation out of a morass of depression and chaotic conditions into which it has fallen during Republican rule." But, he reasoned, recovery would take time. He asked constituents to be patient and to maintain their faith in capitalism and individual initiative. After all, he said, the present depression was not as bad as some previous ones. Sounding like Hoover, he urged the impoverished to look to their local communities for assistance. To rely on the federal government for help, he warned, "is to sacrifice that modicum of freedom and liberty which we now possess."[12]

Arizonans were especially hard-pressed by 1931. Frank Brophy wrote that "the financial situation in our counties and state is deplorable." "Copper," Rawhide Jimmy Douglas succinctly put it, was "on the bum." Red metal prices plummeted from 18 cents per pound in April to 7½ cents in September. Production fell off by 30 percent over the previous year. Some mines shut down permanently. Others, like the UVX in Jerome, closed temporarily. Scores of copper camps faced the possibility of becoming ghost towns. Open mines operated at about one-third of their capacity and workers took a pay cut averaging 9.1 percent. By 1932 the number of men employed in copper-related industries had plunged from 21,000 to 3,000. Farm production was off by two-thirds, nearly half of the state's banks had collapsed, and 78,000 Arizonans required relief.[13]

Arizona producers generally blamed the depressed state of the copper industry on the absence of a protective tariff. "All ferrous metals in this country are protected except copper," Lewis's uncle, Walter Douglas, pointed out. Competitors in Canada, Africa, and South America, Arizonans complained, were capturing much of the foreign and domestic market by underselling Americans. They asked their representatives in Congress to provide relief by seeking an import duty.

This demand for protection against foreign competition posed a dilemma for Douglas. Philosophically, he opposed tariffs. Moreover, in 1930 he had denounced Hawley-Smoot and had rejected efforts to add copper to the list of dutiable imports. He believed that American producers had encouraged foreign production by demanding artificially high prices for copper. As prices sagged and as more and more copper camps became idle, Douglas reassessed his position. "When I saw many of my old friends who had worked with me underground really destitute," he recalled later, "it caused me to have a strong feeling for humanity and a great sympathy for those who were suffering." Douglas was also a realist who understood the political ramifications of continued resistance to a copper tariff. Friends reminded him that his opponents would use his free-trade position to "dynamite" him.

Yielding to public pressure and political reality, Douglas reluctantly came out for a "reasonable tariff on copper." He sacrificed principle, something he rarely did. But he continued to believe that domestic producers in part could not compete because they were greedy and inefficient. "When I consider the extraordinary stupidity of the great copper magnates, I sometimes wonder if it is worthwhile trying to pull the chestnuts out of the fire for them," he wrote Frank Brophy. Yet failure to act would provoke such hardship that violence and perhaps revolution would result. He concluded that there was "nothing to do but to do everything that one can for the magnates, for the state and people whose existence depends upon the copper industry." With his customary energy and penchant for hard work, Douglas spent months working with various groups in the state, including "George the VII Hunt," preparing a case for a copper tariff.[14]

In January, 1932, a month after the Seventy-second Congress convened, Douglas introduced a special joint resolution calling for a duty of 4½ cents per pound on copper imports. Failing to gain passage of the joint resolution, he attached a copper-tariff amendment to the revenue bill of 1932. Appearing before the House Ways and Means Committee and the Senate Finance Committee, Douglas pleaded eloquently for protection. Overseas operators, he explained, produced the metal more cheaply than American developers because of the higher copper content of the ore, lower labor costs, and less burdensome taxes. Foreign competition "has demoralized and is annihilating the copper industry in the United States, is bringing poverty and suffering to thousands of American families, is converting prosperous modern communities into desolate ones, is developing hysteria almost to the extent of open rebellion, and is bankrupting municipalities, counties, and at least one great state." Douglas's efforts and the testimony of representatives from Montana and Michigan brought results. On June 6, 1932, both houses agreed to include in the revenue bill a duty on copper of four cents per pound.[15]

The Bisbee *Sunday Review* credited Douglas with "saving our economic life." Cleve W. Van Dyke, chairman of the Arizona Copper Tariff Commission, acknowledged that the congressman "did a great and noble work for his state . . . and is entitled to a full measure of credit for the successful termination of the copper tariff campaign." Douglas had won a great victory, but he did not relish it. He had turned his back on his convictions, something that honorable men like his grandfather and Clemenceau had admonished him never to do. The betrayal benefited his state and his political career, but he always lamented the decision, calling it one of his major mistakes as a congressman.[16]

While hoping that the tariff would stimulate the Arizona economy, Douglas believed that national recovery depended upon lowering tariffs, reducing Allied war debts, securing bank deposits, and balancing the budget. As the mutual exchange of goods increased, Douglas argued, so did prices, production, purchases, and jobs. To enhance trade, he advocated a reduction in the Hawley-Smoot rates while simultaneously urging a tax on copper imports. He justified the apparent inconsistency by explaining that the latter was a low tariff, which merely enabled Americans to compete, while the former constituted an embargo, which excluded imports and brought retaliation. In January, 1932, he enthusiastically supported a resolution that provided for a bipartisan tariff-making commission, reciprocal trade agreements, and an international conference to discuss tariff reduction. The resolution passed both houses, but Hoover vetoed it.

Reducing Allied war debts and German reparations was another way to revive trade, Douglas contended. Owing to heavy indebtedness, European nations found it difficult to buy goods from the United States. To prevent further financial strain caused by the flight of gold to buy American products, they raised their tariffs to very high levels. When Hoover proposed a one-year moratorium on debt payments in June, 1931, Douglas, like the majority of his colleagues, approved the postponement. His father pressed him to endorse outright cancellation, but he refused on the grounds that it "would mean the political demise" of the legislator who made such a recommendation.[17]

Alarmed by two thousand bank failures in 1931, Douglas supported the establishment of the Reconstruction Finance Corporation. The RFC was authorized to loan $2 billion to floundering banks, railroads, credit associations, and insurance houses. Although he was reluctant to extend public aid to inefficient businesses, Douglas voted for the measure because it would "tend to restore confidence" and curb the number of business failures.[18]

Throughout the depression decade, Lewis Douglas believed that a balanced federal budget was the key to business recovery. In fiscal year 1931 the United States deficit approximated $900 million and it was more than twice that figure the following year. Mindful of the German experience in the 1920s, he argued that massive public indebtedness could bring about an uncontrolled inflation, which, in turn, could cause widespread human suffering and the weakening of democratic institutions. In short, "failure to balance the budget may bring our entire civilization down in ruins." With so much at stake, Douglas believed that a legislator could hardly crusade for a more worthy cause than a balanced budget.

Hoover also feared the consequences of deficit spending. In December, 1931 he asked Congress to balance the budget by enacting additional taxes, pruning appropriations, and reorganizing government agencies. Douglas wholeheartedly supported those recommendations. He despaired, however, when his colleagues moved slowly. "The budget situation remains unchanged—nothing is being done and it appears that nothing will be done," he wrote his father in January, 1932.[19]

A month later, Douglas took to the floor to spur his colleagues to action. If lawmakers continued to spend beyond the government's means, he warned, the nation's credit might collapse, thus "plunging the whole world into darkness because today the United States is the creditor nation of the world." He urged his peers to study each appropriation measure carefully and unselfishly. "We must have the courage," he stated, "to vote against appropriations which might benefit our own districts; to have the courage to go back and face a political fight, but to play our part here honorably."[20]

Douglas tried to do his part. Newly appointed to the Appropriations Committee, he worked "to chop off federal appropriations with the largest, sharpest meat ax" available. In an Interior Department appropriations bill he tried to fix the price of cars purchased for use by that department at a maximum of $750. When representatives from auto-making districts protested that the ceiling was so low it prohibited the purchase of sedans, Douglas responded: "I do not travel in a closed car. I do not see any reason why anybody else should demand that he should be given a closed car." The recommendation failed.[21]

Douglas's zeal for economy troubled some representatives, especially Fiorello La Guardia, who expressed the suspicion that his colleague was attempting to emasculate government agencies "which may step on one's toes." Douglas vehemently denied La Guardia's charges. He pointed out that the government was spending beyond its means and that federal bureaucracy had become bloated, with more than 68,000 employees hired in the last seven years. Privately he assailed lawmakers who resisted large-scale spending cuts as demagogues who were not "sufficiently patriotic to forget their own political welfare." The overwhelming majority of congressmen, he wrote a voter, were unwilling to "look beyond their own districts and their own political future."[22]

Convinced that a balanced budget would revive investment and safeguard democracy, Douglas in February, 1932, introduced a resolution calling for the creation of a special bipartisan committee to investigate ways of reducing federal expenditures and reorganizing government bureaus. The House approved the Douglas resolution by a vote of 215 to 22. Speaker of the House Garner chose John McDuffie of Alabama to head the seven-man bipartisan committee. Douglas was one of four Democrats appointed to the committee.[23]

While the Economy Committee worked on retrenchment, other lawmakers sought to help balance the budget by increasing revenues. In March, 1932, Charles R. Crisp, chairman of the House Ways and Means Committee, introduced a revenue bill designed to raise $1 billion. Over half of the sum was to come from a general sales tax. Douglas actively endorsed the measure, as did the administration and House Democratic leaders. It was assailed, however, by a group of progressive legislators, led by La Guardia. They contended that the levy would diminish mass purchasing power and unjustly burden the poor. Their arguments won over Democratic leaders like Garner, and the sales tax was defeated. Progressives were unsuccessful, however, in their attempt to gain needed revenue through the reimposition of the wartime surtax on all incomes over $100,000. Douglas helped defeat that proposal by arguing that soaking the rich discouraged capital investment. Eventually passed in June, 1932, the revenue bill provided the government with $1 billion by increasing income, corporate, import, gift, and luxury taxes.[24]

Discouraged by the defeat of the sales tax, Douglas still had hopes for the Economy Committee. That body, after two months of study, including meetings with President Hoover, recommended legislation reducing federal spending by more than $250 million. Once again, however, Douglas's colleagues let him down. The House, he complained to his father, "tore the bill to shreds."

The Economy or Omnibus Bill, as the legislation was called, proposed an 11 percent slash in federal salaries, the elimination of Saturday half-workdays, the consolidation of the War and Navy departments, and the reduction of veterans' benefits. The latter item, championed by Douglas, was the most controversial. Despite the fact that approximately 20 percent of Arizona's electorate were ex-servicemen, he believed that veterans' payments had to be reduced significantly in order to balance the budget. "I think what I am doing may defeat me," he wrote his father. "But if it does it will be worth it."[25]

To his colleagues in the House Douglas pointed out that over $1.1 billion yearly was expended on veterans, or 25 cents out of each federal tax dollar. Millions of dollars, he emphasized, were going to veterans who never served overseas and whose injuries were not service related. Congress, he insisted, must eliminate subsidies to nondeserving veterans "without depriving the real war casualty of any benefits to which he may be entitled."

Title IX of the Economy Bill contained ten sections to save the government $48 million in veterans' appropriations. The heart of the measure was section 901, which sought to eliminate compensation for those veterans whose partial disabilities were received outside a combat zone and whose incomes exceeded $1,500 if single, and $3,500 plus $400 for each dependent, if married. Douglas estimated that that provision alone would disqualify 22,000 "gold brikers [sic]."

His recommendations met stiff opposition. Edith Rogers of Massachusetts considered them "a most cruel way of economizing" and John C. Schafer of Wisconsin portrayed Douglas as an "economy god" who "must have blood, and today the disabled veterans of the Nation's wars are to be thrown upon the altar as a sacrifice." It was in this hostile atmosphere that Douglas took to the floor to defend cuts in veterans' benefits.[26]

His speech of May 3, 1932, was one of his most eloquent and courageous. He pleaded with his colleagues to examine the measure "tolerantly, without prejudice—honestly and courageously," keeping in mind that the budget needed to be balanced and that the proposal would not deprive deserving ex-soldiers of any benefits. "This is no time to consider our own petty political careers," he declared. "On the contrary, this is a time when you and I are faced with a crisis, faced with an emergency, when you and I are under the guns. It is for us to decide whether we have the courage to stand under fire." Attacking pressure groups almost as vehemently as economic extravagance, he urged his peers not to be intimidated by the veterans' lobby, otherwise democracy might "crumble into dust."

At the conclusion of Douglas's remarks, his colleagues gave him a long and thunderous standing ovation. When the measure came to a vote, however, it was rejected 211 to 119. "In rising and cheering Mr. Douglas the House was paying tribute to honesty and courage," *New York Times* columnist Arthur Krock wrote. "In voting against him it was recording its belief that these attributes in a politician do not pay. By its vote it was expressing a cynical conviction that the organized minorities have the power to punish and reward at the polls." By the time the House finished amending the Economy Bill, it had reduced the proposed savings from $250 to about $40 million.

Although the veterans' title was defeated, Douglas's speech won national attention. Three of the country's foremost newspaper columnists—Arthur Krock, Frank Kent, and Walter Lippmann—lauded his plea for economy. Douglas's arguments also impressed E. Claude Babcock, the national commander of the Disabled American Veterans of the World War. After listening to his address from the House gallery, Babcock wrote: "I am not authorized by this organization to comment favorably on the fundamental propositions presented by you, but I feel that I owe it to a courageous soldier to tell you of my personal admiration for your splendid presentation of your honest convictions."[27]

Not surprisingly, Douglas's orthodox economic views disturbed many of his constituents. One citizen scored him for downplaying the fact that there was "something wrong with our system of distributing wealth." The American people, he wrote, could not "go on indefinitely" under an economic structure that permitted extreme wealth amidst stark poverty. Douglas, he continued, "seems to be aligned with the Mellons, Morgans, Insulls, Fords and Hoovers more than he does with the vast majority composing the wage earners." Another constituent, an ex-soldier, wrote the editor of a Phoenix newspaper that Douglas "never knew the need of a job or the need of money. His children never cried out for bread and perhaps never will. He has always associated with millions and millionaires and therefore does not know nor appreciate the plight of the common and working people, nor can he have any sympathy for the underdog."[28]

Those assessments carried some truth. Douglas's wealth did shield him from economic deprivation. Moreover, his unyielding adherence to retrenchment, a balanced budget, and limited government caused him to resist federal programs designed to alleviate unemployment and human misery. Ironically, in the midst of deflation, Douglas's greatest fear was runaway inflation, caused by huge budget deficits, which would ruin the middle class and threaten the democratic form of government.

He regarded the high rate of unemployment as a "ghastly thing" which must be remedied. "Society owes no man a living," he asserted, "but society does owe everyone the right to make a living." He recommended the establishment, sometime in the near future, of an unemployment insurance fund to relieve distress. He offered few other remedies for the existing crisis.[29]

Douglas was reluctant to back large-scale public works because they constituted "excessive" federal assistance. When Garner proposed a $2.1 billion federal relief measure in May, 1932, Douglas denounced it as "pork of the most outrageous character." He particularly disliked the public-works provision, pointing out that it called for the construction of buildings in Arizona towns that had been defunct for years. Moreover, spending such vast sums of money on public works, he argued, would increase the deficit, impair the country's credit, and perhaps throw it off the gold standard and "inaugurate an era of greenbacks."

Recognizing that some type of federal relief aid was necessary, Douglas supported a compromise bill introduced by Senator Robert Wagner in July. The Emergency Relief and Construction Act enabled the RFC to loan financially distressed states $300 million for relief and $1.5 billion for income-yielding public construction projects, and it provided $322 million for emergency public-works facilities. These proposals appealed to conservatives like Douglas because state, local, and private agencies rather than the federal government would administer to the needy, because the public works were "self-liquidating" and would not theoretically unbalance the budget, and because the loans would be repaid.[30]

Douglas's views toward federal relief were perhaps most dramatically revealed in his opposition to the controversial veterans' bonus. In 1924 Congress passed the Adjusted Service Compensation Act, which granted each World War I veteran a monetary bonus based on the length of his military service. The bonus, plus 4 percent interest compounded yearly, was redeemable in 1945.

With the onset of the depression, veterans clamored for immediate payment of $3.5 billion. Douglas opposed the demand because it was too costly and worked against the best interests of the veterans. By redeeming the certificates immediately, he pointed out, veterans were surrendering about fifteen years of interest payments. They were also discarding "the insurance which they and their families now have against a day in the future when through disability, sickness, or some other cause, their earning capacity may be *permanently* lower than it is now."[31]

Arizona veterans denounced their congressman's position. They claimed that they needed the cash now and were willing to forgo future benefits in favor of prompt payment. One exercised former serviceman wrote Douglas: "If you accidently walk under a tree and [a] Buzzard Pukes on you—there is no reason to get sore." Congress failed to provide for the immediate payment of the bonus. It did, however, pass a bill over Hoover's veto enabling jobless veterans to obtain loans worth 50 percent of the face value of their bonus. Douglas supported that bill; but it did not satisfy veterans.[32]

In May, 1932, Representative Wright Patman of Texas introduced another resolution authorizing full payment of the bonus. Under the Patman plan the money was to be paid at the 1945 face value through the issuance of new paper currency. Douglas objected to the measure because it allowed "the outright payment to a special group of a gratuity" of over $2 billion in greenback currency. "If the vets want to destroy the country they fought to save," he declared, "let them get another congressman from Arizona."[33]

While the Patman bill was being considered by the House Rules Committee, thousands of veterans converged on Washington to lobby for its passage. By mid-June the Bonus Expeditionary Force totaled about 15,000. Douglas recalled that, when the soldiers "marched down Pennsylvania Avenue, it was one of the most impressive sights" he ever witnessed. The army, he remembered, "marched in perfect order, perfect discipline. These were the same men who 14 years ago marched forward in behalf of their country." The scene, he declared, "made one's heart rise in one's mouth and aroused a full measure of sympathy and emotion." Still, he warned that "grave questions" should never "be decided on emotions." On June 15 the Patman bill passed the House by a margin of 211 to 176. Douglas voted with the minority. Two days later, however, the Senate rejected the measure by a sizable margin.[34]

Despite the defeat of the bonus, many veterans remained in Washington to advertise their grievances. Anxious to remove the demonstrators from the nation's capital, the Washington police department urged the bonus-seekers to return to their homes. Relations between the veterans and police became strained, and on July 28 a skirmish erupted in which two ex-soldiers were killed. Hoover ordered federal troops, under the command of General Douglas MacArthur, to pacify the agitated area. MacArthur moved against the veterans' encampment at Anacostia Flats with tanks, tear gas, and bayonet-brandishing infantrymen. The living quarters of the bonus-marchers were destroyed and Washington was cleared of the veterans' presence.

Douglas denounced Hoover's use of force. He shared, however, the President's objections to the bonus. Like Hoover, he believed that the bonus-seekers were led by radicals. He remembered one leader saying to his followers: "Come the Revolution, you will be smoking black cigars and eating strawberries in the wintertime."[35]

Although Douglas often criticized Hoover's handling of the depression, his views closely coincided with the President's. He shared Hoover's belief that European economic dislocations and financial problems resulting from World War I contributed to the economic collapse. He also supported the view that American recovery depended upon world recovery. He held the Hawley-Smoot tariff largely responsible for the persistence and severity of the depression, and also chided the President for amassing large budget deficits.

Yet the similarities far exceeded the differences. Hoover believed that business confidence and capital investment depended upon a balanced budget, sound money, and stable financial institutions; so did Douglas. Hoover contended that mass buying power and employment would increase once business initiative and investment were restored; Douglas agreed. Both men inveighed against budget deficits and excessive spending, while neither favored soak-the-rich tax schemes that would help make revenues cover expenditures. Hoover and Douglas both acknowledged that the government had to play a positive role in restoring prosperity and relieving distress, yet both wanted that role to be minimal. Finally, both sympathized with the jobless and needy, yet neither was willing to accept unorthodox recovery and relief measures, which might do more harm than good.

Douglas once wrote his father: "However much I dislike and entertain some distrust of H.H., he is playing a more honorable role than is our 'goat herder' from Texas." And in another moment of despondency he wrote: "My feeling is that not only has the Democratic Party done the country harm, but it has also confirmed a generally accepted opinion that in it responsibility cannot be imposed."[36]

Despite his criticism of Garner and his party, Douglas realized that the Democrats would achieve gains at the polls in 1932. He was less confident about his own chances. His crusade for economy hurt him politically, as he knew it would. In January, 1932, the *Arizona Fax* referred to him as "a dud" politically, and in July a group of Arizona veterans pronounced him "unworthy of our further support" in the approaching primary and general election.[37]

Some friends assured Douglas that the loss of the veterans' vote would not defeat him so long as "you continue to be your own natural self, stand your ground, and explain your stand in forceful terms." Others were less sanguine. One advisor, who months earlier had dismissed the possibility of a serious challenge, warned him that summer to expect a difficult race—with good reason, the election of 1932 proved to be the toughest of Douglas's career. It was also his last.[38]

PART THREE
Budget Director

7

Toward the New Deal

BEFORE RETURNING TO ARIZONA TO CAMPAIGN for reelection, Lewis Douglas needed a momentary escape from the grind and frustration of politics. Exhausted by his work on the Economy Committee, he was ordered by his physician to take a complete rest. As he did so often, Douglas relaxed with rod and reel. In June he and John McCloy (husband of Peggy's sister Ellen) spent a week fly fishing for salmon on the St. John River in New Brunswick. Rejuvenated by that expedition, he was ready to fight for another term in office.[1]

On his way West, Douglas stopped in Chicago to attend the Democratic National Convention. He believed that his party would surely capture the presidency so long as it chose "an outstanding man of intelligence and courage," and did "not go off on some sort of questionable tangent." He had mixed feelings about the result. He was deeply disappointed with the Democratic standard-bearers, Governor Franklin D. Roosevelt and Speaker John Nance Garner. Unimpressed with Roosevelt's record as governor, Douglas agreed with columnist Walter Lippmann, who portrayed FDR as a candidate without firm principles, "a pleasant man who, without any important qualifications for office, would very much like to be President." Indeed, Douglas sent copies of Lippmann's unflattering column to the head of the Arizona delegation.

Douglas preferred Newton D. Baker, secretary of war under Woodrow Wilson, or Governor Albert C. Ritchie of Maryland. When the delegates selected Roosevelt, Douglas confided to a friend that "we made a mistake." For the second spot, almost anyone would have been more acceptable to Douglas than Garner. The Speaker, he wrote privately, was "a cheap, yellow political trixster with neither intelligence, mental honesty or courage—a man completely and absolutely unqualified to hold a position of high public responsibility."[2]

The party platform, unlike the nominees, met with Douglas's enthusiastic approval. Stressing states' rights, international cooperation, reciprocal trade, federal retrenchment, and a balanced budget, the platform, Douglas gushed, was "the greatest human document ever framed by a political party." For that reason, he decided to give unstinting support to the two men chosen to execute its provisions. He sent a congratulatory note to FDR and asked to visit the governor in Albany. In a belated reply, Roosevelt wired Douglas that he would be "delighted" to visit with him. Unfortunately, the governor's telegram reached Douglas after he had left for Arizona.[3]

Establishing campaign headquarters in centrally located Jerome, Douglas announced for renomination in late July, 1932. He was running, he reminded voters, to reduce government spending and to lower taxes. Two candidates challenged him in the September primary: Marlin T. Phelps, a conservative judge from Maricopa County, and William Coxon, secretary of the Arizona Corporation Commission and a former state assemblyman from Willcox. Phelps campaigned for decentralized government (he opposed the Reconstruction Finance Corporation), rigid enforcement of national Prohibition, reduced immigration, full repayment of intergovernmental debts, a higher copper tariff, and the veterans' bonus.[4]

"Flamo" Coxon was a young, auburn-haired pepperpot whose views closely resembled those of Phelps. Idealistic, argumentative, and passionate, he appealed mainly to labor groups and veterans for support. "I am fighting my heart out for the common people of this country," he declared. Coxon assailed Douglas and his record without restraint. The incumbent, he charged, was an elitist who was out of step with the wants and needs of the common people. His concern for a balanced budget was "a lot of baloney." Coxon had a similar opinion of Douglas's objections to going off the gold standard and inflating the currency. "I am not so much concerned about remaining on the gold standard as I am on getting off this damned hunger standard," boomed Coxon.

The challenger also denounced Douglas as a politician who had "betrayed his party." He had abandoned Governor Hunt in 1930 and had repeatedly supported Hoover and Republicans on economic issues. Coxon asked voters to consider whether they wanted as their representative a Republican-leaning millionaire's son or a solid Democrat who as the father of seven children knew the meaning of unemployment and hardship: "I have seen that dear, grey-haired mother of mine offer the impoverished nourishment of her breasts to the lips of a hungry babe." Coxon vowed to oppose the Douglas money "until Hades freezes over and then spank them for skating on the ice." Not surprisingly, the challenger's hard-hitting, emotional campaign gained statewide attention and prompted some newspapers to predict a close contest in September.[5]

Douglas worked to fend off his challengers by portraying himself in personal appearances, radio broadcasts, and newspaper advertisements as a scrappy, experienced legislator who battled for the interests of all citizens, not a particular class. He also managed to keep organized labor neutral during the campaign. William Green, president of the American Federation of Labor, considered endorsing Coxon. At Douglas's request, Dean Acheson used his influence with the labor leader to thwart that move.

As always, Douglas made the most of his magnetic personality. Wearing an old gray felt hat, which had become a trademark, he crisscrossed the state by auto, mingling with voters. He was at ease with people and had the ability to converse comfortably with constituents from all walks of life. People liked Lewis Douglas even when they disagreed with him.

He opened his campaign at Library Park in Phoenix on August 5. With a grin, he began his speech by saying: "It seems to me I've heard something about the bonus." Immediately veterans in the audience broke in with boos and catcalls, and throughout the address the congressman was heckled and interrupted. Retaining his composure, he defended his position. Unlike the RFC, which loaned money, he explained, the bonus was a gift, which included $1.6 billion in unearned interest. The former was justified because it reduced bank failures and saved the deposits of large and small investors; the latter was unjustified because it benefited a special group at the risk of jeopardizing the nation's credit. "I do not and won't vote," he said, "to benefit a small group at the expense of all citizens of the United States and through that action deepen and continue the present depression."[6]

Douglas's poise and courage impressed many listeners. The *Arizona Fax*, one of his harshest critics, praised his "courageous attitude" and admitted that he had "made new friends and new votes." His impolite detractors, on the other hand, had "vexed" the audience and done harm to "a worthy cause."

Besides economy, Douglas stressed the necessity of reviving the state's copper industry, calling it "the most important issue before Arizona today." He repeatedly reminded voters of his successful efforts to secure a copper tariff and pledged to work for a higher, permanent duty on the metal during the next legislative session. His advocacy of more protection for copper won praise from heretofore hostile sources, such as Governor Hunt's camp. Douglas further linked his candidacy with the industry that employed about half the state's wage-earners by distributing thousands of small copper campaign cards embossed with his portrait; they read: "Arizona Copper, LEWIS DOUGLAS FOR CONGRESS, DEMOCRAT."[7]

Douglas also declared himself on the still controversial issue of Prohibition. By advocating the repeal of the Eighteenth Amendment he became the only "wet" candidate in the race. Coxon refused to take a stand on the issue and Phelps staunchly supported the Prohibition amendment.[8]

The climax of the sometimes bitter campaign occurred on September 1, when the three candidates appeared before the Young People's Democratic Club in Phoenix. Expecting violence from disgruntled veterans, Arthur Curlee, Douglas's campaign manager, strapped on a six-shooter. Other men in the audience were also armed. But the only fireworks were verbal. Speaking first, Coxon pitched into the incumbent with his usual fervor. His address was interrupted by a vicious dogfight instigated by some of Douglas's Mexican friends. When Robert Stroud, a Douglas aide, asked one Mexican if he had initiated the dogfight, he replied: "Oh Coxon talks too damn much."

Douglas, who spoke next, also encountered distractions. Veterans in the audience once again subjected him to a steady stream of jeers and heckling. As before, he kept his poise and good humor and the tactic backfired. The audience, according to eyewitness accounts, ridiculed the disruptive "hoodlums" and seemed "won over" by Douglas. The third speaker, Phelps, managed to deliver his address without incident.[9]

The results of the September primary showed that Arizonans were dissatisfied with the status quo. Hunt lost his bid for renomination to Benjamin B. Moeur, a politically inexperienced physician from Tempe. Nearly one-third of the state legislators failed to be renominated, and several incumbents were also turned out of office. Senator Carl Hayden won renomination against three opponents, but failed to win a majority of votes. Lewis Douglas also missed a majority, but defeated his nearest rival, William Coxon, by a vote of 33,212 to 28,177.[10]

In a biased but probably accurate postelection assessment, Peggy Douglas attributed her husband's success to the courage of his convictions and his "amazing & compelling personality." She wrote him: "Don't think for a minute that I have forgotten *all* your faults but I am glad to be married to you." Douglas's victory, as usual, was aided by widespread newspaper support and the financial contributions of his father and mother, which totaled nearly $30,000.[11]

Though victorious, Douglas was taxed physically and emotionally by the campaign. Surprised and perhaps hurt by the intense opposition, particularly from veterans preoccupied with "getting their greedy hands" on the bonus, Douglas was relieved when it was over. Despite some "vicious" opposition, he was proud that he "didn't yield a fraction of an inch" on economy or veterans' issues. He remarked to his father that "it takes an awful lot of energy to speak every night to give to it everything one has—to appeal to the finer emotions of people rather than to the baser ones."

Douglas also suffered physically during the campaign. Despite his robust exterior and capacity for work, he had a history of poor health. From childhood through adulthood, he was plagued by sinus troubles. In 1919 his appendix was removed, and in the 1920s he underwent operations for hemorrhoids and a hernia. In 1932 the immediate and most serious ailment was an intense abdominal pain which had bothered him intermittently since the war. Peggy recalled that, as they drove across the state campaigning, her husband would sometimes be in the back of the car writhing in agony, which even morphine could not fully relieve.[12]

Exhausted and ill, Douglas entered a clinic in Santa Barbara, California, for three weeks of tests. The malady, a benign tumor, was incorrectly diagnosed as chronic colitis, and the patient was ordered to rest and adhere strictly to a bland diet. Douglas followed the treatment and quit smoking but his condition improved only slightly. Violating instructions to rest, Douglas left the clinic in late September to prepare for the general election. He planned his departure to coincide with the visit to Arizona of Governor Roosevelt, who had written earlier in the month requesting a meeting during a campaign stop.

Arriving in Phoenix on September 26, Roosevelt made brief speeches at the train station and state capital before heading north by special train to visit the towns of Prescott, Wickenburg, and Williams. From Williams, which he reached about eleven-thirty that night, Roosevelt, his wife, and their son James traveled by rail another ten miles to the 100,000-acre ranch of Isabella Greenway, where they spent the night and the following day. Widow of a wealthy mining magnate, Isabella Greenway had served as a bridesmaid at the Roosevelt wedding and was a lifelong friend of Eleanor Roosevelt. As a delegate to the Democratic convention, she had seconded the nomination of Franklin Roosevelt.[13]

Lewis Douglas and a number of other prominent Democrats, including Senators Key Pittman of Nevada and Thomas Walsh of Montana, Senator Hayden, George Hunt, and B. B. Moeur met Roosevelt for luncheon at the spacious log ranch house, where "coyote pelts adorn the walls and genuine cowpunchers, not the dude ranch variety, go and come in the performance of their actual range duties." In this rustic setting, the Arizona congressman and presidential nominee first talked about the need for government economies. After lunch, Douglas chauffeured Roosevelt to the nearby rodeo grounds and introduced "the next president" to an enthusiastic throng of about five thousand people. Following the rodeo, FDR left by train to carry his campaign into New Mexico.[14]

Shortly after the departure, Douglas wrote Roosevelt that he had "enjoyed beyond words my visit with you at Isabella's ranch." That first meeting eased somewhat his doubts about Roosevelt's ability to combat the depression. Douglas seemed especially pleased by the candidate's support for government economy and general tariff reduction. At the same time, Roosevelt seemed to understand that some American industries, like copper, needed protection from "destructive foreign competition." Douglas was encouraged further when Roosevelt, in subsequent campaign stops, most notably in Pittsburgh in late October, emphasized the need to reduce government spending by 25 percent. By November, Douglas was persuading his recalcitrant father that he should support FDR because his economic ideas were more apt to lead to recovery than Hoover's. Although the Democratic presidential candidate apparently did not record his impressions of Douglas after their initial meeting, he had earlier expressed admiration for Douglas's work in the House.[15]

Douglas realized that victory in the primary almost assured him of reelection to Congress. Still, he campaigned hard, approving a strenuous agenda that called for thirty-three speeches in thirty-one days. He urged Arizonans to vote a straight ticket for the party that held the best hope for economic recovery—which the Democratic platform did by promising to lower the cost of government, balance the budget, reduce taxes, and resuscitate foreign trade through the negotiation of reciprocity agreements. It also urged the repeal of the Eighteenth Amendment in favor of state option, the establishment of an unemployment insurance fund, the use of federal loans to relieve impoverishment, and higher import taxes on some products, such as copper.

A severe intestinal attack prevented Douglas from campaigning during the final week of the contest, but he still overwhelmed his Republican opponent, H. B. Wilkinson, a former state senator from Phoenix, by 75,469 to 29,710. Moeur and Carl Hayden also won handily and Roosevelt outpolled Hoover by 79,264 to 36,104.[16]

When the lame-duck session of the Seventy-second Congress met on December 5, 1932, more than one thousand hunger marchers walked the streets of the capital to remind legislators of the pressing need for relief. In every city, town, and farm community the economic malaise was evident. "No one can live and work in New York this winter without a profound sense of uneasiness," the future New Dealer Rexford Tugwell wrote in December, 1932. "Never, in modern times," he observed, "has there been so widespread unemployment and the distress of sheer hunger and cold." The afflicted cried out for relief during the four-month interregnum period, but Congress and Hoover delayed, bickered, and provided few remedial measures.[17]

The outgoing and incoming presidents differed over the best way to achieve economic recovery—Hoover favoring an international route and Roosevelt preferring a domestic road. Lewis Douglas advocated an approach from both directions at once. For him the domestic path meant slashing expenditures and balancing the federal budget. Alarmed by a four-year deficit surpassing $4 billion, he urged colleagues and influential opinion-makers, such as the Academy of Political Science, to support retrenchment. In Congress, he enthusiastically endorsed Hoover's effort to balance the budget through the imposition of a sales tax. Although the scheme was favored by many conservative Democrats, it was scotched when Roosevelt voiced his disapproval.

Once again Douglas was disheartened by the rejection of the sales tax. Roosevelt's position renewed his doubts concerning the President-elect's commitment to the economy pledge of the Democratic platform. He complained privately that it was discouraging to have a Congress which was "at heart unaware of the seriousness of the situation," but it was worse to have "a President-elect who refused to consider the sales tax and who himself is flirting with the idea of funding a public works program." Foreshadowing a position he would take later as budget director, he criticized Roosevelt's emerging recovery program, which seemed to be based upon experimentation, including farm allotments and public works. Departures from economic orthodoxy, Douglas insisted, should only occur if "we have a firm base on which to rest, namely a budget that is balanced beyond question, and a credit which is impregnable."[18]

Economic recovery could also be reached, Douglas believed, by following an international road, which involved the revival of world trade through reciprocal tariff negotiations, currency stabilization, and the reduction or cancellation of intergovernmental debts. The "point of attack," he wrote privately, "should be the debts." The Roosevelt administration should abandon the Republican policy of "they hired the money" and recognize the necessity of scaling down debt payments. "If the debt question can be readjusted currencies will automatically become stabilized," he wrote. "When currencies are stabilized, tariffs erected in some measure by reason of depreciated currencies can then be lowered."[19]

By 1932 Herbert Hoover had already reached a similar conclusion. Worried that Britain, France, and Belgium might default on their debt payments, which were due in mid-December, he invited Roosevelt to the White House to discuss war debts and the related issues of disarmament and global recovery. Attending the White House conference of November 22 with advisor Raymond Moley, Roosevelt turned aside Hoover's suggestion to name delegates to a special war-debts-revision commission. That evening at a meeting with congressional leaders, including Douglas, FDR explained that he opposed debt cancellation and considered the issue Hoover's responsibility.

Douglas's disappointment was blunted by Roosevelt's invitation to meet with him in Albany sometime in December. Learning of her son's proposed meeting with the President-elect, Josalee Douglas, her body already ravaged by Parkinson's disease, wrote him in a shaky hand: "We have followed your movements in the east and are prouder than ever of your wonderful and extraordinary work. Dear boy—it is truly remarkable what you have done in so short a time. It is almost unprecedented! . . . The only thing that worries me is your health. It is better to give it all up than to have stomach trouble always. You *must rest* more—dear."[20]

But despite occasional painful intestinal attacks, Douglas took little time to rest. On December 7 he wrote Roosevelt: "I have been doing much speculating on economy, the methods by which it may be obtained and about inter-governmental debts. Possibly my speculations may be of some value to you." Three days later Roosevelt asked him to visit over the weekend at Hyde Park.[21]

Douglas arrived at the Hudson River estate on December 18. Other guests included Rexford Tugwell, a Columbia University professor; John Williams, a Harvard economist; and Edmund Day of the Rockefeller Foundation. Williams and Day had been chosen by Hoover to help plan an upcoming international economic conference. Roosevelt asked Douglas to read a telegram Hoover had sent the night before. Disturbed that France and Belgium had defaulted on their December debt obligation, Hoover wanted FDR to work with him on pressing international economic issues. Specifically, he proposed cooperation on a plan to scale down the debts and asked Roosevelt to choose at least two members of a small delegation which would go abroad to discuss debts, disarmament, and economic recovery with European nations. FDR asked Douglas if he could accompany him to Albany, where they could prepare a reply.

Roosevelt, Tugwell, and Douglas drove by automobile over seventy miles of icy roads to Albany, where they spent the evening discussing the President's proposal. Douglas urged cooperation, but FDR demurred. Not wishing to be committed to the policies of a lame-duck President, dubious that debt reduction would restore prosperity, and cognizant of its unpopularity, Roosevelt declined Hoover's offer in a letter of December 19. Apparently at Douglas's request, he did add a clause suggesting an invitation to debtor nations to contact the United States about readjustment. Douglas wrote a friend that FDR's reply "was not what I would have had it but it was a whole lot softer than he would have written it. It left the door ajar."[22]

Hoover too saw hope in Roosevelt's response. On December 20 he sent another long telegram stressing the immediacy of the situation and urging cooperation in the selection of a debt negotiating board. At the suggestion of Secretary of the Treasury Ogden Mills and Secretary of State Henry Stimson, Hoover also enlisted Douglas's help as an intermediary. Stimson wrote in his diary: "Douglas is a perfectly straight high-minded fellow, and the suggestion came up that we should use him to try to get the wires straightened out between the two men." At lunch with Stimson on December 20, Douglas admitted that he was "very anxious about the delay" in debt readjustment negotiations and agreed to approach the President-elect about Hoover's second proposal.

Telephoning Roosevelt from Stimson's home, Douglas raised the possibility of naming one or two men to engage in preliminary discussions with debtor nations. Again FDR refused. If Hoover appointed a committee to begin exploratory discussions, he promised to "keep in touch," but he would not commit himself further. Douglas relayed FDR's disappointing response to Stimson with the remark "There is nothing left to be done." Stimson at last realized that Roosevelt was postponing any real change for debt-revision talks until the change of administration on March 4, 1933. "He would not do what we wanted nor what Douglas wanted," Stimson wrote.[23]

While the Hoover administration assailed Roosevelt for being misinformed and irresponsible on the matter of debt revision, Lewis Douglas sympathized with FDR and remained confident. He wrote a friend: "I got the decided impression that he was going to do something about the debts, that he appreciated their significance in the vicious spiral which is driving us deeper into the depression but that he was reluctant to join in an open cooperative effort with a man who had been repudiated by the country." He made a similar observation to Stimson. His optimism doubtless stemmed from the fact that Roosevelt had informed him confidentially that he planned to invite British and French leaders to Washington to discuss the debt problem shortly after taking office in March.[24]

Although Roosevelt and his closest advisors did not fully share Douglas's internationalist approach to recovery, they respected his grasp of economic issues and valued his counsel. Recording his impressions of the Arizona congressman a week after meeting him at Hyde Park, Tugwell wrote: "Douglas very intelligent, liked him a lot and wondered at it in a congressman."

Roosevelt and Douglas discussed other issues, besides the debts, during their conference in Albany. The two men, Tugwell recalled, talked "at length and fully about changes needed in Washington," especially pertaining to economy and governmental reorganization. Aware that Douglas was an influential member of the Appropriations Committee, FDR asked him to add a provision to a money bill enabling the President "to reduce personnel, abolish functions, transfer, etc., his idea being that he might carry out a reorganization (which Congress will never do) and have it done months before Congress comes back." An incoming President, Roosevelt reminded Douglas, could put this over, "if Congress will come through with blanket permission."[25]

Douglas had some reservations about enhancing the President's power, but he believed that Congress's failure to effect economies necessitated strong executive action. "It is conceivable that civilization itself is hanging in the balance. It can be pushed on the side of recovery or chaos," he fretted to his father. "To me the primary things to be done are clear. First actually balance the budget, second face the question of reviving world trade which of course means debts, stabilizing exchange, and liberalizing tariffs. Yet here men follow their normal instinct to avoid the unpleasant. They talk about inflation instead. When the logic of a situation demands taking one course the fears and stupidity of men are attempting to direct us down the other—the former leads to recovery, the latter to chaos." He concluded this somber letter by stating that he wished he could be more light-hearted because "to be too intense impairs one's effectiveness." Actually, Douglas never fully learned that lesson.[26]

In late December, he forwarded Roosevelt's ideas about reorganization to Senator James F. Byrnes of South Carolina, John Nance Garner, and Representative Joseph Byrns. Those congressional leaders successfully attached a clause increasing the President's power to reorganize to the Post Office–Treasury Department Appropriation Bill.

In December Douglas also heeded FDR's request to work on a measure reducing federal expenditures. Tugwell was troubled by Douglas's approach to economy. "I was struck with the almost vindictive way he spoke of bureaucrats and the way he lingered fondly over the possibilities of economies. He had the same bias, I concluded, as Baruch and others who thought that the federal government was overexpanded and that recovery could be started by reducing its expenditure." Tugwell expressed his misgivings to Roosevelt at Hyde Park two days before Christmas. He also gently scolded the President-elect for being more concerned with reducing the cost of government than he was with improving its efficiency. FDR informed his advisor that he was "quite wrong" and predicted that Douglas would "be helpful" in obtaining reorganization and a balanced budget.[27]

Teaming with Senator Byrnes, Swagar Sherley, former congressman from Kentucky, and Daniel Roper, commissioner of Internal Revenue under Woodrow Wilson, Douglas labored for hours each day on the problem of economy, seldom retiring before midnight. The committee reached "the settled conviction" that upon a balanced budget "depends the hope for early economic recovery of the country." It also urged Roosevelt to include in his inaugural address a pledge "that the spendthrift ways of the government of the past few years are at an end." Failure to make such a pledge, committee members held, might produce "such immediate financial chaos and disaster to the country as to make probably impossible an ending of the depression by ordinary and sane methods." In mid-February the committee forwarded a memorandum to Roosevelt recommending the termination of government grants, subsidies, and research, the elimination of public works, and sharp reductions in veterans' benefits and federal salaries. All told, about $2 billion could be saved. Those recommendations served as the basis for the Economy Bill, drafted by Douglas, and passed into law during the first hundred days of the New Deal.[28]

By early 1933 Lewis Douglas had become an influential member of the President-elect's inner circle. One prominent New Deal historian, Frank Freidel, has characterized him as one of "the most persuasive men around Roosevelt during the formative months of the New Deal."

Encouraged by Roosevelt's receptiveness, Douglas continued cautiously to advance his views on economic policy. In January he informed FDR that the depression's grip could not be loosened until first "we are able to make people feel secure in the possession of their land and their home.... Second, until we make an actual balance of the budget.... Third, until we face frankly and courageously the fundamental question of reviving a dead world trade. This, of course, means facing the question of intergovernmental debts, the stabilization of exchange and the liberalization of commercial policies." He concluded with a grim warning: "I feel very strongly that not only the future of our Party but the future of civilization itself depends upon a bold courageous stand."[29]

In February the collapse of Michigan's banking structure prompted a memorandum from Douglas. The Michigan panic, accompanied by the suspension of all bank payments, he counseled, might become national in scope. He urged Roosevelt and his advisors to formulate "speedily" a policy to deal with such an eventuality. He recommended "a policy of realism" whereby after a review by the RFC "weak and tottering" banks would be allowed to fold, thus bolstering public faith in those banks that remained open. Roosevelt, addressing Douglas as "Dear Lewis," acknowledged the memorandum with thanks, but seemed unalarmed by the Michigan crisis and apparently did not heed Douglas's advice. Four days after he sent the memorandum, however, Douglas was invited to be a member of Roosevelt's administration.[30]

As early as mid-December, 1932, after the Hyde Park meeting, the press speculated on the possibility of Douglas's being offered a cabinet post in the Roosevelt administration. In his nationally syndicated column Ray Tucker wrote in early January that the House member "closest to the President-elect is a man young in years at congressional service." Identifying that man as Douglas, Tucker went on to say that he had impressed Roosevelt and would "probably be heard from in the next administration. He has shown a keen grasp of legislative questions and public problems, and he has a likeable personality. He is handsome, wealthy, personable and intelligent; it seems that all the good fairies were present at his birth."

In the early months of 1933 Douglas was variously rumored to be FDR's choice to head the State, Treasury, or War Department. Characteristically, he downplayed the rumors. He informed Roosevelt: "I am asking you to believe that I have nothing to seek but that I am simply intensely interested in contributing whatever I may be able to contribute . . . toward reversing the vicious direction of the spiral which is spiraling us deeper into the depression." He wrote his father: "There is a little talk about my being somewhere in the Cabinet. I don't believe the talk." Despite his disclaimers, Douglas must have guessed that he was under consideration for some post.[31]

Actually, there was little speculation linking Douglas to the position for which he was best suited, the budget directorship. Swagar Sherley, a Kentucky conservative, was the primary contender for that job, despite the objections of Moley, who preferred an individual with more prestige. In mid-January, 1933, Roosevelt offered Sherley the budget post, which he described as "a key to almost everything else." Sherley, however, declined because of ill health. When Roosevelt asked him to suggest a candidate, Sherley suggested Douglas. Senator Byrnes also recommended the Arizonan.[32]

On February 22, 1933, Roosevelt telephoned Douglas to offer the position, as Peggy listened in on an extension. Douglas believed that he could be of greater service by remaining in Congress. He was also reluctant to leave the House, where he had built a reputation. Finally, he had some doubts about Roosevelt's commitment to economy. He asked for some time to think it over. Although he believed he was ending forever his career in elective politics, his sense of public duty compelled him to accept. He telephoned the next day to say he would take the post if Roosevelt was absolutely committed to economy and a balanced budget. When FDR assured him on those points, Douglas accepted. Informing Governor Moeur of his decision, he wrote that he "could not refuse the responsibility which has been offered for in times like these even more so than in times of war individuals cease to be significant[;] only the common welfare is important."[33]

The appointment was greeted with enthusiasm. Douglas received more than one thousand notes of congratulation, and the nation's leading newspapers called the selection one of Roosevelt's most popular. The New York *Herald Tribune* believed that the congressman was "an ideal choice" to fill a position that was more important than most cabinet posts. Douglas "has shown that he has the sort of two-fisted courage which not only enables a man to stand for the right but to make that right prevail. He has been a gallant figure in the House, and we feel sure that he will make his mark in the Roosevelt regime." In a lighter vein, humorist Will Rogers wrote: " 'Douglas? Douglas? Who in the world is this Douglas that they have appointed night watchman of the budget?' Well, there is one guy I can tell you about. I know him. He is the only Congressman from Arizona. Incidentally, every State ought to have only one. Arizona does better with one than New York does with 45."[34]

Conservatives properly interpreted the appointment as a pledge by the new President for economic orthodoxy. A New York financier was quoted as saying: "With declining markets, today was dark . . . but it was brightened a great deal when word came through of the Douglas selection." Wall Street lawyer John J. McCloy, Douglas's friend, wrote: "The feeling here is that it is the best appointment Roosevelt has yet made." Members of Congress also approved the nomination. Bertrand H. Snell, the Republican floor leader, asserted that it was "one of the outstanding appointments that any President could make at this time," while Joseph Byrns considered the Arizonan "peculiarly qualified for the position." Douglas's sometime nemesis, John Nance Garner, stressed the nominee's courage. "In fact he has got so much courage that he voted with the Democrats about half the time he was in the House and the rest of the time he didn't. That's courage." But it was Douglas's Aunt Ellie who sent perhaps the most satisfying message: "It is a huge job and a great honor. How proud your Grandfather would be."[35]

Working with Roosevelt

ALTHOUGH FRANKLIN D. ROOSEVELT IS OFTEN remembered for enlarging the federal bureaucracy and spending lavishly to stimulate recovery, New Deal scholars have emphasized his concern for economy, government efficiency, and a balanced budget. An example of this early fiscal conservatism was Douglas's appointment. As the President's fiscal representative, he had control over almost every New Deal expenditure, and he proved a stubborn steward of the public purse. More than a financial watchdog, the budget director held wide-ranging responsibilities. He attended cabinet meetings, acted as liaison with Congress, drafted legislation, helped write presidential messages, prepared the budget, and advised the President on a variety of domestic matters. He also coordinated activities among federal bureaus. Executive orders, drafted by various government agencies for the President's consideration, first had to be forwarded to the Budget Office, where they were examined for duplication of effort, cost, and possible departures from administrative policy. After soliciting the views of other departments, Douglas submitted the orders with his recommendation to the Chief Executive.[1]

During the early months of the New Deal perhaps only Raymond Moley had more influence on Roosevelt than Douglas. Columnist Arthur Krock noted that FDR "has affection and admiration for Mr. Douglas and calls him in on nearly every problem for the Executive." Charles Wyzanski, Jr., wrote that his boss, Secretary of Labor Frances Perkins, told him that "every proposition presented at Cabinet meetings is referred to him [Douglas] to see how it affects the Budget and once it is referred his suggestions are generally not limited to finance."[2]

Douglas was also a member of the "Bedside Cabinet"—a small group of advisors including Raymond Moley and Louis Howe who met with the President each morning between 9 and 10 A.M. After breakfasting and glancing through several newspapers, Roosevelt, while still in bed, conferred for fifteen to thirty minutes with first Moley and then Douglas. Those morning sessions, usually devoted to pressing economic problems, were sometimes disrupted by intrusions

84

from Roosevelt's grandchildren, Buzzie and Sisty. Douglas recalled that on one occasion they darted into the bedroom, upset the President's breakfast tray, and spilled marmalade on the bedspread.[3]

Douglas was both exhilarated and humbled by his membership in the inner circle. "It seems queer to telephone at any hour to a President, to go into his bedroom at one in the morning, in fact to have the entré [sic] at any time and to be writing a Presidential message to Congress on the budget," he wrote his father in March. "How strange for an insignificant young man from Arizona to be in such a position. When I stop to think about it all it is quite frightening." Yet, being an insider, he assured his father, would not subvert his independence; indeed, he believed that he might be forced to quit someday because he would be unable to agree with the President on some unorthodox policy.[4]

Douglas's favored position and the attendant publicity disturbed some individuals in the administration. Louis Howe, FDR's long-time friend who lived in the White House, resented Douglas, Moley, and anyone else who got close to the President. Postmaster General James Farley considered it "unprecedented" for the budget director to attend cabinet meetings. Labor Secretary Perkins suspected that Douglas was feeding the press stories about his influence. "He was a person of great charm. He'd been in Washington long enough to know how you get things in the press," Perkins reminisced. "I always have thought that he rather let it be known that he was the President's personal adviser, but the President certainly gave a great deal of color to that because he did see Lewis all the time at odd moments." Indeed, even James S. Douglas expressed surprise at the extensive press coverage and wondered if his son or one of his friends was paying for it. "Of course not," the son shot back. "You can't buy it if you wanted to." He admitted, however, that the glowing publicity was "a little frightening."

For his part, FDR seemed taken with Douglas's intelligence and likable personality. Not only did he meet frequently with the budget director at the White House, but he sometimes conferred with him on the presidential yacht, *Sequoia*. In early April, 1933, Roosevelt wrote Colonel Edward House that Douglas was "in many ways the find of the administration." And he confided to Raymond Moley that in twelve years he "would be a good Democratic candidate for President."[5]

For the first few weeks after the Inauguration on March 4, 1933, Douglas worked at a furious pace. He arrived at his office in the Treasury Building about 8:30 A.M. and sometimes stayed past midnight. "This is the first evening I have been home before midnight for several weeks," he wrote his father in mid-March.

In organizing the Budget Office, Douglas gave top priority to finding a loyal, industrious assistant. James S. Douglas, who continued to subsidize his son, offered one of his aides, Fred Lowery, who had advised Lew during four congressional campaigns. The senior Douglas volunteered to pay Lowery's salary, but the son got him on the government payroll, first as a technical advisor and then as assistant director of the budget. Lewis Douglas also brought in as an assistant Alvin Brown, a graduate of George Washington University Law School. He retained Robert Stroud as his personal secretary.[6]

Besides organizing his own office, Douglas periodically assisted Secretary of Treasury William Woodin with administrative and policy matters. Sixty-six years old, Woodin was a kindly but sickly millionaire industrialist without prior government service. Woodin, Douglas wrote his father, "has no personnel, doesn't know how to get them, and has been relying upon me both to help him and to assist him in getting the proper personnel as undersecretary and assistant secretary." When the New York banker James Warburg turned down the post of under secretary, Douglas recommended his close friend Dean Acheson, a Washington attorney.[7]

The national economic emergency, rather than organizational matters, consumed most of Douglas's time during the spring of 1933. Bank runs had become national in scope by Inauguration Day. The financial crisis demanded immediate attention, and the new President on Sunday, March 5, convened the cabinet in the Oval Room of the White House. At that meeting, which Douglas and congressional leaders attended, the President announced that he was using a World War I act to close the banks temporarily to prevent further gold hoarding and withdrawals. He also said he was calling Congress into special session on March 9 to deal with the banking crisis, the budget deficit, and joblessness.

While some of Roosevelt's advisors prepared emergency legislation to resolve the financial panic, Douglas worked on the final details of the Economy Bill. During the transition, it will be recalled, he and several others had explored ways to cut government spending and had drafted legislation incorporating their recommendations. Douglas submitted the economy measure to Roosevelt on March 2. Five days later, after being sworn in as budget director, he met with the President to review the particulars of the bill. Alarmed by mounting federal deficits, FDR decided to act on the Economy Bill just as soon as Congress disposed of banking legislation and asked Douglas to write a presidential message to accompany the measure.[8]

Douglas spent the following day working with Raymond Moley on the message, and delivered it to FDR the next morning. After a careful reading, the President surprised him by suggesting that the bill include a $300 million appropriation to create jobs in conservation. Douglas demurred, pointing out the inconsistency of the recommendation. "The Congress will either refuse to pass the Economy Act and appropriate the $300 million on the grounds that economy is not necessary," he recalled saying, "or it will pass the Economy Act and refuse the appropriation of $300 million on the grounds that economy is necessary. You shouldn't, Mr. President, go in two directions at the same time. The Congress won't." Smiling, FDR replied: "Lew, I think you are right."[9]

On the afternoon of March 10, Roosevelt forwarded the economic proposal to Congress. He warned that the budget deficit for fiscal year 1933 surpassed $1.2 billion and that the government's credit could not long withstand such a burden. "Too often in recent history," he asserted, "liberal governments have been wrecked on rocks of loose fiscal policy." National economic recovery, he continued, depended upon fiscal responsibility. He asked Congress for authority to reduce expenditures. The cutbacks would require sacrifices, and some groups would be affected more than others, but with the "very stability" of the national government at stake, he warned, "the benefits of some must be subordinated to the needs of all."

The Economy Bill gave the President extensive power to effect economies and reorganization. It empowered him to reduce the salaries of federal employees, including military officers and congressmen, by 15 percent and to reduce veterans' expenditures by reorganizing the pension system. Appropriations for ex-servicemen for fiscal year 1933 totaled $946 million out of an entire budget of $3.6 billion. One percent of the population received about one-quarter of all federal expenditures. The new system would permit the President to reduce payments to veterans with permanent and partial disabilities, and to lower pensions to widows and other dependents of veterans who died from service-related injuries. It also sought to eliminate non-service-connected disability benefits. The Budget Office estimated that about $400 million would be saved through veterans' cuts and $100 million from salary reductions. A saving of $500 million would lower by 13 percent the federal budget for fiscal year 1934.[10]

The economy measure also enhanced the President's authority to institute administrative economies through executive order. It extended the President's reorganization authority from sixty days to two years and allowed executive reorganization to become effective sixty days after the order was submitted to Congress. One political scientist has written that the sweeping authority bestowed upon Roosevelt by the Economy Act "constitutes the most extensive grant of powers to effect administrative reorganization ever entrusted to a President by Congress in peacetime."

Douglas estimated that trimming departmental budgets and eliminating up to 80,000 jobs might save as much as $400 million, thus bringing to $900 million the total savings permitted in the economy legislation. "The extremely onerous reductions in expenditure," he wrote privately, "will break many eggs, but they *will* balance the budget. They *will* insure a sound currency. They *will* lay the foundation for recovery." To those who wondered how recovery could be achieved through retrenchment, he explained that the national government could never equal the private sector in its capacity to create jobs. The government could, however, hinder recovery by allowing large budget deficits to threaten the stability of its currency and destroy the confidence of investors.

Not surprisingly, the economy measure encountered some resistance. Nonetheless, on March 12, the legislation was approved in the House, by 266 to 138. Three days later, the Senate passed it by 62 to 13. On March 20 Roosevelt signed the bill into law and awarded the pen to Douglas. Delighted by the "great victory," Douglas gave most of the credit to the economy-minded President. "Roosevelt has been magnificent," he enthused to his father. "He flirts with ideas, has imagination, is rather slow to come to a definite decision, but when he finally does is willing to go through to the end. This is at least my experience so far."[11]

With the enactment of the economy legislation, Douglas and General Frank T. Hines, head of the Veterans Administration, prepared new veterans' compensation regulations. Numerous individuals and groups tried to persuade the two men to avoid drastic cuts. Isabella Greenway, Douglas's eventual successor in the House, argued that severe reductions not only would be inhumane but would also damage FDR politically. Bill Mathews reminded his friend that if ex-soldiers were dropped from the pension rolls they would burden state relief agencies.

Gordon Browning, a liberal Democratic congressman from Tennessee, "almost got into a fight" with Douglas when he refused to budge on the issue.[12]

Douglas and Hines submitted their directives to the President on March 31 and he issued an executive order announcing them the next day. The new provisions, which were to go into effect on July 1, proposed yearly savings of $400 to $450 million. Pensions to widows, children, and dependent parents of veterans killed in the line of duty went untouched. Payments to the severely disabled—the totally blind, legless, and armless—were reduced only slightly. Compensation for service-related incapacities was lowered by 20 to 40 percent, depending upon the severity of the injury. Rates ranged from $8 monthly for a 10 percent disability to $80 monthly for a 100 percent impairment. Payments were virtually eliminated for presumptive cases—those individuals, mainly with tuberculosis, whose disabilities were presumed to be service-connected. Douglas conceded that the cuts were "nasty," but they were necessary to save the credit of the government. "At any rate," he boasted to his father, "it is over and done with, and nobody has shot me yet."[13]

Although there was no shooting, the issue was hardly settled. The new schedules, far more extreme than ex-soldiers had anticipated, brought a storm of criticism. The Disabled American War Veterans declared that "the one redeeming feature of these new regulations . . . is that the suffering will be such that there will be an early national revulsion when the effects are understood." An American Legion spokesman believed that the directives displayed "a picayune attitude to those who made the sacrifices fifteen years ago, in mud, mire, shell-fire and gas, and who came back unable to stand up to their former jobs and compete in life."

Many of the nation's newspapers assailed the executive cuts as too harsh. Arthur Krock noted in the *New York Times* that "down many Main Streets go armless veterans who used to get $94 a month from the Government, and now get $36." The New York *World Telegram* exclaimed that "to throw wounded veterans into the streets to beg is neither economy nor is it a new deal." The Philadelphia *Record* was thankful that Douglas had not been budget director during World War I: He might have altered General John J. Pershing's inspiring remark "Lafayette, we are coming [sic]" to "Lafayette, we'll be there as soon as we balance the budget."

Throughout April, protests poured into the White House. Louis Johnson, National Commander of the American Legion, pointed out that in some cases amputees would have their pensions cut. One embittered veteran returned his medals and part of his uniform. Another wrote: "This may be a great Country but dam the men that are runing it." Still another wrote Douglas: "Well, you have done it! You have made a name for yourself at the expence of the cripples. You must feel proud. . . . What a man! Brave hero that you are, I dare you to come back to Arizona." Roosevelt responded to the criticism by having Douglas draft replies to the protesters reiterating the point that cuts were necessary to balance the budget and restore prosperity.

If many Americans agreed with Boston Mayor James M. Curley, who called Douglas "the biggest ass of the country," others, probably a majority, shared the budget director's desire to remove undeserving recipients from the veterans' rolls. According to the Baltimore *Evening Sun*, Americans recognized "the fact that much of the money paid out through the Veterans Bureau has been going, not to men who were disabled in defense of the country, but to grafters and panhandlers who were using their military service as an excuse to raid the Treasury."[14]

Veterans who objected to the directives demonstrated their displeasure with a march on Washington. By May 10, hundreds of protesters gathered near the Capitol to denounce the retrenchment program and to demand, as they had done in 1932, immediate payment of the bonus. The presence of the second bonus army and the volume of criticism prompted a reevaluation of the veterans' schedules. After a careful review, Douglas admitted that in some instances, notably the combat-wounded, the reductions were too harsh. Recalling the incident years later, he characterized it as a grievous blunder "for which I will never forgive myself."

Assuming full responsibility for some of the deserved criticism, Douglas asked FDR to consider readjusting some of the provisions before they became effective on July 1. On May 11, after meeting with Douglas and Louis Johnson, Roosevelt announced that the new compensation regulations would be reexamined "to effect more equitable levels of payment." He also revealed that 25,000 veterans would be given jobs with the newly created Civilian Conservation Corps. Those announcements, coupled with Eleanor Roosevelt's visit to the bonus army camp, temporarily blunted the protest movement.[15]

Although Douglas believed that the retrenchment program was sufficient to restore business confidence and revive the economy, the President preferred to do something on the "constructive side" to combat the depression. By the end of March he had proposed the Civilian Conservation Corps (CCC) to fight unemployment, the Agricultural Adjustment Act (AAA) to raise farm prices, and the Federal Emergency Relief Act (FERA) to relieve destitution. He also considered recommending farm and home owners' mortgage relief, and public works.

Funding such projects, FDR conceded to reporters, would probably require public borrowing. To reconcile a policy of additional spending with a stated goal of reduced expenditures, Roosevelt concocted the idea of two budgets. One would be used for everyday governmental expenses, the other would cover emergencies such as destitution and joblessness. The *New York Times* pointed out that, if President Hoover had adopted a separate budget system such as the one FDR was proposing, his administration would have had a healthy surplus instead of a large deficit. Yet Roosevelt refused to acknowledge the incongruity of the system and reaffirmed his commitment to budget equilibrium. He maintained that the supplemental budget was a temporary arrangement, which would be abolished once economic recovery had been reached in one or two years. Knowing that Douglas would have disapproved such an unorthodox scheme, however, he failed to consult him before announcing it at a press conference on March 24. Douglas could do little except insist upon "full disclosure" of all federal expenditures under both the regular and special budgets. FDR agreed.[16]

Privately, Douglas considered the arrangement deceptive and fiscally reckless. Once underway, emergency expenditures would lead to huge deficits and economic calamity. Already press reports indicated that as much as $7 billion would be spent on emergency projects. "Why," he asked himself in a personal memorandum, "should we steel ourselves to the heart-breaking task of saving a billion dollars of ordinary expenditure when with a prodigal hand, we scatter over seven billions upon extraordinary expenditures?'' Congress, he reasoned, would not tolerate such an unsound scheme. But, even if it did, the public would not buy the bonds. He feared that the money would be provided through the issuance of greenbacks. He doubted that large expenditures were necessary, but if they were he wanted to "avoid the fatuity for which the last Administration was notable, of talking soundness and acting looseness." It was impossible, he held, to spend and save at the same time. Moreover, the administration should "not ask people to suffer heartbreaking privation in the interest of a balanced budget if we are to confront them at the next corner with a depreciated currency.''[17]

While disapproving of the dual budget practice, Douglas sympathized with the President's desire to provide relief for the destitute. The budget could withstand modest expenditures to ameliorate human suffering. When Roosevelt, at a White House meeting on March 9, discussed a scheme to spend $300 million to put 500,000 youths to work in reforestation and soil conservation, Douglas gave his enthusiastic support. The Civilian Conservation Corps, as the work-relief agency was called, appealed to him because it performed useful work and provided financial assistance at a reasonable cost. Roosevelt was prepared to float bond issues, but Douglas persuaded him that the program could be initially funded by using unexpected treasury surpluses previously earmarked for public works.[18]

Douglas also approved of direct federal relief assistance. In early March he met over breakfast with Senator Robert La Follette to discuss the possibility of additional measures for the needy. He admitted that the economic crisis made further help imperative and he agreed to recommend to Roosevelt an expenditure of $500 million. The Federal Emergency Relief Act, introduced on March 21 and passed two months later, created a national agency to distribute $500 million in RFC funds to the destitute. Harry Hopkins was chosen to head the organization.[19]

Douglas hesitated to support expenditures beyond the CCC and the emergency relief act. An effort to relieve agricultural distress by enhancing farmers' purchasing power struck an unresponsive chord. Spurred by three years of declining prices and farm strikes in the Midwest, Roosevelt sent a farm relief bill to Congress on March 16. Drafted by Henry Wallace and Rex Tugwell, whom Douglas labeled "a very silly Assistant Secretary," the Agricultural Adjustment Act was a complex measure which sought to please a variety of farm groups. It called for domestic allotments—a scheme to encourage major staple-crop producers to restrict production, thereby increasing prices. Participants in the restriction plan would be rewarded with federal subsidies derived from taxes placed on the processors of various agricultural commodities.

Douglas had serious reservations about the farm bill. He disliked subsidies and production controls, believing that farmers could sell their surpluses abroad if tariffs were reduced. He also worried about the expense. When he and other administrators met at the White House to discuss the farm program, FDR asked how much it would cost. Wallace gave an inflated estimate of $1 billion. The secretary's assistant, Paul Appleby, remembered the President's turning to Douglas and saying: "Lew, remember that figure." Grinning, the budget director replied: "I will, Mr. President. It is a very easy figure to remember."

Privately, the farm subsidy plan evoked grimaces rather than grins from Douglas. James Warburg noted that his friend was "very depressed" by the proposed legislation. Even when he managed to reduce the cost to $300 million, Douglas doubted that the processing tax would yield enough revenue to fund the program. Despite his apprehensions about the cost, he went along with it because even though it would not "do any good," neither would it "do much harm." Moreover, Roosevelt promised to do something to facilitate international trade. At Douglas's request, FDR promised farmers that he would ask Congress to enact reciprocal trade agreements "to break through trade barriers and establish foreign markets for farm and industrial products." That promise was not fulfilled until 1934.[20]

Lewis Douglas, like the President, was troubled by declining commodity prices. Yet inflating the currency would prove an even greater menace. Warburg noted in his diary that Douglas had telephoned "quite excited and very much disturbed by the amount of talk that's going on in Washington about whether or not we should devalue the dollar." Adjusting the currency, Douglas insisted, would only bring runaway inflation and "social disorder." Influential financiers such as Bernard Baruch reinforced his position, calling mild inflation "sheer nonsense. It always starts that way with good intentions, which have been used for the pavements of hell." Deflation could be countered, Douglas believed, if the Federal Reserve discounted paper to make credit easier, if the administration renewed its pledge to balance the budget, and if tariffs were reduced to revitalize foreign trade.[21]

Conservative advisors such as Douglas and Warburg checked the efforts of inflationists by persuading FDR to adhere nominally to the gold standard—but only momentarily. On April 5, under the powers of the Emergency Banking Act passed the previous month, the President relaxed the ban on gold shipments by allowing financial institutions to obtain export licenses from the secretary of treasury to meet foreign business debts. In less than two weeks more than $100 million worth of gold left the country. Realizing that sizable gold losses would contract the domestic money supply further, Roosevelt instructed Secretary Woodin on April 15 to issue no more export licenses after April 18. In effect, the President had decided to abandon the gold standard.

Meanwhile, on Capitol Hill, attempts were underway to obtain currency inflation by amending the Agricultural Adjustment Bill. On April 17 Senator Burton K. Wheeler's proposal for the coinage of silver at a ratio of 16 to 1 was only barely voted down when Roosevelt threatened a veto. That same day, however, Senator Elmer Thomas of Oklahoma introduced an amendment empowering the President to inflate the currency by issuing greenbacks, coining silver, or decreasing the gold content of the dollar. Partial to moderate inflation and anxious to put through the farm proposal as quickly as possible, Roosevelt decided to support the Thomas amendment with some modifications.[22]

On April 18, Roosevelt had scheduled a conference to discuss upcoming economic talks with the British. As each advisor arrived, he announced with glee that the United States was off the gold standard and that his decision was irreversible. Enjoying the startled reactions, he asked for congratulations. FDR then informed the group that he planned to accept the Thomas amendment. After reading its provisions, he asked for comments. After a momentary lull, Raymond Moley has written, "Hell broke loose."

Douglas and Warburg led the fight against the amendment, with tentative support from Hull, Woodin, and Herbert Feis, an economic advisor with the State Department. Warburg considered the amendment "harebrained and irresponsible" and likely to produce "uncontrolled inflation and complete chaos" unless modified. Douglas, who was on the verge of resigning, voiced similar objections. The two men, Moley wrote later, scolded the President "as though he were a perverse and particularly backward schoolboy." Roosevelt seemed to enjoy the outburst and occasionally interjected a question or comment. After nearly three hours of spirited protest, FDR agreed to consider revisions and adjourned the meeting at 11:30 P.M. As the downcast Douglas left the White House en route to Moley's room at the Carlton Hotel, he voiced his now famous remark: "Well, this is the end of western civilization." At the hotel, he continued to despair. He reminded his colleagues of the Oath of the Tennis Court—a response to the unsound monetary policies of the *ancien régime*, which triggered the French Revolution in 1789.[23]

In hindsight, Douglas's gloomy prediction about the future of Western civilization seems rather silly. Yet, as New Deal historian William Leuchtenburg has remarked, "in a certain sense" he was correct, in that "a whole long tradition of limitations on the part of the government had been broken. Once that limit had been broken, then where does the next barrier come? Or were there any barriers anymore?"

Many fiscal conservatives besides Douglas were dispirited in the spring of 1933. Although he did not share the sense of extreme despair, James Warburg felt that "the rug had been pulled out from under us." Bernard Baruch branded the decision to leave gold as "mob rule. Maybe the country doesn't know it yet, but I think we may find that we've been in a revolution more drastic than the French Revolution. The crowd has seized the seat of government and is trying to seize the wealth. Respect for law and order is gone." Even those who supported the departure from gold expressed apprehension. "All of the men there agree," Raymond Moley wrote in his diary, "that it was the most momentous day since the war. We were letting the dollar fall—throwing out the sacred gold standard idol."[24]

As for the Thomas amendment, Douglas and Warburg stayed up all night softening its most "vicious" features, especially the provision permitting the President to issue unlimited quantities of greenbacks. By noon of April 19, they had completed their revisions. They had placed a $3 billion limit on the amount of paper money the President could issue and prohibited the production of greenbacks unless the Federal Reserve had first refused to put an equal amount of currency into circulation by purchasing government securities on the open market. At 3 P.M. that afternoon Douglas submitted the modifications to Roosevelt, and he readily accepted them. Warburg observed that, whereas Roosevelt "had been naughty the night before, had stamped his foot and had his way," he was willing "to be a good boy the next day. So when we built him a bridge so that he still had his damn amendment, but somewhat differently clothed, he was perfectly amenable."

Soothed by the President's willingness to compromise, Douglas no longer felt compelled to resign. Indeed, at FDR's request he even agreed to explain the amendment to the Senate Banking Committee. "Awfully embarrassing for me," he wrote his father, "but I am sure that I must stay on until a real overt act has been committed."

That evening Douglas, Warburg, and Moley met in the Carlton Hotel to rewrite the entire amendment. In final form, the measure not only restricted the amount of greenbacks the President could issue but also authorized him to remonetize silver, to accept $100 million worth of silver as payment on the Allied war obligation, and to lower by as much as 50 percent the amount of gold behind each dollar. Roosevelt accepted the redrafted amendment the following day.

As amended, the Thomas amendment no longer alarmed most conservatives. Warburg boasted that in less than twenty-four hours he and Douglas had "covered up the worst features of the measure" and had averted the possibility of runaway inflation. All circumstances considered, he concluded, "I think we have done a first-rate job in bringing an insane proposal back within the realms of sanity." For Douglas, the amendment was still "pretty discouraging" but it could have been worse. "Of course I do not believe that the President will use either the greenback provision or the power to devalue the dollar except as a result of an international conference," he wrote his father. The farm bill, including the controversial Thomas amendment and the Emergency Farm Mortgage Act, was signed into law on May 12, 1933.[25]

Seeking reform as well as relief and recovery, FDR recommended the Tennessee Valley Authority to assist power users in the American Southeast and the Securities Bill to protect investors. Douglas was cool toward both measures.

The TVA proposal, introduced in early April and signed into law on May 18, 1933, fulfilled a vision of Senator George W. Norris of Nebraska, who had long sought to provide cheap electricity for the residents of the southeastern states through the production and distribution of federal power at a dam on the Tennessee River at Muscle Shoals, Alabama. The idea appealed to FDR because it dramatized the issue of high utility rates and provided enormous economic benefits to the Tennessee Valley. Besides cheap electricity, the measure called for the manufacture of fertilizer, flood control, reforestation, land reclamation, and federal construction of transmission lines to power users. Douglas, who had opposed a similar project at Boulder Canyon in the 1920s as an invasion of states' rights, also objected to the TVA on similar grounds. However, when he learned that the issue had already been settled, he persuaded Norris and FDR to attach to the bill a royalty clause, similar to the one added to the Boulder Dam Act, granting a small percentage of the income from power sales to Alabama and Tennessee.

Shortly before the TVA went into effect, Douglas was asked to review bids for construction of power lines from dams on the river. Copper representatives reminded him that awarding the contract to one of them would stimulate the depressed economies of mining states such as Arizona, Utah, and Montana. Secretary of War George Dern, formerly governor of Utah, also pressed the budget director to award the bid to a copper company. Dern's pressure, Douglas recalled, "was embarrassing for me. I pointed out to him the state from which I came and its interests and that I'd try to be quite objective about it. Nevertheless he wanted me to do it." After careful study, Douglas decided to award the contract to the aluminum company because the white metal was a superior and cheaper method of carrying power. "The sole consideration was what was best in the public interest."[26]

Roosevelt's attempt to purify the stock exchange troubled Douglas more than the TVA. The Securities Bill, enacted into law on May 27, 1933, called for full information to be provided to investors when securities were issued. It also stipulated that before securities could be sold, they had to be registered with the Federal Trade Commission. Like most friends of Wall Street, Douglas agreed in principle with the bill, but had reservations about its specific provisions. He considered the penalties for lack of compliance too severe. He also recalled fearing that it "would have a very serious adverse effect upon the flow of capital and the absorption of the unemployed." While the Securities Bill was under discussion, Congress launched an investigation of Wall Street, including the house of J. P. Morgan. Fearful that an investigation would destroy business confidence, Douglas urged FDR to prevail upon the Senate Banking Committee to postpone it. Roosevelt agreed and asked Douglas to convey his wishes for a delay to Joseph Robinson, head of the committee. When he arrived at Robinson's office, FDR telephoned to inform him that he had changed his mind.

The investigation, which was headed by Ferdinand Pecora, revealed that Morgan had a list of preferred customers, including Bernard Baruch and William Woodin, who were offered stock at reduced prices. Although the practice was not a serious offense, it offended many Americans, including Douglas, who considered it a "deterioration of ethical standards." The Pecora investigation facilitated passage of the Securities Bill.[27]

The economic and political realities that prompted Roosevelt to desert the gold standard and accept the Thomas amendment also compelled him to consider proposals for public works and national industrial planning. Ever mindful of the budget, Roosevelt was initially cool toward huge public-works expenditures. Douglas reinforced the President's bias. He decried large-scale federal works projects because they did not create enough jobs to warrant their expense, they did not greatly stimulate the economy, and they were slow to implement and thus failed to relieve immediate distress. Money spent on direct assistance, he held, would reach more needy individuals. True, direct aid did not give the recipient the satisfaction of earning a living, but it was more important in the long run, he argued, to assure potential investors of the nation's sound credit.[28]

Douglas's stout resistance proved a major obstacle to public-works advocates. Frances Perkins recalled that at virtually every cabinet meeting she would advocate a jobs measure but Douglas politely and deftly managed to deflect the proposal. "The nearest the Cabinet came to hard feelings," she wrote later, "was over Douglas's ability to postpone action by the President on the public works bill." Conservatives such as Warburg worried that Douglas would "make himself politically impossible by being too sound in his opposition to all money-spending programs."

When the topic of public works arose in a cabinet meeting on April 11, Douglas sought to delay discussion. Perkins remembered his saying that he had heard of a plan being prepared that would make a jobs bill unnecessary. Douglas was referring to a national industrial recovery act being worked out under the direction of Senator Robert Wagner. Perkins maintained that he "was using the existence of this planning scheme as a tool to prevent the President from giving assent to a public works program."

Actually, by late April, three separate but interrelated groups were formulating industrial revitalization schemes. Besides the Wagner team, another group was organized within the administration under the guidance of Assistant Secretary of Commerce John Dickinson. Later in the month, at Moley's suggestion, a third group was formed to include Hugh Johnson, an associate of Bernard Baruch, and Donald Richberg, a railroad attorney. Douglas acted as intermediary between the three groups and FDR.

Working closely together, the Wagner and Dickinson teams in late April produced an industrial recovery bill calling for a public-works program of $5 billion. On April 29, several cabinet members and Douglas met with the President to discuss the public-works provision of the draft legislation. The meeting lasted for two and a half hours and Perkins recalled, "We had as hot a debate as I ever heard in cabinet."[29]

Secretary of the Interior Harold Ickes, Secretary of Agriculture Wallace, and Perkins enthusiastically supported massive public-works spending. Douglas argued passionately against it. His plea, Perkins wrote later, "had a sound economic basis" and was compelling. "One could not but share in his concern that heavy expenditures would create a great deficit in the budget and impair the credit of the government." Charles Wyzanski wrote his parents that "Douglas is charming, has real brains and is the soundest man I've met in Washington." Calling him "the real back bone of the conference," Wyzanski predicted that he would one day be "one of the great leaders of the country." At the end of the discussion, Roosevelt announced he would support a limited public-works expenditure of about $1 billion rather than $5 billion, which he considered excessive.[30]

Meanwhile, in early May, Hugh Johnson and Donald Richberg prepared an industrial-recovery bill of their own. Like the Wagner-Dickinson draft, it called for codes of fair business behavior, restrictions on industrial production, restraint of competition to increase prices and wages, and labor's right to bargain collectively. The Johnson-Richberg plan, however, recommended stiffer penalties against unfair business practices, was less sophisticated and downplayed public works.

During the first week of May, the Wagner-Dickinson team had increased to $3.3 billion the proposed expenditures for public works. Douglas informed Roosevelt that such an outlay might not be unbearable if the yearly interest on the debt could be paid. He explained that to meet interest obligations of about $200 million, the administration would be required to obtain additional revenues. FDR agreed. "The last week has been largely devoted to a public works program and a control of industry bill. Both of which I have some doubts of," Douglas told his father. "But the important thing it seems to me if we are to avoid a wild orgy of inflation is to impose taxes sufficient to pay interest and amortization in the obligation to be issued in connection with public works. The president has agreed (I think????) to a 1% general sales tax without exemptions."[31]

When the architects of the two bills could not reach a consensus, Douglas suggested the creation of a subcommittee to blend the two drafts into a single bill. The President appointed a subcommittee and instructed it to convene in the budget director's office until it reached a compromise. According to Donald Richberg, he worked with Douglas, Johnson, and Wagner "almost continuously for several days in the office of the Director of the Budget who kept in close touch with the President until we four had finally completed the bill which became, with a few revisions, the National Industrial Recovery Act."[32]

The compromise measure contained three parts. Title I, dealing with business, provided for codes of fair practice, permitted exemptions from antitrust regulations, promised collective bargaining, and established minimum wages and maximum hours. Title II, relating to public works, established a Public Works Administration to expend $3.3 billion on work relief. Title III authorized Congress to raise $220 million in new revenues to meet the interest payments for bond issues. The experiment was to last for two years.

Despite the hard-fought compromise, Douglas ignobly made one last backdoor maneuver to sabotage the public-works provision. In the hope that Congress would vote it down, he tried to persuade Roosevelt to introduce public works as a separate bill. FDR initially agreed. When Frances Perkins learned of Douglas's action, she became "very angry and thought this wasn't on the level." She telephoned Douglas, who admitted talking privately with Roosevelt. "I think the President thinks it's better to have the public works program in a separate bill," he told her. The next day Perkins convinced Roosevelt that Douglas was trying to abort public works and asked him to restore Title II to the bill. To prevent Douglas from again changing the President's mind, she persuaded him to telephone Wagner immediately with the news that public works would be included in the bill.[33]

On May 17 the President sent the NIRA legislation to Congress. Two days later, Douglas provided the House with four tax plans to gain $220 million for paying the interest on public works. His suggestions included a sales tax of slightly more than 1 percent, hikes in income taxes, larger levies on corporate dividends, and miscellaneous taxes on coffee, tea, cocoa, and gasoline. Congress rejected the idea of a sales tax, but accepted the last three recommendations. After a month's deliberation, the bill was passed on June 16, the last day of the session. Roosevelt selected Hugh Johnson to direct the National Industrial Recovery Administration and Harold Ickes to head the Public Works Administration. To avoid waste and reckless spending in the latter agency, Roosevelt asked Douglas to sit as a member of the Special Board for Public Works.[34]

The abandonment of gold, the Thomas amendment, national industrial planning, and the President's inclination to experiment with unorthodox policies caused Douglas to wonder if the New Deal might not evolve into socialism. "I never know when some new and foolish idea is going to be sprung," he complained to his father. He also worried that FDR might yield to pressure groups and abandon his commitment to restrained spending. He became especially "blue" in early April when he thought the economy program was going to be "butchered."

The retrenchment campaign proved a "hard nut to crack" for many administrators. After a cabinet meeting in late March Harold Ickes confided to his diary: "It was the saddest Cabinet meeting yet. Mr. Douglas . . . had his figures showing how much each department was expected to cut in order to contribute its share toward balancing the budget. . . . This Department is expected for fiscal year 1934 . . . to save over $5 million out of its appropriation. All other departments are cut in greater or less degree."

Ickes was not alone in his criticism. Henry Wallace bewailed the cuts in the Agriculture Department, especially for scientific research. Douglas eliminated research funds because he believed that financing could be obtained from private sources. Wallace called that a "completely impractical approach," especially during a depression. Yet his protests went unheeded because the President was even less supportive of research than the budget director. "Douglas was a very intelligent man—a very likeable fellow," Wallace reminisced. "I would say that he would try to cut with a surgical knife—Roosevelt might use an ax. Neither . . . had any appreciation whatever of scientific work."[35]

Retrenchment also extended to the military. Economies approximated $45 million for the navy and $80 million for the army. General Douglas MacArthur, the army chief of staff, vigorously protested the reductions and requested a hearing before a board of Budget Office personnel headed by Douglas. The latter recalled that the board gathered at a long table in the hearing room to listen to the general's appeal. MacArthur, "regally composed," argued persuasively against lowering the army budget in the interest of national security. At the conclusion of his remarks the room fell silent. Fearful that MacArthur had made his case, Douglas "did one of the meanest things I have ever done in my life." He asked the general if he expected the army to come down with an unusual amount of dysentery in the year 1933–34. MacArthur replied in the negative and asked Douglas the reason for such an inquiry. "Well, General, it's interesting," the budget director remembered saying, "I find on examination of your estimates that you have put in for 378 thousand sheets of toilet paper for every enlisted man and officer in the military establishment." Angered by Douglas's petty tactic, MacArthur stormed out of the room, slamming the louvered doors shut with a bang.

The general complained to the press that the Budget Office's tight-fistedness endangered national security. Douglas responded to the complaint, without mentioning MacArthur directly, in a speech before the American Newspaper Publishers Association in late April. Slashing expenditures, he declared, was a "heartbreaking" but vital task. Most Americans, including those most adversely affected, like veterans and federal employees, recognized the gravity of the problem and gave their cooperation. "But there are some groups that come pounding at the gates of Washington, saying, 'This shall not be done.' To them I say, 'This shall be done.' To those who say, 'You must not cut the army,' . . . I say, 'Which is more important? A national defense which is perfectly futile if the credit of the government collapses or an unimpaired credit of the government?' " For Douglas the choice was obvious.[36]

Called by newspaper columnist Raymond Clapper "The Great High Executioner of Department Spending," Douglas pruned $80 million from the army, $45 million from the navy, $75 million from the Post Office, $12 million from the Commerce Department, $75 million from federal salaries, and $100 million through staff reductions, consolidations, and streamlining. In mid-April, President Roosevelt predicted that savings from veterans' cuts, salary slicing, and reorganization would exceed $1 billion for fiscal year 1934, a 31 percent reduction from the previous year. In early May, FDR announced that the regular budget was only $120 million shy of balancing for fiscal year 1934.

Despite these achievements, the economy program divided Roosevelt's advisors. Conservatives, of course, hailed Douglas's restraining influence. James Warburg referred to him as "the one person in Washington today who has convictions that run in a straight line and who cannot be thrown off this line by political or emotional considerations." Liberals, on the other hand, generally censured him for cutting excessively. Senator Hiram Johnson accused him of having "a heart of stone." Rex Tugwell complained that the President "has got far too dependent on Douglas. It is so easy to like Douglas that his biases tend to be forgotten. But he has them—he is not too liberal."[37]

Meanwhile, turmoil resurfaced over scheduled slashes in veterans' benefits in late May and early June, 1933. Led by Senator Tom Connally of Texas, liberals worked to restore cuts by amending the proposed Independent Offices Bill. Douglas denounced the move as an "outrage" and urged Roosevelt "to stand fast."

Eager to conclude his legislative program before the commencement of the World Economic Conference in mid-June, FDR had Douglas work out a compromise with congressional leaders on June 10. All told, the compromise would cost an additional $77 million, thus reducing veterans' economies from $460 to $383 million.

At the same time, Roosevelt asked congressional approval for an executive order to save $25 million by streamlining certain federal agencies. FDR's action almost jeopardized the veterans' compromise. Congress postponed adjournment for one week and used the interval to seek additional gains for veterans. Roosevelt and Douglas, however, refused to yield further for fear of endangering the economy program. On June 16, the Independent Offices Act passed both houses and was signed into law. With the enactment of that measure and the NIRA, the special session adjourned.[38]

Douglas had ambivalent feelings about the achievements of the Hundred Days. He regarded the Emergency Banking Act, the Economy Act, and relief legislation such as the CCC as positive measures. Such other legislation as the AAA, NIRA, and the Thomas amendment troubled him because he feared it might erode confidence and hinder recovery. When columnist Walter Lippmann congratulated him for his "magnificent fight" to achieve fiscal discipline, Douglas expressed some doubts about his continued success. "I cannot truthfully say that we did win entirely, insofar as discipline is concerned," he wrote the newsman. "There are several deviations that may come back to haunt us. My own judgment is that this is the beginning of a long and bitter struggle with the odds against us, but, notwithstanding, a struggle in which it is well worth while to be a participant."[39]

9

Resistance and Resignation

AT THE CLOSE OF THE HUNDRED DAYS Douglas's doubts about the President's commitment to fiscal restraint were matched by his apprehension over Roosevelt's international economic policy. FDR had failed to fulfill a promise to send Congress a message on tariff reduction. He also refused to scale down the Allied war debts or to commit himself to currency stabilization. As the World Economic Conference opened in London in June, Douglas hoped that agreements could be reached that would avert intense nationalism by reducing impediments to international trade.[1]

The London talks, involving more than sixty nations, focused on currency stabilization. With the dollar fluctuating wildly in relation to the pound, technical advisors from the American delegation worked out a temporary scheme fixing the exchange rate at $4 to the pound. Roosevelt, about to leave Washington for a sailing vacation off the New England coast, refused to be bound to a specific exchange rate and rejected the arrangement.

Although Douglas did not necessarily favor pegging the dollar to the pound or franc, he did support an agreement that would permit fluctuations within a certain range. While in New England to receive honorary doctorate degrees from Amherst and Harvard, he conferred with FDR aboard the schooner *Amberjack II* off Gloucester, Massachusetts, on June 21. He urged the President to agree to the steadying of exchange rates, but Roosevelt remained noncommittal. Dispirited, Douglas feared that the United States was "drifting into a policy of isolation."[2]

His fears seemed confirmed a few days later when Roosevelt disapproved a general declaration framed by the gold-bloc countries in London proposing as a long-term objective the stabilization of currencies and a return to the gold standard. Raymond Moley, the President's liaison in London, recommended accepting the declaration, as did Dean Acheson, William Woodin, and Douglas.

Roosevelt feared that the agreement would impede American recovery by preventing the elevation of domestic prices through the adjustment of the gold content of the dollar. On July 2 he sent his so-called "bombshell" message to London informing the conference that the "sound internal economic system of a nation is a greater factor in its well being than the price of its currency in changing terms of the currencies of other nations." The announcement, in effect, terminated the conference, though for appearances' sake the delegates continued to meet for another two weeks.[3]

Deeply disappointed by the declaration, Douglas met with Roosevelt on July 10. When FDR asked him for his reaction to the bombshell message, Douglas tried to change the subject.

DOUGLAS: "Mr. President, you know what I think of your message. You have sent it, it is gone and is now a part of history. Let's forget it."
FDR: "I would like to know . . . what you think."
DOUGLAS: "I will tell you but you won't like it. You remember I always told you I would tell you what I think, no matter how unacceptable it may be, but I prefer not to, it is too harsh."
FDR: "Tell me."
DOUGLAS: "Mr. President, if you had set out to stimulate nationalism all over the world, you have succeeded. I think you have cast the die for war and I think it will spread over this continent and the world. . . ."
FDR: "Tell me why, in detail."
DOUGLAS: "The Conference in London was an attempt to restore a common currency and reduce impediments to trade. You have botched it and it was the last hope. Hitler is now rising to power on a wave of nationalism. The only way to prevent him from achieving supreme power is by offering an alternative revival of world trade. You sir, have destroyed all hope of that. From now on there will be extreme nationalism, ending up in a war. . . ."
FDR: "That is a pretty violent indictment."
DOUGLAS: "I believe it."
FDR: "You know, Lew, you are seeing ghosts under the bed again."
DOUGLAS: "Perhaps I am, but I will leave it to the historians."

Roosevelt's message also impressed Douglas "as being the most powerful argument for national socialism that one could make."[4]

Meanwhile, Douglas labored in Washington to hold down federal spending. Encouraged by rising commodity prices in June, he believed that recovery would soon be achieved if the administration allowed the market to operate freely. He was especially anxious to restrain spending by the newly created Public Works Administration. Provided with $3.3 billion, the PWA was empowered to launch projects on its own or indirectly through the extension of grants and loans to states, counties, and municipalities.

As a member of the Special Public Works Board, Douglas sought to minimize expenditures, while liberals such as Rex Tugwell favored swift, heavy expenditures to trigger recovery and provide relief. On July 1 Douglas and Tugwell clashed over the rate of interest to be charged state and local governments borrowing money for construction projects. Tugwell favored a rate of 3½ percent, but Douglas considered those terms too generous. He preferred a rate of 4 or 4½ percent in order to minimize borrowing and to give investors a decent return on their money. Moreover, he wanted to withhold grants and loans to those states with unbalanced budgets. Tugwell pointed out that those communities with large budget deficits usually had high rates of unemployment. Douglas's restrictions, he argued, would deny the very purpose of the PWA—namely, to provide work relief. Douglas insisted that virtually every community with an unbalanced budget was controlled by a wasteful political machine and that it would not be unfair to deny them aid until they displayed some fiscal responsibility.

He went on to recommend a slow expenditure of the $3.3 billion appropriation. "I feel that apparently the spiral of deflation has come to an end, and the direction of events has turned, and that the necessity for injecting an artificial factor into the situation no longer exists to the same extent to which it existed in March or April and that therefore we should put on the brakes, deter municipalities, counties and States from borrowing money." Public-works spending would bring the federal deficit to about $6 billion for fiscal year 1935 and Douglas doubted that the government could carry such a burden. "For a depression which has been caused in some measure by excessive debt," he asked Harold Ickes, "how can we hope to pull ourselves out of the depression by increasing the thing that caused it?"

Tugwell said Douglas's recommendation "is that we should not spend what is provided for in the bill, and his reason for not doing it is that recovery has already come or will come if we do not do this." Douglas submitted that the economy had improved to such an extent that the "great gamble" of massive public-works spending no longer seemed necessary. Ickes reminded him that "the Act has been passed and we are called upon to administer it." Douglas dissented, saying that the measure was "entirely permissive . . . and not mandatory at all."

The board concluded that loans for work relief would be made to communities with or without balanced budgets at an interest rate of 3¾ percent. Roosevelt ruled that the entire $3.3 billion would be expended. To the dismay of liberals, however, Douglas was successful in his plea for a cautious approach to avoid graft, waste, and unnecessary expenditures.[5]

During the summer and fall of 1933 Douglas was also troubled by the administration's ill-defined monetary policy. After the abortive London Conference, Roosevelt groped for ways to hike domestic prices. Douglas and James Warburg urged patience and a return to a reanimated gold standard. Unorthodox advisors, represented by economists James Harvey Rogers of Yale and George F. Warren of Cornell, pushed inflationary monetary schemes, which would benefit farmers and debtors.

Warren, a professor of agricultural management, championed a monetary theory called the "commodity dollar." The way out of the depression, he observed, was to raise commodity prices. The cost of wheat, cotton, and other staples was governed, he argued, by the price of another commodity, gold. Increase the value of gold and the price of other commodities would climb proportionately.[6]

The Warren theory appealed to FDR because of its simplicity and practicality. Before committing himself, however, Roosevelt sought Douglas's reaction and found him completely hostile to the scheme. At a bedside conference with the President on June 11 he told FDR he had no use for "rubber dollar men" and that prosperity depended upon sound monetary policy. "I may have been too forceful," he wrote his father, "but I simply won't have these men around. Money and fiscal policy are for the Treasury dept. and not for 2 d—n fools to tinker with."[7]

Worried that Roosevelt's flirtation with monetary experimentation would scare off investors and delay recovery, Douglas urged conservatives within the administration to unite behind a sound currency plan. As Warburg remembered it, Douglas was "very much disturbed," but did "not consider the situation hopeless. He thinks that if we rally the conservative element and make a real effort that we can beat off the commodity dollar boys and the out-and-out inflationists and save the situation once more." Besides Warburg, Douglas enlisted William Woodin, Dean Acheson, and Oliver Sprague in the cause.

Douglas also submitted a memorandum on monetary policy to President Roosevelt. He urged him to discard the theories of "doctrinaire and impractical" economists. The very fact that Warren was advising the President on currency matters, he reported, was unsettling to investors who feared currency inflation. "Whenever a country goes off gold, confidence in the currency of that country is based upon confidence in its management," he declared. "There cannot be, and is not now confidence in the dollar because there is no confidence in the management of it." He implored FDR to look to experienced officials in the Treasury Department and Federal Reserve for advice on monetary management.[8]

During the last week of July Douglas and Warburg met separately with Roosevelt to recommend the elimination of uncertainty over monetary policy. Warburg believed that the "most constructive single action" the President could take would be to appoint Douglas secretary of the treasury. Both men urged FDR to select a group of specialists from Treasury and Federal Reserve to fashion a sound, predictable monetary program and to revitalize an international gold standard. Roosevelt seemed sympathetic to their pleas (Douglas believed that the President had committed himself), but he asked both men to meet with Warren to discuss the commodity dollar.

Douglas saw Warren on July 24, the day before leaving for a summer vacation. As usual, Douglas was personable and accommodating. Instead of denouncing monetary experimentation, he championed the cause of a balanced budget, restrained spending, exchange stabilization, and the gold standard. Although the two men virtually ignored the commodity dollar, Warren came away from the meeting believing that Douglas was "ready to get somewhere near the band wagon if not on it." Douglas, on the other hand, felt that the commodity dollar was a dead issue. Both men badly miscalculated.[9]

Accompanied by Fred Lowery and John J. McCloy, Douglas left Washington in late July for a salmon-fishing holiday on Anticosti Island in Canada. Located in the Gulf of St. Lawrence about fifty miles off the tip of the Gaspé Peninsula, the island was renowned for its fishing and hunting. At their isolated camp on the Jupiter River, the three men fished, tied flies, read, and loafed for more than a week. Lowery eventually recorded their adventure in a small, privately printed book which Douglas always treasured. The trip was cut short when Douglas received an airplane message requesting his presence in Washington.[10]

He had been summoned from the Canadian wilderness by Warburg, who warned him that Roosevelt was about to inflate the currency. Commodity prices, which had been escalating for two months, slid downward in August. To check further deflation, FDR considered utilizing the greenback provision of the Thomas amendment to drive up prices. Roosevelt also conferred with Warren about the commodity-dollar plan.

Fearful that the President would embark upon a monetary experiment that would bring runaway inflation, Douglas met with FDR on August 15 and advised a cautious approach. Only a few days before, Roosevelt had agreed to the formation of an informal group to advise the administration on monetary issues. The Monetary Group included Woodin as chairman, Douglas, Warburg, Sprague, James H. Rogers, Acheson, Walter Stewart, George Harrison, and Eugene Black of the Federal Reserve. Douglas asked Roosevelt to review the recommendations of the Monetary Group before resorting to paper inflation or dollar devaluation.[11]

For the next ten days the Monetary Group labored frantically on the greenback crisis. Douglas went to Hyde Park during the last week of August to warn Roosevelt of the evils of paper inflation. "In the environment of his home where many generations of his family have lived," Douglas wrote his father, "he is a somewhat different man. But even there he flirts with issuing greenbacks—not in the immediate future but within 30 or 60 days."

On August 30 the Monetary Group submitted an interim report advising against devaluing the dollar or issuing greenbacks. The problem of declining prices could be remedied in the short run by encouraging business investment through the expansion of credit and by easing fears against inflation. As a long-term solution the group recommended the reestablishment of a reformed gold standard. To the relief of administration conservatives, Roosevelt decided to scrap temporarily the idea of issuing greenbacks.[12]

Douglas also became disenchanted with the National Recovery Administration. During the summer of 1933, NRA officials headed by General Hugh Johnson worked with business and labor leaders to establish voluntary codes for numerous industries, including oil, coal, automobile, steel, and copper. At his son's insistence, James S. Douglas was consulted about the copper code, but his advice went unheeded. When the codes were issued, he refused to cooperate. He objected to regulations fixing prices and regulating production. "The Code cannot be signed honorably by anybody and the U.V.X. won't sign it," he wrote his son. He denounced the NRA symbol—the blue eagle—as a "G—d— outrage" because it reminded him of the Prussian eagle.

The son shared his father's assessment of the codes. *"Johnson has gone crazy!"* he wrote in late August. The regulations made his "blood boil," because they restrained competition, thwarted antitrust laws, fixed prices, and controlled production. Moreover, by recognizing labor's right to organize and bargain collectively, the NRA encouraged strikes and made unions too powerful. He could readily imagine "labor government" headed by FDR. When Douglas had helped write the NRA bill in the spring of 1933, he had believed that the agency would only regulate hours and wages. By late summer he was convinced that it was "being administered to crush out of existence" the small industrialist who was "the very backbone" of the republic. "I may therefore find it necessary to resign and to tell the public why," he informed his father.[13]

Douglas also considered resignation when Warren's monetary theories resurfaced in the fall of 1933. During September, commodity prices plunged still lower. Farm groups and influential congressmen bombarded the White House with demands to boost prices by inflating the currency. Roosevelt sympathized with hard-pressed farmers and understood the political repercussions if he failed to halt deflation. Moreover, he feared that desperate farmers might revolt.

Douglas was concerned less about revolution and political realities than he was about inflation. "I hope we can avoid drastic inflation and work our way back toward stability and sound economics but I fear my hope is merely a hope." He was so sure that FDR would yield to public pressure to inflate that he suggested stocks the family could buy to protect its interests. "I must admit a real sense of discouragement. This whole show is so silly—much like *Alice in Wonderland*."[14]

Roosevelt, now losing patience with his orthodox advisors, informed Woodin that the latest monetary report was unsatisfactory. "I wish our banking and economist friends would realize the seriousness of the situation from the point of view of the debtor classes,—i.e., 90 per cent of the human beings in this country—and think less from the point of view of the 10 per cent who constitute the creditor class." He told Woodin that if the Monetary Group wanted to be of real service it should advise him how to raise farm prices. It should concern itself with "that objective and that objective only."[15]

Warburg drafted a letter of resignation, but his colleagues persuaded him to stay on. Douglas, too, again considered leaving. "Inwardly I am more and more concerned and more and more inclined to move on," he wrote his father, "but logically I can do so only on the basis of a real principle. And so I must stay and keep on trying to stop the worst—and encourage the best—until the real crisis arises."[16]

Despite his disillusionment, Douglas could not bring himself to resign so long as Roosevelt supported the economy program. And in the fall of 1933 FDR still seemed committed to austerity. At a bedside conference in late September, he asked Douglas to prepare an address on economy for the American Legion in October. In that speech Roosevelt again reminded the Legionnaires that veterans were not entitled to special economic advantages and that those who suffered disabilities long after they had separated from the service could not be compensated by the government.[17]

Meanwhile, Douglas continued to work with the Monetary Group on a remedy for the problem of sagging prices. Before the group could submit its report, however, Roosevelt decided to implement the Warren plan. On October 19 he announced privately that he planned to have the RFC buy gold on the domestic and world markets at prices above the going rate. In consultation with Henry Morgenthau of the Farm Credit Administration and Jesse Jones of the RFC, the President would arbitrarily determine the price of gold. Driving up the price would devalue the currency and push up commodity prices.

On October 20, Roosevelt discussed the gold-purchase plan with Warren, Morgenthau, Acheson, and others. Douglas was notably absent. Acheson, according to Warren, was "nearly hysterical" in opposition. He claimed that the price of gold had been established by law at $20.67 per ounce and any attempt to adjust it was illegal. Roosevelt said that experts had assured him of the legality of the arrangement. Acheson requested written assurances, but the President responded sternly: "I say it is legal."

Two days later Roosevelt announced the plan publicly in his fourth Fireside Chat. "Under the clearly defined authority of existing law," he declared, "I am authorizing the Reconstruction Finance Corporation to buy gold newly mined in the United States at prices to be determined from time to time after consultation with the Secretary of Treasury and the President." Privately, Roosevelt relished the move because for the first time in several decades "Wall Street was not dictating the fiscal policy of the Government."[18]

Not surprisingly, the Monetary Group was appalled by the experiment. Warburg talked over the telephone with Douglas, who "sounded hopelessly sunk and said that Acheson felt likewise." Nor were conservatives consoled by the view of James Cox (who had had FDR as running mate in the presidential election of 1920) that Roosevelt "would never get so far from base that he couldn't slide back without being tagged out."

Douglas outlined his objections to the arrangement in an untendered letter of resignation. He denounced the scheme as a "monetary trick," which might depreciate Treasury bonds, impair government credit, diminish capital investment, increase unemployment, raise tariffs, instigate currency wars, and perhaps "bring down upon the whole world complete chaos." He also condemned the plan as unethical. Only a few days before its implementation, he pointed out, the Treasury Department had issued $500 million in bonds, which would depreciate in value once the dollar was devalued. That act, he wrote, was "so dishonest and so immoral and so unethical that it is beyond my comprehension that you could even contemplate taking it." He concluded by saying that "because I believe your action to be ineffective, because I believe it will intensify human suffering, because I believe it to be dishonest and because I believe it to make impossible of attainment the duties incident to my office, I am herewith submitting my resignation." Upon reflection, Douglas did not send the letter. Instead, he submitted his objections in a toned-down memorandum, minus the resignation.[19]

Douglas and Roosevelt were also at odds over banking policy. The budget director and other conservatives attributed declining prices not only to the threat of inflation and an incoherent monetary policy, but also to a shaky banking system, which the administration refused to rehabilitate. To lift prices and enhance purchasing power, Douglas urged FDR in late September to free more than $1 billion in frozen assets in scores of closed banks. To expand credit and bolster confidence, he also recommended permitting all open banks to qualify for protection under the Federal Deposit Insurance program. The insurance fund, established by the Glass-Steagall Act in June, 1933, was to become operative on January 1, 1934. Only those banks deemed solvent after a careful review by the RFC could participate in the insurance program. Douglas feared that thousands of institutions would be found ineligible, thus triggering another banking collapse.

Under the Emergency Banking Act of 1933 the RFC was empowered to infuse new capital into shaky banks by buying their preferred stock. To avoid charges of government ownership, Jesse Jones, head of the RFC, proceeded cautiously. He preferred, as did Roosevelt, to have local investors buy the preferred stock. Douglas maintained that community investors were not responding, and he implored FDR to let the stock be sold to the RFC. Roosevelt refused, saying that he could find local capital in three days. "I partially lost my temper," Douglas noted in his diary, "and perhaps too vehemently said that neither he nor the holy Trinity could do it in 3 days, 3 weeks or 3 months and that he was going straight into an economic collapse." Douglas considered it odd "to be advocating at least a temporarily and partly socialized banking system. Yet it is the lesser of two evils."[20]

For more than three weeks Roosevelt and Douglas sparred over banking policy. Douglas informed the President that at least two thousand open banks had not been fortified with enough capital to qualify for the federal insurance program on January 1, 1934. Jesse Jones was not getting the job done, he complained to Roosevelt.

At a White House meeting with FDR and Jones in mid-October, Douglas, Eugene Black, governor of the Federal Reserve Board, and Henry Bruère of the Bowery Savings Bank forecast another panic in January unless $600 million was swiftly injected into debilitated banks. Jones, whose job and reputation were on the line, replied that more than $1 billion would be required to achieve solvency and that the RFC would be able to do the job in time. "Boys," Roosevelt concluded, "I am going to back Jess." He asked the four men to work out a suitable arrangement. Douglas wanted to have a New York banker direct the refinancing, but Jones objected. The RFC eventually completed the task, but only after the Treasury Department verified as solvent nearly two thousand doubtful banks.[21]

The criticisms of administration conservatives did not escape the attention of journalists. T.R.B. in the *New Republic* observed that it was common knowledge in Washington "that Acheson and Budget Director Douglas were wholly out of tune with the fiscal direction of the administration." However, "to be fair to the Budget Director, he has not in any way concealed his views from the President, and has been ready to retire at the slightest hint from him."[22]

Irritated by the "growling in public," Roosevelt moved against some of the malcontents. Convinced that Acheson was disloyal and "yellow," Roosevelt asked for his resignation. He also replaced Secretary of the Treasury Woodin, who had been trying to resign for months because of ill health. Woodin recommended Douglas as his successor, but FDR chose instead his Hyde Park friend and neighbor Henry Morgenthau, Jr.

Like most conservatives, Douglas was incensed by Acheson's firing. "Here— things are in a real mess," he wrote his father. "Acheson as you know was asked to resign. Woodin as you know moves to Arizona and Morgenthau is in the saddle. The Administration lost real ability in Acheson, nothing in Woodin, and has acquired stupidity and Hebraic arrogance and conceit in Morgenthau."

Other departures soon followed. On November 21, Oliver Sprague submitted his resignation. Warburg, too, left the administration and published a book assailing its monetary policies. There was expectation that Roosevelt would seek Douglas's resignation. According to Harold Ickes, Douglas "was quite strenuous in expressing his opinion, and . . . in arguing with the President he went a little far both in the substance of what he said and the manner of its expression." Warburg noted that Douglas had "talked much more freely" than Acheson. And Grace Tully, FDR's secretary, claimed that it was Douglas, not Acheson, who was informing the press of the internal disputes.[23]

Nonetheless, Roosevelt apparently never considered purging Douglas. Despite Douglas's outspokenness and his hostility to much of the New Deal program, Roosevelt remained personally fond of him, considered him an able budget director, and respected him for speaking his mind. Indeed, FDR once told Douglas that the reason he fired Acheson was that he never disagreed with him to his face. Nonetheless, although Douglas retained his job, he lost influence as a presidential advisor. "I am pretty well heartbroken over the way things are going here," he wrote a friend. "Whatever usefulness I once had here is now, I think, almost completely gone. The high command is using me now for only two purposes: first to complete the 1935 budget and, secondly, as a decoy to the . . . conservative elements."[24]

Douglas decided "to stick by the ship and take it on the chin as long as I can be of service." Regarding a bloated budget as the chief impediment to recovery, he persistently worked to reduce spending and to prevent the destruction of the currency through inflation. Addressing a group of New England business leaders in late November, he pledged to reduce the national debt and preserve the credit of the government. Further relief expenditures, he warned, would mean additional taxes, which would burden the middle class and hinder recovery. Despite the mention of new taxes, the speech was applauded by the administration. Rex Tugwell described the address as "a beautiful job," which "did more than anything which has happened for a long time to let people know where we stand." He shared Douglas's goal of balancing the budget in fiscal year 1935.[25]

During December, Douglas and Roosevelt conferred often on the budget for fiscal year 1935. Their exchanges sometimes became "quite bitter," with the President growing "considerably irritated." When the press carried stories about the two men being at loggerheads over spending, Roosevelt tried to downplay their differences. "Now there isn't any question of a dispute or a row such as we have heard about," he remarked at a press conference. "Douglas's job is to prevent the Government from spending just as hard as he possibly can. . . . Somewhere between his efforts to spend nothing . . . and the point of view of the people who want to spend ten billions additional on public works, we will get somewhere."[26]

Despite FDR's expression of confidence, Douglas despaired. He complained to his father that in the remaining six months of fiscal year 1934 the government would have to obtain $6 billion to pay for Roosevelt's "mad and reckless" spending programs. As Douglas saw it, there were only three ways to finance such a gigantic debt. First, print greenbacks, which would probably ruin the currency. Second, devalue the dollar by 50 percent and use the profit to meet the debt obligation. Third, borrow the money. Since the first two options were "dishonest," Douglas preferred the third. Public borrowing, however, would only be possible if the government slashed expenditures and assured investors of a balanced budget in fiscal year 1935.[27]

During the final preparation of the budget message on December 29–30, Douglas fought doggedly for the reduction of expenditures. Although the gap could not be closed in fiscal year 1935, FDR promised to seek equilibrium in the following year. He also granted Douglas control over emergency expenditures. He refused, however, to place a ceiling on relief spending. Douglas suggested an expenditure of $1 billion, but Roosevelt insisted upon twice that figure. When Douglas asked him to promise not to exceed $2 billion, the President refused. Douglas again sought to restrict emergency spending to direct relief, saying that there was no need to fund agencies such as the RFC after the current fiscal year. FDR disagreed, claiming that bankers were conspiring to ruin his program by withholding credit. Douglas dissented, arguing that no president since George Washington had "received such hearty, wholehearted support from everyone as he."

The December 29 meeting broke up before the message could be completed. As he left the President's office, Douglas promised FDR a memorandum detailing his opposition to additional expenditures. Roosevelt replied: "Lew (very friendly) it is silly for either you or me to submit memoranda to one another. I know full well what will be in the memorandum before it is submitted."

The following morning FDR again refused Douglas's request to restrict relief spending to $2 billion. By noon the budget message had been completed and the conference adjourned. As he departed, Douglas handed FDR the memorandum he had promised him the day before. Roosevelt reacted "by simply laughing as he was wheeled out of the room on the way to lunch."[28]

The ten-page document was a forceful "last plea" against any emergency expenditures except for "the direct relief of the destitute and the unemployed." As he had during their talks, Douglas warned against paper inflation, "one of the most destructive things a government can do to its people." To safeguard the nation's credit and avoid wild inflation, he advised Roosevelt to phase out agencies like the RFC before they became "permanent fungi" on the taxpayers. Additional appropriations for that agency, he contended, would give it a stranglehold over credit and provide "the medium by which we convert the economic system of this country into a communistic or fascistic one."

He also urged the President to hold the line against additional public-works expenditures because, over the long haul, they failed to stimulate the economy and were not cost-effective. He deemed the CCC a worthwhile agency, but one which could be dissolved. The newly created Civil Works Administration should also be abolished. "We cannot always have what we want," he lectured the President. "We must deny ourselves in the interest of the general welfare." He also derided the idea of a double budget. Such a practice, he stated, "fools no one, for as long as the total expenditures are in excess of total receipts the Government has to borrow as long as its credit permits it to borrow." Finally, Douglas exhorted the President to honor the fiscal principles enunciated in the 1932 party platform, in the campaign speech at Pittsburgh, and in the Economy Message of March 10, 1933. For Douglas, the Roosevelt administration was at a crossroads. It could stop borrowing, restore confidence, and maintain capitalism, or it could "deliberately abolish all private enterprise" and replace it with state socialism.[29]

Roosevelt did not respond to Douglas's memorandum, but did voice displeasure at his habit of recording his objections to administration policy. FDR wondered aloud "whether the man writing such a memorandum wasn't trying to make a written record." In his later years, Douglas denied that he was keeping a record to protect himself, but the evidence indicates otherwise.[30]

Roosevelt delivered the budget message to Congress on January 4. The report showed that for fiscal year 1934 revenues slightly exceeded ordinary expenditures. Emergency spending, on the other hand, created a deficit of approximately $7 billion, thus bringing the national debt to nearly $30 billion, the highest since World War I. The budget for fiscal year 1935 anticipated a deficit of $2 billion, a $5 billion reduction from the previous year. FDR planned "to have a definitely balanced budget" for fiscal year 1936, "and from that time on seek a continuing reduction of the national debt." Roosevelt also announced that he had issued an executive order granting the budget director virtual veto power over emergency expenditures.[31]

While the budget message caused little controversy, the executive order granting Douglas control over emergency expenditures appalled Roosevelt's liberal advisors. Department heads like Ickes and Perkins protested that the directive would permit Douglas to halt expenditures for public works, the CWA, and RFC. He could even disallow spending authorized by the President. Owing to the strong protest, Roosevelt modified the order, which elicited Douglas's complaint that the revised order was so loosely drawn as to be of no value. All in all, the episode proved embarrassing to Douglas and added to his overall disenchantment with the New Deal.[32]

With the completion of the budget, Roosevelt once again turned his attention to the problem of declining prices. The gold-purchase experiment, launched in October, proved a dismal failure. By December virtually every economist had ridiculed the venture. Britain's John Maynard Keynes called the theory "puerile," and Thomas Lamont, a Wall Street financier, referred to Warren as "the greatest living authority on manure."

At a cabinet meeting on January 12, Roosevelt announced that he was discarding the Warren plan in favor of a new gold policy that would permit him to boost commodity prices without resorting to inflation. The Gold Reserve Act, as the legislation was called, transferred to the Treasury Department the gold reserves held by Federal Reserve banks, eliminated gold coin as a means of currency, and prohibited individuals from possessing gold. It also enabled the President to devalue the dollar in terms of gold content by 40 to 50 percent and created a $2 billion Exchange Stabilization Fund with the profits derived from devaluation. The purpose of the fund was to stabilize the dollar in relation to foreign exchange and to permit the government to buy securities.

Having read the proposed legislation, Roosevelt solicited the views of the cabinet. Only Douglas spoke out against it. He was especially critical of the Exchange Stabilization Fund. It was "unethical and immoral," he stated, for the government to maintain the value of securities artificially instead of allowing the law of supply and demand to operate. Besides enhancing the cost of securities, the scheme "beguiled people into a sense of false security with respect to the value of Governments, because it prevented Governments from seeking their normal level." If the administration wished to support securities, he said, it should prune expenditures and balance the budget. He also wondered how Federal Reserve notes could be regarded as anything but scraps of paper since they were no longer redeemable in gold.[33]

Privately, Douglas was even more adamant in his opposition. He complained to a Treasury Department advisor that the purpose of the gold proposal was to replace the Federal Reserve system with a central bank. As for devaluation, he claimed that "it had been a crime since the dawn of history, that they used to hang kings for it, and that citizens used to be boiled in oil whenever found guilty of 'coin clipping.' " He repeated his fears to Carter Glass, chairman of the Senate Appropriations Committee and founder of the Federal Reserve system. Douglas predicted that, if passed, the legislation would foster "one of the largest paper inflations the world has ever known." Glass agreed, but believed the bill would be passed. On January 30, Roosevelt signed the measure into law and the next day fixed the price of gold at $35 per ounce, thus devaluing the dollar to 59.06 cents.[34]

In the succeeding months Douglas grew increasingly disconsolate. He again recommended the dissolution of the fledgling Civil Works Administration, but instead the President asked Congress for an appropriation of $450 million for the CWA and $500 million for direct relief. A month later Douglas voiced his objections to a bill establishing additional regulations over the stock exchange. The Securities Exchange Act of 1934, introduced on February 9, proposed a Securities and Exchange Commission to license and police the stock exchanges. The proposed measure, Douglas wrote a friend, was a masked attempt to "permit the 'Tugwellians' to plan our economy." It would, he insisted, stifle rather than encourage investment in the securities market. To Douglas, the bill was further evidence of the administration's drift toward socialism.[35]

In February, Douglas also criticized Roosevelt's decision to abrogate the federal mail contracts with commercial airlines. Convinced that the contracts had been obtained fraudulently, the President canceled them on February 9 and instructed the army air corps to deliver the mail. Not surprisingly, the airline industry, through its spokesman, Charles Lindbergh, denounced FDR's arbitrary action. Lindbergh, a technical advisor and large stockholder in Pan American Airlines, released to the press a telegram he had sent Roosevelt protesting issuance of the cancellation order without a fair hearing.

Lewis Douglas was at the President's bedside when the telegram arrived. Roosevelt instructed Stephen Early to inform the press that it was in poor taste for Lindbergh to make his wire public before the President received it—and to acknowledge receipt of the telegram under Early's own signature, not the President's. Roosevelt then added: "Don't worry about Lindbergh. We will get that fair-haired boy." Douglas inquired as to the nature of the fraud. Roosevelt replied that the airline companies had conspired to divvy up government business at exorbitant prices instead of bidding competitively. When Douglas maintained that the airlines were entitled to an impartial hearing, the President claimed that the evidence was so overwhelming that a hearing would be a waste of time.

The next day Douglas pointed out that canceling contracts prior to a hearing violated Section 5 of the Independent Offices Act of 1933. Roosevelt, however, would not be deterred. The cancellation of the contracts was "another evidence of an act arbitrarily taken without thought or evidence. There may have been fraud and collusion but it has not been proved," Douglas wrote his father. "It is terribly hard to stay on in the face of distrust and contempt for the ethics of your boss." FDR's threat to "get" Lindbergh made Douglas "shudder—the brutal unscrupulousness of it."[36]

By March, 1934, Douglas was convinced that Roosevelt had surrounded himself with unprincipled, incompetent liberal advisors who were undermining the capitalist system. Privately he made some careless and exaggerated judgments about many New Deal officials. He portrayed Attorney General Homer Cummings as cunning and deceitful. James Farley was "a very ignorant person." Navy Secretary Claude Swanson was "a man of no mental fibre at all, but very pleasant." Henry Wallace had some intellect, but was "very visionary, absolutely financially irresponsible," and unable to stand up to the President. He characterized Rex Tugwell as "cunning, subtle, a Communist at heart . . . who will run for cover at the first sign of danger, but who is unfortunately a vicious influence. He is surrounded with the young Harvard Law School group, all of whom are Communists." Douglas also attacked what he regarded as the "Hebraic influence" within the administration. "Most of the bad things which it has done can be traced to it. As a race they seem to lack the quality of facing an issue squarely." Douglas's bigoted remarks about Morgenthau and other Jews in the administration cannot be defended. Generally, however, he was free of prejudice and cannot be considered an anti-Semite. He enjoyed close associations with Leo Wolman, James Warburg, Herbert Feis, and Walter Lippmann, among others.

Frustrated and discouraged, Douglas again considered resignation but his father, Carter Glass, and Colonel Edward House advised him to stick it out. House wanted him to run for President in 1940 as a Woodrow Wilson Democrat. Douglas was flattered, but did not seem to take the suggestion seriously. He stayed on as budget director because he had not given up the fight as lost. He might yet direct FDR toward "sound" economic policies that would preserve the nation's credit, bring recovery, and safeguard capitalism.[37]

Above all else, he hoped to restrain spending and eventually bring the budget into balance. In late March, however, Congress rebelled against retrenchment. In the Independent Offices Supply Bill of 1934, the administration restored some of the cuts dictated by the Economy Act of the previous year. Congress found the bill too austere and amended it by increasing the appropriations for federal salaries and veterans' benefits by $125 and $228 million, respectively. Douglas considered the amended bill fiscally irresponsible and advised FDR to veto it.

On March 27 Roosevelt disapproved the measure because of its expense. The following day, however, Congress handed FDR his first defeat by overriding the veto. For Douglas, the override was unfortunate but predictable. The veto message, he wrote privately, lacked "conviction" and the President seemed "somewhat indifferent" about the result. Another contemporary observed that after the setback Roosevelt seemed to shun economy in favor of deficit spending.[38]

With the override of the presidential veto, Douglas pressed Roosevelt to restrain spending in other areas. In mid-April, he recommended slashing emergency expenditures by $500 million. Emergency outlays, he argued as he had done earlier, should be limited to direct relief. The dole or relief in kind would fulfill society's obligation to the needy without endangering the nation's credit and the economic security of the vast majority of Americans. Programs such as the CCC, RFC, and public works were "futile, ineffective, costly and wasteful."

Rejecting Douglas's appeal, FDR asked Congress for a public-works appropriation of $500 million. At a meeting on April 23, Douglas protested that such an allocation would prevent a balanced budget in 1936. To his dismay, Roosevelt replied: "That is too far in the future. Why worry about the future?" That response, Douglas noted, "explains much."

He went on to mention that he planned to talk about the importance of a balanced budget to an audience in Chattanooga, Tennessee. FDR asked him not to do it because he was considered "the critic of the Administration" and newspapers would "lift a sentence or two out of its context and play it up as a public criticism. The trouble with the New York Times and Herald Tribune is that in criticizing our spending program they do not speak of the necessity of relieving human suffering—they lack a sense of human needs." Douglas pointed out that he too was disgruntled with the spending program except for direct relief. "Lew," Roosevelt exclaimed, "you are obsessed on this subject." "Perhaps I am, Mr. President," he replied, "but at least it is a conviction and a deep one that we can not spend ourselves into prosperity." To clear the "intense" atmosphere, Douglas agreed not to go to Tennessee.

After this exchange he noted with gloom: "This is a serious situation. The conversation indicates a lack of intent and conviction to bring the budget into balance—to fulfill a promise now four times given—it points to a financially irresponsible mind, and certainly leads me to confirm previous suspicions if not previous convictions. What will the future hold for this country?"[39]

By the end of April, Douglas was convinced that Roosevelt had been won over to the policy of deficit spending advocated by economist John Maynard Keynes and liberal advisors such as Tugwell. "I cannot stomach Tugwell or some of his associates," Douglas wrote privately. As for Keynes, Douglas considered him a misguided thinker whose ideas on government spending would lead to national bankruptcy. When at a cabinet meeting Roosevelt championed the idea of a government old-age, disability, and unemployment program, Douglas privately described the proposal as "bunk."[40]

By May he had become so outspoken in his criticism of the administration that his father admonished him to be more circumspect. The son agreed, and in future correspondence with his father referred to Roosevelt as "Torrence." Douglas refused, however, to hide his opinions from FDR himself. "I do not know how long he will stand for my being around for we are in almost constant disagreement," he wrote his father. He wanted to resign in order to run against Henry Ashurst for the Senate, but abandoned the idea when he realized that veterans, government employees, and high-tariff advocates in the state would combine to defeat him. Moreover, he believed that the administration would use its influence to keep him out of the Senate.[41]

Douglas decided that the battle for economy was lost in early June, when he could not dissuade Roosevelt from seeking additional appropriations—a "kitty" for public works and emergencies. Douglas told the President that he already had a kitty of more than $2 billion and should not need more. Agitated, FDR proclaimed: "I want a kitty and would take a kitty for five billions if Congress would give it to me." Douglas asked if the President planned to spend $300 to $400 million monthly, as some press stories claimed. Roosevelt pounded his fist on the desk and thundered: "I am getting God damned sick of having imputed to me things which I never said." Pointing an accusing finger at Douglas, he exploded: "You have been reading Arthur Krock and Maynard Keynes." Uncowed, Douglas answered: "Yes, I have, and if you aren't going to spend at that rate I don't see what you need the money for." Still irate, FDR exclaimed: "I never said I was going to spend at that rate and I don't like you or anybody else to infer I am going to." Then, his anger subsiding, Roosevelt said: "I am just as Scotch as you. I have some Dutch in me also, and I want to save just as much as you want to save."[42]

For two weeks after that stormy exchange, Roosevelt refused to see Douglas. "Things are certainly getting awfully hot for me here," he wrote his father. "Am inclined to think I should move on soon." On June 28 the President at last summoned Douglas to the White House to help divide funds between public works and relief. At that meeting Douglas asked Roosevelt if it would be possible for him to take a vacation until Congress reconvened in early September. FDR readily agreed. In fact, a few weeks earlier, he had telephoned Peggy Douglas to suggest that Lew take some time off. The meeting ended with the two men shaking hands and wishing each other an enjoyable vacation.[43]

The next day Douglas sent Roosevelt a breakdown of the money available for relief and public works. The President was perturbed when the figures showed that there was not enough money to maintain both programs to the extent that he wished. Roosevelt turned to Harold Ickes and Franklin Roosevelt, Jr., and commented: "There is something I want to say here in the family in case I should die: After I fired Dean Acheson . . . Lew Douglas set out to make a written record. He makes a written record of everything. If things go wrong he wants to be in a position so he can show that on such and such a date he advised the President not to do thus and so. Of course, he makes a very good watchdog of the Treasury, but I don't like it."[44]

On July 9 the embattled Douglas left Washington by train for the West Coast. He had drafted a letter of resignation in late June, but decided to give it further consideration over the summer. "I think the die is pretty well cast," he wrote his father, "but I want to forget it for a while so as to come back to it with a lack of prejudice." He traveled to Los Angeles, deliberately avoiding a visit to Arizona in order to dodge questions about the New Deal.

In California Douglas spent a week visiting with his mother, whose Parkinson's disease had continued to progress. He then went to Montana to join Peggy and the children for a vacation at the Flying D cattle ranch on the Gallatin River. Surrounded by snow-crowned peaks, lush grasslands, and hundreds of white-face cattle, the family fished for trout (catching some of six pounds), rode horses, and crossed the Wyoming border to camp in Yellowstone Park. On one occasion Douglas encountered Herbert Hoover on a trout stream and invited him to their ranch house for dinner. Despite stern warnings the children (there were nine, counting nieces and nephews) misbehaved badly. Hoover seemed unaffected, but

Douglas was horrified. Peggy recalls that after Hoover left, her husband lined up the children and gave them "unshirted hell" while she looked on in well-disguised amusement.

Despite the generally relaxed atmosphere, Douglas fretted about resignation. He told his father that when he returned to Washington he planned to have "a frank talk with Torrence," which would probably result in his departure. "I do not agree with you that having taken the job I must stay on until I am fired. I think on the contrary that when my influence has ended—as I think it has—and when the evidence of continuous and excessive expenditures is at hand—as I think it is—I should resign and state why."[45]

Back in Washington, Douglas decided that "the bell had definitely rung" for him. He learned that Roosevelt had "frittered away" the bulk of a $2.5 billion relief appropriation he had received in June and that he planned to request an additional $600 million. He also discovered that the administration planned to support strikers by allowing them to obtain relief. Finally, he heard Treasury Secretary Morgenthau tell a national radio audience that the administration planned to use the profits from gold devaluation to balance the budget. He branded that statement as "so god damned dishonest that he ought to be ashamed of himself for ever having uttered it." It was, he informed a friend, "absolutely indicative and characteristic of the complete stupidity and utter childishness of the thinking of the high command."[46]

His mind made up, Douglas went to see Roosevelt at Hyde Park on August 30. Arriving at 6 P.M, he was greeted warmly by the President and the two men adjourned to the study. After discussing their respective summer holidays, Douglas came to the point. "Mr. President, this is a sad occasion for me for I am inclined to think that I should move on." Roosevelt believed that Douglas was feeling blue and did not take his statement seriously. "You look as though you were in your grave already and you aren't, nor are you going to resign." Douglas did not indicate that his decision was firm because, as he wrote soon afterward in a long handwritten letter to his father, he "wanted to see his cards." He was perhaps hoping that FDR would make an iron-clad commitment that would permit him to stay on. Roosevelt spent more than two hours trying to dissuade Douglas, but he refused to make promises about a balanced budget.

When FDR asked him why he was considering resignation, Douglas explained that the administration no longer supported the objectives of restrained spending and budget equilibrium. With the abandonment of gold-redeemable money, he asserted, it was "imperative" to adhere to a balanced budget "in order to save the currency and prevent universal misery." Since he could not loyally support a program which he believed would result in paper inflation and the destruction of the economy, he was leaving.

In response, Roosevelt professed his belief in a balanced budget, but emphasized that pressing relief requirements necessitated the delay of that objective for several years. Douglas maintained that the administration had spent so lavishly and had "created [such] powerful vested interests in spending" that the budget might not ever be brought into balance. FDR asked Douglas, "Shall I stop relief expenditures and public works and let people starve?" Once again, Douglas claimed that the administration could have both a balanced budget and social compassion by discontinuing all emergency expenditures except for direct cash relief. The other programs, though politically expedient and uplifting to the recipients, created spiraling deficits, which would destroy the currency and impoverish the majority. Roosevelt replied: "Lew, those are matters which you and I must work out this Fall. I want to study that with you and come to joint conclusions."

Roosevelt then pointed out that the budget for fiscal year 1936 needed to be prepared. Douglas asserted that people in his office were capable of doing the job. He then handed FDR a letter of resignation, which read: "After much thought I have regretfully come to the conclusion that I can not now be of further service either to you or to the public and that in your interests it would be better to replace me with someone who is in more complete accord with your budgetary policies. I am therefore, tendering my resignation. I am deeply grateful for the opportunity you have given me to perform a public service."

Roosevelt hurled the letter on his desk with the remark: "This means the loss of the Congressional elections." Douglas responded: "Oh, no, I am not that important." "Well, that's what it means," the President countered. "There are many people who believe in you—people in all walks of life. They will turn. Your job has been, as I told you, an unpleasant one. Your job is to sit on the lid. When you have come in and criticized after you have gone out I have always said 'There goes dear old Lew doing his job better than anyone could do it.' I should be the one to criticize you for criticizing but I never have. Now, if you go and this letter goes out people who believe in you will turn against me."

The President asked Douglas as a personal favor to delay his departure until the completion of the congressional elections. Douglas refused because it would be dishonest. FDR told him that a decade hence he would regret having left the administration. He requested that Douglas talk with some congressional friends and sleep on the decision overnight. He agreed. The next morning, however, he telephoned to inform the President that his decision was final.

According to observers who visited him the next day, Roosevelt was "terribly upset and hurt" by Douglas's action. FDR called Morgenthau to come over from his nearby estate after Douglas left to tell him of the resignation and ask his advice. That afternoon the President announced the resignations of Douglas and Fred Lowery and the appointment of Daniel Bell as acting budget director. He also sent a terse letter to Douglas accepting the resignation. "It is, of course, with regret that I must accept your resignation as Director of the Budget."[47]

Although hurt by Roosevelt's exceedingly brief letter, Douglas was relieved that the break had finally been made. He was disappointed that he could not bring the budget into balance, but had no regrets about having taken the post. Had he stayed in Congress, he reminded his father, he would have resisted most New Deal measures and would probably have lost his seat. By taking the budget directorship he had exerted some influence during the early New Deal, and served the public during a national crisis. Press stories recounting his service were generally favorable, and hundreds of citizens, including cabinet members and congressmen, congratulated him for a job well done.[48]

After a few weeks, Roosevelt mellowed and sought a reconciliation. He sent a warm letter inviting Lew and Peggy to the White House for a visit. He also expressed his gratitude for Douglas's services. "I do not need to tell you that in spite of the wide divergence of views that developed, our personal friendship continues, and of course I shall always feel grateful for the unselfish valuable contribution you made during those early troubled days when we were getting things back on their feet again." In his reply, Douglas thanked his former chief for the nice letter and the invitation to Washington. He could not resist, however, a final word about the budget. "I hope, and hope most fervently, that you will evidence a real determination to bring the budget into actual balance, for upon this, I think, hangs not only your place in history but conceivably the immediate fate of Western Civilization. Yours, as ever doubtful but so sincerely wishful of success."[49]

Lewis Douglas left the budget directorship because the goal of a balanced budget seemed utterly lost and he could not faithfully serve a President whose policies he believed would lead to economic collapse with intense human suffering. Although in principle Roosevelt never abandoned his orthodox economic convictions, he was flexible enough to postpone the goal of budget equilibrium in favor of unorthodox policies that offered the hope of speeding economic recovery and relieving destitution. An astute politician, FDR also recognized that experimentation and spending were popular. While Roosevelt was willing to play hunches and experiment, Douglas clung rigidly to his economic principles. He considered FDR an intellectual lightweight who played fast and loose with the nation's credit and economic health. He was convinced that the President "never understood the consequences of his actions and was often bewildered by the results of his own actions. He did, however, have supreme confidence in himself to deal with whatever might happen to him tomorrow because of what he might do today."

For Douglas, a balanced budget, sound money, an international gold standard, and low tariffs were articles of faith. "My whole educational foundation rested upon international liberalism," he wrote in his memoirs. In the pursuit of orthodox principles, he often became moralistic, doctrinaire, and emotional. Too often he portrayed those who challenged orthodoxy as incompetent and sinister. A contemporary observer wrote that Douglas saw "disaster at every turn" and "confused the principle of laissez faire with the Word of God." Even Douglas admitted that his convictions were at times an inconvenience because they caused him so much personal difficulty.

Reviewing his decision to resign years later, Douglas admitted that he was "too excessive" and "too unaccommodating" and that his "judgment as to timing was quite wrong." He never questioned, however, his economic convictions and never admitted that he might have been wrong.[50]

PART FOUR

Against the Current

10

Private Man and Public Critic

As a courtesy to Roosevelt, Douglas declined to comment on his resignation until after the November elections. To those who urged him to speak out, he explained: "The act of resigning speaks louder than anything I can say." He also resisted appeals to run for Congress or the Arizona governorship because the political climate did not favor conservatives.[1]

Eager to avoid the limelight, the Douglases spent several weeks at Hastings-on-Hudson, where they relaxed with Peggy's parents and the McCloys. Then on October 6 they sailed to Europe aboard the French liner *Paris*. The couple spent a month touring London, Paris, Brussels, Florence, Rome, and the hill towns of Italy.[2]

Abroad Douglas contemplated his future. Having temporarily forsaken a return to public service, he looked for a job that would be fulfilling and remunerative. Despite hard times he anticipated little difficulty in finding a suitable position. Indeed, one publication named him as one of the twelve outstanding young men of America.

In short order, Douglas received attractive offers in industry, the movies, and education. William B. Bell, head of American Cyanamid, asked him to join the industrial chemical company as vice-president. Bankers who controlled Paramount Pictures invited him to head and reorganize the bankrupt movie company. Trustee Newton Baker wanted him as president of Johns Hopkins University. And James Conant, president of Harvard, offered the position of assistant president of the university. Douglas was inclined to take the American Cyanamid offer, but postponed a decision until he returned from his trip abroad.[3]

After several meetings in New York with Bell and other Cyanamid representatives, Douglas agreed to serve as the company's vice-president and director. He was attracted to academic life, but he also longed to "experience the discipline of the competitive world." Moreover, the Cyanamid post brought $30,000 yearly, nearly twice the salary offered by Harvard. Paramount Pictures offered the most money and Peggy believed the movie business would be exciting, but Lew did not "want to be associated with a company which must produce cheap stuff nor would I be happy with the kind of persons in the operating end." He explained to his father that he had "a reputation for decency and honesty and directness—the most precious thing a man can have—which would be damaged by . . . selling out to the movies."[4]

Unlike Paramount, American Cyanamid was a "clean" and growing company headed by a proper Quaker, William Bell. The Cyanamid chief, whom Lew and Peggy nicknamed Buttonshoes for his style of footwear, admired Douglas and shared his economic conservatism. Indeed, he had offered Douglas a place with the company while he was still budget director. The two men liked and respected one another, but they never reached a first-name basis.[5]

Douglas expected the Cyanamid job to provide his family with financial security. He was now forty, and his comfortable lifestyle had thus far been subsidized by his father. With his son no longer in public service, James repeatedly advised him to acquire a competence. "The period of acquisition of a man's life is comparatively short & in your case it is about half gone & you haven't had much of a chance to really appreciate the value of a dollar, which is not your fault but largely due to my good fortune & the luxurious manner in which we have lived." J.S. reminded him that his "great grandfather's life was ruined because he didn't realize the value of a dollar" and that his grandfather's vast fortune had been virtually dissipated. James urged him to invest at least 5 percent of his yearly income in life insurance and to plan for an old-age pension.

Hurt by his father's admonitions about austerity (J.S. had pointed out the extravagance of sending flowers to Josalee), Lew responded sarcastically that he would henceforth devote "every energy to becoming financially independent." He considered giving up his residence in Arizona to escape income taxes, and in the future he threatened to accept lucrative business directorships from questionable companies such as Paramount. He professed to know the meaning of thrift, but ended his letter by asking his father for a loan of $100,000 to buy three thousand shares of Cyanamid stock.

At a stormy meeting in New York, James Douglas agreed to the loan. In return, however, he asked Lew to restrict his political activities. The father was convinced that Lew's involvement in politics aggravated his son's stomach disorder. Lew dismissed the connection, but consented to the request.[6]

The decision to join American Cyanamid in New York brought the Douglases back to familiar surroundings. Peggy's family lived nearby, and Lew had spent much of his youth and early adulthood in the metropolitan region. With many friends and relatives in the area, the couple did not regret leaving "the City of Dreadful Night," as Lew called the nation's capital. The Douglases obtained a comfortable apartment at 781 Park Avenue to accommodate their children and three dogs. The apartment was within walking distance of Lew's office on the fifty-sixth floor of the RCA building on Fifty-first Street. Peggy brought with her Ninny, the children's governess. And Douglas coaxed his long-time secretary, Robert Stroud, into giving up his office manager's job in Washington to resume service with him.[7]

As in Washington, the Douglases were promptly embraced by the social élite. They attended the opera, ballet, and theatre. But while Douglas appreciated the arts, he lacked his wife's enthusiasm. He preferred to attend sports events, socialize with friends, or spend a quiet evening at home. He was an avid reader of history, biography, and economics, and he excelled at storytelling and extemporaneous speaking. He admired American western art, collecting works by Frederic Remington, Charles Russell, and N. C. Wyeth.

The Douglases were persistently sought out to serve on the boards of charitable, educational, and public-service organizations. Lew accepted affiliations with Amherst, the Teachers Insurance and Annuity Association, the Rockefeller Foundation, and the American Political Science Association. He also accepted membership on the boards of two organizations his grandfather had done much to promote: Memorial Hospital and the Museum of Natural History.

During these years, Peggy Douglas began a lifelong association with the American Red Cross and the Metropolitan Opera, to both of which she made invaluable contributions in fund-raising. In late 1967, George S. Moore, president of the Metropolitan Opera Association, wrote that "the whole Metropolitan Opera 'world' and most of the outside world agree that we would not be in business today if it had not been for Peggy. Her achievements have been fabulous. As a matter of fact I would not have taken the job as President if it hadn't been for her." In the 1970s, Peggy also served as a board member of the Lincoln Center for the Performing Arts. When she resigned that position in 1982, she was accorded a luncheon in her honor, presided over by Walter Cronkite, at which Leontyne Price sang "Peg o' My Heart."[8]

The Douglases had a happy marriage. Although Lew thoroughly enjoyed the company of women, especially beautiful and intelligent ones, was always courtly in his manner toward them, and genuinely respected their observations and opinions, he had but one love—Peggy. She nicely balanced her husband's temperament. Like Lew, she possessed charm, social grace, warmth, and a sense of humor. She was self-assured and intelligent, a fiercely loyal mother and an invaluable helpmate. She occasionally teased or chided her husband. In an address before the Academy of Political Science, Lew referred to the biblical story of David in the lions' den. Peg promptly interrupted to point out that it was actually Daniel who tamed the beasts.

Although Lew never shut Peggy out, he made the major decisions in their life. He often discussed his work with her, but his father served as his closest confidant on business and political matters. Like so many husbands of that time, Lew believed that wives should not be troubled with money matters. It was not until her husband died that Peggy learned the details of their finances. During their fifty-three-year marriage, the couple were seldom separated, but when they were they exchanged love letters, not perfunctory communications. Her letters abound with pride in his achievements, concern for his health, supportiveness, and affection. His letters were affectionate, but not very newsworthy. She once chided him: "Dearest: I love to know you miss me but I would like some news beside—you write the worst letters on earth."[9]

As parents, Lewis and Peggy were loving and indulgent. Lew was away much of the time, but tried to spend weekends and large portions of the summer with Doo, Peter, and Sasselberry, as he nicknamed Sharman. Like his father before him, he had high expectations for his children and tried to instill in them a sense of independence and habits of hard work and perseverance. When the boys were aged three and five, Lewis corresponded with a number of prestigious eastern preparatory schools about enrollment ten years thence. Eventually the boys attended St. Albans in Washington and Groton in Massachusetts before going on to college at Amherst and Yale. Sharman enrolled in the Brearley School in New York and later attended Vassar College.

While his own father had been undemonstrative and distant, Lew was affectionate and fun-loving. He roughhoused with the children, dressed in silly costumes to amuse them, and sometimes instigated water wars and pillow fights. For the parents and children, summers were adventure-filled sojourns in Yellowstone Park, the Grand Tetons, southwestern Montana, the Colorado Rockies, or the family camp in the Adirondacks. Together they rode horses, fished, swam, camped, and canoed. Occasionally they went on family vacations with the McCloys, Achesons, or Davisons. Doo became an accomplished horseman, Peter developed an appreciation for fishing, and Sharman acquired her father's love for the out-of-doors.[10]

At times Lew could be a stern parent, but he was generally not very strict with the children. Nor was Peg. On more than one occasion, James S. Douglas complained of his grandchildren's undisciplined behavior. "To one who sees them only on a short visit your impression is a natural one," Lew protested, "but they do spend a great deal of time during every day reading very quietly and I think have for children an abnormal capacity for quiet." He went on to say that during a visit to Arizona the children showed signs of independence by catching, saddling, and caring for their horses. "To properly bring up children in this day is a problem," he concluded.

Grandfather Douglas believed that religious instruction would help tame his rambunctious grandchildren. He professed shock to learn that on one Sunday morning Douglas had taken his children to the zoo instead of to church. Sunday school was important, he insisted, because it taught young people "to be obedient to the teaching of our Savior." While admitting that he was no saint, Rawhide Jimmy claimed that regular religious instruction during his formative years in Quebec was responsible for "what little character for good I may have." The senior Douglas was convinced "that parents have gotten away from the simple well-known basic things about the upbringing of the young that are of more importance from the time of the cradle than are the choices of supposedly high grade private schools."[11]

Actually, neither parent was very scrupulous about religion. Lew was an Episcopalian and as a youth had regularly attended church and Sunday school. As an adult, he raised the children in the Episcopalian faith but only occasionally attended services himself. He preferred to read the newspaper, golf, ski, ride horseback, or play tennis. Raised in a family of scientists, Peggy was not christened until the late 1940s, when she went to England as the ambassador's wife. Her friends Dot Davison, Sally Brophy, and Lord Halifax, the former envoy to the United States, convinced her that she would not join them in Heaven unless she was baptized. Consequently she was christened at Westminster Abbey with Halifax serving as her godfather. Later, during a visit of the Halifaxes, she was confirmed in the faith at a small church in Nogales, Arizona.[12]

Throughout the 1930s, the Douglases lived comfortably, but not extravagantly. They owned a house in Arizona, but sold the house in Georgetown to finance their living quarters in New York. They traveled, entertained often, and bought well-tailored clothes, but avoided ostentatious displays of wealth. In 1936 the couple's estimated worth, including real estate and 3,000 shares of Cyanamid stock, totaled $178,000.

Douglas was generally well groomed and impeccably dressed. He had little interest in food and would have eaten "nails with ketchup" had Peggy served them. He enjoyed dinner parties for the conversation rather than the food. Perhaps for that reason, he managed to maintain a weight of about 170 pounds on a five-foot-eleven frame. He enjoyed good wine, and with the end of Prohibition he asked his father to order him several cases of French champagne, burgundy, and sherry. He drank vodka regularly, but never to excess. He smoked cigarettes during his early manhood, but quit when doctors convinced him that the use of tobacco irritated his sinuses and aggravated his stomach disorder.

Although he suffered from ill health all his life, Douglas rarely complained. Nor did he often lose his temper. Peg or the children might provoke an occasional outburst, as would a spendthrift New Dealer, but generally he was composed, charitable, and cheerful. He struck some people as being self-righteous and stubborn, but most found in him a determined man of conviction.[13]

Douglas prized good manners and courtesy, but in one respect departed from those gentlemanly qualities by being habitually late. He was rarely tardy for Peg, but kept most other people waiting. Those close to him explained that he had difficulty ending conversations because he did not want to seem abrupt or uninterested. Not surprisingly, his lack of punctuality caused problems for his secretaries. They referred to him teasingly as "the late Mr. Douglas."

As an employer, Douglas was considerate but demanding. He learned subordinates' first names, inquired about their families, helped them with personal problems, and generally treated them kindly. One assistant recalled that most employees adored "Mr. D." and "would bust a gut" for him. Still, he was a taskmaster who drove himself and others hard. He arrived at the office about 9 A.M. and worked until 6 P.M., sometimes later. From his employees, especially the secretaries, he expected, at reasonable but not generous wages, long hours, efficient performance, dedication, and occasional weekend work. He wanted a job to be done his way, though he would accept suggestions when they seemed justified. Inefficient performance seldom resulted in dismissal, however. Instead of firing people, Douglas preferred to demote or transfer them to less-exacting positions.

For much of his career, Douglas's most trusted and valuable assistant was Robert Stroud. For nearly twenty years, Stroud served as secretary, researcher, and advisor. He recalled that during their long association only once did he and Douglas exchange sharp words. On that occasion, Douglas mistakenly blamed his assistant for a foul-up and used his last name as he snapped at him. Later, Douglas realized that he had spoken out of anger and apologized.[14]

While not as extreme as his father, Douglas was cautious with money. He once refused to send a wire to his mother because it cost $1.30. He occasionally saved the expense of buying Christmas presents for parents who had everything.

He declined Dean Acheson's invitation to join the Kedgewick Salmon Club because it was too costly. And he bought expensive clothes, in part, because they lasted for years. He wore some articles of clothing when most people would have discarded them.

Lew indulged Peggy and the children and sometimes bestowed expensive gifts on close friends. When an Amherst classmate died in 1926, Douglas and several other alumni established a trust fund of $8,000 to finance the college education of the man's two sons. When Fred Lowery died in 1936, Douglas helped support his widow. On another occasion he loaned $500 to a former Montclair assistant headmaster who had fallen on hard times. The loan was interest-free, though Douglas did insist upon a promissory note.[15]

Douglas assumed his duties at American Cyanamid on December 10, 1934. As vice-president, he served mainly as a trouble-shooter and economic analyst. He inspected the company's various operations, met with stockholders, and assessed national and international political and economic conditions. In January, 1935, he went to Europe, where he met with cabinet members, politicians, bankers, and opinion-makers. In Great Britain he conferred with Neville Chamberlain, chancellor of the exchequer, and lunched at Chartwell with Winston Churchill, whom he had met at Bernard Baruch's home in New York in the early 1930s.[16]

Despite the extensive travel it entailed, the Cyanamid job afforded Douglas ample opportunity to address public issues. More than anything else, the Democratic sweep in the congressional elections of 1934 convinced him he should speak out. That election, he wrote his father, "confirms my fears that F.D.R. has released forces" that might lead to socialism, "whether he wills it or no." On December 12, he debated the merits of deficit spending with economist Stuart Chase before the New York Economic Club. In the debate, he reiterated his arguments against budget gaps. Conservatives such as James Warburg, who presided over the debate, delighted at "hearing Lew take Mr. Chase apart." Douglas's presentation also brought additional requests to speak out on economic issues.[17]

Throughout the spring and summer of 1935 Douglas lashed out against the excesses and abuses of the New Deal. As always, he advocated laissez-faire remedies for the nation's economic ills. "Am reading Adam Smith's *Wealth of Nations* again," he wrote his father early in the year. "You should read it. As true today—in fact truer—than it was in 1776." In a widely publicized speech before the Wharton School of Finance and Commerce, Douglas stressed the point that swollen budgets had historically paved the way for dictatorship. "It is not unreasonable to suspect," he stated, "that if the mark had not been destroyed by the post-war German inflation, Hitler and Nazism would not now be in Germany." The United States could undergo a similar experience and see its liberties demolished.

The Wharton speech stung Roosevelt. He drafted a reply branding Douglas's remarks "reprehensible" because they came "very close to the kind of lack of patriotism which tends to the destruction of government. In time of war, that kind of lack of patriotism goes under the word 'treason.' In time of peace all that one can do is to call it by the mild appellation of 'lack of patriotic duty.'" After some reflection, FDR decided to ignore Douglas's speech. A month later, however, at the same campus, Harold Ickes assailed the speech.[18]

In early May, Douglas delivered the Godkin Lectures, a series of four talks at Harvard that constituted his most vigorous and ambitious attack against the New Deal. He found a "deadly parallel" between New Deal fiscal policies and "the acts of the Soviet undertaken after the fall of the Kerensky regime." Citing the AAA, NIRA, Wagner Labor Bill, and the Banking Bill of 1935 as examples of unwarranted federal authority, he claimed that "the Administration's design—conscious or unconscious—is that of a Collective system." He urged a return to the "liberal tradition"—those principles of free competition, low tariffs, small government, sound money, and pay as you go, which prevailed during the presidencies of Jefferson and Jackson. Douglas's analysis, enthused New York congressman Richard Scandrett, reflected "good old-fashioned straight Amherst thinking."

But while the call for a return to laissez faire appealed to some Americans, it seemed hopelessly unrealistic to many others. Business executives would have been unwilling to abide by the laws of free trade and uncontrolled competition. Moreover, strict enforcement of the antitrust laws probably would have required a greater degree of government regulation than Douglas and other disciples of Adam Smith would have been willing to tolerate. Throughout the Godkin Lectures, Douglas overstated the extent of government control over the economy. He claimed, for example, that the AAA gave the executive "complete power over agriculture" and that the NRA "vested in the Executive complete powers over all industry and commerce."

Douglas was also mistaken in his assertion that budget deficits inevitably led to currency inflation and then dictatorship—such had not been the case when the United States resorted to greenbacks after the Civil War. And he exaggerated the economic argument in explaining the rise of totalitarianism in Russia and Germany. Like other zealots, he defined issues in terms of black and white. There was no middle ground between private enterprise and state socialism. "We must elect, as our ultimate goal," he wrote, "State ownership of all means of production—a static society and tyranny on the one hand, or we must elect private ownership of property—a progressively rising standard of living, a competitive society, and freedom on the other." The federal government should serve only "as an umpire of a game played by others under a simple set of rules," not as "a player in the game."[19]

Perhaps because the lectures were so widely reported, their publication as a book, *The Liberal Tradition: A Free People and a Free Economy*, failed to arouse much interest. Reviews were generally complimentary, though critical of his penchant for overstatement and alarmism. Lewis Gannett in the New York *Herald Tribune* scored him for his "hysterical gloom, his violent antagonism to everything represented in the New Deal, and his nervous extremism of statement." Even Douglas's close friend William Mathews believed he was crying wolf too often. Douglas, however, did not relax his efforts.[20]

Though one of the most celebrated, Lewis Douglas was certainly not the only Democrat to flail away at the New Deal. Governors Joseph B. Ely of

Massachusetts and Albert Ritchie of Maryland, former Secretary of War Newton Baker, and one-time presidential advisor James Warburg all objected to administration policies. In the Senate, Carter Glass and Harry Byrd of Virginia, Millard Tydings of Maryland and Josiah Bailey of North Carolina counted themselves in the anti–New Deal camp. A gloomy Glass wrote to Douglas in November, 1935, that it was a good time to die "when the country is being taken to hell as fast as a lot of miseducated fools can get it there."

Another group of prominent disaffected citizens, including John W. Davis, Alfred E. Smith, and Jouett Shouse organized the American Liberty League in 1934 to prevent what they saw as the destruction of individual freedom and private enterprise by the Roosevelt administration. Douglas sympathized with its objectives and attended some of its functions, but declined membership in the organization because it attacked the President personally and failed to denounce monopoly, high tariffs, and government paternalism.[21]

Convinced that the New Deal was an attempt "to convert four years into perpetual tenure of office and possession of inclusive power," Douglas yearned to reenter national politics. When Congresswoman Isabella Greenway decided not to run again, Douglas was inclined to announce his candidacy. He dropped his plans when advisors warned that, owing to the strength of New Deal sentiment, running as an anti-Roosevelt candidate "would be like butting your head against a stone wall."[22]

With encouragement from Arthur Krock, Walter Lippmann, and other conservatives, Douglas worked to organize a national meeting of dissident Democrats to "approve of a calm and deliberate document indicting the basic features of the New Deal . . . and reaffirming a faith in the basic philosophy of the Democratic Platform of 1932." He eventually scrapped the idea of a meeting because it might "degenerate into a cheap performance" such as the one sponsored by Governor Eugene Talmadge of Georgia in late January, 1936. He did not, however, abandon the idea of a conservative Democratic manifesto.[23]

Hoping to influence the platform-drafting committees of both major political parties, Douglas joined with Newton Baker and Leo Wolman, a Columbia University economist who had served on the National Labor Advisory Board of the NRA, to write a declaration of principles for conservative Democrats. Published in the *New York Times* on June 3, 1936, the declaration denounced the New Era of the 1920s and the New Deal as "two streams from the same source." The former encouraged "private monopoly in the name of national prosperity." The latter promoted "state-controlled monopolies in the name of the national welfare." Both departed "from the basic principles upon which this nation has grown great and has remained free." The authors sought to revive a "political program" based upon free competition, moderate tariffs, states' rights, and fiscal orthodoxy. Those beliefs, they concluded, "are no more than a reaffirmation of the tradition which comes down to us from the beginnings of the Republic and . . . in them are to be found the safeguards of our security and the guarantees of our freedom."

The laissez-faire appeal received scant public support. The *New York Times* and New York *Herald Tribune* commented favorably, but the Springfield *Republican* declared that had FDR not pushed his party to the left it would have gone the way of the British Liberal party after World War I. Senator Millard Tydings endorsed the principles, but other conservative Democrats, including Dean Acheson, Carter Glass, and Harry Byrd remained silent. The appeal, Arthur Krock and Walter Lippmann accurately predicted, would be rejected as reactionary by most Democrats and as too Jeffersonian by most Republicans. Lippmann wrote that "though the position they take has been the historic position of American liberals and progressives from the time of Jefferson to that of Theodore Roosevelt and Woodrow Wilson, there can be no doubt that since the war the country has lost its grip upon these principles. Whether the revulsion now under way against the New Deal marks a revival of these principles or whether it is merely reactionary, we have yet to learn."[24]

The manifesto and its cool reception may have diminished Douglas's slim chance for a spot on the GOP presidential ticket. With the approach of the convention at Cleveland in June, some Republicans sought to organize a fusion party, similar to the Lincoln-Johnson ticket in 1864. On June 2, the day before the publication of the laissez-faire declaration, the New York *Herald Tribune* ran a front-page editorial imploring party leaders to select a reputable conservative Democrat—Byrd, Ely, Baker, or Douglas—for the second spot on the ticket. Financier Thomas Lamont, B. C. Forbes, publisher of *Forbes Magazine*, Harry Chandler, president of the Los Angeles *Times*, House Minority Leader Bertrand Snell, Congressman Richard Scandrett of New York, and Senators Arthur Vandenberg of Michigan and David Reed of Pennsylvania all endorsed the idea of a coalition party with Douglas as one of the standard-bearers. Yet, as Krock pointed out, Douglas's laissez-faire views were "such that no Republican convention could possibly write a platform on which he could run, and Mr. Douglas is very literal about platforms and pledges. He wholly dislikes the entire Republican economic tradition, and he does not think it will change very much."[25]

While Douglas did not actively seek the vice-presidency, neither did he discourage moves on his behalf. His supporters at the convention informed him that his "democratic label" prevented "open bidding," but that he would definitely be the candidate if party leaders agreed upon a coalition ticket. Governor Alfred M. Landon of Kansas, the front-running contender for the nomination, wanted Douglas as a running mate. And, after Landon's nomination, Douglas prepared a press statement which, though never released, indicated his willingness to serve. He was convinced that the GOP had "been reborn at Cleveland" because it had seemingly abandoned its tradition of supporting monopolies, social privilege, and high tariffs. If it wanted him to serve the republic, he could not refuse.

Despite Landon's preference for Douglas, party chieftains convinced the Kansas governor that the ticket would be stronger with a Republican running mate. Once the election was won, they pointed out, Douglas could be offered a cabinet position, such as Treasury Secretary. Landon eventually selected as his vice-presidential candidate Frank Knox, a Chicago newspaper publisher.[26]

Landon nonetheless sought Douglas's advice. Before his nomination he told an acquaintance that he "would rather talk with Lew Douglas than with any other man in the country." Shortly after the nomination, Landon invited Douglas and James Warburg to visit him in Kansas. After a six-hour visit, Douglas was convinced that Landon was "cautious, thorough, broad, realistic, simple and honest" and favorably disposed toward laissez-faire principles, including low tariffs. Warburg was similarly impressed. "We had a most interesting evening with the Governor and I hope that it may turn out to have been a useful one," he wrote a Landon backer. "I think it will because he impressed Lew Douglas—as he did me all over again—with his clear-headed candor, courage, and intelligence, and Lew is an ally worth having."[27]

At Landon's request, Douglas advised him on the campaign and occasionally commented on the candidate's speeches. The Democratic platform of 1936, which promised a continuation of big government, prompted Douglas's first letter to Landon. He was convinced that political and economic freedom depended on the election of the Landon-Knox ticket. The Democratic platform, he wrote, "is an open plea for the kind of government we have not witnessed in America since the days of the thirteen colonies." He called it "a travesty on the memory and principles of Jefferson," and "a contradiction to real liberalism! It is a reversion to the 'Divine Right of Kings' and the Star Chamber of the Stuarts." He implored Landon "to blaze the trail toward real liberalism."

Douglas made similar appeals to Landon's closest advisors. The only way to defeat Roosevelt, he counseled Lacy Haines of the Kansas City *Star*, was to run on a platform of economic liberalism and to make voters aware of the disastrous results FDR's policies would precipitate. Even if such a campaign did not yield victory, it "will have made a record and laid a foundation which may prove, two or four years later, to be the very things which will save the Republic." Above all else, he advised the Landon camp to run a truthful campaign. "You cannot beat Roosevelt at his own game. You cannot beat Roosevelt by promising the celestial heavens. You cannot beat Roosevelt with a glamorous, dramatic actor. You cannot beat Roosevelt by deceit and guile. He has a monopoly on all of these time-worn, cheap, political instruments. But you can beat Roosevelt by contrast! You can beat Roosevelt by being honest."[28]

Poor health limited Douglas's involvement in the campaign. He suffered a recurrence of intestinal pain—an attack so severe that he submitted to a thorough examination. Admitted to Lenox Hill Hospital in New York on June 30, he underwent surgery for a benign tumor two weeks later. When he left the hospital in early August he weighed only 140 pounds, thirty pounds less than normal. After convalescing for two months on his Aunt Naomi's Tilly Foster Farm near Brewster, New York, he regained his weight and strength.[29]

By September Douglas's faith in the Kansan's candidacy was evaporating. At Des Moines, Iowa, Landon advocated increased aid to farmers. In Minneapolis the governor lambasted Secretary of State Hull's reciprocal trade program and endorsed higher tariffs on farm imports. The assault on reciprocal trade cost Landon the support of such conservative Democrats as Dean Acheson, James Warburg, and Newton Baker.

Despite his dissatisfaction with Landon's Midwest speeches, Douglas never had any doubt about which candidate would receive his vote. "It made no difference to me how bad Mr. Landon might be," he confided to a friend. "I was going to vote against Mr. Roosevelt as a matter of protest." Douglas, however, had doubts about whether he should make his preference public. Friends advised him that a pro-Landon proclamation would probably not affect the outcome of the race and might destroy him politically. Douglas acknowledged FDR's invincibility, but he decided to speak openly. On October 23 he informed the press that he planned to vote for Landon. Explaining his decision to Arthur Krock he wrote privately: "This present outfit in Washington is too unscrupulous and I think it would have been the part of a quitter for me to have remained silent."[30]

He made it clear that he was voting more against the New Deal than he was for Landon. He believed that the public had the right to know that, unlike some conservative Democrats, he would not denounce the administration in public addresses and endorse it in the voting booth. He found it necessary to bolt the Democratic party because its "substance has been corrupted, its virtue has been violated. To support it now is to dishonor the deep convictions of a lifetime."

Privately, he considered Roosevelt unbeatable because he had "bought" hundreds of thousands of votes with relief programs. He also believed that FDR would win because he employed "the technique found to be so successful by Mussolini, Hitler, and Stalin, that is, appeals to class hatred and class warfare." In addition, the incumbent's chances were enhanced by an improved economy. "And he is a consummate actor and an unmitigated liar."[31]

On election day, November 3, 1936, Douglas wrote his friend Frank Brophy: "Today is the day! I think the odds are heavy on Roosevelt but, oh, how I hope I am wrong." He was not wrong. In the most lopsided presidential election to date, Roosevelt won every state except Maine and Vermont, outpolling Landon in the Electoral College by a vote of 523 to 8. In the popular vote, FDR outdistanced his opponent by 11 million ballots.

Douglas was surprised by the President's margin. "Well, it is all over and what a landslide it was," he wrote his father. "While I never doubted R's election I had never contemplated anything like this. What it all means is difficult to say." A few days later, Douglas was still trying to understand the result of the election. He doubted, however, that it meant the Americans wanted socialism.[32]

Roosevelt's victory discouraged but did not deter Douglas. He predicted, accurately as it turned out, that the economic recovery of 1935 and 1936 would not endure. He lashed out against the growth of presidential power, especially when FDR tried to "pack" the Supreme Court in February, 1937. Irritated by the Court's unfavorable decisions against the NRA and AAA, Roosevelt sought unsuccessfully to protect his domestic program by adding as many as six justices to the bench. Douglas denounced that proposal as "a cunning and refined attempt to seize ruthless and unrestrained power."

He also decried the growing power and militancy of organized labor. From his conservative perspective, he censured the sitdown strikers at General Motors in 1937 for trespassing, unlawful seizure of property, and preventing more than 100,000 willing men from working. John L. Lewis, head of the newly formed Congress of Industrial Organizations, drew most of Douglas's wrath. Lewis's power, he claimed, resembled that of the "Duponts, the Sloans, the Rockefellers, the Morgans and all the other so-called predatory interests." While not excusing the abuses of big business, he challenged "any man as a matter of pure fairness to balance the record of John Lewis and what he stands for against the record of General Motors."[33]

For Douglas, the only encouraging aspect of the New Deal was Cordell Hull's continued attempts to reduce trade barriers. At Hull's request, he appeared before the Senate Finance Committee in February, 1937, to advocate the extension of the Reciprocal Trade Agreements Act of 1934. After detailing the drawbacks of protectionism, Douglas emphasized that reciprocity was "one of the few frontal attacks anywhere being made" against the world depression.[34]

In 1937 he once again tried to organize an anti–New Deal coalition under Democratic leadership. "I do not know of anyone in a better position to help develop a coalition than you," Landon wrote the former budget director. At a private dinner party in Washington on December 3, Douglas urged a bipartisan group of senators—Harry Byrd, Josiah Bailey, Royal Copeland, Walter George, Carter Glass, William King, Ellison Smith, John G. Townsend, Frederick Van Nuys, and Arthur Vandenberg—to combine against New Deal legislation. According to Vandenberg of Michigan, Douglas was "bluntly pessimistic" about the chances for economic recovery unless congressional leaders put forth an alternative program that would "give business a chance." After Douglas's talk, the guests decided to prepare a coalition statement.

After additional meetings at the residence of Senator Peter G. Gerry of Rhode Island, the group drafted a Conservative Manifesto. It called for a balanced budget, the elimination of the excess-profits and capital-gains taxes, the end of sit-down strikes, states' rights, and the abolition of governmental interference in the economy. Not surprisingly, partisanship undercut the congressional coalition movement.[35]

Feeling politically impotent, Douglas still longed to return to public service. He preferred politics because it was "a field in which perhaps I have some talent and for which I have a deep liking." Yet he realized that his chances for elective office were slim because "public sentiment" was "at odds with the views that I hold." Friends in Arizona implored him to return to the state to live, but he claimed that he could not earn enough money there, however much he might wish to make the move. "After all," he wrote Arthur Curlee, "it is the place where I would rather live than any place I know. My roots are there and, I think in the final analysis, one finds more real common sense on the curb stone in Arizona than one finds in this city. . . ." Anxious to serve but temporarily blocked from politics, Douglas proved receptive when representatives from higher education sought him out for administrative and teaching positions.[36]

11

An American in Canada

BORED WITH HIS JOB AT AMERICAN CYANAMID, Lewis Douglas was ready for a new challenge. In August, 1937, the president of Amherst offered him the newly created Dwight Morrow chair in political science, but the salary of $8,000 was too modest. Douglas expressed keen interest, however, when Sir Edward Beatty, chancellor of McGill University in Montreal, approached him about heading that institution.[1]

A private university, McGill was founded on the slopes of Mount Royal in 1821. The institution was named for James McGill, a wealthy Montreal merchant, fur trader, and civic leader who in 1811 bequeathed £10,000 and his forty-six-acre estate for the construction of a university. Opened in 1829, the institution eventually became one of the leading English-speaking universities in the western hemisphere. Near the turn of the century, Lord Strathcona, a wealthy financier, established Royal Victoria College within McGill to accommodate female students. And in 1906 Sir William Macdonald, a tobacco titan and one-time chancellor of McGill, donated the land, buildings, and money to establish Macdonald College. Located at Ste. Anne de Bellevue, approximately twenty miles west of Montreal, Macdonald College was endowed with more than $4 million to educate McGill students in the fields of household science, agriculture, and teaching.[2]

Like the most prestigious private colleges in the United States, McGill served the white, male Protestant élite. In 1938, about 20 percent of the university's 3,200 undergraduates were women. They enrolled at Royal Victoria College, but took most of their classes at McGill with the men. Only 3 percent of the student body was French-speaking, even though Montreal, a city of 1.2 million inhabitants, was 80 percent French-Canadian. While Jewish students were not excluded, quotas restricted their numbers. Moreover, Jews had to score 150 points higher than Gentiles on entrance examinations to gain admission. Blacks, too, were restricted on the grounds that preference should be given to Canadian applicants.

The university was controlled by a board of governors made up of twenty-three affluent Protestants. As chancellor of the university, Sir Edward Beatty served as chairman of the board of governors. Crusty and domineering, Beatty was a sixty-year-old bachelor with few intimate friends. He had made his fortune as head of the Canadian Pacific Railway and had been chancellor for nearly twenty years.[3]

Traditionally, McGill principals, the equivalent of American college presidents, served long tenures. In a century of existence, only nine men had held the post. Sir Arthur Currie, who presided from 1920 to 1933, was one of the most successful. He was succeeded, after an interregnum of two years, by Arthur Eustace Morgan, a "megalomaniac," according to Beatty, who lasted only two years.[4]

Beatty hoped to find a tactful, cultivated Canadian academician to replace Morgan. R. C. Wallace (principal of Queens University), Sidney Earle Smith (president of the University of Manitoba), and Carleton Stanley (president of Dalhousie University) headed the list of nearly thirty candidates. Beatty added Douglas's name to the list after hearing him deliver a hard-hitting attack against economic nationalism and big government before the Canadian Club of Montreal in mid-April, 1937. After Douglas completed his address one university governor allegedly remarked to Beatty: "There's our man." From that moment Douglas became the chancellor's first choice. Next to his name on the candidate's list he wrote: "Extraordinarily able, and even eminent. Possibility of securing him remote."[5]

Beatty was aware of Douglas's Canadian heritage. James S. Douglas, who had business connections in Montreal, informed the governors that his son "had a distinct preference for academic work and considered his roots to be in Canada." Moreover, Beatty knew of the many contributions James Douglas had made to McGill. From 1910 to 1918 Lewis's grandfather had served on the board of governors. During that time he donated nearly $320,000 to the university, including $150,000 for the construction of the institution's first men's dormitory. Coincidentally, that dormitory, Douglas Hall, was scheduled to open in the fall of 1937.[6]

In mid-August Beatty asked publisher Edward Crane of the Van Nostrand Company to approach Lewis Douglas about the McGill principalship. When Douglas expressed interest, Beatty traveled to New York to discuss the proposition. At a luncheon meeting, he offered Douglas the job.

Initially, Douglas was inclined to reject the offer. The salary of $20,000 plus $5,000 for expenses was adequate, but less than he was making with Cyanamid. He also wondered if he would be expected to surrender his American citizenship and become a Canadian. He further believed that he would be forfeiting his political future by moving outside the United States. Finally, Peggy was reluctant to move to Canada.[7]

On the other hand, there were many attractions. His father, who secretly planned to move to Montreal, stressed sentimental reasons. It was an "honor," he wrote, "which my father would appreciate in the very highest degree." Besides sentiment, the job offered a chance to reenter the field of public service. He confided to Bill Mathews that he would "never be happy until I feel that I am useful—not useful to a particular group that owns a piece of property—but useful in what, to me, seems to be a broader field. The educational field offers that opportunity." The proposal also appealed to Douglas because prospects in politics were quite dim. His conservative views, plus his stint with big business, virtually negated his chances for elective office. To resume a political career, he would have to return to Arizona, build his fences, and await an opportunity. He feared that the wait, which might take years, would be demoralizing. "It causes one's faculties and talents . . . to deteriorate, stagnate and eventually to die of dry rot. It ends in the spectacle of a broken down, has-been politician who lives bitterly in the past and who has no hope for the future." The McGill post, he concluded, "offers a very real chance for a very real service—not perhaps as great as a life of public service—but almost as great. Besides, *"There comes a time in a man's life when opportunities no longer come."* Douglas did not desire to press his luck.

Douglas now wanted to accept the McGill offer, but feared that the job would drain his resources and jeopardize his family's financial security. Reluctantly, he sought his father's assistance. "As you may realize it is not an easy thing to ask," he wrote. "I do it only because I am, I think, not an unproved quantity and because under all the circumstances surrounding my position it appears to be an appropriate thing to do. I have tried to think of the way in which my grandfather and grandmother would look upon me for making the suggestion—whether they would think less of me for putting the matter to you. I think they would approve of my doing it though they would not necessarily approve of your help." Ever generous toward his eldest son, Rawhide Jimmy decided to provide him with $25,000 yearly for as long as he remained at McGill.[8]

With that assurance, Douglas decided to take the job, provided the board of governors accepted his conditions. Meeting with the board over luncheon at the Mount Royal Club, the candidate set forth his terms. First, he would remain an American citizen. Second, he would educate his children in the United States. Third, he would spend his vacations in the United States and retain his affiliations with American organizations. Last, he would be at liberty to leave the principalship whenever it seemed propitious. The governors agreed to the terms, and Lewis Douglas became the first American to head McGill University.[9]

The appointment, announced on October 4, 1937, was received with enthusiasm in both the United States and Canada. The New York *Herald Tribune* wrote that "of the younger Americans of today, few, if any, stand out as does Mr. Douglas for integrity, ability and sound sense." Sir Edward Beatty wrote privately that "no man whom I have met in recent years has impressed me more." And the Montreal *Star* called him a "man of first-rate calibre" who "will be welcomed here as a Canadian come home."[10]

The McGill faculty approved the decision, but with little enthusiasm. As one former faculty member put it: "After Morgan almost anyone would have looked good." The faculty recognized Douglas as a person of "high stature," but most would have preferred a Canadian scholar. Other professors were convinced, with justification, that the American was "using McGill as a stepping stone to something higher" or as a "refuge until he could get back into politics." Some, disturbed by his conservative views and informality, dubbed him Cactus Lew. "My first recollection of Lewis Douglas," law professor Frank Scott recalled, "was during the inaugural reception for him at the McGill Faculty Club, when he put his arm across my shoulder and said 'Call me Lew.' At that moment I wrote him off as a man suitable for leadership at McGill."[11]

In December, 1937, Lewis and Peggy moved to Montreal with their three children. Lew also took with him Robert Stroud to handle his American interests and do some university-related work. Douglas also retained Dorothy McMurray, who had served as principal's secretary to his two predecessors.

The Douglases adapted readily to their new surroundings. There were two languages and two distinct outlooks on life and society, one unchanged since the days of Richelieu, the other the British tradition. The former dominated government and the latter industry, but they lived in relative compatibility despite some "faint rumblings of yearnings for nationalism on part of the French population." The people, Lewis said, were "most warm and cordial in their welcome. I have seldom, if ever, been in such a friendly community except, of course, Arizona. Peg, I think now is enjoying the experience. It was a good deal of a wrench for her at first but she is thoroughly happy now."

Despite the ease of adjustment, Douglas missed living in the United States and made it clear to those close to him that he did not intend to stay long at McGill. Perhaps anticipating that his father planned to give up his American citizenship, Lew wrote him a long letter expressing his affection for the United States. "You may say that this is my grandfather's country—and so it is; but it is not my country. And I find it difficult to put my heart into the service of a land which, however much I may like it, will always be for me a foreign land. At the first appropriate opportunity I propose to return to my own country." Douglas expressed the same sentiments to Frank Brophy. "Someday," he wrote, "I hope that some foolish University will want me in the States for, after all, however much I decry intense nationalism, I find that I am bound by every emotional tie to the United States, however much I think it is now worshipping false Gods and, indeed, has been for almost seventy years."[12]

Lewis Douglas was installed as McGill's tenth principal on January 7, 1938. The ceremony, performed in full academic regalia, took place in Moyse Hall with the chancellor presiding and the Governor General of Canada, Lord Tweedsmuir (the British novelist John Buchan), attending in his capacity as Visitor of the university. Douglas delivered an inaugural speech over the Canadian Broadcasting Corporation. Stressing a familiar theme, he cautioned against the growth of state power at the expense of individual liberty. He pointed out that "throughout the world in varying degree and with different emphases the ideas and practices of democracy are being threatened by the ideas and practices of absolutism." Universities, he warned, must test ideas and pursue the truth lest democracy perish.[13]

During his two years as principal, Douglas was preoccupied with three issues: First, he worked to make the university financially sound. Second, he sought to counteract the socialist viewpoint within the social sciences without undermining the principle of academic freedom. Third, he defended the right, though not necessarily the propriety, of professors to express opinions on public issues which the outside community considered to be tasteless or unpatriotic.

McGill's financial difficulties proved one of the new principal's most pressing challenges. Throughout the depression decade it operated at an annual deficit. In an attempt to balance the budget, the administration in 1932 had implemented a salary cut of 9 percent for faculty and staff. Despite that move, which saved $87,000 yearly, the shortfall persisted. Under Beatty's direction, the board of governors in 1936 agreed to cover the deficit for the next four years. Beatty himself pledged $10,000 yearly, while Jack McConnell, Sir Herbert Holt, and Herbert Molson each guaranteed $25,000 annually. All told, the governors contributed $371,000 from 1936 through 1939.[14]

At the conclusion of the academic year 1937–38, Douglas reported a deficit of $57,882, the smallest in several years. He also announced that the university had received more than $400,000 in contributions to the general fund, including a $250,000 bequest from the estate of Molson and a $50,000 gift from an anonymous source (Samuel and Allen Bronfman of Seagram's distillery). Although the university community was encouraged by the report, Douglas warned against excessive optimism. He declared that the salary cut would not be restored. Moreover, additional reductions in departmental spending would be forthcoming in order to balance the budget.[15]

As he had during the early New Deal, Douglas worked zealously to chop expenditures. With the support of the board, if not the faculty, he decreased the budgets for nearly every department and office. He reduced the number of telephones, urged the conservation of electricity, delayed the purchase of new equipment, disallowed traveling expenses, and cut back on supplies, printing, stationery, clerical assistance, and janitorial service. He refused to fill most vacancies, eliminated lectureships, closed museums, and curtailed entertainment expenses. He recommended single-space typing, utilizing both sides of paper, and the judicious use of postal privileges, mimeographing, and secretarial help. He frustrated the Physics Department by refusing to finance the construction of a radiology laboratory and a cyclotron. He also proposed to dispose of Macdonald College. Over the course of twenty years that institution had drained the university of about $20,000 yearly, and Douglas persuaded the board to authorize its sale to the province for $4 million. The provincial government, however, turned down the offer.[16]

By the end of 1939, Douglas had slashed spending by more than $125,000. Moreover, during this period of retrenchment, he rescinded the original salary cuts and gave raises to some faculty members. He secured private funds to build the cyclotron and to reorganize the Pathology Department. He also approved the use of general funds to operate the Arthur Currie Memorial Gymnasium, a newly constructed facility funded by Lady Strathcona and McGill graduates. Finally, he worked with Beatty to secure an annual grant of $150,000 for ten years from the provincial government. Douglas initially had philosophical reservations about accepting such a subsidy, but set them aside when the Prime Minister assured him that the money would be given unconditionally.[17]

Besides restoring McGill's financial health, Douglas worked to improve the quality of teaching and to ensure "intellectual balance" in the social-sciences curriculum. Some faculty members, however, considered his pursuit of these goals to be heavy-handed and contrary to the principle of academic freedom. A portion of the faculty became alienated and harshly critical of what they termed Douglas's autocratic leadership.

Douglas professed a firm belief in academic freedom. In too many nations, he informed a group of McGill graduates, educational institutions had become schools of propaganda emphasizing "a particular economic or political philosophy agreeable to the personnel occupying places of public power." The mission of a university, he held, was to promote the pursuit of knowledge and the discovery of the truth. Toward that end, it should serve as a haven where "the inquiring mind can roam untrammelled and unrestricted by conventions." Yet the university must also "be an institution which insists on intellectual competence, on intellectual balance, on mental integrity."[18]

By the end of his first term, Douglas perceived that virtually the entire social-sciences faculty were socialists who were advancing their views in the classroom. Frank Scott and Percy Corbett in law, E. R. Adair in history, and J. C. Hemmeon and Eugene Forsey in economics were considered the most outspoken proponents of socialism. Beatty feared that their attacks on the capitalists of St. James Street might alienate the Montreal business community and impair the solicitation of funds. And, in 1938, Douglas received a memorandum from "D.M." (probably the secretary, Dorothy McMurray) pointing out that since 1933 the number of students studying law had declined by nearly 50 percent. "Some people think that this is because of the radical views held by members of this faculty on social problems." Allowing Professor Forsey, "one of the foremost 'pinks' here," to teach a course in economics, the memorandum continued, would further mar the once-unrivaled reputation of the law faculty.

In the late summer of 1938 Douglas worked to offset what he called the collectivist viewpoint. He recommended bringing to the university prestigious conservative scholars in the general field of political economy to give a series of lectures. Beatty wholeheartedly supported the plan.[19]

In late January and early February, 1939, McGill held a series of nine lectures on the role of the state in society. Professor Robert Warren of the Institute for Advanced Study, Leo Wolman, professor of economics at Columbia University, and Henry Clay, economic advisor to the Bank of England, each delivered three talks criticizing the transfer of responsibility from the individual and local level to the state and federal government.[20]

On the whole, Douglas was pleased with the results of these lectures. Attendance varied from a low of 850 during the second week to a high of 1,300 for the final week. Newspaper accounts were generally favorable, and Oxford University Press agreed to publish the talks as *The State in Society* after McGill offered to subsidize the enterprise. Douglas wrote Beatty that the visiting scholars "are giving some of the collectivists on the staff of the University quite a shock. I hope they are doing them some good, and presenting such a case that they are compelled, however reluctantly, to question some of the premises with which they have been indoctrinated by their high priest, Harold Laski."[21]

Douglas also sought to upgrade the faculty and improve the curriculum. He selected F. Cyril James, a conservative British-born professor of finance at the University of Pennsylvania, to head the Commerce Department and to restructure its curriculum. He also asked several senior professors to take early retirement at emeritus rank. The board agreed to pay the forced retirees their full teaching salaries until their pensions took effect at age sixty-five.[22]

Despite those "reforms," Douglas believed that additional steps were necessary. In February, 1939, he developed a comprehensive plan which would, he hoped, improve the quality of instruction and restore intellectual balance to the liberal-arts curriculum. He devised the plan after viewing firsthand the classroom performances of the social-science faculty. He concluded that "there is not a single man on the staff within the field under discussion competent to present and to support with evidence so plentifully available the alternate point of view to that of the collectivists." McGill, he wrote Beatty, would be shirking its duty if it did not expose students to socialist thought. Yet, he continued, it would also be negligent if it failed to offer courses that challenged collectivist philosophy.

Douglas outlined a three-pronged program to provide the "necessary correctives." First, he would reformulate tenure policy, making job security difficult to obtain for younger faculty members. Second, he would have the deans select a small number of faculty, especially assistant professors, qualified for promotion in rank or salary. Although he did not put it in writing, Douglas's intent was to weed out radicals and replace them with vigorous young instructors with a pro-capitalist slant. The last part of the program called for university-sponsored visiting professorships in the social sciences. The employment of top-notch conservative scholars for a period of two or three years would, Douglas confidently predicted, "have a most beneficial effect on the members of the staff who now, without any competent resistance from any quarter, gaily and irresponsibly present to the students unrefuted, and untested, material."[23]

Although the new academic guidelines were intended to serve as "long-term correctives," they immediately affected some liberal and radical professors. Leonard Marsh, a junior professor who directed McGill's Social Science Research Institute, was terminated in 1939. Eugene Forsey was also forced out. A lecturer for ten years, Forsey was an outspoken, irreverent idealist who sympathized and cooperated with the provincial Communist movement. Occasionally he even dressed in a Russian cap and bloomers. Despite the full support of his department head, J. C. Hemmeon, he was repeatedly denied promotion and eventually dismissed because he lacked a doctorate and was considered injudicious. (Forsey went on to obtain the Ph.D. in 1941 and embarked upon a political career, which led to the Canadian Senate. In 1966 McGill awarded him an honorary LL.D. degree.)[24]

The third component of Douglas's program consisted of visiting professorships. For more than a year, Douglas had been looking for an eminent conservative economist to teach at McGill. When his first choice, Henry Clay, failed to express interest, he turned to T. E. Gregory, an economist at the London School of Economics who was then serving as an advisor to the government of India. With the approval of the board of governors, Douglas offered Gregory a three-year position in mid-February.

The appointment encountered sturdy resistance from the faculty. Dean Ernest Brown of Engineering objected to the way Douglas "sprang" proposals on them without prior consultation. He also believed that the money would be better spent in raising the salaries of professors already on the permanent staff. J. C. Hemmeon protested that he had not been consulted about the Gregory appointment. In response, Douglas pointed out that he was not required by either statute or precedent to confer with department chairmen concerning temporary appointments. Nevertheless, he conceded that he should have consulted with Hemmeon as an act of courtesy and apologized for the oversight.

When Hemmeon learned that the lectureship was to last for three years, he urged Douglas to withdraw the offer. Douglas refused to heed the suggestion because it would be dishonorable to withdraw a tender while it was still under consideration. He again apologized for his lack of consideration. Hemmeon: "Is that as far as you will go?" Douglas: "That is as far as I will go." Hemmeon: "Mr. Douglas, it does no good to say you are sorry." Douglas: "Well, Professor Hemmeon, I think we had better drop the matter." On March 15, the University Senate approved the principal's decision to offer the temporary appointment.[25]

During the next week, several faculty members spoke out against it. The consensus of the faculty, according to Dean C. W. Hendel, was "that people view the Principal as being personally very pleasant and delightful but sometimes autocratic in action."

At last, in the interests of averting discord, Douglas agreed to rescind the invitation. On March 29 he informed Gregory that owing to financial considerations he was compelled to withdraw his offer.[26]

Despite some controversy and resistance, Douglas pronounced his conservative program a success. He had facilitated the removal of elderly or inept teachers; he had launched a public lecture series that championed free-enterprise capitalism; he had appointed James to head the Commerce Department. Those "major moves," he wrote Beatty, were "aimed at minimizing the influence on the student population of certain members of the University staff and at increasing the quality of the scholarship and teaching of its staff members."[27]

However heavy-handed and overzealous Douglas may have been in his attempts to check socialist teaching, he nevertheless resisted public demands to silence outspoken professors who challenged repressive provincial laws. Quebec was governed by an ultra-conservative administration headed by Prime Minister Maurice Duplessis. In the 1930s the provincial legislature had enacted legislation, generally called the Padlock Law, which forbade individuals or institutions to advocate Marxist doctrines or to possess Communist literature, including *Das Kapital*.

When Professors Frank Scott and Percy Corbett spoke out against the Padlock statute, Douglas refused to heed public demands for disciplinary action. He informed the Student Society that if it wanted a Communist to speak on campus, he would not oppose the decision. Moreover, when a graduate asked the principal to recommend ten books which the alumni should purchase for the residence-hall library, he included *Das Kapital* in his selection.[28]

Similarly, Douglas defended the free-speech rights of faculty members who opposed Canada's prospective entry into war on the side of Britain. In various public addresses, Scott and Corbett argued that, if Great Britain went to war with Germany, Canada had a right to remain neutral. Corbett held that in the matter of foreign policy Canada should align herself with the United States. Those arguments infuriated many English-speaking citizens, who labeled them unpatriotic and treasonous.

When board member Jack McConnell complained about Corbett, Douglas defended him. He disagreed with the professor, he told McConnell, but would not try to interfere with his right to free speech. "It would be fatal for me to suggest to Corbett that his views are not wholly acceptable; it would be fatal to the University, it would be fatal to the ideal which the University symbolizes."[29]

The free-speech issue became more controversial after Great Britain went to war with Germany in September, 1939. At a luncheon meeting of the Montreal Rotary Club, history professor E. R. Adair described Poland as a weak, repressive, disunified nation without legitimate territorial boundaries; moreover, he said, the German-Russian alliance and the subsequent invasion of Poland by Hitler's armies were caused by the stupidity and timidity of Britain's Prime Minister, Neville Chamberlain.

Adair's remarks brought a storm of protest. One correspondent called the address "sympathetic to the Communist party," while another described it as "partisan piffle." Another irate citizen telephoned the principal's office with a threat to do violence to the professor. The Montreal *Gazette* described the speech as "inopportune, indiscreet and vexatious at this time." And the Montreal *Star* called it a "lamentable exhibition" which would aid the enemy.

Despite the strength of the protest, Douglas defended Adair's right to speak out. However, when McGill students tried to demonstrate their support for the professor, he dissuaded them. He also discouraged the circulation of a campus petition upholding Adair's right to free speech.[30]

While defending free-speech rights of McGill professors, Douglas did little to combat racial discrimination at the university. True, as noted, he offered a visiting professorship to T. E. Gregory, and also agreed to hire for one year a female physical-education teacher whom he believed to be Jewish. Troubled by the double standard, he wrote Dean Hendel "that the whole question of Jewish admission is one that should be carefully reconsidered." He also "grieved at the treatment meted out" to European Jews. On at least two occasions he tried to find jobs outside the university for Jewish refugees, but without success.

Douglas was a decent, compassionate man, but he failed to review admissions policy. As for refugees, he complained that he was "deluged with appeals on behalf of Jews who seek a new life on this continent. There is not much that I or the University can do."

Actually, alternatives did exist, but Douglas failed to act. Terry MacDermot, a one-time McGill history professor who became principal of Upper Canada College, pointed out that the University of Toronto was adding highly qualified Jewish refugees to its teaching staff and that "they were just about revolutionizing the place, bringing their brilliant minds to work and jacking everyone up." Other individuals pressed McGill to adopt a program similar to one at the University of Toronto that raised money to educate Jewish refugees in Canadian schools. Douglas dismissed both programs. When T. H. Mathews, McGill's registrar, asked Douglas if he could propose as a topic for the national Universities Conference the enrollment of refugee Jews in Canadian colleges, he was discouraged. It was,

Douglas counseled, "a controversial, even dangerous subject, on which much embarrassment might develop from public discussion." For the same reason, he rejected the registrar's suggestion to establish at McGill a "definite University policy" on the subject of admitting Jewish refugees. McGill did not alter its discriminatory policies until the 1950s.[31]

Despite some confrontations with the faculty, economic hard times, discriminatory policies, and Canada's involvement in the war, Douglas enjoyed his job. His informality and vibrant personality made him popular with the administrative staff. His predecessor, one graduate observed, shunned subordinates, but Douglas spoke to and took an interest in them. Dorothy McMurray wrote that "he was so warm and friendly and the atmosphere in the office was so pleasant that the hours passed like a song." And after his departure she thanked "the powers that be for having had the privilege of being associated with you even for a short time."[32]

Douglas was also well liked by the students. He told the incoming class in 1938 that he, too, was a freshman who had much to learn. On occasion he played baseball with students. Once he participated for the Commerce Department team and, according to the student newspaper, showed "classy fielding and some truly fine base-running and stealing." He also told the students that he would always try to be "an understanding and considerate associate."

Only rarely did he lose his patience with students. He became furious when a group of undergraduates, who were celebrating McGill's first football championship in a decade, marched on the German Club on Drummond Street and nearly destroyed it. He also fumed when students balked at his call for frugality and moderation in social activities after the outbreak of the war. With so many citizens making sacrifices to aid the war effort, Douglas believed it would be in poor taste for McGill students to hold lavish parties in downtown hotels, to have the band play at sporting contests, to pull pranks, and to evidence signs of extravagance.

When the *McGill Daily* ran an editorial ridiculing the principal's position, he scolded the editor "like a father." A few days later, he also lectured the student council. Students at other leading Canadian universities had voted to keep activities "on a quiet basis, the bands would not travel, no dances in hotels." Surely, he reminded them, they wanted to avoid having him "forbid this and that as if you were all school boys." The council took the hint.[33]

As they did everywhere they lived, the Douglases enjoyed an active social life. They mingled with the élite in private homes, in vacation retreats, and in downtown hotels such as the Ritz, Mount Royal, and Windsor. They took weekend skiing holidays to Ste. Marguerite, Ste. Agathe, and St. Sauveur in the Laurentians. Douglas fished the St. John and Corneille rivers for salmon. He regarded that fish as "the king of them all, and he who respects him as I do, . . . is not so keen to kill as he is to see and to enjoy the seeing."

Douglas also spent a good deal of time in the United States. Princeton, Brown, Wesleyan, and New York universities awarded him honorary degrees. Alpha Delta Phi fraternity honored Douglas, author Thornton Wilder, and Supreme Court Justice Harlan F. Stone for contributions to the society. As a board member for several organizations, he felt compelled to attend meetings. He also continued to speak out on political and economic issues, delivering speeches at Harvard, Yale, and Amherst, the New York *Herald Tribune* Forum, the Economic Club of New York, and the American Political Science Association. He spent his summers at the Flying D ranch in Montana, in California visiting his mother, and in New York. And when his son Peter became ill in the winter of 1938, he spent several days at Groton comforting him.[34]

The visit of King George VI and Queen Elizabeth proved the major social event of Douglas's principalship. Their Majesties visited Montreal in late May, 1939. The Douglases gave them a tour of the city and attended receptions in their honor in Montreal and Quebec. When the King and Queen toured McGill, Peggy recruited scores of children and her resisting French-speaking maids to line the royal procession route and wave small Canadian flags as the couple passed. Despite the austerity budget, Douglas spared little expense in preparation for the visit. He redecorated the campus and held a garden party attended by a thousand people. Although the Douglases spent only a few days with the King and Queen, they found them a gracious, delightful couple. At a dinner in their honor in Montreal, they joined the Douglases and Mayor Houd in singing "Alouette" and other French songs. The brief encounter between the two couples was prologue to their friendship when Douglas became ambassador to Great Britain less than a decade later.[35]

Although Douglas had never planned to remain long as principal, a rift with his father prompted him to resign sooner than he had intended. In December, 1938, James S. Douglas disposed of his Arizona mining interests, renounced his American citizenship, and moved to Montreal. When the son learned of his father's actions, he was stunned and hurt. The pain turned to anger when he discovered that James had forced Josalee to sign an oath of allegiance to the British Crown. Indeed, that incident nearly severed the close relationship between father and son.

At the British consulate in Los Angeles in early December, 1938, Josalee Douglas, emotional and confused, agreed to become a Canadian citizen out of fear of alienating her domineering, insensitive husband. On December 5 she wrote Peggy: "As you know Father wanted me to become a Canadian citizen in order to avoid paying exorbitant inheritance taxes. I rebelled and said I wouldn't do it. I was an American and wanted to stay one. I have always been very proud of being an American citizen but this was of no avail and he took me in my wheel chair to the English Council [sic] and forced me to sign. I said 'I can't do it Jim,' and he said 'you will do it.'" Declaring that it was "breaking my heart," she implored Peggy to have Lew intercede on her behalf.

After receiving additional information from his mother, Douglas sent his father a reproachful wire via Josalee: "Mother telegraphed your proposed actions. She is profoundly disturbed and asks my advice. I must respond. Needless to say I am deeply disappointed and permanently shaken. You will not find relief you seek. Indeed within three years the burden there will be as great as here." From Douglas, Arizona, the father responded: "All is well and mother not abnormally disturbed, writing." In his letter J.S. tried to calm his son by playing down the incident. Josalee, he reminded Lew, was emotional and prone to exaggeration. In reality, he claimed, she accepted naturalization "without a murmur." He then berated his son for sending such a "shocking" telegram. The next day he sent Lew another letter rebuking him for sending such an "amazingly indiscreet telegram." After reading his father's unrepentant letters, Lew professed to be "more deeply shocked than ever." He warned Rawhide Jimmy that he had advised Josalee to seek legal counsel and that if she decided to fight for the return of her citizenship he would support her.[36]

On December 19, 1938, the father and son discussed their differences at the Windsor Hotel in Montreal. The meeting was heated and emotional. After shaking hands, the father asked his son how he was.

LWD: "As well as could be expected."
JSD: "Why, what is the matter?"
LWD: "What isn't the matter?"
JSD: "Well, certainly nothing is the matter with me. Of that I am sure."
LWD: "Father, what have you done, and what do you propose to do?"

James promptly turned the conversation to the telegram he had received from his son.

JSD: "I will tell you nothing until you come clean with me on that telegram you sent. No father ever received such a telegram. And until you say that you were wrong in sending me that telegram I will tell you nothing. Have you re-read it as I instructed you to do?"
LWD: "Yes, many times."
JSD: "You mean to tell me that you think that telegram was a proper one for a son to send his father?"
LWD: "I consider it to be only dutiful for any son to attempt to persuade his father against making such a serious mistake."
JSD: "You know Mother. She is always disturbed over signing anything. She was disturbed when I made her sign for an annuity. . . . Why . . . many times you have received telegrams from her and have not replied. Therefore, in this instance the only reason for replying as you did was because you hate your father."
LWD: "No. That is not true. . . . Do you not see the distinction, the difference between signing for an annuity and renouncing a nation to which you are devoted."
JSD: "I can see no difference between signing an annuity and what I have done."

Eventually, Lew persuaded his father to discuss the naturalization incident. James admitted that he had forced Josalee to sign the papers. "I told her that she had married me when I was a Canadian, and that when she married me she promised to obey, and that there was no reason why she shouldn't end with me as a Canadian." Pressed to explain his reasons for renouncing his citizenship, James stressed sentiment and heavy taxes. He resented paying $250,000 in taxes in 1938. Moreover, he did not want his heirs to pay sizable inheritance taxes on his estate. But he also acted out of a desire to return to the nation of his birth.

He wanted to be buried next to his mother and father on the banks of the St. Lawrence. He had purchased a farm with a trout stream, which his grandchildren could enjoy in the summers.

James also cited more intimately personal reasons, including a desire to leave Arizona, for his renunciation. "I have slaved all my life for my family. I haven't gone horseracing, but I would have liked to go horseracing. I haven't gone yachting with a great yacht. I haven't played. I haven't had any relief." With most of his friends dead and his "equals" gone, he found it depressing to live in southeastern Arizona. "Now, can you imagine living in Douglas? One walks down the street and one sees one old broken down Juan someone or other, and walking down further one sees another blankety blank destitute friend. Can you imagine living with people who have nothing to offer? Well, that's what Douglas is. And I am going to live with people with whom I want to live." Lew sympathized with his father's position, but observed that he could live and be buried in Canada without forswearing his citizenship. Tax evasion, he insisted, was his father's main reason for leaving the United States.

Subsequently both men refused to budge from their original positions, and the battle of wills endured for a year. Finally, the issue died after Lew refused to discuss it further. Thereafter the relationship between father and son gradually improved, but it was never again as warm and confiding as it had been before.[37]

Meanwhile, Douglas reviewed for his mother the various legal steps she could take to revoke her naturalization statement. He warned her, however, that litigation would involve an emotional strain and would "mean a public disclosure of what father did to you and how he coerced you. It would mean nasty publicity and a real break with father." He advised her to "try to be consoled with the thought that you really are American and that what you did does not represent any transfer of allegiance or affection." Worried that she was upsetting her son and perhaps ruining his career, Josalee accepted his advice. She also took comfort in the opinion of her lawyers, who held that she could not possibly be a Canadian because she had never lived in the country.[38]

In late January, 1939, newspapers broke the story of James Douglas's renunciation of American citizenship. Not surprisingly, press opinion was sharply critical of the decision. Lewis Douglas moved quickly to discourage speculation that he might also repudiate his nation. He confided to Bill Mathews that he was trying "as hard as I can to live down the slur on the name of my family and to give convincing proof that I, at least, am not going to desert my country." He released a press statement which read: "It came as a complete surprise to me and a terrible shock. When I went to Montreal it was public knowledge that I would always remain an American. I was born in Arizona, raised in Arizona, educated in the United States, wore its uniform in time of war, and tried to serve it publicly for more than a decade in time of peace. I repeat now that I can never renounce my American citizenship."[39]

For two months after his father's renunciation, Douglas considered resignation as principal. In a personal memorandum he outlined the advantages and disadvantages of making a move. Staying at McGill might lead to a better relationship with his father and guarantee his future financially. Also, after one or two more years, he might be able to go to an American university as president or professor. On the other hand, returning to the United States would end speculation about his nationality. He would also be able to influence the presidential election of 1940. And if the United States entered World War II, he would be in a position to offer his services. Finally, and most important, he wanted to be financially independent. "For reasons which to me are compelling I can no longer be in a position of financial dependency on you," he wrote James in late January, 1939. "I must, therefore, at the appropriate time return to my own country and concentrate on my financial responsibilities to my family." Douglas feared that unless he accepted responsibility for his mother's emotional distress, James would cut off his subsidy in Canada. "Nothing can be more humiliating, or corrupting of character than to be at the mercy of the whims, fancy or prejudice of another." Financial independence required leaving the field of education and returning to private enterprise while he was still in demand.[40]

Citing personal reasons, Douglas informed Chancellor Beatty in late February, 1939, that he planned to leave at the end of the year. On June 7, 1939, he formally tendered his resignation, to become effective as of December 31. The Board of Governors accepted the resignation with "profound regret" and expressed its appreciation for his accomplishments. It also asked him to serve as a governor upon his retirement from the principalship.

Douglas also helped Edward Beatty search for a successor. When R. C. Wallace, principal of Queens University, turned down the post, Douglas persuaded the governors to appoint someone from within the university. He preferred an individual who would emphasize the importance of the social sciences and who would continue to offer an alternative to the socialist viewpoint. The successful candidate should also be someone who "in making selections within the social sciences, would be guided by my acquaintance with the field and would make use of my associations in that specific area." Douglas and Beatty recommended F. Cyril James, and he proved acceptable.[41]

Douglas left McGill with an uneven record. He shored up the institution financially, secured a generous provincial education grant, restored faculty salary cuts, and oversaw the construction of a new gymnasium. Articulate, gracious, and enthusiastic, he was the embodiment of a successful university head. Yet he had shortcomings. He was overzealous in his efforts to counter socialism, lax in combating racial injustice, and insensitive to the concerns of some department heads and left-liberal faculty members. He defended academic freedom in principle, but at times violated it in deed. He upheld the right of free speech but dismissed as irresponsible professors who criticized the government's foreign policy.

Personally, however, despite his problems with the faculty and the turmoil within his family, Douglas had fond memories of McGill. On more than one occasion he referred to his principalship as "probably the happiest period of my life."[42]

12

Preparing for War

EVEN WHILE STILL AT MCGILL, DOUGLAS HAD RECEIVED numerous job proposals. In 1938 he turned down teaching positions at Amherst and the University of Pennsylvania. He also declined to become a candidate for the presidency of the University of Texas and Ohio State University. Joseph Kennedy, newly appointed ambassador to Great Britain, wanted him to go to London as an assistant, but Douglas refused. He also resisted a tempting offer to preside over the reorganized New York Stock Exchange. For a few weeks he entertained a proposal to head a public policy research association funded by industrialist Alfred P. Sloan, Jr., but withdrew his name from consideration when he learned that the foundation would not be organized to his liking.

Douglas wanted a job in the United States. Anxious to become financially independent, he ruled out academic positions. Only a business organization, he concluded, could offer a substantial income.[1]

When representatives from the Mutual of New York Life Insurance Company approached him about heading that organization, Douglas was responsive. In mid-May he traveled to New York for an interview, and a few days later accepted the presidency of the company at an annual salary of $75,000. News of the appointment brought congratulatory messages from relatives and numerous friends. James S. Douglas, however, felt that his son had "deserted his heritage."[2]

Douglas assumed the presidency of America's oldest and fifth-largest insurance company on January 1, 1940. As usual, he was aided in his tasks by Robert Stroud, who served as assistant to the president and later as company secretary. Douglas succeeded David Houston, secretary of agriculture in the Wilson administration, who had presided over Mutual Life for twelve years before stepping aside to become chairman of the board.

Troubled by reports that Mutual Life was experiencing financial difficulties, Douglas launched a thorough investigation shortly after taking control. He discovered that the financial security of the company had been jeopardized by poor investments in real estate, mortgage loans, and securities. Mutual owned $50 million worth of real estate, mainly in New York City, but had lost $400,000 on that property in 1938. Since 1930 the cost of operating real-estate holdings had exceeded profits by 45 percent.

As for mortgage loans, the new president learned that over the past decade more than 50 percent of all accounts could not fully satisfy interest and amortization payments. He also found an unacceptable number of low-yield and defaulted securities. Comparing Mutual's position with that of eleven competitors, he discovered that his organization had "a higher percentage of securities delinquent in interest or amortization or both generally than any other of the companies examined." Mutual also had a poorer record in terms of yield on securities.

Other problems plagued the company. Over the previous decade costs had remained steady, while the volume of business had dropped substantially. Mutual found it difficult to compete because its insurance prices were comparatively high. Moreover, the selection of policies to underwrite was found wanting. "We have been . . . writing the type of business we should not have been writing," the new president observed.

Douglas also considered the company to have been poorly led. He criticized management's "cavalier" approach toward its workers and the insurance business itself. Employees who basically performed the same tasks did not receive equal pay. An appointment to a position at Mutual too often "was considered to be a pre-empted right to that job for life." The company had little regard for its public image and did not show much concern for accurate record keeping, research, or new techniques. Board meetings usually consisted of "some abacadabra [sic] and then adjournment."[3]

In his first annual report, Douglas revealed some of the problems and announced a plan to remedy them. He decided to focus on improving the company's financial status by locating new investment fields, increasing yields, issuing new kinds of policies, marking down assets to realistic levels, and reducing the annual dividend.

In 1941 Douglas reorganized the company's insurance operations. He recruited Alexander E. Patterson from Penn Mutual to serve as executive vice-president in charge of insurance activities. He also brought in new men to head and revamp the underwriting, actuarial, research, and public-relations departments. He appointed new members to the board of trustees and transformed that group into a hard-working organization. Douglas also had to demote or dismiss some executives, and, as always, found the task difficult to perform. On at least two occasions, he informed terminated officers that if they could not find employment elsewhere they could return to Mutual in a different capacity at half-pay. By 1944 the reorganization efforts had revived company spirit, reduced expenses, and restored financial health. Douglas's ambitious program, one trade journal noted, "has attracted the attention of the entire life insurance business."[4]

Douglas continued to speak out on matters of public policy, especially foreign affairs. In international as well as domestic issues, he was guided by laissez-faire principles. Like Cordell Hull and other internationalists, he believed that peace, prosperity, and freedom resulted from an economically open world. That belief derived mainly from his romantic perception of the nineteenth century. Downplaying the extent of class unrest, colonialism, and militarism, his speeches and writings portrayed the years between 1814 and 1914 as the "Golden Age of modern history." "It was during the Nineteenth Century," he observed, "that freedom progressed furthest along its path and that the greatest number of people in all history enjoyed its fruits." There were a "few backyard duels," but no major conflict that "rocked the universe to its very foundations and unseated the faith of Christian civilization."

That world was destroyed, Douglas asserted, by the rise of unbridled nationalism, which evolved most rapidly in the United States and Germany. Despite the monumental human sacrifices of the Great War, a liberal world order was not reestablished. Douglas blamed that failure on intense postwar nationalism, especially in the United States. After the war Americans "sank back into the embrace of the isolationists and withdrew from that serious acknowledgement of our national responsibility so necessary to international order." By raising tariffs, insisting upon repayment of the Allied debts, abandoning the gold standard, and scuttling the London Economic Conference of 1933, the United States, he wrote a friend, had to be held accountable for the economic and international crises of the 1930s.[5]

Throughout the 1930s Douglas had despaired over the spread of economic nationalism. Such a climate, he pointed out, partially explained Germany's aggressiveness and Italy's foray into Ethiopia. "To talk of peace and disarmament under such conditions," he said, "is to be wholly unrealistic." Peace would be possible, he believed, only with the cessation of economic warfare.

Germany's annexation of Austria in March, 1938, convinced Douglas that another global conflict was "ultimately almost inescapable." When Britain yielded to Nazi demands at Munich a few months later, he wrote Walter Lippmann that appeasement and superior German air power "may have as profound political consequences as the defeat of the [Spanish] Armada." When war erupted in Europe in September, 1939, Douglas was distressed, but not shocked. Immediately he volunteered his services to the State Department, but Hull politely put him off.[6]

Realizing that Great Britain and France needed military assistance, he enthusiastically supported the revision of the American neutrality laws to permit the sale of arms to belligerents on a cash-and-carry basis. Privately he hoped for involvement, but understood that Americans were "slow to move" and not yet "fully aware of the stakes involved in the present struggle." In a commencement address at the University of Arizona, he declared that it was imperative for Americans to increase defense spending and assist the Allies in every possible way.[7]

Douglas realized that strong isolationist sentiment and the upcoming presidential election deterred Roosevelt from taking bold action. As Hitler's troops and panzers smashed into Norway, Denmark, and the Low Countries in the spring of 1940, Roosevelt called for a congressional appropriation of nearly $1.2 billion to bolster the nation's naval and military forces. Douglas heartily approved that measure. Noting the support for increased defense spending by Douglas and other economic conservatives, Press Secretary Stephen Early quipped to FDR: "What can be wrong—something must be?"[8]

In fact, Douglas rarely criticized as Roosevelt tiptoed toward intervention. His one lament was that the administration was not doing enough to meet the foreign threat. He pushed for additional defense measures, including compulsory military service. Influenced by his experience as a "citizen soldier" at the Plattsburg military training camp in 1916, he strongly supported the idea of universal military service. On May 8, 1940, he met with attorney Grenville Clark and seven other Plattsburg veterans at the Harvard Club in New York. At that meeting, and a subsequent meeting two weeks later, Clark persuaded the group to draft a conscription bill. At Clark's urging, Senator Edward Burke of Nebraska and Representative James Wadsworth of New York agreed to introduce the bill in Congress.

Initially, Roosevelt shied away from endorsing the first peacetime draft in history. Privately, however, he encouraged the enterprise. With Clark at the forefront, the Plattsburg veterans spent weeks lobbying for conscription. Noninterventionists like Senator Rush D. Holt of West Virginia pointed out that Clark, Douglas, and other "prime movers" of the draft were the same men who had been lamenting "regimentation in America." Despite the heated protests of noninterventionists, the Burke-Wadsworth Selective Service Bill was enacted in September, 1940.[9]

Alarmed by Hitler's spring offensive, internationalists worked to inform the American public of the threat and the need to assist the Allies. In mid-May, Clark Eichelberger, a prominent internationalist who helped bring a revision of the neutrality law, and William Allen White, the esteemed Kansas journalist, founded the Committee to Defend America by Aiding the Allies (CDAAA). Douglas became an early member.

A nonpartisan group, the committee sought to persuade Americans that their nation's existence depended upon extending generous aid to the Allies. White became chairman and principal spokesman. Eichelberger was named executive director. Within a year, CDAAA had recruited scores of prominent Americans and boasted more than six hundred local branches throughout the country.[10]

Taking an active interest in the work of the committee, Douglas wrote articles and delivered speeches advocating unlimited aid to the Allies. In June he contributed an essay to *Defense for America*, a widely distributed CDAAA volume edited by White.

Douglas portrayed World War II as "a fundamental conflict between two eternally irreconcilable views of mankind." The Allies, representing one view, believed that the individual was the supreme entity in society. The Axis powers held that the state was the ultimate end. Hitler was determined to crush individual freedom wherever it existed. If he conquered Europe he would then turn on the United States. The survival of American democracy, he admonished isolationists, depended upon military preparedness and maximum aid to the Allies. Europe was the western hemisphere's "first line of defense." So long as the Allies resisted and Britain dominated the seas, American security would not be imperiled. At the least, aid to the Allies would give the United States time to build up its defenses. All-out assistance might bring totalitarianism to heel in Europe.[11]

As the final battle for France commenced in early June, Douglas implored Roosevelt to supply the Allies with maximum military aid, especially airplanes. "Should the Allies be brought to their knees before fall, will Germany wait to permit us to build up our defenses? . . . [M]aterial aid to the Allies . . . is the best way of providing protection for our vital national interests." He urged FDR to go directly to the people with a "clear, ringing, forthright statement of the issue that is being decided in Europe, of the consequences to us if the Allies lose, and of the need to give them help during this critical period."

Two days later Roosevelt informed Douglas that he had already initiated action. "Dear Lew: I beat you to it!" FDR chortled. "Very many planes are actually on the way to the Allies. . . . We are turning in old Army and Navy material to the manufacturers who have been given orders for new and up-to-date material. I have a sneaking suspicion that the old material . . . will be on its way to France in a few days." The President declared that he was making every effort to supply the Allies but was "not talking very much about it" because the isolationist press "would undoubtedly pervert it, attack it and confuse the public mind." Roosevelt closed his letter by promising in the near future to address the public on the European crisis.[12]

On June 10, the day Italy declared war on Great Britain and France, FDR delivered the commencement address at the University of Virginia. He denounced Italy for wielding the dagger that "struck . . . the back of its neighbor," and promised publicly for the first time to extend abundant aid to the Allies. For Douglas, the President's speech was "splendid and very moving." He was also pleased when, a week later, Roosevelt named two pro-aid Republicans, Henry Stimson and Frank Knox, as Secretary of War and Secretary of the Navy respectively.[13]

After the fall of France in mid-June, the British position seemed desperate. In less than one year, its destroyer fleet had been reduced from 176 to 68 vessels. Now alone against the Axis powers, Britain appealed to the United States for help. In mid-May, five days after being named Prime Minister, Winston Churchill had asked President Roosevelt for forty or fifty over-age destroyers to defend the home islands. Churchill and King George VI made additional requests in June, but without results. Privately, Roosevelt sympathized with the British appeal, but doubted the legality of a positive response and feared its political consequences, especially if he decided to run again for reelection. Throughout June and July Roosevelt resisted British requests for aid. In early August, however, a small group of individuals who became known as interventionists, or "warhawks," helped prod FDR into action.[14]

With the help of Henry P. Van Dusen of the Union Theological Seminary, Douglas brought together interventionists to discuss ways of providing maximum assistance to Britain. Known as the Century Group, the members held periodic meetings at the Century Association in New York, with Douglas serving as unofficial chairman. Only eleven men attended the first meeting, but the group eventually numbered twenty-eight, mainly from New York. The members privately believed that Britain was fighting America's war and that full-fledged United States intervention would be required to defeat Hitler. Publicly, however, they called for massive assistance short of war. The Century Group was more militant than the Committee to Defend, but the two worked closely together throughout the summer.[15]

Besides Douglas, the initial meeting included Herbert Agar, editor of the

Louisville *Courier-Journal*; William L. Clayton, a Texas cotton broker; Henry Sloane Coffin, president of Union Theological Seminary; Henry H. Hobson, an Ohio bishop; Ernest M. Hopkins, president of Dartmouth College; Henry R. Luce, editor of *Time* and *Life*; Francis P. Miller, director of the Council on Foreign Relations; Whitney H. Shepardson, railroad executive; William H. Standley, retired admiral; and Van Dusen.

The participants agreed that American security would be jeopardized if Germany conquered Britain and seized its fleet. "The British Fleet is indispensable for American security; American assistance is indispensable for British victory." Douglas and Shepardson drafted a memorandum outlining an aid program for Great Britain. The proposal called for the evacuation of British children on United States vessels, the sending of food to Britain in American ships protected by convoys, the granting of credits, the expeditious shipment of munitions, and the deployment of American ships and planes to defend England. The British government, in exchange, should promise never to surrender any portion of its fleet to the enemy, but continue the struggle from American and Commonwealth ports. Finally, the arrangement should be effected by a treaty.

The group also recommended ways of implementing its program. Three members—Luce, Coffin, and Shepardson—would try to win over the administration. Others, principally Miller, were asked to carry "the issues to a carefully selected body of national leaders throughout the country." Douglas was to serve as an intermediary with the CDAAA "for the purpose of pressing on it the necessity of continuing a vigorous educational program in respect of the vital matter of the British Fleet for our defense." He would also be the group's "bridge to Wendell Willkie." Specifically, he was to persuade Willkie, the Republican presidential candidate, "to refrain from attacking" the military-assistance program "and at most to support it."[16]

Soon after the first meeting, Douglas left New York for a ten-day vacation in Sun Valley, Idaho. While he was in the West, the interventionists convened again on July 25. They concocted the idea of exchanging old American destroyers for British bases in the western hemisphere. The *quid pro quo* was to be implemented by executive rather than legislative action. They decided to present the scheme to Roosevelt and to build public support for it by launching an educational program through the CDAAA. Meanwhile, Douglas had met with Willkie in Colorado Springs and informed the group that the GOP candidate would cooperate. On August 1, Herbert Agar, Ward Cheney, and Clark Eichelberger recommended the plan to the President, adding that it had Willkie's blessing. Still Roosevelt made no promises.[17]

The next day FDR discussed the destroyer issue with his cabinet. At that conference Roosevelt decided to offer the vessels to Britain in return for the use of bases in the western hemisphere and for a pledge that England would never surrender its fleet to Hitler. Hoping to obtain legislative approval for the transaction, Roosevelt wanted Willkie to secure the support of the Republican legislative leadership. That evening the President asked William Allen White to approach Willkie. White assured him of the candidate's cooperative spirit, but FDR explained "that Willkie's attitude was not what counted, but that the Republican policy in Congress was the one essential."[18]

Meanwhile, the Committee to Defend bought newspaper space to remind readers that "Between Us and Hitler Stands the British Fleet." Early in August, the Century Group persuaded the World War I hero General John J. Pershing to make a radio broadcast endorsing all-out aid to Britain, including the sale of destroyers. The group also provided a legal justification for consummating the destroyer deal without congressional approval. On August 11, four distinguished attorneys—Charles Burlingham, Thomas Thacher, George Rublee, and Dean Acheson—published an article in the *New York Times* citing the legal means by which the President could effect the destroyers-for-bases transfer through executive action.[19]

Willkie was preparing his acceptance speech to be delivered at his hometown of Elwood, Indiana. Douglas, who stayed in touch by telephone, urged the candidate to include a statement supporting aid to Britain. On August 12, Willkie called Douglas to read him portions of the speech dealing with foreign policy. Forswearing isolationism, the Republican nominee endorsed selective service, strong defense measures, protection of the British fleet, and maximum assistance for besieged England.

Although he favored generous aid to Britain, Willkie was reluctant to exert pressure on Republican congressional leaders to support the destroyers-for-bases deal. His hesitancy prompted Roosevelt to implement the scheme through executive action. Douglas met with Willkie in New York on August 30 and after the meeting informed the Century Group that the candidate would not attack the transaction. After working out the terms of the agreement with the British, the President announced it to the public on September 3.[20]

The arrangement in effect ended neutrality, but a poll showed that 70 percent of those surveyed approved it. Willkie favored transfer in principle, but considered it unfortunate that Roosevelt had failed "to secure the approval of Congress or permit public discussion prior to adoption." Douglas lauded the deal because it attempted to preserve "the most important present element in our present system of defense—the British fleet." He also sent his personal congratulations to the President. "This is to let you know how sincerely I congratulate you on transferring the destroyers to England and receiving, among other things, bases in this hemisphere so important to our national defense. Although I shall not vote for you in November your action in this regard has my complete support."[21]

With the consummation of the destroyer deal, Douglas concentrated on the presidential campaign of 1940. He was pleased with Willkie. He believed that the Republican could win because he was "a great fellow with intelligence, understanding and *courage*!" The nominee had a reciprocally high regard for Douglas. In early 1940 he had written that he "would do any legitimate thing to see Lew Douglas President of the United States."[22]

After his nomination on June 28, Willkie considered naming Douglas as his campaign manager. But Thomas Lamont discouraged this move. "You don't want a giant for that job," he advised. Although there was "no finer man in this country nor a lovelier character," Douglas had drawbacks. His health was uncertain and he was "pretty inflexible." "You don't necessarily want a fellow full of political ideas to run your campaign for you," Lamont concluded. Willkie eventually asked

Minnesota Governor Harold Stassen to head an advisory campaign committee and named House Minority Leader Joseph Martin as Republican national chairman.[23]

At the party convention in Chicago in mid-July, Democrats nominated FDR for a third term. Douglas, who had supported Hull, was disappointed. Dean Acheson taunted him by asking if he planned to support the party nominee. "Hell no! I am not crazy yet," he responded. Lew and Peggy spent a long evening over drinks with the Achesons trying to win them over to Wendell Willkie, but without success. Soon after, Peg sent a teasing note: "I will never speak to you again. I may drink with you . . . but no wine! How could you Dean. You may for some reason think Wilkie [sic] inadequate—but you can't think Roosevelt is all the things you said. I found tears running down my cheeks."

Despite jesting with Acheson, Douglas profoundly deplored this first attempt to violate the two-term tradition. He joined John Hanes, who recently had resigned as under secretary of the treasury, to form an organization called Democrats-for-Willkie. Douglas and Hanes wrote Willkie: "No matter how grave the National Emergency the continuation in authority for three terms of this political machine—clothed as it is with tremendous public power—is a still graver menace to America." The two men hoped to enlist the support of those Democrats whose "loyalty to country takes precedence over loyalty to party."[24]

Angered at the actions of his former associates, Roosevelt struck out at them in a press conference. Hanes and Douglas were "thoroughly honorable and amiable young gentlemen," whose "slant of mind ran more to dollars than to humanity." The President's rebuke was denounced by Douglas's friends. Acheson wrote to say that he resented FDR's "outrageous report" and wanted to go on record as being " 'included out' as a subscriber to it." Judge Learned Hand considered it "a particularly mean slur." "Why in hell does he always, just when one is getting ready to vote for him, do some sonofabitchy thing like that that no gentleman possibly could do? He is a low-down vindictive cuss."

For his part, Douglas shrugged off the presidential censure. To a friend he remarked deferentially that it was "always difficult to see one's self" and therefore there "may be some truth in the President's comment." As always, he refused to engage publicly in personal attacks on Roosevelt.[25]

Democrats-for-Willkie opened its headquarters in New York on August 12. Headed by Douglas, Hanes, Alan Valentine, president of the Rochester Institute of Technology, and Roberta Campbell Lawson, former president of the General Federation of Women's Clubs, the organization adopted the slogan: "Country Before Party—No Third Term." It established a committee to secure one million Democratic vote pledges for Willkie. Refusing financial contributions from the Republican National Committee, the organization solicited funds from private sources. All told, Democrats-for-Willkie raised nearly $400,000 to elect the Republican nominee. Al Smith, Raymond Moley, Isabella Greenway, Pennsylvania Congressman Richard Allen, and other traditional Democrats rallied to the cause.[26]

Toward the end of the campaign, Democrats-for-Willkie was accused of illegal and corrupt activities. Democratic National Chairman Edward J. Flynn charged the organization with violating the Hatch Act by soliciting funds from government employees. Others said the organization was accepting contributions from the Republican National Committee. Still others said Douglas was using his position as head of Mutual Life to pressure employees to support Willkie. The charges, after investigation by the Justice Department and the superintendent of insurance for the State of New York, proved false and were dismissed.[27]

Douglas was initially pleased with Willkie's campaign. During his acceptance speech, the candidate criticized the President's domestic program, especially his failure to conquer unemployment. On the other hand, he basically supported the administration's foreign policy.

In early September, however, Willkie began to drift away from bipartisanship for fear of alienating isolationists. Douglas promptly took him to task, reminding him that party chieftains at the Republican Convention had rejected all isolationist contestants in favor of an ex-Democratic internationalist. "You must be the same type of person, as free, as independent, as courageous, as you were before Philadelphia. This implies that you are not now. The evidence justifies this implication," he bluntly stated. He urged Willkie to shun isolationism and "say in unqualified terms that you believe in and advocate everything that will ensure the survival of the British Empire and the British fleet."[28]

Although his advice went unheeded, Douglas continued to support Willkie. In doing so, he made every effort to counter the influence of isolationists. In late September, shortly after the Battle of Britain, Douglas and about fifty other interventionists flew to Washington to visit Roosevelt and Cordell Hull. There the "flying squadron," as the press called them, presented a petition to the President advocating all-out assistance to Britain short of war. Ever cautious, Roosevelt refused to commit himself.[29]

Throughout September Willkie vacillated between isolationism and intervention. Then in early October he began to attack the administration for warmongering. In a radio broadcast he maintained that "We are being edged toward war by an administration that is alike careless in speech and action." At Boston's Fenway Park he pledged "not to undertake to fight anybody else's war. Our boys shall stay out of European wars." Willkie's remarks infuriated his interventionist supporters. After the Boston speech, Douglas drafted, but did not send, a strongly worded telegram protesting "the change in policy towards what at best can be termed quasi isolationism." Douglas also considered canceling a scheduled crosscountry speaking tour. "I did not come out for you . . . with the understanding that you would move in the direction of isolationism. Indeed I had every reason to believe that you would advocate the opposite policy. . . . This fundamental issue must be immediately clarified with me before I will speak." Apparently he received oral assurances because he stumped for Willkie as planned.[30]

Sponsored by Democrats-for-Willkie, Douglas's national tour began in Baltimore on October 15 and ended in Tucson on November 2. In his speeches, he downplayed Willkie's flirtation with isolationism and stressed the importance of the two-term presidency. By seeking the presidency for the third time, Roosevelt was attempting "to break a fundamental principle of American politics as deeply imbedded in our political structure, as firmly sanctioned by custom and logic, as is the Constitution itself and the Bill of Rights." If democracy was threatened from outside dangers, "a third term may press in on freedom from within." To safeguard democracy from external and internal threats, he implored voters to support Willkie.[31]

For Douglas the outcome of the 1940 election proved disappointing, if not surprising. FDR won a third term by outpolling Willkie 27 to 22 million in the popular vote and 449 to 82 in the Electoral College. The size of Roosevelt's electoral vote stunned Douglas, but he hoped that "the closeness of the popular vote will be a sobering influence." He congratulated FDR and wished him "the fullest success in welding the country together into a strong confident unit, determined to preserve and defend freedom here and wherever it may be lingering in this hazardous world." He also asked to be called upon if the President believed he could be useful in the field of foreign policy.[32]

With the completion of the presidential campaign of 1940, Douglas resumed his activities with the Committee to Defend and the Century Group. He hosted dinners for British dignitaries to learn of England's defense needs. He traveled to Chicago, the heartland of isolationism, to advocate increased aid to Britain before the Council on Foreign Relations. He also helped quash the Hoover food-relief plan. The former President, who had formed an organization to feed Belgians in 1914, sought in 1940 to create an agency to assist millions of hungry people in occupied Europe. Although Douglas sympathized with Hoover's objective, he believed that the supplies would be seized by the Germans and would strengthen "a regime that is wholly hostile to everything in which we believe."[33]

While internationalists like Douglas clamored for increased aid to Britain, isolationists, through the America First Committee, argued for restraint. Founded in September, 1940, to counteract interventionist propaganda, the committee was a nationwide organization with headquarters in Chicago. Headed by General Robert E. Wood, chairman of the board of Sears, Roebuck and Company, America First enlisted the support of many distinguished citizens, including Charles Lindbergh, Edward Rickenbacker, Henry Ford, and Alice Roosevelt Longworth. Isolationists held that extensive aid to Britain would weaken America militarily and involve the United States in a foreign war.

In mid-December Douglas and Wood pressed their respective views before the National Association of Manufacturers in New York. Wood maintained that if the United States informed the British government that under no circumstances would it enter the war against Hitler there would be a negotiated settlement by spring. But, even if Germany conquered Great Britain, the security of the United States would not be jeopardized. Douglas said it was foolish to believe that the United States could coexist with Nazi Germany. Hitler was bent on world domination and would attack America after defeating the British. The United States, he insisted, must take any action to obtain the defeat of the Axis powers. Was it not time, he asked, to "commit ourselves to the proposition that there can be no agreement with violence, no compromise with oppression, and no covenant with tyranny?"[34]

Meanwhile, in early December, Churchill had informed Roosevelt that Britain desperately needed additional planes, naval vessels, and munitions. Unfortunately, he stated, England soon would be unable to pay for such purchases. Churchill asked if there was any way that the supplies could be continued without payment. In a press conference on December 17, Roosevelt buoyed British spirits by expressing interest in a plan to lend or lease supplies to England. At the same time, in a private communication to Harvard president James Conant, FDR announced that he would welcome a letter signed by many individuals supporting the lend-lease idea.

Drafted by Douglas, the letter was signed by 170 prominent Americans. The petitioners declared their "complete approval" for the "recently announced plan for lending armaments to Britain." Professing alarm at the extent of "indifference and apathy" toward the threat to national security, the correspondents asked the President to tell the American people forthrightly "of the possibilities of English failure and of the consequences to us and our children's children should Britain fall." Finally, the signatories urged Roosevelt "to make it the settled policy of this country to do everything that may be necessary to insure the defeat of the Axis powers, and thus to encourage here and everywhere resistance to the plausible but fatal arguments of appeasement."[35]

To gauge public reaction to the idea of lend-lease, Roosevelt released the Douglas-Conant letter to the press on December 27. As expected, isolationists excoriated it. "No one can read that petition," declared Senator Burton K. Wheeler of Montana, "without coming to the definite conclusion that this group wants nothing less than a declaration of war on the part of the United States." Other influential Americans, however, were moved by the appeal and asked to have their names added to it. Doubtless Roosevelt would have proceeded with lend-lease anyway, but the Douglas-Conant appeal made his decision easier. In a fireside chat on December 29, he told Americans that their way of life was gravely imperiled. "The Nazi masters of Germany," he declared, "have made it clear that they intend . . . to enslave the whole of Europe, and then to use the resources of Europe to dominate the rest of the world." That end could never be achieved, he contended, so long as the British fleet controlled the Atlantic. In the interest of national security, the United States "must be the great arsenal of democracy."

Interventionists warmly applauded the address. Douglas sent his personal congratulations, referring to the summons as "one of the great state papers in our history." And he joined Dean Acheson and James Warburg in sending "an open letter to Congress" advocating the speedy implementation of the President's program. On January 6, 1941, Roosevelt reiterated his plea for lend-lease in his State of the Union address. Four days later he transmitted the aid measure, patriotically numbered H.R. 1776, to Congress.[36]

Before interventionists could mobilize public support for lend-lease, however, they first had to resolve internal squabbles, which threatened to destroy their effectiveness. For months the Century Group and the New York chapter of the Committee to Defend America had been dissatisfied with William Allen White's leadership. Anxious not to outdistance public opinion or to run counter to the will of the administration, White insisted upon a cautious course for the CDAAA. Eastern interventionists, including Douglas, favored more aggressive and comprehensive policies, including the extension of financial credit and the convoying of supplies across the Atlantic.

In a December newspaper interview, White portrayed the CDAAA as an antiwar organization opposed to the repeal of the neutrality laws. Convinced that White had repudiated declared policies of the organization, Douglas and other interventionists forced his resignation in early January and replaced him with

Ernest W. Gibson of Vermont. The committee hoped that Gibson, a former Republican United States senator, would use his influence with Congress to speed passage of the Lend-Lease Bill.[37]

To prevent future clashes between the chairman and the national policy board, the committee sharply circumscribed the former's power. Under the new arrangement, a special board was to determine policy, with the chairman operating "within the framework of the policies thus reached." The members elected Douglas chairman of the policy board and awarded him a rank equal to that of the committee chairman. Clark Eichelberger, "the power behind the throne," was selected national director. In practice, Eichelberger and Douglas became the dominant figures in the reorganization. The fact that Douglas was to "figure more prominently" in CDAAA activities seemed to reconcile both extremists and more moderate members, such as Thomas Lamont and Adlai Stevenson.[38]

Under new leadership, the CDAAA took a more aggressive approach toward aid to Britain. Douglas told the Century Group that the policy committee would endorse "whatever is needed to insure the defeat of the Axis" without going to war. Another member declared that the policy staff sought "to be ahead of what the President stands for officially, but at the same time not so far ahead as to embarrass him." The Committee to Defend issued a steady stream of statements urging Americans to support the Lend-Lease Bill. After two months of debate, Congress approved the aid measure on March 8. With that action, historian Robert Divine has written, "the United States took a major step toward war."[39]

Nazi submarines in the Atlantic were sinking more than 500,000 tons of British shipping each month. Such catastrophic losses, interventionists feared, might force the British to surrender. On April 25, Douglas tried to discuss the issue of convoying with Roosevelt, saying that "the critical and decisive struggle for the control of the seas and the freedom of the lines of supply, is going against us." Unable to meet with the President, Douglas decided to release a committee statement endorsing convoying. Such a policy, he admitted, "means shooting, but the risks we take by doing it are incalculably less than by indolently, fearfully, cravenly waiting until we shall stand without a friend on earth in desperate solitude." Cabinet officials also advised the President to escort ships, but without success.[40]

By early May the British position seemed so desperate that the Committee to Defend published yet another policy statement, calling for the "declaration of a full state of national emergency" and the use of American air and naval units to protect the delivery of supplies to the British Isles. A few days after that statement was released, Gibson resigned as chairman to enter military service. He was succeeded by Eichelberger, and for the remainder of the summer the committee agitated relentlessly for convoying.[41]

Throughout 1941 Douglas was plagued by a painful sinus infection. In January he underwent a minor operation on his septum, but surgery brought only temporary relief. In April the infection recurred and he was hospitalized. His doctors sent him to Florida in mid-May, but the condition reappeared when he returned home. In July he again underwent surgery, followed by a recuperative trip to Arizona.

That treatment proved more successful, but the infection was not finally eliminated until 1944, when he again submitted to surgery.[42]

Douglas also suffered the loss of his mother in the summer of 1941. Josalee's last years were filled with pain, loneliness, and worry. She had wasted away from a disease she knew nothing about. Unable to walk, she was confined to bed or a wheelchair. Because of the palsy, her handwriting became so scrawled that she had to dictate her letters. She had once enjoyed taking trips to Arizona by automobile or private railroad car, but she abandoned them when they became too taxing. She lived under the constant care of nurses, in an apartment at the Gaylord Hotel in Los Angeles. Her husband, who was in Montreal, visited infrequently, and even when he did he generally brought little comfort. "I had a consultation of doctors yesterday and immediately afterward Father left for New York, not waiting to hear the results," she wrote Lew. "It all makes me very unhappy and the way he talks about James is a worse shame." Lew visited over the Christmas holidays and at least once during the summer. James, too, made occasional calls. For the most part, however, Josalee was alone.

In mid-June, 1941, she asked Lew to come to her. "I need you more than anyone and I am very lonely with no one to comfort me so you must come and see me if you can. I am very sick tonight. Love, Mother." He arrived in time to be with Josalee at the end. She died from pneumonia on July 6. In her will she left him $250,000.[43]

The United States moved gradually toward military involvement during the summer of 1941. After Germany invaded the Soviet Union on June 22, Roosevelt promised lend-lease aid to the Russians. A few weeks later he dispatched four thousand American marines to Iceland to prevent that island from being captured by Germany. Moreover, in August, Roosevelt permitted American ships to convoy British vessels to Iceland. Douglas approved FDR's policies, but was disappointed that the President did not authorize the convoying of British ships all the way across the Atlantic. To a friend in Britain he wrote that the administration "does not seem to have the toughness of mind or character" to ask Congress to authorize convoying. Until such a policy was adopted, he confided, "I will be on tenterhooks."

In July and August Douglas's policy committee implored Roosevelt to take more aggressive measures to protect British shipping. The CDAAA purchased newspaper space advising FDR to "clear the Atlantic" of German submarines, and sponsored "Battle of Atlantic Week," during which it encouraged citizens to petition the White House. Douglas, Robert Sherwood, and Senator Claude Pepper spoke at the Harvard Club to urge Congress to take action to ensure the delivery of supplies to Britain.[44]

Douglas even considered recommending an outright declaration of war against Germany. On August 20 he brought together Wendell Willkie, Ulric Bell, Ward Cheney, James Conant, Allen Dulles, Clark Eichelberger, Major George F. Eliot, Henry Van Dusen, and Francis Miller. The group agreed that the CDAAA and the recently organized Fight for Freedom Committee should issue a joint statement calling for the United States to declare war against Germany.

After a few days of reflection, Douglas began to have doubts about the advisability of a war statement. He reconvened the group on August 27 to express his misgivings. He argued that advocating war "unsupported by the administration would be construed by the public as an act of aggression, whereas advocacy of measures necessary to our defense would probably be construed by the public . . . as purely protective measures." He realized that his proposals, if implemented by the government, would bring war. He insisted, therefore, that the public should be warned of the risk involved. Specifically, Douglas recommended that the President get congressional authorization to use American military might "to sweep the German menace from the seas." FDR should also seek from Congress the power to permit United States merchant vessels to sail to British ports and to use any force necessary to prevent the Axis powers from acquiring strategic bases in the western hemisphere. Willkie, Bell, and Conant preferred a war declaration, but Douglas's proposal carried.[45]

Douglas's hopes for stronger action were fulfilled early in September when a German U-boat attacked the American destroyer *Greer*. Although it was later revealed that the *Greer* was reporting the position of the Nazi U-boat to British warships, Roosevelt promptly proclaimed the incident an act of aggression. On September 11, he informed the American people of the attack. Branding the German submarines "the rattlesnakes of the Atlantic," he strongly implied that American ships would fire upon Nazi U-boats in the Atlantic. He also announced that American ships would begin convoying merchant vessels in American defensive waters. Douglas immediately congratulated Roosevelt for his "magnificent" speech. "Dear Lew," FDR responded, "My warm and heartfelt thanks for that message of yours."[46]

While pleased with Roosevelt's response to the attack on the *Greer*, Douglas believed that more decisive action was necessary. On September 16, the CDAAA, in effect, urged the President to engage in undeclared war against Germany. The recommendation was for a sweeping policy including (1) the severance of diplomatic relations with Germany; (2) convoying supplies to British ports; (3) preventing an Axis takeover of Atlantic islands or African bases; (4) recognizing the Free French; (5) increasing aid to China and maintaining the embargo against Japan; (6) announcing that the United States would use its armed might to prevent the fall of Singapore, the Dutch East Indies, or Thailand; (7) pledging American participation in a postwar peacekeeping organization.

Throughout the autumn Douglas and other interventionists championed those objectives. Not surprisingly, their position provoked considerable opposition. Charles Lindbergh, speaking in Des Moines, Iowa, on September 11, declared that the British, the Roosevelt administration, and Jews were propelling the United States toward war. As head of the policy committee Douglas responded to the Lone Eagle's remarks. The organization was made up of loyal Americans who believed that the United States must defeat Nazism. "Anti-Semitism," he concluded, "is one of the characteristics of Nazism wherever it has stuck up its ugly head."

Senator Gerald P. Nye of North Dakota denounced Douglas's interventionist speeches. Speaking at an America First rally in New York, Nye threatened to investigate the Mutual Life Insurance Company when Douglas told a group of insurance executives that their policies would "prove as fragile as an empty egg shell unless Hitler is defeated." Informed of Nye's threat, Douglas reiterated his claim "that every American policy-holder has a stake in assuring the defeat of Hitlerism. Neither Senator Nye, nor anybody else, can prevent me from saying that if I believe it."[47]

The combination of military events—German submarine attacks on the American destroyers *Kearny* and *Reuben James*—interventionist propaganda, and favorable public opinion persuaded Congress to act. In November it revised the Neutrality Act to permit the arming of merchant ships and the transportation of supplies in convoyed vessels to belligerent ports. Ultimately such a policy would probably have brought the United States into the war against Germany. But Douglas was impatient. In early December, he advocated a declaration of war against Germany. "Make this war ours," he advised twelve hundred New England educators. His wish was granted when Japan attacked Pearl Harbor on December 7. Noting the "date which will live in infamy," Roosevelt promptly asked Congress for a declaration of war. On December 11, Hitler responded with a declaration of hostilities against the United States.

Like most interventionists, Douglas expressed shock, anger, and relief at the turn of events. "What a disastrous affair Pearl Harbor was!" he wrote his father. He called the naval base commanders, Admiral Husband E. Kimmel and General Walter Short, "dunder heads" for failing to take adequate precautions against an air attack. Despite his anger, Douglas also felt relieved that the United States was in the war. "I, for one," he wrote Henry Morgenthau, "now that the decision had been made irrevocably, feel inwardly happier and more contented." He also took satisfaction in the fact that the sneak attack blasted into obscurity the policy of isolationism. "The Japs did much more than explode bombs in Hawaii," he wrote a friend. "They exploded for all time the whole fabric of the isolationist doctrine."[48]

With his nation at war, Douglas yearned to return to public service. In October, he had accepted an appointment from the Treasury Department at a salary of $1 a year to direct the sale of defense bonds for greater New York. He served only a few months, however, before resigning to assume a position with greater responsibility. Once again he would be a member of the Roosevelt administration.[49]

PART FIVE

The Second World War

13

On Board: The War Shipping Administration

ON JANUARY 26, 1942, LEWIS DOUGLAS WAS FORMALLY OFFERED, and accepted, the position of deputy to W. Averell Harriman, lend-lease representative in England. At an earlier meeting with the President, he had agreed to spend about a month in Washington to acquaint himself with the problems of production and supply, the flow of matériel among the United Nations, and questions of shipping and distribution. He would then proceed to London to become Harriman's alter ego, representing him frequently on the various combined boards that had been set up by the two governments in both capitals and administering the office while Harriman was away traveling in connection with the many tasks his assignment required. Initially, Douglas agreed to take on the job for six months. Soon, however, the overwhelming shipping exigencies of the desperate struggle beginning for the United States were to alter his task and tenure.[1]

Douglas had declined Harriman's approach in November. He was unwilling to leave Mutual Life in the midst of the reorganization and rehabilitation and was convinced, after consultation with, among others, Secretary of War Stimson, that he could make a greater contribution to American preparedness by continuing his work with the Committee to Defend America. But Pearl Harbor dramatically changed his priorities. In early January, Harriman again contacted Douglas, who expressed his willingness to accept. Douglas had already written the President on December 19: "I am yours to command. If there is any task that you think I can do, you know I shall be more than glad to try to do it. . . . No sacrifice is too great to make willingly and cheerfully. And so I offer you my services in the cause." FDR's response was noncommittal: "I have your note and much appreciate your all-out offer of services and will assuredly bear it in mind."[2]

The President's reluctance to accept Douglas's offer was no doubt explained by his irritation, indeed hurt, at his former budget director's activities and rhetoric as a leader of the Democrats-for-Willkie. Although they had been at political odds since 1934 and Douglas had, albeit belatedly and somewhat reluctantly, supported Landon in 1936, his vigorous involvement in 1940 had offended and wounded

Roosevelt, who had regarded Douglas as a personal friend if not a political ally. To be sure, especially since the outbreak of the European war, Douglas had been a firm and often aggressive supporter of the President's foreign policy—often, as has been observed, urging more forceful and early action in assistance to the Allies than the White House was prepared to take.[3]

But the scars of 1940 were still tender. Not only FDR but several of his principal advisors felt strongly about Douglas's lack of loyalty and were reluctant to take him back into the fold. When Harriman urged the President in January to meet with Douglas and offer him the London post, Roosevelt hesitated. Harriman, who had accompanied Churchill to the White House Arcadia Conference over the Christmas holidays, remained for some two weeks after the Prime Minister's departure in order to complete various tasks relating to his own assignment, including the recruitment of Douglas and other personnel for his office. Undeterred by the earlier rebuff, he returned to the President and finally gained his agreement to see Douglas and offer him the London job.[4]

The meeting between Roosevelt and Douglas was later described by Harriman as "touching." Like old friends who had had a serious row but were genuinely fond of each other, they quickly passed over their differences and, in a spirit of mutual affection, settled the question of the appointment. Apparently at that interview Douglas also gave some sort of pledge of future party loyalty. He was scheduled to leave for England in about a month, after thoroughly briefing himself on the issues that would confront him in handling, as FDR wrote, "the affairs of the office while Averell is away from London which will give great continuity to the work which is of such great importance at the present time."[5]

For his part, Douglas was excited at the prospect of contributing to the war effort and, concomitantly, pleased by his reconciliation with the President. The invitation from Roosevelt, accompanied by almost immediate cordiality after the years of estrangement, reflected a largeness of spirit as well as an underlying affection on both sides. This mutual commitment to cooperation and support was to be evidenced over the next two years in the course of activities not anticipated at the time.[6]

In an interview with the New York *Sun*, Douglas characterized his appointment as perhaps the most important to date in his career—one which he looked forward to "with the greatest thrill." But when questioned as to how he and FDR had composed their sometime differences, he typically and diplomatically replied that "the President was most cordial and for my part I was delighted at the opportunity to serve my country at war." Arthur Krock hailed the appointment as an indication that the White House "blacklist" had been breached and expressed the hope that others on it would soon be invited into the government. It is indicative of Douglas's popularity with some members of the opposition party that Congressman Joseph Martin had previously urged Roosevelt to call anti-New Deal Democrats as well as Republicans into national service, specifically naming, among others, Lewis Douglas.[7]

At Mutual Life, it was agreed by the board of trustees that he would continue to function for the time being as president and chief executive officer, with frequent trips to the city to carry out his duties. When, in the coming weeks, it became clear Douglas would remain in Washington, Peggy Douglas planned to join him, leaving Sharman in the care of her long-time and much-trusted nanny. Lew was then able to rent a small house for them in Chevy Chase. But events determined otherwise. After only one night in Washington, the serious illness of the nanny forced Peggy to return to New York to care for their daughter. Lew remained in the Wardman Park Hotel, and the two remained apart, except for his trips to New York on Mutual business and her infrequent visits to Washington, until his resignation in 1944.[8]

Douglas settled into his job on February 5. Immediately he began a round of talks with old associates and new colleagues in the war effort. Within a week, his conversations and the careful perusal of the materials collected for his information had convinced him that "shipping is the real constriction." He wrote Harriman that he had "been deeply concerned with what seems to me to be the over-riding question for the year 1942. All the evidence . . . indicates the meager supply of shipping as the paramount problem." The nation could, he believed, produce the necessary war material, raise, train, and equip a large army, "but without shipping we will be unable to deliver them to the critical theaters of war in sufficient numbers and powerfully enough equipped in time. There are limitations on the amount of shipping that can be added to the pool and the problem is largely how to save shipping for war purposes." The difficulty was compounded by the appalling lack of knowledge concerning the joint and individual resources and requirements of the Americans and the British. "We do not know what all of our tonnage is doing and why it is doing it. . . . The British know much more clearly than we do. . . . I have been in very close touch with Sir Arthur Salter on this problem and with our Maritime Commission."[9]

His investigations had already pointed to the heart of the matter and set him upon a road that would quickly lead to new duties and enhanced responsibilities. A key figure in this development was Sir Arthur Salter, the head of the British Merchant Shipping Mission to Washington, who had worked with British shipping control in the First World War. As the principal representative in America of the Ministry of War Transport (BMWT), he had arrived in the capital the previous March, following the passage of lend-lease, to expedite the use of American shipping to relieve British vessels. By early winter, as a consequence of pressure by the President and Harry Hopkins on the Maritime Commission, American shipbuilding and allocations had dramatically increased. Sir Arthur was well pleased. Then came Pearl Harbor, and the shipping situation almost immediately deteriorated. Overnight America's own war needs in both the Pacific and the Atlantic became competing priorities. American shipping was now equally prey to the enemy submarine. In addition, it was clear that the role of the United States in Allied shipping policy would henceforth be direct and ultimately paramount. Salter was greatly concerned.[10]

It was obvious that new instrumentalities would have to be created for the larger task. This was recognized by Roosevelt and Churchill at the White House Arcadia Conference. In general terms, the leaders had agreed that the shipping resources of the two countries must be pooled and their allocation controlled by a Combined Shipping Adjustment Board (CSAB), with representatives of the U.S. and Britain in both Washington and London. The British side of the operation was handled by the Ministry of War Transport, and the American by the Maritime

Commission under Admiral Emory S. Land. But the organization of the commission did not lend itself to the new demands of a nation at war. Accordingly, after reviewing proposals from the army and navy as well as the commission itself, the President, on February 7, 1942, issued Executive Order 90054, establishing the War Shipping Administration (WSA), following the British prototype time-tested in two world wars.

The new agency had sweeping powers to "Control the operation, purchase, charter, requisition, and use of all ocean vessels under the flag or control of the United States, except (1) combatant vessels of the Army, Navy and Coast Guard; fleet auxiliaries of the Navy; and transports owned by the Army and Navy; and (2) vessels engaged in coastwise, intercoastal and inland transportation. . . ." It was also specifically granted the power to "Allocate vessels under the flag or control of the United States for use by the Army, Navy, other Federal departments and agencies, and the governments of the United Nations." Under the provisions of the Order, the WSA would deal with the British Ministry of War Transport and other Allied agencies on shipping. The administrator was to be directly responsible to the President.[11]

Not surprisingly, the armed services were far from happy with the sweeping powers granted to the administrator to allocate military shipping. Their displeasure was soon to become manifest.[12]

Admiral Land was appointed administrator in recognition of his position as chairman of the Maritime Commission and his personal role, since February, 1941, as the President's principal advisor on shipping. Attempting to reconcile the anomalous relationship between the two agencies he now headed, Land acted "to disturb the Maritime Commission's work as a whole as little as possible, which, in reality, means setting up a War Shipping Administration unit inside the Commission circle." To this end, he delegated two commissioners to the administration: Captain Edward Macauley to oversee merchant-shipping personnel and Captain (later Admiral) Howard L. Vickery to direct new construction. The staff was recruited from existing components of the old agency. Land, wearing his hat as war shipping administrator, was to represent the United States on the Combined Shipping Adjustment Board in Washington, whose first meetings in Washington were held shortly after he assumed his new post.[13]

These actions were a step forward in systematizing and improving shipping which then was in a desperate and openly criticized crisis in allocation and utilization. Before his new appointment, Land had complained that he'd "been kicked all around by the President and also by Harry Hopkins . . . and that if anybody can run the thing better . . . why they're welcome to it." By February, the situation was acute. The dual threat from inefficient organization and sinkings was at that moment worse than any yet experienced in either world war and appeared to be rapidly increasing.[14]

It was this danger to the effective prosecution of the Allied war effort that Douglas had recognized. On February 13, he drafted a memorandum, probably for the Lend-Lease Administration and possibly for Harry Hopkins (but Admiral Land strangely did not see it until April 6), summing up his appreciation of the problem. After an unfavorable comparison with the situation in the First World War and an enumeration of the current demands upon shipping, he wrote: "The only relief that can be hoped for or expected is from careful conservation of our shipping facilities, economizing in their use and planning their employment so as most effectively to serve the essential war requirements. If planning of the use of shipping facilities was necessary to meet the tasks that devolved upon them during the last war, then planning of the use of a far thinner supply of facilities to meet far greater tasks in this war is a thousandfold more essential." After listing in detail data needed to determine requirements, he outlined methods of ascertaining the relevant information and of obtaining greater efficiency. "Unless," he concluded on a somber note, "this sort of program, well organized in personnel, well-planned and well-executed, is immediately installed, the present organization charged with the responsibility of providing shipping facilities may fail in the performance of its high duties; what is more important, we may lose the war in 1942."[15]

Whether or not Douglas had consulted Sir Arthur Salter before writing this memorandum is not clear. Certainly it was about this time that he discussed the problem with him. The two men had met briefly in the 1930s, and Douglas had been greatly impressed with the Englishman. Sir Arthur was convinced that the proper place for Harriman's new assistant was not in London, but in Washington. According to Salter, before undertaking the delicate job of approaching Land with this idea, he spoke to Vickery, whose first words were "I was wanting to see you; I'm convinced that, if this new system [the WSA] is going to work, we need someone like Lew Douglas to act in the same relation to Land for ship allocation as I do for ship building." Encouraged by Vickery's similar conclusion, Salter next turned to Harry Hopkins, who had in the preceding months become his chief contact, champion, and expediter in the White House, acting for and with the President. Hopkins was receptive. He believed that FDR would approve if the request came from Land, an old friend of the President's from the First World War, whom, despite the growing criticism of his management of the crisis, he was anxious to avoid offending. On Salter's suggestion, Vickery spoke to Land, who agreed to the arrangement.[16]

By February 21, Douglas was able to cable Harriman: "The task Hopkins has in mind for me here seems to be immediately important and will be of help to you in London. I have looked forward to joining you but feel that my personal desires should not be considered, therefore I think better remain here." The task was to be chief advisor to Admiral Land.[17]

The work before Douglas was formidable and, with the closer view he was now to have, even more distressing. The situation was to deteriorate further before Douglas's administrative abilities began to show results. Writing to his father on March 8, he described the WSA as "an extraordinary hotspot, for shipping is the key to the whole Allied arch." A month later, deeply immersed in the problems of his new job, he elaborated: "I have certainly landed in a tough spot—shocking—so shocking that I won't write about it. It is discouraging too." At about the same time, he wrote to Harriman in some detail concerning the astonishing deficiencies he had found at WSA—"deplorably little . . . accurate information" about either the requirements or availability of shipping, a "condition of substantially disorderly ignorance," with no attempt having been made to correlate and determine the best use of the statistical material available. In a postscript, he reflected that perhaps he had been too critical, especially when comparing his agency with the British operation. "Remember that the British have been in the war for 2½ years . . . and have developed a workable and effective system. We've been in the war only a short time; naturally, we are not as far along the road to perfection as are the British." He concluded with the hope that another two weeks might see "reasonable accuracy . . . and order emerge from the present state of confusion."[18]

He was overly optimistic. The losses in shipping in the spring and early summer of 1942 were horrifying. By mid-March, the annual rate of sinkings of dry-cargo vessels was over 10 million deadweight tons. In that month alone 788,000 tons went down and by June the monthly toll was 936,000. The tanker toll in March was an unprecedented, and fortunately not repeated, 375,000 tons. Neither the navy nor the army air forces was prepared in ships or equipment to mount a proper antisubmarine defense. Under pressure from the navy to maximize the use of its woefully inadequate escort fleet, convoying began in February and was increased in the following months, but as the above figures indicate, the number of sinkings also grew during the same period. In the first six months of 1942 Allied shipping lost almost equaled the total of 1941. Despite the stepped-up shipbuilding program, it was only at the end of the following summer that new shipping exceeded total losses.[19]

These were facts that only the armed forces and Admiral Vickery's building program could reverse. Douglas's assignment was to allocate the vessel resources available for all types of military and civilian demands, excluding the army's own transport fleet. In that endeavor, he immediately faced a special problem of particular sensitivity, which greatly complicated the already desperate situation—the convoys to meet the promises of aid to the Soviet Union in the First Russian Protocol, signed by the United States in October, 1941. While still preparing for his lend-lease position, Douglas had read the protocol carefully because of its relevance to his task in London. Despite the new requirements after December 7, especially for troops in the Pacific, the President and the Prime Minister at Arcadia had refused to modify the commitment to Russia. Nevertheless, the shortage of tonnage had perforce reduced the number of ships on the northern route in January, and FDR informed Land that he "simply must find some ships that can be diverted at once." Although the flow had improved somewhat by March, it was still far behind schedule, and the President ordered the admiral to find ships "regardless of other considerations." Yet by April, even as the schedule was close to accomplishment, a new development brought disarray. The German forces, surface, air and undersea, which had largely ignored the convoys during 1941 and early 1942, struck with telling results. After the disastrous PQ 17 convoy in June lost 23 out of 36 ships, the British canceled further sailings during the summer, creating a tremendous bottleneck of American ships in Icelandic and Scottish ports assembled for Russia under the pressure of the President's instructions.[20]

Thus the magnitude of the task Douglas faced is difficult to exaggerate. The organization and functioning of the War Shipping Administration was chaotic. Land, who had ably administered the Maritime Commission since 1938 and attempted to carry out the prewar demands upon his agency after the inauguration of lend-lease, realized that the exigencies of his new position required the recruitment of additional professional skills and experience. The assignment of his fellow commissioners, Vickery and Macauley, to ship construction and manpower proved to be splendid appointments. Douglas met the most pressing lack of his organization—managerial skill, combined with an informed world outlook and diplomatic talent to untangle the growing confusion.

Douglas briefed himself and proceeded with all possible speed to reorganize and implement both the procedures and the staff. The system hastily put together, first by the Allied leaders with the Combined Board and then refined by the establishment of the War Shipping Administration on the American side, was in grave difficulty, not from any lack of effort by those attempting to meet its demands, but rather from the lack of clear-cut systems and proper leadership. The cooperative effort of the two principal Allies could not hope to succeed unless a great deal more information was quickly available concerning civilian needs and the demands of the various services. In addition, an accurate accounting of available shipping was urgent. Much of this expertise and knowledge was at the disposal of the British from their experience with the problem in the First World War and during two and one half years of the Second. In the beginning, therefore, Douglas leaned heavily upon their advice and statistics.[21]

Not only was he fully cognizant of Britain's advanced organization and knowledge, he also had the highest personal regard for Sir Arthur Salter. He regarded Salter as an able administrator, whose understanding of the problems facing them both was unequaled. Cutting through the cumbersome machinery of the CSAB, he, therefore, introduced the practice of consulting directly and almost on a day-to-day basis with Sir Arthur on questions of shipping availability and allocation. Often, he turned to Salter on matters not technically of legitimate concern to the British. The offices of both men were in the Department of Commerce building. Their discussions were almost continuous, especially during the first year of Douglas's tenure. So firm was the relationship, and their shared belief that the committee-oriented CSAB could not begin to cope with the urgency of the situation, that, "to the scandal of their respective compatriots," they occasionally sent a joint representative, either British or American, to the board meetings.

Salter was delighted with these developments. In a long letter to his chief, Minister of War Transport Lord Leathers, on April 6, he elaborated at some length on the status, past, present, and anticipated, of Anglo-American cooperation on shipping. He had found Americans "generally good to work with, on certain very definite conditions, and subject to certain very real dangers," namely an inbred suspicion of British motives, overdepartmentalization, lack of foresight and a resentment against being lectured: "they are willing to learn, but not to be taught." Praising Land and his assistants for effort, he faulted them for lack of imagination, planning, and the aptitude "to look at shipping as a whole." Douglas "is a man of quite different type. He is of first rate intellectual, as well as practical ability. He thinks ahead and around his problems; is subtle, industrious and, with a quiet and persuasive manner, strong-willed. . . . He is addressing himself first to the very urgent, obviously important task of expanding the U.S. Administration (now the W.S.A.) for its new tasks. New men are being brought in and *in time* the organization should be immensely improved." Salter felt that now "overwhelmingly the most important general objective to aim at is that of making the 'partnership' idea, implicit in the Combined Board System, a reality . . . this means doing everything to encourage the 'generous' not the 'horse-trading' mood." Meantime, he warned of the continued resistance of the War Department to civilian control, underlining the need for the British to exercise as much influence as possible in disputed cases until a true partnership could emerge under the new, more effective WSA organization.[22]

As an obvious corollary to the personal confidence that quickly developed between Salter and Douglas, there also soon occurred "an affectionate and in-house relationship and terminology" between Douglas's operation in the WSA and the Ministry of War Transport, unequaled in the other points of contact between American and British counterparts, military or civilian. As the official British historian expressed it, they were "endowed as it were with a sense of family solidarity which, however much they might bicker among themselves, made them present a united front against outsiders, whether British or American; and knowledge when combined with proved efficiency, is power; the shipping mysteries, except to those who professed them, were so incomprehensible, that though their respective governments could dictate to the shipping authorities, they could not out-argue them on their own ground. The shipping authorities had to be left to work things out in their own way."[23]

This unique cooperation was to develop and deepen over the months ahead in Douglas's service with the WSA. It generated both successes and problems in his work. He came to his task with some reputation as an Anglophile: indeed, it may well have been a factor in his selection. The value of this sympathy in the conduct of his work and the practicality of the closest possible cooperation with Britain in an area where, at least in the beginning, her knowledge was supreme, is evident. But Douglas exposed himself to the recurrent charge of being pro-British, an accusation that was to be used against him on occasion by his own colleagues and especially by his principal domestic opponents, the military, whose attraction to their opposite numbers was, to say the least, often restrained.[24]

In any case, if the immediate need was to draw heavily upon British expertise, almost simultaneous attention had to be given to the recruitment of able administrators and technicians in the American organization. Retaining such men as Ralph Keating, Richard M. Bissell, and D. F. Houlihan, who had performed yeoman service before his arrival, Douglas reached outside for, in many cases, men of proven ability already known to him. Among these was Franz Schneider of Newmont Mining, who had had considerable experience in this area during the First World War. He joined the WSA in mid-May as Douglas's principal assistant for ship control. Fred Searls, Jr., came aboard as a special advisor. John E. Cushing took over marine, port, and ship operations; B. Brewster Jennings, tankers; and Amyas Ames became administrative officer. Houlihan was eventually succeeded in fiscal affairs by Richard W. Seabury and then Percy Chubb. As he gathered together a dedicated staff in the spring and summer of that year, a notable improvement in the operation of the organization became evident.[25]

Douglas was a tough, demanding, but fair superior. He asked no more of his subordinates than he gave to the job himself. His abilities were then and later fully appreciated by those around him. Commenting that "The hours here in

Lewis's shop are 8 a.m. to 10:30 p.m.'' and that "we work the help in two shifts so as not to kill them off," Fred Searls wrote Douglas's father in July that "Sundays are like any other day." But, he added: "I cannot help but congratulate you on your eldest son. I have, of course, known all along, that he had more than usual ability, but . . . I have come to appreciate what an extraordinary chap he really is. . . . I may say truthfully that he has more ability, judgement, character and solid common sense than anybody I have yet come across in this madhouse of pulling and hauling and good intentions and stupid procedure that is the American war-effort in Washington.''[26]

After almost three months as chief advisor, Douglas's authority had been enlarged and his direct responsibilities increased. The first weeks had indicated to Douglas himself and, more important, to the President and Harry Hopkins that his office must be upgraded, better defined, and given more independence. Accordingly, the President met with Douglas to offer him the close-to-autonomous position of Deputy War Shipping Administrator for Ship Utilization, Planning and Policies. Land's limitations had now become even more evident. The heat from the press was on full blast; the administrator was attacked for the failure to stem the tide of sinkings and to expedite the efficient use of shipping available. Of greater influence, no doubt, was the report on the WSA initiated by Vice-President Wallace, written after a careful investigation by Assistant Budget Director Wayne Coy. It was a damning indictment of Land's administration and emphasized that only since Douglas's arrival had any order at all been achieved in the control of shipping. It recommended that Douglas be appointed War Shipping Administrator and that Land be retained as Chairman of the Maritime Commission in charge of the accelerated ship-construction program.

But Roosevelt, while fully aware of the need for a change, was disposed to keep Land at least in nominal command, moved by old friendship which dated at least as far back as his service as assistant secretary of the navy, by the admiral's previous service in the navy and on the Maritime Commission, and by his own inherent reluctance to fire anyone if he could find another way around a personnel impasse. As a matter of fact, as Douglas later recalled, he was asked by Harry Hopkins, before meeting with the President, whether or not the admiral should be dismissed. "My response was emphatically no." He pointed out that Land was popular in Congress, where he could be extremely helpful, and that, as chairman of the Maritime Commission, he had a permanency that he, Douglas, as "a bird of passage" did not possess. He should be retained. "'But,' I said to Harry, 'keep him out of my hair. I don't have much so it shouldn't be difficult. But don't let him get in my way because he doesn't know really what he is doing. He doesn't know what he's got. He doesn't know how it's employed. Order has to be brought out of this present disorganized administration of shipping. I believe that I can do it. This will be impossible if Jerry [Land] is constantly insinuating himself into the matter.'"

In his subsequent meeting with the President, Douglas apparently covered much of the same ground, especially concerning the retention of Land, no doubt to the President's relief, but reiterating that if Land proved obstructive, he would "put on [his] hat and walk out." He expressed the belief that it was an area in which he could be helpful. "I don't know one end of a ship from another, Mr. President, but I do know something about the movement of commodities in world trade." He might have added, less modestly, that the prime talents he would bring to the position were managerial and diplomatic ability. Roosevelt agreed to give Douglas a free hand, assuring him that there would be no interference from the admiral and that Douglas would have his personal support. He received the President's backing in an even wider arena. He pointed out to Roosevelt that, with the obvious shortage of ships, he would be under fire from all sides: "General Marshall will be on my neck for shipping. Admiral King will be on my neck for shipping . . . the War Production Board will be on my neck for shipping. The Export programs will be on my neck for shipping. The British will; the Russians will. . . . Mr. President, I have got to allocate these ships and I must have your support . . . if I don't have your support, Sir, I can't do it nor can anybody else." In response, the President said: "Lew, I'll give you my word that I will never allocate any ships to anybody and I will never fail to back you up."

Douglas never wavered in his appreciation of FDR's subsequent behavior: "He could not have been more loyal or more true to the commitment he gave me . . . he kept it meticulously." The record confirms Roosevelt's support in the conflicts Douglas foresaw. Of equal if not greater importance to the success of his mission was the role of Hopkins, whose accessibility and confidence, as he functioned as the President's alter ego, were of inestimable value.

In the course of the conversation, an exchange took place in a manner calculated to heal old wounds. Douglas often recalled that, after he had expressed his pleasure and satisfaction at the President's offer, he had remarked: "You know that you and I disagreed once, but this, Sir, is a budget that has to be balanced." "Why do you say that, Lew?" Roosevelt inquired. "Because, Sir, you can't print ships." With that response, the President threw back his head in the familiar gesture with the cigarette holder pointing to the ceiling and roared with laughter. The two were back in harness again.[27]

Douglas's appointment was announced on May 20, in a statement released by Admiral Land. After noting Douglas's service over the past months as his chief advisor on relations between his agency and the British Ministry of War Transport, Land wrote that "Mr. Douglas will now join me in not only planning but directing the use of our merchant marine." His "agreement to become deputy administrator will insure a vigorous and all-out effort to use our ships for the one and only purpose of winning the war." Land also announced the promotion of Vickery to the parallel post of deputy for new construction. The command structure was now in place.[28]

These changes were not unanticipated. In his column of May 18, Drew Pearson had predicted that Douglas was "a good bet for War Shipping Administrator to replace Admiral Land." He reported that "the loading and routing of cargo ships has been under hot inner circle fire for months and the top war chiefs recently reported to the President that this is the sourest spot in the war program." Granting that in his subordinate position Douglas had effected "some improvements," Pearson wrote that, as chief advisor only, Douglas had been "constantly hampered and obstructed" by others in the WSA. Nor was the true relationship between the admiral and his new deputy unsuspected when the announcement was released. The Philadelphia *Record* bluntly stated that the President had "cracked down on the serious shipping muddle by shelving Admiral Emory S. Land. To save Land's face, he was allowed to retain his titles as Chairman of the Maritime Commission and War Shipping Administrator, but two able deputies were appointed who will actually run the agencies." It added that Land was the President's "friend of many years standing and apparently the President did not want to fire him. He therefore resorted to the device of continuing Land as the nominal shipping chief, but giving actual authority to Douglas and Vickery."

In other journals, satisfaction at the appointment of Douglas appeared universal. Personal congratulations poured in from all quarters, by letter and by wire. The British representatives in the United States were delighted at the enhanced authority of a friend who had already demonstrated his sympathy and understanding of their urgent needs.[29]

Obviously, the new relationship between Land and Douglas was a difficult one for both men to carry off without friction. Diminutive, yet athletic and scrappy, a senior naval officer accustomed to command, the sixty-three-year-old administrator was opinionated, outspoken, hot-tempered, sometimes crude, and often tactless. But he recognized his limitations, was certainly acutely aware of the criticism concerning the WSA's efficiency, and realized that changed circumstances after American involvement in the war called for more effective approaches. Initially, then, he showed for the most part a remarkable lack of public resentment or jealousy, and was supportive of Douglas. Nonetheless, the criticism of him and the comments on Douglas's appointment must have hurt. As time went on, the prominence of Douglas's role and the much greater entrée he had to both Harry Hopkins and the President undoubtedly rankled. By the last months of Douglas's tenure, the strain was more obvious than in the beginning. It is safe to say that Land increasingly came to resent Douglas.

Certainly credit is due Douglas for his efforts to minimize the tension. Although he was in fact making the decisions on ship utilization and allocation for the most part alone and personally carrying on the necessary negotiations with civilian and military authorities, he attempted to keep Land informed and even, if only pro forma, to consult with him. Douglas's concern throughout his career to avoid personal antagonisms whenever possible was undoubtedly a factor reducing friction. Yet it is equally clear that Douglas did not greatly respect Land, and occasionally revealed a certain false and even patronizing note in his usually courteous treatment of him. He may in time have unconsciously resented not having the War Shipping Administrator title. Douglas appears to have made little effort to go beyond required formalities in his dealings with the admiral and to have aroused his superior's latent Anglophobe tendencies by his close relations with the British.

Land's simmering antagonism toward Douglas, and Hopkins as well, came to full boil in his autobiography, published in 1958. According high praise to Vickery, Macauley, and Douglas's successor, Captain Granville Conway, Land virtually ignored Douglas, with misleading and perfunctory comments on his appointment and a notation that "We finally broke off relations, due to ill-health on his part and my unwillingness to give the British my shirt," adding bitterly but with no substantiation: "there was an assist from F.D.R., who knew both sides of the story." Land's suspicion of the British had been earlier expressed in a memorandum to the President in April, 1941, following a dinner with the newly arrived Salter. "If we do not watch our step," he wrote, "we shall find the White House en route to England with the Washington Monument as a steering oar." In his autobiography, he also accused Hopkins of being pro-British, alleging that "at times [he] seemed to favor [England] over his own country."

The valiant attempt by the White House to aid Russia was also resented. Hopkins, he charged, had "ultra-Russian leanings." Protesting the sending of Russian convoys in the summer of 1942, Land was close to resigning when Hopkins informed him it was "none of your business what happens to the ships after they leave the United States," but he vowed that "Hopkins was not going to force me out of my job." When he complained to Roosevelt in a private interview about Hopkins's predilection for the English, he got in reply "a long puff on a cigarette, a broad smile; the familiar end of an unsuccessful interview."

In the end, perhaps it can be said that Land won. After the problems had for the most part been mastered and Douglas left the WSA in the spring of 1944, he was succeeded by Conway, who was respected by both, but who gave traditional and appreciated loyalty to the senior naval officer. Land remained, received most of the official credit, and apparently downgraded the awards to Douglas and his principal associates after the war. Douglas never received the Medal of Merit, only the certificate, as did several of his subordinates. Conway, on the other hand, did receive the medal, which he, no doubt, deserved. Perhaps significantly, by the time these decisions were finally made, both Roosevelt and Hopkins were dead. The victim of temporary tenancy and Land's antagonism, as well as an undramatic and little-publicized, though absolutely vital role in the war effort, Douglas never received the recognition he unquestionably deserved for his contribution to Allied victory.[30]

14

The Struggle with the Military

FROM THE BEGINNING OF DOUGLAS'S ACQUAINTANCE with the shipping situation, it was clear to him that the internal problem of organization was closely paralleled by a second urgent priority—to clarify the uneasy relationship between the young civilian agency and the military. This incipient controversy had two separate elements that required resolution if the war effort was not to be crippled: the respective areas of authority and the competing demands of the lend-lease program and the now pressing movement of troops and military matériel overseas.

Within a month of Pearl Harbor, Lieutenant General Brehon B. Somervell, the gifted, aggressive, and ambitious chief of the army's Services of Supply, was putting great pressure upon Admiral Land to increase the allocation of vessels to move troops to both the Atlantic and Pacific theaters. The ships then assigned and in the army transport fleet were, he argued, woefully inadequate for the army's needs. Yet, even as Somervell began his importunities, which were to continue throughout the war, sinkings of ships to Great Britain were reaching alarming proportions, with a resulting drastic drop in imports by March from 30 million tons in 1941 to a projected 22 million tons in 1942. The British were prepared, in the face of new conditions, to accept a reduction, but they estimated an absolute minimum of 26 million tons to survive. Furthermore, Roosevelt was completely unprepared to reduce the commitment to foreign aid, which, in fact, he determined to expand now that the United States was a full partner in the Allied cause. The answer was twofold: to dramatically increase ship construction and to maximize the utilization of the cargo space presently available, a major objective in Douglas's assignment to the WSA.[1]

Within a few weeks of Douglas's first appointment and certainly as he began his second, the WSA had a better grasp of the availability and use of tonnage. Early in his tenure as deputy, he was able to reassure Somervell that the prospects were modestly encouraging for improving the situation. Not only did his office have more accurate information available, but the unexpected curtailment by the British of Russian convoy sailings as the result of greater losses in April had released vessels that could be assigned to both military and civilian needs. In consequence and in anticipation, the army intensified its accumulation of cargo at various loading terminals on the East Coast for the projected Bolero, cross-Channel, operation. With the troops still not ready to depart, the army had decided, with some misgivings, to send its equipment ahead to take advantage of the expected easement in shipping space.

These hopeful signs were the result of better knowledge of ship availability or of unanticipated developments. They did little to alleviate the friction over authority between the WSA and the military. From the beginning the army, and to a lesser degree the navy, had been convinced that control of loading and shipping should be in their hands. With equal determination, based upon his own experience as assistant secretary of the navy and upon the advice and experience of the British in both wars, the President had decided that civilian authority should prevail. His creation of the War Shipping Administration, and perhaps even more decisively, the appointment of Douglas, gave formal emphasis to his conviction. But the army, and especially Somervell, continued to resist and to attempt to erode the authority of the WSA.

During early discussions over congestion at the loading ports, Douglas had clear warning of the difficulties ahead. He presented a plan to improve use of the railroads and terminals by closer collaboration of the WSA, Office of Defense Transportation, the British Ministry of War Transport, and the army. Somervell had objected that this would greatly reduce the authority of his service. A heated argument ensued, with Douglas accusing the military of demanding "absolute power." In the course of the exchange, he also became acutely aware of "the deep anti-British sentiment among Army officers." Reluctantly, Somervell had accepted the proposal, but with the proviso that "it may be modified or withdrawn in its entirety if it fails in its purpose." Clearly a more formal delineation of their respective powers was required.[2]

To this end, Douglas, with his new authority, sat down with Somervell to hammer out an understanding. Somervell wanted to acquire control of military cargo as well as troop carriers; Douglas insisted on retaining supervision of all cargo vessels. Douglas was a determined and skillful negotiator, and a successful one usually, because his final position was often unclear to his opponent until he reached his predetermined point of compromise. Together with his disarming charm, which made it difficult to become angry with him, he had the acknowledged support of the President for ultimate civilian control.[3]

A letter to Somervell shortly before the conclusion of their discussions reflected Douglas's talent for conciliation without retreat. In it he emphasized his determination that the two agencies should enjoy "complete mutual confidence and respect" and assured the general that if that attitude was not yet universal in his administration "it will be very shortly." He acknowledged the validity of several of the criticisms leveled at his organization, but promised to remedy them. He denied any desire to take over the Army Transport Service or to dictate to the military how to load ships at their terminals. Above all, in a determined effort to bridge their differences, he wrote: "I hope that by now you are convinced that the primary ambition of the War Shipping Administration is . . . to do all manner of unpopular things, solely for the purpose of providing the shipping facilities with which men and equipment may be shipped to the critical theaters of war in time to defeat the enemy. On my part, I repeat what I said yesterday—there is going to be no controversy between us. There is a war to be won, and that's the job we ought to get on with." The reassuring words were more easily written than accomplished.[4]

The agreement that emerged from these exchanges was signed by Somervell and Douglas on June 13. It sought to establish an understanding on assignment, loading, and control of cargo vessels. Although it was certainly a compromise in some areas, the ultimate control of the WSA was maintained. The army had pressed for control over the loading and unloading of vessels assigned by the WSA for military operations, including the exclusive use of these ships for their own cargo. Douglas had argued that to conserve space use of these ships should be coordinated for both military and nonmilitary cargo.

The other major issue was allocation. The army wanted vessels turned over to it in guaranteed blocks for stated periods of use, a demand resisted by the WSA as a violation of the pooling principle. It was assured the right to load and unload ships assigned to the service in order to expedite urgent shipments, even if this meant broken or incomplete stowage. The WSA, however, retained control of the assigned vessels by granting the army use of them for only the single outward voyage. Once unloaded, they reverted to WSA supervision. The concessions may have been an effort by Douglas to improve interagency relations. The army was to depend on the WSA for additional terminal facilities and labor. Whenever possible, cargo was to be mixed for tight stowage; freighters could be held at their destinations temporarily in emergencies. Although this protocol did clear the air and further define the jurisdictions of the civilian and military authorities, differences of interpretation were to bring about a renewed confrontation by the end of the year.[5]

Douglas was determined to view the agreement in a hopeful light. He wrote Admiral Land that the settlement was about as good as could be expected. If it had not been negotiated, he declared, there was a real danger of the controversy's becoming a legislative matter with bitterness and danger to both sides. "I took the responsibility, while Somervell was in the mood to settle, to sign finally. . . . The fluidity of the shipping pool has been increased. This, it seems to me, is the basic principle on which we should never yield. On the other hand, we did make concessions to the Army. . . . At this moment we are on the verge of one of the great military movements." Under such circumstances, he concluded, it would be a major error to take the responsibility for upsetting the army's mission. "Indeed to do so might lead to our own defeat." Somervell himself characterized the agreement, in a memorandum to Hopkins, as "eminently satisfactory" and expressed the hope it would "stop some of the sniping that has been going on." Later, Henry Stimson was to sum up Douglas's relations with the military in these and subsequent negotiations by commenting that Douglas was not frightened by "militarism," or "over zealous Army officers," but, "by dealing openly with the War Department . . . he was able to resolve his difficulties." The deserved praise, however, took too little account of Douglas's continuing problems with Stimson's service subordinates.[6]

No sooner had this negotiation been concluded than Douglas was obliged to turn his attention to the conference of British and American war leaders, which got underway in earnest with the arrival of Churchill and Roosevelt in Washington on June 21, after several days of private meetings at Hyde Park. The question that drew Douglas, Land, and Vickery directly into discussion with their chiefs was how and whether to allocate limited steel production between the building of transports in the face of the high rate of sinkings and of additional escort vessels, the latter being urged by Chief of Naval Operations Admiral Ernest King. King began the discussion by stating that "one ship saved was worth two ships sunk," underscoring the importance of escort-vessel construction. Churchill was impressed with the argument. Land replied sharply that the diversion of steel would prevent the building of 100 to 150 cargo ships.

Douglas presented a well-reasoned argument in opposition to King's demand. Pointing out that the period of greatest stringency in shipping was the next six to eight months, he noted that none of the escort vessels planned in the diversion of construction would be available until early the following year. Meantime, the pressure for cargo ships to meet the increased needs of the projected cross-Channel operation and other theaters would intensify. Thus, to meet the submarine threat, "the logic of the position indicated" that the construction of merchant ships, many already on the ways, should be increased. The deficiency in steel, which hampered an advance in escort-vessel construction, should be made up at the expense of domestic consumers of steel plate. Apparently Churchill was more impressed with the force of Douglas's reasoning, turning to King with the remark that although one ship saved was indeed better than two ships sunk, it was far better that one ship delivered needed military cargo than no ships at all.[7]

Although his remarks had appeared in the end persuasive, at least to the Prime Minister, Douglas was concerned that a repetition of Land's blunt opening comments would only exacerbate the dispute. Accordingly, in a memorandum the next day, he warned Land that, however accurate his statement of the case, its tough presentation might arouse the hostility of the military to a point of counterproductivity. He suggested, therefore, that the memorandum Land was drafting for the occasion be toned down so as not "to antagonize so many parties." Douglas's moderating diplomacy was heeded.[8]

In any case, at the White House meeting the following day, there was general agreement that merchant-shipping construction should be interfered with as little as possible and the shortage of steel for escort vessels be alleviated by drawing from other sources. In the event, however, a reduction in merchant-ship building was found necessary, requiring the WSA to cancel a major shipyard contract with a good deal of resultant criticism. The problem persisted through the summer and fall, occasioning continuing pleas from the WSA to the President for War Production Board authorization of the allocation of more steel for both merchantmen and escort vessels.[9]

Meanwhile, Douglas responded to the clamor from Atlantic Seaboard small-boat owners and organizations to use their craft on anti-submarine patrols in-shore. The losses of Allied shipping in coastal waters continued to be appalling. Despite pressure from yacht clubs, chambers of commerce, and the press, the navy argued that the organization of these boats into disciplined patrols would be difficult if not impossible. Supported by the army, which was frustrated by the navy's inability to protect convoys of its troops and cargo, Douglas on June 9 wrote Hopkins about the alarming wastage of tonnage and strongly advocated the utilization of pleasure craft and fishing vessels for anti-submarine patrol in Atlantic and Caribbean coastal waters. The initiative was successful. During the following years, some 2,800 small boats were taken into the coast guard reserve and served with distinction in relieving the navy of much convoy duty by establishing a "picket fence" offshore. Admiral Adolphus Andrews, Commander Eastern Sea Frontier, gave high priority to the organization of these patrols and later glowingly praised their accomplishments.[10]

For Douglas the hectic meetings and conflicts had been aggravated by another bout of physical complications. Sometime early in June, seeking relaxation in a softball game, he had wrenched a muscle and ruptured blood vessels in his leg, putting him on crutches for a month. The debility was accompanied by a painful flare-up of his recurrent sinus infection. Writing despondently to his father, he complained bitterly of Washington as "a hotbed of intrigue, back-biting, rumor, among the hosts of people seeking personal power and position and it is therefore difficult to get things done and at times depressing."[11]

Soon Douglas was off on a journey to London to confer with British shipping colleagues, government and military leaders, and American lend-lease representatives. He arrived on July 25 shortly before General Marshall's departure from London, following the chief of staff's losing battle with the British (and the President) to launch a cross-Channel invasion in 1942 or early 1943 and his reluctant acquiescence in a substitute North African landing sometime in the fall— to be labeled Torch.[12]

Present at 10 Downing Street for the shipping meetings were Churchill; Douglas; Harriman; Lord Leathers; Sir Arthur Salter, who had also returned for the conferences; Lord Cherwell, Churchill's scientific advisor; and several British officers. Churchill raised questions concerning the use of vessels for army cargo and British imports, suggesting that the number of the former was excessive for the needs of the troop buildup in Britain. Since no American officers were present at the first conference, despite the presence in London of Major General Charles P. Gross, Somervell's chief of transportation, a confused report reached the military of what transpired, causing Marshall some embarrassment in his farewell meeting with the Prime Minister and a sharp exchange between Somervell and Douglas upon the latter's return to Washington. Douglas admitted that he had challenged a statement quoted from General Gross that shipping would be easy after August, but denied he had suggested, as charged, any impropriety in army loading or supply. He assured Somervell that the army was for the most part fully represented in subsequent conferences. Obviously, the differences with the military had not ended with the agreement of June 13.[13]

For the remainder of his visit, Douglas was engaged in frequent conferences attempting to forecast the amount of shipping required and available for Bolero or a similar operation, which in the immediate future proved to be Torch. Deficiencies were revealed in the course of examining the data, with which the British were still far better equipped than the Americans. On August 2, Douglas and

Harriman sent a long cablegram to the President, recommending urgently, on the basis of their London discussions and favorable impression of the British organization, that shipping be husbanded by much greater cooperation between the American military and the WSA. Toward that end, they urged a reduction in the scale of equipment reserves and maintenance for American forces in the U.K., closer relations between British and American authorities, more steel for a substantial increase in the United States shipbuilding program, and an improvement in turn-around time. Overall they emphasized that continued or increased shipping aid would be necessary if Britain were to sustain her war effort.[14]

After something over two weeks of taxing meetings and other official engagements, during which he also found time to contact several old friends and to meet General Dwight D. Eisenhower for the first time, Douglas returned to Washington on August 10. However frustrating many of the problems confronted during the whirlwind visit, it was of immense value in providing direct contact with Harriman and his staff and in establishing personal relations with military and civil authorities in England, especially in the Ministry of War Transport and particularly with Lord Leathers.[15]

Leathers was a remarkably able administrator and, for the most part, he and Douglas were to maintain excellent relations at long distance and more notably at the various conferences attended by both. Although he had had only a primary education and a sketchy one at that, his talents were early recognized by the second Lord Inchcape, who had advanced him rapidly in his far-flung Peninsular and Oriental shipping-lines organization. Churchill brought him into the government in 1941 to head the newly formed Ministry of War Transport and later characterized his decision as "one of the most important and fortunate appointments of my war Administration." His diplomatic as well as administrative ability may have come as a surprise to some, for he was far from urbane and his working methods were often baffling. Leathers tended to be uncomfortable with men of intellectual bent. He was a loner, with few if any close friends, uneasy in social situations. Although his reputation for shrewdness and for reaching a correct resolution of problems was well founded, the process was usually mysterious to his associates, some sort of visceral rather than rational method, which could be highly annoying. On occasion, he became too involved in detail. Yet, despite these apparent handicaps to an effective partnership with Douglas, they got along very well, no doubt because of the goodwill on both sides, and generally reached the same answer albeit by different routes.[16]

Of course, Douglas's most intimate British contact was Salter. Following a brilliant academic record at Oxford, Salter had entered the Civil Service and risen rapidly to positions of trust. During the First World War, he was involved in shipping problems, gaining much of the expertise that was to be so valuable in the Second. Brought back into British service on the outbreak of the war after a tour with the League of Nations Secretariat, he was posted to Washington in the spring of 1941 to head the British Merchant Shipping Mission. Judicious, highly intelligent, described by one colleague as "professorial" (he was later to become Gladstone Professor of Government at Oxford and a Fellow of All Souls), somewhat fussy and pedantic, he had skills and a temperament that nevertheless combined well with those of Douglas, who greatly admired him as an economist and elder statesman and leaned heavily upon his counsel and advice. The esteem was mutual. Praising Douglas to Hopkins in September, 1942, Salter wrote: "I am extremely happy in my relations with Lew Douglas who is doing a wonderful job in the W.S.A. and, with adequate support, will do very great things in this war." Salter later hailed Douglas as "one of the most fortunate appointments ever made in the civilian war administration," and as "an administrator . . . of genius. . . . Thank God for Lewis Douglas." He "threw himself into his . . . work with an industry and demonic energy which I have rarely seen equalled . . . [W]orking out . . . allotting . . . American ships as part of the Allied pool . . . was due more to Lewis Douglas than to anyone else in the public service of America." Together they made a tremendously effective team.[17]

Douglas's close and sympathetic relations with Salter and several of his associates in other British missions in Washington, his respect for their experience and knowledge, reinforced his reputation of being pro-British. The charge was leveled again and again, sometimes in jest and on occasion in anger. No doubt there was validity in the accusation. But, in the existing circumstances, it was also a valuable attribute and reflected, rather than prejudice, a breadth of vision required if shipping problems were to be considered and resolved in fairness and with the wider view necessary to a successful conduct of the war. He always first considered the American interest, but perhaps because of his family background, his tenure as principal of McGill, and his appreciation of English culture, he was able to relate to British difficulties and, even more important, to their thought processes far better than were other, more parochial Americans. The British representatives, while finding him always a ready listener to their complaints and briefings, never thought of him as an easy mark. Quite the contrary, he demanded of them, as of his American colleagues, convincing arguments. His questions were often embarrassingly searching, prompting the mission to signal London for more information and detail. Before he made a decision or fought their case before the military or Hopkins and the President, he insisted upon firm evidence. In sum, Douglas's understanding of the British point of view was a positive and indispensable ingredient in the effective utilization and allocation of Allied shipping resources.[18]

Salter and his staff were often accused by their superiors in London of being hopelessly pro-American, bowing too frequently and unnecessarily to the pressures in Washington, to the detriment of British interests. The battles that repeatedly marked relations between the British and American military staffs were in large measure absent from the shipping scene. The flexibility in providing the necessary shipping, which was in the words of Churchill "at once the stranglehold and sole foundation of our war strategy," owed much to the empathy of the central figures, Sir Arthur Salter and Lewis Douglas.[19]

Two themes run through the remainder of the first year of Douglas's tenure at WSA: his efforts to unsnarl and rationalize the utilization of American and Allied shipping on an urgent short-term basis and for the longer struggle ahead, and his increasingly embittered relations with the military over allocation, loading, and consignment, despite the agreement of June 13.

As noted earlier, Douglas began immediately to reorganize the agency, recruiting able administrators. He also introduced office machines, then rather primitive, for record and statistics keeping and retrieval. Another imperative was first to identify, then conscript for the duration, all shipping that could be employed in the war effort, allocate its services effectively, and achieve the maximum efficiency in loading and unloading both civilian and military cargo to ensure that it reached the proper destination. Repair operations had to be drastically improved and turn-around time accelerated.

Shipping in American yards for repair declined from 14 percent in April to under 8 percent in September. By about the same time, ships were being loaded to close to 2 percent of their deadweight capacity and broken stowage greatly reduced. Through increased pooling and an understanding of the division of responsibility for shipping throughout the warring globe, British and American cooperation had grown at a considerable pace. It was reflected in the rearrangement of shipping routes to make better use of the combined merchant fleets and in the mixing of Allied cargoes on the ships of both nations. One of the more interesting innovations inaugurated by Douglas was the use of "strip silhouettes" on each vessel. "The love-life of every ship was documented on that strip and each number of days in transit, in port discharging, being repaired—was clearly identified. Thus we were able to tell how and where ships were being handled, the delinquency in discharging, the delays in repairs and all the things that affected the turnaround. This enabled us to increase the speed of the turnaround."[20]

But an impressive listing of accomplishments ignores the day-to-day difficulties and emergencies that delayed progress or demanded immediate remedy. Perhaps the most striking example in the area of essential war production was the alarming disruption of bauxite shipments from the South American mines in Guiana to Canada and the United States. By August, 1942, submarine sinkings and inadequate port facilities had reduced the supply for the manufacture of aluminum, vital for aircraft production, to what would be used in one week. Douglas moved rapidly to remedy the situation before a disastrous shutdown could occur. Enlisting A. E. Roberts of the Waterman Steamship Company, he gave him sweeping powers to reorganize the entire Caribbean operation. With the cooperation of the navy, which instituted increased patrols, Douglas diverted to Trinidad and St. Thomas vessels bound homeward in ballast or with low-priority cargo from the Indian Ocean, Africa, and the east coast of South America, and transferred new tonnage completed on the Pacific Coast through the Panama Canal to the Caribbean. Meanwhile, Roberts, in Trinidad, got the boats moving and kept them moving. By the end of September, the delivery of the required 300,000 tons a month seemed assured for the future, an increase of several times over the record of the previous months. A herculean effort, but of course at the cost of any smooth development of the long-range organization of shipping so laboriously pursued by the WSA and the British.[21]

Alterations in planning from Bolero to Torch in the Atlantic theater, unexpected high-level commitments, the resumption of the Russian convoys, both to the north and to Persian ports, and the requirements of the Pacific war, all called for drastic changes in WSA planning. Through the spring and early summer of 1942, troop movements and supplies for Bolero had top priority. Then, in midsummer, political and strategic pressures from Russia and Britain prevailed in a decision to launch Torch in North Africa instead. Douglas was obliged to alter ship movements to provide vessels for the forces and cargo in the landing and for the military equipment and provisioning of the area once secured.

On August 20, he assured the army that until further notice shipping previously made available for Bolero would be diverted to the North African operation. At that point the magnitude and the duration of the African campaign was unanticipated, and it was further agreed that the Bolero buildup would be resumed, on receipt of notice from the army, at the rate of one hundred ships a month, sometime in the late fall. The drain of Torch and its aftermath, together with other demands upon shipping, were to lead to a severe crisis by winter. Meantime, as a sort of prologue to this development, Douglas had been forced to provide shipping to carry out the spur-of-the-moment, generous, and life-saving promise of the President to Churchill at the Washington conference in June, upon receipt of the news of the fall of Tobruk, to supply the British forces in Egypt with some 300 tanks and 100 self-propelled guns. To compound the difficulties of this emergency, it was necessary to route the vessels carrying this equipment around the Cape of Good Hope, which absorbed a great deal more shipping time than the direct route.[22]

Added to these problems was the constant pressure from Roosevelt to resume the northern Russian convoys and to increase tonnage to the Soviet Union via the Persian ports. Attempts by the British to reinstate the convoys to Russia in September led to such a disastrous sinking rate that they were discontinued for the remainder of the year, though some attempt was made to run individual ships through the German gauntlet. As to shipments to the Persian Gulf, not only were vessels increasingly in short supply because of the demands of the North African campaign after the November landings, but turn-around time for the ships sent was tremendously increased by completely inadequate unloading facilities. Finally, Douglas took the position that no more cargo except of the highest priority should be sent there. Meantime, he dispatched experts to break the logjam. Under great pressure from the President, who was embarrassed by the virtual halt of Russian deliveries, Douglas released some vessels for the Vladivostok run, despite a concurrent shipping crisis in the Pacific. These almost impossible demands, eclipsing the glimmer of hope for more available shipping that had appeared in midsummer, were paralleled by increased German submarine activity, which reached its climax in November, 1942, threatening all the tenuous lifelines, including the British import program. Only the constant cooperation between Douglas and Salter in pooling and shuffling tonnage between American- and British-controlled shipping alleviated the situation.

Although Roosevelt and Churchill had decided to give the European theater priority, in fact a greater number of American vessels were being used in the Pacific, a problem exacerbated by the longer turn around time for the vast distances of that ocean. To the dismay of the planners, a disproportionate number of vessels in service and of new ships built were being diverted to meet the insatiable demands of the Pacific theater. The navy, determined to take the initiative from the Japanese, obtained the agreement of the army and the concurrence of the President to make marine landings on Guadalcanal and Tulagi, even as the demands upon Allied shipping were facing new challenges in the Atlantic. At the beginning of September, 1942, General Douglas MacArthur, with Australian forces and American airmen, struck at New Guinea. In both operations the fighting was desperate, the odds poor, and the need for supply great. They reflected, in part, the navy's and MacArthur's preference for the Pacific theater.[23]

As early as July, Douglas had become acutely aware of the dangers to his planning from both these sources. Having allocated thirty-six vessels to MacArthur, he now received a request for forty-two additional ships for the exclusive use of the general in Australia. Presaging what was to become a running, albeit formally correct, battle between them for the duration, Douglas, through Somervell, refused. In the future, Douglas was often reluctantly forced to accede to the general's importunities, but almost always at the cost of other Pacific requirements and Atlantic priorities. As if this drain were not sufficient travail, MacArthur more often than not retained the vessels assigned, frequently as floating warehouses. The never-solved struggle over "confiscation" reached a sort of climax in the six months before Douglas's departure from the WSA. Douglas's highly respectful but increasingly urgent requests for MacArthur to release vessels were met with equally correct but noncommittal replies. Finally, in March, 1944, General Marshall, his patience with MacArthur's intransigence at an end, intervened and sent a peremptory cable, which one of his subordinates labeled "a honey."[24]

As if the initial difficulties with MacArthur were not sufficient Pacific diversion, by late October the operation on Guadalcanal faced a final desperate push by the Japanese to regain the island. Roosevelt ordered all available resources to be thrown into the struggle. Specifically, he directed the WSA to allocate twenty additional ships for use in the Southwest Pacific, none of which was to be redirected at the expense of either the Russian run to Vladivostok or the North African expedition. At first glance this appeared an impossible request, inasmuch as there was already a deficit of shipping in the Pacific. But Douglas moved promptly, asking the Joint Chiefs of Staff to indicate the military services in the Pacific from which ships could be taken and assuring the President that the vessels were being allocated "forthwith." By mid-November, he was able to report to Admiral William D. Leahy, Roosevelt's chief of staff, that he had been able to meet all the military and naval requirements for the various areas in the Pacific, a work of "magic" which impressed the services and subsequent historians of the Pacific war.

His accomplishment was even more impressive because of the concurrent bottleneck of shipping at Nouméa, New Caledonia, the principal receiving and distribution center for South Pacific cargo. The inadequate port facilities had led to prolonged turn-around, aggravating the worldwide severe shipping crisis developing in late 1942. Deeply concerned, Douglas enlisted the expertise of Frazer A. Bailey of the Matson Navigation Company, whom he dispatched to survey and make a report on methods of alleviation. By January, 1943, there had been established in San Francisco a joint army-navy-WSA operations committee to coordinate military and lend-lease shipments to the South Pacific; it enjoyed considerable success in improving conditions. In the larger picture of overall wartime strategy, Douglas's constant monitoring of Pacific shipping demands, together with his insistence on civilian control, made a distinct contribution to the maintenance of the Allied decision to give first priority to the Atlantic war, a decision that was continually subject to erosion by certain elements in both American services.[25]

Meanwhile, the agreement of June 13 was disintegrating. By midsummer, 1942, the running battle had begun that was to culminate in a full-scale confrontation in December and January. Sharp disagreements with the army and navy mounted over Douglas's repeated remonstrances against inefficient loading of military cargo, exaggerated demands for space, and jurisdiction over vessel use and the loading and unloading of cargo, complicated by almost independent use of shipping and port facilities. They were answered by countercharges that he was favoring inflated British requirements. Douglas found especially galling the sometimes crude anti-British remarks and innuendoes of some army and navy men with whom he was most closely associated.[26]

In mid-October, the continuing conflict with his military and, to a lesser degree, naval counterparts heated up, punctuated by unpleasant references to the veracity and objectives of the British. Douglas's temper wore increasingly thin as he saw "vicious anti-British sentiment sticking up its nasty head in too many places." The center of this battle was the new demand by the supply services that all cargo, military and civilian, be consigned to the commanding officer of the theater of operations, including that to the British Isles.

Douglas turned to his brother-in-law, Assistant Secretary of War John J. McCloy, who was impressed with his documentation of authority for the WSA, but requested time to consult with Somervell and Gross. Somervell angrily telephoned Douglas and pointed out that the army knew better than the British where lend-lease materials could best be used. Douglas replied that such an arrangement would give the army commander a free hand to divert cargo from its assigned designation to wherever he felt like sending it. Somervell accused Douglas of championing the British, "delivered himself of a tirade against the British," saying that they were "no good," and averred that he and Douglas could never agree because he, Somervell, was "on the American side." Distressed but undeterred, Douglas met with the President, Hopkins, and Land on October 21, and emphasized how much shipping space might be saved by combining cargo. On October 23, McCloy called together Brigadier General Lucius D. Clay, assistant chief of staff for matériel, representing Somervell, and Salter and Douglas to thrash the matter out. After hearing both sides of a heated debate, McCloy opted to support the WSA as consignee for lend-lease cargo. Clay with good grace accepted the decision. He later recalled that, when the military accepted McCloy as mediator, they were not aware he was Douglas's brother-in-law, but nonetheless could not fault the judicious impartiality of his decision-making.[27]

The breach was temporarily closed when Somervell invited Douglas to lunch, and they agreed with surprising conviviality that confrontations were foolish and their letter writing unproductive. Somervell indicated his acceptance of the consignment resolution and agreed to a careful and deliberate execution of that decision. On October 30, McCloy informed Douglas that the army had accepted the WSA proposal. Douglas's emotional strain during this imbroglio was not helped by a simultaneous flare-up of his chronic sinus problem. Writing to a close friend soon after these events, he expressed his opinion that "if the War Department and the Generals would not try to run production, shipping, and transportation, in which they have no experience and for which their restricted and limited intellectual lives make them unfitted; if they would stop trying to grab more and more power, leaving to the civilians the things that are civilian; and if they will only stick to their last of organizing a fighting machine, we might have a better chance of winning sooner."[28]

A skirmish had been won; the major engagement was yet to come. During November, the army and the WSA, in accordance with the Douglas-Somervell understanding, moved toward greater integration in loading, with gratifying results. But disquieting information was beginning to reach Douglas that, despite Somervell's qualified assurances of cooperation, the army and navy were still not reconciled to civilian controls. Then, at the beginning of December, the truce abruptly ended when General Gross, with no warning, informed the WSA that combined loading in New York would cease and that army materials exclusively would henceforth be loaded at army bases. Shocked, Douglas reported this development to Harry Hopkins, pointing out that this would undo all the very hopeful advances of the past month, which had been marked by extraordinarily good loading performances. He would not accede to the general's unilateral decision, which would be "an unconscionable extravagance in the use of shipping." Hopkins supported him completely, asking "what in the world was the matter with those people?" and advising: "I would not yield on that issue at all."[29]

In vain Douglas attempted to obtain a reversal of the army's dictum. Finally, on December 16, he gave a warning to a representative of Gross. He had "been trying to avoid a quarrel, taking personal insults, arrogance, conceits, and a bad record—all in the hope that we would be able to persuade people to do the reasonable thing, but . . . there was a limit to that." In response to an appeal from the general's deputy, Douglas agreed to wait a day or two for the army to reconsider before he moved. He was not sanguine. Shortly after that conversation, he repaired again to the White House, discussed the entire situation with Hopkins, and declared he was at "about the end of my rope." He suggested seeing the President. Hopkins agreed: "Then the President will issue an order and stop it. Don't waste any time. Those fellows will not be persuaded." Reassured, Douglas immediately requested an appointment, which was granted for the 18th.[30]

Armed with a directive for the President's signature, Douglas carefully reviewed the problem with Roosevelt. Would the President sign the directive? It simply reaffirmed, he assured Roosevelt, the initial order establishing the WSA and clearly conformed to the shipping practices of all maritime nations. To the President's query as to whether it should first be shown to the army and navy, Douglas replied negatively: It would only cause "violent dissent." Wayne Coy of the President's staff had approved it; so had Hopkins. Gross and Somervell would only "raise hell." Wouldn't it be well to have a board of some sort including the army and navy? asked Roosevelt. Absolutely not, replied Douglas. It would only weaken the civilian control case in which they both believed. The directive "merely told the Army and Navy to do what he [FDR] had already told them to do." Roosevelt signed with the prophetic comment: "This is right. If this doesn't work you will catch hell." Informed by Douglas of the President's action, Hopkins laughed and said: "Good. Maybe it will raise hell, maybe it won't. They probably will come back."[31]

The directive, formally addressed to Admiral Land, briefly noted the Allied shipping crisis; indicated that no "interference with the most effective use of ships for the war purpose can be tolerated"; affirmed that the responsibility for the "perfect operation of the merchant fleet," in accordance with the executive order of February 7, must be concentrated in one authority; urged the closest cooperation between the WSA and the military services; and directed the admiral to allocate to the army and navy for their exclusive use only "combat loaded vessels," which were to be released to the WSA as soon as they had been discharged, and vessels clearly classified as fleet auxiliaries. He was also to allocate to the army and navy "for the transportation of military and naval personnel and supplies, to be loaded by the War Shipping Administration, space in vessels under the War Shipping Administration, in accordance with the detailed requirements and priorities for their movement established and presented by the Army and Navy." In order that he should have complete information on the "employment of all merchant vessels" for all uses, he requested a monthly report from the WSA on all vessels controlled by them, including "all information" from the army and navy. The document was to have a short fuse.[32]

Douglas had Land dispatch copies of the directive to Secretaries Stimson and Knox, with the suggestion that they appoint representatives to sit down with those designated by the WSA to work out the details of implementation. McCloy soon telephoned Douglas to charge that Roosevelt had signed the directive in an "ex parte hearing." Why had not the military had a chance to present their case? Hopkins reassured Douglas: "Forget it and don't worry." Maybe there would be "no fuss at all." White House aides told Douglas that the "President will stand fast." On December 23, Stimson wrote Land that he "must express his surprise that a matter which so obviously affects the Army should be initiated without anyone in authority from this Department having an opportunity to state his views." Pending clarification of the issue, he was postponing designation of representatives to meet with the WSA. In reply, Land assured Stimson that the directive did not go as far in specifics as did the order of February 7, and that the WSA had no intention of interfering "in the tactical operations of the Army."[33]

The services were not mollified. They requested a meeting of Douglas and Land with the Joint Chiefs of Staff (JCS) in Admiral Leahy's office in the White House on December 28. The Douglas account of the conference suggests that the confrontation was rather more heated than the official transcript indicates. Present were Generals Marshall; Somervell; Henry H. Arnold, chief of the army air forces; and John Deane, secretary to the Joint Chiefs; Admiral King; Rear Admiral Robert M. Griffin, director of the Naval Transport Service; as well as Land and Douglas. Douglas began by repeating the WSA interpretation of the directive, emphasizing that in fact it did not go as far as the February order. He pointed out that recent disagreements concerning loading, combined with a serious worldwide shipping crisis, had necessitated the new directive. He denied any intention to interfere with combat loading. Reflecting both anger and embarrassment, King and Somervell asked why the Joint Chiefs had not been consulted before Douglas went directly to the President. In essence, Douglas's reply was that certain agencies of the military had not been cooperating fully and, since attempts at correction had failed and since the WSA derived its authority directly from the President, it had seemed the appropriate procedure. Leahy concluded the session with the suggestion that representatives of the military and the WSA meet again to arrive at a mutually agreeable interpretation.

According to Douglas's diary of the same day, at one point Somervell implied that the WSA was trying to protect commercial interests, and he also demanded that Douglas "go to the President and have him rescind this Directive, and then we'll sit down." Later in the discussion, Griffin caused Land to "blow up" and say: "The issue then is, Admiral, whether the shipping shall be controlled by the military or by civilians." Griffin replied: "That's precisely what the issue is." Leahy intervened to state: "That's not the issue this morning," though Douglas wrote that "the issue had at last been brought right out so that everybody could look at it." When King argued that the chiefs "have authority in this matter," Douglas expressed surprise at that point of view, and repeated that the authority of the WSA came directly from the President. Finally, according to Douglas, Somervell commented: "I don't want to load any civilian cargo." "Not even if it saves shipping?" Douglas asked. "No," shot back the general, "I don't want to load any civilian cargo."[34]

Although the acrimony at first prompted Douglas to question tartly the propriety of service officers rather than their civilian chiefs dealing further with the WSA, he did agree to continue the discussions requested by Leahy, drafting a series of interpretive memoranda which the service representatives consistently rejected during their meetings. A final memorandum, of December 31, incorporated the concessions both sides were prepared to accept. Specifically, it protected combat and strategic loadings, allowed for civilian cargo on military loadings when possible, and permitted the presence of service advisors when the WSA was loading military cargo. There does not appear to have been any formal acceptance of the document by either side. Rather, the "solution" in the last analysis was more a matter of personal accommodation.[35]

Douglas and Marshall lunched together the day before the next meeting of the Joint Chiefs. Their discussion and an earlier conversation of Douglas with Leahy seem to have been the turning points in the resolution of the problem, largely, or technically at least, in Douglas's favor. Douglas began by disclaiming any intention to restrict the transportation facilities of the army, a concern he feared Marshall harbored in view of his remarks at the meeting with the Joint Chiefs. He then detailed at some length his objectives and reminded Marshall of the many legitimate contestants for shipping among whom he had to adjudicate. Marshall said he understood and agreed on almost all points, but reiterated his distress at Douglas's approach, that is, going directly to the President. Douglas countered that he had only done so after repeated "rebuffs" from the army, even "personal insults," including a "flat declaration . . . that the WSA had no place in the war." When asked pointblank who had made such a statement, Douglas told him it was Gross. Again Marshall suggested, as he had in the Joint Chiefs' meeting, some sort of military inspection service. Douglas repeated that that was already the assigned function of the WSA and emphasized again his conviction that control of the merchant fleet must be in civilian hands. The WSA must be the impartial judge among all claimants; after an admittedly shaky beginning in the spring and summer, it was now competent to make such decisions. The general admitted the validity of these arguments and agreed, in Douglas's words, "to fight our battle for us" if the WSA refrained from going again to the President, which, as he wrote in a follow-up letter, "would lead us to confusions and give us few satisfactions." Douglas insisted his agency, created by the President, must reserve that right, but promised in the future to go to Marshall first, with a view to resolving issues without recourse to the White House.[36]

This direct intervention by Marshall illustrated one of the general's great attributes—the ability to cut through controversy and reconcile the contestants to the achievement of shared goals. The meeting was also a milestone in the growth of a mutual admiration and respect between the two men that was to ripen later during a much closer association of trust and friendship.

The controversy subsided over the next two weeks in a face-saving draw. Somervell conceded that he really didn't care who was the boss as long as the job got done, and Douglas agreed that he did not want to fuss over technicalities as long as ship loading was properly programmed. Somervell deplored the interjection of personalities and recommended that Douglas and Gross "really ought to see more of each other," a suggestion Douglas indicated he would be pleased to follow if Gross "could stand it," no doubt remembering Gross's reported snide reference to him as "Sir Lew" and other unappreciated attacks. Douglas commented favorably on the work under way on the West Coast, where the WSA was cooperating well with the army and navy to unsnarl the South Pacific tangle.

Douglas suspected the army had heard the President would stand firm on the issues between the two agencies. McCloy confirmed this view in a telephone call later in the day, but warned that the navy, especially Admiral King, was still determined to get the order rescinded or altered. The two men predicted that "on sober second thought" the navy would "think better of it." They were correct.[37]

There were some final gasps before the matter was closed. The Joint Chiefs persisted in suggesting to the White House the creation of a joint inspection committee of the WSA, the army, and the navy to ensure maximum use of shipping. Douglas objected, and the President rejected the proposal with the suggestion that he, Gross, and Griffin work out specific procedures. Although McCloy again warned Douglas, on January 16, the morning of the scheduled conference with navy representatives, that "he understood that the Admirals had dropped anchor and had concluded to be very firm," the meeting itself proved to be remarkably conciliatory. In the presence of Forrestal, Douglas once again explained the WSA's objectives: efficient loading, whoever did it, and the release of vessels to WSA control once a mission was completed. On such a basis, the chairman, Vice Admiral Frederick J. Horne, vice chief of naval operations, saw no reason why there could not be "an agreement in principle." But Griffin continued to be contentious and accusatory. Goaded, Douglas responded, "If you insist upon washing linen, I'll do it too—and it will be your linen." Horne gently admonished his colleague and, after some further discussion, agreed that the navy would cooperate as closely as possible with the WSA as well as the army on alleviating the Pacific shipping crisis. Later, Forrestal assured Douglas that he could consider the matter settled. A clear indication of the desire to cooperate quickly came in the replacement of Griffin by Rear Admiral W. W. "Poco" Smith, who worked extremely well with the WSA.[38]

On January 18, Douglas reported to the President that, in accordance with his instructions, he had carried out conversations with the army and navy to clarify the executive order of February 7 and the directive of December 18. "We believe the matter has been satisfactorily settled. The groundwork has been laid for what we sincerely trust will be full and friendly cooperation." Certainly progress had been made, although considerable heat was generated in the process. Greater cooperation between the services and the WSA resulted, but neither won a decisive victory. Disagreements were to continue, but the course of collaboration was never again to be so violently tested. Each side had recognized the mettle of the other. Douglas had won the battle, thanks to the unfailing support of Roosevelt, encouraged by Harry Hopkins, and to the sympathetic civilian leadership of the army and navy, represented by McCloy, Knox, and Forrestal. Credit was also due Leahy and Marshall for rising above parochial interests. The episode probably served best, however, by bringing the smoldering dispute into the open, prompting some compromise on both sides, achieving a greater measure of cooperative rather than competitive exchange, and convincing all concerned that the previous haggling was no way to run a war.[39]

15

From Casablanca to First Quebec

DURING 1943, DOUGLAS CONTINUED TO DETERMINE seemingly insoluble allocations among competing clients for his ships and battle with military encroachments. He also found himself directly involved in the series of Allied conferences that marked that crucial year of the war. Even as his struggle with the army and navy built to its climax in the fall of 1942 and the early days of the new year, another closely related issue was emerging which would come to a head as a result of misunderstandings at a conference he did not attend, Casablanca—in fact, they occurred in large measure because of his absence. It revolved around the precipitate drop in British import levels caused by the military demands upon Allied shipping.

Britain had been generous in anti-submarine-warfare aid, depleting her escort resources and concomitantly reducing the frequency and number of convoys to the United Kingdom. Her shipping lanes were more exposed, her losses proportionately greater, her replacement capacity limited. While the American shipping situation slowly improved, with new construction under the driving leadership of Admiral Vickery, and new and converted shipping more effectively controlled and allocated under Douglas's management, a large proportion of available tonnage was diverted into war services and military lend-lease to meet the needs of Bolero, then Torch, and especially the insatiable demands of the Pacific theater. Striking statistics illustrate the problem: the prewar average of deadweight tons for British imports was 50 million; it fell to 42 million in 1940, 31 million in 1941, and by the end of 1942, to 23 million. By November, U.K. reserves were being rapidly depleted.[1]

The matter was brought home forcefully during Douglas's visit to London in the summer, and his report with Harriman to Roosevelt, on August 2, emphasized the seriousness of the problem. With the increase in military demands in the fall, he realized that an impasse was fast approaching. Meeting with his advisors on October 24, he told them: "The isolationist crowd here in the military establishment will know in a couple of days just how tight our position is. They will demand that British ships be taken out of the British import program to supply these deficits. It is very important that we know what that British program is in detail; that we know more about it than anybody else in Washington, because it is only thru knowledge that we would be able to say to the British 'Yes, we think you should,' or to the military establishment 'If you want to starve them, yes, but if you don't, no.' "

Four days later, accompanied by Admiral Land, Douglas met at the White House with Leahy, carrying a detailed memorandum for the President on the conflict between the military and British requirements. He replied sharply to Leahy's suggestion that ships be taken from the import program to meet the military's demands: "I said the issue was a simple one. Did we want fighting and equipped allies, or did we prefer to fight alone?" In an effort to obtain more reliable information, he urgently cabled Harriman for London statistics on the import program. An encouraging development in an otherwise gloomy picture was the President's approval, on October 21, of a CSAB recommendation that the earlier decision to concentrate Allied ship construction be carried one step further, with the greatly increased rate of shipbuilding, by allocating "an appropriate portion of the net gain in the merchant tonnage of the U.S. . . . to relieve the burden on the war services of each of the other United Nations." Naturally the British would be the major recipients.[2]

Meanwhile, the British themselves, until then reluctant to press their case more dramatically in view of America's own shipping difficulties, had finally reached a level of concern necessitating action. Having exercised every device of economizing and improvising, they faced the imminent possibility of closed factories from lack of raw materials, resulting in unemployment, production paralysis, and a blow to morale, in short, a situation "discreditable in the last degree to his Majesty's Government," in the words of Churchill. After careful consideration of the form increased American aid should take, such as relief on other routes where British shipping was heavily engaged, London decided to ask directly for a guarantee on the import-program level. Accordingly, in November Oliver Lyttelton, minister of production, was dispatched to Washington to put the British case.[3]

The minister was instructed to obtain from the President a definite commitment on the British import program upon which his government could rely during the coming year. According to London's estimates, this would require the assignment of enough American shipping to bring the total dry-cargo figure up to 27 million tons. Although this volume would not restore Britain's depleted stocks, indeed would require further calls upon reserves, it would assure their remaining above a level that would put the economy and war effort in peril. Roosevelt was sympathetic and convinced. On November 30, he replied formally to Lyttelton's proposal in a letter to Churchill, accepting London's figures and promising the shipping needed to meet them. Subtracting the amount carried in British bottoms, this would require about 7 million tons to be supplied by American shipping, approximately 300,000 deadweight tons per month turned over to the program and remaining in its service. However, he hedged his guarantee with a number of qualifications, indicating the various contingencies that might interfere with its accomplishment, especially in the first few months while the demands of military operations in the Mediterranean remained high. He pledged, however, that diversions would be made "only with my personal approval." These reservations were disquieting to the British, but they accepted the guarantee as the best that they could hope for.[4]

Surprisingly, the military and naval authorities were not involved in or informed of these discussions and the President's letter. Even the WSA was not apprised of the precise nature of the communication until some weeks later, at which time Douglas, with the approval of Hopkins, sent an interpretive comment to Salter on its qualifications. In the CSAB meetings of December 29 and 31, Salter directed the attention of the members to the letter and argued that they should inform the JCS of its existence so that together they could proceed with plans for its implementation. Land objected, pointing out that it was up to the President to communicate the contents to the military. Salter persisted, emphasizing that it "was urgent and necessary that the Combined Chiefs of Staff (CCS) should be officially informed . . . and realize its full significance; otherwise plans might be made on a different basis which after being carefully worked upon and completed might be shattered when the letter was in due course transmitted to them." Land stood firm, and the board concurred, agreeing meanwhile to work out its own plans on the basis of the letter's requirements. Specifically, in accordance with their usual practice, Douglas and Salter sat down with the letter, on January 4, 1943, to attempt to understand its commitments and implications. On the same date, at luncheon with Douglas, General Marshall complained that "the only way he had just heard about the communication from the President to the Prime Minister was through the British." In fact, it was only on January 18 that Land was able to inform the CSAB that he had now been "officially" advised of the letter by the President and been asked to plan to implement it. Subject always to the qualifications in the letter, Land then presented a tentative schedule, prepared by Douglas, of tonnage shipments for the period through May. It is not at all clear whether at this point the military, as Marshall indicated, had other than cursory and secondhand information on the communication.[5]

It was under these adverse conditions that the Casablanca Conference, designated "Symbol," got underway January 14. Lord Leathers was present, as a technical advisor, but the WSA was unrepresented. Instead, General Somervell, with his military bias and inadequately informed about the extent and basis of the President's commitment, was sent to handle shipping questions. In retrospect, it seems inconceivable that the two governments, after a year of joint operations and in the face of their past experience concerning the essential importance of shipping to any military planning, should have come together for momentous decisions on future operations with such an ad hoc arrangement for determining its availability. The results were nearly disastrous. Future conferences were to follow a quite different pattern.

Leathers, who assumed more accurate American military information, was confused and frustrated by Somervell's performance. At the beginning of the conference, Roosevelt made a special point of seeing Leathers alone to ask his help "in explaining to our Service Departments the utility and necessity of W.S.A."— a curious request in view of his own failure to invite a representative of the agency to the meeting. Leathers's efforts to comply were in vain. In spite of the recent imbroglio in Washington, Somervell was obviously still unwilling to accept the supremacy of civilian authority. Later in the conference, Leathers complained to Harriman of the great difficulties caused by the "absence of any U.S. representative properly informed on the shipping position." While he was depending on the estimates agreed to by the CSAB, the army and navy were using an independent set of figures and constantly trying to "whittle down or ignore the President's commitment of 27 million tons for the Import Program." One day the military would seem to agree on the overriding necessity to fulfill the presidential commitment, but by the next day they had usually slipped back. When the final American shipping paper was prepared and presented to the British as a "combined" recommendation, it was too late to check many of the assumptions or rewrite the entire document. Among other misconceptions were that the Americans had agreed to replace net British losses rather than guarantee an import tonnage and that the monthly 300,000 tons would be on a month to month basis rather than accumulating in the British service.

In an effort to be as accommodating as possible to the Americans, Leathers reluctantly accepted a provision to commit any surplus British shipping to operation Bolero, which he considered highly unlikely to take place. When Paper CCS 172 was presented to the Combined Chiefs of Staff, it contained, therefore, in Appendix III, a note by the BMWT that "the figures are based on a very rapid estimate and must, of course, be subject to check after detailed examination." Specifically, it insisted that the assistance for Bolero and Husky—the invasion of Sicily—was dependent on the premises that no shipping would be withdrawn from the import program, no reduction required in the minimum requirements for Torch and on the availability of escort vessels. When the paper was accepted in plenary session January 23, it was with the caveat by Churchill that the British commitment should be considered minimal. In the event, the estimate proved to be some 6 million deadweight tons in excess of that actually available. But, when the civilian and military leaders departed from Casablanca on January 24, they were full of optimism for the following year, notably the plans for Husky and the preparation for Bolero, unaware of the "bombshell" ticking away which could blow their calculations out of the water. Compounding the time lag in the explosion, Somervell had chosen to return by a circuitous route, visiting army installations in North Africa, Persia, and India.[6]

On February 11, Douglas handed Salter the outline of a fairly optimistic schedule for British imports for the first five months of 1943. Four days later, Douglas noted in his diary that Hopkins "said he thought I should be informed of [the] Casablanca plans and he would arrange for this either through [the] President or Marshall." But, before such a briefing could be held, Douglas received the first inkling of the giant Casablanca misunderstanding about to unfold. Somervell, finally back from his inspection junket, met with Douglas to request urgently twenty-five additional ships for cargo to General Eisenhower in North Africa. Douglas objected that it would be impossible without removing vessels from other services, principally the British import program, to which the President had made a definite commitment. Was the general aware of that arrangement? "What arrangement?" Somervell replied, in either ignorance or, more likely, irritation.

When Douglas referred to the November 30 letter, the general blandly replied that it had been superseded by Paper CCS 172 at Casablanca and produced that paper for Douglas's inspection. Replying that he neither knew of it nor understood it on such cursory examination, Douglas declared that meantime he was bound by the President's commitment. Concluding this rather strained conversation, Douglas promised to do what he could to meet Somervell's needs—perhaps ten ships.

Douglas immediately called Hopkins for guidance. Somervell's demand could only be met by withdrawals from the British service. Should the President, Hopkins inquired, invoke the reserve clauses in his letter? Douglas refused to advise on this, but reminded Hopkins that such a step would call for consultation with the Prime Minister. He also asked about the advisability of getting the combined chiefs to confirm the necessity of the demand. Hopkins counseled against such action at that time. It was agreed that Douglas would investigate the matter further and inform Hopkins of his findings. Interestingly, apparently Douglas made no effort to ascertain from Hopkins the validity or circumstances of CCS 172, a copy of which he now had in hand. Following this exchange, he conferred with Salter, who assured him he had no knowledge of any commitment at Casablanca that took precedence over the President's letter. When Somervell called him that weekend in New York, Douglas said that his people were carefully checking all convoy schedules and repair, that "we would break our backs," and that he should have an answer the first of the week. He followed with a call to Hopkins, relaying his conversation with the general and emphasizing the necessity of informing the President accurately if there was a conflict. Finally, on February 22, he was able to inform Somervell, Hopkins, and Salter that he could release fifteen (eventually nineteen) vessels for North Africa without damage to the British program. It was a minor miracle, which for the moment satisfied all parties. But the "bombshell" was still not fully exposed.[7]

While Douglas was wrestling with the unexpected army request, Salter had heard from Lord Leathers. "What has happened is that Lord Leathers gave an over optimistic estimate (safeguarded because stated to be subject to check) on an unreal assumption given by General Somervell. It was in any case a provisional estimate (even on that unreal basis) and not a commitment, and it was all on the repeatedly stated (and acknowledged) basis, that it was only an estimate of what—on a given assumption—might be available *after* the British import requirements had been met. There was no acceptance at any stage that shipping should be provided at the expense of a cut in the import programme submitted to the President." Two days later, Gross wrote Douglas: "At the Casablanca Conference, Lord Leathers made certain commitments to General Somervell with reference to British assistance in our efforts to build up forces in the United Kingdom during 1943. Plans for operations . . . are being based on the fulfillment of these commitments. . . . We intend to press for definite scheduling of the troop lift and cargo promised, and will appreciate your help." When Gross asked on March 1 whether he was aware of the British commitment at Casablanca, Douglas acknowledged that he had seen CCS 172, but that it seemed "inconsistent with the pressure placed upon us to allocate American controlled ships to [the] UK service." He was attempting to clarify the issue through Harriman.[8]

A further exchange of cables with Harriman confirmed Douglas's apprehensions, namely that Leathers's unrealistic figures were based on the assumption that British import requirements would otherwise be completely met. It was now clear that the U.K. program was disintegrating so badly that any shipping aid to the U.S. would be quite impossible. Douglas confronted Gross with the bad news, pointing out that the army's stated needs could only be met "at the expense of the UK import program" and that this was a decision that apparently the British were unprepared to make. "Gross seemed very much disturbed and upset," commented Douglas. At this point, Douglas's irritation was directed as much at Leathers's blundering at Casablanca as at the military's excessive demands. Probably it extended also to the President's delay in informing the JCS of his letter of November 30, and the failure to have the WSA represented at the conference. The "bombshell" had burst.[9]

The army's initial shock rapidly turned to anger against the WSA and the British. At a meeting of the Combined Military Transport Committee of the CSAB on March 15, Gross launched an attack principally at the British, but also at the WSA, on the lack of information available to the military at the Casablanca Conference. He accused both of proceeding with plans for the British import program without either the knowledge or approval of the Chiefs of Staff. He answered affirmatively a question from the WSA representative, Ralph Keating, as to whether the agency should consult the chiefs before complying with a directive from the President. Then, greatly to the embarrassment of the British and other members, he charged Leathers with deliberately withholding his knowledge of Roosevelt's letter in his discussions with Somervell. The tone and content of his remarks were so violent and disruptive that the committee agreed to review the official minutes and to consider much of what was said "off the record."

Douglas complained to Harriman that the services were "massing for an attack on the arrangements made in regard to the British Import Program." He told Hopkins that Somervell and Gross were "up to their old tricks . . . trying to make the CCS the allocator of shipping." On the 23rd, Hopkins reviewed with Douglas the conflicting claims and demands of the army and the British and concluded that they could only be resolved by consultation with the British. Douglas reassured Hopkins that the estimates that were being prepared on both sides would be "wed." He was determined, however, as he made clear to Salter, not to permit encroachments on U.K. imports unless agreed to by the British government. The military must not, as he wrote Harriman, be allowed to press home their claims against that program. They must be made to realize it was as important to the success of American arms as any other requirement of the war.[10]

It was Douglas's task to reconcile somehow the seemingly irreconcilable—the British import commitment and the Casablanca military arrangements. Underlining the urgency of his undertaking was the presence in Washington of Foreign Secretary Anthony Eden, sent to Washington in desperation by the Prime Minister, thoroughly alarmed at the deteriorating British import position. He arrived on March 12, armed with a note from Churchill. The Prime Minister declared that U.K. imports must be "an absolute first charge on Allied shipping . . . as vital to the war-effort as supplies to the various theaters. . . . [W]e must know where we stand. We cannot live from hand to mouth on promises limited by provisos."

While Roosevelt and Eden carried on discussions over the next two weeks on this and other wartime matters, Douglas and his aides labored over shipping statistics and procedures.[11]

Meantime, in London, Churchill was further alerted to the degree of bitterness in American military circles by a message from Field Marshal Sir John Dill, the British CCS representative in Washington, who described the "great disappointment at actual shipping situation compared with what CCS were led to believe at Casablanca. Blame for false picture is laid not unnaturally at our door. The strong Bolero advocates are in consequence feeling frustrated." He warned that the Pacific war advocates were as a result once again raising their heads. "We *think* the Americans mis-use ships in the Pacific, but we do not *know*. They *think* we may be using too many ships for British imports, but they do not *know*. In fact, neither side feels the other is being quite open, and there is distrust. I feel very sure that we shall both have to put *all* our shipping cards on the table very soon. . . . On both sides . . . there is a good deal of disappointment and dangerous irritation." Dismayed, Churchill queried Leathers, who responded that "the misunderstandings on shipping are, in my view, due to the division of responsibility on the American side. There is no single control of merchant shipping. . . . The Army and the Navy . . . control large blocks of tonnage, the movements and use of which are almost unknown to us. . . . [The] figures given by General Somervell were very seriously wrong and . . . [recent] statements [by him] . . . indicate he has not yet understood the seriousness of the shipping limitations." Insisting on the accuracy of the BMWT estimates, he asserted: "We have not cards up our sleeve. It is very doubtful if the Americans will ever be able to put all their cards on the table until their shipping is subject to unified control." Leathers's comments were forwarded to Eden by the Prime Minister.[12]

On March 29, Douglas was prepared with his report at a meeting in the White House with the President, Eden, and Hopkins. He had apparently once again achieved the impossible. In answer to Roosevelt's opening question as to whether he had the ships to meet the plans of the Combined Chiefs, Douglas began by enumerating the handicaps under which the WSA operated in attempting estimates of performance. The army never fully informed them of the details, the "inner guts," of their requirements, the type and manner of cargo to be shipped. The navy had not advised them of their needs beyond the second quarter of the year. Finally, and most disconcerting, the army always overstated its requirements—stated military needs had more often than not been maximized to cover all and every contingency. In the light of this history, he had discounted its requirements in several areas, taken into account its recent recommitment to more efficient combining of military and civilian cargo to the UK, and concluded that, at least for the second quarter, the British import program could be met as well as the Combined Chiefs' needs except for Anakim—the plan for the recapture of Burma, scheduled at Casablanca to take place in November.

At this point, Roosevelt interrupted: "And you can do all these things and meet the UK import program?" Yes, Douglas replied, according to the schedule he had submitted, but only if Anakim was delayed. Could the import program be reduced, asked the President? To do so, Douglas responded would mean a "devastating" drop below the estimated overall required figure. "Is that what it means?"

said the President. "That's very serious." "Yes," Eden interjected, "it is very serious." Hopkins drove the point home, asking Douglas how important he considered the import program. It was, he replied, "a very essential and strategic movement." If British production "shrunk to such a level that production declined we would feel . . . [it] ultimately, even though we felt it indirectly, because it would at last come back to us." Even under the schedule he had outlined, committing 7 million tons of American shipping during the year, it was possible that unanticipated British merchant-fleet diversions to North Africa might reduce the total figure as much as 2 million tons below the 27 million estimated figure. The President was convinced. Turning to Eden, he said: "Well, we can consider the import program as settled. You can tell the Prime Minister . . . that we will, for the reasons that have been enumerated here today and for many other reasons, make good our commitment."[13]

Predictably, the army was not happy about the outcome. Somervell and Gross complained to Douglas, on April 7, that the British were getting off "very light [sic]." Douglas's retort was succinct: "I emphasized," he wrote later in the day, "the point that the President had made the arrangement, that it would be a pity if the President, within one week of discussing the matter with Eden, were to call Churchill and to modify the arrangement he had made." When Somervell complained directly to Roosevelt, the President held his ground.[14]

The resolution of the conflict between the military and the British over the 6-million-ton "bombshell" was another milestone in Douglas's fight to maintain the preeminence of the WSA in the allocation of shipping, subject always, of course, to the will of the President. Throughout, he was the beneficiary of his close personal relations with Hopkins and of Roosevelt's continued observance of the pledge of support given when he accepted the task. Not that grumblings and rumblings from the military ceased, but clearly the decision of March 29, and continued evidence of Douglas's growing mastery of his assignment, had taken some of the heart out of their fight.[15]

In any case, actual deployment was considerably better than the pessimistic forebodings of Somervell and Gross. To some extent that was due to Douglas's careful planning, but it was aided immeasurably by the unexpectedly favorable turn of events in anti-submarine warfare. Sinkings in April dropped to less than half those in March, and new construction began to come off the ways in really significant numbers. Net gains over net losses increased and continued to do so through the rest of the war. Exports rose. In retrospect, it is clear that the "heroic" period in the shipping crisis was over. From the gloom of the first quarter of 1943, the second three months saw spirits and expectations rise. In a letter to his father on May 20, Douglas wrote: "For some time the evidence has been mounting which indicates that we may be moving into a period that boasts of more ships than essential for high priority military cargo. We are, for example, during the month of May, and in increasing amounts every month thereafter, putting on enough ships to clear cargo at the rate of between 42 and 45 million long tons a year. . . . This is an export movement far beyond anything the country has ever known." Careful planning would, of course, continue to be essential, and allocation problems between military and civilian needs and among Allies would again cause great difficulties. But if, as Admiral King had said in March, "shipping

[is] at the root of everything," the worst was past. It was an auspicious time for Roosevelt and Churchill to meet again, together with the Combined Chiefs, to plan the further course of the conflict. Profiting from the costly lesson of Casablanca, the leaders made sure that this time their civilian shipping experts were closely involved.[16]

Trident, as the Washington Conference was designated, opened on May 12, 1943, the day after the arrival of Churchill and his party on the *Queen Mary*. While the President and the Prime Minister met frequently, their military and naval staffs were in almost continuous session. The shipping authorities, headed by Lord Leathers and Douglas, reviewed their individual and combined resources and reconciled statistics.

Beginning Saturday morning, a series of meetings were held to assess the shipping requirements, based upon the strategic plans tentatively agreed to by the CCS. As was the case in all the Allied conferences, the shipping authorities were handed the military plans and estimated needs at the very end of the proceedings, with the charge to evaluate in short order the feasibility of their implementation. Conferring first with the American military and naval authorities, principally Generals Somervell and Gross and Admirals Horne and Smith, Douglas and his deputy, Franz Schneider, found it necessary once again to challenge the army's exaggerated figures and deflect a new attack on the British import schedules. At 4 P.M. the meeting became combined with the arrival of Lord Leathers, Salter's deputy John Scott Maclay, and several British officers. They too were exposed to the swollen estimates of the American supply services and to not-so-veiled allusions to the unnecessary requirements of the import program. Somervell was, in the words of the British reporter, "in his trickiest mood." In response, the British pointedly noted that they had, at considerable sacrifice in other theaters, eliminated their shipping deficit to meet the strategic demands of the Joint Chiefs. They suggested the American military "might do some shrinking" and directed attention once again to the fact that the import program was a presidential decision. Douglas made the suggestion that the volume of U.K. imports might be advanced into the summer months when the army needs were at low ebb, thus opening the winter months for a larger number of ships for military cargo.

As the negotiations continued through the night, during which the JCS and the CCS made clear they expected a report by morning, the army requirements gradually came into line with the consolidated statement of the WSA and the BMWT. Attempts of the American military to persuade the British to pick up half of the deficit were without avail, and reluctantly Somervell came around, often in heated argument with Leathers and Douglas, to agree that shrinkages could be accomplished and that the remaining deficit could be eliminated in practice. Late in these harrowing sessions, Maclay produced several bottles of whiskey and some sandwiches. Whether it was fatigue or the stimulant, it was at about this point that the atmosphere began to change, and at 6:45 A.M. the meeting broke up with everyone "well satisfied." Later, Leathers passed the word to Maclay that the President had asked him to thank whoever had provided the whiskey.[17]

Somervell submitted to the Joint Chiefs the paper prepared by Leathers and Douglas. Marshall and King questioned both men closely. Both agreed that the paper deficit shown on the American side was "manageable." That afternoon, Leathers and Douglas reported to the Combined Chiefs that the remaining deficit was "not unmanageable if properly spread." The major factor in meeting both the strategic needs and the British import program was the solution, offered by Douglas and accepted by Leathers, to reorganize sailings and port capacity to swell imports in the summer and facilitate army cargo in the winter. The Combined Chiefs expressed themselves as well pleased. Douglas was particularly gratified by the kudos from the crusty King, noting in his diary: "Before the meeting, Admiral King observed to me that the job had been well done. The British behaved extraordinarily and had shown their anxiety to cooperate and to be helpful. He congratulated the WSA on the part it had played and the way in which it had played it.... He said too, that this was the first statement of shipping that he had ever understood ... and that he wanted to express his appreciation for the way in which it had been prepared."[18]

Along with the success of the shipping calculations at the conference was the growing realization from accumulating statistics that the tide was turning dramatically in the anti-submarine war and that new American construction was rapidly overcoming losses. A striking reflection of this change was not long in coming. In a May 28 letter to the Prime Minister, probably drafted by Douglas, Roosevelt formally confirmed his decision reached during the Washington Conference to transfer, under bare-boat arrangement, fifteen and possibly twenty merchant ships to the British flag during each of the next ten months for temporary wartime duty. Noting that the American fleet "has become larger and will continue to grow at a rapid rate ... [while] the British Merchant fleet has been steadily dwindling [creating] ... in your pool as a consequence about 10,000 [idle] trained seaman and licensed personnel," the President concluded: "Clearly it would be extravagant were this body of experienced men of the sea not to be used as promptly as possible. To fail to use them would result in a wastage of manpower on your side, a wastage of manpower on our side, and what is of equal importance, a wastage of shipping facilities. We cannot afford this waste."[19]

The implication, if not the stated fact, was that the United States was falling short of trained personnel to man the new vessels. Apparently anticipating domestic criticism, or possibly in the interests of wartime secrecy, this decision was not announced as part of the Trident communiqués. But the usual press leakage and public gossip in both capitals encouraged misinformation and potential opposition. Protests from shipping circles that the United States should man its own vessels and from labor leaders that there was no shortage of American merchant seamen appeared in the press and, in time, prompted a strong letter to Land from Joseph Curran, president of the Maritime Union. To discourage such developments, Douglas and Leathers urged the President to authorize an official statement. In addition Churchill, immensely pleased with the President's letter, desired permission to quote from it to strengthen his position in the House of Commons. Bowing to these pressures, Roosevelt cabled Harriman on July 26 to tell Churchill it was "wholly agreeable for him to use whatever phrases and sentences he wishes from my letter to him. I think this is better than putting the whole letter into the record." Three days later, Hopkins telephoned Douglas authorizing release to the press, with a covering explication, of letters to Senator Josiah W. Bailey, chairman of the Senate Commerce Committee and Representative Schuyler Otis Bland, chairman of the House Committee on Merchant Marine and Fisheries, announcing the transfer. Here again, it was considered the better part of wisdom not to publish a copy of the President's letter.[20]

There is some evidence that, whereas Douglas's role was central to the initial decision and subsequent developments, Land, though used as the official spokesman for the public announcement, was not privy to the details and was somewhat chagrined by the affair. Stories appeared in the press implying that some in the WSA suspected that the motive was to help the British maintain their empire rather than conserve Allied manpower. To Douglas, no doubt, the criticism was but one more evidence of the Washington atmosphere of which he had complained some weeks earlier in a plaintive letter to his old congressional chief, John Nance Garner: "If Washington provided an unhappy environment in 1933 and 1934, it offers a nasty one now. . . . The quarrels and squabbles, the ventures for power, jurisdictional disputes, the frivolous way in which the truth is treated by men ambitious for more authority makes one wonder why it is that we seem to get along . . . without bogging down. I suppose it is because there is so much inherent vitality and vigor in the country. . . ."[21]

A new conference between Roosevelt and Churchill, assigned the name Quadrant, was scheduled to take place in Quebec on August 19. It was convened in a mood of optimism, occasioned by the acceleration, expansion, and, consequently, better definition of the Allied advance on several fronts. The Sicilian invasion had been entirely successful; Mussolini had fallen and armistice negotiations were in train with the new Italian government; the CCS had settled upon the following May for the cross-Channel invasion. With these evidences of success in Europe, increased attention also had to be given to the war against Japan and specifically Britain's role in it after the anticipated defeat of Hitler.[22]

Once again, final shipping decisions awaited the proposals of the Combined Chiefs and their approval by the Allied leaders. Of course, Douglas and Leathers conferred on general problems and allocations, preparatory to the expected final flurry of specific accommodation to the requirements presented them. But Douglas also found time to make two new friends, both of whom were to remain close to him and to his family for many years: Major General Sir Hastings "Pug" Ismay, Churchill's chief of staff, and his "girl friday" in the cabinet office, Joan Bright (later Mrs. Philip Astley), who was responsible for many aspects of the organization of this and later conferences. Harriman brought Douglas and Ismay together at luncheon in the Château Frontenac Hotel. "From the first moment that I set eyes upon you," Ismay later wrote, "and we had lunch together . . . I have thought you such a splendid person and staunch ally . . . I have always from the very beginning felt so proud of your friendship." The regard and affection were mutual, and throughout and after the war their relations were marked by frank and intimate meetings and correspondence.[23]

Joan Bright was a friend of Walter Douglas's family in Mexico City, where she had worked some years earlier. Again, a long-lasting note of friendship was struck from the moment Douglas invited her to have a drink with him in the Frontenac. Her recollection of Douglas at Quebec deserves quotation at some length as a snapshot of him in mid-career. ". . . [W]ithin minutes he had me charmed. He was one of those people who did not talk about himself but was genuinely interested in what the other person thought and felt. . . . To look at, he was a man of the open air, a cattleman, sturdily built, with keen brown eyes, easy manners and a relaxed air. He was whimsical, with a subtle wit, courteous, unpunctual—he had no sense of time—and as hard a business man as a hard life could produce. In politics a liberal, he felt passionately about world problems, and was deeply committed to promoting friendship and understanding between Great Britain and the United States. . . . He was powerful and influential, used to getting his own way and will on questions of principle disguised by a soft and hesitant voice. He moved confidentially between the delegations, understood and trusted by the British." The last night of the conference, he persuaded Joan to let him show her the narrow streets of the old French city, where as they walked he forgot the hectic sessions just past to tell her of the land of his forebears. Later, they were to meet again in Cairo, and he and Peggy were to entertain her and Ismay in New York after the Second Quebec Conference. She became a close family friend, seeing the ambassadorial couple often during their London tour and subsequent visits to England, and Peggy when she returned after Douglas's death.[24]

Preliminary to the final report that would be required on shipping capabilities, Douglas met with the President and other members of the American delegation on August 21. He warned that cargo shipping, despite the reduced rate of sinkings, was still very tight. In fact, the lessening of the submarine toll had had the effect of increasing demands from a variety of sources which more than offset the savings. That evening he wrote to Land in Washington: "One of the difficulties of the conference is that it started with the misapprehension that there was a surplus of shipping. . . . [W]e have been spending some time bringing the military face to face with reality. Still, I think that when the demands are all in, properly sifted and related to one another, we will be able to cover them pretty completely."[25]

During the next forty-eight hours, the agreed strategic objectives for the next years reached the shipping men, and they settled down to reconcile requirements and availabilities. Once again, upon the outcome of their unheralded task depended the feasibility of the grand designs of the military chiefs. In all-night sessions, they struggled with the often uncertain facts and eventualities. At times, the demands appeared so astronomical as to put the projected operations seriously in jeopardy. Sharp though constrained exchanges took place between Douglas and Leathers, especially over the availability of British troop transports for Bolero, North Africa, and the Pacific and India, with Douglas challenging his colleague's information. Somewhat grudgingly, Leathers bowed to Douglas's pressure, and accommodation to the military requirements was achieved, although the British continued to have grave reservations concerning the fulfillment of their commitments. Afterward, Somervell patted Douglas on the back with the accolade "Great job, Lew."[26]

On August 24, the CCS received, amended slightly, and approved the plans and reports from the military and civilian shipping experts. Douglas and Leathers added a qualification, pointing out that the anticipated surpluses in shipping resources for the first half of 1944 might be misleading because planned operations for the period could well prove more demanding than contemplated. "We feel it necessary to add this comment,'' the memorandum read, ''lest the figures give rise to misleading interpretations.''[27]

Following the meeting at Quebec, Churchill took advantage of the President's offer to use the White House as his home for the remainder of his stay after Roosevelt's departure for Hyde Park. He convened on September 11 a final session of the British and American service chiefs and certain civilian authorities, including Douglas, to review the strategic situation in all theaters. An immediate problem was the availability of shipping for the buildup of forces for the assault on Salerno, which might well be in conflict with the needs of Bolero. On this score, Douglas was able to reassure the group that "it could probably be managed." Churchill wrote later: "It was an honour to me to preside over this conference of the Combined Chiefs of Staff and of American and British authorities in . . . the White House, and it seemed to be an event in Anglo-American history." Ismay recalled: "It was like a family gathering and every sort of problem was discussed with complete frankness."[28]

About this time, rumors began to circulate that Douglas was in line to succeed Under Secretary of State Sumner Welles. Hull's continuing unhappiness with his deputy's independence, along with reports of his homosexuality, had finally persuaded Roosevelt to part with his old friend. At the President's request, Welles submitted his resignation on August 16, and on September 21 he asked Roosevelt to announce it. The grapevine had it that Douglas was the choice to replace Welles, but he assured questioners that he had no intention of severing his connection with the WSA. Hull made no mention of this speculation in his memoirs. But Henry Stimson indicated in his diary that Douglas was high, perhaps first, on the secretary's personal list for the position. As is often the case, the intricacies of Roosevelt's decision making are unclear. On the morning of September 25, when appointments secretary William Hassett noted to FDR that the press was out with a story about Douglas being made under secretary, Roosevelt responded: "When will newspaper men learn not to climb out on a limb and saw it off?" That evening, with the official announcement of Welles's resignation, he named Lend-Lease Administrator Edward Stettinius to the job. In the opinion of several well-informed reporters, Douglas was Roosevelt's choice until the last minute. If true, his decision may have been motivated by Douglas's virtual indispensability at the WSA, and possibly influenced as well by memories of his independence and past political disaffection.[29]

16

Cairo and Resignation

WHATEVER THE PRESIDENT'S REASONS FOR PASSING over Douglas for under secretary of state, it is certain that his capable hand in dealing with the British on shipping matters was much needed in the ensuing months. Following the invasion of Italy, increasing Anglo-American friction developed around the problem of congestion in Mediterranean ports for the supply of both military and civilian needs and the concomitant and seemingly contradictory demands of London for additional U.S. ships to carry British cargo to the area. Douglas was alarmed at the number of vessels waiting to be unloaded, an estimated one-sixth of those serving the area, but he was suspicious of the BMWT request for more American shipping. WSA authorities, aware that total British tonnage had increased owing to the drop in losses through the summer, noted that the greater part of this windfall was being used in the hitherto neglected crosstrades (trade between ports on neither of which a ship is based) rather than the import program. Were the British, looking toward the postwar restoration of trade, asking for American ships to service the Mediterranean so that their own vessels would be free to build up their shattered commerce? In a letter to Leathers on October 18, 1943, Douglas voiced these doubts, writing: "[W]e think we observe a substantial increase in your tonnage allocated to services that would appear to be commercial. This is raising certain questions in our minds." Leathers's response to this and other expressions of concern was to agree that congestion should be reduced by shipment of only urgently needed supplies, to reiterate that United States bottoms were needed, and to deny any attempt to build up British commercial trade.

In the event, congestion was decreased during the next two months, and less American shipping was requested. As to the crosstrades, the British found that hard facts to convince the Americans were elusive, but could point to the Indian famine as one overriding concern. Distrust would surface again at the Cairo Conference, which was to prove the nadir of Anglo-American shipping relations as well as of strategic controversy.[1]

In the meantime, Douglas was losing Sir Arthur Salter. As early as the Trident

Conference, Leathers had considered "for one reason or another," as Lord Halifax expressed it in a letter to Eden, "bringing Salter home in the not too distant future." Halifax continued: "Salter has done invaluable work here and we all owe him a great debt. . . . He is not everybody's cup of tea but he really has deserved well of the republic." He suggested that Eden explore other useful positions for Salter and have a word with Leathers on the matter. While in Washington, Leathers had also spoken to Douglas and inquired about Salter's deputy, John Scott Maclay, as a replacement. Douglas's response was positive, though expressing some concern over Maclay's lack of seniority. Maclay succeeded Salter in the late fall.[2]

On November 15, Douglas left Washington for the Cairo Conference—Sextant—in company with Sir John Dill, John J. McCloy, Franz Schneider, and several British and American staff officers. Flying in stages, they stopped first at West Palm Beach, then in Puerto Rico, at Georgetown, British Guiana, at Natal, Brazil, which was then literally the air crossroads of the world, and via Ascension Island to Accra, capital of the Gold Coast (now Ghana). There Douglas renewed his acquaintance with Lord Swinton, minister-resident in West Africa, a domain that reached from Dakar to the Congo. Later, during his ambassadorship, and particularly in the years following, Douglas was to become a close friend of Swinton's and a frequent correspondent. On Friday the 19th, they spent the night at Khartoum, where Douglas wrote: "Everything . . . the quiet of the night, the air, its clearness and dryness, the brilliance of the heavens—was so like Arizona." The next afternoon they arrived at Cairo, from which they were driven to their villa at Mena House Hotel, the headquarters of the conference, at the western edge of the valley, almost in the shadow of the pyramids.[3]

Churchill, who traveled with his entourage to Alexandria by way of Malta in H.M.S. *Renown*, was not due to arrive until the afternoon of the 21st. The President, sailing in the U.S.S. *Iowa* to Oran, Algeria, and thence by air, was to land on the 22nd. Generalissimo Chiang Kai-shek and Madame Chiang had already arrived. Taking advantage of the interim before the conference convened, Douglas joined a party of twenty for an all-day flying trip to Jerusalem that Sunday. It proved a hazardous venture: Five minutes after take-off, No. 2 motor sputtered. Fifteen minutes later it failed. Just before landing at Lidda airport, No. 3 engine sputtered but did not die, and the plane landed on three engines.

In fact, Douglas found little to do during "First Cairo," that is the conferences that took place before Roosevelt and Churchill left for their meeting with Stalin at Teheran. The President was much occupied with the Chinese, to the disgust of Churchill, who characterized the "Chinese story . . . [as] lengthy, complicated and minor." The question of a supreme commander for all forces in North Africa and Europe was broached at that time, but not settled. On the 27th, the Anglo-American leaders flew off for Teheran, enabling Douglas to do some sightseeing up the Nile before their return on December 2. Apparently, some word of the discussions and decisions had already reached Egypt, for Joan Bright, who had accompanied Churchill and Ismay, later wrote that Douglas met her at the door of the Mena House Hotel with the words: "Joan, what *have* you done at Teheran? You have set history back many years." Obviously, he was not referring to the welcome agreement on Overlord—the new code name for the cross-Channel invasion in 1944—but rather to the "loose provisions semi-formally discussed" concerning the future of Eastern and Central Europe, provisions which he felt would be taken by Stalin "as a *carte blanche* for future action."[4]

Douglas was more immediately disturbed about the anti-British stance of the Joint Chiefs and, to a lesser degree, of Roosevelt himself, from the beginning of the conference. He was convinced that much of the acrimony had been stimulated by the report of August 4, and especially the letter of August 10, from Stimson to the President, following his trip to England. Both the Joint Chiefs and Douglas had read the letter en route to Cairo. Among the chiefs it had aroused suspicions never far beneath the surface. Douglas was thoroughly angered (and remained so for the rest of his life), for in effect it attacked the Prime Minister and his military staff for obstructionism if not bad faith in regard to planning for Operation Overlord, accusing them at best of halfheartedness and at worst of still pursuing the defeat of Germany "by a series of attritions in northern Italy, in the eastern Mediterranean, in Greece, in the Balkans, in Rumania and other satellite countries." Stimson urged Roosevelt to "assume the responsibility of leadership in this great final movement of the European war" and to insist that command of the operation be given to an American. The details of the political and military discussions at Cairo must be left to other accounts, but there is no doubt that British-American relations were strained, sometimes to the breaking point, or that the leadership did pass westward across the Atlantic. Churchill gave his unqualified support to Overlord, and General Eisenhower was appointed to the Supreme Command. The rapid accumulation of American manpower, material, and experience had finally tipped the scales to favor Roosevelt's preeminence in the coalition councils.

Douglas later recalled a personal experience of flaring tempers and rampant hostility between the delegations. Defending British good faith in conversation with an American admiral, he was appalled to have the officer snap: "Well, Douglas, all you care about doing is to prolong the war." Stung, Douglas replied: "You are quite right, Admiral. This would be the greatest ambition of my life. One son of mine is in the Air Forces. . . . My other son is a forward observer in the Field Artillery. . . . Anything which increases the probability of their death would come, of course, to be my greatest pleasure." Then he added, to his immediate shame, "You close your God damn trap or I will knock your God damn block off," and stalked out of the room. The next day, the admiral apologized.[5]

The acrimony over shipping matters was less intense, though suspicion was ever-present, and the results somewhat inconclusive. Many of the specifics remained to be sorted out in the weeks following. They were, however, spared one problem that had greatly exacerbated Anglo-American relations at the first Cairo meeting. Roosevelt had earlier tentatively agreed with Churchill to aid in the recapture of Burma by an amphibious landing on the Andaman Islands in the Bay of Bengal—code-named Buccaneer. The British chiefs were unhappy at the prospect of this diversion of equipment, especially landing craft, and of cargo shipping from use in the European theater; some of the JCS were anxious to approve the plan of Chiang and Lord Louis Mountbatten (Supreme Allied Commander Southeast Asia). During the absence of the principals in Teheran, and with the knowledge of the complete commitment now to Overlord, Douglas had prepared a memorandum, which indicated very clearly that the Allies did not have sufficient landing craft to support the Buccaneer operation and meet their Western European and Mediterranean requirements. Before the first plenary session of the reconvened conference on December 4, Douglas delivered his memorandum to Hopkins. Apparently, this document played a role in persuading the President and Churchill to abandon Buccaneer.[6]

Most of the shipping meetings were held on the 4th, and especially on the days and nights of the 5th, 6th, and 7th of December. Despite sometimes sharp American questioning on the British use of their tonnage and British unhappiness over the delay of the WSA in producing their figures, tempers at the shipping discussions were mitigated by mutual personal liking. Nevertheless, the exchanges were, like those of their military and political counterparts, the most strained of the wartime conferences. The British estimate for their import schedule for 1944, though lower than that agreed upon at Quadrant, was challenged by the Americans, not on the basis of need, but rather on the ability of ports and internal transport to handle it along with the increased military shipments. The British stood firm and agreed only to reexamine their figures. With some hesitation, the Americans consented to the allocation to the crosstrades of any shipping saved on the import program. Interestingly, in this and other matters of contention at Cairo, Franz Schneider, who was generally more skeptical of British claims, later concluded that they were playing fair and that Douglas, influenced by the overall tensions of the conference as well as the accumulating stresses of the past two years, was at times unduly distrustful. In any case, to relieve British shipping for the Mediterranean, the United States agreed to take over a number of British sailings to the Red Sea and Indian Ocean area and, tentatively, to give some assistance in the shipments of wheat and coal to Italy, where a food crisis had developed. The final report contained a reservation by Douglas and Leathers that military developments after the first half of 1944 were "susceptible of wide and unpredictable changes" that would require "frequent review."[7]

Further accommodations were made on these questions in the weeks following Douglas's return to Washington. Concurrently, he and Leathers made commendable efforts to repair any damage to their personal and official relations suffered at Cairo. Deploring the controversies, Douglas wrote Leathers on January 7, 1944, reviewing their past fine working alliance and asserting that any deterioration would threaten not only the war effort but the "type of arrangement that I deem so necessary between the Commonwealth and ourselves and between us both and others if the promise of preserving the best of Western Civilization is to be kept." He urged that they each keep the other well-informed on their respective shipping situations, especially now that both tended to suspect the other had no shortage of ships. Frankness and candor, rather than trading, should be the order of the day so that they might "recapture that fine relationship that existed between us for so long." Leathers reciprocated Douglas's sentiments of cordiality and cooperation and sent over several of his best men to help develop satisfactory combined programs for meeting the Italian relief requirements, to adjust statistical procedures, and to review their respective positions. By January 23, Douglas was able to inform Hopkins that "we will be able to implement one fleet with the other far more effectively . . . than ever before in our relationship." The depth of Douglas's feelings in the matter are reflected in his closing remarks to Hopkins that "if the British and ourselves are not together, your children's children and my children's children must be prepared to fight another war before the next third of a century has come and gone." For his part, he would "not permit anything serious to happen which will cast a cloud upon the good faith and confidence of the two shipping authorities."[8]

One casualty of these weeks of post-Cairo negotiations was Schneider. Although Douglas had depended heavily upon him as his deputy, there had been stresses and strains between them, largely centering around Schneider's relations with the British Mission, especially Salter. Considerably less inclined than Douglas to be sympathetic to the British case and often particularly irritated by Salter, whom he considered "pushy," he was also somewhat critical of Douglas's hard line toward the military. These differences were aggravated and allowed to fester during the last months of 1943 and early 1944, when Douglas was spending more time in New York at Mutual Life, preparatory to his subsequent resignation in the spring. A great part of day-to-day operations was left to Schneider, whose enhanced position was indicated by his prominence at the Cairo negotiations. At the same time, there is some evidence that almost two years of around-the-clock activity and intragovernment conflict, together with his attempt to oversee the affairs of Mutual Life, had exacted their toll on Douglas's health and nerves. He had returned from Cairo, again by plane, this time in company with Stettinius and Admiral King, to take to his bed briefly with the flu, which worsened his sinus condition. Disturbed by the differences with the British at the conference in January, he resumed a more direct and active role at the WSA to iron out the difficulties. Perhaps unjustly he blamed Schneider's usual anti-British attitudes for some of the problems that had developed, or at least distrusted him to carry on the subsequent negotiations for their resolution. Apparently Schneider's resentment at this intrusion was coupled with his disapproval of Douglas's recent frequent absences in New York and what he viewed as his increasing irascibility and suspicion.

Douglas was aware of Schneider's displeasure. In an effort at conciliation, he praised Schneider for work "superior in quality to any I have seen in any agency of government . . . [or] private institution," declared that their problems stemmed from the terribly heavy tax he had placed on Schneider's physical resources, and suggested that his colleague "relax, rest and take the opportunity . . . to enjoy relief from tension [with a short vacation] so that you can come back to WSA refreshed and eager." Schneider, however, chose to leave, submitting his resignation on February 8, not so much out of pique as in the conviction that his usefulness was at an end and that Douglas himself would soon be departing.

However strained their friendship was at that point, it was soon restored. Later Douglas appointed Schneider to the board of Mutual Life, and they maintained cordial relations until Douglas's death. Schneider was replaced by Captain Granville Conway, who had excellent relations with the British and for whom Douglas had a very high regard as the WSA Atlantic Coast director at the Port of New York.[9]

. . .

As early as June 9, 1943, Douglas had discussed with Hopkins his future at the WSA, prompted by a desire to give the Mutual Life board of directors, meeting the following day, some idea of his plans. In the fall, he would like to be in a position to spend a couple of days each week at the company and to turn over much of the administration of the WSA to others. The end of the war was in sight, and many decisions would have to be made at the company concerning investments in the postwar economy. By spring he hoped to be back with Mutual "most of the time, with occasional visits to Washington." Hopkins agreed, and approved Douglas's so informing his board, but wondered if Douglas would not, when the time came, be somewhat unhappy if he "dropped out of war work entirely before peace had come."[10]

In the late fall of 1943, Douglas devoted more and more time to Mutual Life affairs in New York. By the end of February, 1944, his movements had inspired rumors of his impending resignation. In fact, on March 3 he wrote to the President, asking to be relieved of his duties, effective April 1. Reviewing his service at the WSA and expressing his appreciation to Roosevelt for his "kindness" and "for the support you have extended," gratitude for the opportunity "to try modestly to serve my country," and even noting his "great pleasure" to have been associated with Admiral Land, he indicated that it was imperative for him to "give consideration to other factors. Principal among them is the injunction from my doctor to give serious and continuous attention to an infected sinus" that had reached a critical condition which, if not promptly attended, would lead to a "delicate and radical operation." He offered his services again once his medical problem had been resolved.

Roosevelt expressed his regret and inquired whether he might reconsider his decision. Douglas declined, but indicated he had given the question some thought and would like to withdraw his letter of March 3, and substitute one in which he agreed to stay on as Land's deputy on the CSAB and chairman of the Employment Policy Committee until July 1. He handed the President the new letter incorporating that suggestion, and he commented that Cushing or Conway would probably be his replacement. On March 9, Roosevelt accepted the resignation, adding that, if Land agreed, it was satisfactory to him for Douglas to continue until July 1 in the positions mentioned. As it turned out, Douglas's long hospitalization and recovery, and no doubt Land's opposition, precluded any further active role for him in the WSA. The warm exchange of letters between Douglas and Land belied the scarcely veiled frictions that had often marked their relationship over the previous two years. The antagonism was, however, to be revealed publicly when Douglas a year later published his views on postwar shipping. It was to surface again in the admiral's memoirs.[11]

Pressure to return to an active role at Mutual Life as the war tide was turning toward eventual victory, the very real sinus problem, aggravated by the high level of tension under which he had labored—these were certainly the immediate concerns that prompted Douglas's departure. But he also clearly felt, as he wrote to Harriman, that "the organizational job here has been completed—or as nearly completed as anything ever is. Our relations with the British are better than they have ever been, and rest upon really solid foundations. With the army and navy,

I think we are on friendly terms. The Third Russian Protocol has been more than met. . . . We moved against the U.K. import program last year far more than we undertook to move. . . . The shipping arrangements for the military operations have been completed. From here on, for the next two or three months, there is nothing more that can be done in this regard." His analysis of the situation was echoed by the perhaps reluctant summation of his successes in Land's letter and by Leathers's assertion that Douglas was leaving his post with the "relations between our two organizations . . . on a firm and happy basis." Further confirmation came, ironically, from General Gross, who wrote that: "We shall miss you as the active head of WSA and shall hope that you will again enter the scene courageously as always to support operations by indicating that somehow shipping needs will be 'managed' . . . [T]hough we brought to the Washington scene some of the smell of battle, that was our only approach to the warrior role. In memory only the smiles remain."[12]

Douglas had indeed made a largely unpublicized but absolutely vital contribution to eventual Allied victory and left the WSA in good working order. As so often in his career, he had been handed a difficult task, resolved it successfully, and was ready to move on to new challenges. He found, at least until late in life, little satisfaction in day-to-day operations, once he had tackled and surmounted the pressing problems of the organization or position in which he had been called to serve.

Not that Douglas's work at the WSA went entirely unnoticed. The most elaborate praise came from the *New York Times* and from its Washington correspondent and Douglas's long-time admirer Arthur Krock. On April 1, an editorial entitled "A Job Well Done" reviewed admiringly Douglas's past career and his recent activity at the WSA, where he had assumed the "vital task of transporting America's contribution of troops and munitions across the perilous seas. The assured success of that task, the paper claimed, "gives the United Nations their hope of victory." The editorial further noted: "Political philosophers since Plato's time have liked to paint a picture of the ideal citizen. . . . Many of us have long felt that Mr. Douglas fulfills the specifications . . . the philosophers have in mind . . . [H]e has packed a dozen careers into the space of a few years. May other and still more shining careers await him."

Ten days earlier, in somewhat more measured terms, Krock had enumerated, with surprising accuracy, Douglas's battles and accomplishments in the shipping arena, "without which the Axis would have won the conflict in its early stages. That fact has long been realized, but the proofs will not be known until the war is over." Now, Krock observed, "the task of organizing is done and what remains is operation according to the procedures he evolved." Although Douglas had been labeled "pro-British" by some of his adversaries in government, "he had worked by this plain rule of thumb: it is vital to successful strategy that Britain be kept strong and effective so long as in so doing this nation does not weaken its war or post-war powers." Appropriately, his column appeared under the rubric "Traffic Officer of the Bridge of Ships." But most press announcements of Douglas's departure were more or less perfunctory. Nor did the subsequent appearance of several official histories noting his role greatly enlighten the general public concerning, as Salter later wrote, "the character and scale of this achievement."[13]

Cairo and Resignation

Douglas left Washington for New York on March 27, and four days later entered the hospital for prolonged and often painful treatment of his sinus infection and enforced relief from the contributory stress under which he had labored for so many months. It was not until the beginning of June that he was released and allowed to go West for rest and relaxation. Returning toward the end of July, he was subjected to a second series of penicillin treatments, after which, on August 14, he left to continue his recovery fishing in Montana. On September 7, he was back in New York, and ten days later had the pleasure of entertaining Ismay and Joan Bright, who were returning from the Second Quebec Conference to sail with the Prime Minister on the *Queen Mary*.[14]

During his confinement, Douglas was not spared a painful reminder of his last months at the WSA and his often rocky relationship with Admiral Land. For some time before his departure, Douglas had been concerned about the fiscal and accounting activities of the WSA, which were still to some extent interwoven with those of the Maritime Commission. When evidence began to accumulate that the financial controls were inadequate, he obtained, in October, 1943, with the approval of Land, the services of Eric L. Kohler, a highly regarded public accountant. Kohler's report, submitted on December 14, was extremely critical and recommended that an able accountant be employed to remedy the situation. Douglas warned Land, on January 17, 1944, that the "skin was off his tail, not mine, and I was trying to leave him a cleaner shop." In consequence, in February, J. F. Stone was brought in to take charge of the budget and accounts of the WSA.[15]

By mid-July, Kohler, who had been asked by Land to consult with Stone from time to time, became so disturbed at the lack of organizational support that he complained, whereupon Land subjected him to a tirade against himself and Douglas, "questioning our good faith . . .," while "admitting that the financial affairs of both the Maritime Commission and the War Shipping Administration were well tangled up, yet no worse than the Navy's." He reported this interview to Harold Smith, director of the budget, and forwarded a copy to Douglas. Douglas replied that he did not want to be in a position of casting any shadow on Land. On August 30, as he left the WSA in frustration, Stone made a long report to Land, outlining the many accounting problems and deficiencies and indicating that he had been able to do little to solve them. He also forwarded a copy to Douglas, who acknowledged he had read it "with more than ordinary interest and regret that you have been embarrassed by accepting at my invitation an assignment which I had thought would clarify and order a situation that was confused and disorderly."[16]

Later, in 1946 and 1947, the whole issue was reviewed in rather stormy sessions of the House Committee on the Merchant Marine and Fisheries, which issued a report, on January 3, 1947, highly critical of the Maritime Commission's and War Shipping Administration's accounting practices, but, in essence, exonerating Douglas. As Representative Christian Herter of Massachusetts, a member of the committee, wrote Douglas, it was a "pretty strong indictment," but "I think it is made clear in the report that you did all you could to straighten the situation out without success." As to Admiral Land's defense, it may be found in his memoirs, which took sharp exception to the charges, without any mention of Douglas or his efforts. In justice to both Land and Douglas, it should be emphasized that no fraud was discovered and, most important, that the exigencies of wartime and the tremendous contribution of the WSA to the winning of the conflict go very far indeed to override the errors and oversights leading to loss, waste, and overpayment in the heat of battle.[17]

In April of 1945, Douglas executed a final maritime maneuver, which brought an outraged response from Land and most of the shipping interests—the lead article in the *Atlantic Monthly,* titled "What Shall We Do with the Ships." Both the President and the British authorities had earlier wished to obtain Douglas's views on postwar shipping and to begin plans looking toward the disposal of the huge fleet of merchantmen the United States had constructed during the war. But for various reasons he had not been able to express his opinions formally before his departure from Washington. Not surprisingly, the British were most desirous of obtaining some of this tonnage permanently. As Churchill emphasized to Stettinius during the latter's visit to London in April, 1944, a large merchant fleet was an economic necessity to postwar Britain. With persuasive phrase-making, he pointed out that the " 'love of the sea' of the British and the 'love of the farm' of the Americans will be an important factor." At least part of Stettinius's notes for his conversation with the President following his trip were made available to Douglas. Certainly, the direction of Douglas's thinking on the matter was more than suspected before his resignation. In February, 1944, John O'Donnell, in his New York *Daily News* column, had warned that a battle was developing in Washington, a clash of rival American and British interests for control of commerce after the war. Fearful of the President's pro-British inclinations and possible commitments to hand over a great part of the ships built by the United States to Britain and to other allies, American shipping interests were also highly "distrustful of the warm affection for British shipping competitors nourished in the bosom of Mr. Lewis Douglas." These fears were confirmed over a year later when Douglas, out of office to be sure, aired his views publicly.[18]

    Preparation of the *Atlantic* article began sometime in the late summer or early fall of 1944. In October, he requested from Harry Hopkins, significantly not Land, the last monthly report of the WSA, guaranteeing its security, noting that he was "particularly interested in . . . the tonnage of the world, distributed by flag, before the war and the tonnage now" and revealing that he was working on an article for the January issue of the magazine. In January, he sent a copy of the manuscript to his friend and sometime bauxite expediter for the WSA, A. E. Roberts of the Waterman Steamship Company, who, unlike most of his associates in the industry, shared Douglas's views on the disposition of the fleet and responded with "enthusiasm." "Sorry but can offer no criticism because I think it is excellent," he telegraphed. Whether the opinion of others was solicited at that point is not clear, but advance page proofs were sent to several interested parties shortly before publication. Sir Ashley Sparks, British Shipping Mission representative in New York, not unexpectedly, approved; Ambassador Lord Halifax found it "broad, wise, large minded, and everything it ought to be"; Lord Leathers characterized it as "a very interesting, and to my mind, a fair statement of the position and well timed."[19]

    Admiral Land reacted with scarcely contained anger. After observing sarcastically that "An intelligent discussion of our Merchant Marine problem, even on the basis of widely divergent views, would be a healthy thing," the admiral acidly continued: "Unfortunately, some of the figures which you have used . . . are a bit fantastic, and I am just wondering whether somewhere in the back of your mind a decimal point or two may not have gone astray." He objected vehemently to Douglas's estimate of the subsidies necessary to maintain an American merchant fleet twice its prewar tonnage, corrected derisively his statement on the speed of Liberty ships, and refuted his claim that Britain would emerge from the war without her losses replaced. "The danger is," he gratuitously commented, "that because of your having been Deputy War Shipping Administrator, people who read your 'Atlantic Monthly' article may assume you know whereof you speak." Finally, he expressed personal resentment at Douglas's words "The monopolistic practices that have been established under the administration of the Merchant Marine Act of 1936." Douglas's reply was brief and unsuccessfully calculated to turn away wrath. "I'm terribly sorry you feel a personal resentment," he wrote. "I assure you that I have always had, and still have, a great admiration and affection for you . . . to infer . . . a criticism of you was to infer what was not intended in any way." But this was not to be the end of the matter.[20]

The premise of Douglas's controversial article reflected his allegiance to laissez-faire economics. "The lesson of the last three quarters of a century," he wrote, "is that the more the state interferes with the market place, the more it as a sovereign comes into conflict with other states as sovereigns; the more the state substitutes its own decisions for the decisions of the market place, the more certainly these conflicts will lead to war." To maintain peace following the war, governments must restore the primacy of the marketplaces of the world, freed from government controls, monopolies, and subsidies. It was in this "context that a discussion of the problem of American shipping takes on its real meaning and form." Britain, Norway, and Holland had, since 1939, sustained heavy losses in tonnage, which had not been replaced. "The life of these nations has been drawn from the seas." After its entrance into the war, America became the merchant shipbuilder for the alliance. Thus, at the conclusion of the conflict, "The United States, whose economic life derives little nourishment from the carrying of overseas traffic," would have over five times its prewar tonnage, while "The Allied maritime nations (whose future in large measure depends on the services they perform on the high seas for themselves as well as for others) will have severely depleted merchant marines."

Some argued, Douglas noted, that America should maintain a "huge merchant marine" for national defense. But the experience of "many decades" had shown that operation of ships by the United States was far more expensive than for other maritime states. It must be supported by government subsidies at heavy cost to the taxpayers. He estimated that the maintenance of a fleet only twice the size of the prewar tonnage would cost the country "between $200,000,000 and $300,000,000 each year, depending on the way the subsidy is calculated and the form it takes." It would be "another manifestation of that extreme type of nationalism that has so plagued us throughout the last quarter of a century . . . [and] surely will erode the foundations of the future peace." The answer was, after adequate provision for a fleet train for the navy, to make available to American ship operators, under proper terms and considerations, enough tonnage to carry approximately the same percentage of world and coastwise trade as before the war. If his proposal was properly negotiated, it was possible that no subsidies would be required; thus the "monopolistic practices" which had "been . . . enjoyed by certain overseas operators" under the Merchant Marine Act of 1936 would be eliminated. The remainder of the tonnage should be sold or leased, with attractive arrangements, to other nations, which would guarantee no discrimination against American shippers. Neither Germany nor Japan should be allowed to have a merchant fleet or shipbuilding facilities. The happy consequences of this solution would be the removal of international tensions in the shipping field, a tendency "to restore the market place as an international institution," and to "make ample provision for our national defense."[21]

As presaged by Land's letter, the reaction from the Maritime Commission and from established shipping circles was angry. The commission's statement reiterated much of what Land had written earlier, pointing out that Douglas's official duties had had "no direct connection with the specialized subjects he presumes to discuss" and that "many of his statements are in error." Doubling the size of the prewar fleet would require a maximum subsidy of only $30 million. A recapture clause in the act of 1936 would return as much as 50 percent of that amount to the government over a period of years. Before the war, the merchant marine carried 26, not 20 percent of American foreign trade, while the postwar goal was 50 percent. Why did Douglas refer only to dry-cargo vessels, when the fleet also consisted of "tankers, combination ships and passenger ships"? His figures were "obsolete." "Opinions may differ on this problem . . .," the statement concluded. "But they should rest upon facts not upon error." The *Marine News* editorialized that Douglas's remarks should better have appeared in some " 'Sell America Down the River' alien propaganda 3-sheets-to-the-wind" publication, rather than a journal named for the second greatest ocean. In an article entitled "What Shall We Do with Mr. Douglas?" the honorary president of the Propeller Club of the United States, Arthur M. Tode, called the proposal a "scheme to scuttle the American Merchant Marine, . . . a defeatist argument against American Sea Power."[22]

On the other hand, Douglas was supported by major American manufacturers, who agreed with his objective of foreign nations' obtaining from their carriers American dollar credits with which to make purchases in the United States. Philip D. Reed, chairman of the board of General Electric, was "in complete agreement" with the Douglas thesis. The New York *Herald Tribune* concluded that his statement "though painful, no doubt, to many special interests and anathema to many superpatriots—strikes us as an eminently wise one, both economically and as a practical peace measure." Ironically, in July, a report on the subject by the Harvard Business School, prepared at the request of the navy's Bureau of Ships and the Maritime Commission, substantially supported Douglas's recommendations.[23]

Impressed, indeed overwhelmed, by the furor aroused, editor Edward Weeks opened the pages of the *Atlantic Monthly* for July to a symposium on the article. Basil Harris, president of the United States Lines, and J. F. Gehan, national president of the Propeller Club, challenged Douglas's facts and conclusions. Douglas explained that the large figure he had projected did not cover operating subsidies alone, but also those required for direct operational and construction accounts. Land, permitted the last word, alleged his former deputy's "explanation" was based upon assumptions "none of which has any justification whatever" and concluded that he preferred not to continue the discussion "except to suggest . . . the irresponsibility of his [Douglas's] whole approach to this very important problem." There is an interesting pendant to this controversy and a testimony to Douglas's depth of feeling on the issue. In later years, as a private voyager, Douglas confided to a friend that he refused to travel in the American liner *United States* because its construction had been subsidized by the American government.[24]

17

Recalled to Duty

IN THE THREE YEARS BETWEEN THE COMPLETION of his service with the War Shipping Administration and acceptance of the post of ambassador to Great Britain, Lewis Douglas resumed his duties as president of Mutual Life and devoted his attention to a variety of other interests, private and public. The one official interruption was a tour in occupied Germany as financial advisor to General Lucius D. Clay, in the spring and early summer of 1945.

In early September, 1944, after the long siege in the hospital and a fishing trip to Montana, he rejoined Peggy and Sharman in the New York apartment at 1 East End Avenue, where they had resided since the return from Canada. They were to live there until September of 1946, when they moved to 784 Park Avenue. While Lewis had been in Washington, James had joined the field artillery and Peter the army air forces. He closely followed their wartime careers with pride and concern. James saw hazardous service in Europe, but Peter's long training and eventual commissioning, only in March, 1945, precluded overseas duty before the unexpected conclusion of the conflict. James returned safely, much decorated, to marry Mary Peace Hazard of Rhode Island in March, 1946.[1]

During this period, Douglas also deepened his roots in his native state. He returned often to Arizona for visits of from several days to two or three weeks. He now hoped to realize a dream of owning a large cattle ranch, preferably in the southern part of the state. Several possibilities had been investigated, but his interest narrowed to the Larimore Ranch near Sonoita. The entire transaction was complicated and continued until the middle of February, 1945. When it was completed, Douglas had purchased for approximately $140,000 over 8,500 acres, with a grazing permit for the forest extending into the foothills of the Santa Ritas, including the houses and other buildings on the property and a herd of cattle. His personal satisfaction in the acquisition was matched by the pleasure he knew it would give James, who shared his father's love of the outdoor life and of horses. It would provide a haven for the young man and his bride when he returned from the war and served as manager, and would afford a happy refuge for his parents for many years. The house in Phoenix was sold in 1948 and most of the remaining citrus acreage in 1951. In the mid-1950s, another purchase added over 15,000 acres to the Sonoita property.[2]

Douglas's philanthropic, civic, and corporate affiliations and commitments were resumed and expanded. Since 1935 he had been a trustee of the Rockefeller Foundation and General Board. He was now able to take a more active role in its deliberations, which continued, except for the ambassadorial years, until 1960. The New York Memorial Hospital for Cancer and Allied Diseases had elected him to its board in the same year, and in December, 1944, he assumed the chairmanship; this made him not only the seventh member of his family to serve on the board but the third to lead it, following his grandfather and uncle by marriage, Archibald Douglas.

In August, 1945, the hospital received an initial gift of $4 million from the Alfred P. Sloan Foundation to establish a division to be known as the Sloan-Kettering Institute for Cancer Research, which would incorporate all of the research activities of the hospital. In order to expand proportionately its own facilities, the board launched a Memorial Cancer Fund for an equal amount. The ultimate success of these joint ventures is visible today in the great medical complex on York Avenue. Douglas continued to serve as chairman of the Memorial board and trustee of the institute until 1950. Not unrelated perhaps to these developments was his election in November, 1944, as a trustee of the Sloan Foundation, where he served until his mandatory retirement in 1967.[3]

In 1940, he had become a trustee of the Institute for Advanced Study at Princeton. From 1945 to 1947, he served as a member of the search committee, chaired by Lewis L. Strauss, when the institute sought a replacement for the retiring director, Dr. Frank Aydelotte. Douglas opposed the appointment of a natural scientist and in particular of Dr. J. Robert Oppenheimer, who was at the top of the list. He told Strauss that a natural scientist would take the institute "further and further away from the social studies and may therefore implicitly determine [its] . . . future policy. . . . [T]he advances in the natural sciences have carried us far beyond our ability to control them." Some years later, he elaborated upon his views, noting that "although Oppenheimer might be one of the top scientists, his judgement was not unimpeachable." He had also hoped that the members of the institute would become more closely involved with Princeton University in teaching or lecturing. "It had become my conviction that leisure without responsibility was very apt to become nothing but leisure." Oppenheimer's appointment was confirmed by a special meeting of the board of trustees on April 1, 1947, after Douglas's departure for his post in England. Meantime, Douglas had submitted his resignation because of his anticipated long absence from the country, but the board "utterly refused" to accept it until May, 1951, when he began to spend much of his time in the West.[4]

He had been singularly honored in 1942 by election to the American Philosophical Society. Although he was seldom able to be present at the annual meetings, he served as councillor, from 1953 to 1957, and delivered the R. A. F. Penrose Memorial Lecture in April, 1953.[5]

From a quite different direction came an invitation, in December, 1944, to join the board of directors of General Motors, which he accepted with great pleasure. Throughout his long service in that position, which terminated with his mandatory retirement in 1965, he made a special effort, except when prevented by absence from the country or illness, to attend the stated meetings and take an active part in the affairs of the company.[6]

During his time at the WSA and in the years immediately following, Douglas maintained a cautious public image with regard to party politics, mindful perhaps of his pledge to Roosevelt in 1942, his desire to reenter government service at some point, and certainly reflective of his continuing independent position. He refused a request from James A. Farley, in the fall of 1942, to announce his support for the Democratic candidate for governor of New York against the young Republican district attorney Thomas E. Dewey. Yet he did give Democrat Sidney P. Osborn his warm and enthusiastic backing for the governorship of Arizona during the campaigns of 1940, 1942, and 1944. In February of the last year, he also briefly reentered the arena of an old controversy, writing Governor Osborn to urge that the state legislature finally ratify the Colorado River Compact and accept the proposal of the secretary of the interior that 2.8 million acre-feet of the normal flow and half the surplus be made available by contract with the state. "Without it we stand to get nothing; with it we stand to get much." Although the compact was ratified, the problem of water rights was to remain unresolved for many years to come. In 1946, he was urged by Arizona admirers to run in the primaries against Ernest W. McFarland for the Senate but, though interested, he pleaded his obligations to Mutual Life for at least the next year or so.[7]

His public silence extended also to the national election of 1944. In June, in answer to a friend requesting political guidance, he wrote that his "position of ten years ago on the New Deal . . . has, in the light of my last two and a half years [in Washington] . . . been more than amply confirmed. . . . [T]he New Deal leads . . . to irresponsibility on the part of individuals and irresponsibility on the part of governments. The toll that it will ultimately exact from everybody in the land is, I believe, incalculable. But against all this I don't know with what sense of honor and responsibility the opposition is clothed. . . . I start, unhappily, with a prejudice against Republicans on the one hand and New Dealers on the other, so I am a bad person to whom to put the question you have put." Yet in March he had contributed to the District of Columbia Jackson Day Dinner, and in July, before and during a brief visit to the Democratic National Convention in Chicago, he gave his support to James F. Byrnes, first for the presidency and then the vice-presidency.[8]

Obviously unhappy at the ticket that emerged, he responded to a request for a contribution to the Democratic National Committee with the brief comment: "I vote in the state of Arizona and therefore I have made my contribution to the Democratic National Committee in that state." Later in the same month, he wrote his father that "The political campaign . . . arouses no enthusiasm in me for either side." Toward the end of the campaign, he refused urgent requests from both camps for a public endorsement.[9]

On November 7, in the privacy of a Phoenix voting booth, he registered his support for Dewey. The next week, he indicated to his father his disappointment at the election result: "I expect the outcome will hearten the European people, but I doubt the capacity of this crowd to settle wisely many of the questions, economic as well as political, which must form the basis of a lasting peace." A few days later, he wrote Roosevelt, apologizing for the delay in extending congratulations, "due principally to the fact that I never for a moment questioned the outcome," and expressing "with very deep sincerity the hope that what I think is your great ambition, to establish an enduring peace, will be fully satisfied." Indicative of the success of Douglas's circumspection were the apparently unfounded rumors that circulated soon after the election that he was being seriously considered to replace the retiring Cordell Hull, then, following the announcement of Stettinius's appointment, that he would be the new under secretary. Roosevelt was not likely to appoint other than tractable instruments of his personal foreign policy.[10]

During the remaining few months of Roosevelt's life and the following approximately two years of Truman's tenure, Douglas's attention was devoted primarily to international affairs. But he did keep up his lines to Washington, desirous it would seem of renewed national service but highly selective concerning its character, his doubts about Democratic policies undiminished. The peremptory firing, on January 20, 1945, of Jesse Jones as secretary of commerce to make way for Henry Wallace, as a consolation prize for the denial of the vice-presidency in the fourth term, thoroughly aroused Douglas's anger and prompted a sympathetic letter to Jones. Roosevelt's maneuver, he wrote, was "one of the most misguided ones in the long and tortuous course of the last twelve years." This communication followed closely on the heels of a letter to Robert E. Hannegan, chairman of the Democratic National Committee, acknowledging with pleasure an invitation to the President's fourth inaugural dinner, but declining because of other commitments with the comment: "But I shall be present in absentia."[11]

On April 12, 1945, his complex relationship with Roosevelt came to an abrupt end. Admiration, disillusionment, distrust, bitterness, renewed friendship, and mutual confidence in the face of an external foe, but continuing disagreement on the national purpose—all these facets of their association had been exhibited over the years. The day after Roosevelt's death, Douglas wrote two letters. To Eleanor Roosevelt went a letter of condolence to say "what millions of people all over the world are feeling, that the loss of a great war leader and a great champion for lasting peace is an irreparable one. . . . I feel deeply a sense of personal sorrow." To the new President he reiterated his regrets, offered his services to assist in any way to secure enduring peace, and called upon a "wise Providence" to guide Truman in "concluding successfully the work which President Roosevelt had begun."[12]

Since his departure from the WSA, Douglas had been thinking, speaking, and writing about the reconstruction of the postwar world as the paramount priority in public affairs. It was none too early, he fervently believed, to apply the lessons learned from the policy failures following the First World War, which had contributed directly to the Second. In 1944, addressing the Academy of Political Science of Columbia University, of which he had been a long-time active member and which he served as president from 1942 to 1962, Douglas insisted that the chief threat to permanent peace was intense nationalism. An international peace-keeping agency or a series of "military arrangements" between the United States and other powers was required to "quench" further aggression. Yet it was even more important to establish an international climate in which peace could endure. Such an atmosphere could be created, he contended, by lowering tariff walls, minimizing state interference in the economy, and stabilizing the international monetary system. These thoughts were, of course, not new. Four years earlier, he had put the same case even more succinctly to President James Conant of Harvard. If, after the war, Washington failed to bring about a stable, economically open world in which the United States could "become the dominant power," he wrote, "the jig is up."[13]

Besides economic liberalism, lasting peace depended upon the readiness of Americans to join other nations in preserving world order. In a letter to Grenville Clark, who had proposed a World Congress plan in an article in the *Indiana Law Journal*, Douglas warned: "Unless the world organization is to be superior to, greater than, and possess in its own right [more power] . . . than one nation state, the question of representation . . . is relatively unimportant." The alternative, which he clearly favored, was "the treaty method" among the United States, Great Britain and the Commonwealth, Russia and, eventually, China. "These treaties should provide the force that is necessary to preserve the peace."

Copies of this letter were sent to several of his friends, including Walter Lippmann, who read it "with admiration and complete agreement," commenting that "one other crucial point" must be made: "A world government must enforce its laws, not upon constituent states, but upon individuals." Douglas agreed, and both men feared that the negotiations beginning at Dumbarton Oaks to create a United Nations organization were raising false hopes for the success of a body that would, in fact, have most of the weaknesses of Wilson's League of Nations. Yet partially resigning himself to the course of events, he joined the educational campaign committee for the Dumbarton Oaks proposals. Later, in March, 1945, writing to Harriman, he noted that public reaction to the Dumbarton Oaks agreement was generally favorable and that what criticism existed seemed to be the fear of vesting the new organization with too much power. "I myself, if I had any criticism of it, would take the view that it was clothed with too meager an amount of authority." On July 26, the United Nations Charter was signed in San Francisco.[14]

Although Douglas was certainly in favor of American participation in the United Nations Organization, he was convinced it would be able to function effectively only if it was "supported by a United States unflinchingly committed to the role of the greatest power on earth." The possibly fatal flaws in the charter, he believed, were the inclusion of strife-torn Nationalist China as a permanent member of the Security Council, while the British Commonwealth, except for the United Kingdom, remained unrepresented, and, above all, the right of veto by the permanent members of the Council.[15]

His emphasis upon the necessity for intimate cooperation among the United States, Britain, and the Commonwealth was then as always the cornerstone of his program for the preservation of peace and the achievement of economic stability. "The marrow of our foreign policy," he wrote his father, "should be an extremely close association with the Commonwealth and Empire." To General Sir Hastings Ismay, he asserted "the bald necessity of our playing together, working together, and cementing our relationships by specific engagements and detailed undertakings. . . . The two of us together can lay the foundation for world order, but there can be no world order unless we are together." This was a clear statement of his unqualified international credo.[16]

In 1944 Douglas still entertained hopes that Russia might prove a reliable member of the new world order, but his doubts were manifest. To Ismay, he wrote that the Soviet Union was a "great new lumbering power with whom, without being soft, we must live in peace and friendship." He could not, however, visualize her as a full partner with the Anglo-Saxon nations in any postwar coalition. Russia's history, ideology, and aggressive tendencies, he feared, precluded any real affinity with the Americans and the British. Soon he was writing to James Conant: "I don't mean to be suspicious of Russia, but in view of what seems like an ambition to extend her influence to the Mediterranean and even to the shores of the Atlantic, are you as ready to accept her as a peace-loving nation as you are the British and the Commonwealth of Nations?"[17]

This mixture of hope and skepticism was reflected in his reactions to the Yalta agreements. In March, 1945, he wrote his father: "I am not clear as to the full significance of parts of the Yalta agreement, but on balance I think with you that it holds promise." At the same time, he reassured Harriman in Moscow concerning criticisms of the Polish decisions. "[T]hese, I think, are not very substantial." His cautious optimism concerning Russian cooperation was soon to be shattered by his firsthand observations in Europe during his tour with General Clay later in the year. His experiences as ambassador completed the disillusionment. By the 1950s, he was openly denouncing the accords for their concessions to the Soviet Union in Eastern Europe and their inadequate provisions for the control of occupied Germany.[18]

The series of dramatic events that occurred in July and August had a profound effect upon Douglas. On July 26, Winston Churchill was swept out of power in an overwhelming defeat by the Labour party. To Douglas the elections came as "a great blow and a shock." Attempting to rationalize and moderate his deep concern, he consoled himself, in the letter to his father, with the hope that "the Socialists will not in actual practice [be] as radical as they indicate they will be." In any case, he continued, it was not yet clear that the people really wanted socialism, for the "election was probably influenced by an accumulation of complaints and grievances that piled up during the ten year [sic] period of the Churchill Government. Most people vote against anything rather than for something."[19]

This unsettling and unexpected development was followed closely by the dropping of the two atomic bombs, on August 6 and 9, and the end of the war with Japan on the 14th. Much later, Douglas recalled that he had first learned of the expected success of the atomic experiment as early as mid-April, though he did not reveal the source or circumstances of that information. His reactions in August were both philosophical and prophetic. To Lippmann, he wrote: "What a revolution the last fifty years have been! In a sense, the atomic bomb is perhaps the culmination of what has been going on for the last fifty years, when science has been attempting to bind the world together and politics have been progressively making its integral parts more separated and more hostile." His comment to his father was stark. He was reminded of Abbott Lawrence Lowell's question: "Is the ultimate gift of the natural sciences to man universal destruction?" On the morning of peace, he again wrote his father with more gloom than hope: "At last the end has come after six years—long years in which throughout most of the world every effort of society has been dedicated to the making of war. The state everywhere has assumed the responsibility of directing the lives of men and women for this one purpose.... Will there be any return—now that the end of active war has come—to the ways of the pre-war days? Will the U.S. realize that again it can easily lose what has been won[?]"[20]

That summer and into early 1946, Douglas, together with his economic mentors, Walter Stewart and Leo Wolman, explored the possibility of starting a weekly journal, modeled on *The Economist* of London, to mirror their political philosophy and laissez-faire national and international economic views. He suggested his old friend William Mathews, the editor of the *Arizona Daily Star,* as publisher, and Arizona as the possible seat of the publication. Apparently financial considerations, questions concerning the effect on the public of some of the names suggested for the board, and possibly difficulties over management and policy conspired to prevent the proposal's becoming a reality. Douglas's temporary preoccupation with it was a manifestation of his undiminished alarm over what he considered the fateful course of domestic and international economic and political life.[21]

During July of 1944, the United Nations Monetary and Financial Conference at Bretton Woods, New Hampshire, established an International Monetary Fund and the International Bank for Reconstruction and Development. By the spring of 1946, the organization of the fund and bank had reached a point where the governors were prepared to appoint a president of the World Bank, as it came to be designated. It had been agreed that the president would be an American, since most of the financing would be in the American money market. At their inaugural meeting in Savannah, Georgia, in March, the governors decided that Washington would be the seat of the institutions and that the salary of the bank president would be $30,000, tax free. Soon word was out that the leading candidate was Lewis W. Douglas. By March 15 newspapers reported that he had "the inside track" and noted that his appointment would be "a sop to conservative Democrats." He was regarded as the favored candidate of Secretary of the Treasury Vinson, who had been his close friend and admirer since their service together in Congress.[22]

At least as early as March 25, Douglas had something more than newspaper gossip to alert him to the possibility of an offer. That evening, Secretary of State James Byrnes, apparently at a social occasion, told him that he would get the nod and that he must accept. "I fear we will have to think about it," Douglas wrote his father. Financiers rallied to his support. But New Deal liberals were shocked at the possibility of the orthodox, independent ex-budget director heading such an important international lending institution. Leading the opposition, former treasury secretary Henry Morgenthau wrote Truman and Vinson protesting the choice, because of Douglas's "connections with big business and Wall Street finance, his tie-ins with international financiers, and his general point of view."

By appointing Douglas, Morgenthau asserted, "the Truman administration will be regarded, and justly so, as having by the stroke of a pen handed back control of international finance to Wall Street."[23]

When word of Morgenthau's letter reached the press, conservative newspapers and columnists came to Douglas's defense. Frank Kent, writing in the Baltimore *Sun*, characterized the former secretary's protest as "nonsense." Although Douglas happened presently to be the president of a great insurance company, "the truth is that [he] has spent more of his life since he left Amherst . . . in the public service than in private life. And it is in the former that he made his enviable reputation for ability, character and public spirit."

The *Arizona Daily Star* took a somewhat different tack. To the charge that he was close to Wall Street Douglas would "have to plead guilty." It was as essential for the president of one of the biggest life insurance companies "to have close connections with Wall Street, as it is for a locomotive engineer to have relations with a railroad roundhouse and its gang of workers. . . . Should the job go to a man qualified for it, or should it go to one of Mr. Morgenthau's New Deal friends who might be called upon to follow Mr. Morgenthau's wishes rather than sound banking practice?" But the coup de grâce to the clamor of attack came in the clipped words of the President. Asked, in his news conference of April 11, if he supported Douglas for the presidency of the bank, Truman replied: "Yes." "And, if so, what is your reaction to Mr. Morgenthau's letter of opposition?" pressed the reporter. "Well," remarked the President dryly, "with Mr. Morgenthau no longer in the Treasury, if Mr. Douglas is satisfactory to the Secretary of the Treasury, he is satisfactory to me."[24]

Evidently Douglas was not officially informed until April 13 of the desire of the President, Byrnes, and Vinson to appoint him. He spent much of the day in Washington with Vinson, who convinced him that they were "sincerely anxious that I become the President of the International Bank, and that they want more than merely a 'conservative front.' My doubts on this score have been resolved." Yet he continued to have many reservations. In a long letter to his father, he enumerated them. The authority of the bank president was ill defined, but he admitted that the proposed salary suggested the quality of the person the governors wished to have in that position. Would the bank be a political institution? Several clauses in the charter raised real questions on that score. Certainly it would be "subject to great political pressure." Could the bank properly perform its job "in a world that has fallen under the shadow of disorder"? In the course of the last sixteen years, he had seen various financial and monetary "devices" used as "cures for a malaise." They might be helpful, but "the only basic remedy for the trouble is to work harder and to produce more." Would the bank be only another means of "deceiving people into the belief that production and distribution are not the basic remedies" for recovery? "Under these circumstances loans made by the Bank now may well be in default five years from now." If so, "the President of the Bank will naturally be held responsible." Finally, there were his obligations to Mutual Life and decisions concerning his personal future.[25]

On the same day, he wrote Vinson indicating that he was seriously weighing the invitation. By the 19th, he had made up his mind to refuse the post. Informing Vinson that afternoon, he questioned whether he had "ever been through such a week in my life. I have been torn as I think I have never been torn." But he had concluded that, in the light of his responsibilities to Mutual Life, "my conscience won't let me accept at this juncture." Vinson urged him to delay his decision until he could meet with the President, but Douglas declined, pleading possible embarrassment to Truman and the finality of his decision. To Vinson's further importunities and questions, he exclaimed that he had been "literally . . . on my knees praying," but to go now "would leave certain messes [at Mutual Life]." It was "the most difficult decision I think I ever made in my life." The White House appointment calendar for April 20 scheduled both Douglas and Vinson for a visit with the President. Instead, that day a presidential spokesman announced that Douglas had not accepted the position. Although the official reason was his reluctance to leave the company after having been away for so long in earlier government positions, it is probably fair to say that his concern over the authority of the executive officer and efficacy of the institution to repair economic wounds were of equal if not greater influence on his decision.[26]

On June 4, Eugene Meyer, financier and publisher, aged seventy, with his own long record of public service, was elected president of the World Bank. His tenure ended abruptly six months later with his unexpected resignation. He was succeeded by John J. McCloy, Douglas's brother-in-law, who served with distinction until his resignation in May, 1949 to become High Commissioner for Germany.[27]

Douglas had written to his father: "It was a terribly difficult decision to make, and I suppose that I shall all my life wonder whether it was the right one. The only thing I can say is that it was very close and the best according to my light under the existing circumstances that I could make." Yet, despite this candid filial confession, his declination of the bank presidency proved prologue to another painful episode in their checkered relationship, which had never entirely recovered from the wounds of the last engagement, when his father renounced his American citizenship. Greatly annoyed at his son's decision to refuse a position where he felt much could be done to relieve the financial plight of his beloved Britain and obviously brooding, as often before, on what he considered Lewis's neglect, Rawhide Jimmy, in late July, wrote of his intention to give most of his fortune, and specifically the gold he had in England, to the British government. At Sonoita, where he was spending the month of August on his ranch, Douglas was "too miserable to reply" to his father's letter for several days. When he did, it was to deny that the bank could be "of substantial service . . . to England," and to accuse his father of an attempt "to cut me off and with me my entire family . . . [to] disinherit me [which] has hurt beyond anything I can imagine." He would have "to revise [his] whole life and plans." But most hurtful was the implication that "you think me unworthy of receiving the inheritance" which had been left by his grandfather and augmented by his father. "I have been in public service for the greater portion of my mature years" and unable to "amass a fortune." He had thought "we both agreed" that he should do this because of "my taste and abilities . . . and because you were behind me. I had hoped to enter public life again. . . . All of this must now change."

His father's reply was scarcely reassuring. "Yes, I knew well that my letter of July 29th would be very disturbing. You must not be miserable. Ask for God's help. He will give it." Then, revealing what was undoubtedly the root cause of his unhappiness, he complained of his son's inconsiderate treatment. "I could have written you much during recent years but you were 'too busy' to digest letters on subjects of world wide importance which have concerned me much. . . . [A]fter the shock . . . [of] my letter . . . is passed . . . you will be happier. . . . All is for the best." Rather unconvincingly under the circumstances, he affirmed that his "family affections are [still] deep and fixed." The note of unwarranted martyrdom was not hard to detect. Meantime, Lewis had written a second letter of dismay and bewilderment, delineating his record of public service. His father responded that he felt he had made himself clear—his disappointment stemmed from Lewis's failure to take the bank presidency. "[Y]our decision was a shock. Some shock. Alors, miserable you are, sure, and so am I. Our misery will pass if we pray God for it to pass."

Detecting that the problem lay deeper than the bank decision, but refusing to rise explicitly to the bait of neglect, Douglas answered that "it was a pity" he had not gone up to see his father, but he "had no inkling that you wanted me to take the post." Then, hinting at but not admitting to the heart of the matter, he concluded: "But surely something has happened. I have done something of which I am unaware to mar our relationship. This I regret and it worries me. . . . I shall try my best to come up to see you on Friday for a few days." And so he did, spending the weekend of August 30 and 31 and September 1 in Montreal mending their breach. Again, in October, he visited Montreal. The crisis passed. His father, consoled, did not alienate his fortune or his gold, for which his son had cause to be especially grateful during his ambassadorship.[28]

In his responses to his father's shocking announcement of displeasure, Douglas had countered with the conciliatory comment that, whereas the head of the World Bank could do little for Britain, he hoped in his new position as president of the English-Speaking Union of the United States "to make a substantial contribution to the security of England—indeed of us all." No doubt, for the purpose at hand, he exaggerated the influence of the union, but unquestionably he attached considerable importance to its role in strengthening the bonds of Anglo-American friendship. He advanced the view that, since the war, "the only two powers on earth that have any authority and wield any might west of the Vistula are the British Commonwealth and the United States." In America, only the English-Speaking Union had assumed the task of influencing public opinion in favor of the close relationship he believed must exist to preserve the peace.[29]

It is not clear when Douglas became a member of the union, but in February, 1941, he was elected to the board of directors. In March, 1946, he was urged by the retiring president, James R. Angell, who had served as president of Yale from 1921 to 1937, and by several other members of the board to take over leadership of the organization, which was suffering from a number of debilities. There were serious staffing problems in the main office, the advancing age of the original membership and board was not being offset by the attraction of young new members, and several of the major branches were badly administered. Socially oriented activities had been emphasized to the detriment of efforts to promote understanding and unity of purpose between the United States and the British

Commonwealth. In short, someone of Douglas's organizing ability, energy, and dedication to the union's goals was needed to assume command. After some hesitation, Douglas accepted the challenge. In April, he began the task of revitalization, which was to occupy much of his time before he left the post to assume an official role in Anglo-American relations as Ambassador to the Court of St. James's.[30]

Another instructive prelude to London was the temporary assignment in Germany that Douglas had undertaken for the administration during the last months of the war. Toward the end of March, 1945, he had been surprised in his New York office by a long-distance call from "Deputy President" James F. Byrnes. His old friend alerted him to the possibility he would be offered an appointment as special advisor for financial affairs to General Lucius Clay, slated soon to succeed General Eisenhower as military governor of the American Zone in Germany. Byrnes elaborated, in the words of Douglas, "that the assignment would be a preparatory prelude to picking up and holding the reins of authority when, ultimately, General Clay as the Military Governor of Germany and the actual official military personnel in the occupation organization were to be replaced with civilians." Whether Byrnes was suggesting that Douglas might be slated for the civilian governorship or was speaking only of the general intention, then strongly urged by General Clay, that the military phase of the occupation be terminated as soon as possible and administration turned over to civilian control, is not clear. In any case, on March 30, Byrnes, in the presence of General Clay, again telephoned Douglas, asking that he accept for at least six months the position as advisor and assist in the recruitment of personnel for the permanent organization. Clay's high opinion of Douglas dated from the early years of the New Deal when, stationed at the Army Chief of Engineers Office in Washington, he had worked closely with the White House. His admiration was reinforced by their frequent though often disputatious contacts during the War Shipping Administration period, when he had served as Brehon Somervell's director of matériel.[31]

Douglas was anxious to accept the appointment, because of both his sense of public duty and his concern with postwar policy, especially the rehabilitation of Germany, which he felt had been abysmally mishandled after the First World War. But he was hesitant to seek another leave of absence from Mutual Life so soon after his protracted tour with the War Shipping Administration. He obtained reluctant agreement from Washington to a commitment of only two months, to commence after General Clay had reached Germany. His acceptance was written to Clay on April 4, and his board formally approved the request for leave on April 9.[32]

Within a few days, he was in Washington for a physical examination and a series of briefings. The most significant of these meetings were held with a group whose principal members were William Clayton, Assistant Secretary of State for Economic Affairs, Major General John H. Hilldring, Director of the War Department's Civil Affairs Division and later Assistant Secretary of State for Occupied Areas, General William H. Draper, Jr., Director of the Industry Division of the Office of Military Government for Germany and Harry Dexter White, Assistant to the Secretary of the Treasury. Much of the discussion focused on a policy paper which had apparently been prepared by the Foreign Economic Administration. Douglas was "quite shocked" by this and other proposals that were coming into focus in Washington. They included the movement of industries from economic locations to what he considered uneconomic sites, the amount and form of reparations to be exacted from Germany, and "a variety of other matters, which all together constituted a program of quasi, if not complete, pastoralization."

Although he was fully convinced that Germany "had caused the social fabric of the western world to be seriously tattered twice within the short span of 25 years (and that the German people were not to be trusted) and . . . feared that, given another opportunity, she would again plunge us into one more—and perhaps the last—great catastrophe," Douglas considered it "vitally important that she be welded into the western community of nations." He emphasized that the West had at least a potential enemy to the east of Germany and argued that any program similar to the one that seemed to be taking shape would make it an easy target for the insinuation of Soviet authority. In addition, the removal of industries from Germany, which had been the industrial heart of the Continent, would, he feared, so fragment economic life by their location in areas not natural to their efficient production as to lead to the "imposition of tariffs, quotas or other subventions." It "would produce an economic splintering of Europe rather than an economic unification of Europe . . . for economic unification was a measure which would make each country dependent on the other, thus preventing the development of an autarchical nation-state."

Above all, he was concerned that the policy which seemed to be evolving in Washington failed to "recognize that reparations should be treated as reparations and not as an instrument of control." There seemed to be little or no understanding of the role reparations had played after the First World War "in the widespread economic and political confusion throughout Western Europe which contributed to the collapse of the international monetary mechanism in 1931." To these warnings, members of the group replied that the projected form of reparations, that is the dismantling and transportation of industrial plants, would have an effect quite unlike the previous monetary and commodity exactions after 1918. Douglas was not convinced. In his view, the results would be exactly the same—to deprive Germany of the capacity to acquire exchange. It was essential that Germany export if she were to pay for her essential imports. Otherwise, the United States and other countries would find themselves once again forced to extend financial aid or credit—in essence, to pay the price of the reparations policy contemplated. He found it "almost impossible to persuade the group that, through the machinery of reparations as a medium, we were fixing most of the control policies over Germany and, at least, the basic one, for it implied a policy of scorched earth— almost complete extinction of the industrial heart of Europe." As he wryly noted, "the views I expressed failed miserably to appeal to the rest of those in the group."

In London he met with McCloy and went over much the same ground and presented the same arguments he had advanced in Washington. He also urged that, in view of the conflicting authorities and views in the capital, Clay be given full support by the new President and warned against policy leaks to that segment of the press which advocated a scorched-earth policy and could destroy any reasonable course of action in Germany. From McCloy, who had just returned from a tour of certain parts of liberated Germany, he heard a graphic account of the dislocation and devastation he could expect to find.[33]

The documents Douglas had seen and his consultations in Washington and London reflected the debate that had been underway at least since mid-1944 on Allied policy toward a defeated Germany. The Morgenthau Plan, proposed by the secretary of the treasury in the late summer, had been rather casually accepted by the Allied leaders at Second Quebec. It called for extensive reparations, territorial dismemberment, and the destruction of warmaking and industrial facilities—in short, "pastoralization." But Secretary of State Hull and Secretary of War Stimson strongly opposed Morgenthau's ideas, believing that a vindictive peace would cause economic and social chaos. Their view was that a moderate, constructive peace, which encouraged the revival of non-military-oriented industries, would promote European economic recovery and political stability. From the beginning, though in no official policy-making position, Douglas had questioned the Morgenthau Plan, at first with some hesitancy, but by the spring of 1945, vehemently. As early as October, 1944, he had taken exception to James Conant's apparent support for the extinguishing of German industrial power. He had written Conant that he thoroughly agreed that Germany's warmaking power should be eliminated, but he wondered whether "the social disturbances, indeed upheavals, inherent in a vast reorganization of one of the central industrial powers of all Europe might not also be in itself a cause, perhaps a burning cause, of war." Certainly, after the last war, they had contributed "mightily" to the rise of Hitler. Would not such a policy, he continued, reducing Germany to an agricultural state, "give rise to the same yearnings of revenge"? Furthermore, "might it not throw the German people into the arms of Eastern Europe and remove Germany from the Western World . . ."?

He suggested an alternative: "[W]ouldn't a control of Germany's raw materials, of her coal industry . . . of her organic chemical industry, of her iron and steel, of her fuel oil and synthetic gasoline, of her electrical energy, of her research . . . and of the uses of her raw materials in industrial production, all reinforced by . . . irrevocable commitment that the United States will assume heavy military obligations at the very slightest evidence of her attempting to use . . . her resources for military purposes" be in the long run a safer method of prevention?[34]

Sometime between his acceptance of the German assignment and his arrival on April 18, at Versailles, where General Clay and the German Control Council were located, Douglas found occasion to draft a brief memorandum, dated April 17, elaborating on these views and mirroring his alarm at the continuing punitive direction of official thinking. He advocated as "the first major item in the long term policy toward Germany . . . to arrange hard, fast, riveted commitments that bind the United States and the other powerful members of the United Nations to employ their military strength to crush out forthwith the first signs of a resurgence of military power." This must be accomplished by treaty and by provision for the United States to maintain a military establishment in Europe. Without this guarantee, "the long-term economic policy toward Germany will make little difference except perhaps in terms of time should she ever again harbor designs of conquest."

As to economic policy, he limited comment to a proviso that it "should be formulated in the light of the relationships of the *natural* economic production of Germany to a large part of the Continent of Europe." If, as the evidence indicated, Germany's war potential had been built up behind tariffs and with the assistance of government subsidies, the elimination of these barriers and subventions should not make difficult the formulation of a mutually advantageous long-range economic policy—always with the reservation that it could be effective only if there existed the type of treaty he recommended. The recipient of this memorandum is unknown—probably General Clay. An attached note indicated that it had been seen and used by Byrnes, who became secretary of state on July 3, in his consideration of four-power arrangements for Germany. Whatever its purpose, it is an important milestone in the progress of Douglas's views on the German question as he arrived to take up his new duties.[35]

In Versailles, Douglas was billeted with Robert Murphy, political advisor to General Clay, and several general officers. In the morning, he drove in to Paris for a round of meetings with French officials and Goldthwaite Dorr, assistant to Secretary Stimson, who was visiting France. In a letter to McCloy several days later, Dorr wrote that Douglas was just the special advisor Clay needed "to complement him in wisdom, experience and prestige. The more Douglas can be regarded as a permanent fixture, though having to return to the United States from time to time, the greater his value will be not only in the future but in these initial months."

Douglas spent time with Clay and the heads of the various sections of the military government, acquainting himself with the organization—the German Control Council—to which he was attached. The task proved more formidable than he had anticipated, for, as he later wrote, "in a large measure there was no organization." Through no fault of Clay, who was struggling to put something together in an orderly fashion, the lines of authority in his hands were still badly tangled with the American military command, a not surprising situation in view of the continuing fighting against the crumbling but still active German forces farther to the east. Meantime, it had been decided that Douglas should inspect the deepest sector of the American advance to observe firsthand the extent of the destruction, the supply of foodstuffs, the condition of transport, the agricultural prospect, the state of utilities—everything that had to do with life and living in western Germany.[36]

On a whirlwind nine-day tour, partly by automobile, partly by air, beginning April 22, Douglas visited almost all of the area up to the front lines. Generals Eisenhower, Bradley, Spaatz, Devers, Patch, Patton, Simpson, all briefed him. At Recklinghausen, he was joined by his son James, who as a courtesy was detached to act as his father's aide for ten days. In his later draft reminiscences of the journey, Douglas devoted thirty-two pages to a detailed description of his travels, observations, and conversations, but at the time his major conclusions and recommendations were summed up in a memorandum for Clay. He had viewed a country "completely and absolutely in ruins" and, because of its central position in Europe, economic, political and geographic, "almost tantamount . . . to . . . a continent in ruins."[37]

Douglas's report was grim in its implications. It emphasized the severe shortages of food, fuel, and housing and the totally inadequate transportation facilities. It predicted that such deficiencies, which existed not only in Germany but to a lesser degree throughout Europe, would become much more harsh in the coming winter months unless "the maximum production of critical items can be had out of the productive facilities of Germany that are susceptible of present operation and that lend themselves to speedy rehabilitation." Failure to utilize Germany's productive capacities, he argued, might compel the United States to undertake a massive, long-term European relief program. "The problem is not a German problem. It is one which embraces a very large part of Europe."

Further, to prevent the liberated countries and, to the extent possible, Germany, from "another winter of extreme privation—cold, exposure, and a food supply wholly inadequate for even a low level of subsistence," he recommended two essential measures. First, the German economy should be centrally controlled in all its aspects to permit the equitable distribution of goods and to avoid "wide variations in the standard of living" among the respective zones. Surplus commodities could be transported to liberated areas. Second, the Allies should not restrict "the productive facilities of Germany" for the next eighteen months, "except the obvious ones covering the production of armament and material of this character." This point, of course, raised the question of reparations, specifically the proposed policy of removals. "Any reparations policy during the next eighteen months," he warned, "which contemplates the movement of capital equipment out of Germany as a form of reparations may seriously affect during the period of the pressing emergency the capacity of Germany to produce the commodities necessary for bare living within the peripheral countries and Germany."

That should be the short-term policy. For the long run, he limited himself to the observation that any plan must be "calculated to prevent her [Germany] from again plunging the world into war and, at the same time, make her wealth of *natural* resources and *natural* productive facilities available for the welfare of mankind throughout Europe." His report confirmed and reinforced the opinions he had already formulated before his arrival in Europe and presaged his attitudes when as ambassador to Great Britain he was to play an important role in German reorganization and rejuvenation.[38]

One other consequence of Douglas's journey was the conviction, which deepened in subsequent weeks and years, that the British and Americans should not have withdrawn from their advanced military positions until the problem of Germany and particularly that of Berlin had been settled. At Ninth Army Headquarters, Lieutenant General William H. Simpson told Douglas of his dismay at the order from SHAEF to pull back from the beachhead he had established across the Elbe. General George S. Patton, Jr., went even further in expressing to Douglas his conviction that American troops under his command should have plunged forward into Czechoslovakia and secured Prague, and that, in fact, he favored going as far as Moscow, if need be, to meet the Russian menace he feared.

Douglas reminded the general of Napoleon's unfortunate venture, but he was impressed with the argument for holding Western forces at their furthest advance. Years later he maintained that he had at some point submitted a memorandum to Clay recommending that the American troops on the borders of Czechoslovakia and the British troops on the Baltic not be withdrawn until clear arrangements on Germany had been concluded with the Soviets. According to his account, *"dear Lucius got livid with anger and made the observation that the Soviet were our companions in the postwar period, that they would behave as we expected them to behave."* No contemporary document has been found to verify this recollection.[39]

The receipt at SHAEF, on April 28, of JCS 1067, the basic directive governing U.S. policy in Germany, came as a considerable shock to Clay and to his advisors. Like Douglas, he had been shown drafts of the proposed directive before he left Washington and shared his misgivings, though not so adamantly or, as it turned out, so conclusively. In any case, it was not so much the punitive stipulations of the order that caused dismay but its financial and economic provisions, which failed to take into account the desperate conditions which the occupying forces had found in Germany and which had been amply confirmed by Douglas's recent trip.

As Clay later noted, the military government was "required to stop production in many fields until agreements could be obtained in the Control Council, and such agreement could be blocked by a single veto. The original draft also prohibited financial controls, although the inflation of currency within Germany was already apparent." According to General William H. Draper, chief of Clay's economic division, Douglas's reaction was explosive: "This thing was assembled by economic idiots! It makes no sense to forbid the most skilled workers in Europe from working as much as they can for a continent which is desperately short of everything!" A staff meeting that considered the directive in its various ramifications was unanimous in its conclusion that modifications should be requested to exercise necessary economic and financial controls. Douglas was instructed by Clay to return to Washington to press for these changes. His journey was coincident with the formal surrender of the Germans in the early-morning hours of May 7, and the ending of hostilities at midnight on the 8th.[40]

In the capital, he spent most of the day at the War Department with General John H. Hilldring, director of the Civil Affairs Division, presenting his and Clay's case for the relaxation of some of the immediate restrictions on production as well as those on the long-run problem of reparations. During the afternoon, he went over some of the same ground with Assistant Secretary Robert A. Lovett, introducing also the problem of jurisdiction between the military command and the Control Council in the occupied areas. Later, he flew to New York with Averell Harriman in his private plane; Harriman spoke gloomily to Douglas of the Russian menace and of the necessity for the British and Americans to work together closely in the postwar world. Douglas was both surprised and pleased at what he considered a realistic change in attitude by his old friend, who had, before he became ambassador in Moscow, been far more optimistic about the Soviet Union as a partner in the community of nations.

The next week was a hectic round of meetings with almost everyone of importance to the future of the German problem, including General Marshall, Stimson, and, again, Lovett. Douglas was especially encouraged by James Byrnes's recognition of the dangers in the removal policy and his willingness to press the case with President Truman, although he was warned that the forces favoring a scorched-earth policy were very powerful in and out of the government and that they had private lines of communication to influential columnists able to play very successfully on public opinion.

On May 11, Douglas met with Truman and came away deeply impressed. The President was avid for any and all information Douglas could provide concerning the situation in Germany, listening intently and asking frequent questions. They discussed the inherent dangers in the veto power vested in each national member of the Allied Control Council. On JCS 1067, Douglas said "it was workable only by exception" and, on reparations, submitted that present plans were "bothersome" and might well become "the tail that wags the dog." Truman agreed that the directive "must be flexible and not final" and asked Douglas to see Edwin W. Pauley, whom he had appointed the United States representative on the Allied Commission on Reparations. In the course of their discussion, the President produced maps showing Germany both before Bismarck's unification and in 1945, displaying a surprising knowledge of the evolution of the Reich. Douglas noted later in the day that Truman was "very, very interested in the whole problem and very intelligent . . . very friendly. . . . Also very simple and direct and humble." Later, in his draft memoirs, he added that "the visit gave me a very warm sensation of friendship" and that he had found a man of "courage" and "understanding," whom he had met before but, of course, not in this new capacity. "This very interesting little man," he concluded, had clearly shown unexpected ability in his new position of authority. It was an auspicious beginning of a long relationship, which was soon to become much closer, but also, on occasion, to be strained by Douglas's political independence.

His talk with Pauley later the same day was somewhat reassuring. Upon hearing Douglas's arguments, Pauley indicated no action would be taken on removals until he had a much better idea of the condition of the remaining facilities and the degree of current productive capacity, especially the requirements for maintaining a minimum subsistence level in Germany for the near term. As to JCS 1067, he confirmed it should not be considered the final word.

On Sunday, May 13, and Tuesday, May 15, Douglas met with Assistant Secretary of State for Economic Affairs William Clayton, who "agreed with everything I said." He urged Clayton to delay publicity of JCS 1067, since it would surely be reversed or modified and in its present form would at best be misunderstood and at worst far more difficult to alter subsequently. Leo Crowley, the foreign economic administrator, was also receptive to Douglas's views and complained of the continuing influence on German policy of Henry Morgenthau and his supporters. He had a number of long conversations with McCloy on every aspect of the situation—the influence of American public opinion, further inflamed as more stories of German atrocities came to light; reparations; displaced persons; the role of the Allied Control Council; the need for an exchange of goods between the various zones; Russian intentions; and, in a more philosophical vein, "the struggle for the soul of Germany." The Russians would be trying to win over the

Germans by surpassing the efforts of the western Allies. Should not the West, McCloy suggested, consider imposing a new social structure that would do more for the common man? Douglas made the point that if "the soul is to be won by doing more for the common man, the Economic Directive should be reviewed. Mere distribution of wealth in Germany will not win the struggle if the Economic Directive means what it says. . . . [T]he standard of living has risen through history only because production has risen and more goods have been produced at relatively lower prices."

At the end of the week, he finally met with Henry Morgenthau. From his later account of the interview, it might better be described as a confrontation. "He asked me a number of questions about Germany. I knew, of course, that he was having his recording machine under his desk which would record everything I said. But quite aside from my apprehensions, or rather my knowledge of this, I was quite blunt and told him exactly what my position was. He then, I believe, became, or rather somebody in his office became the informant of Drew Pearson . . . [who criticized] me for advocating a soft policy." Whatever the source, not only Pearson but I. F. Stone in the newspaper *P.M.* soon afterward blasted Douglas as being among the "soft peace crowd," accusing them of responsibility for the delay in publishing the directives on occupied Germany and pressing for a modification of the harsh terms in an effort to rebuild German industry as a "bulwark against bolshevism." Both commentators hinted darkly at some sort of conspiracy among Wall Street lawyers and financiers to revitalize German industry for their own advantage. The charges evoked a considerable number of protesting letters, several of which Douglas answered in some detail, pointing out that the press attacks "were entirely irresponsible and contrary to the facts." He had "had a great dislike for Germany and all its methods for the past twenty-five years," but he was "anxious . . . that the handling of the German situation should not be allowed to impoverish the other friendly nations of Europe, as such a course would be cutting off our nose to spite our face." To his father he admitted wondering "for a while if I should make some kind of a [public] reply, but concluded it is far better to let the matter drop. . . . [T]his is the kind of thing I suppose one must expect."

Douglas had limited success in the short term. Some modifications were made in the directive to permit limited financial and economic controls for preventing inflation. The official and unofficial pressures on the administration for a tough policy were, however, still too strong to allow any overt relaxation.[41]

Back at Versailles, he reported that he had found sympathy and understanding in high places for his message but reluctance to act in the immediate future. He was permitted little time to brood, for General Clay soon dispatched him on a swing through southern Germany to identify and assess elements of local government that had survived the devastation of war and might still be employed if staffed by individuals who had not been members of the Nazi party.

At Munich, Douglas met with local authorities, church dignitaries, and private citizens and was struck by the fact that all "assured me that he or she had no knowledge whatsoever of the ghastly 'camps of death' in which some seven million Jews lost their lives. Yet with almost daily passage through village and city of trains packed to a point of suffocation with poor, emaciated Jews, this ignorance was difficult if not impossible to credit." The next day, they drove to Dachau, where he was horrified at the firsthand evidences of atrocity: the barracks, the gashouse, "a multitude of horrors in what we call a civilized world." "It is difficult to say which was the most horrible of the instruments of torture; possibly the hook upon which men were hung was the most frightful."[42]

Following his trip, Douglas moved his office to General Clay's new headquarters at Frankfurt, where he found himself billeted again with Robert Murphy, this time in a small house. He was soon occupied in the preparation of reports, which detailed for the information of Clay and Washington the severe shortages of food, coal, oil, electric power, textiles, transportation, and leather supplies, which he had found on his inspection trips and gleaned from other intelligence available. He also supplied studies on labor, health, politics, education, and religion. Obviously, other members of the staff did much of the drafting on many of these documents, but two of the reports appear to have been largely Douglas's own work, the "Field Survey on Regional Government in Bavaria," technically written by Lieutenant Colonel Robert Bowie, and "The Reorganization of Germany's Financial System." The Bavarian paper, the product of his recent trip, described the progress in identifying and appointing trustworthy Germans to temporary regional administrative posts and the problems observed in the areas of food supply, finance, education, and denazification. Noting that the denazification teams were greatly understaffed, it called for more personnel and, most important, clear guidelines for a consistent policy. Above all, the report emphasized the continued confusion of authority between the military government representatives and the Third and Seventh Army commands that were in the field.

In the second report, Douglas admitted that his recommendations on Germany's future financial system must obviously be tentative, "principally because of the absence of information necessary to do a thorough-going job," but stated his conviction that "the highly concentrated system of public and private finance, combined with the blocking of exchange . . . constituted the keystone of the arch of Germany's autarchical warmaking power." Thus, he advocated "as great a dispersion of power as is practicable or, stated differently, as great a decentralization of power, public as well as private, as is possible. . . . In the area of finance, it is as important to effect dispersion of power as it is in the political, industrial, or educational fields . . . for each is a facet of the same crystal having a definite relationship to each other."

He recommended vesting broad financial powers in each *Laend* (state) and breaking up the Reichsbank into four independent banks, one for each zone, operating under the authority of the respective Allied military government, with a central banking board of five members, one appointed by each military government and one by the Allied Control Council "to undertake to define national financial policy." Private banking institutions, many of which performed functions for the Nazi party, should be carefully examined and many dissolved. There should be a common currency and completely free trade throughout the country. Finally, he suggested several methods for servicing the public debt.[43]

During what proved to be the last days of his German tour, Douglas had a two-hour conversation with Richard Scandrett, who was visiting Germany as a member of the American Reparations Commission. Scandrett noted that Douglas voiced his strong dissatisfaction with JCS 1067, quoting him as expressing "very deep and genuine apprehension that there was great danger of too great suppression of [the] German economy." When asked if he favored economic rehabilitation so that Germany could serve as a bulwark against the Soviet Union, Douglas, without directly answering the question, declared that he opposed the remilitarization of the country. Scandrett found Douglas's opinions "extremely rigid and predicated upon a deep conviction that there must be a completely 'free-trade Germany.' " Douglas advocated a treaty among the major allies with a definite commitment to use military force at the first sign of a "red light" that Germany was moving toward rearmament. For at least a decade, he believed, the Allies must "strictly supervise" the defeated nation, but they must avoid the error of Versailles "of compelling 'German isolationism' and . . . 'really forcing Germany to become an economic and military aggressor.' " When Scandrett asked if an identity of interests between the United States and Russia was necessary for a peaceful postwar world, Douglas replied that he "considered it important, but that if Russia would not agree, England, France and the United States should go it alone if they had to in reaching an understanding." On the subject of reparations, which was within the purview of Scandrett, Douglas was emphatic that any "negotiations or agreements reached by the Reparations Commission should be made 'subject to the approval of the Control Council,' " which was on the scene and more fully aware of the depth and ramifications of the German devastation.

Scandrett was skeptical of several of Douglas's opinions. He very much doubted that the U.S. Senate would approve the kind of anti-German military alliance Douglas advocated, and he was not satisfied that Douglas was taking a sufficiently hard line toward the defeated nation. It should be rendered, in his own view, completely impotent. "I left," wrote Scandrett after the interview, "with the impression that Douglas had very strong and sincere convictions and a feeling that he has embarked on a crusade to do what he can to have them carried out for the vital interests of the United States and the preservation of peace in the world."[44]

On the same day as the Scandrett interview, June 20, Douglas had his last meeting with Clay before departing again for the United States to bring Washington officialdom up to date on the activities and thinking of the military government. Douglas's understanding with Clay at that point concerning his further service in Germany is ambiguous. He wrote his old friend Leo Wolman that his job in Germany was finished. It had, he thought, been "useful—at least useful from our point of view—[but] there is little more that I can do unless I prepare to stay for an indefinite period. This definitely I cannot and will not undertake." Jean Smith, in her collection of Clay's papers, notes that Douglas resigned in mid-June, but no document has been found to that effect, though in both their books Clay and Murphy speak rather vaguely of Douglas's discouragement over Washington's inflexible policy toward Germany, which led to his resignation. True also, Douglas's two months were up. On the other hand, Clay later recalled that he had been greatly surprised at Douglas's subsequent decision not to come back, that he believed Douglas had always felt a bit guilty about his action, but that it was characteristic of him to avoid an unpleasant face-to-face confrontation if at all possible. Rather, he had chosen to write Clay later from New York. Clay also questioned whether Douglas would have been listened to as carefully in his discussions in Washington with the President and others if it had been known he was not returning to Germany. Clay and Murphy were far less pessimistic about JCS 1067, in that they felt sure when the first flush of vengeance had subsided a much more rational German policy would emerge. Their predictions proved correct. Douglas, Clay speculated, was apparently not prepared to wait it out.

The first hint of Douglas's decision to remain in the States might have been detected by Clay in a letter of July 5, which noted at the conclusion that "conditions here in the company [Mutual Life] are not all they might be, and I am considerably disappointed." But it was only on July 26 that Douglas wrote a long letter, which, after initial pleasantries, continued: "As to my returning, I feel that I should candidly explain the situation here as I find it." Whereupon, he listed several financial developments that would be of fundamental importance to the future of the company. He could not in good conscience absent himself during such a crucial moment in the history of Mutual Life, when "prudent exploitation" of these circumstances might well "increase its yields." Furthermore, his father-in-law had suffered a stroke and the responsibility for many of his affairs had fallen to him. Consequently, he was "suffering from a conflict of desire and responsibility." "I promised you I would return in September. I shall of course keep my promise if you think I should." With Clay's organization developing so "splendidly," he did feel, however, that the general's advisors should now be long-term appointments. "Frankly . . ." he concluded, "I have reached the point where I should, I believe, either resign my position as president of this great life insurance company or abandon extra-lateral excursions. I cannot, now that the European war is over, under the circumstances I have attempted to enumerate above, resign as president, for I committed myself, when I came, to the task of carrying the rehabilitation of this company through to its completion."

Clay's response held out the hope that a later visit for consultation might still be possible. "Of course, whatever your decision . . . I will know that it is all made in good faith and with full appreciation of our problems over here. . . . I want to avoid if possible having to write you off our list of assets." Expressing the hope that the next weeks might so "clarify" Douglas's responsibilities in the States that he would find himself able "to pay us an occasional visit," he added: "If you cannot, I will understand and be ever grateful for what you have already contributed to our task." The fall, however, brought no change in Douglas's decision. In letters to both Clay and Eisenhower, in early October, he reiterated his inability to abdicate his obligations "directly and indirectly" to "three million people," stockholders and company personnel, in the face of fast-moving financial events.[45]

For his trip to Washington in late June Douglas was instructed to discuss the continuing confusion of authority between the field forces and the military government and the need to reactivate German production. On the first question, he had several long talks with McCloy, "who saw the point at once" and suggested he bring the matter to the attention of General Marshall. But, on second thought, they both agreed that this might prove embarrassing to Clay and, in any case, the chief of staff already had his share of problems. They also discussed the questions of coal production, transportation, and food. To Stimson, Douglas painted a "somber picture of the situation in Germany . . . confirming exactly . . . my [Stimson's] first memorandum last summer in the controversy with Morgenthau over 'pastoral Germany.' . . . It all shows the flood of hysteria which was yielded to last year . . . and now we are going to suffer for it." To Morgenthau, whose resignation in anger over his exclusion from the Potsdam delegation Truman was to accept with alacrity soon thereafter, Douglas emphasized the importance of coal not only to Germany but to all of Europe and especially France. He also met with Clayton, Lovett, Assistant Secretary of State Dean Acheson, and Byrnes.

On July 6, he saw the President. During their conversation and in a subsequent letter, Douglas recommended tight Allied supervision over Germany for a number of years, the prompt suppression of "the first manifestation of the resurgence of German military power," the elimination of all forms of economic autarchy, the formation of a central government with limited and dispersed authority, "the sequestering of many of the industrial facilities of Germany . . . and the disposition of them to the governments of liberated areas or their nationals," and the rehabilitation of the German economy to promote continental prosperity. He concluded that the long-term American "policy toward Germany and Europe should aim at the establishment of a relatively free trade area" and the economic interdependence of nation states "so that neither Germany nor any other nation of Western Europe can again become so self-sufficient that she can effectively plunge the world into another and even more devastating struggle."

Specifically, he raised the urgent question of coal to enable the peripheral countries, particularly France, to survive the winter. Its production should "be increased to a maximum for export and consumption of coal in Germany should be held to the very minimum." Truman appeared to share many of Douglas's views, but apparently remained noncommittal on long-term objectives and specific revisions of JCS 1067, although he had just overruled Morgenthau's advice on German coal mining, accepted his resignation, and indicated his rejection of the plan that bore his name.[46]

The German experience was an important landmark in Douglas's career. However brief, it had enabled him to renew important relationships in Washington and abroad and to keep fresh in the minds of those in positions of power and influence an appreciation of his talents. Above all, it had prepared him well for some of the problems he faced during the more memorable mission that awaited him in Britain in less than two years.

PART SIX
Ambassador

18

To the Court of St. James's

IN THE EARLY-MORNING HOURS OF FEBRUARY 6, 1947, O. Max Gardner, scheduled to sail later in the day to London on the *America* to assume his duties as United States ambassador to Great Britain, suffered a fatal heart attack in his New York hotel. The post had been vacant since late September, when Averell Harriman had been called home to become secretary of commerce, following Henry Wallace's abrupt dismissal after his controversial foreign-policy speech in Madison Square Garden on September 12. At that time Harriman had recommended Douglas as his replacement, although his name was not among those prominently mentioned in the press. But in December President Truman and Secretary of State Byrnes had chosen the under secretary of the treasury and former governor of North Carolina for the assignment. Now, with Gardner's death, public speculation did number Douglas among those under consideration, along with William Clayton, James Byrnes, Edward Stettinius, Jr., James Forrestal, Edwin Pauley, and Ambassador to Russia General Walter Bedell Smith. If, indeed, he was aware of the speculation, Douglas probably gave his candidacy little credence, especially after his recent refusal to accept the World Bank presidency.[1]

Meanwhile, General George C. Marshall had been sworn in as secretary of state on January 21, and Dean Acheson had agreed to stay on as under secretary for six months. Acheson and Harriman probably proposed Douglas's nomination to Marshall, who had himself been most favorably impressed by his wartime contacts with Douglas. Certainly his past service and wide acquaintance in official Washington and London, devotion to Anglo-American cooperation, and grasp of international economics fully qualified him for the position. Truman obviously agreed. There was little time to waste. Too many urgent problems demanded the presence of an envoy in London.[2]

The Douglases had been staying at their ranch near Sonoita. On February 8, they drove up to Tucson to hospitalize Peggy, who was suffering from a case of mumps she had contracted from Sharman. Lew checked into the Pioneer Hotel to be near her. On the afternoon of February 12, the telephone rang in his room at the hotel, and Truman and Marshall were on the line. Assuring Douglas that he endorsed all that the secretary was about to say, Truman turned the conversation over to Marshall, who began without preamble: "Douglas, we want you to go to London." "General, what for?" replied the startled Douglas. Somewhat irritated, as was his wont when a message was not immediately understood, Marshall shot back: "Of course, to be ambassador, what did you think?" "Well, General, this comes to me out of the blue; it never occurred to me." Flustered, he added: "Besides, I can't go because Peg is in the hospital with the mumps." "Douglas," Marshall responded rather tartly, "I'm not asking Peg to go to London, I'm asking you."

Later, Douglas wrote that "All of my inclinations were to accept," but that he felt strongly the weight of his obligations to Mutual Life and the need to consult with the board as well as other friends whose counsel he valued and, of course, his family. Collecting his thoughts, he expressed his appreciation for the highly flattering offer, asked for a few days to consider it, and mentioned several conditions that would have to be met if otherwise he found it possible to accept. Chief among these was the assurance that as ambassador he would be no "mere messenger boy," "merely a person with a title," but would be consulted as "someone who has ideas about policy and who would like those concepts about policy at least considered." Informing his father of this conversation and his subsequent deliberations, he affirmed that Marshall had readily agreed and emphasized that "the policy to be followed was wholly consistent with [my] . . . views" on fostering close relations with England. The secretary had urged a prompt decision. There were many matters of great importance that affected relations with Britain and Europe and required the London post to be filled quickly. Douglas was their first choice. It was "a difficult decision to make for the sacrifice is very great," he confessed to his father. Unlike the World Bank presidency, the ambassadorship "is in a field in which there exists complete agreement as to policy and which can be . . . more important in its ultimate effects."[3]

In a fragment of his unpublished memoirs, Douglas also mentioned two other conditions: that a terminal date be put upon his tenure to make it less embarrassing to the President or the secretary if his service was unsatisfactory or if he found the position "inhospitable," and that his appointment not be a political one, "which binds me to any particular political party." He affirmed that he was a Democrat, but that he could not "accept some of the things which the Party has done in the past," had "on occasion voted Republican . . . as a matter of protest rather than as a matter of conviction," and wanted it "clearly understood that this is not a political proposition which binds me without recourse to any political course." The general, Douglas recalled, accepted these propositions as well and promised to explain them to the President. Here the evidence is less clear. In the letter to his father he makes no reference to these stipulations. It would seem, however, that the usual pro forma tender of resignation at the end of the President's term in less than two years would have almost automatically satisfied the first requirement.

The question of political affiliation and loyalty is more complex. Truman and Acheson, and probably Marshall, were already well aware of Douglas's past defections and independent views. Most recently, he had neither publicly endorsed

Roosevelt in 1944 nor made any contribution to the national Democratic campaign. Under the circumstances, the tender of the ambassadorship could hardly have been regarded by Truman as a political appointment or as a reward for financial support. Douglas's disclaimer would have been redundant. The offer was clearly based upon merit and his qualifications. Marshall's own appointment was evidence of the President's ability to rise above political considerations. In fact, one report claimed that, when Douglas was proposed as ambassador, Truman ruefully remarked that the political ramifications would be serious as "Democratic hatchetmen" would object because of his previous political activities. Marshall allegedly replied that they would be "a lot more serious if this Administration appoints an inferior man as Ambassador to Britain at this time."

On the other hand, Douglas's public service had always been as a Democrat, first in Congress, then in Democratic administrations. Noteworthy also was the alleged pledge of loyalty at the time of his last appointment by Roosevelt, and, more relevantly, some inconclusive evidence that a similar commitment was made to Acheson in their conversations before Douglas left for London. Probably no further clarification of the matter will come to light. It deserves mention here, however, in view of the acrimony surrounding Douglas's subsequent actions during the elections of 1948 and 1952.[4]

With a natural disposition to accept the offer, but fully aware of the personal and professional problems to be resolved, Douglas informed Peggy of his unexpected call. Equally startled by the news, her first reaction was also to mention her hospitalization, then quickly to protest leaving the children and to question their ability to afford the post. Through the open window of her ground-floor room, where she was in quarantine, Douglas reassured her that those problems could be surmounted and indicated his desire to give an affirmative reply if he could work out a satisfactory arrangement with Mutual Life. He planned to go to the ranch to think it through and consult by telephone with trusted friends and members of his board. These conversations, including one with former ambassador to Britain and Democratic presidential candidate John W. Davis, encouraged his acceptance and convinced him that his success in rebuilding the company's financial structure and the quality of its personnel since 1940 justified his putting the interests of the country first.[5]

Accordingly, on February 17 Douglas called Marshall and asked that his acceptance be transmitted to the President with the proviso that his nomination not be sent to the Senate until the 26th, which was the earliest date he could arrange a meeting with the Mutual Life directors. He would, he assured the secretary, accept the post even if his board decided not to grant him a leave of absence but asked for his resignation as president. Meantime, considerable and largely successful efforts were made by the State Department to prevent a leak before the nomination went to Congress. At the end of the week, Douglas left by train for New York, where he met with the executive committee of the Mutual board and then the full board. Their decision was to accept his resignation as president, to be succeeded by Alexander E. Patterson, and to elect him chairman of the board with a leave of absence without pay.[6]

Meantime, Douglas had received a letter from the President, dated February 20, expressing pleasure at his acceptance and the "conviction that you are eminently qualified by character and experience to carry the heavy burden of that vitally important office." Sensing in some measure at least the troubled days immediately ahead in foreign relations, Truman wrote that "At no time in our history has it been more essential that the man who speaks for us in London should combine outstanding ability with those qualities which represent all that is best in our American life and tradition." He would have "the entire support of the Secretary of State and myself." The State Department initiated the confidential process of obtaining the approval of the British government and the monarch. Despite the absence of their majesties on a South African tour, Chargé d'Affaires Waldemar J. Gallman was able to report the formal acceptance of Douglas by King George VI on February 27. It was followed by a cable to Marshall from Foreign Secretary Ernest Bevin, reflecting his satisfaction at the nomination of Douglas, "whose high qualifications and friendly attitude toward this country and its people are known to so many here."[7]

The nomination was sent to the Senate on February 26. The same day, Douglas held a news conference in New York, assuring reporters of his optimism concerning Britain's future. Its economic problems could not be viewed in isolation. "It's the spirit of the people that makes people. It was this spirit that made them stand up in the dark days when a great many people with little spirit prophesied their doom. . . . The present crisis is largely due to the dislocations caused by the war and the terrific sufferings and exactions on all of the resources, and otherwise, of the United Kingdom." Asked if, as an insurance man, he considered England a "good risk," he responded sharply: "Yes, Britain is a good risk. Of course she is a good risk. Certainly." On a more personal note, he volunteered that he and Peggy would "live as simply as possible," with due regard to British austerity, and "because otherwise I would wind up in the poorhouse."[8]

On February 28, moving with unaccustomed speed and without hearings, the Senate Foreign Relations Committee, under the chairmanship of Republican Arthur H. Vandenberg, unanimously approved Douglas's nomination. The following week the Senate, by voice vote, followed suit, although William Langer of North Dakota and Tom Stewart of Tennessee publicly announced their reservations about Douglas's Anglophilia. In a typically diplomatic gesture, the ambassador-designate later wrote to each member of the Foreign Relations Committee, expressing appreciation for "the confidence you have displayed in me," and to the two doubting solons disarmingly avowing his complete loyalty "to my flag and to my native land." Both dissenters replied with reserved cordiality.

The afternoon of his confirmation, Douglas and Acheson accompanied General Marshall to the National Airport, where the secretary enplaned for the fruitless Moscow Conference of Foreign Ministers (CFM), which was to prove a prelude for much of Douglas's activity in London. His presence was evidence of his anticipated role in the conduct of American foreign policy.[9]

After Douglas was sworn in on March 8, he was interviewed by John L. Springer of the Associated Press. Reiterating his dedication to the free-enterprise system and his belief that the United States had an obligation to set a good example to reverse the trend toward government-controlled economies, he disclaimed any intention to act as a salesman for his views in Britain, which had, of course, moved in the opposite direction under the Labour government. His job would be to try to "understand differences and establish workable relations [between the two countries] . . . irrespective of their internal political policies." The next day, in the *New York Times Magazine* S. J. Woolf quoted Douglas as stating flatly that it was "up to the English to select their own type of government. Nor does the fact that the Labour Party is in power make any difference in our relations." Britain's form of government "is none of my business."[10]

The appointment received an overwhelmingly favorable response. After reviewing Douglas's record, a *Christian Science Monitor* reporter observed that the nomination "repudiated that oft heard charge that the President can get nobody but second raters and Missourians to take responsible posts." The New York *Herald Tribune* expressed its "congratulations to President Truman . . . on his ability to recognize Mr. Douglas' qualities and to summon them to the public service," and the *New York Times* concluded that "Truman could not possibly have chosen a better man." The Washington *Post* termed the appointment "felicitous," and the neighboring Baltimore *Sun* commented on "the sense of fitness displayed by President Truman in selecting him." The Boston *Traveler* emphasized Douglas's "adaptability": "He is [as] equally at ease in the environment of the mining camp or the ranch corral as he is in the drawing rooms of New York or London." In the Midwest, the Cincinnati *Inquirer* prophesied that he would "improve our relations with Great Britain and also will strengthen Mr. Truman's administration by further defining a middle course between the Roosevelt tradition and that of the GOP." The southern and western press handed out kudos as well. Even Douglas's long-time antagonist Drew Pearson reluctantly conceded that Douglas had "just about the right combination of charm and tact, mixed with mettle, to make an excellent ambassador."[11]

Some voices of dissent were also raised. Chester Bowles, a New Dealer from Connecticut and recently briefly director of the Office of Economic Stabilization, who had coveted the London position, wrote privately that, despite Douglas's inherent decency, he could "think of very few who would have less understanding of what is going on in England." The *Nation* hoped that direct confrontation "with the problems Britain faces" would persuade Douglas that "Ricardo and Mill haven't all the answers." The *New Republic* declared that sending a laissez-faire economist to "the land of Keynes" was akin to "sending a Methodist missionary as ambassador to the Pope." Charles Van Devander in the New York *Post* wondered "whether the best answer to Russian Communism is a retreat into the arch conservatism represented by Lew Douglas."[12]

The range of congratulatory letters and telegrams was equally remarkable. Morgenthau, Ickes, and Frances Perkins hailed the appointment with enthusiasm, as did political opposites Alf Landon and the rising Democratic figure Adlai Stevenson. Former congressional allies and opponents joined the chorus. John McDuffie of Alabama knew "of no man in the country who is better qualified," while Fiorello La Guardia wrote as the "unauthorized spokesman of unorganized America" to indicate his satisfaction. The Supreme Court was represented by Justices Harold Burton and Felix Frankfurter, and Judge Learned Hand of the Second Circuit Court seconded his senior colleagues with an exceedingly bad ode for the occasion.

Canadian admirers were delighted. Prime Minister W. L. Mackenzie King telegraphed: "Your many . . . friends [here] will be sharing my pleasure. . . . It should help to bring all three countries into closer and happier association than ever." Vincent Massey, recent high commissioner to Great Britain, who had been the first Canadian minister to Washington and would later become the first native-born governor general, wrote: "It is a splendid thing to have someone at your Embassy in London who both feels as you do about Great Britain, and at the same time knows the nature of the problem she is facing." In his Montreal *Star*, John McConnell, Douglas's chairman of the board of governors at McGill, welcomed the appointment ecstatically: "No man is better qualified to undertake such a great mission . . . than Lewis Williams Douglas."[13]

Across the water, the press response was mixed and contained an element of surprise. The *Times* of London gave a straightforward and comprehensive account of the new ambassador's career and repeated at some length his favorable comments on Britain and Britain's plight made at the time of his nomination. Its conservative rival, the *Daily Telegraph*, was equally sedate, well informed, and friendly. On the other hand, the liberal Manchester *Guardian* headed its announcement with "An Exponent of Free Enterprise New U.S. Ambassador" and began its write-up with: "How far President Truman has departed from Mr. Roosevelt's philosophy is indicated by his selection of Mr. Lewis Douglas . . . [who] belongs to the extreme conservative wing of the Democratic Party." But, it continued, though the appointment was unexpected, it was "welcomed in London with some warmth," as "Mr. Douglas is not an isolationist and personally he has always been friendly to Britain and the British people." The London *Star*, less restrained, prophesied that Douglas would "become one of the most popular American Ambassadors we have ever had in London" and quoted Sir Arthur Salter to the effect that he was a man of "quite exceptional qualities." The London *News Chronicle* pointed out that during the war "Britain's cause never had a stouter friend."

Some newspapers, perhaps with less extensive files, were caught off guard. The Labour *Daily Herald* commented that the new ambassador was "so little known . . . that American information services had only reference book knowledge of him." In like manner, the conservative *Daily Mail* declared "U.S. Sends 'Unknown' as Envoy." The Glasgow *Herald* labeled his appointment "a complete surprise."

Other British journals, leaning heavily on Douglas's New York interviews, emphasized his and Peggy's empathy for the British people and their intention to share their hardships. Appropriately, the Scottish papers made much of his Lowland antecedents, several featuring the comment of the Duke of Hamilton, head of the Douglas family, that he would welcome the envoy as a member of the clan. The Duke of Buccleuch and Queensberry invited him to visit at Drumlanrig Castle, "the ancestral home of the Douglases."[14]

If Douglas was a comparative unknown to some of the British press and much of the public, he was quickly identified and welcomed by politicians, diplomats, civil servants, and journalists, who were familiar with his wartime service and contributions to Anglo-American accord. Chief among the notables was Winston Churchill, whom he had last seen during the former Prime Minister's visit to the States the previous March, when he had delivered his famous "iron curtain" speech. Replying to Churchill's message of greeting, Douglas wrote: "There is no one on earth with [sic] whom I would rather have a welcoming cable than from yourself. The prospect of seeing you gives me a sense of support and makes the tasks that lie ahead seem lighter." In a BBC interview of February 28, Geoffrey Crowther, influential editor of *The Economist,* waxed eloquent over the appointment: "Mr. Douglas . . . is a man of many parts. . . . I think it will be several degrees warmer in England for the next few years with the presence of Mr. Lewis Douglas in our midst."

The Labour government, despite its awareness of Douglas's economic philosophy, and diplomats and Foreign Office officials were genuinely pleased with the appointment. British Ambassador Lord Inverchapel's congratulatory telegram, "I throw my hat into the air with joy. . . ." was echoed in his report home. At the Foreign Office, F. B. A. Rundall, of the North American Department, minuting the ambassador's dispatches, reassured Bevin that "we have little to fear from Mr. Douglas' alleged conservatism and devotion to free enterprise." He was "fully alive to the strategic implications of our economic difficulties. . . . Nevertheless it would be as well to bear his prejudices in mind and to make sure that he fully understands the objectives as well as the details of our economic planning. From all indications he will be eager to learn and, which is still more important, more than eager to believe well of us."[15]

Douglas spent the next week in intensive briefings at the State Department, in conversations with Arthur Vandenberg and other friends in the Senate, and in visits to the British embassy. He was apprised of and perhaps consulted on what came to be called the Truman Doctrine, the $400 million aid program to Greece and Turkey. It was proposed to Congress by the President on March 12, in response to the sudden British announcement to the United States of its inability to continue financial assistance to those two nations threatened by internal and external Communist pressure. Although Douglas later decried the universal application of the containment policy implied in Truman's address, at the time he fully and enthusiastically supported it. He publicly termed the doctrine "a great State paper," "a clear pronouncement that this time we are not going to withdraw from world affairs," and wrote the President commending the message as "direct, honest, brave and forthright."[16]

He was informed in detail concerning Britain's deepening industrial and financial crisis, exacerbated by the unusually severe winter, which had had an equally disastrous effect upon the already desperate economic plight of all Western Europe. He also learned of the doubtful prospects for successful negotiations concerning Germany at the forthcoming Moscow Council of Foreign Ministers' Conference. Much of what he heard must have come as a shock despite his constant effort to keep abreast of international affairs and his correspondence with friends in England. It was abundantly clear his new assignment was far from routine and much was expected of his talents.[17]

Douglas flew to London March 15. Peggy and Sharman were to follow in late April, after closing the apartment and when Sharman's freshman year at Vassar was near completion. After one of the bitterest winters on record, London welcomed him with a clear, bright, shiny day, which augured well for his future tenure and cheered him on the drive to the residence at 14 Prince's Gate.[18]

This attractive row house, across from Hyde Park, off Kensington Road, had originally been two dwellings, later joined. It had been given to the United States government by J. P. Morgan, Jr. Since the war it had not been occupied except for the six-month sojourn of Averell Harriman, who had redone the third floor to provide a small dining room, living room, and two bedrooms for his single occupancy. The remaining three floors needed some repair and considerable redecoration to be made livable. At some point, probably during Morgan's ownership, four stone Indian heads had been set in over the first-floor front windows, giving the building a distinctly American flavor. It was unpretentious, but gracious and convenient to the embassy, on Grosvenor Square. Recently, however, Barbara Hutton had donated her mansion, Winfield House, to the government as the ambassadorial residence. Beautifully sited in Regent's Park, it was a magnificent gift. The State Department, having set aside almost $800,000 for its renovation, expected the Douglases to move in.

The second day after his arrival, Douglas and Paul Warburg, an attaché and old friend, went to Regent's Park to survey the new premises. They were indeed impressive. But Douglas decided on the spot that the American ambassador need not and should not live in such splendor. In the first place, it would require a personal outlay far above the government allowance, which was already inadequate to maintain the residence at Prince's Gate. Douglas did not consider himself in a position to undertake the financial burden, nor did he think the United States should place such a restriction upon the selection of its future representatives. He was also concerned about reaction to the extravagance and ostentation of Winfield House. England was just recovering from the war; the people's lives were sharply restricted by the rationing of foodstuffs and fuel. For the American ambassador to live in the grand style at that moment in British history would be a great mistake in public relations, almost an affront.

At his first news conference, on March 20, in answer to a direct question as to whether he planned to occupy Winfield House, Douglas replied: "Not if I can help it." It was a "lovely house," but "much too large for me. One cannot live simply there, and I like to live simply." He informed the State Department of his determination to remain at Prince's Gate, which could be suitably remodeled for a mere $18,000. The department objected. Douglas persisted, and finally, only in mid-May, received authorization to proceed with the work at Prince's Gate. Quite apart from the personal considerations that entered into his resolve, Douglas's instincts concerning the propriety of moving into elaborate quarters in the midst of British privation were sound. There is little doubt that much of the popularity of the ambassadorial couple, which contributed greatly to the success of his mission, stemmed from the simplicity and democratic character of their lifestyle, which would have been difficult if not impossible to maintain at Winfield House.[19]

Douglas had reached England on Sunday. Monday morning, promptly at 9 A.M., he arrived at the embassy, met with his staff at the conference held daily, and spent the remainder of the morning and early afternoon consulting the files and acquainting himself with the problems and details of his new responsibilities.

Later, in the absence of Bevin at the Moscow conference, he and Gallman called informally upon Prime Minister Attlee, who was acting foreign secretary.[20]

On Thursday he held a conference with over a hundred members of the British press. From all accounts, he made an excellent initial impression. Setting the stage for the informality he would observe in his relations with reporters and with the public during his tenure, he sat on the edge of his desk and laughed and talked disarmingly throughout the interview. Although properly cautious or noncommittal at that early date in answer to specific questions concerning American policy, he convincingly emphasized the strong bonds of friendship between the two countries. Now, with England far more exhausted by two world wars than most Americans realized, "just as you need us—and I believe you do—so we need you." Placing "no credence" in the "gloomy forecast" for Britain, he expressed complete confidence "that the sun will shine and shine brightly on Britain again, and that she will recover most of her traditional position in the world."[21]

On March 25, Douglas officially assumed his duties with the presentation of his credentials at Buckingham Palace to the Princess Royal and the Duke of Gloucester, Counsellors of State. To Prime Minister Attlee he expressed the hope that Britain would at least continue to bear the cost of her military mission in Greece and deplored the fact that she did not have 20 million tons of coal to export to the Continent. Attlee was agreeable but noncommittal. The principal subject of conversation, however, was the reception to be accorded former vice-president and secretary of commerce Henry Wallace during his forthcoming visit to England. It was a touchy question, for although a distinguished American and a friend of the ambassador, Wallace had been attacking the Truman Doctrine and the idea of containment as imperialistic, a threat to peace, and an attempt to maintain the status quo on a global scale. Pointing out that the trip was unofficial and that he had refused Wallace's request to use the embassy for a press conference, Douglas suggested, no doubt to Attlee's relief, that they both entertain the visitor privately to minimize the anticipated embarrassment of his presence and public statements.

Their apprehensions were well founded, though the disruptive effect of Wallace's speeches, two of which were broadcast, was probably limited to a sympathetic minority. In Manchester, he drew a crowd of four thousand, despite the competition of an international football match, attacking the bellicosity of the United States and the undermining of the United Nations. The *Manchester Guardian* was not impressed, pointing out that Wallace offered no remedies for the problem he raised and criticizing him for indicating that Russia was "passive" while the rest of the world was being "victimized by American expansionism." The editorial concluded that "as an apostle of the one world Mr. Wallace seems a little clumsy." Minister of State Hector McNeil reassured Douglas that whatever temporary influence the speeches may have had would soon wane because "he offered no specific program" and because of "the traditional British view that the citizen of another country should not in England indiscreetly criticize his own government."

Nevertheless, Douglas was disturbed. He expressed his uneasiness to the State Department and wrote his father that he had already discerned in Britain "an extraordinary amount of mental confusion and in some quarters, unfortunately with too much influence, a very deep uneasiness if not in fact an open hostility to Truman's policy." Wallace's comments could only serve to encourage those elements. His views were, to be sure, the products "of a messy mind," but they were "making my task no easier." "How he [Wallace] can reconcile what he said in the United States advising us not to be led by British imperialism and what he has said here in England advising her not to be deceived by American imperialism is difficult for me to understand."

Back in Washington, Wallace's remarks occasioned an exchange in a cabinet meeting, during which James Forrestal inquired why Wallace had not been denied a passport and "why we should not do so now." The President replied that to take such action against a former vice-president and cabinet officer would lead to "severe criticism." Attorney General Tom C. Clark "suggested that it might be even better to weigh carefully the reentry of the gentleman into the United States." In the Senate, Elbert Thomas of Utah raised the possibility of prosecuting Wallace under the Logan Act.[22]

On April 22 Douglas was to make the obligatory speech of every new ambassador before the Society of Pilgrims, an organization promoting Anglo-American understanding. Here he hoped, without directly rebutting Wallace, to reaffirm the cordiality between the two countries and to justify and clarify United States foreign policy. In preparation, he solicited suggestions from, among others, Dean Acheson and R. J. Cruikshank of the *News Chronicle*. It was a distinguished audience, including the Prime Minister, the Archbishop of Canterbury, the Lord Chancellor, and much of the British establishment. In a sense, the occasion was his official introduction to the movers and doers in and out of government. Beyond the hall, many more listened over the BBC.

Douglas's address was received with enthusiasm. He reviewed the historic relations between two great English-speaking countries, their shared values and experiences, which had, in the recent past, "bound us together in the exhausting enterprise of driving into oblivion the ugly forces that were intent upon our destruction." He elaborated upon the economic and institutional ruin of the war. The task of reconstructing "the substance of free government that has been so violently swept away, of reconciling two different codes of human beliefs, of establishing an assured peace is not exceeded in its extent or its intensity in the chronicles of the human race." But, despite the tradition of isolation and the myriad internal wartime financial and economic dislocations which called for repair, America had learned by "the rude shock of experience" that it must assume "the responsibilities that are inescapably associated with our newly acquired authority." Twenty-five years ago, the United States was "faithless to . . . [her] trust." To be so again "would be serving neither ourselves, nor you, nor the cause of peace." "If we now grasp the nettle of authority it is not because we have designs to press our will on others, it is not because we covet new lands. . . . It is rather because we are no less determined than you that by diligence and friendliness, by patience and firmness, peace shall begin to merge out of the dark chaos caused by war."

Speaking specifically to the Truman Doctrine, Douglas declared that America sought only for individuals everywhere the opportunity to "enjoy the privilege freely to select the sort of political and social and economic order of society which seems to them best suited to their national tastes and inclinations, and best adapted to the preservation of the peace." He affirmed his conviction from the example of England's past that "the same energy and resolution which have pulled you through so many difficulties . . . will carry you toward a satisfying and splendid future."[23]

Writing to Acheson the next day, Douglas expressed the modest hope that he had not exposed anyone at home "to embarrassment." "At any rate," he continued, "as nearly as one can tell so far it seems that it has had the effect of repairing some of the damage that Wallace did." Acheson assured him that "All of us in the Department think you did a grand job." Press comment and a number of highly laudatory letters confirmed Acheson's opinion.[24]

His mission had begun well. On May 1, the ambassador met Peggy and Sharman at Southampton. They were to have a decided impact on Anglo-American relations over the next three and a half years. In the mail that day, from New York, in answer to his request, were two books Douglas hoped would prove useful in his quest for knowledge and precedent: Thomas A. Bailey's *A Diplomatic History of the American People* and the biography of his most popular predecessor, Burton J. Hendrick's *The Life and Letters of Walter H. Page*.[25]

19

Launching the Marshall Plan

DOUGLAS'S ROLE IN BRITAIN WAS GREATLY ENHANCED during the first two years while George Marshall was secretary of state. The general had a practice of carefully consulting senior Foreign Service officers in the field as well as in the department and of delegating a good deal of authority, in the military manner, though never evading final decisions or the responsibility for them. Marshall reposed a degree of confidence in the ambassador, equal only, in the opinion of many contemporary observers, to his relationship first with Acheson, then especially with Robert A. Lovett, who succeeded Acheson as under secretary at the end of June, 1947. Marshall had worked with Douglas at the War Shipping Administration, as he had with Lovett as assistant secretary of war for air from 1941 to 1945. The circle of trust was completed by the long friendship between Douglas and Lovett, dating from their college days at Amherst and Yale and extending through association in New York and wartime service in Washington.[1]

Marshall gave Douglas considerable scope in various negotiations, was attentive to his advice on European questions as well as British relations, and depended heavily upon his exceptional rapport with Bevin. Although the general and Bevin held each other in mutually high esteem, Marshall's formality stood in the way of a warm and convivial relationship with the uninhibited foreign secretary. At such times Douglas's presence and intervention proved of value in bridging the personality differences between the two men. Soon on a first-name basis, most unusual between a British foreign secretary and an ambassador, Douglas and Bevin enjoyed a greater degree of intimacy than even the close relations between the two countries at that time would have explained. Despite often heated exchanges and Douglas's sometimes aggressive pursuit of his point of view, their friendship never wavered—perhaps deepened. Douglas had no hesitation about ringing up Bevin directly at the office or at his flat at No. 1 Carlton Gardens or asking to come around to his residence in the evening for an urgent matter. Finally, though Marshall was impeccable in his avoidance of favoritism, evidenced by his invariable use of surnames even with his closest associates, he was obviously warmed by Douglas's charm and gaiety and often able to cast off his otherwise somewhat austere demeanor in the company of the ambassador as well as in the relaxed family atmosphere when he stayed at the residence during his visits to London.[2]

Douglas's exceptional rapport with Bevin was matched by his extraordinary popularity with the British public. His admiration for the country's war effort, compassion for its current privations and faith in its future, reflected in his remarks upon appointment, were harbingers of his actions and activities. His first press conferences and public statements in London reinforced the hopes foreshadowed. His unaffected, thoroughly American personality won the affection of everyone he met, from royalty to coal miners. Peggy, beautiful, witty, yet down to earth, captured the hearts of all classes and ages. Her combination of urbanity and forthrightness struck many Britons as remarkably English—with an American accent. Sharman was soon swept into the social life of the young set around Princess Margaret. The informality and sociability of the Douglas family was widely noted and appreciated. Writing Douglas, on July 31, after a visit, Averell Harriman enthused: "One doesn't have to stay in London long to realize that you are already an institution and so is Peg." By November, Frank McCarthy, wartime Marshall aide and then president of the Motion Picture Association of America, back from a trip to England and equally impressed, wrote Douglas "unanimous expressions of confidence in you in Great Britain. Business associations, old school mates, friends, taxi drivers, diplomats . . . and the Secretary himself—all point to you as the ideal person for your important post. I have never seen more spontaneous and thorough admiration, and I join in the chorus."[3]

Before Douglas left Washington, he was aware of two serious economic problems facing Britain. One was immediate and already crippling—a coal shortage. The other, emerging and deeply distressing, was the mounting evidence that the British loan agreement for $3.75 billion, signed in December, 1945, and approved by Congress only in the following spring after much debate, was woefully inadequate and its effectiveness impaired by the conditions imposed by the American negotiators, principally Will Clayton. Furthermore, the spiraling inflation in the United States was seriously reducing British purchasing power.[4]

The immediate cause of the coal crisis was the terrible winter of 1946–47, which had paralyzed transportation and disrupted the movement of coal. More basic was the shortage of coal stocks which, in part, stemmed from implementation of the Labour government's nationalization of the mines. On February 7, Emanuel Shinwell, minister of fuel, had announced that no power would be furnished to industrial consumers in London and large sections of the southeastern, midland, and northwestern areas of England. Domestic users would have their power cut off for considerable periods each day. Even as Britain desperately needed to increase production for exports, her industrial plant was all but stilled. Although there was strong pressure on the government to request more coal imports to meet the crisis, it was recognized this would have to be approved by the European Coal Organization (ECO), which was aware that the British coal position was if anything better than that of other European countries, with the possible exception of Poland. On February 13, President Truman had offered to divert to England colliers en route to the Continent, but Attlee declined, citing the more pressing needs of Europe. Wryly, F. B. A. Rundall minuted a dispatch from Lord Inverchapel with the comment that, though the proposal was very generous, "The Republicans will probably blame it [the coal crisis] all on our socialism."[5]

Douglas had proposed to Acheson the possibility of recruiting American experts from the coal, steel, and textile industries to evaluate and make recommendations concerning British procedures for increasing production and improving efficiency while reducing costs. After forty-eight hours in London, he was so distressed by personal observation of the British plight that he urged the State Department to support a London request to the ECO for a larger coal allocation from the United States, despite the risk that it would endanger the stability of the ECO and arouse the anger of the French. Marshall refused, barring a personal request from Bevin, citing again the even more urgent needs of the Continent and the bitterness any arrangement outside the ECO would entail toward the British. Douglas agreed and over the next month convinced Attlee of the inadvisability of pursuing the question either with the ECO or the President. He reminded the Prime Minister that the American coal supply was limited, following the damaging effects of the mine strike the previous November. Only in late May was it deemed feasible and appropriate for the United Kingdom to ask for a revised U.S. coal allocation from the ECO, which was negotiated at a rather modest level, largely because of French intransigence.[6]

Meantime, Douglas had made every effort to reassure the British government of American sympathy and of America's desire to be of help, within the confines of larger economic and political considerations. Douglas arranged for Robert P. Koenig, president of the Ayrshire Collieries of Indiana, to come to England to consult and make recommendations on the coal situation. He had also arrived at some conclusions of his own on the British economic crisis and the fuel problem in particular. With due regard for the debilitating effects of the war and the severe climatic conditions just experienced, he placed considerable blame on the socialistic policies and ineptitude of the government.

Writing to Acheson on March 25, he noted that the situation was "not being helped by the five day week for coal miners." Three days later, he cabled that "only lackadaisical efforts appear to have been made toward providing even temporary housing in the more productive coal fields. No action has been undertaken to increase consumer goods . . . for the miners and their families. The system of taxation is such that any increased earnings of the miners resulting from increasing individual production leaves but a small residue in the hands of the miners. . . . Mechanical equipment that is available . . . is not being installed as rapidly as it might be." To John McCloy, now president of the World Bank, he was even more candid: "The coal crisis . . . would have occurred anyhow had there been no cold weather combined with heavy snows. . . . I say this, very conditionally: the Government now being the owner of the coal mines has at best been lackadaisical and amateurish in its approach to this problem; and every issue here in England, of whatsoever kind, can be traced back to original sin—coal. It touches their exports. . . . It touches Britain's exchange position and dollar position. It affects seriously and adversely her political power on the continent of

Europe, and her authority in the Middle East—and, indeed, everywhere throughout the world. If, for example, Britain had 20 million tons of coal to export—Europe would lie in the palm of her hand. The question is more than quantitative; it is qualitative as well. The productivity per man shift is so low . . . that her costs are high; thus affecting the cost of steel and other exports.'' Yet, his abiding faith in the spirit and ultimate good sense of the British people led him to conclude on an optimistic note: "But in spite of this, I am confident that in due course the British will solve their difficulties."[7]

At the end of the year, Douglas was to testify before the Senate Foreign Relations Committee on behalf of the interim aid request for Britain, pending Marshall Plan legislation. Despite his continuing criticisms, in private and to both governments, of the effects of nationalization, outmoded methods, and labor productivity on coal production, he spoke sympathetically of the problems in the industry. Tracing their cause to the tremendous war effort and the terrible winter, he expressed faith in the Labour government's determination to overcome the difficulties. This evidence of good will and a desire to put the best public light on their problems was much appreciated by the Foreign Office. The press echoed the government's gratitude for his remarks. "It is an impressive testimonial. This nation is greatly obliged to him," wrote the *Daily Mirror*.[8]

The dramatic effects of the awful winter of 1946–47 on industry, agriculture, and commerce, coming so soon after the exactions of the war years, had also exacerbated Britain's already acute financial crisis. The ending of lend-lease in August, 1945, had come as a serious blow to Great Britain, leaving her deeply in debt, with her foreign resources and reserves depleted. The American loan of $3.75 billion included a proviso that Britain allow free convertibility of sterling to dollars by July 15, 1947. This would, of course, end the system of imperial preference, which had inhibited trade between countries of the sterling area and the United States. By the time Douglas arrived at his post, evidence was accumulating that the loan was being drawn down much more rapidly than had been anticipated and that the implementation of the convertibility clause could bring financial disaster. The slow European recovery and especially the sharp inflation in America, Britain's chief source of imports, together with the impact of the winter weather and subsequent fuel crisis, were leading to the expenditure of dollars at an alarming rate. The advent of convertibility would accelerate the drain, as the remainder of the loan would go right through London to her creditors in the Commonwealth and sterling area, unless satisfactory arrangements could be made to cancel or defer payment on the balances they held.[9]

When Chancellor of the Exchequer Hugh Dalton first discussed these growing financial problems at "considerable length" with Douglas on May 12, the ambassador expressed doubt that the condition was as serious as outlined. But he asked Dalton to submit a more detailed account of the Treasury estimates. Conversations a week later with Treasury officials apparently convinced Douglas of the validity of Dalton's apprehensions. Writing to Clayton, now under secretary of state for economic affairs, he asserted: "While dollars have been drawn down in very substantial amounts and the rate of drawing on the line of credit is far in excess of any that was anticipated we here cannot find out how these dollars have been used; nor can we determine how they propose to use dollars and the rate at which they contemplate drawing on the line of credit in the future."[10]

By June 18, the British were able to present a fairly detailed accounting of their financial position since the loan agreement and its relation to the world dollar shortage. The situation in 1946 had, in fact, been better than expected, but subsequently the drain upon their resources had rapidly accelerated. They had now used over half of the United States and Canadian credits, which were expected to tide them over until 1949–50, when an equilibrium in balance of payments had been anticipated. This drain had been the result of the fuel and raw-material crisis during the winter and of unfavorable developments in the world economy, particularly the 40 percent increase in American wholesale prices since the loan negotiations. Inflation in the United States had already reduced the buying power of the loan by some $1 billion. Meantime, in aid of world recovery, they had contributed the equivalent of $15 billion in loans and gifts to relief and rehabilitation, with few results so far evident. Their loss of $100 million a month in the second half of 1946 had swelled to over $300 million in April and May, 1947.

These conditions prevented Britain from earning enough dollars from the rest of the world to finance the growing deficit with the United States and Canada. More alarmingly, the imminent implementation of the convertibility pledge would aggravate the problem drastically, for countries short of dollars would attempt to earn sterling from Britain to convert to dollars and thus pass their dollar difficulties on to England. The vital needs of countries holding sterling balances in Europe, but especially in the Commonwealth and colonies, would force them to reduce their sterling balances and constitute a direct drain on British dollars. The world dollar shortage was acute. Britain had to earn dollars to finance her American trade. "If there are not enough dollars in the world to do this, our position becomes critical. Either we are forced into import restrictions on a scale which would . . . [reduce our people's subsistence below] even their present threadbare standards, or we are compelled to abandon our whole concept of multilateral trading and seek to eke out a painful existence on the best terms of bilateral trade which we can secure. Neither of these prospects is tolerable to us." This gloomy appraisal reached Washington two weeks after the secretary of state's memorable speech at Harvard which launched the Marshall Plan. By that time, the plight of Britain was recognized as part of the larger European picture.[11]

In the event, convertibility, inaugurated on July 15, proved to generate the dollar crisis anticipated. By July 25, Douglas was reporting that the British situation was "critical," and that "we run the risk of losing most of Western Europe if the crisis here develops as it seems almost certain to develop." This dispatch was closely followed by an aide-mémoire to Marshall from Chargé d'Affaires Sir John Balfour in Washington, pointing out that the situation was so precarious that any results from the anticipated Marshall Plan might well not come in time to meet Britain's special difficulties. On August 1 Marshall observed to Truman that "the possible developments are most disturbing." Conversations to deal with the critical situation took place in Washington between Secretary of the Treasury Snyder and Sir Wilfred Eady, deputy governor of the Bank of England, on August 18–23, during which the British Treasury suspended sterling convertibility and voluntarily agreed to make no further withdrawals against the American line of credit, which had dwindled to $400 million. This balance was later released, in early December, in recognition of the efforts of the British government to reach bilateral agreements with sterling countries concerning convertibility and of the continuing decline in London of gold and dollar resources.[12]

Although Douglas was gravely concerned that failure to find temporary relief for Britain would jeopardize her role as an effective partner in the leadership of world affairs, he readily admitted that much of the difficulty lay in the failure to "come to grips with their coal problem and other issues." In Washington, where concern was no less acute, opinions were less charitable. In cables to Marshall at the Inter-American Conference in Brazil, Robert Lovett noted: "It begins to appear that Churchill's charge that the loan was largely 'frittered away' is not far off mark." A few days later, he added that the "British must show far more managerial competence and more flexibility in their control measures than heretofore exhibited if they are to operate within the broad terms and purposes of the loan agreement." Treasury Secretary John Snyder's comments were more acid. In a cabinet meeting of August 29, he remarked that: "The crux of the whole matter is that men will only work for incentives, and the British are not producing the incentives, except in the form of dog races, soccer matches and horse racing."[13]

Much has been said and written about the origins of the Marshall Plan and, more specifically, the genesis of the secretary of state's epoch-making address at the Harvard Commencement on June 5, 1947. Among the considerations that contributed to Marshall's decision to speak were the deterioration of the balance-of-payments situation; congressional dissatisfaction with the piecemeal approach to foreign aid, represented by the program for Greece and Turkey; the general economic crisis in Western Europe, exacerbated by the failure to reach agreement in the Moscow Foreign Ministers' Conference on German policy; and Clayton's reports in March and May, emphasizing the hitherto underestimated destruction to the European economy by the war. Input also included reports of the State-War-Navy Coordinating Committee and of George Kennan's Policy Planning Staff. Dean Acheson was responsible for initiating the SWNCC study and enunciated a sort of preview of the plan in his speech to the Delta Council in Cleveland, Mississippi, on May 8, which was much more widely noted in the European than in the American press. Douglas's contribution was at best indirect. His dispatches detailing the deterioration of economic and financial conditions in Europe, specifically in Britain, and implying that the United States would have to act to stem the tide were, however, certainly influential in the reports that were prepared for Marshall.

All of these events and position papers certainly entered into Marshall's decision to speak—which was his own. As to his expectations of its consequences, opinions again differ. The often-heard claim that he had no plan and was vague about the potential of his remarks was challenged by State Department counselor Charles Bohlen, who wrote the original draft and later asserted that Marshall was well aware of what he was saying, carefully not becoming more explicit for fear of alarming the American people about the prospect of some sort of giveaway program and, specifically, to encourage the initiative from Europe. No doubt for the same reasons, there was no background briefing to the press or notice beforehand to European governments or American missions abroad.[14]

As early as May 22, Acheson had, however, hinted to Sir John Balfour, minister at the Washington embassy, that some sort of broad recovery plan for Europe might soon be enunciated. The implications of this calculated leak were weighed by the ambassador, Lord Inverchapel, and his staff at the embassy, and an estimate of its significance was sent to Sir Nevile Butler, head of the North American Department. According to Balfour, the letter reached the Foreign Office the day of Marshall's speech. On May 30, Walter Lippmann, whose access to high places was well known, also confided to Balfour that a plan for "continental rehabilitation" was under consideration and that very probably Douglas would be appointed "a species of diplomatic theater Commander in Europe" to spare Marshall and the department "the difficult task of trying to fit reports from individual Missions into a continental pattern." Lippmann, according to Balfour's second letter to Butler of May 31, had "harped" on the need for a continental, not a "piece-meal" approach. F. B. A. Rundall minuted that dispatch: "it would be greatly to our interest" to have Douglas as coordinator. Butler added that the information tended "to confirm something that I believe the [British] S[ecretary] of S[tate] is already expecting." In his almost illegible scrawl, Bevin confirmed Butler's supposition. Later, when in fact Douglas was offered a similar position, he declined, opting to remain at his London post.[15]

The story of Bevin's alacrity in arranging a meeting with French Foreign Minister Georges Bidault, for June 17, in Paris is well known. On learning of Marshall's remarks via the BBC, he acted, without seeking further information either from Marshall or from the American Mission in London. On June 11, in a conversation with Minister of State Hector McNeil, Paul Porter of Douglas's staff (the ambassador had left that morning for a five-day visit to Germany) admitted that, while the embassy had been forwarding information to be used toward some such an end, apparently Marshall had decided to speak earlier than anticipated. When asked if "he had any precise ideas as to what kind of help Marshall was really thinking of," Porter responded that it appeared to be "a kind of new installment of U.N.R.R.A." As to who should initiate action, Porter was emphatic: "he said that they had all along considered that no one else but us [Great Britain] could do it." By this time, the embassy was, of course, aware of Bevin's communication with Bidault. If Douglas had been taken unawares, he wasted no time in following up on Bevin's action by calling at the French embassy to impress upon Ambassador René Massigli the importance of General Marshall's message. "He feared . . ." Massigli later recalled, "that France might allow to slip away the opportunity to influence, in an important way, the application of the principles enunciated." His apprehensions proved unjustified.[16]

The conversations between Bevin and Bidault on June 17–18 went well, and the two foreign ministers issued an invitation to Foreign Minister Molotov to meet with them at an early date. Although both men agreed to avoid any impression that this was a Western endeavor, American Ambassador Jefferson Caffery reported they "hoped that the Soviets will refuse to cooperate and that in any event they will be prepared 'to go ahead full steam even if the Soviets refuse to do so.' "[17]

Meantime, in Washington, as early as the morning of June 5, preparations had begun on a memorandum for the guidance of Clayton, who was to be sent to Europe for discussions "on the question of further American aid." At Marshall's suggestion, an early draft was revised to give less attention to "American cash" and more to the need for "European organization, however elementary, to facilitate the European states in helping themselves and in making it possible for American aid to be more effective." Armed with this document, Clayton and Douglas carried on conversations in London on June 24–26 with Prime Minister Attlee, Bevin, Dalton, Treasury officials, and representatives of the ministries of Food and of Fuel. Although a good deal of the discussion revolved around Britain's accelerating dollar crisis and the dangers of convertibility, the principal subject was the future development of the Marshall Plan and, specifically, Britain's role in its implementation.

Bevin made two points: He felt Britain was in a different position than the Continent because of her empire and, therefore, hoped to play a partnership role in the American economic solution. He had acted rapidly on Marshall's initiative "without asking questions" because he believed that "it was the quickest way to break down the iron curtain"—Russia's satellites could not resist the allure of assistance toward recovery. He admitted, however, that Dalton's concern about financial resources injected a "caveat" into his plans for a British contribution. Clayton set the tone of the continuing discussions by questioning the distinction between Britain's and Europe's plight and London's ability to share in a financial partnership. The United States could see no justification for a separate status. Furthermore, to bring in the U.K. as a partner would violate the principle that no piecemeal approach be undertaken. As to Russia's Eastern European clients, he expressed reserved confidence in Bevin's assessment.

Bevin returned to the question of why the U.K.'s problems should be lumped together with those of Europe. "We, as the British Empire," could contribute to the economic recovery of Europe. To participate in the program without doing anything would destroy the "little bit of dignity we have left." Clayton was unmoved by the plea. Apparently convinced that this argument was at a dead end, the British asked him to outline present United States thinking on the Marshall program. Clayton responded that he saw several phases in its development: Europe should first explain why they had not made more progress with the help they had already received; second, elaborate in rather specific terms what they had in mind to help themselves individually and collectively; and third, define what assistance they expected from the United States and how long it should continue. He emphasized that it would not be an easy task to sell such a program in the United States. It must be a firm minimal plan, including integration of resources, to convince the Congress. Douglas added that, along with integration, there must be a commitment at least in principle to constructive fiscal policies.

Dalton acidly summed up his impressions of the meetings, giving Douglas good marks. "There has [sic] been too many foreigners in London lately. Mr. Clayton—Doctrinaire Willie, and slightly nervous in manner—with Mr. Douglas, for whom I have an increasing affection and respect, have spent quite a lot of hours with the P.M., Foreign Secretary, myself and P. [President] B. [Board] T. [of Trade]. It is surprising how many hours one can spend with people and yet reach no sharply outlined conclusions. C[layton] has no plan, but we have tried to help him both by giving him large quantities of statistics . . . and by impressing on him that we are something more than just a bit of Europe." Lovett cabled his satisfaction after reading the memoranda of the conversations. In the course of his comment, he indicated his agreement with Douglas "on the importance of steps to straighten out financial chaos, but think that the Brit[ish] are probably right in thinking that we should not press too hard on this from this end." As to timing, he hoped that if Europe had a plan by September 1, there was a possibility of congressional hearings in the fall and approval soon after the first of the year. "This is optimistic," he admitted.[18]

On the evening of the last day of the meetings, Douglas spoke to the American Chamber of Commerce in London. Anticipating the need to make reference to the still nebulous Marshall proposal—not to do so "would be like Hamlet without Hamlet"—he had cabled the secretary for "any advice as to what I might prudently say." Marshall's reply was four pages long, and Douglas incorporated it, with a few stylistic changes, into his address.

Douglas was "enormously encouraged" by the "statesmanlike efforts" which had been made to deal "with the central problem of European reconstruction" and with the early steps taken "in stimulating European initiative and in attracting popular European response." "Some of the major ingredients of peaceful reconstruction have been assembled." It was now clearly recognized that the endeavor would "require large scale assistance from the United States, in terms of both money and materials, over a period of several years." Truman had already appointed three committees to assess the ability of the United States to furnish aid. Meantime, a "second ingredient . . . has been assembled" through the expeditious efforts of Bevin, "an enthusiastic European initiative for coordinated European reconstruction." Any plan "will be unavailing," however, unless it is based on "broad and constructive . . . collaboration . . . evolved by Europeans themselves to make full and integrated use of Europe's resources and its own powers of recovery. . . . The third ingredient . . . is the decision of the Soviet Union to join in the consultations. . . . Given sincere and wholehearted Soviet cooperation the task will be much easier and success far more assured."

But, he continued, in words obviously aimed at the Soviet Union and European Communist parties, other steps were also necessary—"as essential as mortar, nails and good weather are to the building of a house—and these have been in notable short supply of late. . . . [U]nilateral political acts, both by states or by groups within states" must cease. There must be an end also to "propaganda both within the states and among the states, that is designed to arouse fear and hatred, propaganda that preaches the inevitability of war and the decline and disappearance of certain types of economic systems." It was very soon to become clear that these warnings were well taken. In fact, both Department of State counselor Charles E. Bohlen and Policy Planning Staff head George F. Kennan had advised Marshall to include the Soviet Union in his initiative for the sake of world opinion. But both indicated Soviet acceptance might seriously endanger the plan in Congress, and predicted—indeed, probably hoped—Moscow would reject it.[19]

From June 27 to July 2, Soviet Foreign Minister Molotov met with Bevin and Bidault in Paris. The comment of Ambassador Walter Bedell Smith in Moscow before the minister's departure proved correct: "I feel sure," he cabled to Marshall on June 23, "that this participation will be for destructive rather than constructive purposes." Molotov's opening remark to Bidault on his arrival in Paris the evening of the 26th set the tone of the meetings: what had the French foreign minister and Bevin "done behind his back"?[20]

In the abrasive discussions that followed, Molotov was immovable in his position that any inquiry into the resources of the European nations would be a violation of sovereignty, that each nation should make its own study and proposal and these should then be pooled and transmitted to the United States. In vain, Bevin and Bidault argued that this approach ran directly counter to the plan outlined by Marshall. While Ambassador Jefferson Caffery in Paris was reporting these fruitless exchanges directly to Washington, Bevin was sending his daily impressions to Douglas in London for transmittal to Marshall. On July 1, the day before Molotov formally refused to participate in any combined program, Bevin plaintively cabled Douglas: "I have done my best to bridge the difference with the Russians, but it seems to be fundamental and irreconcilable. . . . Molotov's attitude throughout has been cynical, and he certainly has a finger in the uneasy political pie in this country"—a reference to Soviet influence on the strong Communist party in France.[21]

The evening of his return, Bevin had a long conversation with Douglas. Concerned over the ability of the United States to act in time to save a disintegrating Europe, he raised the possibility that the Soviets might torpedo participation not only by their satellites, but by Western countries in exposed positions, such as Norway and Sweden, and even Italy with its strong Communist party. No doubt he was encouraged by the message from Marshall of the same day to him and to Bidault, indicating the secretary's "complete understanding [of] the course of your patient efforts to find agreement with the Soviet Government. . . . At least the Soviet attitude in these questions has been clarified. . . . We here are prepared to do all in our power to support any genuine and constructive efforts toward the restoration of economic health and prosperity in the countries of Europe."[22]

Undeterred by the Soviet rebuff, Great Britain and France issued invitations to all European countries, except Spain, to meet in Paris on July 12. Seventeen states accepted, the U.S.S.R. having vetoed the participation of its satellites. Czechoslovakia, hungry for aid, braved the wrath of its neighbor and responded affirmatively, only to be humiliatingly ordered by Moscow to retract its acceptance. Thus, sixteen nations assembled in Paris, and Bevin was elected chairman. In the first few days, the conference established a Committee on European Economic Cooperation (CEEC), in fact a committee of the whole, a device that permitted closed sessions.[23]

During the first two weeks of the conference, most of the work was conducted by technical committees collecting the required statistics and information. The brilliant economist Sir Oliver Franks was persuaded to leave his post as provost of Queen's College, Oxford, to become Bevin's deputy as chairman of the CEEC. By July 29, he had identified, to the satisfaction of Clayton, the three basic objectives of the conference: a rapid increase in European production of basic commodities, financial stability in balance of payments and internal fiscal policies, and freer trade movements in the European community. He raised two questions that were soon to become central to the progress of the deliberations and deeply involve Douglas in the work of the conference: the relation of German production to European recovery and the degree of American input in the preparation of the report.[24]

The relaxation by the Potsdam Agreement of the rigid financial and economic restrictions of JCS 1067 had led, after tortuous negotiations and an unrealistic assumption that Germany would be an economic unit, to the adoption in 1946 by the Allied Control Council of a Plan for Reparations and the Level of Post-War Industry. This economic program was designed to prevent any German potential for rearmament, develop peaceful industries sufficient to maintain a living standard no higher than those of her neighbors, and provide for reparations. But tension with the Soviet Union (and, less publicly, the obstructionism of the French) had prompted General Clay to halt reparations deliveries to Russia from the American Zone. Further failures to effect unified economic and political policies with their allies persuaded the United States and Great Britain to carry out an economic fusion of their occupation areas into what became known as Bizonia.

Returning from the April, 1947, Moscow Conference, Marshall, thoroughly disillusioned by Soviet intransigence, stopped at Berlin, reviewed with Clay the agreement with Bevin, and instructed Clay "to proceed vigorously with the strengthening of the bizonal organization . . . and to expedite upward the revision of the level of industry to insure the self-sufficiency of the area." Accordingly, Clay and Sir Brian Robertson, his British Zone counterpart, turned to a reorganization of their areas and to the drafting of a higher level-of-industry plan. In the process, a latent economic and political difference came to the fore over British support for the socialization of German industrial enterprises. Up to this point, the State Department had taken a neutral stand on the question. But pressure from the service departments, the Eightieth Congress, and influential political and financial figures persuaded Marshall that socialization was at best untimely. He was also impressed by George Kennan's Policy Planning Staff reports of May 23 and June 2, which emphasized the need for coal not only for German revitalization but for the rehabilitation of Europe. In mid-June, Douglas warned that the British would probably exert considerable pressure for their socialization plan. Clay urged upon Robertson a compromise in the form of German trustees to administer the mines under the control of the combined British and American authorities.[25]

Clayton and Douglas, in their conversations in London with cabinet members and Treasury officials, on June 24–26, made clear that the urgency of increasing German production precluded "experimentation" with the control of the mines. Before learning of British reaction to their remarks and despite Clay's assurance that Robertson and presumably London would reluctantly go along with the trusteeship concept, the State Department called for a coal conference in Washington. It met from mid-August to mid-September and led to the acceptance by both governments of the trusteeship plan, leaving the fate of socialization to the future decision of the Germans.

Throughout this period, Douglas's most important role was in guiding the new level-of-industry plan to acceptance by the reluctant French; it had been agreed upon by Clay and Robertson by July 12, and they proposed to publish it on July 16.[26]

The direction if not the details of the new plan leaked to the French sometime before its projected publication, and they were thoroughly alarmed at its implications. From the beginning of the occupation, they had been fearful of any German resurgence and desirous of becoming the postwar industrial center of Europe. Beset with threats from the de Gaullist right and the Communist left, the insecure French government had been as difficult to deal with as the Soviet Union on questions of German political or economic unity. On July 11, Clayton was subjected to a diatribe from Bidault on the unacceptability of any change in the 1946 level-of-industry agreement that would decrease German coal for export to France by increasing German steel production. In fact, Bidault argued, dismantling should be accelerated and France's share of reparations increased. If, however, Washington and London insisted upon a revision, it should be implemented without an announcement, which would endanger the present French government and doom the European recovery conference scheduled to assemble in Paris the next day. Clayton's dispatch on this conversation was closely followed by an aide-mémoire from the British, advising delay in publication of the plan in view of French representations to them, and by a letter from Bidault to Marshall, indicating that the French government "would be placed in an unexpected and untenable situation if the decisions which are now contemplated were confirmed."[27]

The State Department decided that the French must be placated in order to protect the government internally and to avoid jeopardizing the Paris Conference. The British cabinet reluctantly agreed to hold the plan in abeyance until tripartite talks could take place in London. Douglas was delegated to represent the United States in those talks.[28]

He received explicit instructions from Marshall underlining the delicacy of the forthcoming negotiations. "Whereas the French should be accorded every opportunity to make a full statement . . . [you] should make it clear that in the absence of a fusion of the French zone with the US and UK zones, the US and the UK are responsible for and will take final decisions on all matters regarding the bizonal areas." Douglas was to resist any modification of the Clay-Robertson agreement unless its implementation threatened the "success of the European economic plan or . . . democracy in France," in which case he was to request further instructions. He was not to discuss the resumption of reparations or subsequent plans for the reactivization of German industry or the disposition of the Saar. Any attempt by the French to raise the question of the management of the Ruhr as a "condition" for their acceptance of the agreement should be quashed by pointing out "that 'acceptance' is not involved"—such a broad issue could only be discussed "at or after the November CFM meeting." At the end of the talks a communiqué should be issued, which "will certainly be important from the point of view of the French."[29]

In short, the tripartite conference was to be a face-saving device for the French government, permitting it to accept the level-of-industry agreement after "consultation" and an opportunity to voice its objections and fears. This, in turn, would remove a roadblock to continued French participation in the CEEC and allow for a German contribution to European recovery.

To ensure this outcome, Douglas, Caffery, and Clayton carried on preparatory conversations with Bidault in Paris from August 12 to 19. As expected, Bidault demanded that the Ruhr industry "never again be used for military purposes against France," the production of the Ruhr never be "exclusively" in German hands, and the new level-of-industry plan be withheld until the foreign ministers' meeting in late fall. Moving back and forth between Paris and London, Douglas attempted, with his colleagues, to find some formula that would assuage French fears. Both Lovett and Bevin stood firm: the future of the Ruhr could not stand in the way of the discussions in London and the announcement of the level-of-industry plan. The French, Lovett cabled the negotiators, must agree to proceed "without delay." To Douglas, Bevin confirmed "his belief that we should not, either for the purpose of obtaining acquiescence on the level of industry or for the purpose of satisfying, at the Paris Conference, French apprehensions, pay any price whatsoever except to indicate future sympathetic consideration of the [Ruhr] question."[30]

On August 19, the three Americans informed Bidault bluntly that they had instructions to discontinue discussions on the Ruhr question. In the face of the American stand, the foreign minister gave in. But he warned that the French people would consider the level-of-industry announcement "hope for the Germans and fear for the French."[31]

Meantime, although Marshall and the new secretary of war, Kenneth C. Royall, had been able to resolve their initial conflict over the decision to delay the level-of-industry agreement pending some genuflection to the French, Clay was furious at the postponement. He threatened resignation over State Department interference with the agreement and the kowtowing to French intransigence. Further communications, plus a personal message from Eisenhower as chief of staff— "please remember that now abide Faith, Hope and Charity, these three, and greater than any is a sense of humor"—temporarily dissuaded Clay from any precipitate action. But his opposition to the tripartite talks continued, and his anger was rekindled by instructions to attend the conference as advisor to Douglas. Again he threatened to resign. This time, Murphy warned Marshall, he appeared quite serious. The secretary replied that the department considered Clay's presence "important," and Royall personally "requested" the general to attend. Douglas added his voice to the appeal. Reluctantly Clay complied, accompanied by Murphy.

Clay's distress was occasioned not only by the delay but also, if not more, by State Department interference in his bailiwick and the prominence of Douglas's role in the affair. "I am not willing to accept the responsibility for military government in Germany with operation decisions being made elsewhere." "I will admit," he confided to Major General William Draper in Washington, soon to be appointed assistant secretary of war, "that it is rather humiliating to military government to send its chief representative to London as an advisor to the American representative in discussing the level of industry in Germany for which he has been responsible for two and one-half years. . . . I did not sign up to work for Lew Douglas as much as I like him personally." Four days later, in another transatlantic conversation with Draper, he grumbled: "Lew Douglas likes to run with [the] ball in [an] open field." At the end of the Level of Industry Conference, Clay was constrained to admit that "Douglas handled the matter well," but added: "However, he was helped materially by firm State Department policy instructions for which we are grateful."[32]

The Tripartite Conference of August 22–27 in London was, in essence, a formal replay of the earlier conversations in Paris. Douglas's opening statement was a masterly combination of conciliation and firmness. "I should like to make it unmistakably clear that the Governments of the United States and the United Kingdom are particularly sensitive to the concern of France who three times within the course of 75 years has been invaded by a powerful neighbor." But he also firmly stated, seconded by the British representative Sir Thomas Gilmour Jenkins, joint permanent under secretary of state for German affairs, that "while glad to have French views, in [the] absence of French adherence to bizonal fusion [the] ultimate responsibility for decisions must rest with [the] US and [the] UK."

On August 25, Ambassador Massigli, the principal French delegate, complained privately to British Assistant Under Secretary of State Roger Makins about the "rigid and unbending attitude of the American delegation. He could not understand the position of Mr. Douglas." Attempting to mollify the ambassador, Makins explained that Douglas was much preoccupied with the Marshall Plan Conference and that "any hint that the British and French Governments were not willing to use the productive capacity of the Ruhr to its full extent would prejudice the position with Congress and with the United States [on the Marshall Plan]." Massigli hinted darkly that the American stand might prejudice the Paris Conference "from quite another point of view"—presumably a veiled threat of French governmental collapse or intransigence. On August 28, a final communiqué was issued that papered over the unresolved issues but gave the French the public façade necessary to protect their domestic political position and permitted the British and Americans to publish the new level-of-industry plans and concentrate on the Marshall Plan negotiations. Privately, the French had been assured of further discussions concerning the disposition of the Saar, the control of the Ruhr, and their fusion with the Bizone. Lovett cabled his gratification to Douglas for his "handling" of the discussions. "In view of all the difficulties of the situation you made far greater progress toward an understanding than we had anticipated. The War Department wishes to join us in congratulating you."[33]

20

Marshall Plan Missionary

WHILE THE THREATENED IMPASSE WITH THE FRENCH was building up to the tripartite talks, Douglas continued to be active in both London and Paris, pressuring, explicating, and assisting in the work of the CEEC. His official conversations at Whitehall, together with Clayton, on July 24–26, had followed a warning to Bevin several days earlier, "merely speaking as a personal friend," that he would have difficulty justifying "further direct or indirect expenditure of American dollars to support a country which is unable effectively to manage the most important industry it has so far nationalized"—coal mining. He expected to testify before Congress on behalf of any aid program. While he could make a case for nationalization because of the "dilapidated" state of the industry, he feared he would find it difficult to explain its unsatisfactory production.

Soon after the Clayton visit, Hugh Dalton wrote in his diary that both the Foreign Secretary and the Prime Minister were annoyed at Douglas's somewhat irregular missionary work at dinners in the House of Commons, where he was disabusing members of both parties of any hope that Congress could or would act on any recovery program before the following March. According to Dalton, he was also passing the word, already emphasized to Bevin, that there was "no chance then of their [Congress] doing anything special for the U.K. as distinct from Western Europe," and that if Britain should proceed toward socialization of the Ruhr mines "we [Britain] should be bankrupt in two months and should be handing it all over" to the Americans. Attlee had suggested to the chancellor that perhaps Douglas "had had too much to drink. 'In vino veritas!' " That appears unlikely.[1]

But the government was beginning to recognize Douglas's proclivity on occasion to go beyond his brief. It proved to be at times vexatious to Bevin, who was quick-tempered and subject to passing moments of suspicion. But, in the long run, what might have been an ambassadorial weakness under other circumstances proved an element of strength in relations with Bevin, to whom Douglas spoke directly with equal candor and bluntness. By the time Sir Roderick Barclay became principal private secretary to Bevin early in 1949, he observed between the two men an unprecedented degree of forthrightness and confidence. Bevin responded in kind to Douglas's outspokenness and expressions of personal opinion, even aggressiveness. It was an important ingredient in the growth of their mutual regard and friendship and Douglas's success as an ambassador.[2]

In Paris, Douglas met on August 4–6 with Clayton, Caffery, Murphy, and Paul H. Nitze, who had brought from the State Department the latest memorandum on the Marshall Plan of the Policy Planning Staff. The conferees dealt with the obvious reluctance of the CEEC delegates to face up to a "bold constructive program." Their home governments, for political reasons, shied away from taking the "necessary specific measures" of cooperation. The time had arrived, the Americans recommended to Washington, to extend the "friendly aid" referred to in Marshall's Harvard speech in drafting an acceptable plan.[3]

Lovett responded positively, with the reservation that any advice tendered the CEEC should not be construed as a commitment to any plan nor expose the United States to a charge of dictation. More precise instructions followed, emphasizing principles rather than detailed instructions. The CEEC delegates might be told that a helpful approach would be to begin with the assumption that no outside support was forthcoming and that they must attempt to "work out an acceptable economic future [from] . . . their own resources . . . by the most strenuous individual and collective effort." Then only should they "undertake to define the gaps" which the United States might fill.[4]

Back in London, preparing for the tripartite meeting on Germany, Douglas received another cable from Lovett, who reiterated his concern that the Paris Conference was "Merely adding up separate estimates [which] would obviously result in [an] unacceptable program." Douglas agreed. The time had come to take a more active role. "To hold ourselves aloof from such give-and-take cannot help but encourage other participants to consider that their national plans and requirements should be accepted without examination or discussion. While we perhaps need not take the lead, neither should we hang back." George Kennan and Colonel Charles H. Bonesteel (on assignment to the State Department) were dispatched to Paris to aid in persuading the European delegates "promptly" that "the present plan" near completion "is not acceptable." Clayton had already informed Sir Oliver Franks that the approximately $29 billion figure emerging from the conference was "out of the question." Meanwhile, Lovett stressed the need to have German production and export integrated into the proposal. The Americans were to review the conference's draft plan, not only "to seek explanations and clarifications," but to "guide both content and conclusions." The deadline of September 1 for transmittal to Washington was imminent. With the conclusion of the level of industry meeting, Douglas, on August 28, hastened to join his colleagues in Paris.[5]

The month following, until the delayed report by the CEEC was accepted by the plenary session, on September 22, was a hectic period of active intervention by the Americans. Clayton continued to be the principal negotiator in the triumvirate. He was stern and somewhat forbidding, extremely well-informed on the technicalities and with the best of intentions, but intolerant of what he considered wrong thinking and often difficult in dealing with the Europeans. On the other hand, Douglas was not only appreciative of the positions and problems of the European countries, but, perhaps because of his previous experience, the most sensitive to congressional and public reactions in the United States. While firmly upholding the American point of view and capable of being obstinate when he considered it necessary, he was always receptive to the preoccupations and anxieties of the delegates and reassuring in private contacts. These attributes were of incalculable importance in reaching a satisfactory resolution of differences. Usually deferring to Clayton in the public discussions, he was frequently a moderating influence on him in private. In the words of Lovett, Douglas was "the friendly oil which lubricated the whole affair over there." Indeed, Franks later went so far as to suggest that there might well have been a complete impasse in the negotiations without his presence.[6]

As a consequence of direct American intervention in the preparation of the CEEC plan, the date of the final report was postponed to September 15. Meantime, George Kennan had returned to Washington, sobered by the economic conditions he had encountered in Europe. He counseled the department not to expect, under such circumstances and with jealously guarded national sovereignties, any "bold or original approach to Europe's problems." Rather, after perhaps some scaling down, the report should be accepted as a basis for further discussion and reduction. In other words, the United States would "listen to all that the Europeans had to say, but in the end we would not *ask* them, we would just *tell* them what they would get." He also suggested that consideration be given to some sort of interim aid to get the desperate continent through the winter. On September 10, Marshall and Truman approved a press release from the department, suggesting the possibility that interim aid would be required.[7]

On September 7, Lovett dispatched a circular telegram to American representatives accredited to all the participating governments, instructing them to inform the foreign or prime ministers that the progress of the plan proposed for approval September 15 was unsatisfactory and would encounter great criticism in the United States. The CEEC was advised to delay final action for another ten days to allow time to revise the report along the lines suggested. Clayton, Douglas, and Caffery were directed to use their influence to obtain at least a partial revision. But, anticipating that the request would still be unsatisfactory and publication nevertheless necessary, the department recommended that the proposal be clearly identified as preliminary, "intended as [a] basis for further discussions" to be held in Washington.[8]

Accordingly, Douglas called on Bevin, Roger Makins, and Sir Edmund Hall-Patch, head of the British delegation to the CEEC. He was armed also with a request from Marshall that he raise the possibility of discussing the bizonal economic program at the CEEC, as a contribution to European recovery. The reaction to his remarks was violent. Douglas's report to the department was considerably toned down from Bevin's account of the meeting to Inverchapel. Bevin was angered and surprised when informed by Douglas that all the governments had been circularized, stating flatly that the maneuver was "well calculated to throw the whole conference into disorder and to compromise the program that had been made. . . . I was not prepared to reopen the whole business." Impressed with

Bevin's reaction, Douglas did not even raise the question of a bizonal contribution.[9]

In Paris, he found the French equally disturbed at the extreme pressure for further revision and delay, Bidault characterizing Lovett's action as "intolerable." Yet, on September 11 and 12, the triumvirate, meeting with the conference executive committee in heated debate, prevailed. At Douglas's urging, the explosive German question was not mentioned. The session to accept the final report was to be delayed until September 22. Minimal modifications would be attempted, and the document would not be labeled a final report. In London, Bevin had meantime received confirmation from Inverchapel of the department's firm position. But on Douglas's return to London the following day, the foreign secretary made clear his chagrin at the decision. He was deeply disturbed by the "public consequences" of the previous days' discussions and the decision in Paris. He feared the public would conclude the conference had been unsatisfactory and that European hopes would be undermined, consequences detrimental to the final outcome. Could Douglas or Marshall make a reassuring public statement? Lovett indicated that no useful purpose would be served by an official release, but authorized the ambassador to comment informally in London if it seemed appropriate. Douglas concluded it was unnecessary. The revised report was approved by the conference on September 22.[10]

During these last days of the European meetings, a separate but related problem was explored with the British. It raised the level of Bevin's unhappiness over American pressure. From September 21 to 23 in London, Clayton and Douglas met with Franks concerning the work of the CEEC committees during the forthcoming conference in Washington. They also discussed with Harold Wilson from the Board of Trade, Sir Stafford Cripps, and then Bevin, the British position at the ongoing International Trade Organization conference in Geneva. There were serious difficulties in reaching agreement on the elimination of Commonwealth trade preferences. The British proposals were unsatisfactory to the American negotiators. Cripps and Wilson stood firm. Appealing to Bevin, Clayton hinted at the possible effect of Whitehall's intransigence on Marshall Plan aid to Great Britain. But Douglas, Bevin angrily reported to Inverchapel, "underlined this possibility and said that it might well mean that Great Britain would be left out of any help given under the Marshall offer." Bevin was not impressed by the argument, replying that the Paris Conference was the result of his initiative and that if the United States refused aid because of the Geneva negotiations, "that was their problem." If the Marshall Plan broke down, the United States "would suffer as much as anyone."

Bevin discussed the matter with the cabinet, and Cripps wrote Clayton that the government had gone as far as it could go. Douglas returned the letter to Bevin, suggesting a more conciliatory reply. The Foreign Office refused. The outcome was anticlimactic. Following a pro forma aide-mémoire to London from the State Department deploring the breakdown of negotiations on the question, Douglas met with Bevin on November 1, and agreed, in essence, to drop the issue.[11]

Perhaps that episode, the earlier contretemps with Bevin over the delay in the CEEC report, and the recent warning to the foreign minister that further nationalization of industry or failure to "come to grips with the coal problem" would also seriously endanger Marshall aid prompted an indiscreet letter from Douglas to his old chief at American Cyanamid, William B. Bell. "I can tell you confidentially," he wrote, ". . . that the British Government on the whole is incompetent, blundering and inept." But, he added, softening the charge, "I confidentially believe [this] is but a relatively temporary phase in the postwar life of a tired nation."[12]

Douglas had requested permission to return to Washington briefly for consultation on the results of the Paris Conference and on other developments that had taken place since March. He had often found it difficult from a distance to give a complete picture of events in England and Europe—the "subtleties and nuances" were frequently lost in transit. Accompanied by Clayton, he sailed on the *Queen Elizabeth,* arriving in New York on October 1. Stepping off the *Queen,* he attempted to prepare America for coming decisions. "Most people," he stated to the press, "miscalculated and underestimated the amount of destruction caused by the war in Europe." The damage was "moral, political and economical," as well as physical. The United States must take the lead in rehabilitating those nations as quickly as possible.[13]

In Washington Douglas and Clayton began top-level conferences with State Department officials preparatory to the arrival of the CEEC delegations. They also met with members of the interdepartmental Advisory Steering Committee on European Economic Recovery. The group had been appointed in August to coordinate the work of the earlier committees named by the President, to review the Paris report, and to negotiate with the CEEC representatives. Douglas and Clayton were joined by Walter Bedell Smith from Moscow, Robert Murphy, and General Clay. By then the necessity for early congressional action on European aid had been recognized. Before leaving London, Douglas had warned that the worsening political and economic crisis, especially in France and Italy, might not by spring provide "a democratic area upon which to build a complete recovery program." On September 25 Truman had announced that he was writing the chairmen of the Senate and House foreign affairs committees to convene their memberships. Douglas met with the President twice to emphasize the depth of the crisis. In a closed meeting, he and Lovett briefed seventeen key members of Congress, including Senators Alben W. Barkley, Tom Connally, Bourke Hickenlooper, Scott Lucas, and Representatives Walter H. Judd, Christian A. Herter, and Richard M. Nixon, on the progress of the European recovery discussions.[14]

Douglas returned to London but not for long. While in Washington, he had been alerted to the possibility of an early return to help in the presentation to Congress of the European Recovery Program. On October 28, Colonel Bonesteel reminded Lovett of these discussions and recommended that Douglas be recalled: "He will be a tower of strength to carry the day by day testimony . . . and should take a great load from your shoulders." The Senate and House foreign affairs committees were scheduled to meet in joint hearings on November 10, and the President had called for a special session of Congress to consider the need for interim foreign aid. Less than two weeks after Douglas resumed charge of the embassy, he received a telegram from Lovett, requesting that he come back as near November 10 as possible to appear before the committees.[15]

On November 10 and 11, first Marshall and then Lovett testified at length to the committees on the need for an interim aid program for Europe before the long-range Marshall Plan was considered. The second day Douglas was asked by Senator Vandenberg why Britain, a great coal-producing center, had not been able to obviate the need for coal to be shipped to Western Europe by the United States. Douglas emphasized the "failure, or rather indifference, of the old operators, private operators, to maintain underground operations at a high level of efficiency and to invest that amount of capital which is necessary both for underground and surface operations to achieve the greatest practicable productivity of coal." It was, he noted, a "rather squalid history." (It is noteworthy that he did not volunteer his views concerning the effects of nationalization.) Finally, he warned the committees that they should not count on the United Kingdom's contributing coal to Europe during the period of interim aid.

He also began his testimony on the overall need for both long- and short-term aid. America's "vital national interests are deeply concerned with the restoration of the stability of western Europe. If we achieve our purpose we may . . . be able to establish the foundations for a lasting peace, divesting men of the apprehensions and fears which now bedevil them . . . and restore that kind of stability which is inherent in our traditional views of life." As to the need for interim aid, he prophesied that, if action was not taken, "it is not unlikely that by spring, even early spring, it might be too late to enact a longer range European recovery program with reasonable prospects of its success. The next four or five months are likely to, will prove to, be the most critical ones." He then analyzed in some detail the especially desperate French and Italian situations (the British plight was soon to be temporarily relieved by release of the unexpended funds of the 1946 loan).

France, he predicted, would find it impossible "over a period extending further than approximately sixty to seventy-five days, to provide even the meager bread ration and to purchase that amount of coal which is necessary to keep her factories going to prevent unemployment and the appearance of the sort of chaos and confusion, privation which fosters and provokes all sorts of internal disorders." Conditions in Italy were even more alarming. Both countries had been occupied. Not only had their economic life been gravely disrupted, but their political institutions destroyed. "One can, I think, reasonably assume that the developments will be unfortunate, unhappy and perhaps, very profound [if aid was not forthcoming]."

Douglas's testimony certainly promoted favorable action on the request to Congress. Because of his legislative experience and contacts, he was able to carry on intimate talks with key members which were vital to congressional success. Furthermore, he was free to devote full time to allaying the fears and removing the misunderstandings of individual members. His knowledge, the confidence and favor he enjoyed at the Capitol, and, not least, his personal charm in dealing with men of divergent views without incurring enmity constituted a major contribution to the subsequent passage of the Interim Aid Bill and, later, the Marshall Plan itself.[16]

The British press was enthusiastic about his testimony, and particularly his remarks on conditions in the United Kingdom. On November 13, the *Daily Mirror* hailed his statements in an editorial entitled "Man Who Knows." Noting that too many Americans, after a brief visit, returned to America with "a false message, based partly on ignorance, partly on prejudice," it concluded that "what we have long needed is a powerful witness from the other side. At last we have got him." The following day the *News Chronicle,* under the simple heading "Thanks," expressed the appreciation of the British people for his courage in stating the facts. "Mr. Douglas should know [them] because he has taken the trouble to find out— not just from Whitehall but from the homes and workshops of the ordinary citizen. We are deeply grateful to him for the pains he has taken."[17]

Marshall arrived in London on November 21 for a Council of Foreign Ministers meeting. The omens were not encouraging. Although earlier in the year Douglas had entertained some hope that a strengthening of Western Europe might presage a more fruitful meeting in November after the impasse at the Moscow Conference in April, the intervening months had dimmed his expectations. Indeed, both the British and French governments had informed Washington of their pessimism concerning any agreement at London. Marshall's own impatience with Soviet intransigence at Moscow had not abated. The report of the ministerial deputies, who had been laboring for several weeks on an agenda, did nothing to dispel the gloom. The minutes for their thirteenth and last meeting, on November 22, concluded: "Unable to reach any agreement, it was finally decided to have each Deputy report separately and individually to his Minister." Dining with Marshall and Douglas at the American embassy the night before the opening session, Bevin anticipated the atmosphere to follow. He had met with Molotov earlier in the day and inquired whether the Soviet Union was going to continue the line that all agreements must be unanimous. The Soviet minister's response was evasive and disconcerting—"They [USSR] had been threatened by the United States."[18]

The meetings were largely an abbreviated version of the April debacle— seventeen sessions, as opposed to Moscow's forty-four. Marshall was determined to keep as tight a rein as possible on the discussions, even though it was agreed that the chairmanship should rotate. Whenever possible, he cut off Molotov's attempts to rehash old grievances and replied coldly and succinctly to Soviet propaganda statements. But no agreement could be reached on Austria, the reparations issue remained unresolved, and charges and countercharges were exchanged on the sincerity of Western and Soviet plans for German economic unification. Molotov also took occasion to attack the emerging European Recovery Program (ERP) as a menace to the independence of Western European states.

By December 6, it had become clear that the possibility of any agreement had been reduced to almost zero. Discussions began on how or when to break off the meetings. Bevin and Bidault, even more annoyed than Marshall, assured the latter that, such was the state of British and French opinion, it made little difference whether the pretext was one of procedure or substance. Both, however, were still chary of precipitate action. Marshall also hesitated, fearful that a breakup, though at first "applauded" by the disenchanted American public, might, on reflection, be questioned. Subsequent sessions brought no improvement in content or tone,

Josephine Leah Williams shortly before her marriage to James S. Douglas.

Grandfather Douglas.

Bisbee, Arizona Territory, viewed from the west, 1895.

Lewis with his grandfather Douglas and, at far left, his father.

Lewis and his horse in Nacozari.

Douglas at eighteen, top row on the right, as a freshman at Amherst College, 1912.

Lieutenant Douglas in 1917.

James S. Douglas at midlife.

Congressman Douglas.

James S. Douglas mansion at Jerome, Arizona, with the United Verde Extension mine in the foreground.

At the Isabella Greenway ranch near Williams, Arizona, campaigning with Franklin D. Roosevelt in 1932. Left to right: *Colonel Oscar F. Temple, Adjutant General of Arizona, Governor G. W. P. Hunt, Roosevelt, and Douglas. After taking office the following March, Roosevelt appointed Douglas Director of the Budget.*

SHOT FULL OF HOLES

THERE'S A TIME AND PLACE FOR EVERYTHING — By Jerry Doyle

The Cairo Conference, 1943. Douglas is standing fourth from the right. To his right is Averell Harriman, to his left British Minister of War Transport Lord Leathers, Assistant Secretary of War John J. McCloy, and Harry Hopkins.

Peggy Douglas was a very successful fundraiser for the Red Cross in New York City during the Second World War.

Briefing the new ambassador to Great Britain.

Sharman, Douglas, Peggy, and Lewis Douglas, Jr. at a garden party at the Residence.

Douglas, Secretary of State George C. Marshall, and Foreign Secretary Ernest Bevin at the Residence during the London meeting of the Council of Foreign Ministers, 1947.

Luncheon at the Residence, October 31, 1948. Left to right: Mrs. Bevin, Secretary of State George C. Marshall, Mrs. Attlee, Foreign Secretary Ernest Bevin, Douglas, Sharman, Mrs. Marshall, Lewis's daughter-in-law Mrs. James S. Douglas, Prime Minister Clement Attlee, and Lewis's son James S. Douglas. Reggie, the Douglas family's fox terrier, is the center of attention. Peggy has left the room momentarily.

Douglas and Leader of the Opposition Winston S. Churchill on their way to the House of Commons for the debate on the devaluation of the pound, September, 1949.

Peggy and Douglas arriving in New York on the Queen Elizabeth, *November 21, 1950, at the end of his ambassadorship.*

John J. McCloy and Douglas wearing their wives' hats to protect them from the heat at the dedication of the George C. Marshall Research Library, Lexington, Virginia, May 23, 1964.

Douglas and Frank Brophy, close friends since their boyhoods in Bisbee, reminiscing in their old age.

until Marshall was prompted to accuse Molotov directly of insulting and undignified remarks. The decision was reached by the three Western ministers to call for adjournment. At the next meeting, Marshall reviewed the inability of the council, because of Soviet intransigence, to reach accord on any of the questions thus far discussed. He submitted that no progress could be expected on the items remaining on the agenda and called for adjournment. With dignity and firmness, he concluded: "When we meet again, I hope that it will be in an atmosphere more conducive to the settlement of our differences." Flabbergasted and sputtering, Molotov was forced to acquiesce.[19]

Throughout the council meetings, Marshall leaned heavily upon Douglas for advice and assistance. The ambassador participated actively in the numerous formal and informal conferences of the Western delegates at which policy and strategy were discussed and formulated. At the same time, he was asked by Marshall and Lovett to continue pressure from abroad on Republican House members to expedite passage of the Interim Aid Bill.

In a cable addressed to Representative John M. Vorys, who was authorized to show it to Charles A. Eaton, Christian Herter, and Joseph Martin, he emphasized Marshall's "grave concern" over the situation in France, which was experiencing great pressure from Moscow via the French Communist party. Douglas assured Vorys that his was "not, I promise you, a cry of 'wolf.' This we firmly believe is a brute reality." "Hardly a day [could] be lost" if France was to be saved. By December 11, Lovett was sufficiently concerned about the progress of the bill in Congress to suggest the ambassador's return for further testimony and personal persuasion. Marshall objected in a revealing dispatch. "The situation here is exceedingly critical and Douglas is invaluable, practically irreplaceable, in keeping me in team with Bevin and the British and vice versa. He also serves somewhat the same purpose regarding Bidault. . . . [Douglas and I] both feel it would be a very serious matter for him to be absent during these critical developments." Lovett did not pursue his request.[20]

During the conference, Douglas entertained the other delegations at the embassy, including a luncheon, toward the bitter end, for Marshall, Molotov, and several of their advisors. The atmosphere was distinctly cool, the conversation labored. Turning to Molotov, Douglas observed that since he had been through the revolutionary experience in Russia, he must have a fascinating story to tell. Would he talk about it? Bohlen was dismayed at the indiscretion, and Marshall was shaken. But Molotov, to everyone's surprise, talked for more than an hour, intensely, precisely, and agreeably.[21]

General Clay, who was present at the conference as an advisor, later characterized it a complete failure. But he made note of two benefits. Douglas came away from the meeting with the full background necessary for the "active role he was to play in German affairs" soon thereafter. Second, it expedited movement toward the economic unification of the three Western zones and the transfer to German agencies of greater political authority within the area. Anticipating the absence of agreement at London, the Western leaders had touched upon, but not actively pursued this possibility before and during the conference, fearing that serious discussion would give the Soviet Union ammunition to blame conference failure on collusion. Now the way was open to proceed to the tripartite meetings, in which Douglas was to play a principal role. A third result, which Clay did not mention, was the post-conference conversations between Bevin and Marshall, joined by Douglas, which were to lead to the establishment of NATO in the spring of 1949.[22]

On December 18, Douglas flew back to Washington with General Marshall. He had played a far more significant role than most modern ambassadors even in troubled times. He had also received exceptional public notice. *World Report* had honored him with its cover story on August 12. *Life* followed suit on October 27, its highly laudatory article also giving space to Peggy's contributions and Sharman's social activities. *Time*'s extensive coverage, accompanying a cover picture, was no less complimentary, but included a brusque statement from his brother-in-law, John J. McCloy, calculated to keep the ambassador's constant headgear, a battered gray felt, from needing replacement. "I've known Lew too long to go into ecstasies over him, but then I don't know who I would go into ecstasies over. He's no giant, no genius. He's a sound, solid citizen with a good education and a good start in life who has been bounced to the top in our competitive system. He's no smarter than a lot of other people who haven't leveled out yet. I think that is the way Lew would think of himself."[23]

Interim aid having been obtained, albeit at a reduced figure, it was now necessary to gain approval for the $17 billion four-year recovery program that Truman had asked Congress to authorize. The public presentation before the Senate Foreign Relations Committee started on January 8 with Marshall's formal statement. On January 9 Douglas began his own, more detailed testimony, which lasted for two days. During the next six weeks, he also appeared at the public hearings of the House Foreign Affairs Committee and participated in executive sessions of both committees. Again he served as liaison between Capitol Hill and the State Department. Lovett also continued to be extremely active, both in testimony and especially in maintaining close personal contact with Senator Vandenberg.

Both men were eloquent and convincing. Senator Henry C. Lodge later recalled that they "made arguments for the Marshall Plan which I still remember vividly, more than twenty-five years later. They were there not because their official positions required it, but because of their forensic talent." In the task of convincing Congress of the need for and efficacy of the plan, Douglas drew on his firsthand knowledge of conditions in Europe, past experience in the House and in high government positions, and economic and financial expertise and experience.[24]

There was also some critical reaction. It may have been due to the rather "schoolmasterish" manner with which he presented his material, making extensive use of charts and graphs to explain the plan. Perhaps, too, it was to some extent prompted by the "take it or leave it" note that on occasion crept into his remarks. His personal charm, which was so successful with most members, may have been resented by others as an attempt to divert them from the hard-boiled approach they believed essential. Above all, whereas Marshall's great prestige inhibited blunt questions during his cross-examination, Douglas's very accessibility, as he assumed the burden of presenting in detail the administration's proposals, opened him to sharp interrogation. Interestingly, Senator Connally, the ranking Democratic member of his committee, often proved the most acerbic questioner, while the Republican Vandenberg was obviously sympathetic. The Michigan senator must be given primary credit for piloting the measure successfully through the committee, with Douglas "quarterbacking" the program in Congress for Marshall, while Lovett played a less-visible but active role.[25]

On February 17, the Senate committee unanimously reported favorably on the four-year program, with some modifications in amount and timing. Preparing to leave the next day for England, where he was to represent the United States at the London Conference on Germany, Douglas wrote his father that his task in Washington had been "tedious and exhausting, sitting with the Foreign Relations Committee from 10 in the morning until 5 or 6 in the afternoon; the mornings preparing for the next day or meeting with Senators or Congressmen. The problem has been a perplexing and complicated one. . . . There has been much opposition too. It could not have been successfully concluded had it not been for Vandenberg, who has been superb. He is cast in the mold of the great Senators of the past."[26]

Back in Britain, Douglas reported to Bevin on the progress of the legislation. Bevin sagely commented that his own best contribution would be "to keep right out and to discourage any British intervention, either by personal visits or by publicity. . . . [He] felt the American Administration knew best how to manage their own publicity."[27]

Douglas later spent three weeks in Washington, during the recess of the London Conference, resuming his missionary activities in Congress. On the day of his arrival he accompanied Marshall and Lovett to visit Speaker Joseph W. Martin, Jr., urging haste in consideration by the House. The administration had requested $6.8 billion for the first fifteen months of the plan, but there was considerable pressure for economy in both houses. Fighting attempts to reduce the amount, Vandenberg suggested a compromise to limit the first appropriation to twelve months at a lesser figure. The administration concurred, and the outcome was a first-year appropriation of $4 billion and an eventual expenditure of $13 billion.[28]

Douglas had reason to be pleased with the expected result and his role in its accomplishment. Formal congressional approval of the authorization bill came on April 1, and the presidential signature was affixed two days later. Lovett cabled his congratulations on April 2: "It is a very real personal victory [for you]." On April 13, from Bogotá, where he was attending the Conference of American States, Marshall apologized for being "a little late in the day," and expressed his deep appreciation for "your leading part in passage of ERP."[29]

The most affecting testimonial came from Bevin, who wrote, in a letter to "Dear Lew," on April 3: "I wish I could find words adequate to express the depth of my feeling and the gratitude which I feel towards you for what you have done in connection with the European Recovery Programme. You came to London as Ambassador of the United States at a time when the whole world, and we in Britain, were faced with a host of troubles. You grasped the situation at once. We worked closely together during the crisis last summer arising out of the non-discrimination question. You then helped us smooth out all the difficulties which might so easily have led to division between the English speaking peoples, and which might therefore have seriously affected the whole world situation. . . . I can well understand the great physical and mental strain which has been imposed upon you—not least in flying backwards and forwards between London and Washington. . . . Above all, I should like you to know how very much I have appreciated your advice and help. . . . We shall now strive not to disappoint the people of the United States who have taken this great step to help Europe to get on its feet." In reply, Douglas emphasized that his efforts in Congress were prompted by his conviction "that the moral values which our two countries have thus far so gallantly defended are the very foundation of Christian civilized life. . . . Division between us can only mean a catastrophe for us both."[30]

It remained for the President to name an administrator of cabinet rank to direct the operation of the ERP, to be designated the Economic Cooperation Administration (ECA), and a special representative or "roving ambassador" for Europe to coordinate its implementation, as provided for in the legislation. From the time of his first appearance before the Senate committee in November, Douglas had been prominently and frequently mentioned as an obvious candidate for one of those positions. When he returned after Christmas, James Reston in the *New York Times* revived the rumor, noting that "by bringing Mr. Douglas to the stand with his expert knowledge and his wide business experience, Mr. Marshall seemed to be suggesting an incarnate answer to the Senator's questions. . . . [T]he Marshall-Douglas team so dominated the proceedings that at least several members of the committee thought they saw a solution to the administrative dilemma." Several days later, Secretary of Defense Forrestal, in testimony before the House committee, expressed the opinion that the ambassador, as administrator, would create public confidence that there would be a businesslike administration of the program. Representative Sol Bloom noted that "This committee and everyone else would be assured by the selection of Mr. Douglas that the plan would be managed in a responsible way."[31]

By January 20, Douglas had passed the word that he did not want the job, but speculation did not cease. The *United States News* of January 23, with the ambassador's picture on the cover, captioned an article, "Lewis Douglas . . . Top Man for Marshall Plan." Three days later, Paul Warburg wrote from London that he had been repeatedly asked who the new ambassador would be. "In other words, it is taken for granted that you are going to accept the ERP job. I have told everyone . . . that you intended to remain here." The British embassy in Washington reported to the Foreign Office that Douglas continued "to be evasive when questioned by members of the Senate Foreign Relations Committee on whether he expected to be appointed to either post. Republican leaders in Congress have let it be known that, whilst they consider Douglas eminently well qualified for the post of Administrator, reasons of party politics would make them unwilling to approve his appointment, but that they would gladly see him appointed Special Representative. We should ourselves think that Douglas would prefer . . . to be the Special Representative."[32]

By February 11, when the Senate Foreign Relations Committee voted unanimously to recommend the creation of the two positions, Douglas's disclaimers had apparently taken effect, for speculation on the administrator appointment turned to William Clayton. When Douglas left for London on March 30, he stated flatly that he would not be the administrator and did not know who would be. On April 4, Truman telephoned Acheson to ask if he would consider the position. Acheson refused, citing his political unpopularity in certain congressional quarters, the clear desire of many senators for a nonpolitical businessman, and recommending Paul G. Hoffman, president of the Studebaker Corporation. Truman nominated Hoffman the next day. He was confirmed by the Senate on April 7.[33]

The President had previously called Douglas to offer the post of special representative. Douglas was convinced that the envoy to London could not wear two hats, that it would be a mistake to resign and lose his accumulated effectiveness in the U.K., and that in the new position he would be suspected of partiality toward Britain. He suggested Clayton, who had already indicated he could not accept, or Harriman, as well as several other names. In fact, Hoffman had asked for Harriman or Douglas in that order, but the President had been reluctant to have the secretary of commerce leave the cabinet. But he called Harriman in Bogotá, where he had accompanied Secretary Marshall, and made the offer. Harriman accepted and was confirmed by the Senate on April 26.[34]

In mid-May, Hoffman named Thomas K. Finletter representative in the United Kingdom for the ECA. When Finletter returned to Washington, in 1949, to become secretary of the air force, John W. Kenney, under secretary of the navy, succeeded him. Although these men were directly responsible for Marshall Plan operations in Britain during the remainder of Douglas's tenure, he played an active role during the negotiations with Great Britain, for the bilateral agreement on ERP, which was signed on July 6, and kept in close touch with the subsequent progress of the plan. Frequently serving as interpreter and moderator during periodic American frustration over London's foot dragging on implementation of the plan and British sensitivity concerning their great-power status and Commonwealth relationships, he was often able to forestall unpleasant confrontations. Hoffman succinctly summed up the ambassador's contribution after Douglas had accompanied him and Harriman to a series of meetings with Bevin in October, 1948: "Only as I reviewed mentally the details of our interviews with Mr. Bevin did I realize how superbly you handled the situation. There were at least a half dozen times when if you hadn't come up with the right word and right inclination a real explosion might have taken place. You have my heartfelt thanks."[35]

21

The London Conference

EVEN AS DOUGLAS REAPED KUDOS FOR HIS ROLE in the successful passage of the ERP, two other international problems moved rapidly toward crises. Following the failure of the Council of Foreign Ministers' meeting in December, representatives of the three Western powers and the Benelux countries convened in London on February 23, 1948, to consider the economic and political future of West Germany. Their deliberations, which concluded on June 1 with positive agreements, led directly to the Soviet blockade of Berlin. Douglas was in the center of those events.

Meantime, the partition of Palestine, which had been recommended by the United Nations General Assembly on November 29, 1947, neared implementation, punctuated by increasing violence between Arabs and Jews. The British announced that they would withdraw from the mandate on May 15. In the often frantic preparations for that day and during the hectic diplomatic activity that followed, Douglas served as the principal liaison between the embittered British and the politically racked American government.

In anticipation of a deadlock on Germany, some consideration had been given by the Western powers to tripartite discussions on the future of their zones prior to the CFM meetings. Marshall, however, had decided that prior consultations would be unwise. They would provide the Soviet Union with ammunition for propaganda that the Western powers were not genuinely prepared to negotiate four-power arrangements and would have an adverse psychological effect on the Western delegations to the conference. If, as expected, no understanding was reached at London, formal conversations with the British and French could be undertaken early in the new year.[1]

Accordingly, two days after the abrupt CFM adjournment, Marshall called on Bidault at Claridge's, after Douglas had paved the way for the visit by suggesting the time had come for France, Britain, and the United States to schedule discussions on Germany. Douglas recommended London as the locale for the meeting because he felt that there more pressure could be put upon the British if they proved recalcitrant concerning a change in the status of the Ruhr—an extremely sensitive issue with the French. Bidault agreed and commented that he had spoken to Bevin earlier in the day and found the foreign secretary inclined to place the subject well down on the agenda. His other remarks reflected French anxieties concerning the threat of eventual German industrial competition and military revival, and the instability of the French ministry, menaced from the left and right.

Marshall put the case directly for a tripartite conference to examine the relationship between the Bizone and the French Zone, looking toward possible fusion. He noted the urgency of currency reform in Germany as the value of the mark continued to plummet and emphasized the necessity for increased production in the Ruhr.[2]

That evening, Bevin announced to Marshall that "His own idea [following the failure of the CFM] was that we must devise some western democratic system comprising the Americans, ourselves, France and Italy, etc. and of course the Dominions. This would not be a formal alliance, but an understanding backed by power, money and resolute action. It would be a sort of spiritual federation of the West." He had in mind preliminary "confidential Anglo-American discussions" toward that end. Marshall, though possibly somewhat taken aback by the directness of the foreign secretary's remarks, replied that he had no criticism of their implication. In fact, "He was very willing to have matters discussed with a view to arriving at such an understanding. Indeed there was no choice in the matter. They had to reach an understanding. They must take events at the flood stream and produce a coordinated effort." However, at the moment, he believed they should turn to the pressing problems of Germany—which they proceeded to do. He informed Bevin of his visit with Bidault, who had agreed to an early conference on the subject but was clearly absorbed in the Ruhr question. This conversation marked not only a milestone on the road to a West German government, but of equal or greater importance, the first step toward the achievement of the Brussels Treaty and NATO.

The next day, December 18, Bevin came to Prince's Gate to meet with Marshall, Douglas, Murphy, Clay, and General Sir Brian Robertson, British military governor in Germany. Before and over lunch the group agreed on the course of several future actions. Another attempt would be made to introduce currency reform for all Germany, but failing Soviet cooperation it would be done in the Bizone with expected French adherence. The question of reparation deliveries to the Soviets was left in abeyance for the time being. Closer relations with the French occupation authorities was to be sought, pending a trizonal agreement. Meantime, the powers of the appointive German Bizonal Economic Council were to be expanded by an early election of its representatives. The long-term goal—a West German government including the French Zone—was to be accomplished gradually, unless Soviet actions prompted expedition. The conferees expressed their determination to stay in Berlin and to preserve the Control Council, barring its disruption by the Soviet Union. Clay affirmed that if the Russians became obstructive, the Western Allies "had adequate resources on which to live in Berlin for some time."

Finally, it was agreed that after preliminary conversations with the French a tripartite conference should be held to discuss the future of the Ruhr and other outstanding questions concerning Germany. Inasmuch as the State Department was to play an expanding role in German affairs, hitherto primarily the responsibility of the War Department and Clay, the latter's concluding comment in his report to the Pentagon on the meeting was encouraging: "Our work in London has brought us into a very close relationship with State Department personnel concerned with occupation policy, and there appears to be little real difference in our thinking as to the future."[3]

At Bevin's suggestion, the American and British delegations to the forthcoming conference held three preliminary discussions. With Sir William Strang, permanent under secretary of state for the German section, in the chair, they coordinated a plan of procedure. In general, they accepted the agenda outlined by General Marshall in a letter to Inverchapel of January 30, i.e., the association of the Benelux nations in long-term German policy, the relationship of West Germany to ERP, control of the Ruhr, security against Germany, reparations, and, most important, the evolution of West German political and economic institutions toward a provisional government for the three zones. Douglas, fresh from the Marshall Plan hearings, emphasized the American conviction that the Western zones should enjoy free partnership in ERP and in any European organization to implement it. The long-term disposition of the Ruhr, upon which French feelings ran so high, should be deferred if at all possible, while the security question should await initiatives from Paris, where the nightmare of a German resurgence colored every facet of the problems under consideration.[4]

Events since the CFM had intensified French fears. On January 8, Clay and Robertson had presented to the Bizone *Laender* minister-presidents and officials, meeting at Frankfurt, a plan to strengthen and expand considerably the economic organization of the Bizone. Although both the Foreign Office and the State Department were somewhat taken aback at the "scope" and "dramatic manner" of presentation of the proposals, in general they supported their intent. The French, on the other hand, were alarmed, expressing dismay through their ambassadors in both Washington and London. The recommendations had been made without reference to Paris, which saw in them the first steps toward a West German government, frightening for security reasons and as a possible provocation for the Russians to establish an East German government in Berlin. Attempting to allay the French apprehensions, the United States and Britain pointed out to them that the measures aimed only at clarifying and facilitating the functions of the Bizonal agencies in the face of pressing economic problems. They would be informed of the progress of discussions on the proposals. But they were given to understand that, pending a French decision to fuse with the American and British zones, there was no obligation to have prior consultations with them.[5]

Clay and Robertson issued legislation promulgating their proposals, with some modification, on February 9 and 14. In an effort to be both firm and reassuring before the opening of the tripartite conference, Marshall instructed Caffery, in his conversations with Bidault and other French officials, to emphasize that "French preoccupation with Germany as a major threat at this time seems to us outmoded and unrealistic. . . . [The] real threat to France seems to be another power which will undoubtedly seek to utilize [a] substantial segment of [the] German economy if unable to get control of Germany. In our opinion French security for many years to come will depend upon [the] integration of Western Europe including [the] western German economy. Unless western Germany during [the] coming years is effectively associated with [the] Western European nations, first through economic arrangements, and ultimately perhaps some political way, there is a real danger that [the] whole of Germany will be drawn into [the] eastern orbit, with obvious dire consequences for all of us.'' In rather more detail, Marshall repeated the same message in outlining his views for the guidance of Douglas at the conference. On February 20, the three Western powers signed in Berlin an economic agreement that coal produced in the Saar Territory "shall be considered as a common resource with the coal produced in France," with the understanding that a sum of 70 million Reichsmarks be deducted from the capital reparations due France from the German economy—an inspiriting note to strike for insecure France on the eve of the difficult discussions ahead. Meanwhile, presaging events to come, Soviet Ambassador A. S. Panyushkin, in Washington, had formally protested to Lovett that the forthcoming conference was "a violation of the Potsdam Agreement and of other decisions, adopted by the Four Powers, in accordance with which responsibility for the administration of Germany and for the determination of policy with respect to Germany is borne jointly by the Occupying Powers."[6]

When the tripartite meetings began, on February 23, in the Old India Office, which had become the quarters of the German Section of the Foreign Office, it was agreed that Strang remain in the chair. But it was clear that Douglas, representing the paramount power, would be the leading figure. (The French delegation was headed by Ambassador René Massigli.) The Benelux countries were asked to join in the conversations on items that were of concern to them. Each of the three occupying powers also included in its delegation the military governor of its respective zone. Again, Clay had demurred at attending, but Secretary of the Army Kenneth C. Royall insisted on his presence.[7]

The doubts and differences among the three powers were already well known from the preliminary discussions: French concern about security in the face of a unified West Germany and insistence upon international control of the Ruhr, and British reservations over an indefinite suspension of reparations to the Soviet Union because of the impact of such a decision upon their already strained relations with Moscow. It was left to Douglas to manuever toward some sort of acceptable agreement on these issues. His trump card was the ERP, and he displayed it diplomatically but unmistakably on February 24.

Opening his remarks with an expression of pleasure and satisfaction on the Saar agreement, he proceeded to a pointed review of the recent changes in the European "matrix." On the one hand were the destructive attitudes and actions of the Soviet Union; on the other, the constructive measures initiated at Paris. Congress was now debating the American contribution to European revitalization. A high price had already been paid for the delay in placing Germany on a self-supporting basis. At the moment, Germany constituted no threat, except as it might be used by some other power for its own aims. Without abandoning hope for eventual all-German unity, it was essential that the three Western zones combine at an early date to contribute to Western European political and economic recovery and stability.

Strang agreed on the urgency of action in this direction, but French Ambassador René Massigli expressed reservations about the nature of a reconstructed West Germany and its threat to European security. The experience of Hitler called for caution. France, he said, "approached [the] problem in [the] spirit of [a] traveler entering [a] thick forest full of unknown hazards." Douglas replied that the concept of security had altered in the face of changing circumstances. Delays in German recovery were exacting a tremendous price in American dollars and in the pace of European recovery, which could not long be borne.[8]

Douglas, Murphy, and Clay asked a sympathetic Strang to urge Bevin's reconsideration of the British stand on reparations. Reiterating that the current talks were taking place in the framework of the ERP, Douglas emphasized to Massigli the significance of the Czech crisis, which had ended that day in the formation of a Communist government. He bluntly warned Massigli that they were "under [the] shadow of a situation exemplified by events in Czechoslovakia. The true objective, and the solution of the difficulties would be to weld West Germany with the Western European economy." Massigli agreed, but stressed French concerns over the Ruhr, and the threat of a centralized German government.[9]

Douglas was convinced little progress would be made unless some assurances could be given Paris regarding security against Germany. But the French desire for some sort of three-power German disarmament and demilitarization agreement was considered unrealistic in view of the greater menace to the east. He reminded the French that as long as the occupation continued Paris had every reason to feel secure. With regard to the post-occupation period, a broad Western European pact appeared to offer the strongest bulwark against a revived West Germany and, more significantly, against Russia and her occupation zone. But the French were unconvinced. Advocating international control of the Ruhr and a decentralized West German government as protective measures, Massigli pointed out that France had "drawn certain lessons from history which differ from [the] conclusions drawn by US." He could easily imagine a German government, Communist or not, allying itself with the U.S.S.R. if such an alliance proved advantageous.[10]

Massigli made it known to Strang that his government realized its policy toward Germany must be modified, but was fearful of "something coming out" of the talks that would give the French Communist party an opportunity to accuse the government of insufficiently protecting national interests against a German resurgence. In short, "it was not so important that we should in fact concede anything of substance as that we should appear to do so." Strang said that Douglas was well aware of the problem and was working on Washington for assurances to that end.[11]

By continued pressure upon Washington, Douglas finally received authorization to use both the stick and the carrot. He could inform the French that the United States would make no ERP commitments to the French Zone until Paris was prepared "to make corresponding commitments re closer French association in [the] US-UK organization of Western Germany." Then he could advise Strang,

Massigli, and the Benelux representatives of American support for Bevin's proposals for some kind of Western union and of his government's willingness to find a formula for consultation with France and Great Britain in case of a German threat. He could also state that it was "very unlikely that American forces would be withdrawn from Germany for a very long time—until the threat from the East had disappeared." His colleagues expressed satisfaction.[12]

On the question of the Ruhr, Douglas was able to obtain tentative approval of the establishment of an international control agency at the conclusion of the occupation, composed of the United States, France, Great Britain, West Germany, and the Benelux nations. But the State Department was unprepared to authorize any definite commitment on the details and timing of the proposal. As to reparations delivery to Russia, Douglas, following a number of representations, including not so veiled hints at adverse congressional action on ERP if shipments continued from the British Zone, was able to extract from Bevin an agreement for the time being to review each month's deliveries and not to preclude complete suspension. The future composition of a West German government comprised of the three zones was discussed in some detail, but no final action was taken on the matter. Closer economic cooperation was urged to implement the ERP.[13]

The communiqué at the recess reflected in general terms the progress of these "informal discussions of German problems," and it left little doubt as to the direction of events—toward the creation of a West German government. Despite continuing differences, the atmosphere at the recess was cordial. All parties had made some concessions and were moving toward a consensus.[14]

Back in Washington, Douglas not only resumed his lobbying in Congress for ERP, but, toward the end of his stay, found himself briefly presiding over the birth of the North Atlantic Treaty Organization.

Bevin had wasted little time in following up on his December 17 conversation with Marshall, advancing the concept of some sort of Western alliance. On January 13, Inverchapel wrote Marshall, enclosing a memorandum from Bevin outlining a treaty among France, Great Britain, and the Benelux countries, which could be expanded to include other nations of northern and southern Europe, and, in time Germany. He hoped for "the backing of the Americas and the Dominions." Marshall "warmly applauded" Bevin's initiative. In the next two months, apprehensions in Washington rose sharply because of events such as the Communist takeover in Czechoslovakia, the alarming Soviet pressure upon Norway to negotiate a pact that would put her in a relationship to Russia analogous to that of Finland, Clay's scare telegram of March 5 from Berlin suggesting that war might "come with alarming suddenness" (apparently sent to assist the army in expediting military appropriations through Congress rather than to indicate any dramatic change in the Berlin situation), and the tragic suicide or assassination of Czech Foreign Minister Jan Masaryk.[15]

Bevin had called a conference in Brussels of France, Great Britain, and the Benelux nations, which, on March 17, concluded a fifty-year mutual defense treaty. Meanwhile, the Soviet government, on March 6, had handed to both Marshall and Bevin another long and strong note, protesting the work of the London Conference and the plan of a Western Union, which was being discussed in Brussels, as violations of the existing agreements among the four occupying powers. They were, Moscow charged, not only failing "to promote the establishment of an enduring democratic peace in Europe, but . . . pregnant with such consequences as can suit only all kinds of instigators of a new war." On March 20, the Soviet military governor in Germany, Marshal Vasilii D. Sokolovsky, enhanced the level of anxiety. Calling a meeting of the Allied Control Council, whose proceedings had become increasingly rocky, he demanded full details of the London conversations and, receiving evasive replies, adjourned the session and walked out. It proved to be the last meeting of the council.[16]

With the conclusion of the Brussels treaty, Bevin and Bidault formally requested conversations with United States representatives in Washington on "what further steps may be desirable," i.e., a broader association including the United States. Lovett, burdened by the last-minute ERP legislative push but deputized by Marshall to conduct the meetings, asked Douglas to substitute for him.[17]

Six top-secret sessions were held in the Pentagon between March 22 and April 1. Douglas chaired two of them and John D. Hickerson, director of the Office of European Affairs, presided over the others. George Butler of the Policy Planning Staff, Theodore Achilles, chief of the Division of Western European Affairs, and General Alfred Gruenther, director of the Joint Staff of the Joint Chiefs of Staff, completed the American representation. The British members were Inverchapel, H. M. Gladwyn Jebb, assistant under secretary for the United Nations, who appeared at Lake Success several times as a cover, and Donald Maclean, who was later unmasked as a Soviet agent. The Canadians included Ambassadors Lester B. Pearson to the UN and Hume Wrong to the United States. Over British and Canadian objections, the French had not been invited, owing, as Douglas and Hickerson explained, to possible security risks.

The discussions revolved around recommendations concerning the form that a wider alliance should take, possible participants (including eventually West Germany and Spain), and the steps toward its accomplishment. A draft proposal was approved at the last meeting on April 1, after Douglas's return to London. It contained the basic elements that would surface later in the North Atlantic Treaty of 1949. But it was clearly understood that further progress would require, with the maintenance of strictest secrecy, the approval of Lovett and Marshall, the National Security Council, the Defense Department and the President, and the concurrence of key congressional leaders, especially Senator Vandenberg.

In general, events proceeded along the lines proposed, with the assent of the executive agencies and with the Vandenberg Resolution of June 11, which expressed Senate approval of regional pacts for "collective self-defense," opening the way for exploratory talks, beginning in Washington on July 6, among the ambassadors of the principal signatories. The novelty of such a departure in American foreign policy dictated a strictly bipartisan approach, which in turn required that the Senate Foreign Relations Committee be continuously involved. Thus, subsequent negotiations were handled primarily in Washington, under the direction of Lovett, with Marshall's complete backing, and, after January, 1949, directly by Dean Acheson. The treaty was signed in Washington on April 4, 1949, the same day that Douglas was to suffer his painful eye injury fishing on the River Test.[18]

Coincident with Douglas's return to London, the "consequences" to which the Soviet note of March 6 darkly hinted accelerated. On March 30, the Russian authorities informed the Americans that, effective April 1, they would require inspection of American military and civilian cargo and personnel passing through their zone into Berlin. In addition to a formal protest, Clay requested authority to defy the Soviet order by force if necessary, but Washington gave permission only to attempt passage, not to fire unless fired upon. The Soviet guards stood firm, and as a consequence, American, though not German, rail traffic was canceled, and Clay instituted a modest airlift to supply American personnel in Berlin. Unlike the unfortunately vague arrangements on surface transit, there was a definite written agreement on air corridors. Tension increased sharply on April 5, when a British transport plane and a harassing Soviet fighter collided over Berlin, killing all involved, including two Americans. The Russians apologized, but thenceforth American and British transports were escorted by fighters. For the time being the situation in Berlin remained static but perilous. These events no doubt reinforced Douglas's growing conviction, expressed to Forrestal before his departure from Washington, that it would be extremely dangerous for the United States to view the current crisis as a temporary period of tension. "I think," he warned the secretary of defense, "this will be with us for the next decade." Even that gloomy prediction was optimistic.[19]

During Douglas's absence in Washington, the working party of the three Western military governors in Germany had completed preliminary talks on implementing the tentative decisions of the London Conference on Germany. But the French remained determined on two points: they insisted that elections to the German constituent assembly be on a *Laender* basis and "not in any way . . . in form or substance" by an all-German popular vote, and that proposals for the international control of the Ruhr must include not only management but also ownership.

In London, Douglas found Bevin reluctant to resume as early as April 20, as scheduled, apprehensive that to reconvene before the Italian elections might prompt the Russians to take some precipitate and drastic action to influence their outcome. But Douglas recommended to the department that the risks were fewer to proceed as planned. Lovett agreed, cabling, significantly, that if the action feared was the creation of an East German government, it "would probably enable us to get earliest agreement on similar announcement on part western governments for use shortly thereafter." Massigli concurred with Douglas. On April 6 Bevin consented to "go along," in view of the insistence of the United States and France. In fact, recent events in Berlin had apparently, temporarily at least, markedly affected some French thinking on the timetable for the formation of a West German government. Maurice Couve de Murville, director for political affairs, minimized the influence of French public opinion on German policy and advanced as his personal opinion that "War with the Soviet Union within the next two or three years is inevitable—and that may mean this year."[20]

Preliminary conversations were held by Douglas with the British to attempt a coordination of views before facing their French colleagues. He also had several visits with Churchill, who made some startling suggestions. "If and when the

Soviet develop the atomic bomb, war will become a certainty," he told Douglas, who wrote Lovett: "He believes that now is the time to tell the Soviet that if they do not retire from Berlin and abandon Eastern Germany, withdrawing to the Polish frontier, we will raze their cities. . . . [W]e cannot appease, conciliate or provoke the Soviet." Understanding only force, "they would yield." Blandly, Douglas commented to Lovett: "You know better than I the practical infirmities in the suggestion. They cover quite a wide range, including the political." Less dramatically, Churchill suggested retaliation for Soviet harassment in Berlin, by "a careful examination of the crews of every one of their ships putting into our ports, by annoying their shipping and their use of the Suez and Panama Canals, and by any other method that seems to be appropriate." In Douglas's opinion, such measures would be "to wave a strand of straw, disguised as a club . . . [and] have no effect." Rather, the steps already under way to establish a strong Western Europe, including West Germany, even if "the Soviet may ultimately develop—if they have not already developed—the atomic bomb, may deter them . . . [and] lead to a satisfactory settlement."[21]

The resumed conference faced further clarification of the three principal items on the agenda: the development of the economic and political organization of West Germany, the place of the West German economy in the general European economy and in the recovery program, and the control of the Ruhr. Over all still hung the problem of reconciling French fear of German economic and political resurgence with the need to establish a viable West German government. In the first meeting, Douglas "vigorously" set the tone in response to Massigli's expressions of concern over the effect of a revitalized Germany on public opinion in France. "We face [a] choice at [the] present time," he asserted, "of either taking all reasonable steps to consolidate Western Germany with Western Europe, or admitting this couldn't be done and letting Western Germany move eastward."[22]

Although the three powers were agreed on a federal form of government for Germany, London supported a strong central authority, while France desired a loose confederation. The American position was somewhere in between. By shrewd maneuvering, Douglas was able to reach an acceptable wording for a "democratic constitution . . . of federal type which . . . will protect the rights of the participating states [*Laender*], provide adequate central authority, and contain guarantees of individual rights and freedom." Clay later wrote: "Free-enterprise America, Socialist Britain, and divided France were trying to agree on the principles of a constitution. Ambassador Douglas, with much experience in government and a liberal philosophy of human rights, was well-fitted to head the American delegation and his persuasive powers led to compromises which, although they left many problems to be resolved in Germany, did enable agreement on paper authorizing the military Governors to go ahead with the program."[23]

On the question of the Ruhr, Douglas had to steer a difficult course between the French insistence on strict international control and Clay's and Murphy's determined opposition in principle to its establishment. Clay argued with Douglas that the loss of Silesia to the Eastern Zone and of the Saar to France left West Germany dependent entirely on the Ruhr for its coal supply, and that as long as that situation existed, together with the loss of its major food-producing area to the Soviet Eastern Zone, it would have to depend upon maximum use of its remaining industrial resources to "survive economically." It would be impossible under those conditions for it to develop any surplus to convert to military uses. French fears were at best psychological and unfounded, at worst based upon economic considerations. To submit to the French demands might well, in time, force the new Germany to look to the East for both economic and political alignment. If West Germany was to be brought "into the comity of western nations, then we must do it with two hands which offer friendship, rather than one hand carrying flowers while the other wields a big stick." At the very least, any compromise should not diminish the control of the military authorities during the remaining period of occupation while the United States continued to bear the financial responsibility.[24]

Douglas took Clay's point, but, in view of the need to have French acquiescence in the larger picture of West German political evolution, could not agree "to sink the principle without a trace." He was convinced a satisfactory compromise could be found. Before Clay and Murphy left for Frankfurt, on April 28, Douglas was able to report to Lovett that the general had "evidenced [a] much more cooperative attitude. . . . Rather than precipitate a head-on collision, [I] have adopted the tactics of asking him to suggest methods and language designed to facilitate reaching a satisfactory agreement. Anticipate . . . these tactics will prove . . . successful." During those first strained days within the delegation, Peggy Douglas had done her part to ease the tension by surprising Clay on his birthday, April 23, with a beautiful cake, which obviously touched and pleased him.[25]

A compromise that emerged a week or so later envisaged an international authority making coal allocations in concert with the recovery programs worked out by the OEEC (Organization for European Economic Cooperation, successor to the CEEC) for the participating countries. Douglas found it acceptable, but Clay and Murphy, despite the protective procedures in the proposal, greatly feared it would weaken the predominant financial voice of the military governors and impair German recovery. Both Clay and Douglas appealed to their respective departments in Washington for support, which led to a "statement of principles" that the decisions of the authority "shall be consistent with the programmes of the C.E.E.C. for the recovery of the participating countries," but subject, "during the Control Period," to approval by the military governors, in accordance with existing agreements among the occupying powers "on financial assistance to Germany" and the "allocation of coal and coke." Provision was made for further negotiations on "a more detailed agreement." Clay later noted that "our arguments on this point were frequent and at times bitter." But, he added, "It was impossible for arguments to destroy our friendship. In fact it is impossible to stay angry with Douglas, whose infinite and gracious charm would soothe feelings far more hurt than mine." At the time, however, the disagreement had been keen, Clay describing himself as "the tough so and so injecting the needle," and Douglas admitting to Marshall that he had "lost [his] . . . temper." But even then Clay acknowledged "Lew took the injections and did a masterful job," and Douglas conceded that "after this episode . . . General Clay could not have been more helpful, more considerate, or more reasonable."[26]

The security issue was met by a statement that the three governments would not withdraw their forces from Germany until "the peace of Europe is secured." Bowing to French demands, the "prohibitions on the German Armed Forces and the German General Staff as contained in 4-power agreements . . . [were] reaffirmed" and a military security board was to be established in the Western zones to monitor those provisions. Furthermore, it was agreed that measures would be taken, before the withdrawal of the occupying powers, to prevent any future German remilitarization.[27]

By the middle of May, agreement appeared to have been reached on most issues. But, despite the formal assurances, French concern over security, and especially the reaction of their public opinion, continued to be a specter at the meetings. Then on May 19 came forewarning of an imminent blow to the proceedings. Massigli suggested that in the absence of further Soviet provocations in Berlin it might be advisable to delay implementation of plans for a West German government to forestall a Soviet reaction. Douglas reported to Lovett that he had taken "the responsibility of replying to the effect that delay on our part . . . would be, on the one hand, construed by the Soviet to be evidence of weakness and might inspire them to take the initiative, and on the other hand, delay would have an unfortunate effect on the morale of the Germans." At the same time, he pointed out to the French that the United States was prepared to reaffirm Truman's statement of March 17 and to agree not to withdraw American troops without consultation with the French and British. He also confidentially communicated the text of the proposed Vandenberg Resolution. He hoped the French were reassured. Lovett agreed "that [the] risks of proceeding with [the] establishment [of a] provisional Govt are less than [the] risks of further delay."[28]

The next day, the other shoe fell. In notes to the United States and Britain, France expressed official concern over a Soviet response to the political organization of West Germany and alluded to the weakness of the Western military position in Germany. The French proposed postponement of the announcement of the agreement and a meeting of the three governments at the ministerial level. At a meeting on May 21, Douglas reiterated to Massigli his rejection of the French position, repeated his reassurances and asked acidly if Paris would ever consider the moment propitious to organize the government of West Germany. Strang seconded his remarks. The same day, Douglas recommended to the department that, if necessary, the Americans and British proceed in their zones without the French and "express reservations as to the Ruhr and security considerations qua Germany pending clarification of the French position." "We [the British concurred] recognize," he concluded, "that these recommendations are tough medicine, but we doubt that any milder treatment will produce the result which presumably we seek."

In Washington Lovett spoke roughly to French Ambassador Henri Bonnet: "Eleventh hour demands by the French were threatening all the good work accomplished in the London talks. . . . The German burden must be taken off our backs and the Germans made self-supporting." He authorized Douglas to proceed along the lines suggested in informal conversations with the British, pending top clearance. Two days later, Marshall and Lovett, "with a full understanding of the risks involved," confirmed instructions to go ahead without France if she did not change her position. In London, Bevin informed Douglas he hoped it would not require such drastic action, but he was prepared to proceed and was firmly opposed to a ministerial meeting.

Under this pressure, Paris capitulated, but with the condition that the proposals go before the Foreign Affairs Commission of the French Assembly and then be submitted to a general floor debate by that body. Despite grave reservations concerning the dangers of such an airing, the British and Americans reluctantly accepted this prerequisite to French concurrence. It was agreed, however, that only a very brief communiqué be issued at the end of the conference, with a full communiqué to be released one day before the Assembly debate, in order to minimize the time given to the Soviet government and the French Communists to engage in propaganda.[29]

The conference closed June 1, and a short noncommittal communiqué was issued on June 2. A more detailed statement on the report was released on June 7. Strang delivered a copy to Soviet Ambassador G. N. Zarubin in London and received a protest that the decisions were in violation of previous four-power agreements. The uneasy French then suggested an approach to Moscow, leaving the door open to Soviet Zone association in the proposed German organization. The State Department firmly supported Douglas's opposition, to which Bevin agreed, to any such sign of "vacillation or wavering." When Jean Chauvel, secretary general of the French Foreign Ministry, raised the question again on his visit to London on June 14, the British and American position remained firm.[30]

Although the consideration of the London recommendations by the French Foreign Affairs Commission and the full Assembly was not a matter of ratification but only of debate, Douglas was deeply concerned. Bidault, as their principal supporter in the government, was a weak reed, politically and personally, on which to lean. Writing to his father, Douglas remarked that his "news from France indicates that though the Chamber may take this occasion to get rid of Bidault, it will approve the agreements. Bidault has been hysterical, he has been drinking and talking nonsense in public places. His stock has therefore fallen to a low ebb." But on the evening of June 9, the commission, after defeating two motions to reject the recommendations, approved by one vote its submission for debate in the Assembly.[31]

Alarmed by this narrow margin of victory, Bidault sent Chauvel to London, where he met with Massigli, Douglas, and Strang and called on Bevin in an effort to modify the recommendations to make them more palatable to the Assembly. The suggestion of an approach to Moscow was revived. Chauvel raised again the possibility of a foreign ministers' meeting, asked for an interpretation of the Ruhr agreement to allow French participation in management as well as allocation and for some sort of placating further statements by Britain and the United States that Bidault might use in the Assembly. To all of these importunities, the answer was a firm negative. "I told Chauvel," Douglas cabled Marshall, "that if, after three years of spectacular disunity among [the] four powers, the three last great sanctuaries of freedom were now to present to the world a spectacle of their own disunity, the consequences throughout western Europe and in the western hemisphere might well be incalculable, thus damaging the interests of France and of all those, including my own country, who are attempting to preserve the traditional features of western civilization." Strang argued that the recommendations as drafted gave France the guarantees she needed and rejection might prevent her from ever again obtaining such assurances.[32]

Douglas was amazed at Chauvel's "complete ignorance of the substance" and import of the agreements. "[T]he French delegation," he wrote his father, "had not only failed to inform the government of the meaning of the agreements, but had deliberately given false information to the Government's opponents. Yet they had themselves agreed to the proposal." Some days later, in reply to a letter from John Foster Dulles, he commented that the French had behaved "very curiously." Bidault had "kept no one informed, and some members of the French delegation who returned to Paris not only failed to give the government all the information, but even planted seeds of opposition." It is not clear to whom he alluded. Probably not Massigli, whose integrity he held in high regard, and who, though unhappy about the direction of developments in West Germany, often seemed embarrassed during the conference by the tone of his instructions. Perhaps the reference was to General Koenig or to Couve de Murville and Hervé Alphand, both of whom were also close to de Gaulle. Chauvel departed chastened, enlightened, and apparently reassured that implementation of the agreements would involve further discussions among the signatories. On June 17, the Assembly approved the recommendations, as an "order of the day," by a vote of 300 to 286, with the Communists and Gaullists in opposition.[33]

Two years later, General Clay recorded his estimate of the proceeding and their consequences: "There is no question that this was the most important conference for Germany since Potsdam."[34]

22

The Berlin Blockade

IN 1971, DOUGLAS WROTE TO PHILIP JESSUP, who had been deputy United States representative to the United Nations Security Council in 1948: "It was pretty well known by Clay in Germany and by me, as early as the first of March, 1948, that we were to face serious trouble during the course of the next two or three months. Neither Clay nor anyone else knew what the trouble would be, nor what the manifestation of trouble was to be, but we knew that there would be trouble. We assumed that it would probably take the form of some interference with the access to the city of Berlin, since this was our Achilles Heel."[1]

The imposition of the Soviet mini-blockade and the initiation of the partial airlift by Clay at the beginning of April bore out these apprehensions and foreshadowed coming events. When the London Conference on Germany reconvened, Douglas, Clay, and Murphy were instructed by Lovett to consult with the other heads of delegations and the commanders-in-chief in Germany on the possibility of a "joint approach" which might make the Russians pause before going further in Berlin. Accordingly, conversations were carried on at a luncheon on April 27 among Douglas, Clay, Murphy, Strang, and Robertson and, on the following day, in Strang's room at the Foreign Office, including Patrick Dean, head of the German Political Department, Massigli, General Koenig, and Couve de Murville. From Douglas's and Strang's respective reports of the meetings, it appears clear that the strongest position was taken by Clay, who predicted the Russians would force the issue until the West faced the alternatives "of war or an ignominious retreat from Berlin." Strang and Robertson were not so pessimistic and declined to give a definite answer to Clay's question as to whether Britain was prepared to go to war. But Robertson did volunteer it would be "inconceivable that we should leave Berlin now." The French displayed considerable uneasiness over any action that might precipitate a conflict.

In his memoranda on these conversations, Strang noted that Douglas said little, but apparently "did not altogether share General Clay's extreme views." In the second meeting, Douglas's major contribution to the rather directionless discussion was that "the Russian could so manipulate the position that we might be compelled to use force just in order to protect our position; for instance the use of fighter escort for our transport planes might lead to this." Before the full blockade was instituted, Douglas, according to Clay's recollection, raised the possibility of withdrawal from Berlin as a prudent measure in view of the Western inability to defend the city militarily. He expressed the fear that the Russians might quickly overrun Western Europe and destroy democracy there for a very long time—"he could see the Russians on the English Channel." In Clay's opinion, Douglas overestimated, then and later, Soviet military might and its will to use it. Once the crisis came to a head, however, Clay emphasized, Douglas "was very strong and very determined." In any case, the conversations in April were inconclusive. But they did reveal Clay's determination, British caution, French fears, and Douglas's anxiety.[2]

For some time it had been obvious that a stable German economy, especially as a precondition to a West German contribution to European recovery, required currency reform. The decline in the value of the mark since the end of the war had been dramatic and near catastrophic. Although some effort had been made since the December CFM to coordinate monetary reform with the Russians, it had been half-hearted and unsuccessful. It was therefore agreed, despite some last-minute French reservations, to introduce a new currency in the Western zones immediately following approval of the London recommendations.[3]

On the evening of June 16, 1948, probably in anticipation of this action and possibly as a prelude to the blockade, the Soviet representative, on a transparent pretext, walked out of the meeting of the Allied commanders in Berlin (the Kommandatura), refusing to set a date for the next meeting. In the event, it marked the breakup of the Kommandatura. On June 18, the Western governors informed Marshal Sokolovsky of the terms of the currency reform in their zones, effective June 20, but not applicable to West Berlin. Sokolovsky suspended all surface traffic between West Germany and Berlin and announced the introduction of a new Soviet currency for the Eastern Zone, including Berlin. The Western powers retaliated on June 23 by extending the new currency circulation to their sectors of Berlin but permitting the Soviet Zone Ostmark to have equal legal status. Three days later Clay began a full-scale airlift into the city. Although the Soviet blockade was immediately and ostensibly a reaction to the Western currency reform, previous Russian protests and actions suggested that it was a wider response to the London recommendations, and perhaps to the accumulated frustrations of the Marshall Plan and the CFM stalemate, designed either to force the Western powers out of Berlin or to compel them to reopen four-power ministerial conversations on Germany.[4]

On the 24th, General Clay was in London, as were Under Secretary of War Draper and General Albert Wedemeyer, who had flown to Europe together on an inspection trip. The question was raised of putting an armored column through the blockade at Helmstadt in defiance of the Soviet order. Douglas recalled that he saw merit in the proposal only if it was done immediately. If any time was allowed to elapse, "it would be a foolhardy thing for us and might precipitate some very unfortunate consequences." On the basis of his (and Wedemeyer's) knowledge of the wartime airlift into Chungking from Assam during the war, he strongly supported an expanded airlift, which he "felt quite confident . . . could satisfy the requirements of the western sections of Berlin." Clay, Draper, and Wedemeyer came to the same conclusion, and the plan was put into operation with a mixture of hope and apprehension concerning its success.[5]

On June 25, Bevin made several major recommendations to Douglas, which for the moment he asked not to be transmitted to Washington. Central to Douglas's subsequent activities in the crisis was Bevin's suggestion that it "would be useful if, in addition to the contacts between the two Military Governors in Germany, it could be arranged for discussions on policy to be conducted and decisions taken here in London between myself and a United States representative invested with the necessary authority, who might well be himself [LWD]. This channel had become well established during the recent talks on Germany." In addition, he urged discussion by the Combined Chiefs of Staff in Washington, with possible later inclusion of the French, "to make an appreciation of the situation from a military point of view and of the steps to be taken to meet it," a general survey of the logistical problem in feeding West Berlin by air, consideration of sending an American bomber force to Europe "to help persuade the Russians that we mean business," and, finally, deliberation on the possibility of a joint note of protest to Moscow. The next day, Douglas met first with Strang and again with Bevin, to whom he put the question directly: "What, in . . . [Bevin's] view, would be the consequence of a withdrawal from Berlin?" The foreign secretary replied "without hesitation, that the consequence would be disastrous. We should not be able to hold Western Germany if we quitted Berlin." Douglas responded "that was entirely his view also." He then received permission to pass on to Washington Bevin's remarks of the previous day, with the understanding that they had not yet been discussed in cabinet.[6]

Douglas noted Bevin's conviction that "from here on we will be confronted with a series of issues on which, as promptly as possible, decisions must be taken. . . . This arrangement will . . . provide for complete current information in three places . . . London, Washington and Berlin and . . . accordingly, make feasible discussion in these three places on the basis of complete information. On Bevin's side, he has one reason, in addition . . . for suggesting this sort of arrangement; namely, that it will give him a certain sense of personal and timely association through ability to discuss with the representative of the US Government." Marshall indicated that all of Bevin's points were either accepted or discussion of them in train. He agreed to a "full and complete exchange of relevant information in London" and that Douglas "be furnished copies of all messages on this subject," including those of the Department of the Army. This decision was soon to lead, with the addition of the French representative to the discussions among the Western powers and the emergence of London as the clearing house for information and consultation, to the most taxing ordeal of Douglas's tenure. Undertaken in the midst of the Palestine crisis, to be discussed later, it was a drain upon his time and energy.[7]

In connection with Bevin's request for American bombers, Douglas was later to claim that as early as the end of March he had suggested to Marshall the deployment of two more divisions in Germany and the basing of B-29s in Britain.

On his return to London he had broached the subject informally to Bevin. However accurate this memory of prescience, Bevin's query of June 25 was followed up with remarkable alacrity two days later at a meeting of State Department and military officials, who agreed to instruct the ambassador to explore the "possibility we may wish to send 2 or 3 B-29 bomber groups to Great Britain." He was to request clearance. Bevin received immediate cabinet approval, enabling Douglas to inform Washington of British authorization to send eighty-two fighter aircraft and two bomber groups through the U.K. to Germany and to base one bomber group in England.[8]

On June 28, Truman, meeting with Lovett, Royall, and Forrestal, made clear his intention to stay in Berlin at all costs, supplying "the city by air as a beleaguered garrison." If the Russians persisted, the United States, Great Britain, and "if possible," the French should send a joint note to Moscow, "asserting our rights in Berlin and stressing Sov[iet] responsibility for, and callousness to [the] threatened starvation of [the] civilian population." Every effort should be made to appeal to world opinion by diplomatic exchanges and publicity, "not excluding ultimate reference of [the] case to [the] UN at [the] appropriate time." Informing Douglas of these decisions, Marshall indicated that he would shortly receive a draft note emphasizing the humanitarian and peace-threatening rather than the legalistic aspects of the crisis. He was to discuss the text with the British government and Massigli. Fortunately for the future of joint action, the French that day, after initial irresolution, "urgently requested" three-power consultations in London. Both the Foreign Office and the State Department took immediate advantage of this welcome if belated approach to urge their representatives in Paris and Berlin "to infuse courage into the French and to convince them that we have both the will and the ability to carry this thing through."[9]

Meantime, Bevin continued to impress upon Douglas, and upon the State Department through Sir Oliver Franks, the new ambassador, "the imperative necessity for the United Kingdom, the United States and French representatives in London to concert together so that there would be no unilateral action. It should be definitely assigned to the three in London to discuss all German matters, including Berlin, and report to their governments so that prompt and decisive action might be taken." By June 30, it was agreed that Douglas, Strang, and Massigli "would together form a standing body which would meet to consider political aspects of the present Berlin crisis in order to facilitate the taking of joint decisions." But Bevin had meantime made clear his view that any note should be delayed until "proposals for increasing the airlift to Berlin and the bomber force was [sic] more advanced" and that the three powers should not permit the Berlin crisis to go to the United Nations "as long as it could be dealt with on a technical basis."[10]

On June 30, Marshall dispatched to Douglas the draft note from the United States to the Soviet government for consideration in London as a joint endeavor and issued a public statement indicating the American determination to remain in Berlin and to supply the population with fuel and food by air. The stage was set for the around-the-clock consultations which were to occupy most of Douglas's time over the next three months.

On June 30, Douglas met with Attlee and Bevin at 10 Downing Street to discuss the proposed note. The ministers expressed two reservations. They suggested allowing some time to elapse in order to assess Soviet reaction to Marshall's statement and to similar statements to be made by Bevin and by Anthony Eden, for the opposition, in the House of Commons that night. The ministers also took exception to the last two paragraphs of the draft note, which suggested a CFM meeting, once the blockade was lifted, to negotiate any problems concerning quadripartite administration of Berlin and, failing resolution there, submission of the matter to the UN. Objecting to bypassing the military governors, they feared the ramifications of opening "any other channel for consultation or discussion" until it was evident that the Allied Control Council was unable to resolve the problem.

Douglas agreed. He could understand why, for the sake of American domestic opinion, it might be necessary to suggest the UN "as a suitable forum for settlement of the issue." But he preferred to let the Soviet Union suggest the next move. As to a CFM conference "for this particular purpose, we can be reasonably certain that the Soviet will construe it as a sign of weakness, will therefore snap at it, and will extend the area of discussions far beyond the domain of the controversy in Berlin. Any evidence of softness on our part may at this particular juncture when there is evidence of Soviet irresolution, react to our serious disadvantage. . . . At this particular moment, when we are trying to put into effect the program in Western Germany . . . the Soviet would use it as a platform for propaganda which might adversely affect German response to our program . . . impair our influence . . . [and] possibly defeat our objectives."[11]

Later that night or the next morning, the "standing committee" of Douglas, Strang, and Massigli met for the first time. Massigli seconded the reservations of Bevin, Attlee, and Douglas on the last paragraphs. Meantime, reacting to the ambassador's report on the British position and his personal recommendations, the State Department offered, on July 1, to modify the draft to call for Control Council negotiations in the first instance and eliminate mention of a CFM meeting, but to retain reference to the UN in case of failure by the military governors.[12]

Over the next week, the three diplomats were in continual session, attempting to reconcile the differing views. The French, with the most exposed geographical position and precarious domestic political balance, shied away from a statement that might be too provocative. The British too wavered, temporarily reversing their stand on mentioning a CFM meeting, and then urging a meeting of the Western military governors with Sokolovsky before a note was dispatched. Following up on the latter suggestion, Clay and Robertson called on the Soviet general on July 5. Stating their case for reopening the issue at their level, they received clear evidence that the London Conference was at the root of the Soviet blockade. "He [Sokolovsky] made it quite clear," Murphy reported, "that he was not prepared to answer any question on the resumption of traffic unless the results of the London Conference were also discussed. . . . It is clear that further action here by the three west military governors would serve no useful purpose." On receipt of the report from Berlin, Marshall urged speed on textual agreement and delivery of the Western note to Moscow. Now thoroughly persuaded by Bevin's initial argument and Douglas's strong concurrence, he considered it "clearly inadvisable" to refer to the CFM in the message.

On the evening of July 5, agreement was reached. The next day, the British and Americans delivered identical notes to the Soviet ambassadors in their capitals; the French, ever cautious, handed a separate communication, with a slightly different wording, to the Soviet ambassador in Paris. The final paragraph of each note was left purposely vague, requiring as a prerequisite to any negotiations the lifting of Soviet restrictions, indicating willingness then to discuss the dispute at the level of the military governors and, in general, noting that "such disagreements . . . should be settled by negotiation or by any of the other peaceful methods provided for in Article 33 of the Charter in keeping with our mutual pledges as copartners in the United Nation."[13]

Writing to his father on July 7, Douglas described the hectic days just past. "The task of . . . reconciling our views with the views of France and Britain . . . was not easy . . . particularly because of a note of arrogance which has crept into our dealings with other countries. By that I mean the disposition to demand that other countries bow to us and accept, without question, our view, and what is worse, our precise language. To break through this front of intolerance, suspicion and arrogance in Washington, was as difficult as it was unpleasant."

Because of the need for absolute secrecy, it was not possible to use the telephone to the United States and Germany; they had to depend on the teleconference instrument in the embassy. Thus, because of the time difference, then and during later urgent moments in the continuing crisis, Strang and Massigli had to join Douglas at the machine during the late night and early morning. Often Douglas and Massigli slept at the embassy, and on occasion it was necessary to arouse Bevin in the middle of the night for an opinion. Douglas's colleagues recalled these vigils with a mixture of pain and pleasure—pain at the physical strain, the need for quick decisions, and frequent confusion over the communications from Washington, pleasure at the occasion they afforded for the growth of mutual respect and friendship. To his father Douglas complained of another handicap—the absence at that time of any person on his staff "of sufficient competence and experience with whom I can test my own thinking and against whose mind I can rub mine." Waldemar Gallman had just been named ambassador to Poland. Julius Holmes, who was the replacement as counselor and who was to prove of inestimable assistance in the future, did not arrive until late in the summer.[14]

During the week that followed delivery of the notes to the Soviet Union, speculation was lively in Western foreign offices and in Berlin concerning the nature of Moscow's response and alternative reactions to it. Douglas flew to Berlin for consultation with Clay. In London he suggested to Bevin a joint inquiry to Moscow as to when a reply might be expected. Bevin thought such action might be interpreted as a show of weakness or produce a "violent Soviet reaction," for which the West was not yet sufficiently prepared. If the time lengthened, he would reconsider the proposal.[15]

The suspense ended on July 14, when the Soviet ambassadors handed identical notes to the American, British, and French governments. Accusing the Western powers of activities at the London Conference "directed towards the division and dismemberment of Germany including the preparations which are now in progress for the designation of a separate Government for the western zones of Germany and the separate currency reform for the western zones of occupation carried out on June 18 of this year," Moscow refused to "link" any negotiations "with the fulfilling of any preliminary conditions whatsoever," i.e., the lifting of the blockade. While open to four-power conversations, Moscow emphatically stated that they "could be effective only in the event that they were not limited to the question of the administration of Berlin, since that question cannot be severed from the general question of four-power control in regard to Germany."[16]

Douglas, Strang, and Massigli were instructed by their governments to examine carefully the Soviet note's implications and begin work on a draft reply. Meantime, Douglas sent a long dispatch to Lovett, listing six alternative responses that had occurred to him. One he rejected out of hand—to abandon Berlin. "The effect of this action . . . would, I think, be a calamity of the first order." His tentative conclusion, provided that the Western powers did not negotiate "under duress," was "to agree to discussions commencing with the situation in Berlin, but without closing the door to discussion of such other matters as may seem to be appropriate in the light of Soviet behavior during the discussions on the Berlin situation." Almost as an afterthought, he inquired whether the department had considered "the advisability of some oral representation to the Kremlin to obtain some indication as to whether it is the Soviet intention to resolve the issue by forceful means."[17]

The decision was to make a direct oral approach to Stalin. It would be a joint approach by the three governments, dealing with the Berlin situation only, but leaving the door open for further discussion on German matters "in the appropriate place and in the appropriate manner." If Stalin's response was "negative," then a written reply would be sent and the matter referred to the United Nations. Marshall instructed Douglas to ascertain Bevin's views on the proposal. He did not wish to inform the French government directly until he had received Bevin's reaction in view of the cabinet crisis in Paris (from which Robert Schuman emerged as the new foreign minister). Accordingly, Douglas asked Strang to notify Bevin, attending a Benelux conference at The Hague, before Bevin's meeting with Douglas the next day.[18]

Bevin's initial reaction was strongly adverse. To approach Stalin directly would elevate the issue "prematurely" to the level of the heads of state and give the Soviet leader the initiative in setting the time, place, and scope of further discussions. He also opposed as fruitless taking the case to the United Nations. At the most, he would consider an oral communication to Molotov by the Western ambassadors individually in Moscow. Over the next three days, Douglas persisted in his attempts to persuade the foreign secretary to modify his position, both men occasionally becoming extremely testy. In an effort to force Bevin's hand, he suggested the possibility of an individual approach to Stalin by Bedell Smith on behalf of all three powers. Bevin firmly rejected that proposal. Meantime, both men were acutely aware of the difficulties in carrying along, in Bevin's words, a "fearful and bankrupt France," whose timidity was clearly reflected in Massigli's reservations. It was hoped that the new French government that would take office in a few days would be in a position to act more decisively.

On July 25 Douglas flew to Berlin to confer with Clay, who had just returned, accompanied by State Department counselor Bohlen, from a National Security Council meeting in Washington, where he had been promised more planes. Smith came in from Moscow. The next day, Bohlen and Smith went with Douglas to London. There, in almost continuous meetings, Douglas's persistence wore down the opposition of Bevin and others in the Foreign Office, as well as the resistance of the French. Bevin received cabinet approval for the approach urged by Marshall and agreed upon by the Berlin conferees. The envoys of the Western powers in Moscow were to present individually an identical aide-mémoire to the Soviet Foreign Office, requesting a personal meeting with Stalin and Molotov. Despite their eventual concurrence under American pressure, French and British anxiety that hasty action might precipitate war was clearly evident in remarks to Bohlen by Massigli and by Bevin, the latter at one point commenting in only "semijocular fashion": "I know all of you Americans want war, but I'm not going to let you 'ave it."[19]

Douglas's fatigue led not surprisingly to self-doubts. Writing a personal letter to Marshall on July 28, hand carried by Bohlen, he expressed concern over his handling of the negotiations. His major error, he believed, was to have transmitted to Bevin at The Hague the substance of the department's dispatch recommending an oral approach before he had the opportunity to discuss the proposal face to face. Perhaps he was mistaken, but he had sensed "a note of suppressed irritation or disquiet" in Washington at his conduct of the complicated discussions with the French and British. Sometimes he felt "as lonely as a pine tree on a bald granite mountain." Marshall's reply was prompt and reassuring, suggesting that Douglas was entirely too sensitive. "I have been under the impression that 95% of the entire State Department cable traffic has been directly with you on an 'eyes only' basis and you have been too busy to be lonely. For my part, if I did not have people like you and Lovett to carry me along, I would be the lonely one. Please be of stout heart . . . everything you have been doing is exactly the way we would have wanted it, and I don't know what in the world we would do without you in London. Literally, you have rendered a very great service to your country." He closed with "Affectionately," a new level of intimacy in their correspondence.[20]

Earlier, in the midst of those hectic days, Douglas had somehow found time to reply at length to a letter from Senator Vandenberg. It reflected his recognition of the senator's influence on American foreign policy and domestic politics, hinted in passing at his own ambivalence concerning the forthcoming presidential campaign, and revealed his current views on the origins of the Berlin crisis. Commenting on Truman's call, during his recent nomination-acceptance speech, for a special session of the Eightieth Congress, he expressed his "great doubts about political tricks." The burden of his remarks, however, dealt with the blockade. He did "not think it fair to say . . . that either currency reform . . . or the London Agreements, or both, are the cause of the Soviet interference with normal transportation facilities to . . . Berlin." Rather, it was the inevitable outcome, sooner or later, of the arrangements made in 1945, primarily "at Soviet insistence," to establish a four-power government of Germany. Different languages, different philosophies, the requirement to govern by unanimous consent, the "establishment of the seat of this extraordinary government in a city to which only one of four powers had undisputed territorial right of access," and subsequent Soviet intransigence in all areas of possible cooperation were "the reasons for recent Soviet behavior. . . . The division of Germany, however permanent or temporary, became a fait accompli three years ago."[21]

With the agreement to approach Stalin directly, there was a momentary pause in Douglas's concentrated activity, but he was soon again deeply involved in the crisis. Stalin and Molotov, after a calculated delay, met with the Western ambassadors in Moscow on August 2. The Soviet leader appeared remarkably affable and suggested further discussions between Molotov and the envoys. These lasted another three weeks, during which the Soviet foreign minister raised conditions that were completely unacceptable to the Western powers. Despairing of progress, the ambassadors requested and were granted a second meeting with Stalin on August 23. Again he was conciliatory, and it was agreed to turn the technical questions of currency and the Berlin traffic over to the military governors in Berlin. There again an impasse resulted.

Throughout all these diplomatic maneuvers, while the currency question as cause for the blockade was ostensibly the issue, it was made clear in oblique and, on occasion, direct remarks by the Soviet negotiators that the real problem was their objection to the formation of a West German government. The talks in Berlin broke down on September 7, with Robert Murphy informing Marshall that "he could see no sign of a desire on their part to reach agreement." On September 14, Smith and his colleagues presented to Molotov an aide-mémoire delineating the questions on which the military governors had been unable to agree. The Soviet reply of September 18 rejected the Western note as giving "a unilateral account of the course of discussions" and as presenting "incorrectly" the position of the Soviet representatives in Berlin. It appeared that Moscow was counting on either a forced change of direction in the institution of a West German government or a breakdown in the airlift over the winter, or both.[22]

From the beginning of the negotiations in Moscow and then in Berlin, the British, and initially possibly Ambassador Smith, had been more optimistic about a solution than the State Department, Clay, or Douglas. Anticipating failure, Douglas early put pressure on Bevin to agree to threaten to go to the United Nations if the talks broke down. Reluctantly, Bevin concurred if and when it seemed appropriate, but "with . . . misgivings." Any such announcement to Stalin would be "a damp squib," he told Douglas. But, "if the United States Government wanted it, I would acquiesce." As the discussions in Berlin neared a deadlock, Douglas was able to report to Lovett that the British were prepared to go to the United Nations, probably the Security Council, although some in the Foreign Office feared the veto there, but that the French government, in the midst of another cabinet crisis, was willing only to consider the possibility.[23]

When the Allied Control Council talks in Berlin had broken down completely on September 7, Murphy observed: "It is clear that [the] Soviets are making only those proposals which would give them complete control so as to make our acceptance impossible." The next day, Douglas was instructed to prepare with the British and French the aide-mémoire to be presented to Molotov in Moscow. These discussions proved to be exceptionally difficult and at times acrimonious. The United States, in the words of Marshall, wished to give "clear evidence of our willingness to break if they persist in their attitude." The British and the

French wanted to "leave the issues blurred and offer the Russians an opportunity to prolong the discussions on what we would regard an unsatisfactory basis and under most humiliating conditions."

Douglas pressed his case with vigor. Bevin stood firm: "It was quite impossible for me . . . to commit His Majesty's Government to something that might mean war. There was a very strong feeling, deeply resented here, that the United States were trying to boss us. That was something that neither the Cabinet or Parliament would accept." Douglas, drafting and redrafting the document in conference with Bevin, Strang, and Massigli and nightly on the telecon with Washington, "looked," Bevin observed to Franks, "tired and ill." In Washington, Franks approached Marshall to present the British case personally to see if it were "not possible to improve matters." In consequence, after consultation that day with Vandenberg, Royall, and Draper, Marshall decided "[t]o put the importance of three-power unity ahead of everything else." In his diary the night before, Forrestal had written: "This is the seventy-ninth day of negotiations and all persons concerned are close to a state of exhaustion—telecon conversations with Douglas in London ceased at 2 o'clock this morning, which was seven o'clock London time, and were resumed this morning at 8:30." On September 12, a mutually acceptable aide-mémoire was drafted, which listed the conditions under which the three powers would agree to resume discussions among the military governors, thus leaving the door slightly open. The Soviet reply, on September 18, effectively closed it.[24]

At that point, the United States government was in favor of recognizing a break and referring the matter to the United Nations, then meeting in Paris. Bevin complained that Douglas "in his usual manner tried to make me commit myself in advance to decisions which I had made it clear could best . . . be taken in Paris by the three Ministers together. . . . He put questions about it which seemed to suggest that one of my motives might be to delay proceedings." He denied the implication and expressed the hope that the issue was not going to lead to another wrangle with Washington.[25]

The three foreign ministers met in Paris on September 20. Meantime, the "standing committee" in London had prepared a draft reply to the Soviet note of the 18th. The following day, it was reviewed by Marshall, Schuman, and Bevin. Douglas, Strang, Patrick Dean, head of the German Political Department in the Foreign Office, and Massigli withdrew to revise it in accordance with the changes agreed upon. It was brief, reviewing the position of the Western powers and inquiring if Moscow was prepared to lift the blockade in order that discussions might continue. The Soviet answer, considerably longer and more involuted, was negative. Accordingly, the three ministers accepted the drafting committee's text of a new note, which delineated the previous discussions and exchanges and informed the Soviet government that its action in Berlin would be referred to the Security Council under Article 33 of the Charter. Douglas raised with Philip Jessup and Marshall the crucial question as to whether the United States was taking the case to the UN for "moral backing" for whatever further measures it might feel obliged to take, including force, or whether the submission was "sincerely designed to assist in reaching some kind of a solution." Marshall indicated that the

United States had "to recognize the implication of the step" and, barring a completely unacceptable resolution, should "be prepared to carry through."[26]

On October 4, the Berlin question was placed on the agenda of the Security Council. The ensuing debate led to a proposal by several neutral powers looking toward a resolution of the problem. When put to a vote, on October 25, it was supported by nine members including the Western powers, but vetoed by the Soviet Union. Thereafter, sporadic attempts were made and suggestions advanced for breaking the deadlock. The work of a United Nations Technical Committee on Berlin Currency and Trade proved fruitless. Meantime, the airlift continued through the winter with remarkable success, despite periods of miserable weather.[27]

Clay continued to be convinced that the Russians would not push the issue to the point of conflict and was cheered by the remarkable performance of the airlift. To visiting author-diarist Harold Nicolson, he put the odds of war at "one in ten." "The Russians know they would be licked. If they cut our air-route, they know it is an act of war. They won't cut our air-route," he stated flatly. Douglas was not so sanguine. Through the fall, he suggested several compromise solutions in conversations with the British and communications to the State Department. He admitted that some of his ideas "might be construed as a retreat on our part and therefore be taken as a sign of weakness. But if the neutrals were to ask us if we would accept something along these lines, this objection might be met at least in part." "I hope," he wrote to his father, "we can find some way out of the Berlin dilemma. The danger is so great should it become a casus belli nothing could prevent the Soviet armies from sweeping across the continent to the Atlantic littoral—occupying France, the Low Countries. A horrible spectacle to contemplate for the Soviet would ruthlessly exterminate all the friends and every element of civilization in the west." Back in the United States on a brief visit in early November, he told a dinner party at the Forrestals', which included Allen Dulles, that it was "essential to get a settlement of the Berlin impasse." He thought the Russians were also seeking "some face-saving formula."[28]

Speaking to Walter Lippmann, who was in London in December, Douglas revealed his afterthoughts about the State Department's handling of the crisis in the summer and his fears for the future. Somewhat belatedly, he now questioned the wisdom of the London Conference decision on an early formation of a West German government, since it had probably triggered the blockade. Looking back on the subsequent negotiations, he felt that agreement might have been reached by the military governors if the matter had been referred back to them after the breakdown, on September 7, of their discussions. Instead, in essence, the Western powers ceased to negotiate. He was convinced that the situation in Berlin would worsen rather than improve, as Clay predicted. Certainly, Berlin was not worth a war. He blamed much of the difficulty on Clay's independence from the State Department and felt that Bohlen's influence on Marshall had been unfortunate in persuading him to take too intransigent a position during the negotiations. Clay's cognizance of these apprehensions was later acknowledged when he wrote that though Douglas agreed that they must stay in Berlin "up to the point of war . . . he felt that war must be avoided at all costs as a Soviet holocaust would destroy the remaining liberal thought in Europe."[29]

Whatever Douglas's later doubts about the haste in forming a West German government, the movement was already well under way as he expressed his views to Lippmann. In September, a constituent assembly had been convened in Bonn, which was to adopt in May, 1949 a "Basic Law for the Federal Republic of Germany." Moreover, on March 20, at the urging of West German officials, the Western military governors had declared the Deutschmark the only legal tender in West Berlin, despite British and French reluctance and Douglas's fear the action would produce additional Soviet countermeasures. As to the blockade, the logjam began to move only after Marshall had left office and was succeeded by Dean Acheson. In late January, 1949, Stalin gave a hint of compromise in answer to a question put by an American journalist. Jessup picked up the ball in secret talks with Soviet UN Representative Yakov Malik, which led to a public announcement on May 5 by the Four Powers that the blockade would be raised in return for a lifting of the counter-blockade and a reconvening of the Council of Foreign Ministers. That CFM meeting, which took place in Paris between May 23 and June 20, accomplished nothing, but was a face-saving device for the Russians.[30]

During the height of the Berlin crisis from June through September, London had been the center of activity in coordinating Western policy and drafting the various diplomatic notes in a manner acceptable to all parties. Douglas always considered it the most difficult and demanding period of his tenure. Much later, Sir Patrick Dean, who had meantime served as ambassador to the United States, described Douglas's contribution succinctly: "He did more than anybody else on the American side to bring both firmness and wisdom to bear at a very critical time."[31]

23

Palestine and Presidential Politics

THE RESOLUTION OF ARAB AND JEWISH CLAIMS in Britain's Palestine Mandate and the sharp Anglo-American differences over their solution were to occupy much of Lewis Douglas's time and energy during 1948, concurrently with the Berlin crisis. In fact, as early as the eve of his ambassadorial nomination to the Senate there had been a display of the growing British bitterness over politicization of the issue in the United States. On February 25, 1947, Ernest Bevin, frustrated by his unsuccessful recent attempt to reach a solution by a conference of Arabs and Jews in London, lashed out in the House of Commons at what he called Truman's exploitation of the issue for domestic political gain. Harking back to President Truman's support of increased Jewish immigration and especially his statement of October 4, 1946, before the congressional elections, favoring the concept of a separate Jewish state, Bevin blamed the failure of his talks with Jewish leaders in Paris that fall and at the later London conference on American interference. He disclosed that he had begged Secretary Byrnes to dissuade the President from speaking out, but was told that if Truman did not Thomas Dewey would. Angrily he concluded: "I really must point out that in international affairs I cannot settle things if my problem is made the subject of local elections."

Although he disclaimed any intention of arousing ill-feeling in the United States, Bevin's remarks most certainly did so, in the White House and among many segments of American opinion. The episode was a sobering foretaste for Douglas of the difficulties he was to face on the problem.[1]

Unable to resolve the issues unilaterally, the British referred the Palestinian question to the General Assembly of the United Nations, which met in its first special session in New York on April 28, 1947. There, a special committee was appointed to make recommendations to the regular session in September. During this period, and in fact throughout 1947, most of the discussions on the problem between the British and American governments were carried out in Washington.

Although Douglas was not directly involved, he did, on at least two occasions, make his predilections clear. Speaking to the British-American Parliamentary Group on May 5, he deplored the Zionist campaign in America. He thought it was doing great harm to Great Britain and hinted darkly that other anti-British influences were pouring money into the movement. Somewhat baffled by the ambassador's veiled accusations, neither the Foreign Office nor the Washington embassy was able to identify his targets. "Still," as one Foreign Office official minuted, "Mr. Douglas should know what he is talking about." Whatever Douglas's sources, his comments may have reflected State Department fears of Soviet intrusion into the Palestine problem.[2]

A month later, Douglas assured Bevin that "he was doing everything in his power to bring pressure to bear against the subversive activities of the Jews in the United States." Bevin welcomed his remarks. On September 9, Bevin complained to Douglas and Loy Henderson, director of the State Department Office of Near Eastern and African Affairs, that Washington had contributed to British problems in Palestine. His efforts to make progress had been complicated by statements urging the admission of 100,000 immigrants. Illegal immigration had received "financial and moral support" in the United States, and "publicity campaigns" had been carried on in support of Jewish terrorists. Referring to the recent recommendation for partition by the United Nations Special Committee, he gave clear warning of Britain's reluctance, in fact inability, to carry out the overseer role assigned to it by the majority plan.[3]

The report, issued on August 31, consisted of a majority and a minority plan. The first recommended partition into a Jewish and an Arab state, each to become independent after a transitional period of two years, and with the city of Jerusalem to be placed under the trusteeship of the United Nations. The minority plan called for a unitary federal state with Jerusalem as the capital, with a three-year transitional period under the supervision of an agency of the UN. Under a provision of the majority plan, Britain was to continue the administration of Palestine during the transitional period and admit into the Jewish area 150,000 immigrants.[4]

The report was submitted to the General Assembly for a decision at its regular session at Lake Success, New York, in mid-September. During the next two and one-half months, tensions on the issue were high in that body, in the United States, Britain, and the Near East—and in the White House. The President supported partition. He was moved by deep sympathy with the plight of Jewish refugees in Europe, influenced by a great deal of often-resented political pressure from pro-Zionist groups in the United States, and swayed by the friendly persuasion of his one-time business partner, Eddie Jacobson, as well as by respect for the personality and arguments of Chaim Weizmann, the distinguished British chemist who was to become the first President of Israel. The Arabs opposed partition. They were supported by a number of career State Department officials, including Henderson, who feared it would be a vehicle for Soviet penetration into the area and were convinced it could only be accomplished by force, which would alienate the U.S. from the Arab states, whose oil America coveted. On October 11, the United States officially announced its support for partition. During the ensuing weeks there was further controversy over the precise lines of the demarcation, and considerable acrimony over American pressure on other delegates to support partition. The final vote on November 29 was 33 to 13 in favor of partition, with 10 abstentions. The outcome was certainly influenced by the Soviet decision to cast its ballot and influence with the majority. Conflict between Arabs and Jews broke out immediately. The British reaffirmed their intention to withdraw from the mandate, setting the date of May 15, 1948, and not to oversee the division.[5]

During the last days of the debate in the UN, Marshall was attending the Council of Foreign Ministers meeting in London. Although the burden of discussions was on the issues before the council, he was exposed to several monologues by Bevin on British concern over developing events in Palestine. On the evening of November 24, at a dinner for Marshall, Douglas, and several other guests, Bevin elaborated on the British position. According to Marshall, the foreign secretary stated that "the unanimous political reaction" in his country was opposed to "Jewish influence in Palestine," that "anti-Jewish feeling in England now was greater than it had been in a hundred years," that Jewish pressures in the United States had sabotaged his earlier efforts to find a solution, and reminded his guests that the Balfour Declaration had called for a Jewish home, not a Jewish state. "I made no answer to his various statements," Marshall wrote Lovett, "other than to say that I had sympathy for the British in their difficulties in Palestine and under the pressures of the American Jew."[6]

After the vote at Lake Success, Bevin gave Marshall an informal note, confirming that the British would leave their mandate on May 15 and commenting on the difficulties he anticipated in implementing the withdrawal. He emphasized the necessity of stopping illegal immigration in the interim. Otherwise, Arabs would massacre Jews, and outside forces would be required to preserve order. If the United States was requested to provide troops, would not the Soviet government also demand participation? Marshall confessed this was of great concern to the American military establishment, but he doubted the Jews would press the immigration issue now that partition was near at hand. Bevin disagreed: "He had no confidence in the Jewish Agency."[7]

When Marshall paid his farewell call on December 17, Bevin returned to the subject by commenting that the Arab reactions were even more violent than had been expected. He was attempting to calm them. As to the Soviet support of partition, he saw it as a calculated maneuver to incite violence in the area, which would provide an excuse for them to intervene. Marshall suggested that the situation was not as serious as Bevin painted. Apparently dissatisfied with this reaction, Bevin sent an amplification of his remarks in a memorandum to the State Department, reiterating his alarm. "It would be dangerous to underrate Arab resentment. . . . [A]ll possible steps should be taken by the United States Government, not only to reassure the Arabs, but also to persuade the Jews, even tho it means the exercise by the latter of considerable restraint, to make good in deeds their words of friendship to the Arabs."[8]

While Marshall tended to discount Bevin's apprehensions, others in the State Department, impressed with the increasing level of conflict in Palestine and already predisposed to question the wisdom of partition, were exploring alternatives. Although it is difficult to believe that Douglas was unaware of this activity during his sojourn in Washington working with Congress for ERP, he does not seem to have discussed it in his conversation with Bevin on his return to London, February 19, 1948. Ten days later, he commented that he had heard nothing from the State

Department on the issue, but, according to Bevin's version, added: "The United States Government was trying to extricate itself from the impossible position they had gotten into." Bevin offered to help Marshall privately if he could. "Perhaps, however, everyone has been put in such a difficult position owing to U.S. policy that they might all like to get out of it," he noted.[9]

As the prospects for a relatively peaceful accomplishment of partition rapidly deteriorated, Washington began to reassess its position. The Arab League nations had made clear their determination to oppose the decision by force and threatened to refuse American access to oil pipelines. The British not only had announced their determination to leave the mandate on May 15, but in the interim had refused the Jews the right to raise and train an army to defend themselves. Meantime, as the spring wore on, the Czechoslovakian crisis and the ominous developments in Berlin presaged the possibility of other calls on America's limited military resources if she was asked to help enforce partition. Douglas's remarks to Bevin probably reflected his knowledge that the State Department had already moved a considerable distance in a decision to abandon partition temporarily and opt for a United Nations trusteeship. The White House, however, vacillated between recognition of the necessity to change course and sympathy for the Jewish cause, combined with domestic political considerations in an election year and tremendous Zionist pressure inside and outside the country.

On March 19 U.S. ambassador to the United Nations Warren Austin recommended to the Security Council that the matter be referred back to the General Assembly and that meanwhile Palestine be placed under a United Nations trusteeship. The violent reaction from the Jewish community was most embarrassing to Truman. In the end, however, he stood by the decision, declaring that prevailing conditions in Palestine precluded a peaceful solution and that the United States was not prepared to commit troops to enforce partition. Trusteeship would be only a temporary measure to maintain order following the British withdrawal. Partition remained the ultimate aim of the American government.[10]

By the time these events took place, Douglas was again in Washington, lobbying for the Marshall Plan. Waldemar Gallman, as chargé d'affaires, cabled the initial British reaction to the U.S. action, which was far from reassuring. Although the Foreign Office was sympathetic to the American attempt to maintain peace in Palestine and desired to be helpful, domestic considerations, for the time being at least, precluded British participation in policing a trusteeship. The "British Cabinet and British politicians are deeply sensible of [the] overwhelming popular demand in [the] UK to get 'the boys' home from Palestine," and any attempt to keep British troops there, however briefly and for whatever reason, in the face of terrorist attacks, would produce a violent response. On April 1, the Security Council passed two resolutions, the first calling for a truce in Palestine and creating a truce commission, the second convening a special session of the General Assembly, which Austin made clear would receive a trusteeship proposal from the United States.[11]

Before Douglas returned to London, certain members of the State Department drafted a personal letter from Truman to Attlee, to be carried by the ambassador, appealing for British cooperation in the trusteeship plan, including the provision of troops. For whatever reason, it was not approved by Robert Lovett, possibly in consultation with the President. Instead, Lovett sent a circular telegram to diplomatic representatives accredited to concerned countries, instructing them to discuss the proposed UN trusteeship with the prime minister or foreign minister. It would be a "temporary" arrangement, "without prejudice . . . to the eventual political settlement . . . whenever the Arab and Jewish communities agree upon the future government." A more specific request for British and French participation in maintaining security during the trusteeship was dispatched by Lovett to Douglas three days later. Douglas was to point out the increasing irritation of other UN members at Britain's refusal, having handed the problem to that body, to participate in finding a solution. American public opinion was particularly aroused and Anglo-American cooperation in other areas endangered.[12]

Bevin's response to Douglas was sharp. London would await the discussion in the General Assembly before making any decisions. But, he emphasized, the United States request for a continued active British role must remain secret. If it became "publicly known, it would arouse such hostility here that it would endanger the relations" between the two countries. "If any statesman in this country suggested that His Majesty's Government should take further responsibility for Palestine, he would not survive for a moment." He told Douglas the British government had no alternative suggestions to make. Meantime, other sources in the Foreign Office, Douglas reported, were "unanimously" of the opinion that the use of French troops would "be disastrous," provoking a "violent reaction because of [the] general Arab attitude towards France."[13]

Disappointed but persistent, Lovett instructed Douglas to return to the charge. Over the next two weeks, his pressure on Bevin and Attlee, who the State Department apparently hoped would be more flexible, were of no avail. On April 28, replying to Douglas's expression of concern that Abdullah of Trans-Jordan might invade Palestine, Attlee sharply asked: "What was aggression? Was it aggression for Arabs to come into Palestine from their own countries, and non-aggression for Jews to come in by sea to the tune of thousands?" But the Jews were unarmed, Douglas protested. Attlee responded that was "Hitler's method": put people in as "tourists," then arm them. Finally, however, the ministers agreed that if the Jews would restrain themselves, Britain would try to restrain the Arabs. Douglas assured Lovett of his conviction that "Bevin is deeply concerned" and was not "deliberately adopting a 'Dog-in-the manger' attitude. . . . He is, however, at his wits' end to know what to do." Furthermore, the Conservative party was also "vigorously opposed" to the retention of British troops in the mandate. Churchill had personally assured him of this position "in unqualified terms." "This political situation," Douglas concluded, "which I am confident I accurately assess, makes Bevin's position doubly difficult."[14]

Meantime, at the General Assembly the trusteeship idea was getting nowhere. The call for a truce had been ignored by both sides. Trusteeship was seen by the Arabs as a prelude to partition, by the Jews as a denial of statehood. In desperation, as the May 15 deadline drew near, Truman proposed a ten-day cease-fire, during which the mandate would be extended, the General Assembly recessed, and on-the-spot truce negotiations take place. The Arab reaction was highly qualified, the Jewish response negative. The British government refused to change its decision to give up the mandate on May 15.[15]

With time running out and neither UN trusteeship nor an extension of the mandate in sight, pressure was building up in the White House to recognize the new state which the Jews were clearly determined to declare on the termination of British control. It was generated, in part certainly, by fear that the Russians would do so, providing a pretext to inject themselves into the area by coming to the aid of the Jews. But undoubtedly the most pressing consideration was political. Several of Truman's advisors, especially David Niles, administrative assistant for minorities, and Clark Clifford, special counsel to the President, urged recognition, both from personal conviction and to attract the Jewish vote in the coming presidential election. On the other hand, the State Department, with Marshall and Lovett in the forefront, firmly opposed the recommendation.

In a high-level strategy meeting at the White House on May 12, the two sides confronted each other before the President. Lovett bluntly warned that it would be an act of bad faith to recognize while the matter of a truce was still before the General Assembly, and he disparaged the political considerations as both unethical and counterproductive. Marshall was even more forthright: "I said bluntly that if the President were to follow Mr. Clifford's advice and if in the elections I were to vote, I would vote against the President." This was strong language, which probably Truman would have accepted only from the general, who did not, however, go so far as to deny the President's right to recognize nor threaten to resign if he did so. Truman was dissuaded from any early announcement of his intentions.[16]

The next twenty-four hours were marked by hectic activity on the part of the Jewish Agency in behalf of immediate recognition and by the State Department to prevent it. But at 6:11 P.M., Washington time, May 14, minutes after the Jewish Act of Independence came into force, the White House announced de facto recognition of the state of Israel. Consternation reigned at the State Department and at the General Assembly, especially within the United States delegation. Marshall, though deeply chagrined, remained loyally at his post.[17]

In London, reflecting the disarray in the State Department and the speed of the action, the first communication from the embassy to the Foreign Office was a note to Bevin, indicating that "The Ambassador has been instructed" to inform him that the Provisional Jewish State was expected to request recognition from the United States and that "in the present circumstances we feel that we should grant recognition . . . as the de facto authority." It was scornfully minuted by a Foreign Office official: "Written the day *after* the U.S. President granted de facto recognition."[18]

Bevin dispatched a note to his Washington embassy and the U.K. delegation at the UN, which in first draft began: "We do not wish to enter into recriminations with [the] U.S. Government about their recognition of the Jewish State without any warning to us . . . ," but was toned down to "Without dealing at present with other aspects of . . . [the] recognition. . . ." The gist of that message and a second one of the same day was to inquire of Washington the status of the truce negotiations and to make clear to the American authorities that Britain not only had no intention of following suit on recognition but would veto any attempt to obtain Israeli membership in the United Nations. The latter step seemed unlikely,

Bevin admitted. "But American policy over Palestine is so wild and unpredictable that it may help you to have this indication of my present views."[19]

Douglas made his views clear to both the Foreign Office and his own government. Lunching with Superintending Under Secretary of State Michael Wright on May 21, he expressed the fear that decisions in Washington were being taken without "adequate thought or understanding of their consequences." Perhaps together they "could succeed in impressing on Washington the dangerous results of their continuing on their present course . . . and then be able to work backwards toward some more sensible line in common." He cabled Lovett that "irrespective of rights and wrongs of question, I believe worst shock so far to general Anglo-American concert of policy since I have been here was sudden US de facto recognition of Jewish state without previous notice of our intentions to British Government." To his father he expressed his consternation even more bluntly. "What an unholy mess we have made of it [the Palestine question], solely because of political considerations at home. It is a shocking performance, and I confess that the behavior of my country in this respect is the cause of no little sense of personal shame."[20]

Over the next month, however, the tension between the two countries began to ease. On May 22, Douglas had a long conversation with Bevin, which cleared the air somewhat. Two days later, Truman, on Marshall's urging, accepted the recommendation of Douglas and Bevin that no attempt be made to raise the arms embargo to the Middle East to assist the Jews. Douglas met with concerned members of the government, including Bevin, Attlee, Minister of Defence A. V. Alexander, as well as the heads of the military, naval, and air establishments, to review the political and strategic situation in Palestine. Afterward, he expressed to Washington his "genuine hope of US-UK cooperation" in solving the problem "only if neither government is so carried away with emotional factors as to back either one or other side for military victory." With a truce, the two governments should approach the Arabs and the Jews on an "equal footing and in close collaboration." On May 14, the General Assembly had called for a truce, to be implemented by the Security Council, and Count Folke Bernadotte, president of the Swedish Red Cross, accepted the position of mediator. On May 29, the Security Council called for a four-week cease-fire, which was accepted by both sides three days later and was to go into effect June 11.[21]

Fences were further mended in conversations by Douglas with Michael Wright and Bevin. Both emphasized that "renewed divergences" over Palestine would present "formidable risks." The two countries must concert their actions, "exchange and pool all information," and, if the mediator requested counsel, offer "joint advice." Douglas thoroughly agreed and urged the State Department to consider the conversations an "extension" of his earlier meeting with the cabinet members and Service Chiefs and welcome evidence of the British desire to keep Britain and the United States "in step re Palestine." By June 19 he was reporting encouraging evidence throughout the Foreign Office "and among English Arab experts outside government that early establishment small compact Jewish state be in best interest Arabs." It was, he believed, a "milestone in British thinking."[22]

Marshall's response to these communications was entirely affirmative. Close collaboration was essential. The department also favored redrawing the Israeli boundaries "to make a compact and homogeneous state, the remainder to go largely to Transjordan with appropriate transfer of populations," the frontiers to be guaranteed by mutual agreement and the UN. Jerusalem would remain an international city. Wright "warmly welcomed" the agreement to concert the views and recommendations of the two countries. Most important to Douglas's future involvement, Wright suggested that the "main channel" of communication be the London embassy. Douglas cabled Marshall he would "be the goat," if the department wished. Lovett agreed. "Neither Cadogan [Sir Alexander, British representative to the Security Council] nor the Embassy here have as direct and as influential access to Bevin as you and . . . [while your description of yourself as 'the goat'] is painfully correct, we shall be glad to look to you as our principal negotiator with the UK. . . . We are gratified by the energy and skill which you have displayed in treating with Bevin on this problem which is so surcharged with emotion as well as difficulty and would welcome your views as to an eventual *modus vivendi* and any comment you may have in mind on our own ideas in this regard."[23]

Bevin had meanwhile recommended to Douglas that he be the principal channel of communication with the Foreign Office on the Berlin blockade. By July 7, Douglas had received further departmental authorization to act on his own in decisions on Palestine demanding haste, "so long as HMG sticks to the generally established line." He was now at the center of both crises.[24]

The confidence in Douglas was certainly not shared by the Jewish community and pro-Zionist opinion in the United States. Understandably suspicious of Britain's and Bevin's pro-Arab sympathies, Zionists viewed with alarm Douglas's collaboration with the Foreign Office, representing a State Department that they perceived as anti-Israel. Through private and public sources, they were well aware of the department's opposition to immediate recognition and accused it of continuing to work with "oil and British interests to thwart the President." In letters to Les Biffle, secretary of the Senate, who forwarded it to Matthew J. Connelly, Truman's confidential secretary, and to Senator J. Howard McGrath, chairman of the Democratic National Committee, Lillie Shultz, director of the *Nation* Associates, warned of the pro-Arab influence in the State Department. She also angrily reported a meeting in the last week of May of Douglas with prominent Labour party representatives. Her informant in London had written: "Douglas agreed that Truman was stupid in recognizing Israel and that Bevin was quite right that the Morrison-Grady plan [for a federative state, proposed by the Anglo-American negotiators in July, 1946] was best. . . . It was so bad that Michael Foot (a Labor Party M.P. and journalist) was defending Truman while Douglas was defending Bevin. . . . Everybody assumes that the State Department is completely with the British."[25]

Whatever the truth of this story, it probably did come close to representing Douglas's views. Bevin's position was starkly revealed in indiscreet remarks to Harold Nicolson after a dinner at the Iranian embassy. He was, in Nicolson's words, "in good form—noisy and vulgar." As to Palestine: "He says that he pays no attention at all to the attacks of the American press. What do they matter?

After all, it is the principle that counts, and nobody is going to tell him that in principle it does not pay better to remain friends with 200 million Moslems than with 200 thousand Jews, 'to say nothing of all the oil.' " But the die had been cast—there was a Jewish state, and it had been recognized by the United States. Now it was necessary for the two countries to make the best of what had occurred and to seek some viable solution in Palestine with a minimum of violence, through British pressure on their Arab clients and American influence on Israel.[26]

During the summer, in the face of frequent violations of the extended cease-fire, Bernadotte tried to formulate mutually acceptable peace terms. Meantime, in London, Douglas worked to coordinate the views of Marshall and Bevin. The British dilemma lay in how much pressure they could put on the Arab states, with whom their long-term influence was in jeopardy. On several occasions, Douglas was asked to join the foreign secretary in meetings with his top advisors on the Middle East. Reporting on these and other discussions at Whitehall, Douglas gave as his view that "it would be a calamity" for all parties concerned "were Britain to lose such vestiges of influence as she still possessed with the Arab governments. The game being played by HMG is one requiring courage and it may be lost if remaining British influence among the Arabs vanished from the Middle East. There is little doubt that the Soviet is ready to take Britain's place." "Lurking in the background," Douglas cabled Lovett, "is the menace of Soviet behavior and the consequences thereof if our side allows the matter to go by default." When the Security Council considered a resolution to renew the cease-fire, which would, Douglas reported, cause a "most unfortunate anti-British local impression in Arab states," Bevin, after much hesitation, decided to vote affirmatively with the United States, "because I think it is right." It was noteworthy that both the Soviet Union and Ukraine abstained. The concurrent Berlin crisis only heightened Western fears of Russian intervention.[27]

By early August, the surprising success of the Jewish forces and the occupation by both sides of territory not assigned to them under the original partition plan had convinced the British that the only solution was to work closely with the United States to legitimize borders approximating the de facto lines that had arisen out of the fighting. Divergence between the U.S. and Great Britain would inspire the Arabs to believe intransigence would induce London to support their attempts to eject the Jews from territory they then held. As Douglas put it to Marshall, "HMG cold-shouldered the Arabs in order to secure their acquiescence to [the] truce" and was ready to do so again to gain their agreement to the de facto situation in Palestine, "provided USG for its part is willing to base its own policy on realities and if necessary, cold-shoulder the Jews."[28]

A few days later, Bevin somberly—"I have never seen him in a more solemn—not petulant mood," cabled Douglas—again raised the Soviet spectre. Past history, he said, confirmed that when the USSR was "thwarted at one point [it] soon transfers its attentions to another." If stopped in Berlin, it might well turn to the attractive "soft spot" of the Middle East. "It would be naive to suppose USSR would refuse to take advantage of a personality such as [Menachem] Beigin [sic] [leader of the Irgun] and of the apparent determination on the part of Jews generally not to let truce work." The Palestine situation was as dangerous as that in Berlin and the same dangers applied—"If US and UK go slack, we lose."

Marshall indicated his general agreement and soon advanced some specific suggestions of his own.[29]

In the midst of these attempts at coordination, a disconcerting and revealing episode occurred with the passage through London of the newly appointed special representative to Israel, James Grover McDonald. A former member of the Anglo-American Committee of Inquiry on Palestine, McDonald had been named to the post by Truman without reference to the State Department, which was both offended by the slight and appalled at the dispatch of a person so clearly identified with the Jewish cause. Arriving in England on July 28, he was informed by Douglas that an appointment had been arranged with Bevin for August 3. Accompanied by the ambassador, McDonald met not only a cool reception from the foreign secretary, but by his own account a diatribe against Truman and the Jews. He was shocked at the attack and dismayed by Douglas's lack of rejoinder. Speaking on the telephone from Geneva two days later to Clark Clifford, he described Bevin's "feeling toward the President [as] . . . something that is difficult to describe. . . . [S]tronger than that [Clifford had suggested "bitter"]. And I haven't met anyone since Hitler who seems to me to have such a mental complex as he has. He's arrogant—opinionated—and he would put the whole responsibility on your Chief." And Douglas had "Just let it pass. . . . He had larger fish to fry. But my own feeling is the way to deal with a man like that is not to let things like that go by." In his "thank you" letter to Douglas, McDonald expressed the same dismay at Bevin's "unwarranted charge of bad faith against the head of a great state," but refrained from any criticism of the ambassador.[30]

On June 28, Bernadotte had offered his first "suggestions" for consideration by the two parties. They envisaged two states, with the Arab areas of Palestine as part of Trans-Jordan, joined in a union to deal with common economic matters, foreign policy, and defense. Bernadotte recommended a change in the original partition plan to give the Negev to the Arabs and to include all or part of western Galilee in the Jewish state. The arrangement was satisfactory to neither side and discussions continued.[31]

By mid-August, Marshall agreed with Bevin that their two countries should take a more active and coordinated role in devising "general principles of settlement" to present to Bernadotte. Dr. Ralph Bunche, the number-two man on the mediation team, had made clear to Marshall that Bernadotte was hesitant to make further recommendations without the assurance that Britain and the United States were "in agreement on [the] general lines of an equitable settlement." Only then did he feel there was a chance to move toward a peaceful solution.[32]

Accordingly, in the greatest secrecy, with Douglas acting as principal negotiator, the State Department and the Foreign Office began to put together a set of proposals for Bernadotte. By August 27, Douglas was able to transmit the essence of the British views, incorporating their understanding of the thinking of their American counterparts. The principal components were the abandonment of the idea of union and approval of the award of the Negev to the Arabs and of western Galilee to the Jews. Jerusalem would be autonomous under UN rule, with the Arab and Jewish areas each having their own municipal administration and with free access to the city by both. The Arab territory would be incorporated into Trans-Jordan. The plan should be submitted directly by Bernadotte to the

Security Council, which would be responsible for its enforcement. At that point, the British and American governments would put pressure on both sides to accept the proposals. Marshall replied that the conclusions of the United States were "practically identical with those suggested in [the] British working paper."[33]

It was, Douglas urged Washington, important to get the recommendations to Bernadotte as quickly as possible. Premature leaks would smack of collusion and jeopardize any hope of success. Quoting Foreign Office officials, he emphasized that "from moment proposals become known they should carry label 'Mediator-made in Sweden.' " "[N]ow cat is half out of bag, quicker bag is handed to Mediator the better." The source of concern was the decision of the State Department to inform the Israeli government of the gist of the understanding on September 6.[34]

American and British diplomats conferred with Count Bernadotte on Rhodes and found that his first draft was remarkably close to their joint recommendations. On September 16, Bernadotte forwarded his report to Secretary-General Trygve Lie, urging that it be put before the General Assembly, not the Security Council as advocated by the United States and Britain, because of the need for prompt action. The following day, on a tour of Jerusalem, Bernadotte and the French UN observer riding with him were assassinated by members of the Stern Gang, a Jewish terrorist group. Three days later, Bernadotte's plan was released in Paris, where the General Assembly was convening.[35]

Douglas was convinced that Bernadotte's report reflected an acceptable compromise that had emerged from the weeks of work in London—"no small achievement." He urged public statements by Marshall and Bevin accepting the proposals as a proper basis of settlement. "When one reviews the situation in its historic perspective, the progress that has been made, however tedious, is not far short of being a miracle." Although Britain was not entirely happy with some points, the plan should "stand or fall as a whole," in the interests of a "solid US-UK front." Britain was, in Bevin's words, prepared "once and for all [to] put His Majesty's Government flatly on record as favoring partition as a permanent solution for Palestine and thus burn His Majesty's boats with the Arabs." But he rejected a joint statement, which would suggest an Anglo-American "deal." A prior British release would encourage the charge that American policy was made in London. Rather, he advised an American statement of unqualified support, followed by one from himself in the House of Commons. Douglas recommended, "with all the force at his disposal," acceptance of that procedure. Marshall, then attending the UN session in Paris, concurred. Having already received Truman's approval of the Negev-Galilee territorial change, and after advising the President of his text, the secretary issued a statement on September 21 urging "the parties and the General Assembly to accept the proposals in their entirety." Bevin made a similar announcement on September 22.[36]

Almost immediately, the Israeli government and the Arab League (with Trans-Jordan confidentially expressing its qualified support of the plan) voiced their disapproval on a variety of opposing points. Of great significance to the subsequent course of events, the Jewish community in the United States responded negatively to the Negev proposal as a betrayal of the promise of the Democratic Convention platform (also the Republican platform) to abide by the November 29, 1947, partition boundaries, unless changes were acceptable to the Israeli government.[37]

Whatever Truman's understanding of his previous approvals, he was now crossing the country on his campaign train, appalled at the possible political repercussions among American Jewish groups. For the moment, however, he was dissuaded by Lovett from demanding a modification or at worst a reversal of Marshall's statement, either by Marshall himself or by a personal presidential message to Jewish leaders. Meantime, the clamor from Jewish organizations, who were publishing full-page advertisements protesting the plan, continued to exert great pressure on the President. Marshall came back to Washington to convince the President that any action would torpedo the plan. In the end Truman was persuaded, in Lovett's words, "that we had better say nothing than say something wrong." For the moment the President was content to insist that the American delegation bend every effort to defer debate and voting in Paris on the plan until after the election—an assignment that Marshall found increasingly embarrassing.[38]

Douglas was horrified at the prospect of a retreat and a breach in the Anglo-American concert. He cabled Marshall on October 14 that it "would turn back the clock many months . . . cause a rebirth of doubts as to the stability of US policy, and hazard the outward recurrence of a serious menace to our national interests. . . . [The President] himself would be the first to realize that no political position, however high—no public office, however great its prestige, is worth gambling with the vital interests of the United States. I would not be serving you, the President, and my country to the best of my ability were I to withhold what I realize is a blunt but considered statement of my best opinion." He wrote his father: "Also Palestine had stuck up its ugly head again in the form of an endeavor on the part of the President to squirm out of our agreement with H.M.G. on the Bernadotte proposals. But I hope we have frustrated the President's plan." As to the decision to avoid a UN vote before the election, Bevin reluctantly agreed to cooperate on Douglas's advice that it was the lesser of several evils. Several days later, Permanent Under Secretary of State for Foreign Affairs Sir Orme Sargent expressed grave doubts as to whether it would "be possible to revive the Bernadotte plan after all this delay." It appeared the Jews would soon force the Egyptians out of the Negev "and [they] will be far too cock-a-hoop to be willing to retreat." As a consequence, the plan, being unenforceable, could no longer gain a two-thirds majority in the Assembly.[39]

Then, on October 22, despite earlier indications that he would not inject the issue into the campaign, the Republican candidate, Thomas E. Dewey, released a letter to the chairman of the American Christian Palestine Committee, accusing Truman of repudiating his previous policy by support of the Bernadotte plan. Truman's answer, Lovett warned Marshall in Paris, was sure to be "immediate and aggressive." "You may wish [to] inform Douglas," he added, "so he can batten down hatches." Two days later, the President, deploring the injection of partisan politics into the Palestine question, publicly reaffirmed his support of the Democratic platform, including rejection of any changes in the boundaries set by the UN partition vote without agreement by Israel and favoring a revision of the current arms embargo. He added that he had instructed government agencies to expedite consideration of Israeli applications for financial aid. Anglo-American cooperation and unity for which Douglas had labored so skillfully and successfully was now seriously endangered.[40]

But, though undoubtedly disheartened and probably angered, Douglas attempted to minimize the damage. With as yet only the press reports on the Dewey-Truman exchange in hand, he reassured Wright that he "did not attach . . . great importance to the statement [of the President]." The two candidates were engaging in the usual campaign exchanges. He was sorry Palestine had to get into it, but he hoped London would not feel obliged to comment. He reiterated his personal dedication to joint support of the plan and his fears of Soviet interference. Wright was not sanguine. In his dispatch to the British UN delegation, he commented that they had already been asked to "meet American wishes in [a] dangerous postponement of [the] discussion of Palestine before the Assembly. On top of this we are now asked to close our ears to irresponsible and harmful public statements."[41]

Although the campaign rhetoric and the concurrent Israeli successes against Egyptian arms in the Negev were seriously eroding the Bernadotte plan, Douglas struggled to convince the State Department that no suggestion should be made at the General Assembly that the United States had, in fact, modified its support. To do so would be "playing directly into Soviet hands. . . . Nothing would please the USSR more than to have another year of turmoil in Palestine and this is an almost certain prospect unless the US and UK by standing shoulder to shoulder can command a 2/3 majority in favor of Bernadotte's proposals." His "understanding" with Bevin was that if the United States took a pro-Israeli position, Britain would be free to take a similar pro-Arab step. "[The] Palestine situation [was]," he warned, "probably as dangerous to our national interests as Berlin." Whereas the German danger had been given wide press coverage, the situation in Palestine had been largely ignored. This had allowed "the Soviet to play her game in the Middle East without attracting attention." Douglas reported that Lieutenant General Gerald Templer, vice-chief of the Imperial General Staff, had called on him to report evidences of greatly increased Soviet influence and activity in the Middle East with the development of the Palestine issue.[42]

On October 29 Marshall flew to London to confer with Douglas, Attlee, Bevin, and others in the Foreign Office. While there, he received commiseration from Lovett, who cabled: "I am sure you agree that our past experience with formally approved positions and instructions which are subsequently and suddenly altered or revoked is increasingly dangerous and intolerable. I can imagine what you have been through in Paris. It has been absolute hell here." The reference was not only to the general vacillation on the Bernadotte plan, but to the immediate instructions to avoid, before the elections, any commitment by the United States on the Security Council resolution to place sanctions on the Jews if they did not withdraw their troops from advanced positions in the Negev.[43]

Douglas arrived in the United States on November 3 to visit his gravely ill father in Montreal, but also, perhaps of equal or greater urgency, to attempt to persuade the President not to desert the Bernadotte plan. It is possible Marshall had encouraged the mission. On November 6 Lovett and Douglas met with Truman, who was still glowing from the upset election victory. Douglas argued vehemently for complete United States support for an unamended Bernadotte plan, which, he emphasized, provided machinery for later adjustments. To offer modifications beforehand would be to open "the flood gates . . . to amendments from all sources, and there would be little if anything left of the cheese when the rats got through [Douglas noted this was a badly mixed metaphor]." He pointed out that the British clearly understood and accepted the need for territorial adjustments for both the Arabs and the Jews, but this should be the work of the conciliatory commission after the acceptance of the entire plan. But the President stood by his platform commitment and subsequent announcement of October 24. He could not support the plan "in its entirety"—a reference to Marshall's statement of September 21—without the concurrence of the Israeli government. Frustrated and angry, Douglas bluntly told the President, to the consternation of Lovett, that he was "taking an action which will come back to haunt our country, if not the whole western world. . . . [T]hree million votes in New York State are not a good enough reason for playing ducks and drakes with our future." Flushed and indignant, Truman rose from his chair to respond, then sat down and said: "I am afraid perhaps you may be right, Lew, but I have gone so far I cannot change now."[44]

Although the Security Council had finally voted to call on the Jews and the Arabs to withdraw to the positions held on October 14, neither side complied. To all intents and purposes the Bernadotte plan was dying and would soon be officially dead. After his return to London on November 10, Douglas continued his labors to keep the United States and Great Britain in harness, but it was a painful and embarrassing exercise. On November 20, Philip Jessup, speaking before the United Nations, declared that, although the United States agreed with the essence of the Bernadotte plan, Israel should have the boundaries laid down in the Partition Resolution of November 29, subject only to her agreement for change. Queried informally by the American embassy as to their reaction, the Foreign Office replied they "were greatly disappointed by the speech which was even worse than we had been led to expect." In Washington, Lovett told the British minister he could hold out no hope of the United States "modifying their attitude."[45]

By the beginning of December, Douglas had notified the State Department of his conviction that it would be inappropriate to discuss further any territorial changes with the British government unless he was specifically instructed to do so. If that should occur, he continued sarcastically, "I hope that it will be borne in mind that any chance of success with [the] UK will depend upon convincing [the] UK that there is a southern frontier somewhere in [the] Negev beyond which [the] US will not support Israeli claims." The official demise of the Bernadotte plan took place on December 11, when the General Assembly passed a resolution that avoided all mention of the partition plan and the Bernadotte proposals, and set up a conciliation commission to assume the previous function of the mediator and the truce commission.[46]

On December 20, two days before his departure for the United States, Douglas was invited by Bevin to a "Palestine" luncheon with the minister of defence, the leading military and naval authorities, and minister of state in the Foreign Office

Hector McNeil. The conversation was in the nature of a post-mortem on their previous efforts and the Bernadotte plan. It was obviously a depressing affair, with Bevin expressing his concern over Communist penetration into the Middle East and his hope that the two governments might still agree on a southern frontier for Israel that they could recommend to the Arabs and Jews with unwavering unanimity. Soon after his arrival in Washington, Douglas discussed this with State Department officials, who made it clear such an arrangement was not presently feasible.[47]

Over the next four months, under the aegis of Dr. Ralph Bunche, who continued as acting mediator under the conciliation commission, armistices were concluded between Israel and Egypt, Syria, Trans-Jordan, and Lebanon along the generally established lines of their respective forces. Most non-Arab states, including the United Kingdom, granted recognition to Israel. But the Palestinian problem was far from solved, and continued over the years to threaten the peace of the area and of the world.

Writing to Brendan Bracken, in 1958, Douglas noted sadly: "Although Truman did many brave and courageous things in international politics, most people have forgotten that he not only condoned but supported the use of force by the Israelis to push their frontiers far beyond anything which the UN had contemplated. . . . [This convinced] the Arab world that we were hostile to them. This is one of the considerations that makes the area so difficult for us to deal with now." Until the end of his life, Douglas was strongly antagonistic to Israeli ambitions and activities and to the continued American commitment to her policies.[48]

24

Personal Misfortune and Diplomatic Tensions

DOUGLAS'S LAST TWO YEARS IN LONDON WERE somewhat less hectic diplomatically than the first two, but were marred by personal loss and misfortune. The Marshall Plan was underway, the Berlin blockade was resolved through other channels, the formation of a West German government was proceeding on schedule, and the Palestine situation was temporarily under some control. Negotiations toward a North Atlantic Treaty had continued largely in Washington and were brought to fruition there, under the aegis of Dean Acheson, in April, 1949. The new secretary of state, who took office on January 21, 1949, was less inclined than his predecessor to delegate authority and more apt to work with London through the extremely able Sir Oliver Franks, with whom he had a splendid relationship. He and Bevin also soon established a remarkable degree of mutual confidence and camaraderie, despite their disparate backgrounds; this further diminished Douglas's role as an intermediary between his principals.[1]

Early in January, 1949, James Stuart Douglas died in Montreal after a lingering illness. On April 4, Douglas suffered a painful, dangerous, and debilitating eye accident that virtually incapacitated him for some months and severely limited his activities from time to time until the end of his tenure. From then on resignation was periodically discussed, but, at the urging of Acheson and the President, he remained at his post for another eighteen months.

Palestine had not been Lewis Douglas's only brush with presidential politics in the campaign of 1948. On June 25, the day after Thomas Dewey's nomination at the Republican convention in Philadelphia, he wrote the governor a warm letter of congratulations, concluding with the interesting comment that he had communicated with reservations, "lest you construe . . . [the letter] and interpret it, to state the case quite frankly, as an expression of hope, on my part, that I would be one of the beneficiaries of the patronage which may soon be yours, but the ties of friendship were stronger than fears you will misunderstand. Of one thing you may be sure, I seek nothing for myself." Dewey's cordial reply invited

Douglas to call on him if he should return to the country in the next few months. Douglas promised to do so.

A few days later, writing to Arthur Vandenberg, he confessed that "You, of course, were my favorite [candidate]," but that he would have hated to see the Senate deprived of his "authority" and "great talents of persuasiveness." Shortly afterward, Walter Lippmann wrote that if Vandenberg had been nominated the senator had planned to keep Douglas in London "as the chief symbol of the continuation of the bi-partisan policy." At the end of July, playwright and friend Robert Sherwood told Douglas that everyone in England feared a Truman defeat would mean his replacement, a tragedy from the British viewpoint. But in mid-October Douglas wrote his father that John Foster Dulles, the Republican member of the United Nations Delegation, had recently assured him in Paris "that Dewey—if elected would ask me to remain on in London at least for several months—possibly a year or more."[2]

Meanwhile, Douglas was approached by the Democratic party for financial support. In early September, National Chairman J. Howard McGrath cabled him requesting a donation then or later during the campaign. There is no reply in the files.[3]

On October 13, Louis Johnson, party finance chairman, cabled then called Douglas in Paris on the "most urgent" need for a contribution to the President's depleted campaign coffers. Over the telephone and in a letter, Douglas explained his refusal. "In the first place, I am a poor man and not a wealthy man." His ambassadorship had required him to dip deeply into his capital. In any case, his resources had never permitted him to make "the sort of contribution which I expect you want." Secondly, "I came to London not because I wanted to come, for the title of Ambassador holds for me no allurements whatsoever. . . . It was understood that I would be completely nonpolitical." He would, as he had always done in the past, make a "modest contribution of between $250 and $500 to the Democratic Committee in Arizona [he, in fact, eventually sent $500]." In conclusion, he reassured Johnson that this position in no way reflected any "lack of respect for the Democratic Party or the President for whom I have a very warm feeling of affection."[4]

Apparently, on October 20, he discussed this exchange with General Marshall. The secretary's comments are unrecorded, but they were probably sympathetic. Some of the party faithful saw Douglas's refusal as disloyal, a violation of his reported earlier pledge or pledges not to stray from the Democratic fold and as evidence of his desire to stay at his post after Truman's expected defeat. Others, who found Louis Johnson's personality and importunities objectionable, did not fault him.[5]

In the event, Douglas voted for Dewey by absentee ballot. A loyal, effective, and influential instrument of Truman's foreign policy, he was nevertheless still opposed to Democratic domestic programs and convinced that under Dewey, partisanship would stop at the water's edge. Much later, commenting on the campaign, he noted that "sixteen years was too long for one party to stay in power." But the day after the election, having just arrived in New York from London, he hastened to telegraph his congratulations to the victorious Truman. At his meeting with Truman at the White House on November 6 and in a follow-up letter on November 9, just before his return to England, he assured the President: "In our entire political history there has been no parallel to the almost single-handed campaign that you carried on to such a successful conclusion. Viewed from afar it was a really amazing performance." In a congratulatory letter of the same date to successful vice-presidential candidate Alben Barkley, he termed the Truman campaign "a magnificent performance."[6]

His letter to Johnson was to prove an embarrassment to Douglas, but there is little reason to believe, as alleged by various journalists shortly afterward, that it was the decisive factor in being passed over as Marshall's successor as secretary of state. The general, who was nearing seventy and in poor health, had made known his desire to retire, even if Truman was reelected. The knowledge of his intention was public, and speculation had begun in early November on his replacement. Among those prominently mentioned and recommended to the President were Averell Harriman, Justice William O. Douglas, Chief Justice Fred M. Vinson, Dean Acheson, and Lewis Douglas.[7]

The matter apparently came up during Douglas's conference with the President on November 6, for three days later he wrote his father: "The question of my succeeding Marshall as Secretary of State will, I fear, become very real and I shall have to answer it. It is very annoying, but I suppose it will have to be reached by my conception of public duty and the sort of commitments the President is prepared to give." Back in London, he responded to an inquiry on the matter from William Campbell, his father's man of business in Montreal: "I am afraid that I may be pressed [on the secretaryship], for in the last conversation I had with Mr. Marshall on Tuesday in Paris, he expressed a very strong opinion that I should not only be asked, but that I should accept. *I assure you I don't look forward to it with any pleasure at all.* On the other hand, I know I am in the dog house with certain of the Democratic politicians, because I took the position during the campaign that I was a part of a non-partisan, non-political group charged with the responsibility of foreign policy, and that I would not in any way contaminate my position in this respect. This may provide me with relief."[8]

By that time Truman had been informed of Douglas's exchange with Johnson and it was soon to be aired in the press. Then and later, some commentators attributed the choice of Acheson to the President's resentment. But the burden of evidence suggests that, to whatever extent Marshall may have urged Douglas's appointment to Truman and however dismayed the President may have been at his refusal of campaign support, Acheson was his first choice from the outset. Even as Douglas wrote Campbell, Truman had prevailed upon Acheson to return from the private practice of the law to take over from Marshall at the beginning of the new term. His acceptance was to be kept secret until January 7. No doubt Douglas and the others named were considered as alternatives if Acheson could not be persuaded to accept. Whether Douglas ever formally expressed his reluctance to assume the task is not clear, but later he stated flatly he had at some point indicated that if the position was offered he would not accept.[9]

Meanwhile, in accordance with custom and practice and "perhaps the President's wishes," as he wrote Secretary Marshall, Douglas had submitted his resignation to Truman, "to take effect at your pleasure," before the beginning of the new term. Apparently, unlike his reaction in some similar cases, the President, aware of Douglas's history of political independence as well as his great value in London, had taken little umbrage at the ambassador's lack of campaign support. To Douglas Fairbanks, Jr., dining at the White House early in December, he made a point of praising Douglas warmly. There is no record of his replying to the resignation letter of December 17.[10]

When Douglas met Truman on January 24, he raised the question again, citing "personal problems which [he thought] . . . required his resigning"—referring probably to his duties at Mutual Life. Truman refused, saying he was "most anxious" for him to retain his post. Douglas agreed to stay on at least four or five months. Informed of this conversation, Acheson told Truman he hoped Douglas could be persuaded to stay much longer. The problems of Germany, Palestine, and the Marshall Plan, and the work toward a North Atlantic Treaty were all still in the "acutely active stage." "It would be a great detriment to have Mr. Douglas leave." Accordingly, he was authorized by Truman "to do everything possible to induce Ambassador Douglas to stay as long as possible."[11]

On January 2, 1949, James Stuart Douglas died in Montreal of congestive heart disease. He was buried in Mt. Hermon Cemetery in Quebec beside the rest of his family. Since late 1947, he had been in failing health, a source of constant concern to his son, absent in London with so few opportunities to visit his father. Douglas had written as often as his hectic schedule permitted, and it was now his father's correspondence that diminished as his energy declined. But the son was in continual receipt of information on his father's condition from Campbell and the physicians in attendance. Early in 1948, James Douglas had been well enough to undertake a last trip to Arizona to visit old haunts and see his surviving friends and associates. But, by mid-year, he was largely confined to his home and frequently to his bed. Lewis's two days in Montreal in November were the first time he had seen his father in eight months and their last reunion before his death.[12]

Rawhide Jimmy had been a difficult father, but their mutual devotion was unquestioned. With his passing, a formidable but loving influence disappeared from Douglas's life. As one Arizona obituary aptly described his character: "He sometimes exhibited a harshness that chilled those closest to him, then his sympathetic nature would unfold like a benediction, sweeping every trace of resentment away." Certainly his pride in his son's accomplishments was matched by his generosity during Douglas's years of public service, in the Congress, as principal of McGill, and finally as ambassador. During the first year at his London post, Douglas received £6000 from his father and, in October, 1948, an additional £20,000. This support was of great assistance in maintaining the expensive London post, however modest the Douglases attempted to keep their establishment.[13]

In the last decade of his life, James Douglas's generosity also extended to universities, hospitals, and churches in Canada, to which he gave large benefactions, admittedly a subject of some concern to his heirs. In consequence, his estate was considerably less than might have been expected. In his last will, drawn up in November, 1948, he left further large sums to charity and a number of individual bequests to relatives and friends, the remainder going equally to his two sons, amounting eventually to approximately $750,000 each. This inheritance was to ease greatly Douglas's pecuniary problems and to allow him soon to consider seriously a financial opportunity in Tucson—purchase of a controlling interest in the Southern Arizona Bank.[14]

On February 3, Douglas returned to his post, where there were two questions that demanded his immediate attention. He was to attempt to reach agreement with the British and French on a reassessment of the dismantling program and on the prohibitions and restrictions to be placed on industry, in connection with the ongoing negotiations for the formation of the West German state. At the same time, he was to chair preliminary discussions looking toward a military assistance program to the Western Union nations, coincident with the forthcoming North Atlantic Treaty.[15]

After the London Conference on Germany, the Western military governors had been unable to agree on the specifics of further dismantling for reparations or the extent of continued limitations and restrictions on remaining industries. In the fall, a team of American industrialists, chaired by George Humphrey, had conducted a survey and made recommendations, which were referred to an intergovernmental conference in London. Since the majority of the plants were in the British Zone, Douglas's task, to gain acceptance of the Humphrey list of retained plants without the imposition of an inordinate number of restrictions on the amount and nature of their production, was a touchy one. The French and the British were both deeply concerned about security, and the British were alive to the implications of industrial competition. But the State Department, with Clay's strong support, was convinced that a more lenient and realistic approach was necessary if West Germany was to provide for her own needs and make a contribution to ERP.[16]

Initially, the British balked at the number of retained plants recommended by Humphrey and insisted upon a firm linkage between the dismantling decision and definite agreements on prohibitions and limitations. The United States wished to defer final arrangements on the latter issue until a peace treaty and to take care of the former, which it considered more urgent, immediately. When Douglas pushed this position with Bevin, British displeasure at the pressure reached Attlee, who complained of "his growing irritation at the American practice of demanding decisions and replies from us at ridiculously short notice," citing specifically "Mr. Douglas's latest representations on dismantling." Douglas hoped that an assurance that the negotiations on prohibited and restricted industries would be initiated at an early date might reduce British objections to handling the issues separately. But Bevin and the cabinet remained determined to conduct the two negotiations together.[17]

When Douglas passed the word to Bevin that Congress might cut economic recovery funds to countries receiving reparations payments if they refused to proceed with only the dismantling settlement alone, the foreign secretary at first suggested they might well accept that risk, but then agreed to go back to the cabinet with the problem. In the face of the British, and to a lesser degree French, adamancy on the subject, Douglas was finally instructed to agree to discuss both issues. But it was to be understood that any agreement on prohibited and restricted industries would be limited to the period preceding the peace treaty and that, if agreement was not reached in four or five days, the United States would revert to dealing with the two subjects separately.[18]

Douglas, Bevin, and Schuman began their meetings on March 14. They were painful and at times acrimonious sessions. Schuman said "little," but Bevin was "generally petulant," Douglas reported. Clay was fearful that Douglas would go too far in placating the British and French. "Lew is a grand fellow," he commented, "but he likes to be liked and is always [an] eager beaver to reach agreement in which everyone is happy." When Douglas requested his presence and advice, Clay at first declined: "Mr. Douglas has infinite confidence in his knowledge of Germany. . . . I am afraid my visit would be helpful neither to Mr. Douglas nor to me and would wind up in further disagreement between us." Later he consented to come.[19]

In the end, concessions were made by all parties, with the final recommendation adhering closely to the American position: only 8 of the 167 plants recommended by Humphrey for retention were to be dismantled, and final long-term prohibitions on German industry would be deferred until the peace treaty. The short-term prohibitions in the interests of security were somewhat less sweeping than the original British and French demands. Agreements were reached on March 31 and forwarded to the military governors, who soon put them into effect. "There is a very good feeling here [in Washington]," Robert Murphy, now acting director of the German and Austrian Office in the department, wrote the ambassador in a letter marked "Personal and Secret," "about the skillful way in which you handled PRI [Prohibited and Restricted Industries] and REP [Reparations] in London." As often in the past, Douglas's success belied Clay's initial ire and expectations. Later, rather grudgingly, he wrote that Douglas "had a difficult negotiation to conclude." He had been able, however, "to obtain some major concessions from both the British and French representatives." But there was a price to be paid for virtual American victory, as Douglas reported during the discussions. "Perhaps," he wrote Murphy, "my reports have not given you [the] full flavor of [the] diet here, the heat to which we have subjected Bevin and Schuman, the unwillingness with which they permitted me to extract concessions and [the] bitterness which remains."[20]

Simultaneously with the discussions on Germany, Douglas was assigned the task of coordinating the formal negotiations between the United States and the Western Union countries concerning the military assistance program that was proposed to go hand in hand with the North Atlantic Treaty. To assist him, Brigadier General Marshall S. Carter, who had been Marshall's special assistant, was ordered to the London embassy staff with the rank of minister. The decision to move on this issue parallel to the North Atlantic Treaty negotiations had been made in Washington in July, 1948, and informal discussions had already taken place between American military authorities and Field Marshal Lord Montgomery's Western Union military headquarters at Fontainebleau. The ominous Soviet activities in Czechoslovakia and Berlin in 1948 and the woefully inadequate European military capability to withstand any onslaught by the some thirty Soviet divisions in Eastern Europe seemed clearly to indicate the need for American aid in strengthening Western European forces as well as in promoting economic recovery.[21]

On March 1, 1949, Douglas and Harriman presented to Bevin the "broad outlines" of the program as then envisaged, which included furnishing both financial aid and matériel. There was complete agreement that this assistance should not interfere with or reduce the ERP program. At this early date, Bevin, foreshadowing the future of NATO, indicated that, if the program led to a unified military establishment, it should be under the command of an American officer. He also urged immediate consultation with the French, who had not yet been approached, since they were "supersensitive" to any concerted action by the British and Americans before their own involvement. The following day, Douglas and Harriman met with Attlee, Bevin, Minister of Defence A. V. Alexander, Chancellor of the Exchequer Sir Stafford Cripps, Lord President of the Council Herbert Morrison, and Roger Makins, who gave their approval to the concept as outlined. Meanwhile, Ambassador Caffery presented the projected plan to Foreign Minister Schuman, who expressed general agreement. The way was now clear to formal discussions with the full Western Union Consultative Council, made up of foreign ministers, defense ministers, and, in some cases, finance ministers of the five Brussels Treaty powers.[22]

Meeting individually and collectively with that group in London on March 15, Douglas was pleased to receive a generally favorable response to the American proposal. The questions raised then would subsequently be the subject of further clarification as the negotiations between the Americans and Europeans progressed: American aid other than financial and matériel, i.e., the inclusion of United States forces in the European military establishment; the addition of other than Brussels Pact European nations in the program; resentment over the American warning to the Netherlands that aid should not be used in their colonial difficulties in Indonesia (which could apply also to France in Indochina and Britain in Malaya) and the delicacy of the timing on this issue in relation to the signing of the Atlantic Treaty.

Over the next two weeks Douglas was able to ensure that the formal request from the Western Union powers would be acceptable to Washington. Heeding his strong recommendation that the United States not insist on reservations concerning the Dutch in Indonesia, or any other bilateral military or economic conditions, but rely on the zealousness of all members of the program to police themselves—"If they do not hang together they will be hanged separately"—Washington accepted the general assurance that the assistance would be predicated on principles of "self-help, mutual aid and common action." For their part, the Brussels Treaty powers made no mention of the inclusion of other European nations or of assistance other than financial and matériel. The request was formally submitted April 5, the day after the signing of the North Atlantic Treaty, and acknowledged the following day with the assurance that it would be put before Congress.[23]

Later in the month and in early June, Douglas expressed his deep concern over the forthcoming congressional reception and handling of the Mutual Defense Assistance Bill. It was submitted to Congress on July 25, the day the President signed the ratification of the North Atlantic Treaty. The ambassador warned against attempts to finance the program at the expense of the ERP, against any "unilateral or onerous conditions . . . unrelated to the defense of Western Europe . . . [or any] indication that [the] UK should curtail social welfare and housing or similar expenditures and redeploy Government expenditures to [the] defense fund as an imposed legislative condition of US aid." He was also alarmed at rumors Congress might put over the legislation until its next session. "[This] would have [a] serious adverse effect on [the] total situation in Western Europe." "The British 'will to resist' Russia is so strong that it would take much more than one shock to affect it," but the "psychological consequences" in France and on the continent might be serious indeed.

In fact, Acheson did encounter congressional problems over the legislation on a variety of counts. But the Russians came to the rescue. On September 23, Truman announced that the Soviet Union had exploded an atomic device. The bill passed Congress quickly and was signed into law by the President on October 6. On November 15, Douglas had the satisfaction of presiding over the first meeting, in London, of representatives of the State and Defense departments and of the Brussels Pact powers to discuss the specific military requirements of the recipient countries. Simultaneous conferences were held at Oslo and Rome for the Scandinavian countries (except Sweden) and for Italy and Portugal, who were also signatories of the North Atlantic Treaty.[24]

On April 4, 1949, the North Atlantic Treaty was signed in Washington by the ten European powers, the United States, and Canada at a ceremony that included remarks by all the participating foreign ministers and an address by President Truman. The same day, about noon, near Nursling on the River Test, while fishing for salmon, Douglas suffered his fateful eye injury. It was to color the rest of his life.[25]

Since his grandfather had first introduced him to the art, fly fishing had been his principal recreational passion and source of relaxation. "[A] haven—an escape from the troubles of the day—a sanctuary in which the concentration which it requires washes the mind clean as new linen" was his description of its delights and therapeutic value. Leaving for his London post in 1947, he looked forward to new challenges on the rivers and lochs of Scotland and the chalk streams of the southern counties. He included in his baggage not only his fine tackle, but a recent article in *Fortune* on fly fishing, and fly tying, carefully marked in his own hand "take to England." Before his departure, he had ordered rods handmade like his own by the great craftsman Everett Garrison as gifts to be delivered to fellow devotees, Generals Marshall and Bedell Smith, Frank Brophy, and Dr. Girard Oberrender, his sinus specialist in New York. In the fall of the year, he ordered another for Sir Richard Fairey, a prominent airplane manufacturer, whose water at Bassington House on the Test he had fished that summer and who was with him at the time of his accident.[26]

In fact, the earliest opportunity to wet his line in England apparently came at Fairey's, in July, with son Peter, who was making his first visit to the family in London. He fished on occasion at Fairey's and elsewhere before and after the accident and was elected an honorary member of two British fishing societies. But his most cherished hours as an angler were at the Houghton Club at Stockbridge on the Test in Hampshire, halfway between Winchester and Salisbury.[27]

"[I]t is my favorite spot in the world," he wrote Sir Anthony Eden, in 1971, of Stockbridge, the club, and its water. Situated in a lovely river valley, with its meeting and dining room in the Grosvenor Hotel, appropriately furnished and appointed, the Houghton, founded in 1823, claimed to be the oldest trout-fishing club in the world. Generals Eisenhower and Smith had been guests there during the war years, and it was the latter who wrote from Moscow, in April, 1947, to Sir Robert Sinclair, a long-time member, suggesting the pleasure Douglas would derive from a day or two of fishing on the river. Before receipt of that letter, however, Sinclair, who had known Douglas in Washington during the war, asked him to fish the club water as his guest. It was not until the next spring, when the mayflies were again rising, that he was able to find time to accept the invitation, accompanied by Peter. Within a week of his visit, he was elected an honorary member. At that time the membership varied from sixteen to nineteen. Before his departure from the ambassadorship, he was uniquely designated an "overseas member," and in 1972, to his immense gratification, elected a full member, the only American to be accorded either distinction.[28]

It was not at Stockbridge but at Fairey's salmon-fishing water downstream below Nursling that Douglas experienced the appalling injury to his eye. Casting against a strong wind, with a very heavy wet salmon fly, which he found difficult to control, he had just about decided to transfer to spinning equipment, when a sudden gust blew the line back and drove the hook into his left eye. His ghillie immediately ran to fetch Sir Richard, who was fishing some distance away. By the time Sir Richard and his man reached Douglas, he was in agony. Cutting the line close to the eye and wrapping a scarf around Douglas's head, his host, helped by the two ghillies, half carried the injured man across three-quarters of a mile of rough water-soaked ground to the car and drove the fifteen miles on back roads to Southampton. There, more time was lost in locating the Free Eye Hospital, where finally E. C. Zorab, an ophthalmic surgeon, administered an injection to relieve the pain and removed the hook.[29]

In London, Peggy was entertaining Stella, Lady Reading at lunch when she was telephoned about the accident. She rushed south by car to the small hospital, where Douglas had been placed in one of the two private rooms. The next day, Maurice Whiting, a London eye specialist, was called in on the case, and on April 7 Sir Stewart Duke-Elder, surgeon-oculist to the King, was brought down for consultation. That day the bandages were first removed and the prognosis was uncertain. It was too early to tell whether his sight could be saved and, if not, whether the eye should be removed. Douglas was in considerable pain. Peggy stayed at a nearby small hotel, spending most of her time in her husband's darkened room, with occasional quick trips to London to meet pressing obligations. Sharman came down for frequent visits and John McCloy flew over from the States to see Douglas and comfort Peggy. By April 16, although there was little change in the condition of the eye, his general health was sufficiently improved to move him by ambulance to Prince's Gate.[30]

For some weeks the fate of his eye was in doubt. Despite the continuing pain, the doctors wished to save it. Since some light was coming through, that would allow for a corneal transplant if, in the future, that was possible and anything should happen to his good eye. Gradually, despite recurring crises, it became evident that the need for removal had passed. But his ordeal was not over. On May 12 he was operated on to remove an adhesion, and at the end of July it was necessary to perform a cataract operation on the injured eye, which, though successful, was painful and debilitating. He was ten days in the hospital and at home in bed for another two weeks. Later, after the bandages were removed, he began, with increasing frequency, and finally permanently, to wear a black patch, which became a distinguished and distinguishing mark.[31]

Douglas had offered to resign in a telephone conversation with Acheson on May 3, citing his month's absence from duty and at least a month more of expected relative inactivity. But the secretary and the President rejected the suggestion, urging him to remain at his post as long as possible, at least until the end of the year. Both men wanted him to "stay right where he is." Even on a reduced schedule, his presence in London was "necessary." In his press conference on June 9, Truman, asked whether he contemplated a change in London, replied, "No. Mr. Douglas has agreed to stay. He has recovered from his eye injury, and is going to stay there." Despite another flat denial of resignation, after a meeting with the President on September 13, Douglas, on the basis of further medical advice and his unwillingness to perform at any level less demanding than that he felt required by his post, had begun serious discussions on a date for his retirement. Because of the reluctance of Acheson and Truman to replace him and of his deceptively improved health in the late winter, it did not, in fact, take place until November, 1950. However, his eye continued to trouble him considerably and interfere from time to time with his work.[32]

As might be expected, colleagues and friends in high places were quick to express their concern and sympathy. Bevin called on Peggy when he landed at Southampton on April 15, returning from the North Atlantic Treaty ceremony. Attlee kept in constant touch. Churchill wept on hearing the news, and he and Mrs. Churchill telegraphed their grief and concern. Mrs. Churchill wrote a touching letter to Peggy, and both sent flowers and called at the residence several times. Sitting beside the invalid's bed, the former Prime Minister presented Douglas with autographed copies of his books, patted his knee, and said: "My dear Lew, you must not let this disturb you. You must remember that Nelson had only one eye." Lovett, now back as a partner in Brown Brothers, Harriman, wrote: "Frankly, I know of no replacement of adequate stature to meet the challenge of these vitally important days and months ahead. I don't ask for a bit of magic like producing a 'successor'; I would consider it lucky to find a 'substitute' to play an unimportant quarter after we have piled up a commanding lead."[33]

But perhaps most moving was the outpouring of affection and esteem by admirers in Britain, the United States, and, indeed, many other parts of the world. It was evidenced by articles in the press, by an influx of letters of sympathy, offers of assistance and advice and simple gifts to him and Peggy, as well as by popular demonstrations of goodwill. Many correspondents offered eye donations. A Hampshire man proposed to give his in gratitude to the American people for all they had done for Europe and his country during and after the war. From Jerome, Arizona, an eighty-four-year-old declared he could die happy if Douglas could use his eye. Public concern was demonstrated on one occasion in London soon after the return from Southampton. His car was stopped at a red light next to a double-decker bus. The passengers recognized him by the bandage, the bus emptied, and the occupants crowded around to express their solicitude. Throughout the spring and summer, the British and American papers assiduously reported the details of his treatment and progress.[34]

Despite his opposition to socialized medicine, he found that most of his treatment and all of his hospital costs were covered by the National Health Service. He was pleased to accept an invitation to hand out the prizes for the School of Nursing at the Middlesex Hospital, which gave him opportunity to publicly express his gratitude. "Had it not been for the time I spent in the hospital at Southampton, and later at Middlesex [where he had the London operations], I would never from my own experience have known the competence, skill, technical ability, cheerfulness and eternal vigilance of the doctors, surgeons and nurses who performed a miracle." He had an electromagnet especially designed to use for removing metal particles from the eye, which he presented to the Southampton Free Eye Hospital in October, 1950. As he remarked shortly afterward, "Since they wouldn't let me pay for the room in the hospital where I was treated, and I saw no reason why anyone else should carry the burden."[35]

Despite his continual discomfort and reduced working hours, Douglas was keeping close watch on what rapidly was threatening to become a British financial crisis as serious as that which had developed in 1947, if not more so. Since sterling was not convertible into dollars, other members of the sterling bloc were drawing on their deposits in London for needed exports, and this caused a deceptive industrial boom accompanied by high employment and high prices. This protected market was not competitive with the United States, the result being in a sharp decline in American buying from the U.K. and parts of the Commonwealth, aggravated by a recession in the United States. As a consequence, Britain was rapidly using up her gold and dollar reserves for purchases of raw materials and food from the United States and other countries. As early as June 16, after a confidential conference with Sir Stafford Cripps, and again on June 22, Douglas alerted Washington to the alarming drain in reserves indicated by the figures for the second quarter of 1949. If some remedy was not applied, the Labour government would soon face virtual bankruptcy with concomitant danger to its own political future.[36]

The principal remedies, as Douglas saw them, and Harriman from Paris agreed, were an austerity program, including a sharp reduction in dollar imports, and possible further assistance from the International Monetary Fund or the United States and/or devaluation of the pound. Within the British government, Cripps was adamantly opposed to devaluation as, in the later words of Attlee, "something not quite honorable. He was rather a silly ass that way." Attlee himself saw no other way out. Without American assistance, "one just had to do it. . . . We were in the position of playing a game in which all the chips were in the hands of one player—and he kept them in his pockets." The Americans, it was clear, had no intention of further bailing out the British. Whitehall would have to sort out the various solutions and reach its own decisions. Douglas's great concern was that the process would bring acrimonious debate between the two countries "in which the UK blames [the] adverse developments on the US recession and the US blames the UK for socialist mismanagement of its affairs."[37]

In July Secretary of the Treasury John W. Snyder came to London and met, accompanied by Douglas and Harriman, with Attlee, Bevin, Cripps, the Commonwealth minister, and the Canadian finance minister. The Americans listened to Cripps's various proposals, but did not indicate concurrence or willingness to accept any responsibility for them. Snyder suggested that further talks be held in Washington at the time of the International Monetary Fund meeting in September and came back to Washington fearful of further British financial importunities. He assured the Senate Foreign Relations Committee that the United States would not consider further American largess. Acheson was more sympathetic to the British plight and cognizant of its implications to the larger picture of Anglo-American relations, but for reasons not entirely clear, the next round of talks in Washington were to be presided over by Snyder.[38]

Like Acheson, Douglas saw the larger picture. But he was no apologist for the British dilemma. In a frank letter to Lippmann, he asserted that he "honestly [did] not see how their own democratic institutions can stand up if they don't make up their minds here that they have to work like blazes and that many of the dreams they have been dreaming over the course of the last thirty years are unfulfillable." Yet, he continued: "Democratic institutions can't stand up if they are subjected to the disillusionment which is inevitable if Britain is to recover." Thus, Britain was "on the horns of a dilemma." He wrote in much the same vein to Vandenberg, stating flatly that: "I, myself, feel that we should extend to the British during the forthcoming talks no additional direct dollar assistance . . . [though perhaps there are other things we could do] that will make it easier for the British to earn dollars and to face up to some of their own internal difficulties which they, and they alone must resolve." It should be noted that the British harbored a good deal of ill-will toward continuing American pressure, especially as ardently promoted by Marshall Plan Administrator Paul Hoffman, for greater British participation in European economic integration. This, among other actions, entailed free convertibility, which had been so disastrous in 1947. Hoffman constantly accused the British of having an overvalued pound.[39]

Douglas sailed to New York on the *Queen Elizabeth* on August 27, to spend about a month in the United States to participate in the financial talks and to attend to personal affairs, including consultations with New York ophthalmologists. Before his departure, the embassy dispatched a paper to the State Department on the forthcoming meetings, reviewing the problems and options and emphasizing again "the delicacy of the psychological situation in the UK" and the necessity "not only [to] avoid telling the British what they should do in their internal affairs, but also [to] avoid giving the impression that we have done so."[40]

In a confidential letter to Acheson, Douglas offered less formally much the same advice. The British would be "rather desperate. . . . They will probably, unfortunately, look to us to provide the answers. . . . [T]hey will, I fear, be sensitive, very suspicious and perhaps unreceptive." But the American negotiators must show "great self-restraint and even though we may not feel it completely, show real sympathy. . . . We should try to avoid . . . insisting on asking the

British what they propose to do about it . . . [and refrain] from making any commitments as to what we propose to do about it." Above all, "ideological differences" must not develop and there should be no lasting impression that the United States wished to see the downfall of the Labour government, which was expected soon to call for new elections. Labour might then run on an anti-American platform, which could be successful. "It is not their return to power which is perhaps so important as their return to power on an anti-American platform."

A candid postscript pointed out that with all the American talk about multilateral trade and nondiscrimination "intellectual honesty" would reveal that "we don't enjoy a particularly pure record. We want multilateral trade, and we object to discrimination in respect of all things we do well, but reserve the right to discriminate in those matters which we do inefficiently. Shipping, for example." With his signature, he jotted: "This sounds awfully preachy to me."[41]

As it turned out, following the apprehension on both sides, the Washington meetings proved something of an anticlimax. The first days were marked by tense exchanges, including an American denial of the British request to waive the requirement of the 1946 loan agreement, which prohibited discrimination against American exports, an attempt to stem the drain on dollars. Then the London negotiators informed their American counterparts, in the greatest of confidence, that a decision had been made before their departure to devalue the pound. They asked no advice, but now the United States officials did know—a rather awkward position, for they could be, and were, accused, when it was announced, of having forced the decision. Acheson and Douglas believed it had to be done. Snyder was fearful "of upsetting the applecart." But the Americans awaited the official announcement and prepared, in Sir Oliver Franks's words, "to extend a helping hand in a decent and friendly fashion" in the circumstances flowing from it. The Americans refrained from suggesting a figure.[42]

On September 18, Cripps broadcast the decision to the nation. The devaluation was somewhat more than 30 percent, from $4.03 to $2.80. The reaction was one of surprise and shock, ranging from approval by the Manchester *Guardian* and the Labour *Daily Herald* to not surprising accusations of deception by Cripps from the Conservative *Daily Telegraph*. As to international ramifications, the French, though angry at not having been warned, revalued the franc on September 20 by 10 percent in relation to sterling. Shortly afterward sixteen other countries, including the dominions and the other members of the Western Union, devalued their currencies in relation to the dollar. From London, Julius Holmes predicted the decision would probably require an early election, for the government needed a fresh mandate to carry out the various economic and fiscal policies the devaluation demanded. In fact, the results proved more efficacious than anticipated, for the United States recovered quickly from the spring recession and the recovery, together with the cheaper pound, made it possible for American buying in Great Britain to quicken and relieve the dollar shortage.[43]

Douglas remained a week longer to discuss his future relationship with Mutual Life and to take care of some of the details of his father's will. Arriving in Southampton aboard the *Queen Elizabeth* on September 26, he attended the debate on devaluation in the House of Commons the next day, then immediately flew to

Paris, no doubt to help mend French fences damaged by the recent monetary decision. From there he went to Frankfurt to consult with McCloy, who had, to Douglas's pleasure, in May accepted the position of American high commissioner to the new German Federal Republic.[44]

From Frankfurt, he flew to Lausanne, where he met Peggy, Sharman, and the young family friend Lord Westmorland, who had left London by car on the 26th for a long-awaited holiday in Switzerland and Italy. In later years, Westmorland recalled the journey as one of his most pleasant memories. Douglas was the perfect host, kind, considerate, unfailingly good-humored, insistent, with Baedeker in hand, on tracking down little-known points of interest and politely turning aside the persistent questions of the press, who hoped to detect a romance between Westmorland and Sharman. For Douglas and his family, it was a well-deserved and much-needed respite after the personal pain and shared anxieties of the past six months.[45]

But within days he was off to Paris, where the United States ambassadors to Western Europe, including McCloy and Harriman, met with representatives from the State Department to discuss major problems in the countries to which they were accredited and in the community as a whole. With Douglas leading off the discussions, they generally agreed that the most pressing issue was the British government's unwillingness to participate in the economic integration of Western Europe, which contributed to a growing rift with the continental powers, exacerbated by the recent devaluation. While Douglas was convinced closer integration could not proceed without the U.K., he saw no evidence that the current government was prepared to move in that direction. Beset with internal economic problems, dedicated to socialist doctrines of highly centralized domestic controls that did not permit "too intimate foreign economic intercourse," and concerned with its relationship to the Commonwealth, "the present regime," in Douglas's opinion, "[was] a very poor prospect as a major element in what we know must be done." However, the United States should "press ahead. . . . The situation was not hopeless." He expected elections in the near future, and there were "elements there [the Conservatives?] who are acutely aware of the necessity for further British cooperation."[46]

On November 10-11, Douglas was back in Paris as an advisor to Acheson, who met with Bevin and Schuman in a marathon conference—couches were brought into nearby rooms for the weary to take brief rests—to iron out problems connected with the establishment of the German Federal Republic. The future course of dismantling, satisfactory assurances to the French for security, the interpretation and implementation of the occupation statute, integration of the new state and the Saar into the Council of Europe, admission of the Federal Republic to the International Authority for the Ruhr, eventual termination of the state of war with Germany, and relations with the Soviet-sponsored East German Democratic Republic were all discussed "with," in Acheson's report to the President, "very satisfactory results." As to the difficult question of commercial relations by the Western European countries with the East German regime, it was agreed that Douglas should sit with the permanent commission of the Brussels Pact nations when the matter was under consideration.[47]

. . .

This is not the place to review United States China policy in 1949, at which time it became a major issue in Anglo-American relations. Suffice it to say that, after October 1, when the Communists proclaimed the People's Democratic Republic of China, Douglas's role was, in his later words, to use "every argument I had in my bag to dissuade" Bevin from recognizing the new regime.[48]

Serious consideration of the attitude of the Western powers toward the advancing Chinese Communist forces began in May, when the State Department made clear that any decision must await events. Although Bevin concurred and agreed to give the question "full consideration," his jocular remark reported by Douglas, "Do you want us to go as slow on this as we have in the case of Israel?" was an early reflection of the divergence in the positions of the two governments. In late July, Bevin agreed in conversations and correspondence with Douglas that "our officials should consult together" on the problem, but was "non-committal" on common action.[49]

Whitehall was particularly concerned about the future of British interests in Southeast Asia and in Hong Kong. The growing divergence was further evidenced on August 26, when Bevin, in discussion with Douglas, referred to the volume of British and American trade with China and its potential for influencing the Communists "in our favor." He added: "We believe, too, that the Chinese Communists were first and foremost Chinese and that they were not capable of becoming Russians overnight." He made the same point to Acheson during the financial meetings in Washington in September. But both men seemed determined that their differences over this issue not be allowed to interfere with their common policies in other areas and agreed to consult about any future actions on the question by either party.[50]

Although the Truman administration was exploring various approaches to the rapidly changing Chinese situation, a number of factors militated against following the apparent direction of British policy toward recognition. Already accused by a vocal China Lobby of having "lost China" by insufficient aid to Chiang, it was also faced by an influential body of opinion within Congress that opposed recognition. A voluminous white paper issued by the State Department in August, covering relations with China since 1947, was intended to show the futility of American efforts to save Chiang in the light of his ineffective, corrupt, and unpopular regime. But the volume was used by its critics as ammunition for further attacks on the administration for failure to give sufficient aid to Chiang against the Communists. The situation was further complicated by the continuance of the Nationalist government on Formosa. Under the gun of these domestic pressures and the reluctance in certain quarters of the Truman administration to consider Mao anything other than a Kremlin puppet, recognition by the United States of the People's Democratic Republic was out of the question, at least for the time being.

Then, with what appeared to be a breach of the agreement on consultation, the British government, without notification to Washington, replied, on October 5, to the Chinese Communist announcement, on October 1, of their new government. In a formally addressed note, it expressed the hope that the "Friendly and mutually advantageous relations" that had previously existed between the two countries "will continue in the future" and that "informal relations should be established between His Majesty's Consular offices" and the authorities of the new "Central peoples government" for mutual convenience "and the promotion of trade." The note was first brought to the attention of the State Department by the French embassy. Greatly disturbed by the turn of events, the department requested the London embassy to ascertain the authenticity of the information and an explanation.[51]

The Foreign Office replies were less than satisfactory. When confronted by Douglas, Bevin expressed surprise that Acheson had not been consulted and attempted to place the blame on his staff. Julius Holmes found it "difficult [to] escape [the] conclusion such failure [was] deliberate." First Secretary Arthur Ringwalt informed the Foreign Office he feared it had "pulled a fast one," and that he "personally was not too impressed by what seemed . . . to be specious arguments." President Truman, Acheson recorded, "thought that the British had not played very squarely with us in the matter." All and all, it was an unpleasant episode.[52]

In any case, it proved to be the prelude to British de jure recognition of the People's Democratic Republic, soon followed by most of the other North Atlantic Treaty states and Commonwealth governments. On December 1 in a personal letter, Douglas warned Acheson that a decision was probably imminent. Acknowledging the inevitable, Acheson, in conversation with Franks on December 8, asked that the United States be given "maximum notice of our [British] intentions in order that [American] public opinion be properly prepared" and be assured the action "does not mean that fundamentally our aims are divergent." On December 15, the British cabinet reached a definite decision to extend recognition to the Chinese Communists, de jure, and to withdraw it from the Nationalist government. The action was formally taken on January 6, 1950.[53]

When Douglas was in New York in September, an examination by Dr. Edmund Goodman, who had for some years been his physician and surgeon, had revealed that the varicose veins in both legs that had been giving him increasing discomfort over the past seven or eight years were now in a dangerous condition. It was arranged then that the veins would be stripped and the arteries tied off. He entered the hospital on December 9, for an anticipated stay of one week. But the operation proved to be a good deal more difficult than expected, and as late as December 22, still in the hospital, he complained to Acheson that his legs looked "like two totem poles." He was allowed to go home on the 24th, then on Christmas Day returned, complaining of discomfort, which was diagnosed as a pulmonary embolism. He remained in the hospital until the end of January, 1950. He finally left New York by train on February 4 for the long-delayed vacation and continued recuperation in Arizona. Three days before his release, George Marshall paid him a prearranged visit, which was much appreciated and certainly an indication of the general's affection and regard.[54]

25

The End of the Mission

IMPROVED IN HEALTH AND SPIRIT AFTER SOME THREE weeks in Arizona, Douglas returned to Washington in early March, 1950. He assured Acheson and the President, who expressed "great gratification," that he was prepared to stay in London as long as his services were useful and desired. On the evening of March 7, he was to join Acheson at dinner with Sir Oliver Franks for one of the wide-ranging personal discussions that the secretary and the British ambassador had initiated soon after the latter's arrival in Washington. That afternoon, Acheson and Douglas sought counsel from State Department officials and High Commissioner McCloy on the approach they should take. Reviewing the current sources of tension between the two countries, including British recalcitrance on increasing military production under the Mutual Defense Assistance Program and on cooperating in the European Payments Union, Douglas urged the importance of establishing whether or not London was really prepared to "pursue a common policy and objectives." If not, "It might be desirable to suggest . . . we would have to reexamine our whole foreign policy." Deputy Under Secretary of State Dean Rusk hesitated to support such a "drastic" line. McCloy emphasized the need for a vigorous move in the direction of "political unity such as the establishment of confederation for Europe" and urged "the inclusion of Germany in the North Atlantic Treaty framework." Douglas voiced reservations on confederation as "a practicable proposal." Director of the Bureau of German Affairs Henry A. Byroade noted that the British must "recognize that they had lost their old position of power and would have to face up to a changed status in the world."

Acheson left the briefing intending to point out to Franks that the great steps taken since 1947 in strengthening the "Western cause" had "lost their momentum and we seem to have slowed down to a point where we are on the defensive while the Soviets are apparently showing more self confidence." Some imaginative "new idea or new step [was needed] which would regain the initiative." Douglas agreed with Acheson that both Bevin and Strang "had distinct limitations along this line." He suggested, however, that there were others in the Foreign Office who might have constructive ideas and some among the Conservatives, especially Eden, although it was "a very ticklish matter to talk to the opposition." There was a general consensus that Franks himself had an ingenious mind and might make helpful suggestions "for eliciting new ideas or a response to new ideas in the UK."[1]

Douglas returned to London on March 17. He had little time to touch base with either the embassy or the Foreign Office before he was off to a periodic meeting in Rome of United States ambassadors. The envoys' discussions included the means by which the United States could contribute to a closer association of the Western European countries, politically, economically, and, by inference, militarily; the relation of the U.K. to European unity; the role and contribution of West Germany; and the future of the North Atlantic Treaty Organization. Like Acheson, the ambassadors were concerned by what they perceived as inertia in the West and by the rising tide of Soviet activity.

It was generally agreed that NATO offered the most hopeful vehicle for strengthening Western political integration to counter the Russian presence but that the expansion of its military aspects would, perforce, involve German manpower, which, for political reasons, was presently "impracticable." Perhaps, however, West Germany might "contribute to the defense of Europe by furnishing material and supplies as distinguished from military equipment for the purpose."

Douglas's assessment of Anglo-American relations and British cooperation in European unity was mixed, but on the whole pessimistic. Essentially, he reiterated the problems previously raised at the October, 1949, ambassadorial meeting and in Washington before his departure. On February 20 the elections in Britain had returned Labour to power but with a slim majority. In consequence, the government was paying more attention to Conservative opinion. Though Douglas doubted new elections could be expected in the near future, "Careful briefing of Conservative members would make it possible for us to get decisions on important matters in this period of finely balanced power."

But Britain's role in Europe continued to be "limited" by her commitment to the Commonwealth and her colonies and by her misconception of the "special relationship" with the United States, which inhibited her cooperation on the Continent. Above all, as long as Labour was in office, there was a "basic conflict between the requirements of a Socialist society and of an international society as we conceived it. The Socialist was a planner and could not tolerate any external influences." "Perhaps," he added in some exasperation, "we had been a little tender with the British. The time might come when we should tell them that we would have to review our whole policy unless they would do their part in maintaining the principle of US/UK cooperation in prosecuting the cold war."[2]

Douglas's remarks on expanding relations with the Conservative leadership were somewhat misleading. In fact, from the beginning of his tenure he had kept in close touch with Churchill and, to a lesser extent, with Eden, as well as with many Conservative back-benchers. His acquaintance with Churchill before and during the war had quickly ripened, after his arrival in London, into a warm friendship, marked by frequent social contacts, political conversations, and correspondence. His esteem for the wartime leader was unbounded. He invariably excused or defended Churchill's gaffes and foibles, always listed him, along with Clemenceau, as a savior of the Western world in the twentieth century, and regarded him as a symbol of all he admired in the British.

Douglas's affection was appreciated and reciprocated. In or out of office, Churchill made a point of knowing and getting along with all American ambassadors, but his friendship with Douglas was exceptional and continued until the end of his life. Douglas was not in the crony class of Churchill's friends, some of whom were a bit disreputable, nor was he probably considered a high-flier by the great man. But Churchill was very close and always accessible, found Douglas's views sound, his instincts fine, and his personality attractive and compatible. Lew and Peggy were, in the later words of Sir Winston's grandson, in the "family circle." Perhaps the most obvious evidence of Churchill's attachment was his approval of Douglas's membership, in 1950, in The Other Club, the only American ever to be so honored. Formed in 1911 by the then Liberal Churchill and his Conservative friend F. E. Smith (later first Earl of Birkenhead) to foster interparty social relationships, by the 1940s the club's membership, limited to fifty, also included outstanding men from nonpolitical areas of national life. Since the death of Birkenhead in 1930, it had become a Churchillian coterie.

There is evidence that Douglas's political contacts with Churchill became more frequent in the spring of 1950. For example, he informed Acheson that he had spent several hours with the Conservative party leader discussing the substance of his speech on foreign policy delivered in the House of Commons on March 28. On the advice of Douglas, Churchill played down his advocacy of German rearmament, though he refused to retract his earlier remarks on the subject, which had aroused considerable controversy. He also welcomed the suggestion that he couple his "generous observation" about Acheson with a favorable comment on Senator Vandenberg to avoid "any charge of interfering in American politics." This recommendation was motivated by a desire to avert any further embarrassment to Acheson, who, since the beginning of the year, had been subjected to a mounting series of partisan attacks. These had been prompted by the President's statement of January 5, and the secretary's follow-up press conference of January 6, both denying military aid to Formosa and rejecting any American involvement in the Chinese civil war; his Far Eastern perimeter speech of January 12; his refusal to turn his back on Alger Hiss; and the opening of Senator Joseph McCarthy's "Communists in government" campaign. In fact, in reporting to Acheson on his conversation with Churchill, Douglas recalled his own efforts "with my friends on the Hill" before leaving Washington to blunt the critical onslaught against Acheson and offered, if he could be of further help, to "pop into a plane and return."

Although some dialogue with the opposition was not at all unusual for an ambassador and had particular advantages in the light of the new parliamentary composition, it also presented certain dangers to both governments, especially as it involved Churchill, whose unpredictability and indiscretions were a source of concern. Indeed, Bevin was very close to Eden, had often sided with him against Churchill on foreign policy in the war cabinet, periodically called him in for consultation, and made Foreign Office telegrams of interest available to him. On the other hand, while he had been a loyal member of the 1940–45 coalition government and greatly admired Churchill's wartime leadership, Bevin had by 1949 begun to resent his former chief's meddling in foreign affairs. Always quick to be suspicious, he occasionally became resentful of the Douglas-Churchill relationship. Such a moment of passing pique is recorded in Hugh Dalton's diary of September 2, 1950, following a conversation in the Commons lobby: "Ernie doesn't trust Lew Douglas any more. He thinks he sees too much of Churchill and tells him too much." But there is no reason to believe that such an isolated outburst revealed any lasting diminution of Bevin's regard and affection for Douglas.[3]

There are indications, however, that Douglas's affinity with Conservative views and political and social circles and his unconcealed criticism of Labour party domestic policies were considered inappropriate and counterproductive by some officials in the State Department, including Acheson. The origins and extent of Acheson's possible misgivings about the diplomatic ramifications of Douglas's intimacy with the Conservative leadership are difficult to document, but they probably began soon after the secretary took office and may have been a factor in his disenchantment with Douglas that culminated in their estrangement during and after the 1952 elections. There are also some grounds for believing that Harriman shared these apprehensions. He too was later alienated by Douglas's support of Eisenhower in 1952, but their breach was healed. Both men were apparently concerned, rightly or wrongly, that Douglas's effectiveness in dealing with the British government had been weakened or warped by his sympathy and close association with the Conservatives.

But the preponderance of evidence suggests that these fears were unfounded or at least exaggerated and oversimplified. In 1958, Admiral Richard L. Conolly, commander-in-chief, U.S. Naval Forces, Eastern Atlantic and Mediterranean, whose tour of duty coincided almost exactly with that of Douglas, summed up his observations succinctly. "He [Douglas] was made to order to be Ambassador to Britain at that time. He got along wonderfully well with the Labor [sic] Government, in spite of the fact that they knew he disapproved of every damned thing they stood for . . . right across the board. And he used to tell them so. But they like straightforward speech of that sort, and difference of opinion. They're used to it, they adjust to it, and if you're not . . . objectionable about it, they accept it."

Whether or not Acheson's perceived doubts about Douglas's objectivity in dealing with the Foreign Office was the motivation, the latter was not assigned to head the delegation to carry on preparatory talks with the British and French nor to act as principal advisor during the scheduled meetings of the three foreign ministers and of the NATO council which took place in London from late April to mid-May. Instead, to the surprise of the Foreign Office, he appointed Ambassador-at-Large Philip C. Jessup.

It could be argued that the decision was prompted by Acheson's consideration for Douglas's health and his realization of the heavy workload these duties would entail. But that explanation would only partly account for the Jessup appointment. In any case, some members of the embassy and, no doubt, the ambassador himself, were also disconcerted by the size of the staff accompanying Jessup and Acheson and the degree to which it ignored them in negotiations that followed. Later,

Acheson implied to a member of the embassy that these peculiar arrangements were, in fact, the result of his growing doubts about Douglas's circumspection in discussing in unofficial quarters the sensitive matters under consideration.[4]

Douglas was, however, kept informed of the course of the preparatory meetings and probably saw most of the position papers and cable traffic. He appears to have interjected his views most vehemently concerning the question of a "special relationship" between the United Kingdom and the United States that was acknowledged in one of the bilateral position papers. From Paris, Ambassador David Bruce, also privy to the document, took exception to the statement as an "established US policy . . . [because of its] consequences in regard to our other partners in the Atlantic community [which] will be extremely harmful. . . . It would be regarded on the continent as the abandonment by the US of any serious attempt at European or even Atlantic community integration in favor of an Anglo-American world alliance as a cornerstone of US foreign policy." The British would then presume to act as an intermediary between Washington and Europe. London's "desire for [a] special relationship," he warned, ". . . is in fact indissolubly linked with their unwillingness with respect to greater participation in European affairs and will inevitably be so interpreted by Continental European Powers."

Douglas's lengthy cabled reaction was widely addressed—not only to Bruce and his minister Charles Bohlen, but also to Acheson, Harriman, and Jessup. Granting the validity of some of Bruce's arguments and the need to exercise "a certain amount of caution in acknowledging the existence of the relationship, and a certain amount of discretion in dealing with specific questions which arise out of [it]," he rejected the view that it should not be recognized "solely because it might possibly interfere with the smooth working of the North Atlantic community." "A special relationship . . . [is] as inescapable as the facts themselves." The problem was not whether Britain would attempt to act as an intermediary between the United States and the Continent. "If she would become a good intermediary and exert the sort of leadership we want, what harm would this do? . . . The issue is not whether the UK would attempt to be Mr. Bones in a minstrel show but whether the UK would be a good Mr. Bones." In equally colorful language, he concluded: "I do not for a moment imply that the UK's desire to have a special relationship . . . is as pure as Castile Soap or as clean as Snow White. Her motives are no worse than ours, and no better, but I do not agree with the view that the primary reason which moves her to attempt to establish a special US-UK relationship is because of her unwillingness to join in molding a more closely knit Western Europe. Her principal motive is to buy insurance." His comments were vintage Douglas, but appeared to be in some conflict with the doubts he had earlier expressed in Rome.

They also pointed up what was possibly another source of Acheson's misgivings—Douglas's unalloyed Anglophilism. Soon after reaching London, Acheson saw the position paper to which Bruce had objected. He was horrified that "the wretched paper existed." It would arouse suspicion and dissension among the European allies and give the opposition at home ammunition for the charge American foreign policy was dictated by a foreign power. He castigated his colleagues for their "naïveté" and ordered all copies that could be found burned. He admitted that he was pro-British, that a "special relationship" did exist, though he would characterize it over the years as "unique" rather than "affectionate." But it was madness to put it into writing, stirring up trouble on both sides of the Atlantic. He would express any "sentimental impulses" in his speech to the Society of Pilgrims. It had no place in diplomatic discourse. Very likely he believed Douglas too often overstepped this line to the detriment of practical American interests.[5]

Acheson arrived in London on May 9, following a two-day visit in Paris, where Foreign Minister Robert Schuman in great confidence had disclosed his coal and steel plan for Western Europe. When Ambassador Massigli informed both Bevin and Acheson that the French foreign minister had presented his plan to the Chamber of Deputies, Bevin was furious, charging Acheson and Schuman with colluding in Paris to formulate the plan and then keep it from him until it was made public. With some difficulty, Acheson was able to disabuse Bevin of the first charge and explain his embarrassing position on the second. In the event, the Labour government, seeing the threat to its domestic socialist economy as greater than the potential losses to its continental markets, refused to join in the European negotiations, which were successfully concluded with discreet American encouragement in April, 1951. Acheson always considered that Britain's decision was "her great mistake of the post-war period." Douglas agreed, writing to a friend his conviction that "Socialism advanced as an international regime must in practice be intensely nationalistic. The experience of Britain confirms that beyond almost any question of a doubt. . . . Internal planning [does not] admit of any external factors."[6]

The foreign ministers' sessions, which began with Schuman's arrival on May 11, were far-ranging, covering not only Europe, but China, Southeast Asia, and the Middle East. Positions were clarified and agreements to disagree established on some issues. But unquestionably Acheson's main objective was to emphasize, as he did in his first conversation with Bevin, that they must get their peoples to realize "that resistance to the Russian danger must have absolute priority and furthermore we had only a few years in which to organize and strengthen ourselves."

At the NATO council meetings that followed, for the first time the basic problems of the new entity were brought out on the table: the need for a common plan for the defense of Western Europe, though the details were left purposely vague, and the role of Germany. A step toward military integration was the agreement to establish a permanent council of deputies of the foreign ministers to meet continuously in London to plan for balanced collective forces. Although the long-term objectives and methods to this end were still unclear, the groundwork was laid for what was to become, after the attack on South Korea, a functioning North Atlantic Treaty Organization.[7]

Whatever doubts Acheson may have entertained about Douglas in the spring of 1950, he apparently retained considerable respect for his abilities and his influence abroad and at home. The night before leaving London, he discussed the possibility of the ambassador's assuming the chairmanship of the new NATO Council of Deputies, an appointment which they enigmatically referred to in subsequent personal correspondence as "Operation Bisbee." Douglas was not anxious to accept the new responsibility, foreseeing difficulties in wearing two hats and apprehensive about the added strain upon his uncertain health. But he expressed willingness to undertake the task "for a reasonable period" if Acheson and Truman considered it the "best solution."

By June 9, he had given the question further thought, especially in relation to his physical condition, which was proving an ever greater handicap to his current duties. "I say, therefore, quite bluntly," he wrote Acheson, "that I do not want to participate in Operation Bisbee." In fact, he noted, his energy had so noticeably diminished over the last year and a half that he should consider retiring from the ambassadorship in the next few months. Yet he left the door slightly open. If the secretary and President still felt his appointment was "the best immediate answer," he would "very reluctantly" take on the double duty for four to six months, however detrimental to his health. On June 13, Acheson cabled enigmatically: "Our effort in operation BISBEE failed, so no progress has been made by us. . . . I shall talk with you further about the matter." A week later, Bevin sent a message to Acheson, urging action on the naming of an American deputy, as the other NATO countries were waiting for Washington to take the lead in constituting the council. On June 24, Acheson notified the signatories of the North Atlantic Pact that Charles M. Spofford had been designated the United States deputy.[8]

Douglas's letter of June 9 was the harbinger of a more direct request for the acceptance of his resignation by the end of the year. In a telephone conversation with Acheson on June 16, and a "Purely Personal and Confidential" letter of June 20, he enumerated the reasons that had "impelled" him earlier in the year to agree to remain at his post and why they were no longer valid. First, Acheson had then been the object of an "assault" to discredit him and through him the authority of the President. A resignation might at worst have been interpreted as a repudiation of the administration, or at least would have placed Truman in an awkward position in choosing a successor. Now Acheson had "met the attack and repelled it." Second, "the importance of the task to be done here in London is, as I view it, decreasing in its relation to the world situation." The hub of negotiations on European problems was shifting to other capitals. It is not clear whether Douglas was referring to Bonn or Paris or whether it was a veiled reference to the concentration of power in Washington and his own diminished role in the recent negotiations. He did add that the arrival of Spofford would relieve him of many of the "responsibilities" he had previously assumed.

Finally, the eye injury followed by the operation on his legs and the continued painful treatment of both problems had sapped his strength. In the last two weeks he had been free of pain in his eye only three days. All these circumstances had convinced him that "the need for my remaining on indefinitely has . . . fallen very substantially when measured by the need to retire, catch my breath and try to meet my responsibilities to my family." At some point Acheson had suggested the alternative of trips to Arizona every other month or periodically for three months. Douglas rejected that "generous and considerate" proposal as inviting criticism of them both. He asked to be relieved between the first of October and the first of January, preferably during the former month.

They discussed the matter again by telephone on June 23. The next day North Korean forces crossed the 38th parallel. Somehow finding time in the midst of the emerging crisis, Acheson wrote Douglas on June 27 that the subject of resignation must be put aside until the course of events was clarified. He expressed himself as "more grateful than I shall ever be able to tell you" for the reasons pertaining to his own situation that had prompted Douglas to stay on and urged him, even if there should be an early return to "normal times," to delay his decision until after the fall elections and nearer the time Congress would reconvene. Meantime, while understanding and accepting Douglas's arguments, he would not agree to his request, so that he could in good conscience say that they had no arrangement. He would keep the matter to himself. Otherwise, "rumors," "difficulties," and "maneuvers" would begin, "which in no way could be in the public interest." Douglas responded by cable that he was in "complete accord." For the time being the matter was dropped.[9]

Even as Acheson wrote, Douglas was himself involved in the Korean affair. That morning, together with Julius Holmes, he had cabled urging that the presidential statement on the crisis omit any reference to Soviet association with the Korean action. Although he was confident "that the Soviet has not only approved . . . the aggression and has provided the North Koreans with the implements of war," he feared that to "express it publicly" would be "so committing the Soviet that they will find it difficult to save their face" in case Moscow decided to disassociate itself from the action. That advice, which had also come from Ambassador Alan G. Kirk in Moscow, was followed. Accusing only "Communism" of moving now from "subversion" to "armed invasion," Truman declared that, since the North Koreans had not withdrawn to the 38th parallel in conformity with the Security Council resolution of June 25, American forces had been ordered to provide "cover and support" to South Korean troops and the Seventh Fleet directed to prevent any attack on Formosa by the Chinese Communists and any further sea or air action by the Nationalist Chinese against the mainland. The future of Formosa awaited "restoration of security in the Pacific," a Japanese peace treaty, or resolution by the UN—a considerable shift in emphasis from his statement on Formosa of January 5, which had emphasized noninterference in the Chinese civil war. Acheson acknowledged in his letter that Douglas's recommendation had "saved us from making a serious error. Your help and guidance is invaluable."[10]

That evening the Security Council passed, with the Soviet representative still absent (he had boycotted the council since January in protest against its refusal to seat Communist China in place of Nationalist China), its second resolution, calling on members of the United Nations to "furnish such assistance to the Republic of Korea as may be necessary to repel the armed attack." Following the Security Council resolution, the British put their naval vessels in adjacent waters at General MacArthur's disposal. Soon they would supply a contingent of troops. They also began, through their ambassador in Moscow, attempts to find a peaceful solution. Their "unsolicited diplomatic initiative," as Acheson later described it, led to several weeks of strained relations between Washington and London. Douglas found himself in the midst of this contretemps.

When British Ambassador Sir David Kelly was finally able to see Andrei Gromyko on July 6, the Soviet deputy foreign minister gave some enigmatic evidence of seeking a peaceful solution. Detecting in Bevin's report of this conversation to him a willingness on the part of Britain to make unacceptable concessions to end hostilities, Acheson instructed Douglas to make it clear that any response should not involve either the question of Formosa or of Chinese Communist representation at the UN, but only the withdrawal of North Korean forces from South Korea. Bevin was ill, so Douglas spoke, first with Minister of State Kenneth Younger (Hector McNeil had earlier been appointed secretary of state for Scotland) and then with Attlee, who had unobtrusively come up from Chequers for the meeting, and received assurances that Kelly's instructions would be in conformity with Acheson's wishes. Acheson received this information on the morning of July 8, but later the same day was handed by Franks a message from Bevin, dated July 7, suggesting that the United States might wish to rethink its position on Formosa if that was the price the Soviet government asked for aid in restoring the status quo in Korea.[11]

Although the next day Acheson received and approved, with a few reservations, Bevin's instructions to Kelly, he and the President were sufficiently alarmed by the earlier message to send a very strong reply on July 10, to be delivered personally by Douglas. It was a long, vigorous, and detailed statement on why the "Soviets [should] not be paid any price whatsoever for calling off an attack which they should never have started." Recalling the lesson of the thirties that appeasement can never halt aggression, he continued: "There can be little doubt but that Communism, with Chi[na] as one spearhead, has now embarked upon an assault against Asia." The United States could not and would not alter its stands on Formosa, Chinese Communist recognition, or admission to the UN. Douglas was to make clear orally that the note represented the President's as well as Acheson's views, to remind Bevin that in May he himself had privately expressed doubts about the U.K.'s China policy, and to "ask him frankly what possible practical advantages he sees in trying to get Communist China into S[ecurity] C[ouncil] and return to SC of USSR in present situation." "I want you," Acheson instructed Douglas, "to leave him no doubt of seriousness with which I view implications of his message and their possible effect on our whole future relationship."[12]

As directed, Douglas called on the ailing Bevin at the hospital and delivered Acheson's letter with the accompanying oral comments, which he also put in writing. Bevin, Douglas reported to Acheson, was "somewhat surprised and a little taken aback at the vigor of your response." Bevin noted that Kelly's instructions remained as agreed upon. He was "rather defensive" about his own communication, which was simply to explore the American reaction if the Soviet response offered "proposals which on the surface might appear to be honest and inviting." He wished to study Acheson's letter and consider the oral representations before making any definite reply. In view of Bevin's reaction, Douglas questioned whether the foreign secretary had fully appreciated the import of his message to Acheson and "whether Bevin himself initiated message or . . . [it had been] some subordinate's handiwork—probably Strang's. It has marks of Strang's spoor."[13]

Deputy Under Secretary of State Sir Pierson Dixon commented that the "tone" of Douglas's remarks "reflects the mood when the Americans feel they have shouldered the burden of the world and are being criticized by others whose burden they are carrying." He thought Douglas should be asked to "explain this obscurely worded menace" in the last paragraph of his remarks. Sir Oliver Franks told Acheson that Bevin was "disturbed" by the words "serious consequences" which Douglas had used. Acheson assured Franks they were meant only to avoid the possibility "of our policies drifting apart." The upshot of the affair was that Bevin dispatched a long reply reviewing the British position on Formosa, Chinese Communist admission, and the Soviet return to the Security Council, but reiterating solidarity in not submitting to Soviet blackmail on Korea. The matter ended there.

Meantime, Franks had given the Foreign Office sound advice. Waxing eloquent on the United States response to the North Korean challenge, he commented that, in the face of the invasion, action was the order of the day in Washington. "Thought is the enemy of action." He advised playing "the exchange of thoughts between the two Secretary's [sic] of State long rather than short. Let a little time go by . . . [until] the Americans have recovered their poise." The Kelly-Gromyko conversation came to naught. But Douglas appears to have been the scapegoat in the Washington-London imbroglio.[14]

What were Douglas's private views on the motivation and implications of the North Korean attack? No contemporary comments have been found except for his advice to Washington not to make any public reference to the USSR in the President's statement. But, less than two years later, in a letter to presidential candidate Eisenhower, while warning against overspending for defense, he dismissed any inference, which he accused the administration of fostering from the outset, that the North Korean attack revealed Soviet intentions to make war. Rather, he asserted, the withdrawal of U.S. troops from South Korea in 1949, the White Paper on China, Truman's statement on Formosa of January 5, Acheson's elaboration to the press on January 6, 1949, and the premeditated leaks of the Joint Chiefs' judgment that Korea had no strategic value had all combined to convince the North Koreans that they "could cross the 38th parallel without any danger whatsoever of interference." He did not believe that "Soviet intentions and the Korean episode . . . [were] irrevocably associated." Concluding his letter to Eisenhower, Douglas declared that the Truman administration continued to use the Korean War as evidence of the Soviet "desire to precipitate a war" because it lacked the "moral character to admit a mistake."[15]

Douglas did not wait long after the North Korean invasion to resubmit his request for relief. On July 27, he wrote Acheson, reiterating and updating the reasons advanced in his earlier letter. He had been reexamined by his physicians, who advised "time and rest" as the only "effective remedies" for the "constant discomfort" and "at times . . . fairly intense pain" he continued to experience in his eye. Despite their diagnosis, he would be willing to continue at his post "if there were a real need to do so." But "the responsibilities which were formerly lodged in this Embassy . . . have gradually and very properly diminished." With "the clouds of war gathering," the emphasis was increasingly on military and defense matters. Spofford, now in London chairing the Council of Deputies, could, with his colleagues, deal with these problems and their political ramifications. "Only the routine reporting, combined with an occasional task of some significance, remains for this Embassy to do." If there should be a general war, he would like to be of service, but this could only be possible if he had some time to recover his health.

He asked that the resignation be effective November 1 and that the announcement be made soon after the first of August rather than later, when it might be misinterpreted so near the fall elections. He and Peggy needed at least a couple of months after the announcement to "make our departure decent and courteous." If it was delayed until after the elections, his resignation could not be effective before January 1, which might endanger his health. He enclosed the draft of an official resignation to the President for the secretary's comment and suggestions, as well as a brief personal letter to Truman.[16]

Further communications by letter, cable, and telephone continued over the next month, ironing out the details, while Acheson sounded out possible successors. Douglas elaborated that, despite his intense aversion to causing the administration embarrassment, a delay in obtaining relief might lead to his right eye's becoming affected or to the excision of the left. Earlier, in April, Acheson, anticipating Douglas's resignation and impressed with Thomas Dewey's public attempts to stop the vicious partisan Republican attacks on Truman's foreign policy by McCarthy, Taft, and others, had confidentially sounded out his friend and former presidential candidate as a possible replacement. Dewey had declined. Now, in mid-August, he turned to Robert Lovett, who also declined as being "temperamentally" unsuited for the "ambassadorial life." He suggested, among others, Walter S. Gifford, a Republican and president of the American Telephone and Telegraph Company, who had performed distinguished government service in both world wars. Sometime in September Gifford accepted the appointment.[17]

Meantime, Acheson had ordered Douglas home, along with McCloy, for consultation on the strengthening of NATO and particularly on the military role of Germany, preliminary to another series of tripartite foreign ministers' and NATO council meetings in New York beginning in mid-September. Douglas had also requested an opportunity to discuss the details of his impending resignation with the President and secretary.[18]

The question of German participation, of an American troop contribution, and of an American commander as components in vitalizing NATO and hastening Western European integration had been in the air for almost a year. With the fear of a Soviet strike elsewhere after Korea, they came to the fore. Acheson believed he now had the leverage to persuade reluctant Europeans and American critics to advance NATO to a new stage of development. He preferred to delay the highly controversial issue of German military participation until the European NATO buildup was agreed upon and under way. But during August he was under pressure from the Joint Chiefs and a "steady stream of cables" from McCloy, Bruce, and Douglas to speed up the process. Douglas, who was chairing an international study group on Germany, after discussions with McCloy and Spofford in London, wrote: "There are, it seems to me, three essential requirements to the creation of a European army of which German units would form an integral part instead of . . . a purely national German army. . . . [They] are . . . the assumption of command by an American . . . three or four American divisions in Europe . . . and the dispatch of several . . . more British divisions to the Continent." Acheson decided to couple some form of German rearmament with the promise of an

American military contingent and leadership in the recommendations he put before the foreign ministers and NATO council in New York.

Douglas's and McCloy's further advice on reaching Washington August 31 certainly contributed to the secretary's resolution. The New York meetings did, in fact, begin that long and difficult course. They led to the appointment in December of General Eisenhower to command a combined NATO force, congressional approval, after a "Great Debate" in 1951, of an American troop contribution, and eventually, following prolonged French opposition, to a rearmed Germany in NATO in 1955.[19]

26

Farewells

DOUGLAS, SOON JOINED BY PEGGY AND SHARMAN, spent the month of September in Washington, Arizona, and in New York, though he did not attend the conferences there. On September 26, Franks was called to the State Department, where Under Secretary of State James E. Webb, in the presence of Douglas and Assistant Secretary George W. Perkins, informed him officially that the ambassador had resigned for reasons of health, effective about November 1. Douglas emphasized to Franks that "his only reason for withdrawal was that he was simply unable to continue longer at the post." The President wished to appoint Walter S. Gifford and requested rapid agreement on the nomination from the British government and the King.

Franks expressed the "deep appreciation of the British people and his Majesty's Government for the splendid way in which Mr. Douglas had represented the United States and indicated that Mr. Douglas had earned a lasting place in the hearts of the people as well." Explaining to the Foreign Office that Truman had "gone outside all party considerations" in naming Gifford, he speculated on the department's entreaty for speed. The administration, he cabled, "evidently dread the pressures which will develop on the President once the resignation of Lew Douglas is known. . . . I have no doubt that the domestic political campaign now at full blast makes things very difficult for the President if he tries to hold up publication of the name of the new Ambassador." The affirmative answer from London was prompt. A few days later, a member of the British embassy wrote Superintending Under Secretary of State for Foreign Affairs Michael R. Wright that "Gifford will be more like the American Ambassadors we used to have in London before the War—Bingham, etc.—and that while he will be an admirable representative and do all the public side of things very well, he will be much less interested in the day to day work than Lew Douglas and will not intervene himself in nearly so many detailed problems as has his predecessor. That may be no bad thing!" In fact, Gifford proved a very active and effective envoy.[1]

On the afternoon of September 26, Douglas met with Truman, and their official exchange of correspondence was released. Douglas based his request upon health, emphasized that a continuing close relationship with Britain and the Commonwealth was "one of the solid corner-stones of the civilized world," and offered, once he was rested and recovered, to serve the President again. In reply, Truman stressed "the great courage and devotion you have shown in sticking on at your post in the face of such compelling reasons of health," and expressed the hope that, after a "speedy and complete recovery," he might "at some early date call upon you once again to help meet our country's needs." Noting the "loyal service" Douglas had performed "in such a vital spot," the "wise counsel" he had given in the solution "of all the complex problems of the day," and his "broad appreciation of the fundamentals of our relationship to the British Commonwealth," the President concluded that the London assignment "rounds out a career of singular versatility and usefulness. It has been given to few of our citizens to render such high service in fields of responsibility so varied and diverse." That day Truman also received Douglas's personal note, thanking the President for his "faith" in his abilities and the "extraordinary experience you have given me. I can never adequately express my gratitude." Truman acknowledged it separately, briefly but warmly, reiterating: "I'll count on you as soon as you are back in shape."[2]

News of Douglas's impending departure from London elicited an outpouring of praise and regret from both sides of the Atlantic. The New York *Herald Tribune* editorialized that Douglas had "touched greatness again and again. . . . One likes to think of him as the complete American—equipped with that perfect balance of horse-sense and principle, of humor and wisdom, which have formed the character of our nation's best." Under the heading "Deep Regret in London," the *Times*, commenting on Douglas's firm commitment to the "continuing close relationship" between the two countries, praised him as a "scrupulously fair and honest interpreter of post-war Britain to the Government and the people of the United States . . . [whose] independence of judgment . . . has helped to smooth the path of the two countries through many contentious issues." "Britain loses perhaps her greatest—certainly her best-informed—American friend," wrote Alec Collett, in his *Evening News* column. Pointing out that "Few American Ambassadors to Britain have earned as much respect and good-will as has Mr. Douglas," a *Manchester Guardian* editorial emphasized that he had been more than an "Ambassador to one country," he had been "chiefly responsible on the American side for the handling of the Berlin crisis . . . played an important part in other matters of German policy and, above all, in the building of the Atlantic Pact." His friend Brendan Bracken's *Financial Times* went one step further: "London has been lucky in the eminent Ambassadors sent to us by the United States but among them Mr. Douglas is surely pre-eminent." Anticipating the event, the *News Chronicle* of September 17 had been equally emphatic. Douglas was "possibly the most successful American Ambassador we have ever had."[3]

Still in New York for the foreign ministers' and council meetings, Ernest Bevin sent by hand to Douglas at his office at Mutual Life a letter expressing "shock" at the news of his resignation and sorrow at its cause—the condition of his eye. "It has been a great joy working with you, especially during the period when we have had so many terrific difficulties to overcome. . . . I can only express my thanks for your cooperation and for the great confidence that existed between us and, what is more important, for the firm permanent friendship that has been established." Replying in kind, the ambassador characterized their work together "as the most satisfying period of my life." His decision had been difficult: "I wanted desperately to stay in England. Actually, however, I had no choice." From the other side of the House of Commons, Anthony Eden, in London, voiced his regret at Douglas's leaving. Citing his "tact and patience," but "above all his qualities of character," he predicted that the ambassador would "hold a special place in history as the man whose skill as the interpreter between the two nations has nourished understanding at a critical hour."[4]

From the beginning of his tenure, Douglas had received remarkably wide and favorable coverage in the British press. Even the left-wing papers remained more than kind, despite his known conservative views. As his first private secretary wrote soon after their arrival, "LWD has an air of simplicity and utter genuineness that has completely captivated the local newspaper boys." Not only were his official actions and statements carefully noted, but human-interest items were also frequently reported. Hearing that he was an ardent bicycler, the British Cycle and Motor Cycle Manufacturers presented him, in 1947, with an Armstrong Peerless Comfort. A year later, he was described as "leisurely pedaling" through Hyde Park on the way to the embassy, not because of the petrol shortage, but because he liked "the air and exercise." Animal-conscious Britons were delighted to read that, when an unruly horse with a frightened woman rider reared in front of the ambassador's car at Hyde Park's Albert Gate, Douglas jumped out and led the plunging horse to the nearby Rotten Row bridle path. Following a session of the conference on Germany in the spring of 1948, the *Daily Telegraph* ran a picture of the ambassador and a London bobby pushing his car out of an icy rut in the snow. The caption read: "From Tripartite talks through unilateral effort."[5]

Douglas addressed British audiences often and well, not only in London but throughout the United Kingdom. His speeches were usually personally prepared. In his files for this period are voluminous notes and drafts in his own hand, together with lists of books he had drawn and read from the library on the subject of his remarks. His speaking voice was rather soft, but carrying and compelling. His texts varied from the simple and straightforward to the sentimental and moving, depending upon the occasion and the audience.[6]

To the American Society in London July 4, 1950, he presented a concise, factual account of the background, course, and implications of the Korean crisis, praised by Harold Macmillan for "both the form and content." "It was," he wrote Douglas, "a model of clear and convincing argument; it will prove historic." The next month, at the Edinburgh Festival, accepting the freedom of the city, among other honors during his visit, he gave an extremely affecting and effective address. Recalling his great-grandfather's, grandfather's, and grandmother's connections with the city, he said that "in vain [those of Scottish descent] . . . try to still the shiver of excitement, the sense of pride, the glow of inner warmth . . . [when they] return at last to the Scotland of their ancestors and to its capital. I am no different." Praising the "many Scots and men of Scottish lineage [who] have played their parts and earned a place of great distinction in the annals of

America . . . [and] exercised such a powerful influence in the molding of American institutions," he then turned to a brief but powerful peroration on the need for cooperation between their two countries. Young America had been forced by circumstance to "a new position of authority." Great Britain's "centuries and generations of experience in international affairs had clothed her with a wisdom in international affairs so necessary" to America. If " 'freedom's holy light' " was to be protected and continued "burning brightly to future generations . . . we must remain united." This was, in fact, the major theme in most of his addresses, sometimes in the face of demonstrations, usually from members of the Communist party.[7]

During the two-day visit to Edinburgh, he also received an honorary degree from the university. It was the last of his many British academic honors. Along with Edinburgh, where both his great-grandfather and grandfather had been students, perhaps he took most pleasure, for quite different reasons, in his degrees from the universities of Bristol and Oxford. Churchill was chancellor of Bristol and personally conferred the Doctor of Laws. Oxford had granted the Doctor of Civil Law to several American statesmen and some but not all American ambassadors, but Douglas's came rather early in his tenure, June, 1948. The chancellor was his old friend Lord Halifax, and the university was representative of much that he admired in British life. He cherished the association. In June of the last year of his life, with the warm encouragement of the current chancellor, Harold Macmillan, and at some physical inconvenience, he again participated proudly in Encaenia.[8]

The residence quickly became one of the centers of London social life. The dangers and hardships of the war and the two drab years of privation that followed had left the city starved for gaiety. Under wartime ambassador John Winant, a most retiring man, and briefly Averell Harriman, who was in London alone, 14 Prince's Gate had stood largely silent. Peggy was determined to end that hiatus, while observing the continuing rationing restrictions and with due sensitivity to the severe economic conditions under which Britain still suffered. When thoughtful friends in the States sent such luxuries as butter and meats to the Douglases, they were shared as special treats with their guests. The warmth and hospitality at the residence was a welcoming oasis in postwar London.[9]

There were many formal occasions, of course, but it was the unconventionality of so many entertainments that delighted their guests. They included a broad spectrum of politicians in and out of government and representatives of other areas of British and American life, including the stage, academia, finance, and the press. Often served from a buffet and placed at small tables, young and old, royalty, peers, and commoners, the famous and unknown were seated together, and initial restraint soon vanished. Charades frequently followed, sweeping away remaining inhibitions and allowing Douglas to throw decorum to the winds and indulge in his love of high-jinks. Later, perhaps, Danny Kaye, a close family friend, would drop in to further enliven the party and present a few skits.[10]

Twice a week Peggy gave a cocktail party for as many as a hundred and fifty guests, which Douglas seldom attended because of his official duties. Mixing Britons and Americans and calling on unattached young officers from the nearby barracks to help entertain, she attempted to memorize the names and interests of the guests to make the affair as friendly and personal as possible. If she had a formal dinner following and some of the guests had lingered past the appointed time, the ambassador's aide, Paul Warburg, would blow a little whistle and merrily announce: "The party's over, Mum has to dress." Essential to the smooth functioning of all of these events was the firm but unobtrusive hand of the incomparable butler, Epps, and the efficiency of Peggy's personal secretary, Elizabeth Jackson (later Lady Cowdray).

There were also frequent intimate Sunday-night suppers at the residence, usually including Brendan Bracken, to whom Douglas had become very close; Alexander Korda, the extraordinary film magnate; and sometimes W. S. Robinson, the Australian mining entrepreneur, who played an important role behind the scenes in British financial and political life. The conversation, Douglas later recalled, was always "fascinating," for Bracken had an "extraordinary range of knowledge and—what few people with a wide range of knowledge possessed— a great capacity to interpret what he knew." Often Douglas would spend an evening with Bracken in his home at 8 Lord North Street, remodeled to create a lovely semicircular library lined with crowded bookshelves, and on the wall, Romney's portrait of Edmund Burke, an intellectual hero to them both.[11]

Peggy's activities were by no means restricted to the purely social. At the invitation of Lady Reading, head of the Women's Voluntary Services during the war, Peggy accompanied her on a number of trips throughout the British Isles to talk to Women's Institutes about the work of women in America and to answer questions concerning the United States. During the first eight months, she visited a great many communities. After that, she was forced to restrict her institute speaking to four or five days every two months. In the midst of one appearance, in Inverness, she had to take a transatlantic telephone call and came back to the meeting to announce the birth in Tucson of another James Stuart Douglas. The Scots ring of the name was an instantaneous hit with the audience. Afterward, as she walked through the town, shopkeepers presented her with little kilt pins, blouses, kilts, and caps for her first grandson. Later, she encouraged other embassy wives to carry on her work, which was praised in the *Daily Telegraph* as "of lasting educational value."[12]

She took a particular interest in the care of the sick, especially children. In 1949, she arranged through American friends funds for the importation from the United States of hospital equipment not otherwise available because of the dollar shortage. It included one hundred electrical devices for turning pages of books read by military amputees and twenty-five microfilm projectors for ceiling reading by paralyzed soldiers who were forced to lie flat on their backs. Children's Hospital in Great Ormand Street became a special object of her attentions. For two years she was able to provide for a special baby food essential to the young patients' health. As she prepared to leave England, the press commented on "how much we are going to miss her," her contributions to Anglo-American friendship, her "warm humanity" and, in a charming touch, "her smile. . . . Le sourire, c'était la femme."[13]

The ambassadorial couple made a host of close friends from many walks of life—though the majority were, not unnaturally, from the socially prominent aristocracy—whom they continued to see on their subsequent, almost annual visits to England. Unfortunately, the two men with whom Douglas had been most intimate in the Labour government, Ernest Bevin and Minister of State Hector McNeil, did not live long after his departure. Bevin's deteriorating heart condition forced him to leave the Foreign Office in early 1951, and in a few weeks the "old ticker," as he always put it, gave out. McNeil died in 1955. Bracken succumbed to throat cancer in 1958, a great loss for Douglas, whose own recent very serious surgery had forced him to cancel a flying trip to visit his dying friend. Churchill, of course, lived until 1965, and their frequent reunions were always stimulating and, toward the end, often sentimental. The Douglases were among the few Americans, including ex-Presidents Truman and Eisenhower and their wives and Bernard Baruch, who were personally invited by the Churchill family to Sir Winston's state funeral. Lewis Douglas was unable to accept, but Peggy and Sharman attended, flying with the official delegation, headed by Vice-President Humphrey, on the President's plane. With the passing of many of their contemporaries, the younger generations, together with a continuum of new friends, welcomed them and, after Lew's death, Peggy to their second home.[14]

The Douglases' relations with the Royal Family must, of course, be considered in a special category, for however cordial, even warm, the friendship, a certain formality had always to be observed. King George VI, a shy and retiring man, seems to have been unusually comfortable in the company of the relaxed and affable ambassador, whose wisdom and experience he admired. Queen Elizabeth enjoyed Douglas's sense of humor, which was very similar to her own. The Queen, much more gregarious and outgoing than the King, saw the ambassadorial couple quite often and became particularly close to Peggy, whose animation and "English" forthrightness she found very attractive. On a number of occasions she spent an informal evening at Prince's Gate playing canasta, then all the rage in America, which she had been taught by Peggy and Lew. Princess Elizabeth, Prince Philip, and Princess Margaret were frequent guests at the residence when other young people were being entertained. From the palace came not only the usual invitations to various formal functions, but some for lunching or dining *en famille* and others for weekends at Windsor.

During the later part of 1948 and much of 1949, the King's illness and subsequent surgery for early arteriosclerosis, which had affected his legs, greatly limited his official and social activities. Douglas received a number of letters from physicians and friends in the States suggesting possible treatment for His Majesty's condition. Some of these suggestions he passed on to Sir Alan Lascelles, the King's private secretary, for whatever benefit they might have for the physicians in attendance. Lascelles expressed gratitude, commenting on the treatments suggested. No stranger to illness and pain himself, Douglas undoubtedly empathized more acutely than most with the suffering of the monarch, whom he regarded with great affection and respect. The day following the King's death on February 6, 1952, Douglas broadcast a brief but moving tribute from New York over the Voice of America, praising his courage, high sense of duty, and humanity. He had been a "kind and generous host whom we shall never forget."[15]

A strong bond between the two families, and evidence of the royal couple's confidence in the Douglases, was the friendship that quickly developed between Sharman and Princess Margaret. By the time she was presented at the royal garden party on June 10, she had been written up several times in the London papers and described as "already such a tremendous success among the younger set over here." She was photographed with the King and Queen, the Princesses, and Prince Philip (Elizabeth and Philip were then engaged and were married on November 20) at the Eton–Harrow cricket match in mid-July. A few days later, she was off at 3 A.M. with Princess Margaret's party to tour the night clubs following a large dance at the palace. Asserting that, aside from the Royal Princesses, she was the most photographed young woman in England, including screen stars, the London correspondent of a Texas paper explained in August that her "breathless eagerness, her broad smile, her smart—but not too smart—clothes provide a dash of color that the drab post-war social scene sadly needs." She was soon routinely described as one of Princess Margaret's closest friends, and the London and American press avidly followed her activities. It was not long before the gossip columnists were erroneously linking her romantically with several of her escorts, including the Marquess of Blandford, the Marquess of Milford-Haven, Mark Bonham-Carter, Lord Westmorland, and Peter Lawford. Her devoted father, who had long ago, for some obscure reason, dubbed her Sassleberry, was somewhat dismayed at the flood of publicity.[16]

In October, 1949, the *News Review* had Sharman on the cover in full color over the caption "Good Will Girl," with a long write-up and interview inside. In December, the Hasty Pudding Club of Harvard gave her its "Woman of the Year" award because "she has done more for international good will than many a diplomat, fully equipped with striped pants and portfolio." Yet, somehow, in the midst of her social whirl, Sharman had been able to complete by 1949 the full course at Queen's Secretarial College, which she had taken at her father's request.[17]

The weeks before the Douglases sailed for home were filled with sad farewells and marked by innumerable tributes to them both from all quarters of Britain. At the top of their social calendar were a "very private, very family dinner" for the Royal Family at Prince's Gate on October 27 and an intimate dinner party and later a family luncheon at the palace a few days before their departure.[18]

Foreign Secretary and Mrs. Bevin gave a formal dinner for the Douglases at the ministerial residence. Attended by Prime Minister and Mrs. Attlee and several other members of the cabinet, it also included some leaders of the opposition (though not Churchill, who declined at the last minute because of an altercation with Bevin in the House of Commons the night before, which he felt might cause embarrassment to them both), senior members of the Foreign Office and the embassy staff, financial and business executives, and such old friends as Lord Leathers. It was an unusual gesture. Bevin spoke without notes in a striking and emotional tribute to Douglas's contribution to Anglo-American relations. The next day, Douglas paid his farewell call on Attlee. Meanwhile, there was a flurry of minutes at the Foreign Office as to whether or not Bevin should take the unusual step of going to Southampton to bid the Douglases farewell. As one proponent noted: "Mr. Douglas is rather a special case." But conservative opinion prevailed with the decision that the Bevins would call on the ambassador and Peggy at Prince's Gate the morning of the departure as a special mark of favor.[19]

Churchill's leave-taking had taken place several nights before the Bevin function. With only Lord and Lady Salisbury as the other guests at Hyde Park Gate, the Churchills' London home since 1945, the Douglases dined and reminisced. Toward the end of the nostalgic evening, Churchill slyly asked if they would like to see his newest decoration, the Order of the Elephant from Denmark. As they admired it, he ordered a footman to draw the draperies at one window, revealing on the sill his own painting of performing circus elephants, which had long been a favorite of Douglas. "My dear Lew, I do not give my children away lightly, but I want you and Peggy to have that." Peggy and the host tearfully embraced.[20]

There were many other gifts, of course, but perhaps the most distinctive, apart from the Churchill painting, was sent after their departure by a group of House of Commons members concerned with Anglo-American relations with whom Douglas had often dined. It was a stone griffin, weighing over five hundred pounds, from outside the House, which had survived the bombing of Westminster during the war, but had been taken down when Victoria Tower was repaired. Placed first at the Sonoita ranch, it later presided over the front garden of the Douglas home, Pantano Farm, in Tucson.[21]

From the French government, Douglas received formal appreciation of his diplomatic contributions in the European arena and especially to France. Ambassador Massigli inquired if he would accept the highest order of the Légion d'Honneur and expressed the hope that he might confer it. Before responding, Douglas made sure that acceptance would constitute no breach of State Department rules, pointing out that, since the investiture would take place after he had made his adieux to the King and government, he would "to all intents and purposes" be out of the service. No objection was raised. The Grand Croix was conferred by Massigli at the French embassy on November 15. For Douglas, the honor had a special sentimental value: both his grandfather and his father had been members of the order. Later, he was awarded the Grand Croix de l'Ordre de la Couronne by Belgium. The British government considered giving him a decoration in 1949 and again in 1950, but no action was taken. That distinction was to come in 1957 at the hand of Queen Elizabeth II during her visit to the United States.[22]

The ambassador's public valedictory was his speech to the Society of Pilgrims on November 6. Broadcast over American as well as British radio networks, it was preceded by messages from John W. Davis, president of the Pilgrims in the United States, and from Sir Oliver Franks in Washington. Referring to the Atlantic as "the great river of Anglo-American association" and of their embassies as the "two great channels through which the lively waters run," Franks praised the "superb skill with which the American faucet had been managed in London [which] has greatly helped the pressures on the British tap in Washington." "The United States has been very fortunate in her servant, but not more fortunate than Britain in her friend." Lord Halifax, as president of the Pilgrims, reviewed Douglas's distinguished career and paid tribute to his "singular capacity for dealing with all kinds of men and things." So far as he could tell, the ambassador during his tenure "had never put a foot wrong." He suspected that Douglas had experienced difficulties on occasion explaining British actions to Washington and, similarly, that there had been times "when he might have wished his own official chiefs had thought or spoken somewhat differently. . . . The debt we owe him for all this business of generous interpretation is very great."

In his address, Douglas reviewed the amazing changes that had taken place in the relations between his country and Britain and Europe during his years in London. In consequence, "The march of Communism in Europe has been arrested and turned back." The Marshall Plan had assisted Europe and the United Kingdom to help themselves in restoring economic and political stability. But continued Soviet activities soon made it clear that further measures would have to be taken to ensure the defense of the Western community. Out of this threat the North Atlantic Treaty had been negotiated—a dramatic reversal in the foreign policy of the United States. "If there is to be an adequate common defense for our community," Douglas warned, "the momentum which has been achieved by the events in Korea and by common understanding of its urgency cannot be allowed to slacken." Essential to this objective, he emphasized, was a reconciliation between France and Germany, which, he was convinced, could be begun in the Schuman plan. This should prepare the way for a "genuine international military and defense organization" that would, while involving Germany, include guarantees against a "resurgence of purely national German military might." In this task, he concluded, "the British Commonwealth of Nations and my country must bear a heavy responsibility together. You need us and we need you." His remarks were received with prolonged standing applause and cheers, much pounding on the tables, and a rendition, led by Lord Halifax, of "For He's a Jolly Good Fellow," by over five hundred Pilgrims in white ties, tails, and decorations.[23]

The *Times*, commenting on his Pilgrim speech, pointed out that he had "borne [a] . . . burden of work which the old masters of a more leisurely diplomacy would have considered an intolerable imposition. . . . Yet . . . Mr. Douglas . . . has appeared in surprisingly many places, and has brought to many multitudes of people a fuller comprehension of the mind of modern America." The *News Chronicle* asserted that "The U.S. Embassy in Grosvenor Square during Mr. Douglas's term was the focal point for decisions which have changed the whole world outlook." With Labour in power there were "yawning gulfs of misunderstanding to be bridged" between the two capitals. As an interpreter, he had performed "so skilfully that few realize how well it has been done."

The *Daily Express* affirmed that "The people of Britain—people who have never been near an official function—feel that a good friend is leaving," while "Peregrine," in the *A.B.C. London News-Letter* a month after Douglas's departure, wrote that the "English people have lost a diplomatic guest who may well go down to History as the most revered United States Ambassador London has ever had. . . . He has walked with Kings and not lost the common touch. I have never met a man more truly lovable." Paul Hoffman, greatly impressed with the comments he had heard and read during his visit to London in mid-October, wrote Douglas: "Your leaving for America has filled . . . [the British people] with almost as much sadness as did the death of Queen Victoria. This I consider quite extraordinary, because, after all, you might return."[24]

Farewells

. . .

Arriving in New York on November 21, Douglas traveled to Washington three days later to "pay his respects" to the President and call in at the State Department. He returned to New York on the 25th and left by air for Arizona December 1. Peggy, after a visit with her parents in Hastings-on-Hudson, followed by train on December 6. He was home at last for a much-deserved rest.

But his energy, though diminished, would not allow him long to remain idle. He was soon again deeply involved in his private financial concerns and in civic activities. Nor was he forgotten in Whitehall. In the spring, Hector McNeil wrote from London: "We all miss you badly. We have all suffered from your absence and our relationship has suffered. René Massigli and I found ourselves moping in a corner the other night and agreed that the world had fallen to pieces since you took your hand from it."[25]

PART SEVEN

The Later Years

27

Home

DOUGLAS'S FIRST MAJOR PUBLIC APPEARANCE after his return was, appropriately, before the Pilgrims in New York on January 24, 1951. Pleading for military and financial support to Western Europe, he cautioned that the nation must be careful not to "violate the second principle of foreign policy and impose upon our own resources a burden which, over a long period of time, may undo the American scheme." There were "two ways . . . by which our future may be seriously damaged. The first is by failing to be strong enough, and the second is by imposing upon ourselves a burden which is heavier than we can carry." The United States did not have the resources to defend "every part of the world." It was essential that "we identify in our own mind the critical areas. . . . Clearly one of these critical areas—indeed the most critical area—is the Atlantic Community."

He then introduced another theme. We should not "be timid . . . in inventing new devices, if they be necessary, by which and through which we may have communications once more with the Soviets." To depend only on force "is to engage in a practice hazardous to our peaceful purpose." A meeting with a "responsible and high official of the Soviet" with a free and frank exchange of views might lead to no obvious result. On the other hand, "it might convince the Soviet that we are not guided by aggressive designs and are not behaving in faithful accord with the Marxist belief that the capitalist world must go to war in its final desperate effort to save itself."[1]

Two months later Douglas reiterated the same points and added others at the Charter Day ceremonies at the University of California, Berkeley. Comparing the nineteenth century as a "period of peace unparalleled in modern history," marked by the free movement of men and goods, to the contemporary international environment of virulent nationalism, economic disruption, revolution, and the threat of another world war, he offered "three basic propositions" that might be useful in facing the future. First, "American impatience for a speedy settlement will not . . . be satisfied. . . . A span of many years will probably be required." Second, "war . . . will resolve none of the liabilities we have inherited. . . . The aftermath of war . . . is often more devastating than the lives that are sacrificed and the property that is destroyed during the period of open hostilities.'' Third, ''the [present] unsettled state of world affairs . . . is derived largely from the imbalance of power which the war produced and the division of Germany which our inexperience unwittingly sanctioned.''

The United States must, therefore, do everything necessary to redress the balance of power peacefully "within the capacity of our national resources and the essential nature of a free society . . . over a protracted period of time." It should muster only enough military power "to deter the Soviet from making the decision to go to war," but not attempt to arm sufficiently "to invade the Soviet sphere or even to prevent communist forces from advancing at all against the West." If America undertook the latter goals, it would entail "a burden which probably no free society can carry." Speaking in the midst of the "Great Debate" on sending four American divisions to strengthen NATO, Douglas stated that their dispatch "will not only stimulate . . . [Western European] faith in themselves and in us, but . . . will have a restraining influence on the Soviets if in fact they contemplate military action." A limited rearmament program must, however, be "paralleled with continuous efforts to restore communications with the Soviet [or] it may produce, as almost all other rearmament programs have produced, the war which it is our primary purpose honorably to avoid." If "a nice combination" of these two tactics were employed, it was not "too much to hope yes to expect that one by one the problems . . . and dangers . . . will slowly disappear. Peace may descend on the land and its peoples once more."[2]

Throughout the decade—in fact for the rest of his life—he voiced these views. Strength must be combined with continued efforts at negotiation. War would be beyond any conflagration yet experienced and not halt the ideologies it sought to check. Excessive arms expenditures would bring internal controls and taxation that would threaten the free society America was trying to preserve. Again and again, he expressed doubts that "the Soviet is prepared and is anxious to plunge the world into another great convulsion." Rather, he envisaged a long period, even through the lives of his grandchildren, of Communist-inspired "disturbances, of civil wars, of inspired rebellions, of limited armed conflicts in the distant lands across the seas" in an "attempt to sabotage the system which they believe to be repugnant to their own." But, if the West persevered in its attempts to redress the balance of power by the means he outlined, "it was not unlikely" the world would be spared the horrors of a great war and that Soviet influence would begin to disintegrate.[3]

Like many other conservatives, Douglas opposed American globalism. The United States had neither the resources nor the resolve to contain Communism throughout the world. He rejected the domino theory and policies, such as liberation, which sought to counter Soviet influence in Eastern Europe. Nor should the United States, acting as the world's policeman, use military means to combat nationalist uprisings. He later opposed the Eisenhower Doctrine, the sending of marines to Lebanon in 1958, and American intervention in Vietnam. The United States, he maintained, must draw the distinction between defending its vital interests and resisting changes in the status quo.

In another and related area, he continued to advocate freer trade and convertible currency as a means of strengthening the U.S. economy and the rest of the world and of opening other avenues of communication between East and West. The first step was for America to simplify the "intricate maze of restrictions and regulations with which tariff rates are associated," then "to make it known that there would be no elevation or increase of the restrictions which presently exist." Foreign importers should be assured that their investments in the United States would be secure. Speaking to the American Petroleum Institute in 1953, he said "it would not be imprudent or unwise—in view of the great benefits to the country as a whole arising out of convertible currency—for us to devise a sort of scheme extending over half a century which would provide for a very low, a very modest, annual reduction of rates so that we would depart . . . from the policy of exclusionism which began to creep into a modified policy of protection after the close of World War I." He then outlined policies other countries might pursue to facilitate progress toward the same ends. "This is," he asserted in the commencement address at MIT in the same year, "the only policy which may bind the nations of the Free World together and enable them to achieve a solid sense of security and stability."[4]

In 1958, in a written statement to the Senate Appropriations Committee and in a speech to the Life Managers' Association of New York, discussing the necessary role of foreign aid, he emphasized the same points. Foreign aid must be continued, he argued, "to insure us against the probable unpleasant internal consequences of a depreciation of major world currencies against the dollar." But, in the long run, only "a gradual reduction of our own protective barriers in consideration for compensating reductions elsewhere of barriers, including, it is hoped, exchange restrictions" would achieve the essential goal of permitting other countries to earn enough dollars to preserve stability of exchange rates.[5]

He also urged consideration of the benefits of East-West trade, especially for West Germany's and Japan's economic well-being. If those countries were not to become permanently dependent upon America, should they not be allowed to resume their prewar commerce with Eastern Europe and the Asian mainland? Were France, Great Britain, or the United States prepared to receive German products and would the United States or other powers allow Japan "to invade" their markets in the Pacific? Would the United States "accept Japanese goods"? He reminded his audiences that the Marshall Plan had assumed that by 1952 East-West trade in Europe would be restored to its earlier level.[6]

Early in his first year home, Douglas accepted an offer to lead a new endeavor in public policy-making. During the war, Eisenhower had been disturbed by the lack of knowledge among his troops of the American principles for which they were fighting overseas. On becoming president of Columbia, he initiated discussions inside and outside the university to establish an organization that would disseminate information and inspire discussion of national issues. He wrote Douglas, on November 20, 1950, to urge him to assume a major role in the undertaking. On the eve of the general's departure to take up his new duties as supreme commander at NATO, Douglas somewhat reluctantly agreed to serve as chairman of the American Assembly's National Policy Board. The board and the participants in the assembly's periodic meetings included distinguished representatives from business, agriculture, labor, government, education, and politics. It was financed by contributions from companies, unions, foundations, and individuals. It met at Arden House, at Harriman, New York, a gift of W. Averell Harriman to Columbia for conference purposes. The first meeting was held from May 21 to 26, 1951, on United States–Western European relations, with Senators Paul Douglas of Illinois and Robert Taft of Ohio opening the discussions with statements of the problems and alternative solutions. Subsequent meetings in 1952 and 1953 were held on inflation and on economic security.[7]

Although Douglas was active in the decision-making on the topics to be discussed, most of the detail work was handled by the executive director, Dean Philip Young of the Columbia Graduate School of Business. Douglas set the agenda for the first two assemblies, writing a friend that, with Congress passing requests for billions of dollars for defense "without inquiring about the details," it was essential to address the "devastating effects of tremendous public spending." He rejected a suggestion from a group of Columbia alumni that the third meeting be on "The Effects on this Nation of Discrimination Against Persons of Color," noting that the topic was "ineptly stated . . . [and] premature. Although it has aroused considerable emotion, it is not as important a matter for the nation as some of the others [recommended]."[8]

Douglas submitted his resignation from the board and the chairmanship in a letter to President Grayson Kirk of Columbia in April, 1953. He gave as his reason the recent acceptance of a special mission for President Eisenhower to study the sterling-dollar problem, but it seems clear that he had initially agreed to take on the assembly task only because of his friendship for Eisenhower and the latter's intense interest in the project. Indeed, as late as November, 1952, the general had written Douglas that he still considered the establishment of the American Assembly as "perhaps the most important step he had taken while president of the University." Douglas's own enthusiasm for the undertaking had, however, always been limited and perhaps dimmed by the suspicion of a sensitive man that the effusiveness of the invitations by Eisenhower and others to participate had been prompted primarily by sympathy and affection for someone who had been forced by ill-health to step down from an important post of public responsibility. In any case, he had seen the program off to an auspicious beginning and was probably ready to step aside even if he had not received the assignment from the new President.[9]

Douglas's rejection of racial discrimination as a timely subject for an assembly meeting raises the question of his generally ambivalent record on the civil-rights movement, then and later. Soon after the Supreme Court school desegregation decision of 1954, he confided to Senator Harry Byrd of Virginia: "It seems to me that it has put back the resolution of this most perplexing problem by more than half a century, for it revives the almost dormant prejudices and emotions that were so justly born during that black post–civil war period." In 1957, writing to Byrd's Virginia colleague in the Senate, A. Willis Robertson, he described federal civil-rights activity in behalf of black Americans as a "vicious encroachment on the rights . . . of the respective states, as well as upon the rights of individuals." Ironically, that December President Eisenhower asked him to serve as chairman of the Civil Rights Commission. After reading the enabling statute and discussing the post with Presidential Assistant Sherman Adams and the attorney general, he declined, pointing out that his experience did not fit him for the position. His views sprang, however, not from lack of sympathy for the plight of the blacks nor for their betterment through gradual societal change, but rather from his overriding commitment to states' rights and his opposition to legislation as an answer to social problems. Given his philosophy, he did practice his beliefs on equal rights and in tolerance. In 1964, he and Peggy received the National Human Relations Award of the National Conference of Christians and Jews. Toward the end of his life, he contributed liberally to the United Negro College Fund, and Peggy was an active member of the board.[10]

When Douglas accepted the ambassadorial appointment, he believed the affairs of the Mutual Life Insurance Company of New York were in good hands with the appointment of Alexander E. Patterson as president. But in September, 1948, Patterson died suddenly of a stroke. From London Douglas strongly recommended that Louis W. Dawson, vice-president and general counsel, be designated acting executive head of the company. The board immediately followed his advice, despite doubts based on Dawson's retiring personality and lack of administrative experience. Some members of the board considered going outside for a permanent appointment, but Douglas obviously desired an interim arrangement, leaving the door open for his own return as chairman and president or as chairman and chief executive officer, with an outsider brought in as president if Dawson did not carry out his responsibilities to the satisfaction of the board. At that time, of course, the national presidential election was on the horizon, and there was considerable question in Douglas's mind whether he would still be in London in the new year.[11]

The unexpected Truman victory and the continuation of Douglas's tenure, then the eye accident in May, 1949, prompted some members of the board, led by Gilbert H. Scribner, to initiate action in early June for a permanent reorganization of the company's major executive offices. The move seems clearly to have had as its object to bypass Douglas and the executive committee and probably to appoint Dawson, who had done an admirable job, permanently as president and chief executive officer. Dawson himself appears to have been entirely innocent in the matter. In any case, Douglas was furious. A flurry of angry and hurt correspondence ensued from London. He fully intended to return as chief executive officer, whatever other title he might hold. In the event, the board, including Scribner, voted to rescind the motion to consider reorganization. It had been a most unpleasant episode for all concerned. Leo Wolman, Douglas's old friend and fellow board member, reassured him, however, that "The Board is yours, lock, stock, and barrel, and so are the officers in the field. . . . The defections of the Board, if that is what they are, are minor and have always been there." On his visits to the States Douglas reiterated his desire to return to his old position, indicating in great confidence his intention to resign as ambassador sometime in the spring of 1950.[12]

But early in 1950 circumstances combined to convince Douglas that he could not resume his duties as chief executive officer. After his vascular surgery and its complications in December and January and with his continued eye problem, his doctors advised him not to assume such a burden. Furthermore, despite those disabilities, he had agreed, at the request of Acheson and Truman, to stay on in London as long as he was needed. He, therefore, reluctantly recommended to the board Dawson's permanent appointment, which occurred in March. Douglas continued as chairman, "not," as he wrote one trustee, "to occupy an empty position, but really to discharge the duties of adviser to the officers and the members of the Board." It was, no doubt, a painful decision for Douglas, for he found it very difficult, then and later, to relinquish the reins of power in a company he had worked so hard and successfully to restore to a position of financial prosperity.[13]

His unhappiness was intensified in June, when the New York State Insurance Department questioned the enhanced authority of the chairman of the board, agreed to, at Douglas's insistence, in the March meeting. Dawson attempted to calm Douglas's fears that he was being pushed to one side, emphasizing that "Because of our personal relations and my respect for your judgment I am sure you know that from my own desires this would result in securing your views on major matters." Douglas was not placated. He argued that the new code of reorganization under consideration did not adequately describe the responsibilities he should enjoy. "Either you or I continue to attempt to reconcile our differences . . .," he telegraphed Dawson, "or I will yield to you and resign from the Board entirely. . . . I [am] . . . not interested in merely a title and . . . I desire to participate in formation of major policy and the nomination of the important senior officers and in the selection of members of the Board of Trustees." He reminded the new president and chief executive officer of the part he had played in his selection and of his own "great success" in that position. It was "not fair" to place him in the position, as he described it to Wolman, of a "mere figurehead." After this exchange, the executive committee took no final action on the code, appointing a committee to reexamine it and recommend new wording. There the matter stood until Douglas's return from England, when the future relationship between the two officers was worked out to their mutual satisfaction. In 1959, at the mandatory age of sixty-five, Douglas was named honorary chairman and retired from an active role on the board. Dawson became chairman and Roger Hall was elected president.[14]

Meanwhile, in 1949, Douglas had assumed a major financial undertaking with his purchase of a controlling interest in the Southern Arizona Bank and Trust Company of Tucson from the estate of an old friend. Hubert d'Autremont's death in April, 1947, ended a distinguished career as a banker, mine developer, civic leader, philanthropist, and politician; he had been elected president of the Arizona state senate the previous January. Before Douglas's sudden appointment to London, he had discussed with d'Autremont the possibility of acquiring some or all of his proprietary rights in the bank. At about the same time he had arranged for his son James to begin work at the bank, in addition to his duties overseeing the Sonoita ranch. But, following Douglas's departure and immersion in his new duties, the purchase had been in abeyance. The death of the owner and president reopened the question, as his widow wished to dispose of the shares inherited by her, her daughters-in-law, and minor grandchildren, in accordance with her husband's desire that the bank remain under competent local control.[15]

Correspondence between Douglas and Helen d'Autremont concerning the purchase began during the summer of 1947. The transaction was completed and publicly announced in September, 1949. Isabella Greenway King and her husband, Harry King, had also early expressed an interest in purchasing some of the d'Autremont stock, and a mutually satisfactory arrangement was reached at the same time between Douglas and the Kings. Of the then 2,500 shares outstanding, Helen d'Autremont and her family owned 1,050. Douglas purchased 800, the King family, including Mrs. King's son Jack Greenway, 250. In a separate understanding, Douglas and the Kings agreed not to sell their holdings without first offering them to the other party and to vote their stock as a unit. Upon his return from Europe, Douglas would serve as chairman of the board, on which Harry and Isabella King would also sit.[16]

Both purchasing parties indicated to Helen d'Autremont their intention to maintain the local character, ownership, and control of the bank. But they also pointed out that they could not foresee the future, which might bring conditions under which their own interests, those of other stockholders, the depositors, and the community might be better served by disposing of the stock to some other banking institution. Unfortunately, in the light of later events, that qualification, which appeared in Douglas's first draft of the press release of the sale, was eliminated in the published announcement on September 16, 1949.[17]

On January 9, 1951, Douglas was formally elected chairman of the board and indicated his plans to spend a substantial amount of his time in Tucson and take a "reasonably active" interest in the management of the bank. In fact, soon after the bank sale in 1949, he purchased a 167-acre tract of land on East Fort Lowell Road, where in 1953–54 he built his Tucson home, Pantano Farm, in order to be closer to his downtown office than the ranch, some forty miles to the southeast. In the future, he and Peggy divided their time between Tucson and New York, generally spending much of the winter in Arizona.[18]

Also in 1951, Brendan Bracken, who had in 1945 become chairman of the board of the Union Corporation, an influential gold and metal finance company with large overseas holdings, especially in South Africa, invited Douglas to become a director. This provided him with a financial interest in London at the corporation's headquarters and required periodic trips to South Africa. During these visits he became well acquainted not only with mining and banking officials but with most of the important members of the South African government. He deplored apartheid, and predicted it would "produce over a long period of time an explosion that will be heard around the world." But he was hopeful that foreign investment would create the "economic pressures to upgrade the training and quality of the natives." In the same year, he was elected a director of the International Nickel Company of Canada, whose board was composed of equal numbers of Canadians, Britons, and Americans. These two were among the most enjoyable and active of his many outside corporate affiliations.[19]

Within a year of assuming the chairmanship of the Southern Arizona Bank, Douglas was faced with his first decision affecting his commitment to Helen d'Autremont. His oldest friend, Frank Brophy, offered to sell him his ownership interest in the Bank of Douglas. After some correspondence, Douglas decided that acceptance would, if not technically, at least morally, be a violation of his and the Kings' obligation.[20]

Then in 1954, the Phoenix-based First National Bank of Arizona, a subsidiary of the Transamerica Corporation, threatened to move aggressively into southern Arizona by opening a branch in Tucson. In an effort to meet this competition, Douglas unsuccessfully explored various arrangements that would strengthen the capital position of the Southern Arizona Bank and still maintain its independence or at least preserve its intrastate character. In the summer of 1955, Transamerica made a direct offer to Douglas, which involved exchanging Southern Arizona Bank stock for its own corporate shares if 80 percent of the stockholders agreed. Both Douglas and son James, who had become assistant to the president and was active as his father's personal representative during the former's frequent absences, had grave reservations about the arrangement. They hoped independence might be maintained by increasing the capital of the bank through a large issue of common stock or some other device, which would, however, entail a considerable financial burden on the stockholders for the next decade.[21]

As the summer wore on, the terms of Transamerica's offer became progressively more attractive and the difficulties of remaining independent in the face of the anticipated competition more obvious. After agonizing over the implications of the dilemma, Douglas called an informal meeting of the stockholders, on August 25, to present the latest Transamerica proposal and the alternative of "going it alone." Seventy-five percent of the stockholders were represented. The financial advantages of the Transamerica offer, which was open only until August 30, were overwhelming. It would also provide, Douglas pointed out, research resources, opportunities for large national accounts, and better services and interest rates for customers. Nor could the stockholders overlook the force of the "wave of mergers and consolidations of banks throughout the U.S." "There are," he continued, "on the other side of the coin, weighty sentimental, emotional and philosophical considerations," not the least of which was the moral obligation to the d'Autremonts. Those "points of view," he admitted, "move me very deeply and weigh with me very heavily." Yet he had a clear responsibility to present the proposal to the stockholders, since it entailed "such a substantial sum of money" to all of them.

He stated he was "perfectly willing to go any way the stockholders want to go," to accept or reject the offer. But he could not "recommend that you decline this offer on financial and economic grounds." He indicated that the name of the bank would remain the same for the foreseeable future, the majority of directors would be local, and the tenure of the present officers and other personnel ensured. At the end of the meeting, every person present, including Charles Maurice d'Autremont, a major stockholder, who voiced his conviction that his brother Hubert would have recognized that changed conditions justified acceptance of the offer, indicated support for the proposal. By the end of November, the transaction was completed, and the Southern Arizona Bank and Trust Company became a subsidiary of Transamerica. Also, in consequence, Douglas became the largest individual stockholder in Transamerica and was elected to its board of directors and executive committee.[22]

On August 31, Douglas wrote Helen d'Autremont, who had been out of town when the Transamerica proposal had to be considered. Admitting that his initial mistake had been to decline Frank Brophy's offer in 1951, he emphasized his and his family's willingness to go it alone if the other stockholders had rejected the bid from Transamerica and related the many advantages that would accrue to the bank from the merger while it retained its essentially local character. "Of course," he wrote, "the ghost of Hubert hovered over me throughout. Emotionally, it was not an easy matter for me to bring this proposal to the stockholders." Unconvinced, Helen d'Autremont was greatly disturbed by the transaction, and some members of her family were indignant. She aired her unhappiness publicly in a letter to the editor of the *Arizona Daily Star*, published on October 5. Douglas, who valued his reputation for probity, was deeply hurt by the implications of improper conduct. Unfortunately, the bitterness of some of the d'Autremonts and their sympathizers and the distress at what Douglas and his family considered unwarranted criticism lingered even beyond the deaths of the principals.[23]

After the merger, the Southern Arizona Bank prospered. A large measure of local control of its operations was maintained. An elegant new building in the Italian Renaissance style was completed in 1958. In 1965, Douglas retired to become honorary chairman of the board (though he noted to a friend he would "continue to do approximately the same things I have always done, except to preside at Board meetings"), and three years later James was named president.

In 1972, the Western Bancorporation, successor to Transamerica, began discussions to merge the Southern Arizona Bank with the First National Bank of Phoenix. This was accomplished the year after Douglas's death, with James becoming a vice-chairman of the board, along with Edward M. Carson, in charge of overseeing its southern Arizona operations, and Robert D. Williams of Phoenix, named president and chief executive officer of the combined institutions. Some years later, the Western Bancorporation changed its name and those of its subsidiaries throughout the West to First Interstate Bank. James was unhappy that his new position entailed working in Phoenix and soon resigned as vice-chairman, but remained an active member of the board.[24]

Before leaving London, Douglas had accepted an invitation by a group of southern Arizona ranchers and businessmen to become president of the Southeast Arizona Weather Research Corporation, which had been organized to explore ways to increase precipitation in that part of the state. In December of 1950, the group granted a contract to Dr. Irving Krick, head of the Water Resources Development Corporation of Denver, to carry out cloud-seeding operations in the area in 1951. The results, though inconclusive, were sufficiently encouraging for the group to renew the contract for 1952. But Douglas and other members of the organization had meantime come to the conclusion that it was premature to continue attempts at increasing rainfall without further basic scientific research in meteorology, especially as applied to their region. To this end, he entered into an extended correspondence with leading meteorologists in the United States and abroad for advice and support, as well as with the Ford, Rockefeller, and Sloan foundations (he was a trustee of the last two) for possible financial assistance in the research.[25]

On the basis of advice from the experts and the foundations as well as assurances from President Richard A. Harvill that the University of Arizona would cooperate in setting up a program within that institution, Douglas invited a group of distinguished atmospheric physicists to Tucson in January, 1953, to formulate a proposal. From there, the group moved to Schenectady, New York, to meet with representatives from the Department of Meteorology of the University of Chicago and other interested scientists. During the year, the University of Chicago's Cloud Physics Project agreed to cooperate with the University of Arizona in recruiting qualified personnel for an institute at Tucson. The Sloan Foundation approved a grant of $50,000 a year over a three-year period, beginning in 1954. This support was approximately matched by the university. The National Science Foundation granted $50,000 for the period through 1956, and the Air Force Cambridge Research Center gave assistance in the form of essential equipment. A number of other government agencies provided nonfinancial support to the program.[26]

The Institute of Atmospheric Physics was formally established in early 1954 at the University of Arizona with Dr. Roscoe R. Braham, Jr., of the University of Chicago Cloud Physics Program as director, sharing his time between the two institutions. Lewis Douglas was named consulting administrative director, without a salary, a position he held until his death. The institute introduced courses for both undergraduates and graduates and offered advanced degrees in meteorology, later under the direction of the academic Department of Atmospheric Sciences. Its research on the fundamental mechanisms that govern weather processes is internationally recognized.[27]

Douglas's interest in weather modification coincided with congressional concern with its potential, manifested in the creation, in 1953, of the Advisory Committee on Weather Control. Douglas was appointed a private member by President Eisenhower in December. Despite some promising evaluation and encouragement of ongoing experiments, the brief existence of the committee was marred by competition and suspicion among the government agencies over jurisdiction. The final report concluded that there was no need at that time for federal regulatory legislation. No new funding was forthcoming, and the committee ceased to exist at the end of 1957. But Douglas's tenure in the committee had provided him with contacts that were invaluable in forwarding the work of the institute at the university.[28]

Douglas also took an active role in the emerging field of solar energy, in which Arizona became an early center with the formation of the Association for Applied Solar Energy in Phoenix in 1954. The new organization, in which Douglas was a director, in cooperation with the Stanford Research Institute and with financial support from several private foundations and government agencies, planned a World Symposium on Applied Solar Energy to be held in Phoenix November 1–15, 1955. The invited scientists, some 500, of whom 130 were from almost forty countries outside the United States, insisted upon a purely scientific meeting before the Phoenix conference, which was to include approximately 600 laymen primarily interested in the possible practical uses of solar energy. The preliminary conference on Solar Energy—Scientific Basis was held at the University of Arizona, with Douglas presiding, on October 31 and November 1. The group then moved to Phoenix, where a number of the same papers were repeated and others presented on applied aspects of the subject. Again Douglas served as general chairman, reading, in his opening remarks, a letter from Eisenhower, expressing the President's gratification that the United States was "host country" for efforts to explore "further practical applications of laboratory discoveries . . . toward a fuller use of the virtually unlimited energy of the sun."

Unfortunately, the future of the association was discouraging as interest in solar energy waned and research received little private or official support. In 1958, Douglas tried unsuccessfully to interest the University of Arizona in "absorbing the work of the Association," including its library and publications. Arizona State College was more receptive, and in 1959 the executive committee voted to establish its headquarters at Tempe. Although unhappy with the association's decision, which he believed was influenced by Phoenix members, and doubtful about the scientific competence at the state college, Douglas continued as a director and financial supporter. Diminution of support and membership led to a reorganization in 1963 as a professional association, renamed the Solar Energy Society, with a much more international and less Arizona-dominated leadership. Eventually, in 1970, it moved to Melbourne, Australia. By a twist of fate named OPEC, the society prospered in its new home.[29]

Douglas's concern with the utilization and preservation of natural resources ranged beyond climate control and solar power, locally and nationally. In 1953 he accepted the chairmanship of the Mid-Century Conference on Resources for the Future, sponsored by Resources for the Future, Inc., funded by the Ford Foundation. He characterized its task as a "collective attempt to divine some of the issues which are implicit in the subject of raw materials—the raw materials of the atmosphere, the raw materials of the seas and of the waters and the raw materials of the land—and which are relevant to their businesslike employment, a wise and appropriate conservation of them, and to replenish them by new discovery of new sources or new substitutes." Addressed by President Eisenhower, members of the cabinet and Congress, as well as academic and industrial specialists, the conference discussed the points he had raised.[30]

From 1957 to 1963, he headed the Arizona Water Resources Committee of businessmen, cattlemen, farmers, scientific experts, and political figures. The most important work of the committee was the encouragement of watershed programs to improve the flow of water from forested areas, for which it obtained over $300,000 from the Department of Agriculture. Throughout its existence, it received active cooperation from the University of Arizona's College of Agriculture, Institute of Atmospheric Physics, and several departments. Projects were undertaken in six of the state's fourteen counties.[31]

As the city's leading banker, Douglas was involved in attracting new industry to Tucson and southern Arizona. He was among the first to recognize the importance of the Kitt Peak National Observatory, established near Tucson in 1957, the army's electronic proving ground at Fort Huachuca, the ongoing research at the university, and the climate as attractions for companies, especially in the electronics field.

In 1958, he announced a three-year $90,000 program, financed by the Southern Arizona Bank, Tucson Gas and Electric, and the Tucson newspapers to publicize the advantages for light industry in the area. It was one modest beginning to an enterprise that, over the next quarter century, grew in scope and participation to contribute greatly to Tucson's impressive growth. A number of light industries, many electronic, moved large and important branches there.[32]

Douglas had critics in Tucson who resented his prominence and financial shrewdness and, on occasion, privately accused him of hubris, but even they deferred in public to his warmth, intelligence, and experience. His counsel was sought and his participation solicited in many statewide undertakings. He seemed to know and be known by everyone in the region. Nowhere was this better exemplified than locally in his daily walk down Stone Avenue from the bank to lunch at the Old Pueblo Club. He was slowed by greetings and conversations with everyone he encountered from shoeshine boys to city fathers.

As late as 1963, despite his independent political views, he was approached by fellow Arizonan Stewart Udall, then President Kennedy's secretary of the interior, on the possibility of running for governor. He gave the proposal serious if brief consideration, but decided his health precluded undertaking the arduous tasks of campaigning and two strenuous years in the statehouse. It was not the first time the suggestion had been made over the years that he stand for either senator or governor, but it was the last. Previously he had been uninterested because of other obligations or an accurate assessment that his opposition to the current national Democratic administration would prevent success. In the case of the governorship, his reluctance was reinforced by conviction that the state constitution had created a weak executive. Probably his momentary interest in 1963 reflected his recently acquired regard for President Kennedy and the attraction of a final stint of public service.[33]

On his and Peggy's annual trips to England and in correspondence, Douglas continued a lively interest in British affairs and in Anglo-American relations. In New York, he resumed an active role in the English-Speaking Union as chairman of the board. His visits to London always included meetings with political leaders and influential figures in other walks of life, usually a few days of fishing at the Houghton Club, and often, if the season was open, some grouse shooting at the estate of his old friend and sometime Prince's Gate neighbor, Lord Swinton. Frequently, the couple stayed at the Hyde Park Hotel, but on occasion rented a house or flat for several weeks in order to reciprocate the hospitality always accorded them.[34]

As ambassador, he had been disappointed at the narrow Conservative party loss in 1950. Back home, he awaited the outcome of the next election, in October, 1951, with hope and fear. Writing to Churchill before polling day, he expressed concern that another Labour victory would have "consequences . . . incalculable for the whole of Christendom." When the Conservatives did triumph, he was elated over Churchill's return to power and impressed with the caliber of the new cabinet, but lamented the slim majority the party had obtained. When Sir Winston stepped down in 1955, he commiserated with Brendan (by then Lord) Bracken. He could understand how "the beloved Boss" felt isolated "from the stream of events." "I wish," he wrote, "he were boss of the civilized world. . . . There is no one anywhere who speaks with the voice of the turtle, except himself." But he was enormously cheered by the decisive sanction the Conservatives received when Sir Anthony Eden went to the country shortly after his succession to the premiership. "I was," he wrote Sir Winston, ". . . as enthusiastic about the outcome as though several generations of migrant Scots had not accidentally made of me an American."[35]

When British friends and exalted guests visited the United States, the Douglases made every effort to entertain them either in New York or Arizona. Lord and Lady Halifax, on a nostalgic tour of the country under the auspices of the Commonwealth Fund, in the fall of 1951, "stole," in the words of the former British ambassador, "a delightful ten days to stay with Lew and Peggy Douglas on their ranch in Arizona." It was impossible to find a pair of jeans long enough for the very tall visitor. With those he wore reaching far above his ankles and a disreputable straw hat for protection from the sun as he rode the range, his attire was a far cry from the usual apparel of a proper English gentleman. It was during this visit that the devout Anglican insisted on completing Peggy's preparation for eternity by confirmation at a small Episcopal chapel in Nogales.[36]

The Queen Mother came to the United States in the fall of 1954. Douglas had arranged for her to speak before the English-Speaking Union. The gala dinner at the Waldorf-Astoria on November 3, which he chaired, attracted over three thousand guests. Her Majesty was presented with a gift of $433,481 for the King George VI Fellowship Fund. For the Douglases, no doubt the high point was, however, the night before, when she spent a quiet dinner and evening at their apartment, "with a game of canasta thrown in."[37]

Three years later, Queen Elizabeth and Prince Philip made a ceremonial visit. On that occasion, Douglas arranged for a joint dinner of the English-Speaking Union and the Pilgrims at the Waldorf the evening of October 21. But before that event Douglas was informed by Sir Harold Caccia, the British ambassador, that Her Majesty had been pleased to appoint him a Knight Grand Cross of the Most Excellent Order of the British Empire "in recognition of your outstanding services in the cause of Anglo-American understanding." On October 19 in the British embassy in Washington, Douglas knelt before the Queen for his investiture. Before the dinner two days later the Queen and Prince Philip, led by seven pipers of the Canadian Black Watch, proceeded through the several dining rooms to greet some 4,000 guests. Douglas, resplendent in the riband and insignia of his new dignity, presided over the glittering affair.[38]

Later in the year Douglas underwent extensive and serious surgery. In fact, the years since Douglas's return had already been marred by several hospitalizations and two relatively minor but uncomfortable surgical procedures in 1952 and 1954. His left eye had continued to be a source of periodic discomfort, but there was one amusing consequence. When Harry W. Wallace, president of Hathaway Shirts, and his wife were crossing together with the Douglases on one of the *Queens*, they observed the ambassador with his patch. Mrs. Wallace, impressed with the distinction it gave Douglas, persuaded her husband to use the idea in advertising his product. The first advertisements appeared in 1951, using Baron George Wrangel as the model. They were an almost instantaneous success. Somewhat belatedly, in 1955, admitting Douglas had been the inspiration of the ads, Wallace offered to send him the gift of a "modest quantity of Hathaways" in appreciation. Douglas responded with his neck and sleeve size, but there is some doubt as to whether the shirts ever arrived.[39]

Intestinal surgery in late December, 1957, following some weeks of discomfort, revealed a malignancy, which was successfully and permanently removed but left Douglas with a colostomy. It was a source of great inconvenience, which he bore with fortitude in the years that followed.[40]

His convalescence prevented the annual trip to England in 1958. But June of 1959 found the Douglases back in London for a month; he was to participate, as honorary chairman of the American delegation, in the first meeting of the Atlantic Congress. An unofficial offshoot of NATO, the congress had been organized to mark the first decade of the organization and to discuss and make recommendations for the second. Formed by a group of leading citizens from the countries in the alliance and financed by foundations and corporations, it included 650 representatives. The delegates attended as individuals but had the strong support of their member governments and the patronage of President Eisenhower and Queen Elizabeth.

The recommendations of the Congress were not unexpected: increased consultation among the member governments, a buildup of military strength to earlier agreed minimum standards and greater integration of forces, promotion of economic growth and cooperation, and the establishment of a permanent private organization to study and disseminate information on questions vital to the Atlantic community. The last proposal led to the creation of the Atlantic Council and the Atlantic Institute, which are located in Washington and continue to perform a useful function in providing an intellectual focus on NATO affairs. Douglas played an active role in both organizations until the early 1970s, when his health limited his participation.

Addressing the assembly in a special plenary session on June 9, Douglas spoke of the unique accomplishment their deliberations celebrated. NATO was "perhaps the most startling novelty of the first half of this century. . . . That the North American part of the new world is irrevocably committed to the preservation of the civilization of which it is an integral part is, I suggest, the most important of the international developments since the turn of the century." Had such an institution existed in 1914 or 1939, two great and terrible wars might well have been averted. Now, however, as they met to find new ways of strengthening this "society of freedom," the world was faced with a frightening and perplexing predicament. Science had developed a new knowledge, the use of nuclear energy, which could immensely benefit mankind but also lead to its destruction. "At the same time . . . the political behavior of man has, on balance, been lagging behind, if in many respects it has not deteriorated. Many new manifestations of excessive nationalism—not patriotism—are emerging in almost every part of the world—old and new." The delegates must persuade their governments "that time is pressing, that politics must take control of the forces science has generated, that unrestrained sovereignty, *once constrained* for almost the stretch of a century from Waterloo to the Marne, must once again subject itself to self discipline and to wholesome restraints." Only when these contradictions and dangers were met, he concluded, could "an enduring peace finally be fashioned out of a period of uneasiness."[41]

His words, though perhaps obvious, rose above the details of the deliberations to pose the truly overriding question of his and succeeding generations. They reflected his growing pessimism, as the decade ended, that mankind would find the answer.

Monitoring Eisenhower

ALTHOUGH DOUGLAS DID NOT FORMALLY ENDORSE Dwight Eisenhower's presidential candidacy until late September, 1952, his actions and statements made his decision obvious long before that date. In July, 1951, he met with Eisenhower at NATO headquarters in Versailles. Whether he raised the question of a political future for the general in the course of their discussions is not known. Speculation concerning Eisenhower's availability was certainly in the air, and Douglas had met with Dewey, an early supporter, shortly before his departure. Six months later, the general announced from Paris that he would accept the Republican nomination if offered and authorized his name to be entered in the New Hampshire primary. In May, 1952, running neck and neck with Taft in the primaries, he resigned his command to return to the United States to conduct his campaign in person.[1]

Earlier that month, Douglas foreshadowed his decision before a joint dinner in Tucson of the Pima County Democratic Committee and the Young Democrats Club of Arizona. He described the basic principles of the party as resistance to "an unnecessary investiture of government with too wide an authority over the affairs of the individual . . . and [belief in] the frugal use of public credit." "Every Democrat," he continued, "must be more concerned with his country's future than with success of the party at the polls. . . . Every American has . . . three loyalties. The first is to his country, the second to his state, and the third to his party. Whenever these three conflict . . . [he must] resolve the conflict in favor of the higher loyalty. This, I believe, is the essence of being a good Democrat . . . [and of] being a good American."[2]

It was a remarkable statement to a gathering of the party faithful, but, knowing Douglas's political history, his listeners should not have been completely surprised. The *Arizona Republic* the next day gleefully reported "Douglas's Truths Shock Democrats," and the *Arizona Plain Talk*, a Democratic organ, deplored the speaker's taste in using "the occasion to announce his de facto membership in the

Republican Party." The audience, it continued, had the right to expect their principal speaker "to praise the Party not to bury it."[3]

Douglas had already begun his voluminous correspondence—and frequent meetings—with Eisenhower; he continued to offer advice and counsel over the next nine years. Concerned over Eisenhower's statement, while still at SHAPE, in support of the administration's request for increased foreign economic and military aid, he questioned "our frantic effort to build up a defense system." No one, he asserted, was more aware of the Soviet threat than he. But inflated budgets risked "destroying not only the economies of Europe, but of modifying beyond recognition the peculiar sort of system that has been characteristic of our own country." That danger was "at least as great as the danger from a hostile power." Eisenhower responded "instantly," because of "the profound importance" of the subject. He firmly agreed that *"the financial solvency and the economic soundness of the United States constitute together the first requisite to collective security in the free world,"* but he was convinced that, after all that America had poured into Europe, to decrease the appropriation bill sharply might dangerously slow the momentum.

Douglas disagreed. Pentagon budgets were always padded. He also feared saddling Europe with a burden of rearmament that would undo the economic advances since 1948. The United States was trying to do more than was necessary or possible, financially and militarily. He then enumerated the mistakes he believed had contributed to the North Korean invasion and charged the administration with subsequent exaggeration of the Soviet intention to make war. The NATO defense program should be "selective" and only large enough to "deter" any Russian temptation to attack.[4]

In June Douglas raised a domestic issue long an object of his conservative concern—the growth and power of the national trade union movement. It represented, he warned Eisenhower, "the growth of private power in a form which the country has not experienced . . . since corporate monopolies first put in their appearance." In some ways it was an even "more dangerous . . . [threat] to the freedom of the Republic." The important goal of labor legislation was to guarantee every worker the right to join or not to join a union. The Taft-Hartley Act of 1947 was a step forward, but more specific measures were needed. He would very much like an opportunity to talk to Eisenhower about the matter.[5]

Douglas objected to the candidate's speech before the American Federation of Labor, which he considered a "futile effort to gain the votes of trade union leaders." Eisenhower already had the chance to get the support of 50 percent of the workers who were non-union and of many of those who were union and chafed under the power of their organizations. If he took a forthright position on the labor question, Douglas advised, he would be "branded a brave man. The American people want bravery." There was no need to court labor leaders. He returned to the issue in conversations and communications with the President, members of Congress, and friends of like mind on a number of occasions during the Eisenhower administration—and throughout the rest of his life. Dedicated to the "right to work" principle, he deplored any amendments to the Taft-Hartley Act that he saw as weakening its effectiveness or as not further strengthening its provisions.

He expressed doubts to friends that the President understood the implications of the labor movement. Douglas was an active member of the De Mille Foundation, set up to promote "right to work" legislation, opposed the AFL-CIO merger in 1955, and continued to urge that unions be subject to the provisions of the antitrust laws. In a letter to Arthur Krock in 1962, he wrote: "If any administration, whether it be this one [Kennedy's] or a subsequent one, is interested in dealing with the problem of the trade union leader, they should repeal the Norris-LaGuardia Act and bar national unions."[6]

After a bitter battle with Taft supporters over the seating of delegates, Eisenhower was nominated at the Republican Convention on July 11. Two weeks later Governor Adlai Stevenson of Illinois, the reluctant candidate, accepted the Democratic Convention's endorsement for President. Douglas had as yet made no public announcement of his choice. On August 30, at his request, he met with Stevenson in New York to inform him, "as an ordinary act of decent courtesy" and because of their "friendly relationship," that he would support Eisenhower. Apparently he gave as the reason his disagreement with the Democratic domestic, especially fiscal, policies, the need for a change in party administrations, and his confidence in Eisenhower's internationalism. Privately, his comments were more personal. To Lord Salisbury he wrote that Stevenson had "no depth, and . . . the greatest capacity for indecision of almost anybody I have ever known." More bluntly, to Brendan Bracken he commented: "Stevenson does have wit, but so did Oscar Wilde. . . . I like him. I have fun with him. But I think he is a sham. There is a bogus quality about him."[7]

Douglas was not, however, happy about the Republican platform plank on liberation policy nor the Eisenhower speech to the American Legion, on August 25. To say that the United States would never be satisfied until the satellite states had an opportunity to determine their own form of government, he told and then wrote the general at length, was "to say that the present restrictions . . . must . . . be removed as a result of our efforts." It was a dangerous pronouncement, promising more than we could or should undertake and quite "likely to be another step in the direction of a third world war. . . . Almost certainly [it] will produce retaliatory steps . . . [and] an environment which makes war much more likely, if not inevitable." "It may very well be," he added, "that the mere declaration of this policy will make more secure Communist hold on the satellite areas." In any case, it was an intrusion of a "moral basis" for national policy that, in the past, had led the country into great difficulties not in accord with its "enlightened national interest."[8]

Douglas discussed his objections with John Foster Dulles and thought the area of disagreement had been substantially reduced, only to have the liberation policy more stridently repeated in Dulles's speech in St. Louis on September 26, accompanied by what he considered an unfair attack upon George Kennan's containment policy. He telegraphed Dulles three days later, charging that his remarks could at worst lead "only to another war and at best to distrust among thoughtful members of the Western European Community of our wisdom, if not our intentions." Such statements would "do considerable damage to Eisenhower's cause . . . [and make] it almost impossible to seize the opportunity as I had hoped you would seize it, to make the Republican Party the party of peace." Dulles's four-page telegraphed reply that his policy did not necessarily mean war and that "it is not possible to have a foreign policy debate without disturbing friends abroad" did little to assuage Douglas's distress.[9]

Despite these reservations, Douglas finally spoke in Phoenix in support of Eisenhower and the Republican nominees for Arizona senator and governor, Barry Goldwater and Howard Pyle. He cited his disagreements with Truman's fiscal and labor policies, especially the "dangerous doctrine of unlimited executive authority" as demonstrated in the President's steel-plant seizure during the recent strike. Notwithstanding the "pulls of party loyalty, the sentiments of friendship and . . . old associations," he had concluded "that the interest of the nation and the world will be best served by the election" of the Republican candidates. A month earlier, after some hesitation, pleading health problems, he had turned down the general's invitation to chair the organization of Democrats and independents being formed to support his campaign. At that time, he had reassured Eisenhower of his intention to vote for him.[10]

Eisenhower was pleased with the Phoenix address, which received national coverage—"That was a terrific speech you made." On October 21, in New York, before the New York *Herald Tribune* Forum, Douglas made his only other major statement, which was primarily an indictment of Democratic policies. After predictable criticism of Roosevelt's and Truman's domestic leadership, he devoted most of his remarks to foreign policy. During the war, "sensible precautions" had not been taken to prevent the Soviet Union from taking every advantage to increase and expand its dominion. Yalta was a disaster. The division of Germany was "the most fantastic arrangement ever made about any large and populous area in the history of modern politics. For it the highest Democratic officials forever must be held accountable." The Berlin crisis was the direct consequence of "inexcusable negligence of our government in not making proper arrangement[s]." The "loss of China" stemmed from the errors of wartime diplomacy. The division of Korea after the Communists had fought against Japan only six days "set the stage for the present costly and bloody and frightful war in the Orient." The recapture by their rightful owners of lost territories could, however, only be achieved by "patient efforts, unfailing wisdom" that would prevent "the final desperate device, another call to arms." "Whatever the argument or excuse," he concluded, "the blunt and inescapable fact remains that these . . . agreements . . . were made . . . by the highest officials of the Democratic Administration. It must be held forever accountable for them and their ghastly consequences." On the other hand, "Mr. Eisenhower, who was not at Yalta . . . will bring unusual experience and a wholly objective and fresh mind to these questions. . . . He has the qualities and talents . . . to hold the coalition of our allies in complete and harmonious accord and to mold the internal coalition which is so essential to the resolution of the issues which we face."[11]

Not surprisingly, the reactions of leading Democrats to these attacks ranged from dismay to anger. Considering Douglas's past history, they were no doubt prepared for another ballot-box defection and private criticism of their domestic regime. But they considered his previous pledges of loyalty still operative. They were unhappy at his public support of Eisenhower and particularly indignant at his virulent and unsubstantiated charges on foreign policy for the period when he had served Democratic administrations in WSA, as General Clay's advisor, and as ambassador. Whether or not he realized it, Douglas's remarks were also an attack upon his beloved Winston Churchill, who participated in or approved of many of the decisions he deplored. Truman wrote philosophically to James Farley: "I, myself, can't understand Lew Douglas. As you say, some people take everything from the Party and give nothing." In the 1956 election, when Douglas repeated his performance, Truman was more vitriolic: "Lewis Douglas was never a Democrat until after he got his job under the Democrats. He's a copper millionaire." However, Truman was never personally unpleasant to Douglas in later years; in fact, he apparently retained a certain grudging respect for his wisdom and probity.[12]

Two long-standing and intimate relationships did suffer—one temporarily, one permanently. Averell Harriman, who had persuaded Roosevelt to invite Douglas back into his administration in 1942 and, with Acheson, promoted him for the ambassadorship, was distressed at what he considered a breach of faith. But two years later he put political differences aside and held out the hand of reconciliation. Their relations were cordial until Douglas's death.[13]

Acheson, on the other hand, was incensed at what he considered Douglas's disloyalty, not so much to the party, with which he had on occasion become disenchanted himself, but to Truman personally. He was devoted to the President. That Douglas would lend his name and voice to a campaign that attacked Truman so viciously was inexcusable. Although the two men continued to exchange formal greetings at Christmas and to see each other occasionally socially, the breach was never healed. Terribly hurt by Acheson's attitude, which he considered unfair, Douglas made a number of unsuccessful attempts to restore their friendship, both directly and through the good offices of mutual friends. Two of many evidences of his chagrin and sadness at Acheson's estrangement are found in a note to the former secretary on October 22, 1969: "I miss you and our old association more than I can say," and in a letter to Truman shortly after Acheson's death, in which he commented that his breach with Acheson had been "one of my sorrows as I approach the winter of my discontent, for I have always been loyal to Dean and one of his most affectionate admirers." The depth of Acheson's resentment was reflected in the detailed autobiographical account of his State Department service, in which Douglas was mentioned by name only twice in passing, while other less-important figures received considerable and usually laudatory comment. Douglas was offended by the omission in *Present at the Creation* of any references to his role in the ERP, the Berlin blockade, the creation of West Germany, and the beginnings of NATO. He could, he wrote former State Department advisor Herbert Feis, "write volumes" on what had been left out of the book. In later years, Acheson commented acidly to a mutual friend: "Lew Douglas changes his politics as often as he changes his shirt." It is noteworthy and relevant that Acheson's fierce loyalty to Truman also led to his bitterness toward Adlai Stevenson for what he considered the candidate's attempt to disassociate himself from Truman during the 1952 campaign.[14]

Eisenhower was elected by the largest popular vote in history to that date and carried with him both houses of Congress. Meeting with the President-elect several times over the next weeks in New York, Douglas urged him, on December

26, to try to establish "some method of continuous communication between our government and the Kremlin" as soon as possible after the inauguration. Otherwise, it would be difficult to avoid a war in the next few years. Formal notes between foreign ministers through embassies and vitriolic charges in the United Nations, the prevailing methods of exchanging views, were obviously unfruitful. In particular, he advocated a meeting between Eisenhower and Stalin alone. Whatever the general's personal reaction to the advice, no doubt the more militant John Foster Dulles, soon to be secretary of state, found it unpalatable.[15]

Meantime, cabinet making was in progress. Eisenhower had designated General Clay and Herbert Brownell as the core of a small committee to make suggestions on appointments. There were rumors that Douglas was being considered for under secretary of state or secretary of commerce, but according to Clay's later recollections his name was never seriously considered. His minimal activity in the campaign did not outweigh the fact that he had been a member of the two preceding Democratic administrations, making his selection unlikely with so many office-hungry Republicans clamoring for positions. When asked himself on November 25, after a meeting with Eisenhower, Douglas replied categorically: "I was offered nothing and I sought nothing."[16]

But soon after the inauguration the President enlisted Douglas to serve as Dulles's deputy in conversations in Washington with British Foreign Secretary Anthony Eden and Chancellor of the Exchequer R. A. Butler, principally on financial and economic questions. The participants agreed, among other decisions, that the United States would undertake over the next months an investigation of the courses of action that would facilitate the exchange of currencies and trade in the free world and especially between the United States and the Commonwealth. Back in Arizona, Douglas accepted an invitation from Dulles, "In accordance with the desire of the President," to head up the proposed study. Although he was pleased to have available the services of experts in government departments and agencies, he wished to restrict his immediate staff to Professor John H. Williams of Harvard and his old friend Dr. Walter Stewart of the Institute for Advanced Study, both distinguished conservative economists. After initial consultations in New York and Washington the following month, he left for London and, briefly, Paris in early May, joined later by Stewart.[17]

Appropriately, his most exhaustive conversations were with Butler, to whom he sent an outline of his proposed report for comment. Reporting to the President on the progress of his work immediately on his return to the United States, he received appreciation and praise from Eisenhower by return mail. Most significantly, reflecting their friendship and his confidence in Douglas, the President concluded: "You understand, of course, so far as I am concerned you have one job which will never be finished as long as I am occupying this office—that job is to help keep my thinking on the rails."[18]

Except for two brief visits to Washington in June, Douglas remained in New York, deliberately isolated from protectionist influences, especially in the Treasury and the Senate, to write the report himself, with the assistance only of Stewart and Williams. It was brief—only seven typewritten pages, submitted to the President in the form of a letter dated July 14. It dealt primarily with the continued imbalance between the dollar and other currencies and very specifically sterling.

He identified the causes of the problem as, among others, the change in the U.K.'s position from the leading creditor to the leading debtor nation, the increased resources she had been forced to devote to defense and overseas commitments, the high level of government expenditure for social services and the concomitant heavy taxation and resulting shortage of private savings for investment, and the American trade policies of protection and subsidization of services which could be more cheaply rendered by foreign enterprise. The report concluded that monetary measures alone could not change the American surplus-payment position with reference to the rest of the world, and especially with Britain.

The pressures on sterling were such that a change to free convertibility might well be fatal, as it had come close to being when instituted at the United States' insistence in 1947. But the British Conservative government was attempting to improve the situation. It had reduced inflation and taxes to free money for investment, denationalized some industries, derationed many articles, and was in the process of reopening a number of commodity markets. More remained to be done. Meanwhile, the United States must assist the process by reducing protectionism, which was the policy of a debtor, not a creditor, nation. Pending achievement of this policy by legislation, Washington should announce it as an aim. Another positive step would be additional American investment in foreign countries. He concluded that the need for prompt action was indicated by the speed with which he had made his investigation and submitted his report.

His findings were predictable. They were a condemnation of the policies of the previous British socialist regime, praise for Conservative efforts to remedy them, and a powerful plea for a determined drive to end American protectionism. Eisenhower was impressed with its "vein of candor, both with respect to the United Kingdom's position and our own, which is, I think, refreshing and very useful." He asked his friend to serve on the Commission of Foreign Trade Policy that he was establishing, but Douglas declined—possibly anticipating that its work and recommendations might not be as forthrightly free trade–oriented as his own.[19]

When the report was released on August 24, the reactions were, as might be expected, favorable in Britain, mixed in the United States. The *Times* and the *Economist* gave it high marks, the latter pointing out that it was "the biggest dose of liberal realism that could wisely be administered, at this stage in the making of American policy, within one document." According to Ambassador Winthrop Aldrich, Gifford's successor in London, there was "no doubt that the report itself, together with the President's comments on it, have created the best possible impression here." The *New York Times* hailed it as "economically unimpeachable," while the *Herald Tribune* maintained that it "brilliantly illuminates the core of the free world's trading problem." On the other hand, protectionist circles, as represented by the Hearst New York *Journal-American*, attacked its findings as based on "an impertinent and fallacious theory that the economic health of other nations is so important to us that our own economic well-being must not be of any concern to us." When Vermont Royster of the *Wall Street Journal*, which supported the report in general, mildly objected that it had not placed sufficient blame for the current sterling-dollar imbalance on previous British policies, Douglas admitted he had, for diplomatic reasons (as he had pointed out in a letter to the President), been gentle in his accusations. "Possibly I should have said much more bluntly what I intended," he wrote Royster, but it was noteworthy that "a number of [British] Socialists have communicated with me, to take me to task for my criticism of Socialist policy."[20]

During the latter months of 1953 and in early 1954, Douglas turned down two other appointments offered by the President. In November, he was asked to assume the American co-chairmanship of the Permanent Joint Board on Defense, U.S. and Canada. He was definitely interested, but having just accepted an assignment on the Weather Control Commission, he reluctantly declined—"were I to do more, I would do nothing well." Again, in March, probably for the same reason, he turned down a proffered post on the Commission on Inter-Governmental Relations.[21]

In 1954, Douglas's long-standing disgust at McCarthyism, dating from the initial attacks upon Acheson, the State Department, and the Democratic administration in general in 1950, reached a high point of revulsion and alarm. Although he had earlier attributed much of the appeal of the slanders of Senator McCarthy and his cohorts to the anti-Communist hysteria whipped up by the Truman regime, he was no less "horrified" at its rising tide and implications. "The injustice that has been committed against individuals is bad enough and is cause for real concern," he wrote a friend in February, 1954, "but much more important is the impediment which the witch hunts are placing upon the expression of opinions and because they aggravate the hysteria about Communism and the Soviet and make it difficult for wise men to make wise decisions."[22]

Harking back to past grievances, he tended to equate the contemporary tactics he deplored with those "used in the days of the New Deal, both by Congressional committees and by Executive agencies—tactics aimed at destroying the reputation of almost every person who had some mark of distinction in the business community." They were two sides of the same fraudulent coin. There is no evidence, however, to indicate whether or not he faulted the new administration for its outwardly permissive attitude toward McCarthy, including the refusal of Eisenhower during the campaign to repudiate McCarthy's attacks upon Douglas's revered General Marshall.[23]

His first public pronouncement on the subject appears to have been an address to the English-Speaking Union at the dinner in his honor in London on May 11, 1954. It was a powerful statement. First, he reviewed for his British audience the history of similar political aberrations in the American past in order to explain "the strange and bewildering spectacle that has been developing upon the American political stage." The excuse in the past and present that such methods were justified by the ends was totally unacceptable. "It is because the issues of treason and loyalty have become mixed up with the issues of wisdom and folly that this recent display of injustice, intolerance, vituperation and invective has tended to impose restraints upon that easy possession of individual rights . . . that are such indispensable characteristics of a free society. . . . By invoking all the devices of irresponsibility, by lodging in the same place the functions of the prosecutor, the jury and the judge, by defaming the honest, by perverting and destroying all of the rules of just procedure, by making neighbor suspicious of neighbor, by pitting brother against brother, fear is spread across the land, deep incisions are cut across nations and between nations." Yet, he assured his listeners, "the deep-seated and abiding sense of justice and fair play" which characterized the American people, would "prevail against all odds." The London press hailed his remarks as "courageous." Harold Nicolson, who was present, wrote his wife, Vita Sackville-West, the next morning: "My word, he made a good speech! A direct all-out attack on McCarthy. I enjoyed it, and you know I do not enjoy public dinners."[24]

On his return to the United States, Douglas urged Republicans to denounce McCarthyism, lest their embrace lead to the demise of the two-party system and "the restoration of the American Socialist Party [the Democrats!] to a position of prolonged domination." The Republican party must "purge itself of this cancerous disease" by denying funds to the senator's committee, removing him as chairman, or withdrawing his power of subpoena, or all three. He was one of twenty-three prominent Americans to sign a public telegram supporting the resolution of Senator Ralph E. Flanders of Vermont that led to the censure of the Wisconsin senator by his colleagues in December. Later in the year he presented the Freedom House award to journalist Edward R. Murrow for his exposés of McCarthy's tactics.[25]

Inevitably, his opposition to McCarthy led to rebukes and attacks from the senator's supporters, ranging from his oldest friend, Frank Brophy, to Barry Goldwater, Westbrook Pegler, Alfred Kohlberg of the China Lobby, and several agents and policyholders of Mutual Life. To those he knew, he replied carefully and courteously, outlining his position. To other correspondents, he used what was in fact a form letter, emphasizing his "deep conviction . . . that unfairness [from whatever source] . . . is offensive to the basic principles of our society." Writing to Senator J. William Fulbright of Arkansas to congratulate him on his vote in favor of censure, Douglas contributed another dimension to his view of the whole episode. "Back of the McCarthy Affair," he wrote, ". . . I suspect there lurks a very fundamental general issue . . . the amount of power that has migrated to the Pentagon. . . . At some point . . . somebody must reassert the authority of the civilian agencies . . . and prevent this authority from forming public policy. . . . I imply that the issue of power exercised by the military is associated with McCarthy because of the extent to which the military brains, retired as well as active, support his activities." It was a perceptive but ironic comment in view of the fact that the senator's undoing dated from his abortive attack against the army.[26]

As 1954 progressed, Douglas also became increasingly concerned about the public bellicosity on foreign affairs of some Republican leaders and the rumored hard line of several of the President's advisors, especially concerning Indochina. The speeches in Congress by Senator William Knowland of California and the reported views of military leaders, especially Admiral Arthur W. Radford, chairman of the Joint Chiefs of Staff, urging intervention by the United States to save the French at Dienbienphu, had alarmed him. The apparent reluctance of Dulles to negotiate at the ongoing Geneva Conference on Vietnam was a further cause for anxiety. "The people are jittery about war," he wrote presidential secretary Thomas Stephens; "they are fearful that the Administration is moving toward it." The impression was abroad that the "Republican Party is the party of belligerency. . . . [A]fter being pulled out of the frying pan in Korea, the country does not want to be plunked into the fires of Southeast Asia.'' He suggested that he and several other "strong supporters of the President" see Eisenhower on the dangerous developing situation. With the difficulties in arranging a convenient time and with the Geneva Agreement, reached on July 21, the meeting did not take place.[27]

Douglas's apprehensions did not disappear. In October, he wrote Eisenhower that the "narrowness by which we escaped entanglement in a protracted, bloody, cruel, and, at best, indecisive test in the jungles of Southeast Asia, the implications at one time that we should intervene with force" (undoubtedly a reference to the advice of Vice-President Nixon and of Dulles, though no names were mentioned), continuing warlike statements, and the power of the Pentagon "altogether tend to increase this undercurrent of uneasiness.'' Eisenhower's reply was reassuring: "With practically all of what you say I am in complete agreement."[28]

But no sooner had his fears about Indochina been allayed than a new threat loomed over Formosa and the offshore islands of Matsu and Quemoy. In the face of evidence that the Chinese Communist government was preparing an attack on the Nationalist base and the two small islands it held near the mainland, Congress, at the request of Eisenhower, passed on January 29, 1955, the Formosa Resolution. It was a blank check, authorizing the President to use the armed forces to protect Formosa and the nearby Pescadores. Specific mention of Matsu and Quemoy was deliberately omitted. In great consternation, Douglas wired Senator Walter George of Georgia, chairman of the Senate Foreign Relations Committee, urging great restraint in the resolution's wording. Advancing the view that, while Matsu and Quemoy belonged to one of the two Chinas and the title to Formosa and the Pescadores was hazy, he urged that the issue of the possession of the latter territories be put into the hands of the United Nations by the establishment of a temporary trusteeship. This would discourage Chinese Communist aggression and prevent the United States from becoming directly involved. Following the resolution's approval and the presidential assent, he wired George again, suggesting as a solution receiving two Chinese governments in the United Nations, warning against forcing the administration into inflexible positions, and deploring the continued inflammatory remarks of Senator Knowland.[29]

As the potential for a dangerous confrontation continued, Douglas began a lengthy correspondence with Eisenhower and Dulles on American policy in the area. He directed the President's attention to the absence of any references in administration pronouncements to the legal position in the area of the Formosa Straits. "The whole case [of the United States] . . . rested upon strategic considerations." This position was, he asserted, "very perilous." It could be used against the United States "with frightful results" by the Soviet to justify the seizure of the rest of Germany and "practically all of Western Europe [and] . . . Southeast Asia . . . [and] the attack by the North Koreans." Strategic considerations were important, but "they ought to be reinforced by legal considerations." Only a treaty or other international action could remove the area from legal limbo. As to Matsu and Quemoy, they had always been a part of China and, with recent developments, two Chinese governments contested their sovereignty. "We are taking sides in a civil war. Is this precisely what the administration wants to do?"

To remain "indifferent" to the legalities of the situation would be to "aggravate the forces in England that are determined to unhorse the Conservative Party." The administration was "relatively compatible" with the present British government; a "wide chasm between us might very well develop" if Labour came to power.

Eisenhower admitted the logic of Douglas's arguments on the dangers in pursuing a "doctrine of strategic convenience," but pointed out that "our enemies" had acted "without any semblance of justification in international law." There was, furthermore, a legal justification for assisting in the defense of Formosa, as it was occupied by a government that the United States recognized. As to Matsu and Quemoy, their evacuation would be disastrous to the morale of the Chinese Nationalist forces. He had turned Douglas's letter over to Dulles, who he hoped would also have time to frame an answer.

Indeed the secretary did, writing in stronger language than Eisenhower. If the Communists launched an attack on Formosa and the Pescadores, then the United States had the right to defend its ally "wherever it is appropriate," including the offshore islands. He could not understand why the Nationalist government, which the United States recognized as the legitimate government of China, had any "better title" to Formosa and the Pescadores than to Matsu and Quemoy. True, U.S. policy might "involve us in a civil dispute . . . [but] we have to take that risk" as had already been the case in Korea, Germany, Austria, Vietnam, and Laos.

Douglas was not convinced by either response, reiterating to the President his earlier points and adding that if American forces were engaged in a Chinese civil war, it would have an unfavorable "influence upon the morale of Oriental people everywhere." Douglas's arguments were "persuasive," Eisenhower replied, but "you do not tell me *what to do if we lose Formosa.*" Would the United States enhance Asian morale if it urged "gradual abandonment of area after area to the greed of the Communists[?]. . . . The central fact of today's life is that we are in a life and death struggle of ideologies." There were, he concluded, "important facets of this whole tangled question that you have not stared squarely in the eye." No, we should not and need not lose Formosa, Douglas wrote back, but we must protect it with the sanction and support "of a substantial number of our Allies," not go it alone. This defense should not, however, apply to Matsu and Quemoy.

After a final round of correspondence, Eisenhower suggested "we had better continue our discussion when you are here in Washington [in late May]." They did meet on May 27. Whether or not they reconciled their viewpoints is not known. In any case, the Chinese Communists did not attack and the tension in the Formosa Straits gradually eased.[30]

That summer, Douglas did have reason to rejoice as he saw one of his cherished policies advanced. On July 18, 1955, the Big Four, now represented by Eisenhower, Eden, French Premier Edgar Faure, and Russian Prime Minister Nikolai A. Bulganin, with Party Secretary Nikita S. Khrushchev close beside him, met for a week in Geneva, for the first time since Potsdam. Although no progress was made on the major outstanding issues, the atmosphere was warmed by the President's friendliness, and the other leaders were startled by his open-skies inspection proposal. The Soviets rejected the plan with their usual suspicion, but it was well received by the rest of the world as evidence of America's desire for peace. Returning from a trip to London and Paris, Douglas informed Eisenhower that he had made a tremendous impression upon the peoples of Europe, "a greater impression . . . than any President, including . . . Woodrow Wilson . . . in the spring of 1919." "It was a great achievement." It was an answer to his long-time plea for communication with the Kremlin and, he hoped, "a precedent . . . [for a] successful restoration of orderly and courteous communication . . . [to] facilitate the resolution of some of the issues which perplex us." Though Douglas's hopes were not to any measurable degree fulfilled, the conference did indeed lead to a period of relative relaxation, highlighted by Khrushchev's visit to America in 1959, and lasting until the fateful U-2 incident in 1960.[31]

But Dulles's usually glum countenance in the photographs of the Geneva meeting no doubt reinforced Douglas's long-held view that America's foreign policy was in uncertain, perhaps dangerous, hands as long as Dulles was secretary of state. Confiding his concern to London friends in the summer of 1955, he speculated "that Foster Dulles suffers from an inferiority complex, and therefore always tries to say the thing that will please his audience without reflecting that by so doing he causes offense to other people and destroys confidence in his own good faith."[32]

Dulles's *Life* article on January 16, 1956, in which he congratulated himself for having dared to go to the brink of nuclear war to preserve peace, shocked Douglas and confirmed all of his suspicions. He was constrained to indicate his displeasure directly. "My dear, dear Foster," he wrote on January 18, "I have read your article in Life Magazine. You do make it extremely difficult for your friends and for those whose whole disposition is to support the Administration. Particularly you make it difficult for the great mass of independent people and for the large number who crossed from the shore of one party to the shore of another in 1952. I write this to you as a friend, and not in any spirit of carping criticism." The same day, he sent a copy of the letter to presidential assistant Sherman Adams, with instructions to show it to Eisenhower "in the greatest of confidence." Unless the President "clarifies the position . . .," he wrote, "[and] the implications of the expressed statements of the *Life* article, we will be in real difficulty." Adams's reply carefully refrained from indicating whether Eisenhower had been shown the letter, but commented that the "matter . . . is in better perspective now than it was a while ago, though I agree in many respects it was most unfortunate."[33]

In later years, Douglas put his case against Dulles more bluntly. "Foster was a difficult man to get on with," he told an interviewer. "As a result, I think that Foster did the cause of the Western world a great deal of damage. . . . The fact is, that Foster Dulles was club-footed. He couldn't say something in a nice persuasive way. He was very conscious of power, and also he was very conceited." Unfortunately, Douglas recalled, the President "let Foster Dulles do about what Foster Dulles wanted to do," as he did with all his cabinet officers.[34]

To Douglas the most egregious example of Dulles's muddling was the Suez crisis of 1956—an episode that was especially painful to him because neither could he defend the actions of his old friend Sir Anthony Eden and the Conservative government. He faulted Dulles for his unnecessarily insulting manner of canceling American financial support for the Aswan Dam in July. Egyptian President Gamal Abdel Nasser retaliated four days later by proclaiming the nationalization of the Suez Canal to use the revenues to finance the dam. Eden's immediate reaction was to initiate plans to seize the canal. The French reaction was equally militant. Eisenhower demanded a meeting of the signatories of the 1888 canal convention before any further action was taken. Dulles flew to London for the conference, urging patience and international action. Douglas was momentarily impressed with the secretary's skill in the presentation of the American case. Dulles had achieved a vote of eighteen to four for his proposal to create an organization of canal users that would temporarily operate the canal, overriding Eisenhower's concern that the plan would be unacceptable.[35]

But Nasser, as Eisenhower had predicted, paid no attention to the conference. London and Paris, determined on military action and well aware of American opposition to the use of force, simply left Washington in limbo as their plans, in collusion with Israel, went forward.

On October 29, in a preemptive strike, Israel moved deep into the Egyptian Sinai. The next day, Britain and France issued an ultimatum, obviously overwhelmingly unfavorable to Egypt, that both sides withdraw ten miles from the canal or they would intervene, and vetoed two Security Council resolutions demanding Israeli withdrawal. Two days later, British and French air forces attacked the Egyptian positions with devastating results. A seaborne assault force was en route. Horrified, Douglas wrote the President: "I had never thought I could be so angry with the British as I am. . . . [T]hey have tricked us and deceived us in a way that is reminiscent of the 18th century. To have behaved toward us—their best friend on earth—in this manner, shocks me very much indeed. . . . I have no doubt we have made mistakes . . . that we messed up the Middle East, but . . . this is no excuse."[36]

Eisenhower's response was more mellow, more regretful than outraged: Douglas's letter "quite accurately expresses the feelings I have toward our British friends. We must remember, of course, that in spite of all that has happened, Britain must continue to be our best friend—so I have no intention of using the British Government as a whipping boy. The worst thing about it all . . . they have been stupid." The President's dilemma was further complicated by the almost simultaneous Soviet armed suppression of the Hungarian revolt and its declared support for Egypt—all this just five days before the American presidential election. To add to his difficulties, during the night of November 3, Secretary Dulles was rushed to the hospital in great pain with what was soon diagnosed as abdominal cancer.[37]

Despite UN cease-fire demands, the Anglo-French naval task force opened fire on Egyptian positions on November 6, but, under great internal and external political pressure, Eden ordered the shelling to stop as of midnight. The same day Eisenhower won an overwhelming election victory. Douglas wired the President, suggesting that he propose to the British and French a publicly announced withdrawal, if the Soviet Union would simultaneously withdraw all their forces from Hungary. Eisenhower answered that "we now have enough complications in the United Nations without adding another." First, the Suez must be contained, then, through the UN, "we should raise quite a storm of exhortation . . . to get Russia to withdraw."[38]

Gradually the crisis subsided. The Soviets did not intervene in the Suez, but the British and French forces remained. The Egyptians had blocked the canal with sunken ships on November 1, and the other Arab nations had cut off the flow in their pipelines. Rumor was abroad that Eisenhower might refuse them American oil until the British and French withdrew. Gravely concerned that the President was seriously considering such pressure, Douglas telegraphed and then wrote a plea for him to reexamine its consequences. It would "reduce Europe to the condition in which we found her in 1947." It would, by further humiliating the British, "create in the Middle East a void into which only the Soviet will move." It would restore Nasser's position. It would undermine NATO. It might well bring about the "fall of the Conservative Government and the restoration to power of the Socialists. . . . I urgently ask now that you review this policy immediately and at least talk with the British and our western allies about the most effective and speedy means of coming to their aid in the vital matter of oil."[39]

On November 30, Eisenhower did order emergency oil shipments to Britain and Europe and answered Douglas's telegram and letter at some length. Douglas, he gently admonished, had exaggerated the harshness of United States policy toward Britain and France. The government was doing all in its power to assist its allies in finding solutions to their problems and was only awaiting action by them to make public a joint program. When the Israeli invasion occurred and British and French intervention followed, he wrote, there was no choice but to uphold America's obligations under the United Nations Charter. But it was also necessary to protect the oil supply to Western Europe for the future. To this end, the United States had to maintain relations with the Arab countries which would dissuade them, in their anger, from destroying their oil industry. The United States was able to do that by guaranteeing that until the British and French withdrawal none of the oil from the still-operating American-controlled Tapline would go to them. If successful, this policy would preserve the Arabs' European market. The British and French now appreciated the American endeavor and were moving toward the necessary steps. Meanwhile, Eisenhower emphasized, he had repeatedly made it clear publicly that despite the recent sharp differences the British and the French were still America's friends.[40]

Following a long and rather rambling reply, Douglas added what must have been a painful postscript. "I hate to say that British power is waning, and I fear will continue to wane, but it is of some importance that it should not evaporate suddenly, for great voids will be created and an imbalance of power which we may not be willing quickly enough to redress. . . . [T]he difference between an abrupt disappearance of British power and the gradual diminution is the difference between revolution and evolution."[41]

Douglas also exhorted his English friends, frankly but kindly. To Lord Salisbury, then lord president of the Council, he sent a cable on November 4, recognizing that American "mistakes" had contributed to the unfortunate dénouement, but pointing out that the "clear sentiment . . . in this country" was that the situation did "not justify the action which has been taken." Writing the next day to Lord Swinton, until recently the secretary of state for Commonwealth relations, he again accepted a degree of American responsibility: "Foster Dulles," he said, "began to mess up the situation a long time ago," and the Republicans had inherited "from President Truman the very unpleasant and disagreeable situation" that led to the intervention. Even so, was the British and French action "prudent?" Swinton tended to agree that the method chosen by his former cabinet colleagues was unfortunate, but emphasized the immediate need to heal the wounds inflicted on the Anglo-American relationship. Sir Pierson Dixon, British UN representative, after dining with Douglas in New York on November 28, wrote Foreign Secretary Selwyn Lloyd that the former ambassador acknowledged "the errors on the United States' side were at least as great as the errors on our side and that we must now get together, pick up the bits, restore the old basis of alliance and make it firmer and more realistic than it was before."[42]

Later, when Eden resigned as Prime Minister, in January, 1957, to be replaced by Harold Macmillan, Douglas agreed with Brendan Bracken that the Conservative government had botched the affair, but "the provocation," he reaffirmed, "was very great and . . . there were a lot of bumblings, stumblings and rumblings by Mr. Dulles that became completely unintelligible." He was sorry about Eden, but there was no other escape for him. "I am deeply saddened that a career should have been so badly battered at the end."[43]

The following spring, he and Salisbury corresponded again on the subject. Salisbury still defended the action on the basis of British experience: "Anthony, I and other members of the government belong to a generation which had twice seen a world war break out which could almost certainly have been prevented if steps had been taken in time. . . . Now we saw much the same situation rising again. . . . I still believe that the policy itself was right." Douglas was understanding, but remained convinced that the measures Britain had taken were counterproductive.[44]

In July, 1958, Douglas confided to Walter Lippmann that the Anglo-French intrusion in Egypt made more sense to him than Eisenhower's 1958 armed intervention in Lebanon that summer to prevent a threatened Nasser-inspired Iraqi invasion. Much later, several British leaders and commentators of the era speculated that if Douglas had been ambassador at the time, communications between the two governments would never have been allowed to deteriorate as they had in the early fall of 1956, and the debacle might well have been avoided.[45]

These tragic events took place during the last ten days of Eisenhower's campaign for a second term. At the end of February, despite his heart attack the previous September, he had announced his intention to run again, and despite surgery for ileitis in June, he soon after reconfirmed his decision. Douglas was delighted, assuring the President that his operation for a similar complaint twenty years earlier had left him "a very much stronger person than I had been before." He apparently gave no consideration at all to the idea of supporting Stevenson, who was once more the Democratic nominee. When he announced his endorsement of Eisenhower, he repeated as he had in 1952 that "loyalty to one's country takes precedence over loyalty to one's party." The President had ended one conflict, Korea, and kept the United States out of further "futile wars," his "whole career

[was] ... mute evidence of his dedication to Grover Cleveland's famous proposition that 'public office is a public trust.'" In Arizona, he added, he would work for the reelection to the Senate of "my old friend and colleague [Democrat] Carl Hayden." Taking a more active role than he had in the previous election, he participated, as a member of Citizens for Eisenhower-Nixon, in a number of events and rallies staged for the President's campaign.[46]

In early October, Douglas was shocked to learn that the *Arizona Daily Star* would come out for Stevenson. In indignation, he wrote his old friend, editor and publisher William Mathews, after many drafts, that the Democrat was an "irresponsible—even reckless—candidate," alluding possibly to Stevenson's suggestion that the draft be reduced and his advocacy of a cessation of nuclear-bomb tests. If the paper persisted in its intention, it would not only be a grave error of judgment, but be construed "as a personal repudiation of myself." The public would assume an open break between the two men. Mathews stood his ground: "To imply that if I act contrary to your wishes our friendship will cease, but will continue if I bow to your command, puts our relationship on the basis of master servant." He enclosed the editorial for the next day, October 14, headed "Stevenson for President." Douglas replied, though still aggrieved, that he "did not intend to imply that ... our friendship would cease. ... [It] will continue quite irrespective." But their relationship had suffered a serious wound.[47]

Their political differences erupted again in 1958, when the newspaper supported Ernest McFarland against Goldwater for the Senate. Because of the responsibility represented by his 2 percent interest in the *Star*, Douglas claimed the courtesy of consultation, if not the right to determine policy. Mathews denied the claim, citing past editorial decisions on which Douglas, without any objections, had not been consulted. He then gratuitously charged that Douglas and the Kings had struck a "hard bargain" with Helen d'Autremont and that the Transamerica sale violated the moral principles to which he had assumed they both subscribed. Angered and hurt, Douglas responded with seven pages of detailed facts on both transactions. Mathews was not convinced. Douglas drafted a heated reply: "The intolerance and conceit of your letter, combined with the other implications have consequences to our friendship which are clearly your responsibility." It was not sent. A week later, he dispatched a more conciliatory message, asking that they put aside recriminations. It concluded: "Your friend, who has been deeply hurt, but who wants always to be your friend." On June 18 they lunched together. Douglas in a memorandum on the meeting wrote: "He apologized for the written matter that hurt my feelings. He agreed that I was a very honorable man and accepted as a statement of fact that I have never tried to drive a hard bargain with Mrs. D'Autremont. So we agreed mutually to do our best to restore our old relationship which rested on mutual confidence and respect." It was restored perhaps, but badly tattered.[48]

Soon after Eisenhower's reelection, Douglas accepted appointments on two committees. The first, honorary chairman of the Committee for Hungarian Relief, was of brief duration, ending in mid-May, 1957, when he and his colleagues submitted to the President a final report on their activities in behalf of Hungarian refugees in the United States. Although Tracy Voorhees, the active chairman, undertook most of the work of coordinating voluntary and government agencies for relief and rehabilitation, Douglas played a significant role.[49]

More important and long-lasting was his service as a member of the United States Advisory Commission on Information. In November, he agreed to fill out the unexpired term of a resigning member, beginning in January, 1957. He was reappointed to a second three-year term in 1959. He was not very happy with the leadership of the incumbent director of the United States Information Agency, Arthur Larson, an Eisenhower appointee, but delighted when President Kennedy named Edward R. Murrow to the post in January, 1961, and disgusted with the right-wing criticism that accompanied it. Throughout his tenure, he deplored the agency's independent status, convinced it should be incorporated into the State Department for better coordination of foreign-policy statements. Too often, he believed, it was unduly influenced by the views of the National Security Council. "Above all," he commented some years afterward, "the USIA must abide meticulously to the truth. The minute it departs from an accurate presentation of the facts it loses credibility."

During his service, he prepared two studies on the agency's work, one on the United Kingdom, the other on South Africa, where he frequently traveled in connection with his directorship of the Union Corporation. In Great Britain he was pleased with what he found. The libraries, speakers, and exchange-of-persons program were all doing valuable work. He recommended increased funding. In South Africa, he felt the agency's activities were as successful as possible under the repressive Nationalist regime. Unless the racist policies of the ruling party were changed, however, he anticipated "a quite violent explosion . . . within three years, five years, or ten years." To meliorate the prevailing and dangerous climate of opinion there, he urged that agency activity be stepped up, especially the exchange of persons.[50]

Although Douglas continued to be described as a member of the President's "inner circle" of informal advisors, along with Generals Gruenther, Clay, and Bedell Smith, banker Robert Cutler, John J. McCloy, President Ralph Cordiner of General Electric, President Benjamin Fairless of U.S. Steel, Chairman Eugene Holman of Standard Oil of New Jersey, and several other prominent financiers and businessmen, his contacts and counsel were less frequent and significant in the second administration than in the first. Early in the term, he expressed his dissatisfaction with the President's performance and his concern about White House fascination with men of great wealth—with whom he did not identify himself. To Brendan Bracken, he wrote in the spring of 1957: "It seems to me that since the election something has happened. . . . [F]rom my side of the continent [he appears to have] . . . abdicated to a pretty second-rate group of people—if not in whole, at least in part. At any rate, it is all disturbing, if this should be the case."[51]

However, about the same time, he was mentioned as a possible successor to Secretary of the Treasury George Humphrey, who was said to be planning to resign—a rumor apparently without foundation. In any case, after his major surgery in December of that year and the long recovery and accommodation to a new lifestyle, his chances of either being asked or accepting any official position were slight.[52]

When the Formosa problem flared up again in August, 1958, Douglas could not forbear again offering advice to the President. He urged that Formosa be placed under a United Nations mandate or by "some other method" prevented from falling into Communist hands until its status was settled by an appropriate *"international process and accepted international instrument."* "As an inseparable part of a proposal of this sort," he then added, "I suggest that Quemoy, Matsu and the offshore islands be conceded to be a part of the mainland." Eisenhower, quoting a State Department brief, answered that the actions envisaged by Douglas would be interpreted as "appeasement and an indication of weakness by the United States." Matsu and Quemoy had always been under the jurisdiction of the Republic of China. The United States could not " 'concede' territory of a sovereign state." Douglas probably expected nothing more, but he could not refrain from labeling to the President the department's arguments as "sophistry."[53]

In 1972, three years after Eisenhower's death, Douglas commented candidly on his friend's administration. "He had a very poor understanding of the structure of American federal government. I think he looked upon the Presidency as though perhaps it was somewhat analogous to a crown." He had tried to talk to the President about this misconception, but "I think he never really understood." Though his own instincts were excellent, Eisenhower continued not to lead, but to let his cabinet officers do "about what [they] . . . wanted to do," especially Dulles, whose policies were disastrous in a number of instances. Sadly, he concluded: "I don't think Ike was a great president."[54]

Considering Douglas's political allegiances from 1948 onward and his greatly resented attacks on the Truman administration, this was a fascinating appraisal. It is especially striking when compared with a letter to Harry Truman in 1969. "As I scan the behavior of Presidents in the area of foreign policy," he wrote his old boss, "and try to make objective judgments of their attitudes and leadership in this field . . . I come to the conclusion that you will be rated by objective historians as the finest President we have ever had." In the face of unprecedented problems for America, he continued, "you made bold, brave and valid decisions which, on balance, have helped in the past to shape the world in a better mold and which, as one looks down the corridor of time, will probably make the future a more livable world for mankind. . . . I want you to know how deeply I feel . . . I am taking this opportunity to put it in black and white." Truman's reply was characteristic. "I was deeply moved by your assessment of the period. History, in due course, will make its own personal decision and I have never given any thought to it. What is important to me is to have a judgment from one I hold in high esteem and whose opinion has a special meaning for me."[55]

29

Sunset

AS THE PRESIDENTIAL YEAR OF 1960 ADVANCED, Douglas veered momentarily toward the Democrats when it appeared their candidate might be Lyndon B. Johnson, who, he wrote to Sam Rayburn, was "the most experienced and by long odds the most equipped man on the horizon." The Speaker showed the letter to Johnson, who replied with appreciation. But with the nomination of John F. Kennedy, Douglas opted, with reservations, to support Richard Nixon.

He approved the vice-president's statement that it was important to keep the negotiating lines open to Moscow, however strained current relations after the U-2 incident, and whether or not settlements on great issues were immediately forthcoming. On the other hand, he deplored Nixon's hard line on the continuing questions of Matsu and Quemoy. "[A]s a personal friend and Democrat who had intended to vote for you," he wired Nixon, "I want to suggest inflexible position you have taken . . . [on the islands] not only unsound in principle but politically damaging. . . . Moreover I am confident it is losing you thousands and thousands of votes." Above all, he obviously still entertained serious reservations concerning the vice-president's political ethics and the bellicose advice on foreign policy he was reputed to have given Eisenhower.[1]

He delayed until almost the last minute giving the Republican candidate his public endorsement, which outlined the reasons for his difficult choice. Released to the press on November 3, it expressed his earlier hope to support the Democratic ticket, but concluded that the course of the campaign had convinced him that Nixon and his running mate, Henry Cabot Lodge, "because of their wider and richer experience in foreign affairs are better able to preserve the peace in a world in which the great issue is war or peace." He attacked the fiscal and monetary policies "of the dominant wing of the Democratic Party" that would prevent the government from dealing effectively with "the problems of inflation or recession should either develop." Nixon's announced policies were more flexible and also better suited to "preserve stability of international exchange . . . vital to our own internal economic health and to the integrity of the western alliance." He contributed $5,000 to the Volunteers for Nixon-Lodge Finance Committee.[2]

Nevertheless, he hastened to write John F. Kennedy, the successful candidate, on November 11, admitting that he had not voted for him but offering his congratulations and support with advice on any matter on which he might be helpful. He received an invitation to the inauguration. Unable to attend, Douglas sent a check for $500 to help defray the expenses of the festivities. Only in late December did he find time to write a letter of condolence to Nixon, indicating his regret at the outcome of the election and his admiration for the vice-president's "extraordinary discretion and generosity since it was held."[3]

He also wrote Johnson, offering him and Kennedy his "help on any problem that is on your platter." "This does not imply that I want a job, Lyndon. I do not want a job. I merely want to be of assistance." He was later greatly impressed with Kennedy's inaugural speech, terming it the "nicest piece of English that has come out of the White House since Woodrow Wilson." "The one note . . . absent . . . was humility." Commenting on the new cabinet, he found it "on the whole . . . far better than I expected." Dean Rusk was "competent," if "unglamorous," but Robert McNamara, he speculated, might well "turn out to be the most powerful person in the group."[4]

As time went on, Douglas became increasingly favorable in his assessments of Kennedy's administration, especially in the area of foreign policy. He strongly supported the President's efforts for a Limited Test Ban Treaty. Telegraphing Kennedy in late July, 1963, he offered to use his influence with Goldwater and other opposition leaders to persuade them to approve ratification of the treaty. National Security Advisor McGeorge Bundy responded that the White House would be very grateful if he would "pitch in with Senator Goldwater and possibly with one or two others of the doubtful and uncommitted senators." Douglas did so, but with limited success. Though the Senate gave its approval on September 24, Goldwater voted with the minority. Claiming success with several others whom he had contacted, Douglas commented wryly to Bundy on Goldwater: "Although I like him very much and have known him since he was a baby—[he is] a rather dangerous man."[5]

Apparently, he had earlier communicated with the White House on several other occasions and received no reply, for, about the same time, he confided to the new secretary of the interior, Stewart Udall, whom he had supported as congressman, his doubts that the President "is sufficiently friendly to me." He was not, he pointed out, "a novice" in foreign affairs and believed he was "entitled to more courteous consideration." Nevertheless, he confirmed in two follow-up letters to Udall, apologizing for his earlier "pompous" and "conceited" remarks, that he intended to support Kennedy for reelection in 1964. He would do so because "although I am not a particularly constant one in national elections, I am a registered Democrat and believe the Party to be more lively than its opposition . . . [and] because I think the President has discharged exceptionally well his responsibilities."[6]

He was shocked by Kennedy's tragic death. Five months later he summed up his appreciation of the young President in a letter to Robert Kennedy. "I had not voted for your brother," he wrote, "but I learned, during the period of his administration, to have for him an increasingly great respect and admiration. His quality of mind was very rare. We had not had anyone in the White House of that particular intellectual capacity since, I think, Woodrow Wilson. His increasingly thorough grasp of the problems of foreign policy commanded my deep respect."[7]

Not surprisingly, since he had favored the Texan for the nomination in 1960, Douglas was an early supporter of President Johnson's candidacy in 1964. In January, he wrote Johnson, reminding him of their earlier contacts in Washington, when Johnson was an assistant to Congressman Kleberg of Texas, and offering his services in any capacity that might be useful. "I have learned so much from my mistakes. The process of education might be helpful to you on specific issues. I seek no permanent position. I merely want to help during what must be for you a trying period." He received a polite reply from a presidential aide. Six months later, a congratulatory letter on one of the President's speeches gained for him a personal note of appreciation.[8]

Meantime, he had firmly rebuffed efforts to obtain his endorsement for Goldwater's Republican nomination. In answer to a solicitation for financial aid, he wrote to a Goldwater supporter that, although he had an affectionate regard for the senator and agreed with some of his views, "I doubt that he does his homework well enough to be in the White House. I think I have told Barry this. . . . I spoke as a friend." After Goldwater's nomination at the emotion-charged San Francisco Convention in July, Douglas informed Averell Harriman that he was "back in the fold, even if Goldwater had not been nominated." The Arizona senator "would be a disaster as President." A few days later, he released a public statement. Acknowledging his long friendship with Goldwater, he warned the voters that the election of the Republican candidate would increase the possibility of the United States being plunged into "the most frightful, destructive and completely devastating catastrophe of modern history"—namely, a full-scale conflict in Vietnam, or worse.[9]

His relations with the President by that time had warmed to the point of a personal meeting on July 30, during which he assured him of his support for the nomination and for the election. Both Stewart Udall and McGeorge Bundy had briefed Johnson beforehand. They reminded him that Douglas, though a nominal Democrat, had not supported a Democratic presidential candidate since 1932 and had backed Goldwater for the Senate in 1952 and 1958. But now, Udall informed the President, Douglas considered the senator's nomination a "tragic mistake" and was committed to the cause of peace. Because of his corporate connections, his endorsement "would undoubtedly have an impact in the business community similar to that of . . . Henry Ford II." Bundy was less kind in his assessment. Douglas, he noted, "talks a better game than he plays. He is getting on. He also loves the importance of visiting the White House." He might be "helpful on a Committee of Citizens for Johnson," but he should probably not be asked "to do any major executive job."[10]

After the meeting, Douglas issued a statement emphasizing that "The pursuit of policies which may lead to war or peace is, I believe, the essential issue of this campaign. It reduces all other questions to insignificant dimensions." To be sure, he continued, "Many view with alarm what they call a 'slow drift toward socialism [referring to Johnson's "Great Society" programs].' But how much of the American society which we would like to preserve will remain should brinksmanship carry us over the brink[?]" Soviet society, like all societies, he emphasized, was constantly changing. "It is, therefore, imprudent to base policy on the presumption that the communist societies will *never* change." It was necessary to search constantly "for every avenue that may lead to a more effective *modus vivendi* for the free world as well as for the several communist orbits of authority, without, of course, letting our guard down." Johnson was far "better equipped, intellectually and by experience" to deal with these great issues and "to avoid the holocaust of a major international conflict."[11]

Following Johnson's nomination on August 26, Douglas contributed liberally to the campaign in Arizona, to the President's Club of the Democratic National Committee, and to the National Independent Committee for Johnson and Humphrey. He corresponded with the President and met with him on at least one occasion to discuss campaign strategy. His advice elicited from Johnson, after one long letter, the flattering comment: "As always, you drove directly to the hub of the matter in your analysis of the campaign. I place high value on your comments and sincerely hope you will continue to let me have the benefit of your wisdom." When Johnson won in November with an overwhelming and unprecedented 61.1 percent of the vote, Douglas telegraphed and wrote with congratulations and asked for an appointment around the first of December, when he would be back on the East Coast. He would appreciate an opportunity to confer with Johnson before the forthcoming visit of British Prime Minister Harold Wilson. The President's reply was warm and complimentary: "You always have been a man who puts his country first, the mark of quiet and sincere patriotism." But, despite further correspondence with a presidential assistant, no appointment was arranged. Douglas did, however, attend the formal dinner on December 7 honoring Wilson.[12]

Douglas's belated admiration for Kennedy and his enthusiasm for Johnson's campaign reflected not only genuine support for the new Democratic administrations, but even more, fear of the bellicosity of the dominant Republican right wing. It was accompanied by hesitant indications that he would welcome some sort of appointment in the government. The earlier correspondence with Stewart Udall on the governorship had hinted at that desire. With his health reasonably stabilized and his active duties with Mutual Life terminated, he was willing and, he believed, able to return to at least limited public service. He was pleased to be back in the Democratic "fold." He believed he had much to offer in the way of experience and, despite the handicap of his past close relationship with Eisenhower, felt his abilities were not being fully recognized or utilized. He broached the subject tentatively to J. William Fulbright during the 1964 campaign, but had immediate second thoughts about the appropriateness of his remarks. "I am really ashamed at myself," he wrote the senator, "for asking you the question which I asked in my last conversation with you. I really want nothing—I seek no position and I want no privilege." He affirmed that he only wanted to see Johnson win and "to be helpful to him and I hope he knows that whatever talents I have, modest though they may be, are at his disposal." He then outlined the considerable knowledge and practice in foreign affairs which prompted him to offer his services. "I could not serve in any permanent job, nor would it be possible to even suggest me," but perhaps he might be of assistance in some "ad hoc temporary capacity"—preferably in the foreign-policy area. He was "terribly keen to be of help to the President."[13]

That correspondence highlighted the mixture of modesty and pride, even vanity, that characterized Douglas, especially in his declining years—a condition not unknown among elder statesmen who feel neglected. His own case was, of course, complicated by a history of erratic political allegiance. Those nearest him sensed his feeling of being "left out" or courteously ignored. Fulbright was sympathetic and somewhat encouraging, but no call came from the President. Douglas's only service to the administration was membership, at the request of Stewart Udall, on a special presidential task force in 1966–67, to make recommendations concerning policy toward American Indians. The final report urged the federal government to find ways to lead the Indian to "equal citizenship, maximum self-sufficiency and full participation in American life." Local governments should cooperate with Washington in finding a "greater range of alternatives" for Indians.[14]

In any case, Douglas soon became disenchanted with the Johnson administration, as its actions in Vietnam belied the moderation advocated by the President during his campaign. Long concerned that the United States "not become entangled up [sic] in a protracted and bloody war in the jungles of Southeast Asia," as he wrote Arthur Krock in 1961, Douglas had been appalled at Goldwater's belligerent statements. Johnson's apparent desire to limit the Vietnam engagement had been the central reason for Douglas's support. Two days after the Vietcong struck at the American barracks at Pleiku on February 7, 1965, Douglas called on the President to urge not retaliation but negotiation. To reinforce his remarks he sent a long telegram the next day. He posed a series of percipient questions. "[I]t is legitimate to ask oneself, how can we win? Is there a sufficient will in South Viet Nam to resist? We can win a war whether further massive action does or does not produce massive retaliation from China. But what do we do after we have won the war? Without an indigenous will to resist does not American military success mean American occupation? And will American occupation create hostility throughout most of Asia and Africa?" Considering the tension between China and the Soviet Union, he suggested that submission of the question to the United Nations might be worth "serious consideration." He received a reassuring but noncommittal reply from McGeorge Bundy that the President's "Underlying objective and his are the same."[15]

But Johnson did order in retaliation a series of devastating bombing raids on North Vietnam. Writing to Arthur Krock, Douglas termed the American action "nuts." "Why we think we can do better than the French who were fifteen years at it and had to give up, I don't understand." Then the President sent two battalions of marines, the first American combat troops, to South Vietnam. This decision was followed, early in the summer, by the dispatch of additional army units. Douglas was increasingly alarmed. "That we are there at all," he wrote Lord

Swinton, "is one of the residual heritages from John Foster Dulles." It was becoming more and more difficult to disengage, he acknowledged, but the United States must find a way to do so. It must find a way to make "some sort of settlement with both North Viet Nam and the Viet Cong regarding South Viet Nam. . . . We, I fear have the rather antiquated idea that the Communist state is part of—what was 20 years ago—the massive Communist order of society that extended all the way from the Elbe to the South China Seas. We have not yet fully understood that the massive and gargantuan Communist order is splintered into many bits—some small, some large."[16]

These comments were only the beginning of Douglas's long and fruitless campaign, from a position of political impotence and in declining health, to prevent the growing involvement and ultimate disaster in Vietnam. Early in 1966, he opened a correspondence with Senator Fulbright, chairman of the Foreign Relations Committee, who had become an outspoken critic of the war, offering advice and support in his efforts. He asked: "Is it Communism [we are fighting]? Isn't it rather an intense and firmly held sense of nationalism. . . . There is, I suppose, a co-mingling of Communist sentiment with national sentiment but I suspect the dominant feeling is nationalism. I have no doubt that all systems in primitive countries would like to be collectivist; but they are also, I think, going to be nationalist."[17]

He found kindred spirits in George F. Kennan and General James M. Gavin and urged that they unite with a few others of like mind in a public statement of their opposition to Johnson's policies. But Kennan sadly discouraged the move. "I just don't think it would do any good. . . . [W]e have reached the point where only the other presidential candidates, and eventually the voters, can help." In 1967, after reading an article by Walter Lippmann in *Newsweek* advocating withdrawal, Douglas sent his congratulations. "Here," he confided to Lord Swinton, "we are engaged in one of the most foolhardy adventures we have ever been engaged in in South Viet Nam. I think it is contaminating our relationships in Europe where our vital national interests are concerned. I can't agree with the 'domino' theory. It just doesn't make sense to me." Late that fall, in collaboration with his new friend George Backer, he telegraphed Ambassador Ellsworth Bunker in Saigon, with a copy to the President, urging a detailed program of land reform and the encouragement of small private enterprise in South Vietnam as a way of strengthening the government. No reply was apparently ever received from either recipient. Efforts to see the President were unavailing.[18]

Thoroughly disillusioned by 1968, Douglas, without much hope, turned once again to the Republican candidate for President, who had at least announced a "secret" plan for ending the war. "Our choices this year are intolerably bad. Two squareheads—one a limpid mimic of L.B.J., the other the product of his own inadequacies." Thus did he characterize his dilemma to Lord Swinton. He liked Hubert Humphrey personally, later sent his sympathy for the loss of a close election, and contributed $1,000 to help defray his campaign debts. To Nixon, he pledged his support, if the Republican was elected, for "every possible device . . . to bring our participation in the war in Vietnam to a reasonable and speedy termination." The candidate's response attempted to be reassuring, but Douglas found it exasperatingly vague: "I cannot find anything in your public statements which indicate that you agree [with me]." In the end, he grudgingly cast his ballot for the Republican.[19]

In May, 1969, discouraged at the lack of progress to end the engagement, he spoke out at a dinner of the Pilgrims in New York, declaring that "our vital national interests seem to be obscure" in Vietnam and that the domestic economic strain was "immeasurable." He wrote to Fulbright in September: "What a botch Nixon is making of Vietnam. He is following in the footsteps of his predecessor. There seems to be no imagination and no real determination to bring the war in Vietnam to a close." A month later he asked Fulbright to arrange a meeting for him with Senate Minority Leader Hugh Scott to urge upon the President confidential talks with the Soviets to enlist their assistance, through some concessions in Germany, to help "disentangle ourselves" from Vietnam. Failing that endeavor, he advocated telling the Saigon government "we were no longer under any obligation to continue to lose American lives . . . [and would] withdraw all American troops within a relatively short period of time." Fulbright replied that he no longer had any influence with the Republican leadership or the President. "They would be more likely to listen to you than to me," but he held out little hope of success against the mind-set of the administration.[20]

While many Americans expressed alarm over college disturbances, Douglas defended the demonstrations against the war as legitimate exercises of the "right of assembly and the right to seek redress which is deeply embedded in our Constitution." He wrote a concerned George Kennan that student unrest was "related primarily to a deep shadowing distrust of the establishment in regard to Vietnam." And to Calvin Plimpton, president of Amherst College, he attributed campus upheavals to "one of the craziest, maddest adventures the country has ever embarked upon."[21]

In May, 1970, he was "stunned" by the invasion of Cambodia and the resumption of bombing, publishing a telegram to Senator John Sherman Cooper of Kentucky, supporting his amendment to an appropriations bill co-sponsored by Frank Church of Idaho, refusing funds to support a war undeclared by Congress. His protests and efforts, like those of so many others, seemed to fall on deaf ears in the seats of power. He remained frustrated, agitated, and profoundly depressed over the continued embroilment in Southeast Asia.[22]

Nor was he very happy over Nixon's cabinet appointments. William Rogers, the new secretary of state, he respected and liked personally, but considered unqualified for his post; the actual direction of foreign policy would, he prophesied, fall to Henry Kissinger, the National Security Advisor. Except for George Shultz as secretary of labor, he found the cabinet without distinction of any kind. He was particularly alarmed by the appointment of Maurice Stans as secretary of commerce and had warned Nixon directly of his misgivings immediately after the election, giving an unsatisfactory appraisal of Stans's character and abilities, based on the latter's earlier employment with the Western Bank Corporation. He was distressed again at Nixon's ill-fated nominees for the Supreme Court in the spring of 1970. "He is now displaying the characteristics of the old Tricky Dick," he wrote Lord Swinton, "an angry Dick, to the misfortune of his country and of the rest of the world. But, alas, I am afraid he was always made this way and now can't be remade."[23]

Discouraged, he wrote Senate Majority Leader Mike Mansfield in July, 1970, that he would enthusiastically support a bid by him for the 1972 Democratic presidential nomination. The Montana senator replied with deep appreciation, but made clear that he had never "had and never will have ambitions in that direction." In November, he wrote Senator Edmund Muskie of Maine, offering to do anything necessary to "further your fortunes for the year 1972—I am at your disposal to command." The senator was grateful, but indicated he had not yet made up his mind to run. They lunched together in the spring, and Douglas sent a generous check to support Muskie's pre-announcement activities. He rejoiced at the senator's subsequent decision and, with Peggy, attended a kick-off Dinner for Muskie in New York on January 5, 1972. When Muskie's campaign faltered and Senator George McGovern forged ahead, he urged the Maine senator to remain in the race and to state emphatically that the time had come for the United States to leave Vietnam. After Muskie's withdrawal, Douglas wrote him sadly: "[You had the] . . . character and intelligence to become one of our outstanding Presidents."[24]

As election day approached, he was obviously torn between his dislike and distrust of Nixon and his qualms about what he saw as McGovern's inexperience and irresponsibility. It is possible that he was still undecided as he approached the polling booth. But he was denied the right to cast a ballot. Some mixup in his registration had removed him from the rolls. He protested vigorously to county authorities but to no avail. The only clue to his intention was a congratulatory letter to Nixon. "You and I have not always agreed in the past but I think the country is well served by the outcome of the election yesterday." Indeed, a cease-fire was already being negotiated, and was signed on January 27, 1973, by the United States, South Vietnam, North Vietnam, and the Vietcong. It called for the withdrawal of American troops. But over 50,000 American lives had been lost. Hostilities between the North and the South soon resumed and led in two years to the victory of North Vietnam.[25]

Meantime, the Watergate scandal was unfolding. Whatever Douglas's initial reactions to press reports of the break-in and the possible involvement by the White House, by April, 1973, he was thoroughly alarmed at the evidence presented before the special Senate investigating committee under Senator Sam Ervin of North Carolina. As he wrote the senator, he laid much of the blame on the migration of power to the White House since the New Deal and the resultant activity of anonymous and unaccountable "young men" around the presidents. But he "did not then foresee such a perfectly outrageously stupid and incalculably great act of deception and dishonesty as the Watergate affair." By May 1, in a letter marked "eyes only," he informed the committee chairman that he saw only two ways out of the situation: The President could announce that in view of the "great constitutional crisis which throws a shadow over the great position of the Presidency," which should have no "question mark" concerning its integrity, he was resigning. "But I doubt that Nixon is made of this sort of impersonal objective stuff." "The other alternative, and it would seem to me that this is one which ought to be seized, is to institute impeachment proceedings."[26]

He was, however, prepared to wait for the independent report of special prosecutor Archibald Cox, whose credentials he found impeccable. He was stunned when, in October, the President fired Cox over the objections and resignations of Attorney General Elliot Richardson and Deputy Attorney General William D. Ruckelshaus, writing all three of them letters praising their courage and integrity. To Lady Swinton (Lord Swinton had died in 1972), he summed up, at the end of the year, his long-standing assessment of the President: "But I must say that his troubles are largely of his own making. I have known him for a good many years. I have worked with him. I have never trusted him. I voted for him [in 1968] because he was better in my opinion than his alternative." Douglas did not live to see the dénouement of the affair in the following summer, when Nixon opted for the first alternative—resignation—earlier suggested by the Arizonan, but only in the face of irrefutable evidence of wrongdoing and of inevitable impeachment.[27]

In Arizona, in the 1960s, Douglas once again became gravely concerned about developments on the issue which had marked his debut in state politics—the use by the state of the Colorado River waters. With the belated ratification of the Colorado River Compact by the state in 1944, Arizona had moved to implement a long-considered canal system to bring water to central and southern Arizona by a 241-mile-long aqueduct from Lake Havasu. Legislation was introduced in Congress for the Central Arizona Project (CAP). But there was opposition to what many congressmen considered an extravagant and unnecessary boondoggle. Above all, California contended that Arizona would be using water that had not been allocated to it. Under these circumstances, Arizona finally decided to take its case to the Supreme Court once again to obtain a settlement of the lower-basin water rights. It was one of the most complicated and long-drawn-out litigations in the Court's history, with a 1963 decision that was based not on the Colorado River Compact, but on the Boulder Canyon Act of 1928. It reaffirmed the congressional division of the first 7.5 million acre-feet, allocating 4.4 million to California, 2.8 million to Arizona, and 300,000 to Nevada, and the right of the secretary of the interior to determine the division of surpluses or shortages above or below these basic figures.

It appeared to be a victory for Arizona, and the state's congressional delegation moved to push ahead with the CAP. But there were still two serious problems that Douglas, from his vantage point of long association with the question, emphasized in sometimes heated correspondence with the Arizona delegation and others over the next five years. He was convinced that the average river flow at Lee's Ferry, the dividing line between the upper and lower basins, used as an official measure of water available, was misleading. With the current and anticipated use in the upper basin and the great variation in stream flow from year to year, he maintained that the 4.4 million guarantee to California could well prove disastrous for the Arizona project. Secondly, he questioned whether the federal government would continue to appropriate, even after authorization of the project, the large sums necessary to complete the CAP. The state, he believed, must find some efficacious way to fund the anticipated shortfall in federal support or even the entire expense.

He, therefore, vehemently urged that the CAP legislation not include the guarantee of 4.4 million acre-feet to California and that Arizona be permitted to build a low dam at Bridge Canyon or Marble Canyon, which would generate needed electric power, the revenues from which could pay a large part or all of the cost of the CAP in lieu of federal funding. On the first issue, his efforts were in vain, for the Arizona delegation found it impossible to obtain support for CAP from the California representatives without the guarantee, and were forced to compromise for the sake of approval of the project by Congress in 1968. As to the proposed state-constructed dams, conservationists argued that they would do great damage to the river and especially to the Grand Canyon. Douglas contested their arguments, but they won the day.[28]

If, in his last decade, Douglas was distressed by United States involvement in Vietnam, the developing Watergate scandal, and the decisions regarding the future use of his state's water resources, there were also happy occasions and rewarding undertakings to brighten his days. Certainly, the visit to Tucson of Princess Margaret and the Earl of Snowden in 1965 was an exciting and joyous event. Following a good deal of personal and official planning—the Princess had long wanted to see America and make a personal visit to Sharman—the couple arrived in New York on November 4. They departed almost immediately for San Francisco for a few days, then flew to Los Angeles for a series of social events featuring film celebrities, planned by Sharman, who accompanied them on the entire trip.

On November 10, they came to Tucson, and were "whisked," as one disappointed onlooker complained, to the Douglases' Pantano Farm. In fact, every effort was made to preserve the privacy of the visit. The evening of their arrival, the Douglases gave a reception at the Arizona Inn. Danny Kaye flew in and sang after the buffet supper and, in Douglas's words, "did his stunts." The following day, the couple were taken to Kitt Peak National Observatory and an open-pit copper mine. Then the Douglases and the Snowdens flew over the Grand Canyon to Page, Arizona, where they spent the night and went boating on Lake Powell. The weekend was spent quietly at the farm, and Monday morning the visitors journeyed on to Washington and New York in a plane provided by President Johnson. As their flight disappeared, Peggy was heard to exclaim: "It's been a glorious vacation for them. Now I can get some rest." But she hastened to add: "There wasn't a minute that wasn't fun. . . . It was a magical three days."[29]

During his final years he found great personal satisfaction and fulfillment from a new assignment—leadership of the Winston Churchill Foundation of the United States in support of Churchill College at Cambridge University. The idea for a British institution emphasizing science and technology grew out of Sir Winston's conversations, soon after his retirement from office in 1955, with Lord Cherwell and Sir John Colville. He had been much impressed by his visits to the Massachusetts Institute of Technology and deplored the fact that so many of the great British inventions of the century had been perfected and developed in the United States because of the greater availability of technological skills. He wanted to see an institution comparable to MIT founded in the United Kingdom and, because of his familial and public ties with America, have it emphasize a close association with scientists and technologists from the United States.[30]

It soon became evident, however, that it would be more sensible to found a college in an existing university than to attempt to establish a separate institution. Cambridge was a logical choice, with its outstanding tradition in science and its great existing laboratories. Douglas first learned of these plans from Sir John in 1957 and, in May, 1958, agreed to be a trustee of the Winston Churchill Foundation in the United States, under the presidency of Carl Gilbert, chairman of the Gillette Corporation. Its task would be to raise an endowment to support American students and visiting fellows at the college. In 1959, the Cambridge University Senate gave official approval for the college, and Sir John Cockroft, director of the British Atomic Energy Authority, was named master.[31]

Gilbert went to Washington in the late 1960s as special representative for trade negotiations, and new leadership for the American foundation was obviously required. Reluctantly, as his health was declining, Douglas agreed to take on the task if he could have an active second in command. He was elected president in March, 1970, and a year later Harold Epstein left his position as vice-president of the Institute for International Education to become executive director and relieve Douglas of much of the day-to-day work. Meantime, in 1968, Sir William Hawthorne had become master of the college. He and Douglas quickly found a beneficial meeting of minds on college affairs.[32]

Under Douglas's leadership, the work of the foundation was revitalized. Among his first acts was to broaden the membership of the board by invitations to a number of prominent figures in the United States and Britain. On March 31, 1971, he organized a solicitation dinner in New York, at which Winston Churchill, as the main speaker, declared that the college was "a living memorial to . . . [his grandfather] far greater than any statue, memorial or mausoleum, at the same time forging another link between our two peoples." The most ambitious and gala effort to publicize and raise funds for the work of the foundation was the subscription premier performance in the United States, on October 10, 1972, of the film *Young Winston,* followed by a formal dinner dance at the Plaza. The showing was attended by the Duke and Duchess of Kent. By late 1973, Douglas had succeeded in raising $500,000 of his goal of $2.5 million to fund scholarship and fellowship programs in perpetuity. He had begun planning for a commemorative event in 1974 to celebrate the centennial of Sir Winston's birth.[33]

In the fall of 1973, the trustees, impressed by the success of Douglas's activities in the face of failing health, proposed a dinner in his honor. He declined. Writing to Honorary Trustee Bess Truman, he apologized for his intransigence. "I simply cannot go through with this proposal. I would, I think, crawl under the table and disappear during the course of the dinner were it to be held. . . ." Mrs. Truman's reply was brief and to the point. "I understand and think you have done the right thing. . . . Too bad there aren't more like you."[34]

Two special projects for the college enlisted Douglas's personal attention. Brendan Bracken had left some of his furniture, silver, and paintings to Churchill College. This gift inspired Lord Drogheda to propose a memorial at the college to his friend and benefactor. The idea was greeted with enthusiasm and a generous contribution by Douglas and by other admirers of Bracken in England and in the United States. After some discussion, it was decided to use the funds collected to endow the main reading room in the college library.[35]

Very shortly after Douglas became president of the American foundation, Colville informed him of the necessity for an archives section of the library to house Sir Winston's papers and the papers of many of his associates, which were to be given to the college. Again, Douglas's response was enthusiastic. It was quickly decided that the archives centre be funded by a distinctly American contribution, presented and funded by recent ambassadors to the Court of St. James's or their heirs and other eminent Americans. Douglas spearheaded the collection of funds and took a particular interest in arranging for the casting of the magnificent ceremonial nickel-bronze doors for the centre.[36]

That summer of 1973, Douglas had much cause for happiness and satisfaction. In England, he had participated once again in Encaenia at Oxford, with Peggy spent a weekend with the Queen Mother at Royal Lodge, Windsor, taken another record fish at Stockbridge, visited with many old friends, and seen the archives centre dedicated. His son James was now president of the Southern Arizona Bank. Lewis, Jr. (Peter), after graduating from Yale in 1948, had gone on, under the initial tutelage of Douglas's old friend oilman Everett DeGolyer, to stake out a successful career first in mining and petroleum exploration and later, on the West Coast, in large-scale real-estate development. One sad note, Peter's wife, Virginia Welch Lang, whom he had married in 1956, had died in 1971 after a short illness. Sharman, after a career in public relations on the West and East coasts, had, in 1968, married Andrew MacKenzie Hay, an English businessman working in New York.[37]

But over the previous five years his health had noticeably declined and he had been subjected to several surgical procedures, including a cataract operation on his good eye in 1972. Periodically, he was plagued with a distressing rash. After his return from England, he suffered a premonitory attack of abdominal pain, which disappeared, however, without complications. He tired easily and found walking more difficult, but, never complaining, insisted upon trying to carry out his myriad undertakings. He even attempted some hunting and fishing in the fall of 1973.[38]

He was staying with friends on Long Island when, just after New Year's Day, 1974, he was struck by the agonizing pain that was the beginning of his last illness. At Columbia-Presbyterian Hospital, preliminary tests and examinations indicated he had a small intestinal obstruction. But, after some initial relief and general improvement, he experienced a chill, his fever rose, and his condition rapidly deteriorated. An operation on January 12 disclosed massive adhesions from previous surgery, causing a major obstruction and necessitating excision of some of the small and most of the remaining large intestine. At first, he rallied from the surgery remarkably well. But then he began to fail rapidly. The great resources of endurance that had brought him through so many physical crises were exhausted. After artificial feeding was discontinued, he was unable to take nourishment and rapidly weakened. Under the circumstances, the attending physicians saw little hope of recovery.[39]

When she was informed of the prognosis, Peggy immediately notified James, and arrangements were made to fly Lew to Tucson. His wishes were well known. He had expressed them eloquently to William Allen White many years before:

"[Arizona] . . . is a beautiful country, and its people are nice people. Their point of view, I think, is my point of view because I was born and raised there. They are, as it were, a part of me. Their country is my country. . . . I shall go [there] during the closing days of my life, if I can anticipate sufficiently the coming of the end." Early on the morning of February 27, he was moved by ambulance to Kennedy Airport, where he was flown by American Airlines in a section curtained off for him, Peggy, and Sharman. His physician and friend Dr. Edmund Goodman, who had been attending him since the early 1940s, followed.[40]

In Tucson, he lingered for nine days, up in a wheelchair some of the time and able to go out to feed his horses at the fence. One of his favorite mares had just foaled and brought her offspring for his inspection. Sometimes, especially during the nights, his mind wandered, to his own and his family's distress. But for the most part he was serene and without pain as his life ebbed. His heart stopped beating on the morning of March 7 in his eightieth year.[41]

The services were held at St. Philip's in the Hills Episcopal Church, which was crowded with old friends from all walks of life and state and local officials, including the governor. The only music was "America the Beautiful" and "The Battle Hymn of the Republic." Through the great window behind the altar the mourners watched a thunderstorm playing over the Santa Catalina Mountains, but "just as the service ended," in the words of John J. McCloy to their Amherst classmates, "the sun came out and it made the mountains glisten. I felt that I was sensing the passing of Lew's spirit and I am sure that most of the congregation felt the same way." His ashes were scattered over the hills at Jerome, where he began his public service and where he had brought his bride so many years before.[42]

The condolences that flooded in, from royalty and government leaders, from miners, ranch hands, and casual acquaintances, praised his contributions to the state and nation and recalled his indomitable spirit and many acts of kindness. Representative of their tone was the brief and moving message from Omar N. Bradley: "The world has lost a giant. I have lost a friend." From closer to home came a tribute Lew would, perhaps, have cherished most. The *Arizona Republic* mourned his passing in an editorial entitled, from Chaucer's line: "Parfit gentil knight." Reviewing his amazing career, which "spanned the seemingly unbridgeable distance between the saloons of frontier Arizona and the sophisticated salons of London," it identified "his chief commodity in trade" as "rugged independence." He could, it concluded, also be called "the perfect Arizonan."[43]

Notes and Bibliography

Notes

LIST OF ABBREVIATIONS

BMWT	British Ministry of War Transport
COHC	Columbia University Oral History Collection
DDEL	Dwight D. Eisenhower Presidential Library
DP	Douglas Papers, Special Collections, The University of Arizona Library
ERP	European Recovery Plan
FDRL	Franklin D. Roosevelt Presidential Library
F.O.	Foreign Office Files, Public Record Office, Kew, England
FRUS	*Foreign Relations of the United States*
HLHP	Harry L. Hopkins Papers, FDRL
HSTL	Harry S. Truman Presidential Library
I	Interview
JFKL	John F. Kennedy Presidential Library
LBJL	Lyndon B. Johnson Presidential Library
LC	Library of Congress
MT	Ministry of Transport Papers, Public Record Office, Kew, England
NA	National Archives, Washington, D.C.
OF	Official File, Presidential Papers
PPF	President's Personal File
PREM	Prime Minister's Papers, Public Record Office, Kew, England
PSF	President's Secretary's File
RG	Record Group, National Archives
RR	LWD's "Random Reminiscences"

Notes

CHAPTER 1 *The Family and the Frontier*

1. James S. Douglas I; LWD, "Reminiscences," 2–4, COHC; JSD diary, Nov. 7, 8, 11, 12, 1907. DP 28; JSD to JD, Nov. 8, 1907, DP 6; Douglas *Daily International*, Nov. 8, 1907. Don Dedera and Bob Robles use a similar version of the London anecdote, which Douglas often recounted, to introduce their moving and detailed account of the event, in Spanish and English, *Goodbye, Garcia, Adios* (Flagstaff, Ariz., 1976). Jesús would have been twenty-four years old on November 13, 1907.

2. Federal Writers Project, *Arizona: The Grand Canyon State* (rev. ed., New York, 1956), 171–175; "Bisbee, Arizona, Feb. 4th 1900" (unpublished manuscript presented by Mrs. Kimball on May 24, 1930), Arizona Historical Society Library (hereafter AHSL); Opie Rundle Burgess, "Bisbee," *Arizona Highways*, XXVIII (Feb., 1952), 12–13, 32–35.

3. Joseph Miller, *Arizona: The Last Frontier* (New York, 1952), 32, 35; Annie M. Cox, "History of Bisbee, 1877 to 1937" (Master's thesis, University of Arizona, 1938), 80–81, 118–124; Joe Chisholm, *Brewery Gulch: Frontier Days of Old Arizona* (San Antonio, Tex., 1949).

4. Frank Brophy interview with Bernice Cosulich, July 1, 1952, Miscellaneous Notebook, box 5, Bernice Cosulich Collection, AHSL; Robert G. Cleland, *A History of Phelps-Dodge, 1834–1950* (New York, 1952), 106–110, 160–162; Cox, "Bisbee," 35, 87, 96–101, 133–143; LWD to Frank Brophy, Aug. 31, 1973, box 65, Brophy Papers, AHSL; James B. Allen, *The Company Town in the American West* (Norman, Okla., 1966), 4–5.

5. Bernice Cosulich, "Mr. Douglas of Arizona: Friend of Cowboys and Kings," *Arizona Highways*, XXIX (Sept., 1953), 3.

6. Cox, "Bisbee," 17–20; Ira B. Joralemon, *Copper: The Encompassing Story of Mankind's First Metal* (Berkeley, California, 1973), 123–124; " 'Don Luis' of Mule Pass," Los Angeles *Times*, March 24, 1907; Brophy 1.

7. JSD to LWD, Sept. 21, 1937, DP 32.

8. James Douglas, Jr., ed., *The Journals and Reminiscences of James Douglas, M.D.* (New York, 1910), 26–253; Colin K. Russell, "Dr. James Douglas, 1800–1886, Adventurer," *Transactions of the American Neurological Association* (1935), 2–6; Alfred Hasbrouck, "Gregor McGregor and the Colonization of Poyais, Between 1820 and 1824," *Hispanic American Historical Review*, VII (Nov., 1927), 450.

9. Douglas D. Martin, "The Douglas Family of Arizona," unpublished manuscript in Special Collections, University of Arizona Library; Joe Chisholm, "Dr. James Douglas," *Arizona Historical Review*, IV (Oct., 1932), 5–19; P. B. McDonald, "James Douglas," *Dictionary of American Biography*, V, 396–397. James Douglas, autobiographical recollections, folders 3–6, DP 2; T. Sterry Hunt, "The Hunt and Douglas Copper Process," *Engineering and Mining Journal*, 14 (July 2, 1872), 10–11; James Douglas, "The Copper Queen Mine, Arizona," *Transactions of the American Institute of Mining Engineers*, XXIX (Feb., 1899), 511–546; James Douglas, "The Copper Queen Mines and Works, Arizona, U.S.A.," *Transactions of the Institute of Mining and Metallurgy*, XXIII (1912–1913), 532–550; Hugh Langton, *James Douglas: A Memoir* (Toronto, 1940), 19–64; Joralemon, *Copper*, 119–142; Lewis W. Douglas, "Dr. James Douglas: An Appreciation," in American Geo-

graphical Society, Occasional Publication No. 3, *The Golden Spike: A Centennial Remembrance* (New York, 1969), 49–53; Walter Douglas, "The Life of James Douglas," *University of Arizona Bulletin*, XI (July 1, 1940), 68–79; Otis E. Young, Jr., "Origins of the American Copper Industry," *Journal of the Early Republic*, 3 (Summer, 1983), 135–137.

10. Langton, *James Douglas*, 63.

11. Ibid., 64–74, 87, 90–100; Cleland, *Phelps-Dodge*, 99–107, 117–148, 161–162; Mary Kidder Rak, "Douglas," *Arizona Highways*, XXVI (Jan., 1950), 4–11; Cox, "Bisbee," 40–43, 102–110, 114–115.

12. Ibid., 105–111, 116–119; James Douglas, autobiographical recollections, folder 6, DP 2; James W. Byrkit, *Forging the Copper Collar: Arizona's Labor-Management War of 1901–1921* (Tucson, 1982), 26–33, 64–68.

13. Melvyn Dubofsky, *We Shall Be All: A History of the Industrial Workers of the World* (Chicago, 1969), 370; Byrkit, *Copper Collar*, 187–215.

14. Philip Taft, "Bisbee Deportation," *Labor History*, XIII (Winter, 1972), 12.

15. Ibid., 3–40; Dubofsky, *We Shall Be All*, 385–391; Byrkit, *Copper Collar*, 183–186, 288–289.

16. *New York Times*, Oct. 24, 25, Dec. 18, 20, 28, 1913, Jan. 27, May 2, 1914, Jan. 28, 1915, July 3, Aug. 21, Nov. 11, 1918, Aug. 14, 1927; *Milestones of Memorial Hospital* (New York, 1934), 8–9; Lewis Douglas, "Dr. James Douglas," 52–53; Langton, *James Douglas*, 102–110; Cleland, *Phelps-Dodge*, 162–163; James Douglas, diary entries for Feb. 14, Nov. 30, Dec. 23, 28–29, 1916, DP 4. A list of Douglas's philanthropies may be found in DP 19. See also "James Douglas," *Engineering and Mining Journal*, CVI (July 6, 1918), 18–19. There is no suitable biography of James Douglas.

17. LWD, "Reminiscences," 4–5, COHC; LWD to Hugh Langton, Sept. 8, 1939, DP 23; LWD to Samuel Rosenman, Oct. 26, 1972, DP 118.

18. Lewis W. Douglas, unpublished biography of Dr. James Douglas, 264–265, 330–332, DP 23.

19. LWD to John M. Gaus, Feb. 27, 1934, DP 202; LWD, unpublished biography, 240–290; LWD 1; Brophy 1; Peggy Douglas 1.

20. LWD, "Reminiscences," 5, COHC.

21. Ibid.; Bernice Cosulich, "Mr. Douglas," 3; *Arizona Daily Star*, Nov. 11, 1891; R. D. Leisk, "James S. Douglas: An Appreciation," *Journal of Metals*, I (April, 1949), 177–178; JSD to JD, Sept. 6, 1914, DP 6.

22. JSD to JD, March 8, 1916, DP 6; T. A. Rickard, "The Story of the UVX Bonanza—I," *Mining and Scientific Press*, CXVI (Jan. 5, 1918), 9–17; Herbert V. Young, *Ghosts of Cleopatra Hill* (Jerome, Ariz., 1974), 123–124; Cleland, *Phelps-Dodge*, 132.

23. JSD to LWD, Nov. 9, 1916, DP 31; Rickard, "The Story of the UVX," 13–17.

24. Brophy 1; *New York Times*, Jan. 3, 1949; JSD, last will and testament, Nov. 10, 1948, DP 57. He left his sons, Lewis and James, about $750,000 apiece.

25. Brophy 1; Frank Brophy, "The Reluctant Banker; From the Reminiscences of Frank Cullen Brophy," *Journal of Arizona History*, XV (Summer, 1974), 177; C. F. Lowery to LWD, June 8, 1930, DP 81.

26. Brophy 1; Peggy Douglas 1.

27. JSD to chairman, House Committee on Military Affairs, Feb. 7, 1916, John Greenway Papers, AHSL; Brophy 1; *Phoenix Messenger*, Dec. 20, 1924; *Arizona Magazine* (undated), box 5, Cosulich Papers; JSD to LWD, Jan. 14, 1917, DP 31. The Jerome mansion, which James S. Douglas deeded to Lew soon after he moved to Canada, became something of a white elephant. It was finally donated to the State of Arizona and opened as a historical museum in 1965, DP 109, 110.

28. Brophy, "Reluctant Banker," 177.

29. LWD to Mrs. S. Randall Detwiler, Sept. 4, 1956, DP 50; LWD to C. J. Beale, Feb. 5, 1957, DP 109; *New York Times*, Jan. 10, 1949; Lee Scott Theisen, "Two Kindly Grouches: A Note by Stephen Bonsal on James Douglas and Georges Clemenceau," *Journal of Arizona History*, 18 (Spring, 1977), 93–98; Georges Wormser to Robert Paul Browder, March 1, April 29, 1977.

30. LWD 1; JSD to LWD, May 7, 1925, DP 31.

31. Peggy Douglas 1; Frank Brophy interview with Bernice Cosulich, July 1, 1952, box 5, Cosulich Papers; Brophy 1; McCloy 1; Schneider 1.

32. JSD to LWD, Nov. 9, 1916, DP 31; JSD to John Greenway, Feb. 7, 1916, Greenway Papers.

33. Lewis Douglas, "Clemenceau," in Lord Longford and Sir John Wheeler-Bennett, eds., *The History Makers: Leaders and Statesmen of the 20th Century* (New York, 1973), 8–33.

34. Peggy Douglas 1; Brophy 1.

35. LWD to JSD, May 13, 1922, DP 31.

36. Frank Brophy interview with Bernice Cosulich, July 1, 1952, box 5, Cosulich Papers; Astley 1; Brophy 1; Flora Rhind to TGS, Aug. 12, 1973.

37. Cox, "Bisbee," 80–81; LWD to Samuel Rosenman, Oct. 26, 1972, DP 118; LWD address before the Arizona National Livestock Show, Phoenix, Arizona, Sept. 30, 1952, DP 319. Douglas also spent some of his youth in Prescott, Arizona.

38. Josephine Douglas to JD, May 6, 1902, DP 7. (Hereafter Josephine will be called Josalee.)

39. LWD, "Reminiscences," 2, COHC;

Charles Stephens to LWD, Aug. 2, 1908, and unnamed newsclips dated Aug., 1908, DP 62; Brophy to his mother, Aug. 23, 1904, LWD to Brophy, Aug. 10, 1905, box 4, Brophy Papers; Bernice Cosulich, "Mr. Douglas," 4, 6.

40. Glenn S. Dumke, "Douglas, Border Town," *Pacific Historical Review*, XVII (Aug., 1948), 291; LWD to Brendan Bracken, Sept. 2, 1948, DP 301; *New York Times*, April 18, 22, 1913.

41. LWD, "Reminiscences," 1–2, COHC.

42. "Bisbee, Feb. 4th, 1900," AHSL; Mr. and Mrs. Ned B. Cowles to LWD, Dec. 20, 1947, DP 281; RPB, conversation with a Mexican traveler, March 25, 1975; Brophy I.

43. LWD to William A. White, July 25, 1943, DP 227.

CHAPTER 2 *Education, War, and Marriage*

1. Brophy I; LWD, "Reminiscences," 7–8, COHC. Before going East Douglas received some formal education in California public schools. For the most part, however, he was educated during his early years by his mother. In early 1902, at the age of eight, he wrote Frank Brophy: "I have my lessons every day. I study reading, spelling writing and arithmetic and mother teaches me." LWD to Brophy, Feb. 25, 1902, box 4, Brophy Papers, AHSL; JSD to JD, Jan. 5, 1900, Jan. 21, Aug. 4, 1903, June 14, Dec. 30, 1904, DP 6.

2. Hackley School catalogs for the years 1904–1909, Hackley School Archives (hereafter cited as HSA); "Hackley's 75th Anniversary," *Hackley Review*, IX (Fall, 1974), 4–7; Brophy 1906, JSD to Henry White Callahan, Feb. 6, April 28, JD to Callahan, April 8, 1908, folder 1908, HSA. Rawhide Jimmy visited Lewis only periodically. JSD diary entries, April 28, May 4–5, 1907, DP 28.

3. Walter B. Gage (headmaster at Hackley) to John G. MacVicar, Sept. 10, 1908, folder 1908, HSA; Dilworth Lupton, "Lewis Douglas Was a Fine Boy," Cleveland *Press*, March 4, 1947, DP 62. For Douglas's formative years, see Thomas G. Smith, "Lewis Douglas Grows Up," *Journal of Arizona History*, XX (Summer, 1979), 223–238.

4. LWD, "Reminiscences," 9–10, COHC.

5. JSD to Walter B. Gage, May 1, 21, June 1, July 24, 1908, folder 1908, HSA; JSD to JD, July 25, 1908, DP 6.

6. LWD, "Reminiscences," 10, COHC; LWD to MacVicar, Nov. 3, 1936, DP 62.

7. MacVicar to JSD, June 10, 1909, Feb. 22, 1910, Feb. 6, 1911, DP 62.

8. JSD to LWD, March 2, 1914, DP 63.

9. LWD to JSD, Nov. 10, 1909, April 26, Oct. 31, 1910, MacVicar to JSD, Oct. 7, 1910, DP 62.

10. LWD to JSD, April 26, 1910, MacVicar to JSD, June 9, 1911, DP 62; JSD to JD, Jan. 6, 1912, DP 6; JSD to Samuel P. Applewhite, June 9, 1912, box 9, Samuel Applewhite Papers, AHSL, Phoenix Chapter.

11. Montclair *Times*, June 8, 1912, DP 62.

12. *Ye Yeare Booke, 1912*, 31, 65, 69, 71, 82, 85–86, 91, 94–95, 100; Archibald C. Merrill to TGS, Feb. 3, 1976. Frank Brophy, who attended Montclair for one year in 1911–1912, complained that Lewis was so busy with school affairs that he seldom saw him. Brophy to his mother, Feb. 11, 1912, box 4, Brophy Papers.

13. James Douglas (LWD's brother) to TGS, June 7, 1974; Peggy Douglas 1.

14. Bixler I; McCloy I; Bixler to TGS, March 17, Aug. 23, 25, 1979.

15. Bixler I; Charles Weeden to TGS, July 5, 1981; LWD to Hugh C. Weed, Feb. 28, 1945, LWD to JSD, Feb. 7, 1913, Feb. 2, 1914, DP 63; Bixler to TGS, July 8, 1981.

16. LWD to Josalee Douglas, Feb. 17, JSD to LWD, March 12, LWD to JSD, April 4, 1914, DP 63; *Olio* (college yearbook) 1916; *Amherst Student* (college newspaper), Sept. 26, Oct. 2, 3, 10, 21, 24, 28, Nov. 4, 18, 1912; Feb. 27, March 13, 24, April 17, 1913.

17. JD diary entries, July 6, 15–16, 20–22, 24–31, 1913, DP 4; JD to JSD, May 14, 28, June 2, 1913, DP 6; LWD, unpublished biography, introduction; LWD to JSD, Feb. 7, 1913, April 4, 1914, DP 63.

18. LWD, "Reminiscences," 11–12, COHC; J. Alfred Guest to LWD, Dec. 5, 1972, DP 63.

19. *Amherst Student*, Oct. 17, 1912; Claude M. Fuess, *Amherst: The Story of a New England College* (Boston, 1935), 309–310; Julius S. Bixler, "Alexander Meiklejohn: The Making of an Amherst Mind," *The New England Quarterly*, LVII (June, 1974), 179–195.

20. LWD to Cullen Murphy, Aug. 23, 1973, DP 63.

21. *Olio*, 1916; Bixler I; *Amherst Student*, May 12, 18, 1916, Oct. 14, 1937.

22. Springfield *Republican*, March 5, 1933; *Olio*, 1916; McCloy I; Wheeler-Bennett 1.

23. LWD to JSD, Aug. 28, 1916, DP 63.

24. LWD, "Reminiscences," 16, COHC; LWD to JSD, April 10, 1916, DP 63, JSD to LWD, Jan. 14, 1917, DP 31; LWD to James "Doo" Douglas (his son), Dec. 31, 1956, DP 69.

25. LWD to JSD, June 22, 1917, DP 31; LWD to Frank Brophy, Sept. 2, 1936, DP 77; JSD to Josalee, Oct. 16, 1917, DP 29; Brophy to his mother, Sept. 9, Oct. 16, 22, 28, Nov. 8, Dec.[?], 1917; Brophy to his father, July 1, 1917; Brophy to parents, Sept. 5, 22, 1917, box 4, Brophy Papers.

26. "Military Record of Lewis W. Douglas," DP 61; LWD to JD, Dec. 9, 1917, DP 65. Douglas's military service records, held at the National Personnel Records Center in St. Louis,

Missouri, were destroyed by fire on July 12, 1973.

27. LWD to JSD, Aug. 10, Sept. 3, 1918, DP 31.

28. H. J. Brees to LWD, Dec. 28, 1920, DP 61; LWD, RR, 25–27, 63, DP 118; 91st Division Publication Committee, *The Story of the 91st Division* (San Francisco, 1919), 39–46; "Military Record of Lewis W. Douglas," DP 61; Douglas *International*, July 8, 1919; Douglas *Daily Dispatch*, July 9, 1919.

29. LWD to Josalee Douglas, June 15, 1922, DP 65.

30. LWD, unpublished biography, 241–242; LWD I; Wheeler-Bennett I. Many Americans besides Douglas resented Germany for destroying what they considered the ideal world order of the prewar years. See Henry F. May, *The End of American Innocence: A Study of the First Years of Our Own Time, 1912–1917* (New York, 1959).

31. LWD, "Reminiscences," 20–21, COHC; Walter R. Agard to RPB, June 9, 1975.

32. LWD, "Reminiscences," 23, COHC.

33. Peggy Douglas I.

34. Smith College *Yearbook*, 1919.

35. Peggy Douglas I; John A. Williams, Hackley School Director of Development and Alumni Affairs, to TGS, May 30, 1984.

36. Brophy I; LWD to JSD, Jan. 24, 1920 [1921], DP 31.

37. LWD to JSD, Feb. 4, 1921, DP 31. James S. Douglas's letter to Lewis of Jan. 29, 1921 is missing from the files. Its contents are clear from Lewis's reply of Feb. 4, 1921.

38. LWD to JSD, Feb. 6, Peggy Douglas to JSD, Feb. 6, 1921, DP 31; JSD to Greenway, Feb. 26, 1921, Greenway Papers.

39. Peggy Douglas I; LWD to John M. Gaus [June or July], 1921, DP 23.

40. Peggy Douglas I; LWD to JSD, July 18, 1921, DP 31; LWD to John C. Greenway, Feb. 11, 1921, Greenway Papers.

CHAPTER 3 *State Representative*

1. United States Department of Commerce, *Fourteenth Census of the United States: 1920* (Washington, D.C., 1922), I, 180, III, 81; Herbert V. Young, *Ghosts of Cleopatra Hill: Men and Legends of Old Jerome* (Jerome, Ariz., 1974), 119–128; James W. Brewer, Jr., *Jerome: A Story of Mines, Men and Money* (Globe, Ariz., 1970), 1–12; Thomas Campbell, typescript, "I.W.W. Jerome," box 1, Thomas Campbell Papers, AHSL; Jerome *News*, Aug. 30, Sept. 29, Dec. 11, 1919, Oct. 14, Dec. 9, 1921, Jan. 10, Feb. 3, 28, 1922.

2. Ibid., Aug. 23, 1923; Peggy Douglas I.

3. LWD interview with Nann Novinski, in Verde *Independent*, April 15, 1965; Peggy Douglas I; W. F. Staunton, unpublished memoirs, II, 86–88, W. F. Staunton Papers, University of Arizona Library.

4. Peggy Douglas I; Jerome *News*, Sept. 30, 1921; LWD to Louis Cates, Nov. 29, 1938, DP 109.

5. Peggy Douglas I; LWD to JSD, May 9, 1922, DP 31.

6. LWD to Josalee Douglas, June 15, 1922, DP 65; LWD to JSD, June 12, July 4, 10, 1922, DP 31. In early July Grandmother Naomi Douglas died, leaving Lew $4,000. Last Will and Testament of Naomi Douglas, March 24, 1918, DP 58; Jerome *News*, June 23, July 7, 1922.

7. LWD to JSD, Sept. 9, 1922, DP 31.

8. Jerome *News*, April 4, May 12, Aug. 11, 23, Sept. 5, 1922; LWD, "Reminiscences," 25, COHC.

9. LWD to JSD, Sept. 9, 1922, DP 31; Jerome *News*, Sept. 13, 26, 1922; Yavapai County Board of Supervisors, Election Statistics, 1923, Court House, Prescott, Arizona.

10. LWD to JSD, Oct. 9, 1922, DP 31.

11. Marjorie Haines Wilson, "The Gubernatorial Career of George W. P. Hunt of Arizona" (Ph.D. dissertation, Arizona State University, 1973), 21–26, 33–34, 58–66, 195–234; Tucson *Arizona Daily Star*, May 14, 16, 17, 19, 25, 1922; Jerome *News*, June 30, Aug. 1, 4, 1922.

12. LWD to JSD, Oct. 9, 1922, DP 31; Jerome *News*, Nov. 3, 1922.

13. Ibid., Oct. 6, 13, 17, Nov. 8, 14, 1922; Yavapai County, Election Statistics, 1923.

14. Peggy Douglas I. The Douglases lived on Holly Street for two years and then moved into a home on Seventh Street, which they occupied until the 1940s.

15. Peggy Douglas I.

16. LWD to JSD, Sept. 12, 1924, DP 31.

17. *Journal of the House of Representatives of the Sixth State Legislature of Arizona, 1923* (Phoenix, 1923; hereafter cited as *Arizona House Journal*), 100–101, 104, 123, 175, 185, 338, 342, 363–364; LWD notes on Highway Investigating Committee, DP 122; Phoenix *Arizona Republican*, Jan. 23, 1923.

18. *Arizona House Journal, 1923*, 68, 80, 95–96, 112, 119–120, 139, 179, 226, 238–239, 361–363, 411, 432, 496, 573–574, 579.

19. Ibid., 37–40, 46, 87, 106–107, 140, 206, 225–227, 233, 254–256, 316, 436, 454, 464, 482, 494; *Arizona Daily Star*, Jan. 20, 21, Feb. 8, 11, 1923; *Arizona Republican*, Jan. 24, 25, 28, Feb. 1, 7, 8, March 3, 1923.

20. Jerome *News*, Feb. 2, 1923; Thomas G. Smith, "Lewis Douglas, Arizona Politics and the Colorado River Controversy," *Arizona and the West*, 22 (Summer, 1980), 125–162.

21. Background material on the Colorado River controversy is in Lewis W. Douglas, "The Colorado River: From Its Sources to the Sea," *Arizona Highways*, XLIV (May, 1968), 4–6, 39;

Norris Hundley, Jr., *Dividing the Waters: A Century of Controversy Between the United States and Mexico* (Berkeley, 1966); and Hundley, *Water and the West: The Colorado River Compact and the Politics of Water in the American West* (Berkeley, 1974). Bisbee *Daily Review* editorial in *Arizona Daily Star*, June 13, 1922.

22. The definitive study of the Colorado River Compact is Hundley, *Water and the West*. See especially chapters 5–7.

23. Arizona Democrats were hardly unanimous in their skepticism. Those from western counties, where the dam would be built, favored the compact. Democratic Congressman Carl Hayden also supported the agreement. Thomas Campbell, typescript, "The True Story of The Colorado River Compact," box 1, Campbell Papers; *Arizona House Journal, 1923*, 25; *Jerome News*, May 9, Oct. 6, 1922; *Arizona Daily Star*, Dec. 23, 1922; *Arizona Republican*, Feb. 8, 1923; Malcolm B. Parsons, "Origins of the Colorado River Controversy in Arizona Politics, 1922–1923," *Arizona and the West*, IV (Spring, 1962), 27–28, 38; Parsons, "Party and Pressure Politics in Arizona's Opposition to Colorado River Development," *Pacific Historical Review*, XIX (Feb., 1950), 58, 61–62; Donald R. Van Petten, "Arizona's Stand on the Santa Fe Compact and the Boulder Dam Project Act," *New Mexico Historical Review*, XVII (Jan., 1942), 8–10; Dwight E. Mayo, "Arizona and the Colorado River Compact" (M.A. thesis, Arizona State University, 1964), 30–39; Hundley, *Water and the West*, 140–142, 159–164, 194–203, 238–240; Walter Rusinek, "Against the Compact: The Critical Opposition of George W. P. Hunt," *Journal of Arizona History*, XXV (Summer, 1984), 155–170.

24. LWD to Marcus Smith, May 1, 1923; LWD typescript "What Will Determine the Merits" and notes on the Colorado River Compact, DP 122. For a detailed treatment of Douglas's position on the compact, see Smith, "Douglas," 125–140.

25. *Arizona House Journal, 1923*, 70, 75, 110–111, 176–177, 210–211, 221–222; *Arizona Republican*, Jan. 20, Feb. 1, 1923; *Jerome News*, Jan. 26, Feb. 9, 13, 1923; *Arizona Daily Star*, Jan. 17, 20, 1923; LWD to John C. Greenway, Feb. 8, 1923, DP 122; Tucson *Citizen* quoted in Mayo, "Arizona and the Colorado River Compact," 38.

26. *Arizona Republican*, Feb. 10, 1923.

27. *Arizona Daily Star*, Jan. 28, 1923; *Jerome News*, Jan. 30, 1923; Parsons, "Party and Pressure Politics," 55.

28. *Jerome News*, Feb. 13, 27, 1923; *Arizona Republican*, Feb. 17, 1923.

29. *Arizona Daily Star*, Feb. 16, 1923; *Arizona Republican*, Feb. 1, 9, 10, June 13, 20, Aug. 3, 1923; Ross R. Rice interview with LWD for the Carl Hayden Project, March 23, 1973, DP 119.

30. LWD notes on the Colorado River Compact, DP 122.

31. *Arizona House Journal, 1923*, 301–305, 565–570; *Arizona Republican*, Feb. 16, March 9, 1923; *Arizona Daily Star*, Feb. 28, March 8, 1923; Parsons, "Colorado River Controversy," 40. During the 1923 session, some twenty bills for qualified or unqualified ratification of the compact were introduced.

32. LWD, "Merits," DP 122; LWD, "Reminiscences," 27, COHC.

33. *Arizona Daily Star*, April 29, 1923; Phoenix *Arizona Gazette*, May 9, 1923; LWD to Herbert Hoover, May 12, LWD to Harold Elliott, May 24, LWD to A. G. McGregor, June 19, 20, 1923, Statement Before the Federal Power Commission by the Arizona-Colorado River Conference Committee Concerning the Development and Utilization of the Resources of the Colorado River, DP 122; *Arizona Republican*, Sept. 25, 26, 1923, Jan. 5, March 2, 23, 1924.

CHAPTER 4 *The Road to Washington*

1. *Jerome News*, Feb. 8, 1923.
2. Ibid., Aug. 26, 1924; Peggy Douglas I.
3. LWD to Harold A. Elliott, Oct. 24, Howard Cornick to LWD, Oct. 31, 1923, DP 122; LWD I.
4. *Arizona Daily Star*, June 21, 1923; *Jerome News*, July 31, Sept. 9, 16, 1923, Dec. 22, 1924, June 22, 1926.
5. Brophy to TGS, June 5, Oct. 28, 1974, June 11, July 9, 1975; Peggy Douglas I; Records of the Grand Central Mining Company, DP 446; Brophy to LWD, May 21, 1926, DP 77; *Arizona Daily Star*, March 23, 1926, May 29, 1928.
6. LWD to Governor Hunt, March 5, A. T. Kilcrease to LWD, Feb. 28, March 7, LWD to Kilcrease, April 5, 1926, DP 123; LWD I; Peggy Douglas I; Phoenix *Messenger*, April 7, 1926; LWD to William Mathews, June 9, 1930, DP 168.
7. *Arizona Daily Star*, May 22, 1926.
8. Peggy Douglas I; JSD to LWD, May 24, 26, 1926, DP 31.
9. Jingle is in DP 123.
10. United States Congress, House, *Senatorial Campaign Expenditures: Hearings before a Special Committee Investigating Expenditures in Senatorial Primary and General Elections*, 69 Cong., 1 Sess., part 4, 2510–2511, 2680–2687; Ellinwood I.
11. Peggy Douglas I; Peggy Douglas to Miss Eggelston, July 29, 1926, DP 123.
12. *Jerome News*, June 22, 1926.
13. LWD interview with James Sargent, DP 119. Another rival, H. A. Davis, also tried to use the copper connection against Douglas. See *Arizona Republican*, Sept. 4, 1926.
14. *Arizona Daily Star*, Aug. 7, 1926. Poem printed in *Arizona Republican*, Sept. 5, 1926.

15. *Arizona Daily Star*, June 13, July 28, Aug. 6, 1926; Benson *News* quoted in ibid., Aug. 17, 1926; "Straight Talk," flyer issued by the Douglas-for-Congress Club, Sept. 1, 1926, DP 123.

16. Mrs. R. C. Arnold to LWD, July 3, 1926, DP 123; *Arizona Daily Star*, Sept. 11, 14, 1926; John Reilly to LWD, Aug. 16, 1926, DP 123; JSD to LWD, Aug. 17, 1926, DP 31.

17. LWD to Jackson Nored, Aug. 31, 1926, DP 123.

18. LWD interview with James Sargent, DP 119; Peggy Douglas 1.

19. Jerome *News*, June 25, 1926; *Arizona Daily Star*, June 13, 28, 1926; *Arizona Republican*, Sept. 3, 1926; "Straight Talk."

20. Jerome *News*, June 22, 1926.

21. LWD to Carl Hayden, April 26, May 11, 1926, DP 123.

22. *Arizona Republican*, Sept. 7–10, 17, Oct. 3, 1926.

23. Jerome *News*, Oct. 26, 1926; *Arizona Republican*, Oct. 10, Nov. 1, 1926.

24. LWD interview with James Sargent, DP 119; *Arizona Daily Star*, Oct. 10, 13, 15, 16, 1926.

25. *Arizona Republican*, Oct. 31, 1926.

26. Howard Cornick to F. W. Lowery, Oct. 14, Lowery to LWD, Oct. 14, 1926, DP 123.

27. *Arizona Daily Star*, May 21, 1926; LWD, "Reminiscences," 27–28, COHC; LWD 1, April 26, 1973.

28. United States Congress, Senate, "Senatorial Campaign Expenditures," *Senate Report* 1197, 69 Cong., 2 Sess., 1926, parts 3 and 4; *New York Times*, Oct. 27, 1926.

29. *Arizona Republican*, Oct. 31, 1926.

30. "Campaign Expenditures," *SR* 1197, 69 Cong., 2 Sess., part 3, 1, 4–5; *Senatorial Campaign Hearings*, 69 Cong., 1 Sess., part 4, 2344.

31. Ibid., 2518.

32. Ibid., 2516–2520, 2522–2524, 2504–2514; *Arizona Republican*, *Arizona Daily Star*, and *New York Times*, Nov. 1, 1926.

33. *Senatorial Campaign Hearings*, 69 Cong., 1 Sess., part 4, 2774–2788, 2740–2748, 2805–2821, 2887–2900; LWD, Campaign Expense Statements for 1926, DP 123.

34. Jerome *News*, Nov. 5, 1926; *Arizona Republican*, Nov. 3, 1926; General Election Returns, State of Arizona, Nov. 2, 1926, DP 123.

35. *Senatorial Campaign Hearings*, 69 Cong., 1 Sess., part 4, 2507–2509, 2513; *Arizona Daily Star*, Sept. 18, 1926.

CHAPTER 5 *Congress and the Colorado River*

1. Peggy Douglas 1; B. F. Gavin to LWD, Nov. 16, 1926, Oct. 3, 1927, LWD to John N. Garner, March 11, LWD to James W. Collier et al., Nov. 10, LWD to Dispersing Clerk of House of Representatives, July 7, 1927, DP 124.

2. *Arizona Gazette*, Sept. 12, 15, 1927.

3. *Arizona Daily Star*, Sept. 15, 1927; P. W. O'Sullivan to LWD, Sept. 15, 1927, DP 124; *Arizona Gazette*, Sept. 15, 1927. Unidentified newsclip found in Douglas file, James H. McClintock Collection, Phoenix Public Library; Coconino *Sun* editorial reprinted in *Arizona Daily Star*, Sept. 27, 1927.

4. Diary of Governor George W. P. Hunt, Sept. 14, 15, 1927, Arizona State University Library (courtesy of Dr. Marjorie Haines Wilson); *Arizona Gazette*, Sept. 16, 1927.

5. *Arizona Daily Star*, Jan. 20, Feb. 1, 22, Sept. 22, 1927.

6. Peggy Douglas 1; Brophy 1; LWD to JSD, May 30, June 8, 1927, DP 31; James Douglas (brother) to LWD, Feb. 17, Nov. 23, 1928, Jan. 24, 1940, DP 66.

7. Josalee Douglas to LWD (twice), June 15, 1927, DP 65.

8. LWD to JSD, July 27, 1928, DP 31.

9. Peggy Douglas 1; *New York Times*, obituary, May 1, 1980.

10. LWD diary entry for Dec. 5, 1927, DP 124; *Congressional Record*, 70 Cong., 1 Sess., 8–11; *New York Times*, Dec. 5, 6, 1927.

11. LWD diary entries for Dec. 6, 7, 9, 12, 1927, DP 124. The diary ends with the entry for Dec. 16.

12. *Arizona Daily Star*, April 4, May 11, 1930; *New York Sun*, Sept. 8, 1931; Representative Gordon Browning (Tennessee), "Reminiscences," 10–11, COHC; Henry L. Stimson Diary, June 4, 1932, Yale University Library; Wheeler-Bennett 1; LWD interview with James Sargent, DP 119.

13. Ibid.

14. Ibid.; Peggy Douglas 1; LWD to Cordell Hull, May 13, 1948, DP 302; *Cong. Rec.*, 72 Cong., 1 Sess., 4070, 6009. Douglas once wrote his father: "Poor Henry! Poor as he is I think he is a better man than Hayden—who votes as demogically as Henry, but who hides his demogoguery beneath an oily unctuous exterior of self-satisfied virtue." LWD to JSD, March 9, 1937, DP 32.

15. LWD to JSD, Feb. 25, 1928, DP 31; Clarence B. Kelland, "Reminiscences," COHC; Representative John W. McCormack to RPB, Sept. 24, 1975; confidential remarks of Hon. Joseph Martin and Hon. Samuel Rayburn to Frank McNaughton, Nov. 19, 1947, Frank McNaughton Papers, HSTL.

16. LWD to JSD, Feb. 6, 1928, DP 31; Peggy Douglas 1; Davison 1; Drew Pearson, *Washington Merry Go Round* (New York, 1931), 22–23. Columnist Robert Choate wrote in 1933 that Douglas "is undoubtedly the most popular single personality in the House. He is respected

in the Senate. He is the friend of everybody in Washington's social life." Choate, unidentified newsclip, Feb. 26, 1933, DP 234.

17. Peggy Douglas I; LWD to Carl Hayden, Sept. 25, 1928, DP 148; Frank Brophy to LWD, Oct. 8, 1928, DP 77; *Arizona Daily Star*, Oct. 30, 1928.

18. George F. Sparks, ed., *A Many-Colored Toga: The Diary of Henry Fountain Ashurst* (Tucson, 1962), 258; Beverly B. Moeller, *Phil Swing and Boulder Dam* (Berkeley, 1971), 90, 94-96, 105; Norris Hundley, *Water and the West: The Colorado River Compact and the Politics of Water in the American West* (Berkeley, 1974), 267-270.

19. LWD to JSD, April 6, Feb. 6, 1928, DP 31; Sparks, ed., *Diary of Henry Fountain Ashurst*, 254, 258.

20. United States Congress, House, Committee on Irrigation and Reclamation, *Hearings on Protection and Development of the Lower Colorado River Basin*, 70 Cong., 1 Sess., 1928, 105; LWD to JSD, Feb. 6, 1928, DP 31. See also LWD to Robert Tally, Dec. 22, 1927, LWD to Thomas Peters, Feb. 20, 1928, DP 132.

21. LWD to Owen Young, Jan. 17, 1928, DP 132; LWD to JSD, March 18, 1928, DP 31; United States Congress, House, Committee on Irrigation and Reclamation, "Boulder Canyon Project," House Report 918, 70 Cong., 1 Sess., 1928, part 2, 1-45; *Cong. Rec.*, 70 Cong., 1 Sess., 6248. Douglas blamed Garner, the ranking member of the Ways and Means Committee, for the progress of the bill. He privately accused Garner of making a deal with the Democratic backers of the measure, in return for support for the Speakership. See LWD to Sidney Osborn, May 16, LWD to Everett Johnson, March 31, 1928, DP 148.

22. *New York Times*, May 24, 1928. For additional favorable press reports, see Salt Lake Tribune, Arizona Daily Star, Arizona Republican for May 24, 1928. Governor Hunt also praised the speech, see Hunt Diary, May 23, 1928, Arizona State University Library (courtesy of Dr. Marjorie Haines Wilson).

23. Thomas G. Smith, "Lewis Douglas, Arizona Politics and the Colorado River Controversy," *Arizona and the West*, 22 (Summer, 1980), 152-162; *Cong. Rec.*, 70 Cong., 1 Sess., 9623-9635.

24. Ibid., 9489, 9760, 9770. Douglas introduced a substitute bill more palatable to Arizona, but it failed to come to a vote.

25. Ibid., 9771-9772. Douglas introduced several amendments in an attempt to bury the bill, but they were all rejected.

26. Ibid., 9775-9780, 9985, 9988-9989.

27. LWD to Malcolm Beranger, May 25, LWD to Oscar Irvin, May 30, 1928, DP 132; LWD to Howard Cornick, May 30, 1928, DP 148.

28. LWD to JSD, March 18, 1928, DP 31; LWD to Arthur Curlee, March 7, LWD to M. T. Phelps, March 17, LWD to Sidney Osborn, April 24, LWD to Evan S. Stallup, May 21, LWD to A. T. Kilcrease, May 30, 1928, DP 148; *Arizona Daily Star*, Aug. 27, Sept. 1, 2, 1928; Bisbee *Review*, Aug. 28, 29, 1928; Florence *Blade-Tribune*, July 28, 1928.

29. Undated editorial, Mesa *Journal-Tribune* in DP 148; "Official Canvass General Election Returns, November 6, 1928," DP 148; *Arizona Daily Star*, Nov. 7, 8, 1928.

30. "Report of the Colorado River Board on the Boulder Dam Project," House Document 446, 70 Cong., 1 Sess., 1-15; LWD to Ralph Ellinwood, Dec. 5, 1928, DP 132; Hundley, *Water and the West*, 173-175.

31. LWD to Secretary of the Interior, Nov. 26, 1928, DP 133.

32. *Cong. Rec.*, 70 Cong., 1 Sess., 823-824; *United States Statutes at Large* (Washington, 1929), XLV, 1057-1066; J. E. Gavin to Dwight B. Heard, Dec. 14, 1928, DP 132.

33. *Cong. Rec.*, 70 Cong., 1 Sess., 836; LWD, quoted in Coconino *Sun*, Oct. 24, 1930.

34. *Cong. Rec.*, 71 Cong., 3 Sess., 5564. See also LWD to Frank Brophy, April 12, 1930, DP 77; LWD to P. G. Spilsburg, Jan. 14, 1931, DP 160; LWD to the Douglas, Arizona, League of Women Voters, Oct. 8, 1930, DP 173.

35. LWD to Daniel C. Green, Jan. 19, 1929, DP 132; LWD to John G. Phillips, Jan. 9, 1929, DP 133.

36. LWD I; LWD to Dean Acheson, April 5, Acheson to LWD, April 6, John M. Ross to LWD, April 26, LWD to K. Berry Peterson, April 30, 1929, DP 157.

37. *Hearings on Second Deficiency Appropriation Bill for 1930*, 71 Cong., 1 Sess., 1012-1013, 1058-1076; *Cong. Rec.*, 71 Cong., 2 Sess., 9576, 11040-11044, 11247-11248; Los Angeles *Times* editorial reprinted in the Coolidge [Arizona] *News*, Sept. 4, 1930.

38. LWD to Carl Hayden, Oct. 23, LWD to W. C. Mullendore, Nov. 4, 1929, LWD to William R. Mathews, March 14, Dean Acheson to LWD, May 18, 1931, DP 157; *Arizona v. California*, 283 U.S. Reports 463-464 (1931).

39. *Cong. Rec.*, 70 Cong., 1 Sess., 9629; ibid., 71 Cong., 3 Sess., 5564; Bisbee *Review* editorial in *Arizona Daily Star*, May 29, 1928. In July, 1940, Swing-Johnson was amended to give $300,000 annually to both Arizona and Nevada for the remainder of the 50-year amortization period ending in May, 1987. Through May 31, 1973, Arizona had received a total of $336.1 million from surplus power profits. See G. G. Stam, Commissioner, Bureau of Reclamation, U.S. Department of Interior to Congressman Morris K. Udall, Jan. 8, 1975, attached to undated memorandum from Udall to TGS.

CHAPTER 6 *A Remedy for Hard Times*

1. *Congressional Record*, 71 Cong., 1 Sess., 2143, 572–573; Joan Hoff Wilson, *Herbert Hoover: Forgotten Progressive* (Boston, 1975), 133–135; Harris Gaylord Warren, *Herbert Hoover and the Great Depression* (New York, 1967), 169–172; Ellis W. Hawley, *The Great War and the Search for a Modern Order: A History of the American People and Their Institutions, 1919–1933* (New York, 1979), 178–180.

2. *Cong. Rec.*, 71 Cong., 1 Sess., 2143–2144; LWD to P. Parrish, June 27, 1930, DP 163; LWD to editor of the *Arizona Daily Star*, Oct. 27, 1971, DP 60; LWD interview with James Sargent, DP 119; Lewis W. Douglas, *The Liberal Tradition: A Free People and a Free Economy* (New York, reprint edition, 1972), 1–14.

3. LWD to JSD, June 25, 1929, DP 31; Peggy Douglas I, April 28, 1975; LWD to Frank Brophy, Oct. 5, 1929, DP 77; Lewis W. Douglas, "Clemenceau," in Lord Longford and Sir John Wheeler-Bennett, eds., *The History Makers: Leaders and Statesmen of the 20th Century* (New York, 1973), 29–32; Lewis Douglas, *RR*, DP 118; Lee Scott Theisen, ed., "Two Kindly Grouches: A Note by Stephen Bonsal on James Douglas and Georges Clemenceau," *Journal of Arizona History*, 18 (Spring, 1977), 93–98; LWD diary entries, Sept. 13–18, 1929, DP 95; Pierre Brive, ed., *Georges Clemenceau: Lettres à une amie, 1923–1929* (Paris, 1970), 638–639.

4. LWD interview with James Sargent, DP 119.

5. Peggy Douglas I; Stroud I; LWD to JSD, Feb. 20, April 18, 1930, Jan. 16, 1932, DP 31.

6. *Cong. Rec.*, 71 Cong., 2 Sess., 2248–2249.

7. Ibid., 2975–2976, 3105; LWD to JSD, Feb. 6, 1930, DP 31.

8. George W. P. Hunt to LWD, March 13, LWD to Hunt, March 19, LWD to John J. Durkin, May 30, 1928, and numerous other letters in DP 142; LWD to William Mathews, June 9, 1930, DP 168; U.S. Congress, House, Committee on Irrigation and Naturalization, *Hearings on Immigration from Countries of the Western Hemisphere*, 70 Cong., 1 Sess., 1928, 355–365; *Cong. Rec.*, 71 Cong., 2 Sess., 6614, 7210, 7277, 7321, 7600, 8842–8843, 8891, 8968.

9. Frank Brophy to LWD, Nov. 12, 25, 1930, DP 77; Henry R. Curran to LWD, May 26, LWD to Curran, June 27, 1930 (not sent), DP 168; LWD to Brophy, Nov. 26, Dec. 2, 1930, DP 77; LWD to Mrs. Leora L. Brewer, Dec. 14, 1931, and numerous other letters in DP 197; *Cong. Rec.*, 72 Cong., 1 Sess., 6004; ibid., 72 Cong., 2 Sess., 12, 4508–4516.

10. *Arizona Daily Star*, July 25, Aug. 28, Sept. 1, 1930; *Yuma Sentinel*, Aug. 12, 1930; Douglas *Dispatch*, Aug. 21, 23, 31, 1930; Ellinwood I; Peggy Douglas I.

11. For Douglas's campaign statements, see Winslow *Mail*, Oct. 21, 1930; *Coconino Sun*, Oct. 24, 1930; Prescott *Courier*, Oct. 25, 29, 1930; Bisbee *Ore*, Oct. 29, 1930; LWD to A. H. Favour, Dec. 4, 1930, DP 173; William Mathews to LWD, Dec. 1, 1930, DP 78; Oscar Irvin to LWD, Nov. 7, M. Alice Patterson to LWD, Nov. 9, 1930, DP 173; Coolidge *News*, Sept. 4, 1930; Arizona Secretary of State, "Official Canvass of Votes Cast at the General Election Held on November 4, 1930," DP 173.

12. E. Pendleton Herring, "First Session of the Seventy-second Congress," *American Political Science Review*, 26 (Oct., 1932), 848, 854; LWD to Mrs. L. J. Tuttle, Oct. 8, 1930, DP 173; *Arizona Daily Star*, Nov. 6, 14, Dec. 1, 1931.

13. Ibid., April 12, Sept. 15, 1931, May 14, 1932; Brophy to LWD, Dec. 16, 1931, DP 77; Lewis W. Douglas, testimony before the House Ways and Means Committee, reprinted in *Cong. Rec.*, 72 Cong., 1 Sess., 7525–7526; Lewis W. Douglas, testimony before the Senate Committee on Finance, reprinted in ibid., 13808–13809. For the depression in Arizona, see William H. Jervey, Jr., "When the Banks Closed: Arizona's Bank Holiday of 1933," *Arizona and the West*, 10 (Summer, 1968), 127–152; C. L. Sonnichsen, "Hard Times in Tucson," *Journal of Arizona History*, 22 (Spring, 1981), 23–62.

14. Bisbee *Daily Review*, Dec. 13, 1931. For additional pro-tariff sentiment, see numerous newsclips in DP 164, 207. LWD interview with James Sargent, DP 119; William Mathews to LWD, March 6, 1932, DP 78; *Arizona Daily Star*, April 15, 16, 1931; LWD to Frank Brophy, Dec. 10, 1931, DP 77; LWD to Cleve W. Van Dyke, Arizona Copper Commission, Jan. 19, Feb. 2, 1932, DP 203; *Dunbar's Weekly*, Oct. 24, 1931.

15. *Cong. Rec.*, 72 Cong., 1 Sess., 2852, 4841, 7525–7526, 13809–13810, 10943–10945; LWD to Charles Crisp, acting chairman, House Ways and Means Committee, March 18, 1932, DP 203; *Arizona Daily Star*, March 18, 29, 30, 1932; LWD interview with Ross R. Rice for the Carl Hayden Project, March 23, 1973, DP 119.

16. LWD to Dr. John Bacon, Feb. 10, 1932, DP 205; *Cong. Rec.*, 72 Cong., 1 Sess., 1035–1039, 1635; *Arizona Daily Star*, Jan. 9, 10, 1932; Bisbee *Sunday Review*, Sept. 11, 1932; Van Dyke quoted in Prescott *Courier*, Sept. 30, 1932. For Douglas's regrets, see Lewis Douglas, *The Liberal Tradition*, viii–ix; H. B. Elliston, "Crusader and Budgeteer," *Christian Science Monitor*, Nov. 27, 1935.

17. Albert U. Romasco, *The Poverty of Abundance: Hoover, the Nation, the Depression* (New York, 1965), 184–187; Hawley, *Search for a Modern Order*, 191, 197; Bernard Baruch

to LWD, March 4, 1932, DP 205; LWD to Frank Brophy, Dec. 29, 1932, DP 77; LWD to M. R. Aumas, Jan. 25, 1929, DP 148; *Cong. Rec.*, 72 Cong., 1 Sess., 867; LWD to JSD, March 1, 1932, DP 31.

18. Frederick L. Allen, *Since Yesterday: The Nineteen-Thirties in America, Sept. 3, 1929–Sept. 3, 1939* (New York, 1940), 37–41; Arthur M. Schlesinger, Jr., *The Age of Roosevelt: The Crisis of the Old Order, 1919–1933* (Boston, 1957), 474–476; Broadus Mitchell, *Depression Decade: From New Era Through New Deal, 1929–1941* (New York, 1947), 13–14, 127–129; LWD to James B. Ray, May 17, LWD to F. L. J. Carroll, May 24, 1932, DP 210; *Arizona Daily Star*, Aug. 23, 1932; LWD to Newton D. Baker, Dec. 24, 1934, DP 252.

19. Warren, *Hoover*, 158–159; Wilson, *Hoover*, 149–157; LWD to Sidney Sapp, May 31, 1932, DP 197; LWD to J. G. Flynn, March 22, 1932, DP 205; LWD to JSD, Jan. 16, 25, 1932, DP 31.

20. *Cong. Rec.*, 72 Cong., 1 Sess., 4067–4070.

21. LWD to the editor of the Haverhill (Mass.) *Gazette*, March 12, 1932, DP 214; *Cong. Rec.*, 72 Cong., 1 Sess., 232, 4093–4094, 4467–4470, 6009, 10484–10485.

22. Ibid., 6006–6009; LWD to William Mathews, March 22, 1932, DP 205; LWD to Walter Martin, March 12, 1932, DP 232.

23. Besides McDuffie and Douglas, other Democrats on the Economy Committee were Joseph Byrns and John J. Cochran of Missouri. Republicans included William Wood of Indiana, William Williamson of South Dakota, and C. William Ramseyer of Iowa. LWD to JSD, March 1, 26, 1932, DP 31; *Cong. Rec.*, 72 Cong., 1 Sess., 4407, 6011; William Starr Myers and Walter H. Newton, *The Hoover Administration: A Documented Narrative* (New York, 1936), 178, 192. At the same time Douglas was introducing his economy resolution in the House, attorney Grenville Clark was organizing the National Economy League. See Lewis W. Douglas, "Grenny in the 1930s and 1940s," in *Memoirs of a Man: Grenville Clark*, collected by Mary Clark Dimond, edited by Norman Cousins and J. Garry Clifford (New York, 1975), 195–196.

24. *Cong. Rec.*, 72 Cong., 1 Sess., 7325; Jordan A. Schwarz, *The Interregnum of Despair: Hoover, Congress, and the Depression* (Urbana, Ill., 1970), 106–141; Howard Zinn, *La Guardia in Congress* (Ithaca, N.Y., 1959), 220–226; Arthur Mann, *La Guardia: A Fighter Against His Times, 1882–1933* (Philadelphia, 1959), 303–305; Francis E. Brown, "Congress Wrestles with the Budget," *Current History* (May, 1932), 205–213; "The 'Soak-the-Rich' Drive in Washington," *Literary Digest* (April 2, 1932), 8–9.

25. LWD to JSD [n.d.], March 16, May 22, 1932, DP 31; *Cong. Rec.*, 72 Cong., 1 Sess., 7980, 7999, 9312; U.S. Congress, House, *To Effect Economies in National Government*, House Report 1126, 72 Cong., 1 Sess., 1932.

26. *Cong. Rec.*, 72 Cong., 1 Sess., 9504–9505; 9491–9493.

27. Ibid., 9504–9520; *New York Times*, May 4, 5, 1932; Walter Lippmann to LWD, May 9, 1932, DP 280; Frank Kent in Baltimore *Sun*, May 5, 1932; E. Claude Babcock to LWD, May 3, 1932, quoted in *Arizona Daily Star*, May 14, 1932.

28. B. M. Stanley to William Mathews in *Arizona Daily Star*, May 15, 1932; letter from "A Real Ex-Serviceman" to the editor of an unidentified Phoenix newspaper, Lewis W. Douglas File, James H. McClintock Papers, Phoenix Public Library.

29. LWD interview with James Sargent, DP 119; *Arizona Daily Star*, April 25, 1931; LWD to P. Parrish, June 27, 1930, DP 163.

30. LWD to JSD, May 28, June 14, 1932, DP 31; *Cong. Rec.*, 72 Cong., 1 Sess., 12243–12244, 14684–14692, 15232–15233; Warren, *Hoover*, 205–207; Hawley, *Search for a Modern Order*, 209.

31. Donald J. Lisio, *The President and Protest: Hoover, Conspiracy, and the Bonus Riot* (Columbia, Mo., 1974), passim; Roger Daniels, *The Bonus March: An Episode of the Great Depression* (Westport, Connecticut, 1971), 37–40; LWD to Vernon F. Roy, Dec. 19, 1930, DP 166.

32. Christopher Totten to LWD, Jan. 3, 1931, DP 166; *Cong. Rec.*, 71 Cong., 2 Sess., 9870–9871; ibid., 71 Cong., 3 Sess., 6170–6172. See also DP 166 for additional letters of protest.

33. LWD to F. L. J. Carroll, May 24, LWD to James B. Ray, May 17, LWD to F. E. Norris, May 19, 1932, DP 210; LWD handwritten comments on margins of William Mathews to LWD, April 27, 1932, DP 78.

34. Daniels, *Bonus March*, 99, 101, 117; *Arizona Daily Star*, Aug. 12, 1932; *Cong. Rec.*, 72 Cong., 1 Sess., 13053.

35. Daniels, *Bonus March*, 123–181; LWD interview with James Sargent, DP 119.

36. LWD to JSD, May 14, March 26, 1932, DP 31. For Hoover's ideology and presidential policies, see Warren, *Hoover*, 148–167; Wilson, *Hoover*, 122–167; Richard Hofstadter, "Herbert Hoover and the Crisis of American Individualism," in *The American Political Tradition and the Men Who Made It* (New York, 1951), 279–310.

37. *Arizona Fax*, Jan. 22, 1932; *Arizona Daily Star*, May 15, 1932; Irving L. Gibson, adjutant of the Mathew B. Juan Post No. 35, Chandler, Arizona to LWD, July (no date), 1932, DP 210.

38. William Mathews to LWD, May 13, 1932, DP 78; Evan S. Stallup to LWD, Oct. 21, 1931, July 13, 1932, DP 210; Stroud 1.

CHAPTER 7 *Toward the New Deal*

1. LWD to JSD, June 14, 1932, DP 31; LWD to Dr. W. P. Sims, July 14, 1932, DP 232.

2. LWD's comments on the convention are quoted in L. J. Bugg to Louis H. Howe, Nov. 26, 1931, PPF 1914, FDRL; LWD to William J. Donovan, Nov. 22, 1930, DP 173; Ronald Steel, *Walter Lippmann and the American Century* (Boston, 1980), 292; LWD to B. J. McKinney, Feb. 13, LWD to Samuel Applewhite, July 12, 1932, DP 232.

3. Miami, Arizona, *Silver Belt*, Sept. 9, 1932; LWD to FDR, July 14, FDR to LWD, July 20, 28, 1932, DP 174.

4. *Arizona Republic* (formerly the *Republican*), July 29, Aug. 3, 11, 1932; *Arizona Daily Star*, Aug. 11, 12, Sept. 1, 1932.

5. Benson *News*, Dec. 4, 1931; William Coxon, speech delivered at Phoenix, Arizona, Aug. 2, 1932, DP 231; *Arizona Fax*, July 29, 1932.

6. Dean Acheson to LWD, Sept. 7, LWD to Acheson, Sept. 21, 1932, box 9, Acheson Papers, Yale University; Clarence B. Kelland, "Reminiscences," COHC; Robert C. McManus, "Best Apple in the Barrel," *North American Review*, 234 (Sept., 1932), 275-279; *Arizona Gazette*, Aug. 6, 1932.

7. *Arizona Fax*, Aug. 12, Prescott *Courier*, Aug. 17, *Arizona Republic*, Sept. 3, 4, Miami *Silver Belt*, Aug. 19, Bisbee *Sunday Review*, Aug. 21, Arizona *Globe Record*, Sept. 9, 1932; R. J. Prochow to LWD, Aug. 30, E. Ross Housholder to LWD, Sept. 1, 1932, DP 232.

8. Yuma *Sentinel*, Sept. 13, 1932.

9. Frank Brophy to TGS, Jan. 9, 1975; Stroud I; LWD to Dean Acheson, Sept. 21, 1932, box 9, Acheson Papers; *Arizona Republic* and Miami *Silver Belt*, Sept. 2, 1932.

10. *Arizona Republic*, Sept. 14-16, 1932.

11. Peggy Douglas to LWD, Sept. 10, 1932, DP 68; campaign contributions of James and Josalee Douglas, DP 27.

12. LWD to Dean Acheson, Sept. 21, 1932, box 9, Acheson Papers; LWD to JSD, Sept. 21, 1932, Jan. 21, 1933, DP 31; Peggy Douglas 1.

13. LWD to JSD, Sept. 21, Nov. 8, 1932, DP 31; FDR to LWD, Sept. 6, 1932, DP 174; William Mathews to Louis Howe, Sept. 17, 1932, box 16, Democratic National Committee Papers, FDRL; Isabella Greenway, diary entry Aug. 26, 1932, box 42, Isabella Greenway Papers, AHSL.

14. *Arizona Gazette*, Sept. 27, 1932; Williams *News*, Sept. 30, 1932; Lorena A. Hickok, *Eleanor Roosevelt: Reluctant First Lady* (New York, 1962), 37-38.

15. LWD to FDR, Sept. 30, 1932, DP 174; LWD to JSD, Nov. 8, 1932, DP 31; FDR to Bishop Atwood, Nov. 2, 1931, in Elliott Roosevelt, ed., *FDR: His Personal Letters, 1928-1945* (2 vols., New York, 1950), I, 226-227; Frank Freidel, *Franklin D. Roosevelt: The Triumph* (Boston, 1956), 361-363; Samuel P. Applewhite to FDR, Sept. 15, 1932, box 15, Democratic National Committee Papers, FDRL. Nearly a year after the visit to Arizona an acquaintance wrote Roosevelt: "I doubt if Isabella, with all her remarkable intuition, realized what she was doing when she brought Lewis Douglas in contact with you that day. I had a feeling at the time that we were listening to the next president but not the least suspicion that he was talking to the Director of the Budget." Grosvenor Atterbury to FDR, Aug. 8, 1933, PPF 741, FDRL.

16. Democratic State Central Committee, Campaign Itinerary for LWD and B. B. Moeur, Sept. 28, 1932, DP 232: *Arizona Daily Star*, Oct. 16, *Arizona Republic*, Oct. 26, 1932; Yuma *Sentinel*, Oct. 5, 7, Bisbee *Ore*, Oct. 5, Arizona *Globe Democrat*, Oct. 7, Florence *Blade*, Oct. 14, Graham County *Guardian*, Oct. 28, 1932; *Statistics of the Congressional and Presidential Election of November 8, 1932*, DP 232.

17. Rexford Tugwell diary, Dec. 23, 1932, Tugwell Papers, FDRL; Arthur Schlesinger, Jr., *The Age of Roosevelt: The Crisis of the Old Order: 1919-1933* (Boston, 1957), 448-449; Jordan A. Schwarz, *The Interregnum of Despair: Hoover, Congress, and the Depression* (Urbana, Ill., 1970), 205-229.

18. LWD, "Economy in Federal Government," *Proceedings of the Academy of Political Science*, XV (Jan., 1933), 172-177; Frank Freidel, *Franklin D. Roosevelt: Launching the New Deal* (Boston, 1973), 51-54; LWD to JSD, Nov. 8, 1932, DP 31; LWD to William Mathews, Dec. 29, 1932, DP 78.

19. LWD to Frank Brophy, Dec. 29, 1932, DP 77; LWD to Walter Lippmann, Nov. 30, 1932, box 67, Lippmann Papers, Yale University.

20. Freidel, *Launching*, 31-39; James MacGregor Burns, *Roosevelt: The Lion and the Fox* (New York, 1956), 145-146; LWD to JSD, Nov. 24, 1932, DP 31; Josalee Douglas to LWD, Nov. 25, 1932, DP 65.

21. LWD to FDR, Dec. 7, Guernsey T. Cross (Secretary to Governor Roosevelt) to LWD, Dec. 10, 1932, DP 174. LWD to JSD, Dec. 18, 1932, DP 31.

22. LWD to Walter Stewart, Dec. 14, 1932, LWD to Colonel Edward House, Jan. 14, 1933, DP 174; LWD to William Mathews, Dec. 29, 1932, DP 78; LWD to Raymond Moley, May 4, 1964, DP 118; LWD to FDR, Dec. 19, 1932, PPF 820, FDRL; *New York Times*, Dec. 19, 20, 1932; Freidel, *Launching*, 40-42; Paul K. Conkin, *The New Deal* (New York, 1967), 30-33; William E. Leuchtenburg, *Franklin D. Roosevelt and the New Deal, 1932-1940* (New York, 1963), 31-32.

23. Henry L. Stimson diary, Dec. 21, 1932,

Yale University; Herbert Feis, *1933: Characters in Crisis* (Boston, 1966), 47; *New York Times*, Dec. 21, 22, 1932.

24. LWD to William Mathews, Dec. 29, 1932, DP 78; Stimson diary, Dec. 21, 1932.

25. Tugwell diary, Dec. 25, 1932, FDRL.

26. LWD to JSD, Jan. 21, 1933, DP 31.

27. LWD to FDR, Dec. 30, 1932, DP 174; *Congressional Record*, 72 Cong., 2 Sess., 4589–4613; Rexford Tugwell, *In Search of Roosevelt* (Cambridge, Mass., 1972), 216.

28. LWD to JSD, March 12, 1933, DP 31; Douglas, Roper, and Sherley to FDR, Feb. 19, 1933, DP 237; LWD to Raymond Moley, May 4, 1964, DP 118; The Unofficial Observer (J. F. Carter), *The New Dealers* (New York, 1934), 266; Freidel, *Launching*, 241–242. The committee prepared more than two hundred memoranda dealing with government economy. See National Archives, Record Group 51, Bureau of the Budget Series 32.2, boxes 1–3. Douglas worked mainly on reducing veterans expenditures. He wrote a friend: "If I had my way I would cut the veterans four hundred million dollars and I think I am going to have my way." LWD to William Mathews, Feb. 15, 1933, DP 78.

29. Freidel, *Launching*, 70; LWD to FDR, Jan. 19, FDR to LWD, Feb. 3, 1933, DP 174; LWD to JSD, Jan. 21, 30, 1933, DP 31.

30. LWD, memorandum for FDR, Feb. 18, 1933, DP 236. For the banking crisis, see Leuchtenburg, *Franklin D. Roosevelt*, 38–39.

31. Washington *Daily News*, Jan. 5, *Arizona Fax*, Jan. 13, *Buckeye Review*, Jan. 20, *Dunbar's Weekly*, Feb. 3, 1933; LWD to JSD, Jan. 21, 30, 1933, DP 31; LWD to FDR, Dec. 30, 1932, DP 174.

32. FDR to Swagar Sherley, Jan. 17, 1933, box 2, Special File, Governor's Correspondence, FDRL; Tugwell diary, Dec. 29, 1932, FDRL; James F. Byrnes, *All in One Lifetime* (New York, 1958), 67.

33. Peggy Douglas I; LWD to Raymond Moley, May 4, 1964, DP 118; LWD to Governor B. B. Moeur, Feb. 24, 1933, DP 233.

34. New York *Herald Tribune*, Feb. 24, 1933; "Will Rogers Says," Washington *Times*, Feb. 25, 1933. For letters of congratulation and press comment, see DP 234, 235.

35. *New York Times*, Feb. 24, *Wall Street Journal*, Feb. 24, 1933; McCloy to LWD, Feb. 24, 1933, DP 234; *Congressional Record*, 72 Cong., 2 Sess., 5552; Garner quoted in unidentified newsclip. DP 234; *Arizona Daily Star, Arizona Republic, Dunbar's Weekly*, Feb. 23–25, 1933; Elizabeth (Ellie) Douglas to LWD, Feb. 23, 1933, DP 234. Someone wrote on a newsclip: "Dear Peg: Proud as you always have justly been of him, & convinced of his superlative qualities, this must give you an extra little flutter in your warm heart!," ibid.

CHAPTER 8 *Working with Roosevelt*

1. Howard Zinn, *New Deal Thought* (New York, 1966); Paul K. Conkin, *The New Deal* (New York, 1967); Barton J. Bernstein, "The New Deal: The Conservative Achievements of Liberal Reform," in Bernstein, ed., *Towards a New Past: Dissenting Essays in American History* (New York, 1968); Frank Freidel, *Franklin D. Roosevelt: Launching the New Deal* (Boston, 1973); James E. Sargent, *Roosevelt and the Hundred Days: Struggle for the Early New Deal* (New York, 1981); Milton Katz, "From Hoover to Roosevelt," in Katie Louchheim, ed., *The Making of the New Deal: The Insiders Speak* (Cambridge, Mass., 1983); 121–122. For the importance of the Budget Office in the early New Deal, see A. J. Wann, *The President as Chief Administrator: A Study of Franklin D. Roosevelt* (Washington, D.C., 1968), 16, 40–46; Lewis H. Kimmel, *Federal Budget and Fiscal Policy, 1789–1958* (Washington, D.C., 1959), 175–176, 215; Arthur Krock, *Memoirs: Sixty Years on the Firing Line* (New York, 1968), 159; Rexford Tugwell, *The Democratic Roosevelt: A Biography* (Garden City, N.Y., 1957), 265.

2. For Douglas's influence, see William E. Leuchtenburg, *Franklin D. Roosevelt and the New Deal* (New York, 1963), 36–37, 45; James MacGregor Burns, *Roosevelt: The Lion and the Fox* (New York, 1956), 172, 234–237; James E. Sargent, "FDR and Lewis W. Douglas: Budget Balancing and the Early New Deal," *Prologue*, 6 (Spring, 1974), 33–43; Albert Shaw, "Executives in the New Deal," *Review of Reviews*, LXXXVII (April, 1933), 30; James P. Warburg, *The Long Road Home: The Autobiography of a Maverick* (Garden City, N.Y., 1964), 113; Arthur Krock in the *New York Times*, April 28, May 19, 1933; Charles Wyzanski, Jr., to Judge Learned Hand, May 11, 1933; box 108, Learned Hand Papers, Harvard Law School; Charles G. Ross, "A Man Who Can Say No with a Smile," *Literary Digest*, CXVI (July 8, 1933), 3–4; Turner Catledge, "A Hard-Hitter Strikes at the Budget," *New York Times Magazine*, March 19, 1933; Russell Owen, "The 'Brain Trust' Mirrors Many Minds," *New York Times Magazine*, June 11, 1933; William Hurd, "The Nation's New Leaders," *Current History*, 38 (May, 1933), 146; *Newsweek*, 1 (June 24, 1933), 5; Morris Markey, "He's Got His Hand in Your Pocket," *American Magazine*, CXVI (June, 1933), 22–23.

3. Ernest K. Lindley, *The Roosevelt Revolution: First Phase* (New York, 1933), 286; The Unofficial Observer (J. F. Carter), *The New Dealers* (New York, 1934), 125; Raymond Moley, *After Seven Years* (New York, 1939), 166; Raymond Moley, assisted by Elliot A. Rosen, *The First New Deal* (New York, 1966), 238;

Rexford Tugwell, *Roosevelt's Revolution: The First Year—A Personal Perspective* (New York, 1977), 98–100; Peggy Douglas 1.

4. LWD to JSD, March 12, 1933, DP 31.

5. James Warburg, diary, July 23, 1933, 1177–1178, 1180, COHC; James A. Farley, *Behind the Ballots: The Personal History of a Politician* (New York, 1938), 217–218; Frances Perkins, "Reminiscences," book 5, 26, COHC; JSD to LWD, March 16, 1933, DP 31. Douglas's tart reply to his father was written on the margin of the March 16 letter. FDR to Colonel Edward M. House, April 5, 1933, in Elliott Roosevelt, ed., *FDR: His Personal Letters, 1928–1945* (2 vols., New York, 1950), I, 342; Moley, *First New Deal*, 352; Raymond Moley, *27 Masters of Politics: In a Personal Perspective* (New York, 1949), 41; Harold L. Ickes, *The Secret Diary of Harold L. Ickes* (3 vols., New York, 1953–1954), II, 518.

6. New York *World Telegram*, March 15, 25, 1933; "In the Saddle," *Collier's* (July 29, 1933), 26–27; LWD to JSD, March 5, 12, April 5, 16, JSD to LWD, March 16, 1933, DP 31; Stroud 1.

7. LWD to JSD, April 5, 1933, DP 31; LWD interview with James Sargent, DP 119; Unofficial Observer, *The New Dealers*, 121, 320, Boston *Herald*, April 28, 1933. Charles Wyzanski called Douglas "the real Secretary of the Treasury," and Charles S. Hamlin of the Federal Reserve Board expected Douglas to succeed Woodin. See Wyzanski to Judge Learned Hand, May 11, 1933, box 108, Hand Papers; Charles S. Hamlin, diary, May 18, 1933, 73, vol. 23, Hamlin Papers, Library of Congress.

8. Ickes, *Diary*, I, 3; George Martin, *Madam Secretary: Frances Perkins* (Boston, 1976), 16; Freidel, *Launching*, 175–195, 213–215; LWD to JSD, March 5, 1933, DP 31; *Arizona Daily Star*, March 3, *New York Times*, March 8, 1933; LWD, personal memorandum, "The Final Report to Governor Roosevelt," Feb., 1933, DP 200; Lewis W. Douglas, "Grenny in the 1930s and 1940s," in *Memoirs of a Man: Grenville Clark*, collected by Mary Clark Dimond, ed. by Norman Cousins and J. Garry Clifford (New York, 1975), 196–197.

9. LWD to Raymond Moley, May 4, 1964, DP 118; LWD interview with James Sargent, DP 119.

10. Franklin D. Roosevelt, *The Public Papers and Addresses of Franklin D. Roosevelt*, compiled by Samuel I. Rosenman (13 vols., New York, 1938–1950), II, 49–51; LWD draft of Economy Bill, DP 200; *New York Times*, March 11, 1933; James E. Sargent, "Roosevelt's Economy Act: Fiscal Conservatism and the Early New Deal," *Congressional Studies*, VII (Winter, 1980), 33–51; Burns, *The Lion and the Fox*, 167–168; Leuchtenburg, *Franklin D. Roosevelt*, 45.

11. Wann, *The President as Chief Administrator*, 24; Barry Dean Karl, *Executive Reorganization and Reform in the New Deal: The Genesis of Administrative Management, 1900–1939* (Cambridge, Mass., 1963), 190–191; LWD to JSD, March 12, 16, 1933, DP 31; LWD, personal memorandum, March 29, 1933, DP 200; Sargent, *Hundred Days*, 112–113, 117–118; LWD, radio broadcast typescript, "Economy and Human Values," DP 200; *New York Times*, March 19, 24, 1933. Conservatives were delighted with the legislation, but some liberals feared that Douglas's cuts would be excessive. James Warburg, diary, May 30, 1933, 861, COHC. See also Thomas Lamont to Lady Sibyl Colefax, April 14, 1933, box 87, Thomas Lamont Papers, Harvard Business School; *Wall Street Journal*, March 14, 1933; Felix Frankfurter to Acheson, March 13, 18, 22, Acheson to Frankfurter, March 13, 24, 1933, box 11, Acheson Papers, Yale University; Alan Brinkley, *Voices of Protest: Huey Long, Father Coughlin and the Great Depression* (New York, 1982), 59–60.

12. Executive assistant, A. D. Hiller, memorandum for the administrator, General Frank T. Hines, March 20, 1933, DP 206; William Mathews to LWD, April 1, 1933, DP 69; LWD to JSD, April 5, 1933, DP 31; Gordon Browning, "Reminiscences," 134, COHC; *New York Times*, March 31, 1933.

13. *Public Papers*, II, 99–100; *New York Times*, April 1–2, *New York Herald Tribune*, April 2, 1933; Roger Burlingame, "Counter-Attack," *Atlantic Monthly*, CLII (November, 1933), 533; Freidel, *Launching*, 448; *Newsweek*, I (March 25, 1933), 7–8; Ann Hard, "A Veteran Cuts the Budget," New York *Herald Tribune Magazine*, (April 16, 1933); LWD to JSD, April 5, 1933, DP 31.

14. *New York Times*, April 2, 1933; newspaper comments may be found in "Whittling Down Roosevelt Economy," *The Literary Digest*, CXV (June 17, 1933), 3–4; Frank Hines to FDR, May 6, LWD to FDR, May 8, Louis Johnson to FDR, April 10, Wallace O. Adkins to FDR, June 7, LWD, draft reply for FDR to James O. Turner, April 15, 1933, OF 95-D, FDRL; "Fraidy Cat" to LWD, March 23, 1933, and numerous other letters of complaint in DP 201; Boston *Globe*, Aug. 1, 1933.

15. LWD interview with James Sargent, DP 119, LWD to Raymond Moley, May 4, 1964, DP 118; Roosevelt, *Public Papers*, II, 168; *New York Times*, May 11, 1933; Sargent, *Hundred Days*, 211; Freidel, *Launching*, 449.

16. Ibid., 252–253, 260–261; LWD interview with James Sargent, DP 119; FDR press conferences, March 22, 24, 1933, I, 62–64, 77–79, FDRL; Sargent, "FDR and Lewis W. Douglas," 36–37.

17. LWD, personal memorandum, March 27, 1933, DP 200.

18. Colonel Kyle Rucker, memorandum for the Secretary of War, March 11, 1933, OF 268, FDRL; Rucker, memorandum for Secretary of War, April 3, 1933, box 69, Louis Howe Papers, FDRL; LWD to FDR, April 2, 1933, OF 8, FDRL; CCC newspaper *Happy Days*, Sept. 30, 1933, RG 35, NA; Edgar B. Nixon, ed., *Franklin D. Roosevelt and Conservation, 1911–1945* (2 vols., New York, 1957), I, 138–139; LWD interview with James Sargent, DP 119; *New York Times*, March 25, 1933; Sargent, *Hundred Days*, 108; Freidel, *Launching*, 255–260.

19. LWD, *RR*, 23–25.

20. Van L. Perkins, *Crisis in Agriculture: The Agricultural Adjustment Administration and the New Deal, 1933* (Berkeley and Los Angeles, 1969), 36–37; Theodore Salutous, *The American Farmer and the New Deal* (Ames, Iowa, 1982), 3–33; Freidel, *Launching*, 83–101, 229–308; LWD to JSD, April 5, 1933, DP 31; Paul Appleby "Reminiscences," COHC; Warburg, diary, March 23, 1933, 207, 210, COHC; LWD interview with James Sargent, DP 119; Roosevelt, *Public Papers*, II, 74–79, 175–183.

21. LWD to JSD, April 5, 1933, DP 31; Warburg, diary, April 13, 14, 1933, 460, COHC; Bernard Baruch to LWD, April 22, 1933, Bernard Baruch Papers, Princeton University.

22. Freidel, *Launching*, 323, 330–332; Leuchtenburg, *Franklin D. Roosevelt*, 50–51.

23. LWD interview with James Sargent, DP 119; Warburg, diary, April 18, 1933, 497–499, COHC; Warburg, *Long Road Home*, 119–120; Ickes, *Diary*, I, 658–659; Moley, *First New Deal*, 302–303; Moley, *After Seven Years*, 158–161; Herbert Feis, *1933: Characters in Crisis* (Boston, 1966), 124–131; Adolf Berle, memorandum, April 24, 1933, box 15, Adolf Berle Papers, FDRL.

24. William E. Leuchtenburg, "Reminiscences," 24–25, COHC; Leuchtenburg, *Franklin D. Roosevelt*, 51; Warburg, diary, April 18, 1933, 504, COHC; Baruch quoted in Arthur Schlesinger, Jr., *The Age of Roosevelt: The Coming of the New Deal* (Boston, 1958), 201; Moley quoted in Sargent, *Hundred Days*, 178; LWD, *RR*, 4–5.

25. LWD to JSD, April 23, 1933, DP 31; LWD, personal memorandum, "Notes on Greenbacks," DP 211; Warburg, diary, April 19, 1933, 509–511, 512–517, COHC; Thomas Lamont to G. Fummi, April 28, 1933, box 138, Lamont Papers.

26. LWD interview with James Sargent, DP 119.

27. Ibid.; LWD to JSD, May 27, 1933, DP 31.

28. Freidel, *Launching*, 416–421; Warburg, diary, March 19, 23, 1933, 183, 207, COHC; LWD, *RR*, 23–25.

29. Frances Perkins, *The Roosevelt I Knew* (New York, 1946), 197–198, 269–271; Warburg, Diary, April 3, 1933, 333, COHC; Perkins, "Reminiscences," book 4, 535–536, book 5, 1–3, COHC.

30. Freidel, *Launching*, 422–435; Perkins, *Roosevelt*, 272–273; Perkins, "Reminiscences," book 5, 10, COHC; Ickes, *Diary*, I, 28; Charles Wyzanski, Jr., to parents, April 29, 1933, quoted in Freidel, *Launching*, 431.

31. Sargent, *Hundred Days*, 205–206; LWD to JSD, May 7, 1933, DP 31.

32. Robert F. Himmelberg, *The Origins of the National Recovery Administration: Business, Government, and the Trade Association Issue, 1921–1933* (New York, 1976), 190, 200–201; Ellis W. Hawley, *The New Deal and the Problem of Monopoly: A Study in Economic Ambivalence* (Princeton, 1966), 25, 42; Donald Richberg, *My Hero: The Indiscreet Memoirs of an Eventful but Unheroic Life* (New York, 1954), 164–165; Donald Richberg, *The Rainbow* (New York, 1936), 106–114; Ickes, *Diary*, I, 35; Hugh S. Johnson, *The Blue Eagle from Egg to Earth* (Garden City, N.Y., 1935), 193–195; *New York Times*, May 9, 14, 1933.

33. Perkins, "Reminiscences," book 5, 75–85, COHC.

34. *New York Times*, May 19, 1933; FDR press conference, June 16, 1933, 398, FDRL; Tugwell, *Roosevelt's Revolution*, 165, 169; Sargent, "FDR and Lewis W. Douglas," 38.

35. LWD to JSD, April 23, 1933, DP 31; Warburg, Diary, April 3, 1933, 133, 346, COHC; Ickes, *Diary*, I, 11, 14; Henry Wallace, "Reminiscences," 199–200, COHC; Rex Tugwell, Addendum to Diary for the Hundred Days, 3–4, box 19, Tugwell Papers; Henry Morgenthau, Farm Credit Administration Diary, May 24, 29, June 5, 12, 1933, 34–35, 37, 40, 44, Morgenthau Papers, FDRL; Mordecai Ezekiel, memorandum for Secretary of Agriculture, May 27, 1933, box 1, Ezekiel Papers, FDRL.

36. LWD, *RR*, 1–5; Douglas MacArthur, *Reminiscences: General of the Army Douglas MacArthur* (New York, 1964), 100–101; *New York Times*, April 27, 1933.

37. Newsclip, LWD folder, box 127, Clapper Papers, LC; Sargent, *Hundred Days*, 41; *New York Times*, April 13, May 4, 1933; Charles E. Wyzanski, Jr., to Judge Learned Hand, May 11, 1933, box 108, Hand Papers; Warburg, Diary, May 30, 1933, 364, COHC; Tugwell, Diary, May 31, 1933; Freidel, *Launching*, 452–453.

38. Ibid., 252, 448–453; Sargent, *Hundred Days*, 242–248, 250–262; *New York Times*, May 27, June 6, 1933; Burlingame, "Counter-Attack," 527–538; LWD to JSD, June 8, 1933, DP 31; Roosevelt, *Public Papers*, II, 222–225; Karl, *Executive Reorganization*, 190–191; Wann, *President as Chief Administrator*, 25; FDR press conferences, March 22, May 19, 1933, 62, 281, FDRL.

39. Walter Lippmann to LWD, June 16, LWD to Lippmann, June 27, 1933, DP 201.

CHAPTER 9 *Resistance and Resignation*

1. LWD to JSD, April 23, May 7, 27, 1933, DP 31. In early April Roosevelt invited representatives from Great Britain, France, and nine other nations to Washington for bilateral economic talks. Those discussions, in which Douglas was a major participant, proved a failure. LWD, RR, 6–7; Sir Frederick Leith-Ross, *Money Talks: Fifty Years of International Finance* (London, 1968), 166–167; Raymond Moley, *After Seven Years* (New York, 1939), 210–212.

2. James P. Warburg, *The Money Muddle* (New York, 1934), 120–127; James P. Warburg, *The Long Road Home* (New York, 1964), 132, 139–140; *New York Times*, June 22, 1933; LWD to Walter Lippmann, June 27, 1933, DP 238.

3. Moley, *After Seven Years*, 245–253. For accounts of the London Conference, see Frank Freidel, *Franklin D. Roosevelt: Launching the New Deal* (Boston, 1973), 470–489; Robert Dallek, *Franklin D. Roosevelt and American Foreign Policy, 1932–1945* (New York, 1979), 49–58; Arthur Schlesinger, Jr., *The Age of Roosevelt: The Coming of the New Deal* (Boston, 1958), 213–232; Paul K. Conkin, *The New Deal* (New York, 1967), 45.

4. LWD, RR, folder 8; James E. Sargent, "Oral History, Franklin D. Roosevelt, and the New Deal: Some Recollections of Adolf A. Berle, Jr., Lewis W. Douglas, and Raymond Moley," *Oral History Review* (1973), 102; LWD interview with James Sargent, DP 119.

5. LWD, personal memorandum, June 30, 1933, DP 236; confidential proceedings, executive session, Special Board for Public Works, July 1, 1933, DP 244; *New York Times*, July 7, 1933; LWD to JSD, July 8, 23, 1933, DP 31; Harold Ickes, *Back to Work* (New York, 1935), 23–27; Rexford Tugwell, *Roosevelt's Revolution: The First Year—A Personal Perspective* (New York, 1977), 165, 169–173; "Diogenes, The Controversy," *Literary Digest*, 116 (July 15, 1933), 10; William E. Leuchtenburg, *Franklin D. Roosevelt and the New Deal* (New York, 1963), 70.

6. George Warren, Diary, March 5, April 12, July 10, George Warren to FDR, March 16, 25, April 24, 1933, Warren Papers, Cornell University; Warburg, *Money Muddle*, 66–70; Freidel, *Launching*, 88, 325; Schlesinger, *Coming of the New Deal*, 234; The Unofficial Observer, *The New Dealers* (New York, 1934), 133–139; Leuchtenburg, *Franklin D. Roosevelt*, 78–79.

7. LWD to JSD, July 11, 1933, DP 31.

8. James Warburg, Diary, July 12, 20, 1933, 1128, 1165–1166, COHC; LWD, memorandum for FDR, July 20, 1933, DP 236.

9. Warburg, Diary, July 23, 24, 1933, 1177–1180, 1183–1195, COHC; LWD to JSD, July 23, 1933, DP 31; Warren, Diary, July 24, 1933.

10. LWD to JSD, Aug. 20, 1933, DP 31; John J. McCloy to LWD, Oct. 17, 1933, DP 75; Fred Lowery, *History of a Fishing Trip* (privately printed, 1934).

11. LWD to JSD, Aug. 20, 1933, DP 31; Schlesinger, *Coming of the New Deal*, 236; Warburg, Diary, August 8, 1933, 1251–1254, COHC; Warburg, *Long Road Home*, 144–145; Herbert Feis, *1933: Characters in Crisis* (Boston, 1966), 280–282.

12. Warburg, suggested agenda for Monetary Group, with LWD's penciled comments, Aug. 14, 1933, DP 248; LWD, Memorandum Regarding Issue of Thomas Amendment Notes for Purpose of Retiring Maturing Public Debt, Aug. 18, 1933, box 7, Warburg Papers, JFKL; Oliver Sprague to Warburg, Aug. 30, 1933, Warburg to Sprague, Aug. 31, 1933, ibid.; LWD to JSD, Aug. 30, 1933, DP 31; Interim Monetary Report, Aug. 30, 1933, DP 248; Feis, *Characters*, 282–283.

13. JSD to LWD, June 30, Aug. 4, Sept. 23, LWD to JSD, June 26, Aug. 31, Sept. 29, 1933, DP 31; LWD interview with James Sargent, DP 119.

14. Schlesinger, *Coming of the New Deal*, 236–237; LWD to JSD, Sept. 14, 1933, DP 31.

15. Warburg, Diary, Sept. 21, 1933, 1458–1463, COHC; LWD, Diary, Sept. 27, 1933, DP 31; New York *Herald Tribune*, Sept. 25, 1933; William Woodin, "Report for the President," Sept. 28, 1933, DP 248; FDR to Woodin, Sept. 30, 1933, quoted in Schlesinger, *Coming of the New Deal*, 238.

16. Warburg to FDR, Sept. 29, 1933 (not sent), box 6, Warburg Papers, JFKL; LWD to JSD, Sept. 29, 1933, DP 31; LWD to Frank Brophy, Sept. 30, 1933, DP 77.

17. LWD, Diary, Sept. 25, LWD to JSD, Sept. 29, 1933, DP 31; LWD, draft of American Legion Speech, Sept. 27, 1933, DP 236; FDR, before the American Legion Convention, Oct. 2, 1933, DP 243.

18. James Warburg to Dean Acheson, Oct. 12, 13, 1933, DP 247; Monetary Group, draft documents, Oct. 16, 20, 1933, DP 248; Dean Acheson, *Morning and Noon* (Boston, 1965), 174–194; Warren, Diary, Oct. 6, 20, Warren to FDR, Oct. 16, 1933, Warren Papers; Harold L. Ickes, *The Secret Diary of Harold L. Ickes* (3 vols., New York, 1953), I, 110, 113; Feis, *Characters*, 285–286.

19. Warren, Diary, Oct. 22, 1933; Warburg, Diary, Oct. 25, 1933, 1644–1645, COHC; Warburg to James Cox, Oct. 30, Cox to Warburg, Nov. 1, 1933 (not sent), DP 236; LWD, memorandum for FDR, Oct. 21, 1933, Record Group 51, Bureau of Budget, Series 21.1, box I-7, NA.

20. LWD, Diary, Sept. 27, 1933, DP 31.

Notes to Chapter 9

21. Ickes, *Diary*, I, 108–109; J. F. T. O'Connor, Diary, Oct. 6, 16, 1933, FDRL; Jesse Jones and Edward Angly, *Fifty Billion Dollars* (New York, 1951), 30ff; Bascom Timmons, *Jesse H. Jones* (New York, 1956), 198–200; Freidel, *Launching*, 235–236; Schlesinger, *Coming of the New Deal*, 429–430.

22. *New Republic*, LXXVI (Nov. 29, 1933), 71.

23. Ickes, *Diary*, I, 115; Warren, Diary, Oct. 25, 29, 1933; Henry Morgenthau, Farm Credit Diary, Oct. 27, 1933, 101; Morgenthau Papers, FDRL; Charles Hamlin, Diary, Nov. 15, 18, 1933, Hamlin Papers, LC; LWD to JSD, Nov. 20, 1933, DP 31; Warburg, Diary, Nov. 17, 1933, 1759, COHC; Grace Tully, *F.D.R., My Boss* (New York, 1949), 178; Schlesinger, *Coming of the New Deal*, 242–245; Burns, *The Lion and the Fox*, 206.

24. LWD, personal memorandum, Jan. 12 1934, DP 236; LWD to William Mathews, Dec. 1, 1933, DP 78; LWD to Parker Corning, Dec. 2, 1933, DP 237.

25. LWD to Representative John McDuffie, Dec. 2, 1933, DP 237; LWD to Walter Lippmann, Dec. 17, 1933, DP 238; LWD, address before the Ninth New England Conference, Nov. 23, 1933, DP 237; *New York Times*, Nov. 24, 1933; Rex Tugwell to LWD, Nov. 27, 1933, DP 238.

26. FDR press conference, Dec. 13, 1933, II, 538, FDRL; LWD, personal memorandum, Dec. 13, 1933, DP 237; *New York Times*, Dec. 12, 1933; Walter Lippmann, "Today and Tomorrow," New York *Herald Tribune*, Dec. 14, 1933.

27. LWD to JSD, Dec. 22, 1933, DP 31.

28. LWD, memorandum on conversation with the President, Dec. 29, 30, 1933, LWD, draft number 15 of Budget Message, DP 236.

29. LWD, memorandum for FDR, Dec. 30, 1933, DP 236.

30. Ickes, *Diary*, I, 134; LWD to Arthur Schlesinger, Jr., Aug. 4, 1959, DP 306; LWD to JSD, Jan. 26, 1934, DP 31.

31. FDR, press conference, Jan. 3, 1934, III, 25–29, FDRL; *New York Times*, Jan. 5, 1934; Unofficial Observer, *New Dealers*, 127.

32. FDR, executive orders of Jan. 3, 6, LWD, memorandum on conference with the President, Jan. 9, 1934, DP 236; Ickes, *Diary*, I, 134–136; *New Republic*, LXXVII (Jan. 24, 1934), 307; Dean Acheson to James Warburg, Jan. 7, Warburg to Acheson, Jan. 11, 1934, box 13, Warburg Papers.

33. Keynes quoted in Leuchtenburg, *Franklin D. Roosevelt*, 81; Thomas Lamont, personal memorandum, Dec. 7, 1933, box 107, Lamont Papers; Ickes, *Diary*, I, 140; LWD, personal memorandum, Jan. 12, 1934, DP 236.

34. LWD, personal memorandum, Jan. 13, 16, 1934, DP 236; Schlesinger, *Coming of the New Deal*, 246; Albert U. Romasco, *The Politics of Recovery: Roosevelt's New Deal* (New York, 1983), 91–118.

35. LWD, memorandum for FDR, Jan. 24, 1934, DP 236; Ickes, *Diary*, I, 143; *New York Times*, Jan. 28, 1934; LWD, personal memorandum, Feb. 1, 1934, DP 236; LWD to Harry Hopkins attached to letter to Henry Morgenthau, Feb. 16, 1934, box 79, Morgenthau Papers; LWD to William Mathews, April 7, 1934, DP 78.

36. LWD, memorandum on Cabinet Meeting of Feb. 9, LWD, notes on meeting at the President's bedside, Feb. 12, LWD, notes on meeting of Executive Council, Feb. 13, LWD, to JSD, Feb. 11, 1934, DP 31; Schlesinger, *Coming of the New Deal*, 446–452.

37. LWD to JSD, March 2, 28, April 5, 15, LWD, memorandum of a conversation with Colonel Edward House, Feb. 22, 1934, DP 31; LWD to House, April 16, 1934, DP 238. Liberals were growing increasingly disenchanted with the budget director. Disturbed that a man of Douglas's ability was "so insensitive to the intellectual currents of his generation," the Pulitzer-prize-winning poet Archibald MacLeish planned a critical appraisal in an article in *Fortune*. Dean Acheson dissuaded MacLeish, describing Douglas as "one of the only living conservatives of the time." For Acheson's defense of Douglas, see Acheson to MacLeish, April 6, 1934, reprinted in David S. McLellan and David C. Acheson, eds., *Among Friends: Personal Letters of Dean Acheson* (New York, 1980), 20–22.

38. LWD, memorandum as to possible veto of Independent Offices Bill, March 27, FDR, veto message to Congress, March 27, 1934, DP 243; LWD to JSD, March 28, 1934, DP 31; James Byrnes, *All in One Lifetime* (New York, 1958), 75–76.

39. LWD, personal memorandum, April 5, 1934, DP 237; LWD, memorandum for FDR, April 13, 1934, OF 79, FDRL; LWD, memorandum on White House Conference, April 23, 1934, DP 236.

40. LWD to JSD, April 27, May 4, 1934, DP 31; Ickes, *Diary*, I, 163; LWD to Walter Lippmann, May 28, 1934, DP 238; Tugwell, *Roosevelt's Revolution*, 96–97. Dean Acheson, who shared Douglas's fears of central planning, referred to him as "a leader" who grasped "perfectly what the advocates of a planned and regimented national life want to achieve." But his loyalty to FDR and his fleeting hope "that the situation may swing around to his point of view, makes it impossible for him to lead in public debate in opposition to the whole program." Acheson to MacLeish, April 6, 1934, as found in McLellan and Acheson, eds., *Among Friends*, 20–22.

41. LWD to Arthur Curlee, May 9, 1934, DP 238; LWD to JSD, May 4, 12, 25, JSD to LWD, May 17, 1934, DP 31.

42. LWD, memorandum on conference at the White House, June 7, LWD, personal mem-

oranda, June 11, 12, 14, 15, 1934, DP 236; Sargent, "FDR and Lewis W. Douglas," 40–42.

43. LWD to JSD, June 6, 30, 1934, DP 31; LWD, personal memorandum, June 28, 1934, DP 236; Peggy Douglas I.

44. LWD, memorandum for FDR, June 29, 1934, DP 236; Ickes, *Diary*, I, 173–174.

45. LWD to FDR, June 29, 1934 (not sent), DP 236; LWD to JSD, July 9, 10, 11, 18, Aug. 6, 16, 19, 1934, DP 31; LWD to Swagar Sherley, Aug. 19, 1934, DP 238; Peggy Douglas I.

46. LWD to JSD, Aug. 26, Sept. 3, 1934, DP 31; LWD to Charles E. Perkins, Sept. 6, 1934, DP 237; LWD to William Mathews, Sept. 6, 12, 1934, DP 78.

47. LWD, copy of longhand notes on visit with President, Thursday, Aug. 30, LWD to JSD, Sept. 3, 1934, DP 31; LWD to FDR, Aug. 30, FDR to LWD, Sept. 1, 1934, PPF 1914, FDRL; Morgenthau, Diary, Aug. 31, 1934, vol. 2, 60–61; Jacob Viner, "Reminiscences," 52, COHC. Douglas recounted the details of his resignation to several correspondents in DP 236. In his later years, Douglas insisted that Roosevelt offered him the Treasury secretaryship or another cabinet post if he would stay on. He did not mention that offer in any of his many letters written at the time. See LWD to M. E. McMillen, March 17, 1966, DP 60.

48. LWD to JSD, Aug. 6, Sept. 8, 1934, DP 31; Harold Ickes to LWD, Sept. 8, 1934, and numerous other letters in DP 236; Hamlin, diary, Sept. 7, 1934, Hamlin Papers, LC; J. F. T. O'Connor, diary, Sept. 1, 1934, O'Connor Papers, FDRL; Frances Perkins, *The Roosevelt I Knew* (New York, 1946), 274; Perkins, "Reminiscences," book 5, 85–86, COHC.

49. FDR to LWD, Nov. 5, LWD to FDR, Nov. 28, 1934, DP 236.

50. LWD to Brendan Bracken, April 17, 1957, DP 307; LWD, RR, 4–5; Unofficial Observer, *New Dealers*, 126–128; LWD to Harold Ickes, Sept. 8, 1934, DP 236; LWD to James Byrnes, Nov. 11, 1969, DP 328; LWD to Arthur Schlesinger, Jr., Aug. 4, 1959, DP 306; LWD to Arthur Krock, Sept. 27, 1968, March 14, 1973, DP 330; LWD interview with James Sargent, DP 119.

CHAPTER 10 *Private Man and Public Critic*

1. *New York Times*, Sept. 3, 4, LWD to JSD, Sept. 8, 1934, DP 31; Isabella Greenway to LWD, Sept. 9, LWD to Greenway, Sept. 10, William C. Joyner to LWD, Sept. 15, 1934, DP 239.

2. *New York Times*, Oct. 7, 1934; LWD to JSD, Oct. 24, 30, 1934, DP 31.

3. Durwood Howes, editor of "The Youngmen's Who's Who" in the Minneapolis *Journal*, Dec. 20, 1934; LWD to JSD, Nov. 5, 1934, DP 31; James Conant to LWD, June 28,

LWD to W. B. Bell, Sept. 12, Newton Baker to LWD, Oct. 4, 1934, DP 236.

4. *New York Times*, Nov. 22, 1934; LWD to JSD, Nov. 21, 28, Dec. 25, 1934, Jan. 4, 1935, DP 31; LWD to Frank A. Vanderlip, Dec. 28, 1934, DP 236; Peggy Douglas I; LWD to W. P. Sturtevant, Dec. 4, 1934, DP 250; LWD to Newton Baker, Dec. 26, 1934, DP 252.

5. Peggy Douglas I.

6. JSD to LWD, Jan. 18, 1935, Dec. 28, 1933, DP 32, 31; LWD to JSD, Sept. 21, Oct. 11, Nov. 6, 22, Dec. 22, 1936, DP 32.

7. LWD to Robert Stroud, Nov. 30, 1934, DP 250; Stroud I; LWD I; Peggy Douglas I.

8. Don Hardy to LWD, June 23, 1935, DP 63; Raymond D. Fosdick to LWD, Dec. 18, 1934, John D. Rockefeller, Jr., to LWD, Jan. 18, 1935, DP 405; H. Morton Merriman to LWD, Nov. 20, Dr. James Ewing to LWD, Nov. 26, 1935, DP 404; *New York Times*, Nov. 1, 1936, May 4, 1937; George S. Moore to LWD, Nov. 16, 1967, DP 68; Peggy Douglas I; Rosemary Holusha, "The Douglas Art Collection," *Arizona Highways Magazine*, 56 (Nov., 1980), 38–43.

9. Brophy I; Wheeler-Bennett I; Ellinwood I; Peggy Douglas I; Astley I; Peggy Douglas to LWD, Oct. 20, 1937, DP 64. The lions' den story appeared in LWD, "Industrial Organization and the American Ideal of Living," *Proceedings of the Academy of Political Science*, XVII (Jan., 1939), 122–123.

10. Douglas's inquiries to preparatory schools are found in DP 65; Peggy Douglas I; LWD to Acheson, [n.d.] box 9, Acheson Papers, Yale University. All the summers were not funfilled. In 1937 the Davisons lost their young son Trubee to leukemia. LWD to Acheson, Sept. 15, 1937, ibid.

11. LWD to JSD, Sept. 21, 1932, JSD to LWD, Jan. 10, 1932, DP 31.

12. Peggy Douglas I; Brophy I; JSD to LWD, Nov. 28, 1932, LWD to JSD, Dec. 8 1932, April 23, May 7, 1933, DP 31.

13. Peggy Douglas I; LWD to JSD, Oct. 5, 1933, DP 31; "L. W. and P. Z. Douglas, Combined Comparative Balance Sheet, Dec. 31, 1935 and 1936," DP 319; A. C. Nussbaumer to James P. Warburg, Nov. 8, 1933, box 6, Warburg Papers, JFKL; Unofficial Observer [J. F. Carter], *The New Dealers* (New York, 1934), 125; James Landis, "Reminiscences," 238, COHC; McCloy I; Harriman I.

14. Stroud I; Smith I; Beaton I; Damsky I.

15. LWD to Josalee Douglas, June 15, 1922, DP 63; Brophy I; LWD to Brophy, Sept. 16, 1936, DP 77; Smith I; LWD to William Miller, Aug. 7, 1940, Jan. 6, 1941, DP 62; LWD to Acheson, Dec. 22, 1934, April 16, 1935, Acheson to LWD, April 18, 1935, June 30, 1936, box 9, Acheson Papers.

16. LWD to Robert Stroud, Nov. 30, 1934,

DP 250; *New York Times*, Dec. 11, 1934; LWD, Diary of a Trip Abroad, Jan., 1935, DP 250.

17. LWD to JSD, Nov. 8, 1934, DP 31; LWD, "A Policy of Recovery," *Vital Speeches of the Day*, I (Jan. 14, 1935), 229–234; *New York Times*, Dec. 13, 1934; Dean Acheson to James Warburg, Dec. 15, Warburg to Acheson, Dec. 17, 1934, box 13, Warburg Papers, JFKL; Frank Knox to Warburg, Jan. 2, 5, 1935, box 9, ibid.

18. LWD to JSD, Jan. 24, 1935, DP 32; LWD, "The Relationship between Federal Fiscal Policy and Economic and Social Stability," DP 255; *New York Times*, March 15, 1935; Henry Morgenthau, Diary of Henry Morgenthau, March 14, 1935, IV, 89–90, Morgenthau Papers; draft of reply, box 4, Stephen Early Papers, FDRL; Harold L. Ickes, *The Secret Diary of Harold L. Ickes* (3 vols., New York, 1953–1954), I, 345; Ickes, address before the Wharton School of Finance and Commerce, April 15, 1935, DP 251.

19. LWD, *The Liberal Tradition: A Free People and a Free Economy* (New York, reprint edition, 1972), xvi, 53, 102, 1–14, 101–106; LWD to Frank Brophy, Sept. 2, 1936, DP 77; LWD to J. R. Finlay, March 18, 1935, DP 255; Richard Scandrett to Charles B. Bugg, March 7, 1935, vol. 2, Scandrett Papers, Cornell University.

20. Henry Hazlitt in the *New York Times*, July 28, 1935; Nicholas Roosevelt in the New York *Herald Tribune*, Oct. 13, 1935; J. Philip Wernette in the *Harvard Business Review*, XIV (Winter, 1936), 248; Walter Lippmann to LWD, July 9, 1935, DP 253; Lewis Gannett, "Books and Things," *Herald Tribune*, July 15, 1935; William Mathews to LWD, Nov. 13, 1935, DP 78. For Douglas's published attacks against the New Deal, see his works cited in the Bibliography. *New York Times*, June 15, Sept. 26, Oct. 15, 16, Nov. 15, 26, 1935; LWD, "Why Employment Is Retarded," *Vital Speeches*, II (Nov. 4, 1935), 86–88; LWD, "There IS One Way Out: Saving—Not Spending—Will Bring Reemployment," *Atlantic Monthly*, CLVI (Sept., 1935), 267–272; LWD, "Can Government Spending Cure Unemployment?" *Atlantic Monthly*, CLVI (Oct., 1935), 408–412; LWD, "The Danger of Mounting Deficits," *Atlantic Monthly*, CLVI (Nov., 1935), 561–567; LWD, "Sound Recovery Through a Balanced Budget," *Atlantic Monthly*, CLVI (Dec., 1935), 676–680; LWD, "Blowing the Bubble!" *Atlantic Monthly*, CLVII (Jan., 1936), 40–45. The *Atlantic Monthly* articles were eventually collected under the title *There Is One Way Out* (Boston, 1936). LWD, "The Planning of Taxation, Currency and Finance," *Proceedings of the Academy of Political Science*, XVI (Jan., 1936), 491–499; H. B. Elliston, "Crusader and Budgeteer," *Christian Science Monitor Magazine*, Nov. 27, 1935; James Farley to FDR, Sept. 17, 1935, DP 251.

21. For the conservative opposition, see George Wolfskill, *The Revolt of the Conservatives* (Boston, 1962); George Wolfskill and John A. Hudson, *All But the People: Franklin D. Roosevelt and His Critics, 1933–1939* (New York, 1969); James T. Patterson, *Congressional Conservatism and the New Deal: The Growth of the Conservative Coalition in Congress, 1933–1939* (Lexington, Ky., 1967); James Warburg, *Hell Bent for Election* (New York, 1935); Arthur Schlesinger, Jr., *The Age of Roosevelt: The Politics of Upheaval* (Boston, 1960), 515–520; James MacGregor Burns, *Roosevelt: The Lion and the Fox* (New York, 1956), 240–243; Glass to LWD, Nov. 26, 1935, DP 252; LWD I; LWD to Fred Lowery, Dec. 3, 1935, DP 81.

22. LWD to Albert Simms, May 18, 1936, DP 251; LWD to Ellery Sedgwick, June 15, 1936, DP 253; LWD to Arthur Curlee, Dec. 5, 19, 1935, March 28, 1936, Curlee to LWD, Dec. 15, 1935, May 14, 1936, DP 252; William Mathews to LWD, Nov. 4, 1936, DP 78.

23. Arthur Krock to LWD, May 19, 1936, LWD to Walter Lippmann, March 23, 28, April 2, 1936, DP 253; Schlesinger, *The Politics of Upheaval*, 520–523.

24. Ibid., 515–516, LWD to Newton Baker, April 25, June 1, 1936, Baker to LWD, May 1, 1936, DP 252; *New York Times*, June 3, 4, 5, 7, 8, 1936; Walter Lippmann, "Today and Tomorrow," *New York Herald Tribune*, June 4, 1936; C. H. Cramer, *Newton D. Baker: A Biography* (Cleveland, 1961), 267–268; Springfield *Republican*, June 5, 1936. Actually Lippmann was not an impartial observer, because he participated in the planning of the declaration and commented on early drafts. See Lippmann to Baker, April 20, Baker to Lippmann, April 20, 1936, box 54, Lippmann Papers, Yale University; Lippmann to LWD, draft statement, April 16, 1936, box 67, ibid.

25. New York *Herald Tribune*, June 2, 1936; Thomas Lamont to LWD, June 3, 1936, B. C. Forbes to LWD, May 15, 1935, Harry Chandler to LWD, May 12, 1936, DP 251; Richard Scandrett to LWD, March 6, 1935, Scandrett to Jesse Barrett, March 13, 1935, volume 2, Scandrett Papers, Cornell University; Wolfskill, *Revolt of the Conservatives*, 199; Arthur Krock in the *New York Times*, June 3, 1936.

26. Unsigned telegram to LWD, June 9, 1936, Robert Stroud, memorandum for files, "Tuesday" [June 9, 1936], LWD, press statement (not released), June 11, 1936, DP 251; Alfred Landon, "Reminiscences," 26, COHC; Donald R. McCoy, *Landon of Kansas* (Lincoln, Neb., 1966), 258–259.

27. James A. Garfield to LWD, May 23, LWD to Lacy Haines, June 19, 1936, DP 251; LWD to William Mathews, June 26, 1936, DP 78; Warburg to Judge George T. McDermott, June 19, 24, Warburg to Landon, June 25, 1936, box 10, Warburg Papers, JFKL.

28. LWD to Landon, June 29, 1936, DP 253; LWD to Haines, July 4, 1936, DP 251.

29. LWD to DDE, July 12, 1956, DP 311; LWD to JSD, Sept. 1, 4, 1936, DP 32; LWD to Frank Brophy, Sept. 2, 1936, DP 77; LWD to Samuel Applewhite, Sept. 16, 1936, DP 79; O. C. Pickhardt, M.D., "Report on Lewis W. Douglas," July, 1939, DP 60; Goodman I; Lenox Hill Hospital, operative records, July 13, 1936, DP 60; *New York Times*, July 14, 1936.

30. Warburg to W. W. Cumberland, Aug. 11, 27, Landon to Warburg, Sept. 18, Warburg to Landon, Oct. 13, 1936, box 10, Warburg Papers, JFKL; Acheson to LWD, Oct. 19, 1936, DP 79; LWD to Grenville Clark, Oct. 30, LWD to Arthur Curlee, Nov. 3, 1936, DP 252; LWD to Krock, Oct. 23, 1936, DP 253; Schlesinger, *Politics of Upheaval*, 634.

31. *New York Times*, Oct. 23, 1936; LWD to JSD, Oct. 21, 24, 1936, DP 32; LWD to Krock, Oct. 23, 1936, DP 253; Acheson to LWD, Oct. 23, 1936, DP 79; Mathews to LWD, Oct. 24, 1936, DP 78.

32. LWD to Brophy, Nov. 3, 1936, DP 77; LWD to JSD, Nov. 4, 9, 1936, DP 32.

33. LWD typewritten draft of press statement, Feb. 9, 1937, DP 252; LWD to Lippmann, Jan 30, 1937, DP 253.

34. LWD to Hull, Jan. 22, 28, Hull to LWD, Jan. 26, Feb. 4, 1937, LWD, statement before the Senate Finance Committee, Feb. 15, 1937, DP 252; *New York Times*, Feb. 16, 1937.

35. LWD to Landon, March 22, April 16, Landon to LWD, April 1, 1937, DP 253; LWD to John F. Carr, March 2, 1937, DP 252; John Janney, "Keeper of the Middle Road," *American Magazine*, CXXVI (July, 1938), 36–37 ff.; Patterson, *Congressional Conservatism*, 202–206; C. David Tompkins, *Senator Arthur J. Vandenberg: The Evolution of a Modern Republican, 1884–1945* (Lansing, Mich., 1970), 154; John Robert Moore, *Senator Josiah William Bailey of North Carolina: A Political Biography* (Durham, N.C., 1968), 151–159.

36. LWD to Brophy, Sept. 16, 1936, DP 77; LWD to Curlee, May 19, 1937, DP 252.

CHAPTER 11 *An American in Canada*

1. Stanley King to LWD, Aug. 6, 1937, DP 62; LWD to JSD, Aug. 17, 1937, DP 32; LWD to Dean Acheson, Sept. 15, 1937, DP 79.

2. Cyrus MacMillan, *McGill and Its Story, 1821–1921* (London, 1921), 15–37; "Royal Victoria College," folder in box 294, and "Macdonald College," several folders in boxes 300, 301, Principal's File, McGill University Archives (hereafter PF followed by the appropriate box number).

3. For the student population, see folder "registration," PF 283; *McGill Graduate's Bulletin* 2 (Nov., 1937), DP 257; LWD interview with Carolyn Cox, March 15, 1938, PF 283; Carolyn Cox, "A Private Canadian University with a Public Service," *Christian Science Monitor*, May 24, 1938; J. C. Simpson, Associate Dean of Medicine, to LWD, Jan. 14, C. W. Hendel, Dean of Arts and Sciences, to LWD, Oct. 11, 1938, PF 272; Hon. H. Carl Goldenberg to TGS, Oct. 17, 1979; Gales I; Frost I; D. H. Miller-Barstow, *Beatty of the C.P.R.* (Toronto, 1951).

4. Eleni Bakopanos, "Arthur Eustace Morgan: The Wrong Man at the Wrong Time," *McGilliana: The History of McGill Project*, No. 9 (Double number, March-Sept., 1980), 1–6; Edgar A. Collard, ed., *The McGill You Knew: An Anthology of Memoirs 1920–1960* (Don Mills, Ontario, 1975), 236–238; Grimson I; Edward Beatty to T. R. Loudon, May 14, 1937, vol. 163, Edward Beatty Papers, Canadian Pacific Railroad Office, Montreal, Quebec.

5. Edward Beatty to T. R. Loudon, May 14, Beatty to W. Sherwood Fox, May 14, Beatty to W. Harold Taylor, May 25, 1937, vol. 163, Beatty Papers; Montreal *Gazette*, April 20, 1937; "Luncheon Speech Lands New Head in Old McGill," undated newsclip from *The Financial Post*, PF 281; McGill University, Candidates' List for Principal, ibid.

6. Edward Beatty to Floyd S. Chalmers, Oct. 12, 1937, vol. 166, Beatty Papers; Montreal *Daily Star*, Oct. 7, 1937. For Lewis's grandfather's contributions to McGill, see accession 640, letterbooks 18, 27, 31, 39, 40, 41, 43, 51, 57, 59, 61, McGill University Archives (hereafter cited as MUA); LWD to D. Lorne Gales, Sept. 5, 1973, DP 258; W. B. Howell, "James Douglas, A Benefactor of McGill," *The McGill News* (Dec., 1931), 33–37. James Douglas also served as chancellor of Queens University and donated $250,000 to that institution.

7. Robert Stroud, "Recollections of Events Leading Up to Mr. Douglas's Coming to McGill University," Jan. 10, 1939, DP 258; LWD, "A Host of Golden Recollections," in Collard, ed., *The McGill You Knew*, 240–241; LWD to JSD, Sept. 7, 1937, DP 32; Peggy Douglas I.

8. JSD to LWD, comments written on the margins of LWD to JSD, Aug. 17, and returned, JSD to LWD, Aug. 26, Sept. 15, Nov. 23, LWD to JSD, Sept. 1, 7, 21, 28, 1937, DP 32; LWD to William Mathews, Oct. 1, 1937, DP 78; LWD to John Nance Garner, Sept. 24, 1937, DP 252.

9. LWD, personal memorandum, Sept. 22, LWD to Edward Beatty, Sept. 28, Oct. 1, 5, 1937, DP 257; minutes, McGill University board of governors, Oct. 4, 1937, 991–992, MUA.

10. See numerous congratulatory messages in DP 257; New York *Herald Tribune*, Oct. 5, 1937; Montreal *Daily Star*, Oct. 5, 1937; *McGill Daily*, Oct. 5, 1937; Edward Beatty to Floyd Chalmers, Oct. 12, 1937, and several other letters in vol. 166, Beatty Papers.

Notes to Chapter 11

11. Nicholls I; Grimson I; Frank Scott to TGS, Sept. 3, 1975; J. C. Hemmeon to Eugene Forsey, June 13, 1939, accession 1707, Forsey Papers, MUA; Charles Hendel to LWD, Nov. 8, LWD to Hendel, Nov. 12, 1937, PF 285.

12. LWD to Edward Beatty, Nov. 8, 9, 19, 1937, DP 257; Peggy Douglas I; Stroud I; LWD, "A Host of Golden Recollections," 242; Dorothy McMurray, *Four Principals of McGill: A Memoir, 1929–1939* (Montreal, 1940), 41; LWD to Brophy, March 30, 1938, DP 77; LWD to JSD, May 6, 1938, DP 32; LWD to Dean Acheson, Feb. 24, 1938, box 9, Acheson Papers, Yale University.

13. Edward Beatty to LWD, Dec. 10, 1937, vol. 168, Beatty to LWD, Jan. 4, 1938, vol. 169, Beatty Papers; LWD, inaugural address, Jan. 7, 1938, PF 282; *McGill Daily*, Jan. 17, 1938.

14. Gales I; Frost I; Grimson I; Beatty to J. W. McConnell, Nov. 10, 1937, vol. 167, Beatty to B. M. Hallward, Feb. 10, 1938, vol. 170, Beatty Papers; Beatty to F. O. Stredder, bursar, June 1, 1938, PF 281; Beatty to Stredder, July 8, Stredder to Beatty, June 27, 1939, PF 279.

15. LWD, *Annual Report of McGill University for 1937–1938* (Montreal, 1938), 20–21; Montreal *Gazette*, undated newsclip, PF 283; McMurray, *Four Principals*, 41–42.

16. Grimson I; Gales I; Nicholls I; LWD to Beatty, Sept. 21, 1939, LWD to members of McGill University Finance Committee, Oct. 3, 1938, PF 281; LWD, memorandum "Suggested Budget Savings for 1939–40," Nov. 9, LWD, undated memorandum, "Talking Points," confidential minutes of a meeting between principal and deans, Sept. 22, LWD to deans and heads of departments, Nov. 8, 21, 1939, PF 279; Stanley Frost, "Lewis William [sic] Douglas: Right Man at the Right Time?" *McGilliana*, no. 9 (double number, March–Sept., 1980), 8. For the proposed sale of Macdonald College, see LWD to Beatty, Oct. 11 (not sent), Oct. 26, Nov. 3, Beatty to LWD, Oct. 31, Nov. 14, 1938, PF 301; W. H. Brittain to LWD, Dec. 13, 1938, March 16, 27, 1939, LWD to Brittain, March 23, 1939, PF 301; LWD, principal's private memorandum for the file, March 29, LWD, memorandum of a meeting, May 11, 1939, Beatty to Prime Minister M. L. Duplessis, Nov. 15, 1938, Duplessis to Beatty, Dec. 20, 1938, PF 301.

17. Frost, "The Right Man," 8; LWD, *Annual Report of McGill University for Period June 1, 1938 to January 1, 1940* (Montreal, 1940), 7–8; board of governors, minutes, Dec. 16, 1938, 1013, May 9, 1939, 1026–1028, Nov. 14, 1939, 1056–1057, MUA; LWD to heads of departments, Nov. 21, 1939, PF 279; LWD to Beatty, undated, PF 288; Beatty to LWD, March 14, 1938, vol. 171, Beatty to LWD, Jan. 12, 17, 1939, vol. 179, Beatty to M. L. Duplessis, Dec. 21, 1938, vol. 178, Beatty to Duplessis, May 1, 1939, vol. 183, Beatty Papers.

18. LWD, Founder's Day Dinner address, *The McGill News* (Winter, 1938), 20–24; LWD to Beatty, Oct. 5, 1937, DP 257; Toronto *Daily Star*, Oct. 6, 1937.

19. Beatty to A. E. Morgan, Feb. 18, 1936, PF 279; Beatty to W. H. Brittain, Dec. 2, 1937, vol. 168, Beatty to LWD, Jan. 22, 1938, vol. 169, Beatty Papers; undated memorandum, initialed "D.M." to LWD, PF 280; undated, unsigned memorandum concerning declining Law School enrollments, PF 293; Beatty to LWD, Sept. 6, 1938, PF 267. Douglas's letter to Beatty of Aug. 22, 1938 is missing from the files.

20. LWD to Henry Clay, Sept. 20, 1938, DP 258; Beatty to F. Cyril James, April 15, 1940, PF 272; LWD, preliminary draft of the foreword to *the State in Society*, DP 258; LWD to Lord Tweedsmuir, Dec. 16, 1938, PF 265.

21. Memorandum on attendance at Moyse Hall, Feb. 14, 1939, Robert Stroud to Oxford University Press, July 25, 1939, PF 272; Robert Warren, Leo Wolman, and Henry Clay, *The State in Society* (London, 1940); LWD to Beatty, Feb. 1, 1939, PF 279.

22. Peggy Douglas I; Stroud I; Beatty to George McDonald, April 23, 28, 1938, vol. 171, Beatty to LWD, May 5, 1938, vol. 173, Beatty Papers; undated memorandum on retirements in PF 283; board of governors, minutes, May 9, 1939, 1027, MUA.

23. LWD to Beatty, Feb. 3, 1939, PF 279.

24. Stanley Frost, "The Right Man," 10; Eugene Forsey to TGS, Sept. 26, 1979; D. Lorne Gales, taped interview with Eugene Forsey, Accession 2087, box 6, MUA; Dean C. W. Hendel to Forsey, June 9, 15, Oct. 17, 30, Forsey to Hendel, June 9, Oct. 17 (not sent), 20, 1939, J. C. Hemmeon to Forsey, June 13, 19, 1939, Accession 1707, folder 1, Forsey Papers, MUA; Forsey to D. Lorne Gales, Sept. 17, 1973, folder 4, ibid.

25. LWD, memorandum of conversation between principal and Dean Brown, May 5, 1939, DP 257; LWD to Henry Clay, March 3, Clay to LWD, March 21, 1938, LWD to T. E. Gregory, Feb. 22, 1939, PF 286; LWD to J. C. Hemmeon, March 1, 15, Hemmeon to LWD, March 2, 1939, LWD, principal's private memorandum for the file, March 15, 1939, PF 286; board of governors, minutes, May 9, 1939, 1037–1038, MUA.

26. Dorothy McMurray, "Notes Taken Down on the Typewriter from Dean Hendel, Sunday, March 19, 1939," meeting of heads of Departments of Faculty of Arts and Science, March 20, 1939, LWD to T. E. Gregory, March 29, 1939, PF 286.

27. LWD to Beatty, Nov. 23, 1939, PF 279.

28. *New York Times*, Jan. 7, 8, 9, 11, 1938; Stanley Frost, "The Right Man," 9, LWD, "A Host of Golden Recollections," 242–243; *McGill*

Daily, March 2, 1938; G. H. Fletcher to LWD, Feb. 22, 1938, PF 276; LWD to G. B. Glassco, March 29, 1939, PF 280; Montreal *Gazette*, Aug. 15, 17, 24, 1938; Beatty to LWD, Aug. 18, Sept. 6, 1938, PF 267.

29. LWD to Jack McConnell, Jan. 4, 1939, PF 267. A newspaper which echoed the views of the provincial government also denounced Corbett's remarks. See the Quebec *Chronicle-Telegraph*, Jan. 11, 1939, Beatty to LWD, Jan. 12, 30, LWD to Beatty, Jan. 16, April 27, 1939, PF 267; Beatty to Arthur G. Penny, Feb. 15, 1939, vol. 180, Beatty Papers.

30. Montreal *Gazette*, Nov. 15, 16, 1939; Montreal *Daily Star*, Nov. 15, 1939; memorandum of telephone conversation, Nov. 23, 1939, PF 288; undated memorandum of conversation between LWD and "the boys," PF 288; LWD, "A Host of Golden Recollections," 244–245; LWD to Russell Merifield, Nov. 28, 1939, PF 288.

31. LWD to A. S. Lamb, July 20, 1938, PF 301; LWD to Charles Hendel, Oct. 12, LWD to T. A. Crerar, Nov. 29, LWD to R. G. C. Belz, Nov. 26, 1938, PF 272; Beatty to LWD, Nov. 29, 1938, vol. 177, Beatty Papers; memorandum of conversation with Terry MacDermot, July 4, 1938, PF 273; LWD to T. H. Mathews, Jan. 26, 1939, PF 272.

32. Gales I; Grimson I; McMurray, *Four Principals*, 41–42; McMurray to LWD, Dec. 29, 1939, PF 283; McMurray to LWD, Oct. 8, 1964, DP 259.

33. LWD, baccalaureate address to graduating class of McGill University, May 22, 1938, DP 257; undated newsclips from *McGill Daily*, PF 280; LWD to W. Bruce Ross, Oct. 27, Ross to LWD, Nov. 6, 1938; *McGill Daily*, May 25, 1939; D. Lorne Gales to TGS, Oct. 26, 1979, Sept. 15, 1980; newsclips on German Club raid in PF 276; LWD to Hugh Crombie, April 1, 1939, PF 269; LWD to Russell Merifield, Oct. 13, 26 (not sent), 1939, LWD, "Points for Student Meeting," Oct., 1939, LWD, memorandum for the file, Oct. 16, 1939, PF 276.

34. Peggy Douglas I; Montreal *Daily Star*, Feb. 1, 1938; LWD to JSD, March 16, Aug. 15, 1938, DP 32; LWD to J. G. Harrison, July 20, 1938, PF 277; LWD to George McDonald, July 6, 1939, PF 281. For honorary degrees, see DP 73.

35. LWD, *Annual Report for 1939–1940*, 5; Peggy Douglas I; Wheeler-Bennett I.

36. Josalee Douglas to Peggy Douglas, Dec. 5, Josalee Douglas to LWD, Dec. 6, 7, 9, 10, LWD to Josalee Douglas, Dec. 7, 12, 1938, DP 63; LWD to JSD, Dec. 8, 13, JSD to LWD, Dec. 8, 9, 1938, DP 32; James Douglas (Lewis's brother) to LWD, Jan. 19, 1939, DP 63.

37. LWD, memorandum of telephone conversation, Tuesday morning, Dec. 20, LWD, memorandum of conversation, Wednesday, Dec. 21, 1938, LWD, summary of conversation at Windsor Hotel, Jan. 14, 1939, JSD to LWD, Dec. 20, 21, 1938, June 15, July 22, 1939, LWD to JSD, Dec. 20, 1938, Jan. 14, 27, Feb. 28, June 13, July 9, Sept. 8, 1939, DP 32.

38. LWD to Josalee Douglas, Dec. 12, 1938, Jan. 14, 16, 1939, March 5, 1939, Josalee Douglas to LWD, Feb. 27, March 25, 1939, Michael F. Shannon and Thomas A. Wood, attorneys at law, to Josalee Douglas, March 18, 1939, DP 63; LWD to Dean Acheson, Feb. 16, Acheson to LWD, Feb. 14, 20, 1939, DP 79.

39. Comments from various American and Canadian newspapers may be found in DP 32; LWD to Mathews, Jan. 12, 1939, DP 78; LWD, press statement, DP 32.

40. LWD to JSD, Jan. 27, Feb. 28, 1939, DP 32; LWD, undated personal memorandum, DP 257; LWD to Victor Cazelit, July 18, 1939, DP 258; Peggy Douglas I; Brophy I; Stroud I.

41. Board of governors, minutes, June 7, 1939, 1046, MUA; Beatty to LWD, June 8, 1939, vol. 184, Beatty to Robert C. Wallace, July 8, 1939, vol. 185, Beatty Papers; LWD, memorandum of meeting in principal's office, May 29, LWD, minutes of a conference between representatives of the executive committee of the board of governors and the committee of deans, June 9, LWD to Beatty, June 12, 1939, PF 282; Stanley Frost, "The Right Man," 10–11.

42. LWD to Eustace Seligman, Nov. 14, 1972, DP 62; LWD, address before the McGill Society of Great Britain, Sept. 24, 1947, DP 287. Peggy, too, left McGill with fond memories. Peggy Douglas I, April 28, 1975.

CHAPTER 12 *Preparing for War*

1. LWD to Dean Acheson, Aug. 8, 1940, DP 79. In 1938, Douglas agreed to write a book on the state of the nation for Yale University Press, but the project was never undertaken. For the many employment opportunities, see DP 258.

2. Leon Fraser to LWD, May 8, LWD to Fraser, May 10, LWD to David Houston, May 20, June 12, LWD, memoranda of telephone conversations with Houston, May 22, June 8, LWD to Frederick S. Stevenson, July 7, numerous congratulatory letters, 1939, DP 413; New York *Herald Tribune* and *New York Times*, June 9, 1939; Josalee Douglas to LWD, June 9, 1939, DP 65; William Mathews to LWD, Aug. 9, 1939, DP 78; JSD to LWD, June 15, 1939, DP 32.

3. Stroud I; LWD memorandum of telephone conversation with Robert T. Stevens, Oct. 26, Leon Fraser to LWD, Oct. 31, LWD to Fraser, Nov. 2, 1939, DP 413, LWD remarks at managers' meeting, Ponte Vedra Beach, Florida, Nov. 10, 1941, DP 427.

4. M. S. Rukeyser in New York *Journal-American*, March 9, New York *Sun*, March 7, *Wall Street Journal*, March 7, 1941; LWD to the board of trustees, April 26, 1944, DP 417;

The Eastern Underwriter, Aug. 25, 1944; A. L. Kirkpatrick, "Along the Row," *The Chicago Journal of Commerce*, May 31, 1944; Stroud 1.

5. LWD to JSD, Sept. 27, 1940, DP 32. Douglas based his interpretation of the nineteenth century on John Maynard Keynes's *Economic Consequences of the Peace* (New York, 1920). He pronounced Keynes's work "the finest thing he ever did, indeed . . . the only fine thing he ever did." LWD to JSD, Feb. 2, 1945, DP 242; LWD to Arthur Schlesinger, Jr., Feb. 18, 1952, DP 306; LWD to Philip Young, Jan. 5, 1953, DP 313. For Douglas's views of the nineteenth century, see LWD, Lamont Lecture, Yale University, May 9, 1939, DP 256; LWD, "Economic Isolation and Its Consequences," *The Phillips [Academy] Bulletin*, XXX (July, 1936), 4-10; LWD address before the National Association of Life Underwriters, Montreal *Daily Star*, Sept. 18, 1941; LWD, "External Policy and Our Internal Problems," *Proceedings of the Academy of Political Science*, XIX (May, 1940), 68-77; LWD to William Mathews, June 1, 1943, DP 78.

6. LWD, "Economic Isolation," 9-10; LWD to JSD, March 16, 1938, DP 32; LWD to Lippmann, Nov. 11, 1938, DP 253; LWD to Hull, Sept. 3, Hull to LWD, Sept. 4, 1939, DP 252.

7. LWD to Edward Beatty, March 28, 1940, DP 257; *New York Times*, May 3, 1940; LWD, "If the Allies Lose, What of the U.S.?" *Current History*, LI (June, 1940), 47-49; LWD, Commencement Address, University of Arizona, May 29, 1940, DP 104.

8. LWD to Victor Cazelit, May 1, 1940, DP 262; LWD to FDR, April 15, FDR to LWD, April 18, 1940, PPF 1914, FDRL; Stephen Early, memorandum for the President, May 17, 1940, Early Papers, box 4, ibid. For Roosevelt's foreign policy in the spring of 1940, see Robert Divine, *The Reluctant Belligerent: American Entry into World War II* (2nd ed., New York, 1970), 86-88; Robert Dallek, *Franklin D. Roosevelt and American Foreign Policy, 1932-1945* (New York, 1979), 218-221.

9. Clark to LWD, June 5, 13, LWD to Clark, June 14, drafts of Training Camps Association Bill on Selective Service, June 12, 18, 21, 1940, Frank Kent to LWD, April 16, LWD to Archibald Thacher, May 18, 1946, DP 266; *New York Herald Tribune*, Aug. 7, 1940; LWD, "Grenny in the 1930s and 1940s," in *Memoirs of a Man: Grenville Clark*, collected by Mary Clark Dimond, edited by Norman Cousins and J. Garry Clifford (New York, 1975), 197-198; John G. Clifford, "Grenville Clark and the Origins of Selective Service," *Review of Politics*, XXXV (Jan., 1973), 17-40; Martin L. Fausold, *James W. Wadsworth, Jr.: The Gentleman from New York* (Syracuse, 1975), 311.

10. Walter Johnson, *The Battle Against Isolation* (Chicago, 1944), 62-74; Divine, *Reluctant Belligerent*, 86-90; John D. McKee, *William Allen White: Maverick on Main Street* (Westport, Conn., 1975), 186.

11. LWD, "Defense Today," in William A. White, ed., *Defense for America* (New York, 1940), 139-147.

12. LWD to FDR, June 5, FDR to LWD, June 7, 1940, PPF 1914, FDRL.

13. Dallek, *Roosevelt and American Foreign Policy*, 228; Robert Divine, *Roosevelt and World War II* (Baltimore, 1969), 31; LWD to FDR, June 11, 1940, PPF 1914, FDRL; LWD to Frank Knox, June 22, 1940, DP 261; LWD, "Grenny," 198.

14. Lord Lothian to Whitney Shepardson with attached memorandum, July 28, 1940, Shepardson Papers, box 7, FDRL; Divine, *Reluctant Belligerent*, 93-94; David Reynolds, *The Creation of the Anglo-American Alliance, 1937-41: A Study in Competitive Cooperation* (Chapel Hill, N.C., 1981), 112-120.

15. LWD to Robert E. Cleary, July 21, 1961, DP 347; Van Dusen to LWD, July 3, LWD to Van Dusen, July 12, 1940, DP 265; Van Dusen, letter to the editor, *New York Times*, March 6, 1949; Johnson, *Isolation*, 115; J. R. M. Butler, *Lord Lothian (Philip Kerr) 1882-1940* (New York, 1960), 292-294. For the best works on the formation and activities of the Century Group, see Charles Ross in the St. Louis *Post-Dispatch*, Sept. 22, 1940, Shepardson Papers, box 3, FDRL, and Mark Lincoln Chadwin, *The Warhawks: American Interventionists Before Pearl Harbor* (New York, 1970), 43-73.

16. "Meeting at Columbia Club, July 11, 7:30," "Notes on Supper Meeting, Century Association," July 11, 1940, "Memorandum on American Aid for Great Britain," DP 265; Chadwin, *Warhawks*, 74-80; Francis P. Miller, *Man from the Valley: Memoirs of a Twentieth Century Virginian* (Chapel Hill, N.C., 1971), 93-97.

17. Herbert Agar, *Britain Alone: June 1940-June 1941* (London, 1972), 155-156; Charles Ross in St. Louis *Post-Dispatch*, Sept. 22, 1940; Chadwin, *Warhawks*, 80-86; Miller, *Man from the Valley*, 98-102; Miller to Henry Luce, July 23, 1940, DP 265. Douglas recalled that the destroyers-for-bases deal was first discussed at the Century Association meeting of July 11, 1940. While it is possible that the group discussed such a scheme, the minutes do not record the conversation. See LWD to Shepardson, Feb. 20, 1948, DP 280; LWD to Robert Cleary, July 21, 1961, DP 347.

18. Henry Stimson, Diary, Aug. 2, 1940, Yale University; William L. Langer and S. Everett Gleason, *The Challenge to Isolation, 1937-1940* (New York, 1952), 749-754.

19. Ibid., 755-757; *New York Times*, Aug. 11, 1940; Chadwin, *Warhawks*, 89-93.

20. Ibid., 94-96; *New York Times*, Aug. 12, 30, 1940; Agar, *Britain Alone*, 159; Langer and Gleason, *Challenge to Isolation*, 757-770; Reynolds, *Anglo-American Alliance*, 121-132;

Philip Goodhart, *Fifty Ships That Saved the World: The Foundation of the Anglo-American Alliance* (Garden City, N.Y., 1965), 159–190.

21. Wendell Willkie, undated working paper, "National Defense Since Conventions," Presidential Campaign Papers, box 3, Willkie Papers, Yale University; Divine, *Reluctant Belligerent*, 96; Dallek, *Roosevelt and American Foreign Policy*, 244–245; LWD, statement for CDAAA, Sept. 3, 1940, DP 265; LWD to FDR, Sept. 4, 1940, PPF 1914, FDRL.

22. LWD to Ellery Sedgwick, June 4, LWD to Alf Landon, July 3, 1940, DP 263; Herbert S. Parmet and Marie B. Hecht, *Never Again: A President Runs for a Third Term* (New York, 1968), 65.

23. Thomas Lamont, undated memorandum recounting telephone conversation, box 124, Lamont Papers, Harvard Business School Library; Robert E. Burke, "Election of 1940," in Arthur Schlesinger, Jr., and Fred I. Israel, eds., *History of American Presidential Elections, 1789–1968* (4 vols., New York, 1971), IV, 2937.

24. Undated note from Acheson with LWD's response on the reverse side, Peggy Douglas to Acheson, undated, box 9, Acheson Papers, Yale University; Hanes and LWD to Willkie, July 20, Willkie to Hanes and LWD, July 22, 1940, DP 264; Ellsworth Barnard, *Wendell Willkie: Fighter for Freedom* (Marquette, Mich., 1966), 209.

25. FDR press conference, July 23, 1940, XVI, 54, FDRL; *New York Times*, July 24, 25, 28, Aug. 1, 1940; Acheson to LWD, July 25, LWD to Acheson, Aug. 8, 1940, DP 79; Learned Hand to Acheson, July 24, 1940, box 15, Acheson Papers, Yale University; New York *World Telegram*, July 27, 1940.

26. *New York Times*, Aug. 13, 1940; I. W. Diggs, memorandum on the activities and organization of Democrats-for-Willkie, Oct. 3, 1940, Langbourne M. Williams, Jr., chairman of the finance committee of Democrats-for-Willkie, to LWD, April 9, 1941, DP 263.

27. Grand jury investigation, 1940–1941, DP 263; LWD to Louis H. Pink, Dec. 13, 1940, DP 413; *New York Times*, Sept. 26, Oct. 23, 1940; *New York Post*, Oct. 22, 1940. Douglas also was falsely accused of associating with a group of life-insurance executives who claimed that the value of policies would diminish greatly with Roosevelt's election. Hubbard Hoover to LWD, Nov. 28, LWD to Hoover, Dec. 3, 1940, DP 263.

28. Wendell Willkie, undated working paper, "National Defense Since Conventions," Presidential Campaign Papers, box 3, Acceptance Speech, Aug. 12, 1940, box 5, Willkie Papers, Yale University; LWD to Willkie, Sept. 6, 1940, DP 264.

29. *New York Times*, Sept. 28, 1940; Ulric Bell to General "Pa" Watson, Sept. 25, 1940, PPF 1914, FDRL.

30. Burke, "Election of 1940," 2941–2943; LWD to Willkie (not sent), Oct. 11, LWD to Russell Davenport, Oct. 21, 1940, DP 264. For the views of other interventionists who were baffled by Willkie's foreign-policy statements, see Grenville Clark to LWD, Oct. 30, Whitney Shepardson to LWD, Nov. 1, 1940, DP 263; Ronald Steel, *Walter Lippmann and the American Century* (Boston, 1980), 386–387.

31. LWD interview with Baltimore *Evening Sun*, Oct. 15, 1940; LWD, numerous speeches and newspaper clippings in DP 264; LWD, "No Third Term," *Saturday Evening Post*, CCXIII (Nov. 2, 1940), 27 ff.

32. LWD to John B. Elliott, Nov. 12, 1940, DP 263; LWD to FDR, Nov. 11, 1940, PPF 1914, FDRL; LWD to Henry Morgenthau, Jr., Nov. 12, 1940, box 80, Morgenthau Papers, FDRL; FDR to LWD, Nov. 20, 1940, DP 261.

33. Dinner at University Club, Dec. 2, LWD address before the Chicago Council on Foreign Relations, Nov. 11, 1940, DP 270; Francis Miller to LWD, Sept. 27, Nov. 25, LWD to Miller, Sept. 28, The Commission for Relief in Belgium, et al., "Statement of a Vital Question to the American People," Sept. 20, "Britain and the Famine Situation," memorandum attached to Ulric Bell to LWD, Nov. 1, Bell notes on Century Club meeting of Nov. 20, 1940, DP 265; The American Forum, "Shall America Feed the Conquered Nations of Europe?" New York *Post*, Nov. 23, 1940; Chadwin, *Warhawks*, 134–143.

34. Ibid., 118–120; Wayne S. Cole, *Roosevelt & the Isolationists, 1932–45* (Lincoln, Neb., 1983), 379–382; Wayne S. Cole, *America First: The Battle Against Intervention, 1940–41* (Madison, Wis., 1953), 10–31; Johnson, *Isolation*, 161–167; *New York Times*, Dec. 14, 1940.

35. Dallek, *Roosevelt and American Foreign Policy*, 254; Conant to FDR, Dec. 16, FDR to Conant (with Conant's comments to LWD on the margins), Dec. 19, LWD to Ulric Bell, Dec. 23, William Agar to LWD, Dec. 24, Douglas, Conant et al., to FDR, Dec. 25, 1940, DP 265; James B. Conant, *My Several Lives: Memoirs of a Social Inventor* (New York, 1970), 228.

36. *New York Times*, Dec. 28, 30, 31, 1940, Jan. 3, 1941; LWD to FDR, Dec. 29, 30, 1940, Jan. 7, 1941, PPF 1914, FDRL; Frederic Coudert to LWD, Dec. 31, 1940, DP 265; Dallek, *Roosevelt and American Foreign Policy*, 257–258; Chadwin, *Warhawks*, 151–152; James P. Warburg, *The Long Road Home: The Autobiography of a Maverick* (Garden City, N.Y., 1964), 185–186.

37. Johnson, *Isolation*, 171–190; New York *World Telegram*, Dec. 28, New York *Herald Tribune*, Dec. 29, 1940; LWD and Eichelberger to White, Dec. 24, LWD to White, Dec. 26, White to LWD, Dec. 28, Frederic Coudert to LWD, Dec. 25, LWD to Coudert, Dec. 28, 1940, White to LWD, Jan. 1, LWD to White, Jan. 1, White to Coudert, Jan. 9, 1941, White to Duncan

Grover, Jan. 3, 1942, White to LWD, May 17, 1943, DP 265; White to Walter Lippmann, Jan. 11, 1941, box 109, Lippmann Papers; [Herbert] Bayard [Swope] to FDR, Dec. 24, 1940, OF 4230, box 1, FDRL. Conservative members, headed by Thomas Lamont, appealed to the White House to save White's job but without success. See Lamont, telephone message for Cordell Hull, Dec. 28, 1940, box 21, Lamont Papers; Lamont to FDR, Jan. 3, 1941, OF 4230, box 1, FDRL.

38. Adlai Stevenson to LWD, Jan. 4, 11, LWD to Stevenson, Jan. 7, Frederic Coudert to LWD, Jan. 13, 1941, DP 265; Lamont to LWD, Jan. 10, 1941, box 21, Lamont Papers; LWD I, April 26, 1973; John Bartlow Martin, *Adlai Stevenson of Illinois: The Life of Adlai Stevenson* (New York, 1976), 183–184.

39. LWD to Edgar Hunt, Feb. 10, 1941, DP 265; Stimson, Diary, March 8, 1941, Yale University; Johnson, *Isolation*, 206–210; Chadwin, *Warhawks*, 163; Divine, *Reluctant Belligerent*, 110–111; Mrs. Kermit Roosevelt, memorandum for General Watson, May 1, 1941, OF 4230, box 1, FDRL. For the close cooperation between the CDAAA and the White House, see numerous communications in OF 4230, FDRL.

40. LWD to John Cowles, March 27, 1941, DP 265; Grenville Clark to Ernest Gibson, March 28, 31, John Perry Wood to Gibson, April 21, William A. White to Gibson, March 31, 1941, Gibson Papers, University of Vermont; Johnson, *Isolation*, 211; LWD to FDR, April 25, 1941, PPF 1914, FDRL; *New York Times*, April 28, 1941; Divine, *Reluctant Belligerent*, 113–115; Cole, *Roosevelt & the Isolationists*, 424–426. White resigned his position as honorary chairman when the committee advocated convoying. McKee, *White*, 194–195.

41. CDAAA, "Statement of Policy," May 7, 1941, DP 265; Gibson to Hugh Moore, May 12, Gibson to LWD, May 19, CDAAA, *Progress Bulletin*, May 15, 1941, Gibson Papers.

42. Goodman 1; Robert Stroud to James Conant, Jan. 15, Claude Pepper to LWD, May 9, Stroud to John D. Rockefeller, Jr., May 14, Stroud to Alexander Sachs, July 14, LWD to Sachs, July 18, 22, LWD to Eve Currie, July 19, 1941, DP 265.

43. Josalee Douglas to LWD, May 5, 1939, June 11, 1941, LWD to Josalee, June 11, 1941, undated memorandum, S. P. Applewhite, DP 63; *Arizona Daily Star*, July 7, 1941.

44. LWD to Henry Clay, July 22, 1941, DP 261; LWD, address at Harvard Club, Aug. 13, 1941, DP 265; Divine, *Reluctant Belligerent*, 127–133; Johnson, *Isolation*, 214–216.

45. LWD to Ulric Bell, Aug. 18, Grenville Clark to LWD, Aug. 20, 25, Henry P. Van Dusen to LWD, Aug. 25, 31, LWD to Van Dusen, Aug. 28, Sept. 3, LWD to Ernest Hopkins, Aug. 28, James Conant to Bell, Sept. 5, 1941, DP 265.

46. William L. Langer and S. Everett Gleason, *The Undeclared War, 1940–1941* (New York, 1953), 744–746; Divine, *Reluctant Belligerent*, 148–149; LWD to FDR, Sept. 12, FDR to LWD, Sept. 16, 1941, DP 261.

47. CDAAA, "Statement of Policy," Sept. 16, 1941, DP 265; *New York Times*, Sept. 12, 19, 30, Oct. 2, 1941. Douglas also scolded the timid within his own organization, see LWD to Livingston Hartley, Sept. 29, 1941, DP 265.

48. Divine, *Reluctant Belligerent*, 147–153; Johnson, *Isolation*, 218–222; Boston *Herald*, Dec. 6, 1941; LWD to JSD, Jan. 26, 1942, DP 33; LWD to Henry Morgenthau, Jr., Dec. 19, 1941, box 80, Morgenthau Papers; LWD to Claire Ellinwood, Dec. 15, 1941, DP 265.

49. Richard C. Patterson, Jr., to LWD, Oct. 10, Charles S. Bell to LWD, Oct. 31, 1941, LWD radio address, Jan. 2, LWD to Morgenthau, Jan. 28, Morgenthau to LWD, Feb. 2, 1942, DP 266.

CHAPTER 13 *On Board: The War Shipping Administration*

1. LWD to JSD, Jan. 26, 1942, DP 32b.
2. Stimson, Diary, Nov. 27, 1941, Stimson Papers, Yale University Library; Harriman 1; LWD appt. diary, Nov. 27, 1941, DP 113; LWD to FDR, Dec. 19, FDR to LWD, Dec. 23, 1941, DP 261.
3. See Chap. 12.
4. Harriman 1.
5. Ibid., W. Averell Harriman and Elie Abel, *Special Envoy to Churchill and Stalin, 1941–1946* (New York, 1975), pp. 121–122; Harriman to Mrs. R. B. Shipley, Jan. 27, Harriman to LWD, Jan. 26, R. P. Meiklejohn to LWD, Jan. 26, R. P. Meiklejohn to Monnet B. Davis, Jan. 27, FDR to LWD, Jan. 26, LWD to FDR, Jan. 27, LWD to Harriman, Jan. 31, 1942, DP 267.
6. Peggy Douglas 1.
7. *New York Sun*, Jan. 29, 1942; Arthur Krock, "A Great Deal of Talent Is Still Outside," *New York Times*, Feb. 20, 1942; Binghamton, New York, *Sun*, Jan. 13, 1942.
8. LWD to JSD, Jan. 26, 1942, DP 32b. Later, on May 25, after he had accepted appointment as Deputy War Shipping Administrator, the board voted to continue the same arrangement with a reduction in salary from $60,000 per annum to $50,000, DP 416. Peggy Douglas 1; Stroud 1.
9. LWD to Harriman, Jan. 31, Feb. 10, Feb. 17, 1942, DP 267.
10. Arthur Salter, *Slave of the Lamp: A Public Servant's Notebook* (London, 1967), 151–172; C. B. A. Behrens, *Merchant Shipping and the Demands of War* (London and Nendeln, 1978), 263, 285. Unfortunately, Salter's private papers were inexplicably destroyed while in temporary storage in a London depository.
11. Behrens, *Merchant Shipping*, 287–88.

A detailed account of the work of the Combined Shipping Adjustment Board can be found in S. McKee Rosen, *The Combined Boards of the Second World War: An Experiment in International Administration* (New York, 1951), 71–130; NA/RG 248/LWD/18/ Executive Orders WSA; Richard M. Leighton and Robert W. Coakley, *Global Logistics and Strategy, 1940–1943* (Washington, D.C., 1955), 215–217.

12. Ibid., 217–218. At a meeting of the Joint Chiefs of Staff on January 13, 1942, General Marshall had expressed his view that "the Chiefs of Staff should have control over shipping resources" so that they could apply them to the best strategic purposes. C.O.S. (42)79, Annex XXXIV, p. 85, as cited in Behrens, *Merchant Shipping*, 288, 5 n.

13. Frederic C. Lane, *Ships for Victory: A History of Shipbuilding Under the U.S. Maritime Commission in World War II* (Baltimore, 1951), 162, 754 passim; NA/RG 248/LWD/5/ Combined Shipping Adjustment Board Agenda.

14. John Morton Blum, *From the Morgenthau Diaries: Years of War, 1941–1945* (Boston, 1967), 80–81; Behrens, *Merchant Shipping*, 263. "Everything . . . turns upon shipping . . . the shipping shortage will be the stranglehold," Churchill wrote Roosevelt in a message on March 5, 1942, MT 62/35.

15. On April 6, Douglas sent a copy of the memorandum "for your eye and your eye alone," to Land with a covering letter, which noted that it had been "scribbled off on Feb. 13 and modified somewhat during the latter days of that month. Doubtless it needs further amplification and some relatively unimportant modification. For better or for worse, it was this view of the matter that in large measure landed me here with you. May I say quite candidly that what I wrote on Feb. 13, as a result of a very superficial knowledge of the problem, is borne home to me now as a temperate statement more than amply confirmed by wider observation of fact and a better understanding of the nature of your problem." On the routing slip, Land commented: "Read and re-read with the greatest interest—also I concur." DP 267. See also Robert Sherwood interview with LWD, London, June 20, 1947, Sherwood Papers, folder 188, Houghton Library, Harvard University.

16. Salter, *Slave of the Lamp*, 174–175; Emory S. Land, *Winning the War with Ships: Land, Sea, and Air—Mostly Land* (New York, 1958), 210; Harriman 1. John Scott Maclay, who was Salter's deputy and successor as head of the British Mission, recalled that Salter consulted Winston Churchill, who had known Douglas since the early thirties, about recruiting him for the shipping organization. No corroborative evidence has been found, but it is possible the exchange occurred. Muirshiel 1. Churchill's deep concern with the problem at this time is reflected in his *The Hinge of Fate* (Boston, 1950), chap. 11, "The Shipping Stranglehold."

17. LWD to Harriman, Feb. 21, and Land to LWD, March 16, 1942, DP 267; NA/RG248/LWD/5/ Combined Shipping Adjustment Board Agenda.

18. LWD to JSD, March 8 and April 6, 1942, DP 32b; LWD to Harriman, March 22, 1942, DP 267. Bissell's later evaluation of the problem at that time is essentially the same. Bissell 1.

19. Leighton and Coakley, *Global Logistics*, 206–208, 211.

20. Ibid., 552–558; FDR to Land (by hand), March 17, 1942, HLHP, box 309, F.4, FDRL; Gen. J. H. Burns to Hopkins, May 19, Land to Rear Admiral Akulin, May 20, 1942, HLHP, box 326, Russian Requirements, ibid.; LWD to R. J. Lynch, Feb. 11, 1942, DP 267. In a letter of May 12, 1942, to Hugh Fulton, LWD recounts in fascinating detail the peregrinations of one ship stranded in Scotland, ibid. G. S. Nyberg to Land and LWD, July 13, 1942, NA/RG248/LWD/15/ Russian Shipping.

21. Bissell to RPB, July 24, 1978; Muirshiel 1; LWD to Hopkins, June 17, 1942, HLHP, box 320, FDRL; Behrens, *Merchant Shipping*, 288 ff.

22. Ibid., 288–290, 449 n.; Bissell to RPB, July 24, 1978, and 1; Muirshiel 1; *Boston Herald*, May 22, 1942. The closeness of the relationship is evidenced in the office diary kept by LWD with fair regularity and often in considerable detail from June 23, 1942 to March 13, 1944, hereafter cited as "Diary" in the account of LWD's service with WSA. Salter to Leathers, April 6, 1942, MT 62/58.

23. Behrens, *Merchant Shipping*, 449.

24. Bissell to RPB, July 24, 1978, and 1; Muirshiel 1; F. Schneider 1. The "pro-British" charges are amply documented below.

25. LWD to Franz Schneider, March 21, 1942, DP 267; NA/RG248/LWD/13/Personnel and 18/Administration, General, passim; LWD to chairman Medal of Merit Board, March 12, 1947, DP 268; LWD memorandum "Good Men in the War Shipping Administration," April 22, 1944, DP 267; Lane, *Ships for Victory*, 754 ff.

26. Bissell to RPB, July 24, 1978; Fred Searls, Jr., to JSD, July 12, 1942, DP 39.

27. For a summary of newspaper criticism of the WSA, see San Francisco *Chronicle*, May 24, 1942. Wallace to Coy, April 14, memorandum report to the President and Vice-President on the wartime transportation situation [undated], box 14, Coy appointment and telephone conversations journal, April 20–29, 1942, box 3, Coy Papers, FDRL. This account of Douglas's meetings with Hopkins and the President is drawn from Douglas's notes for his projected memoirs "Random Reminiscences," DP 118. It appears essentially the same in various correspondence

and conversations over the years and in LWD I. LWD dated the meetings in early April, but since the Coy report was not submitted until at least late April and the appointment was not announced until May 20, it is more likely they took place in early May. As evidence of Hopkins's role, see HLHP, FDRL, passim, and NA/RG248/LWD/8/ Harry Hopkins, passim. Land, *Winning the War*, 92, 31.

28. Land to FDR, May 16, 1942, OF 4772, FDRL; *New York Sun*, May 20, 1942. It is clear that Douglas and Vickery had a high regard for each other personally and professionally, and worked well together. Bissell to RPB, July 24, 1978; LWD to Mrs. Vickery, March 21, and Mrs. Vickery to LWD, Aug. 12, 1946, DP 267.

29. "Washington Merry-Go-Round," Philadelphia *Record*, May 18, and news release under by-line of Robert S. Allen, May 21, 1942. See also the Philadelphia *Inquirer*, May 22, St. Louis *Post-Dispatch*, May 22, Boston *Herald*, May 22, "Today and Tomorrow," Los Angeles *Times*, May 26, 1942, and *New York Times*, March 21, 1944; DP 267, passim.

30. Lincoln Barnett, "Land of the Seven Seas," *Life*, XII (May 18, 1942), 32–40; "Tactless Talk," *Time*, XL (Nov. 2, 1942), 83; Salter, *Slave of the Lamp*, 175; Harriman I; Muirshiel I; Ames I; F. Schneider I; Bissell to RPB, July 24, 1978, and I; Peggy Douglas I; Diary, DP 268 passim; Peggy Douglas to LWD, April or May [n.d.], 1945, DP 68; Land, *Winning the War*, 209–210; Land to FDR, April 11, 1941, HLHP, box 320, list 1, Shipping, FDRL; LWD to Chairman Medal of Merit Board, March 12, Schneider to LWD, Oct. 19, LWD to Schneider, Nov. 5, 1947, DP 268; Secretary of Medal of Merit Board to LWD, July 16, 1947, DP 267. We are indebted to Professor Frank Freidel for information from his interview with Land, who complained that it was almost impossible for him to get in to see Roosevelt during this period. Freidel to RPB, Dec. 11, 1978.

CHAPTER 14 *The Struggle with the Military*

1. Richard M. Leighton and Robert W. Coakley, *Global Logistics and Strategy, 1940–1943* (Washington, D.C., 1955), 208–211; C. B. A. Behrens, *Merchant Shipping and the Demands of War* (London and Nendeln, 1978), 289; Frederic C. Lane, *Ships for Victory: A History of Shipbuilding Under the U.S. Maritime Commission in World War II* (Baltimore, 1951), 144.

2. Leighton and Coakley, *Global Logistics*, 368–369; LWD to Hopkins, NA/RG248/LWD/1/ Army Requirements; Joseph P. Eastman to LWD, March 18, meeting with General Somervell, March 18, Somervell to Douglas, March 19, memorandum re conversation with War Department, March 19, 1942, NA/RG248/LWD/6 Correspondence.

3. McCloy I; Clay I; Leighton and Coakley, *Global Logistics*, 218–219.

4. LWD to Somervell, June 10, 1942, NA/RG248/LWD/19/ Reading File, June, 1942.

5. NA/RG248/LWD/1/ Agreement Between WSA and War Department (S.O.S.); Leighton and Coakley, *Global Logistics*, 218–219.

6. LWD to Land, June 15, 1942, NA/RG248/LWD/19/ Reading File, June, 1942; Somervell to Hopkins, June 14, 1942, HLHP, box 321, FDRL; Henry L. Stimson and McGeorge Bundy, *On Active Service in Peace and War* (New York, 1948), 494.

7. Winston S. Churchill, *The Hinge of Fate* (Boston, 1950), chap. 22; Diary, June 23, 1942, DP 268.

8. LWD to Land, June 24, 1942, NA/RG248/LWD/19/ Reading File, June, 1942.

9. Diary, June 24, Oct. 21, 23, 1942, DP 268; *New York Times*, June 24, 1942; Lane, *Ships for Victory*, 178–184, 190–201, 311; LWD to FDR, Oct. 16, 1942, OF 4772, FDRL; Leighton and Coakley, *Global Logistics*, 624.

10. Stimson, Diary, June 7, 1942, Stimson Papers, Yale University Library; LWD to Hopkins, June 9, with attached memorandum of June 8 and enclosures, LWD to Hopkins, June 10, 1942, HLHP, box 5, FDRL; Searls to Land, June 18, Andrews to All Task Force Commanders, Oct. 24, 1942, memorandum of W. H. Labrot, Jan. 15, 1944, NA/RG248/LWD/5/ Coastal Patrol; Ames I; Arthur Salter, *Slave of the Lamp: A Public Servant's Notebook* (London, 1967), 181.

11. LWD to JSD, July 9, 1942, DP 32b.

12. Bissell to RPB, July 24, 1978; LWD to Capt. A. P. Werner, Civil Aeronautics Authority, July 15, 1942, DP 267; Forrest C. Pogue, *George C. Marshall: Ordeal and Hope* (New York, 1966), 334–349.

13. Meetings at 10 Downing Street, July 25, 31, 1942, NA/RG248/LWD/10/ Misc. London Papers; Chief of Transportation, Services of Supply, London, to Somervell, July 26, Somervell to LWD, with enclosure, July 29, LWD to Somervell, Aug. 11, 1942, not sent, but makes reference to a telephone conversation of same day to Somervell giving same information, NA/RG248/LWD/1/ Army Requirements, May 1–Dec. 31, 1942.

14. Bissell to RPB, July 24, 1978; LWD and Harriman to FDR, Aug. 2, 1942, NA/RG248/LWD/10/ Misc. London Papers.

15. Minutes of CSB meetings, London, July 29, Aug. 3, 6, 7, 1942, NA/RG248/LWD/6/ CSB Minutes, Feb. 27–Dec. 31, 1942; Robert Rhodes James, *Victor Cazalet: A Portrait* (London, 1976), 279; LWD to Eisenhower, Sept. 5, Eisenhower

to LWD, Sept. 16, 1942, DP 267; Diary, Aug. 13, 1942, DP 268.

16. Winston S. Churchill, *The Grand Alliance* (Cambridge, Mass., 1950), 152–153; Muirshiel I; Harriman I; Keenlyside (who was Leathers's principal private secretary) to RPB, March 1, 1977; Bissell to RPB, July 24, 1978; Sinclair I. According to *A Guide to the Papers of British Cabinet Ministers, 1900–1951*, compiled by Cameron Hazlehurst and Christine Woodland (London, 1974), 89, Lord Leathers left no personal papers relating to his ministerial career.

17. Salter, *Slave of the Lamp*, 175 and passim; Muirshiel I; Bissell to RPB, July 24, 1978; Ames I; F. Schneider I; Sinclair I; Salter to Hopkins, Sept. 12, 1942, HLHP, box 219, FDRL; Arthur Salter, *Memoirs of a Public Servant* (London, 1961), 271 and passim; Arthur Salter, "Lewis Douglas," *The Spectator*, 85 (Nov. 17, 1950), 505; Diary, Oct. 7, 1942, DP 268.

18. Bissell I and Bissell to RPB, July 24, 1978; Muirshiel I; Sinclair I; Keenlyside to RPB, March 1, 1977; Harriman I; F. Schneider I.

19. Salter to Leathers, April 6, 1942, MT 62/58; Muirshiel I; Churchill, *Hinge of Fate*, 199.

20. F. Schneider I; Ames I; Bissell I and Bissell to RPB, July 24, 1978; Leighton and Coakley, *Global Logistics*, 616–617; Behrens, *Merchant Shipping*, 288; LWD to Brig. Gen. Hal C. Pattison, Feb. 28, 1969, DP 267.

21. LWD to Knox, June 18, Knox to LWD, June 24, W. L. Batt to Under Secretary of War Patterson and Under Secretary of the Navy Forrestal, Aug. 11, LWD to E. A. Roberts, Aug. 24, 1942, NA/RG248/LWD/2/ Bauxite; Diary, Aug. 13, 21, 25, 1942, LWD to Peggy Douglas, Nov. 19, 1943, LWD to chairman Medal of Merit Board, March 12, 1947, DP 268; LWD to editor, New Orleans *Times-Picayune*, March 12, 1962, LWD to Brig. Gen. Hal C. Pattison, Feb. 28, 1969, DP 267.

22. Diary, Aug. 20, 1942, DP 268; Leighton and Coakley, *Global Logistics*, 457, 372–374; Behrens, *Merchant Shipping*, 313–317; LWD to F. Schneider, July 20, F. Schneider to LWD, July 22, 1949, DP 279.

23. Diary, Aug. 21, Oct. 10, 1942, DP 268; Leighton and Coakley, *Global Logistics*, 272–274, 461–462, 560–563, 580–591, 616; NA/RG248/LWD/15/ Russian Shipping, passim; LWD to Brig. Gen. Hal C. Pattison, Feb. 28, 1969, DP 267.

24. Behrens, *Merchant Shipping*, 290; Diary, Aug. 31, Dec. 7, 1942, DP 268. In the entry on the latter date, Douglas reported Hopkins's remarks that "the Navy had made up its mind that it was going to throw every monkey wrench it could into the machinery for fighting the war in the Atlantic. Its view of the war, he thought, was that it must be fought in the Pacific, and that it would do everything it could to resolve the issue accordingly." LWD to Somervell, July 19, 1942, NA/RG248/LWD/19/ Reading File, July-Aug., 1942; Keating to Gross, Aug. 6, 1943, NA/RG248/LWD/1/ Army Requirements; Muirshiel I; Ames I; LWD to MacArthur, July 22, 1943, DP 267; MacArthur to LWD, Aug. 17, 1943, LWD to Charles E. Brown, Feb. 18, 1944, NA/RG248/LWD/1/ Australia; Diary, Mar. 4, 1944, DP 268.

25. Leahy to LWD, Oct. 26, LWD to Leahy, Oct. 28, 1942, NA/RG248/LWD/19/ Reading File, Oct.-Nov., 1942; Pogue, *George C. Marshall: Ordeal and Hope*, 393–394; William D. Leahy, *I Was There: The Personal Story of the Chief of Staff to Presidents Roosevelt and Truman, Based on His Notes and Diaries Made at the Time* (New York, 1950), 117–118; LWD to Leahy with memorandum for the President attached, Nov. 17, 1942, PSF, War Shipping File, FDRL; Leighton and Coakley, *Global Logistics*, 395–396, 398–402; "Program to speed up turnaround of ships operating to South and Southwest Pacific," Jan. 12, 1943, NA/RG248/LWD/18/ WSA Directive, Dec. 18, 1942; LWD to Brig. Gen. Hal C. Pattison, Feb. 28, 1969, DP 267; Muirshiel to RPB, July 7, 1981.

26. Somervell to Land, Aug. 5, LWD to Somervell (two letters, neither sent), Aug. 15, Keating memorandum to LWD, Aug. 12, LWD to Gross (marked "Personal and Confidential"), Aug. 21, 1942, NA/RG248/LWD/1/ Army Requirements, July 1–Dec. 31, 1942; Diary, Aug. 20, 31, Sept. 2, 1942, DP 268; Muirshiel I; Sinclair I; Bissell I; F. Schneider I; LWD to JSD, Oct. 14, Nov. 2, 1942, DP 32b.

27. LWD to JSD, Oct. 14, 1942, ibid.; Leighton and Coakley, *Global Logistics*, 616–618; Diary, Aug. 13, 21, Sept. 9, 12, 14, 17, 19, 21, 23, 1942, DP 268; McCloy I; Clay I.

28. Diary, Oct. 27, 30, 1942, DP 268; LWD to JSD, Oct. 14, 1942, DP 32b; LWD to William Mathews, Nov. 5, 1942, DP 78.

29. Leighton and Coakley, *Global Logistics*, 618; McCloy to LWD, Nov. 14, LWD to McCloy, Nov. 19, 1942, NA/RG248/LWD/19/ Reading File, Oct.-Nov., 1942; memorandum of David E. Scholl to LWD, Nov. 25, 1942, NA/RG248/LWD/1/ Army Requirements, April 1, 1942–Dec. 31, 1942; Diary, Dec. 7, 1942, DP 268.

30. Diary, Dec. 16, 1942, ibid.; LWD to FDR, Dec. 16, 1942, PPF, 1914, FDRL.

31. Diary, Dec. 18, 1942, DP 268.

32. "Directive from the President to Admiral E. S. Land, Administrator, War Shipping Administration," Dec. 18, 1942, NA/RG248/LWD/18/ WSA Directive, Dec. 18, 1942.

33. LWD to Stimson and Knox, Dec. 18, Stimson to Land, Dec. 23, Land to Stimson, Dec. 29, 1942, ibid.; Diary, Dec. 21, 1942, DP 268.

34. Deane to LWD, Dec. 24, 1942, "Minutes of a Meeting at Admiral Leahy's Office

Between the Joint Chiefs of Staff and the Administrator and Deputy Administrator of the War Shipping Administration, on Monday, December 28, 1942, 10:00 A.M.,'' NA/RG248/LWD/18/ WSA Directive, Dec. 18, 1942; Diary, Dec. 28, 1942, DP 268.

35. Ibid.; LWD to Hopkins, "Proposal Submitted to General Somervell and Admiral Griffin," Dec. 29, with Somervell's and Griffin's handwritten changes, "Memorandum to Give Effect to Certain of the Provisions of the Executive Order of February 7, 1942," Dec. 31, 1942, NA/RG248/LWD/18/ WSA Directive, Dec. 18, 1942; LWD to FDR, "Personal and Confidential," Dec. 30, 1942, OF 4772, FDRL.

36. Diary, Dec. 31, 1942, DP 267; Jan. 4, 1943, DP 268; Marshall to LWD, Jan. 8, 1943, NA/RG248/LWD/18/ WSA Directive, Dec. 18, 1942.

37. Diary, Jan. 8, 1943, F. Schneider to LWD, Feb. [n.d.], 1948, DP 268.

38. "Proposal for an Inspection Committee," submitted by Joint Chiefs of Staff, [n.d.], LWD memorandum to the President, Jan. 9, 1943, NA/RG248/LWD/18/ WSA Directive, Dec. 18, 1942; Diary, Jan. 9, 16, 1943, DP 268. In his Diary of Feb. 17, and in a letter to Capt. H. A. Flanigan of July 25, 1943, LWD commented on his fine relations with Admiral Smith. An entry of Jan. 18 noted that before the meeting of Jan. 16, the navy seriously considered submitting a bill to Congress asking for construction of one million tons of fleet auxiliaries, obviously to free itself from WSA dependence. After the meeting, it withdrew its request. Ibid.

39. LWD to FDR, Jan. 18, 1943, OF 4772, FDRL. Diary entries of March 12, 13, 16, and April 1, 1943, indicate much-improved relations over combined loading operations with the army. DP 268.

CHAPTER 15 *From Casablanca to First Quebec*

1. Richard M. Leighton and Robert W. Coakley, *Global Logistics and Strategy, 1940–1943* (Washington, 1955), 677–678; C. B. A. Behrens, *Merchant Shipping and the Demands of War* (London and Nendeln, 1978), 315–317.

2. Diary, Oct. 21, 24, 28, 1942, DP 268; LWD to Harriman, Oct. 28, 1942, NA/RG248/LWD/3/ Cables; memorandum for the President, Oct. 8, Memorandum of U.S. Tonnage to Make Good Losses of Other United Nations, Oct. 6, 1942, OF 4772, FDRL.

3. Behrens, *Merchant Shipping*, 317 ff.; Diary, Nov. 17, 1942, DP 268. On Oct. 29, 1942, Salter wrote Sir Cyril Hurcomb at the BMWT on the gravity of the danger to the British import program from U.S. military demands. MT 62/68.

4. U.S. Shipping Assistance (marked "Brief for Mr. Lyttleton"), Oct. 30, F. H. Keenlyside to Salter, Oct. 31, Leathers to Salter, Dec. 10, Churchill to FDR, Dec. 30, 1942, MT 62/68; Leighton and Coakley, *Global Logistics*, 679–680. These commitments appear to be based on the estimates in LWD to Hopkins and FDR, Nov. 19, 20, 1942, HLHP, box 320, Shipping, FDRL.

5. LWD memoranda to Hopkins and to Salter, Dec. 11, approved by Hopkins, Dec. 14, 1942, HLHP, box 321, Shipping, FDRL; NA/RG248/LWD/5/ CSAB Minutes, 2/27/42–12/31/42 and 6/ CSAB Minutes, 1/1/43–; Diary, Jan. 4, 1943, DP 268; memorandum to CSAB from WSA, Jan. 18, 1943, DP 267.

6. Leighton and Coakley, *Global Logistics*, 675–677, 680–682; Behrens, *Merchant Shipping*, chap. 15; Casablanca Conference: Report on Shipping Aspects, MT 62/75; "Symbol," MT 62/86.

7. LWD memorandum to Salter on schedule of shipping to U.K., DP 267; Diary, Feb. 15, 19, 20, 1943, DP 268; Leighton and Coakley, *Global Logistics*, 515.

8. Salter to LWD, Feb. 25, Gross to LWD, Feb. 27, 1943, NA/RG248/LWD/1/ Allocations General; Diary, March 1, 1943, DP 268.

9. LWD to Harriman, March 3, Harriman to LWD, March 10, 1943, NA/RG248/LWD/1/ Allocations General; Diary, March 12, 1943, DP 268.

10. Keating to LWD, March 30, 1943, NA/RG248/LWD/5/ Combined Military Transport Committee; Diary, March 16, 23, 27, 1943, DP 268; LWD to Harriman, March 27, 1943, NA/RG248/LWD/19/ Reading File, Jan., Feb., March, 1943.

11. Behrens, *Merchant Shipping*, 363–365.

12. Dill to British Chiefs of Staff, March 18, Churchill Minute to Leathers, March 13, Leathers to Churchill, March 19, 1943, MT 62/79.

13. Diary, March 29, 1943, DP 268; Eden to Churchill, March 30, 1943 (two messages), MT 62/89.

14. Diary, March 29, April 7, 1943, DP 268.

15. See ibid., May 7, 1943, for an account of a meeting of LWD, Hopkins, Somervell, Gross, and Smith at which the army retreated in some disarray.

16. Leighton and Coakley, *Global Logistics*, 697; LWD to JSD, May 20, 1943, DP 32b.

17. Diary, May 22, 23, 1943, DP 268; Annex III, Strategic Discussions, "Trident," MT 62/83; Muirshiel 1.

18. Diary, May 23, 1943, DP 268.

19. LWD to JSD, June 12, 1943, DP 32b; Hopkins to LWD, May 24, 1943, HLHP, box 178, F. 540, Gr. Brit., FDRL; Roosevelt to Churchill, May 28, 1943, DP 267.

20. *Journal of Commerce*, July 21, 1943; Joseph Curran to Land, July 26, Harriman to LWD and LWD to Harriman, July 19, Harriman to LWD and LWD to Harriman, July 24, 1943,

NA/RG248/LWD/2/ BMSM-Msc.; LWD to Hopkins, July 22, FDR to Harriman, July 26, memo of Hopkins to FDR, July 26, Hopkins to LWD, July 29, memorandum for the President, July 26, and file memo, July 29, 1943, PSF, 192, WSA Folder, FDRL; Land press release and letters to Bailey and Bland, July 27, 1943, DP 267.

21. Drew Pearson, "Washington Merry-Go-Round," Aug. 15, 1943; LWD to Garner, July 1, 1943, DP 26.

22. The DP, NA/RG248/LWD, and MT all have remarkably little material on this conference. See FRUS: Conferences at Washington and Quebec, 1943 (Washington, D.C., 1970) and Winston S. Churchill, Closing the Ring (Boston, 1951), chap. 5.

23. Ismay to LWD, April 7, 1944, DP 261; Ismay to LWD, Sept. 27, 1950, DP 301.

24. Joan Bright Astley, The Inner Circle: A View of War at the Top (Boston, 1971), 111 and Astley 1.

25. FRUS: Conferences at Washington and Quebec, 1943, 843; LWD to Land, Aug. 21, 1943, NA/RG248/LWD/12/ Quebec (Douglas).

26. Astley, Inner Circle, 110, described shipping as "the overriding factor." General Lord Ismay, Memoirs (London, 1960), 315–316. In the transportation of troops, the Queen Mary and the Queen Elizabeth each played an "indispensable role," carrying, without escort because of their speed, over 130,000 troops to Europe. LWD to Commodore Marr on the occasion of his retirement, Oct. 11, 1968, DP 354. "Washington Merry-Go-Round," Sept. 27, 1943; Quadrant Report, MT 62/84; Twenty-Second Periodical Survey for Minister of State (Cairo), Aug.-Sept., 1943, MT 62/28.

27. FRUS: Conferences at Washington and Quebec, 1943, 1153.

28. Ibid., 1229–1233, 1236; Ismay, Memoirs, 319–320.

29. Orville H. Bullitt, ed., For the President: Personal and Secret: Correspondence Between Franklin D. Roosevelt and William C. Bullitt (Boston, 1972), 514–517; LWD to Chalmers G. Graham, Sept. 18, LWD to Stettinius, Oct. 3, 1943, DP 267; Stimson Diary, Sept. 7, 1943, Stimson Papers, Yale University Library; New York Times, Sept. 25, 1943; Cecil B. Dickson in Elmira, New York, Advertiser, Sept. 25, 1943; Danton Walker "Broadway," New York Daily News, Oct. 1, 1943; Drew Pearson, "Washington Merry-Go-Round," Oct. 18, 1943; William Hassett, Off the Record with FDR, 1942–1945 (New Brunswick, N.J., 1958), 208–209.

CHAPTER 16 Cairo and Resignation

1. Robert W. Coakley and Richard M. Leighton, Global Logistics and Strategy, 1943–1945 (Washington, D.C., 1968), 236–240; Twenty-third and Twenty-fourth Periodical Survey for Minister of State (Cairo), Oct., Nov., 1943, MT 62/28; LWD to Leathers, Oct. 18, 1943, NA/RG248/LWD/2/ BMSM-Msc.; Leathers to LWD, Nov. 1, 1943, HLHP, box 210, Post-War Shipping, FDRL.

2. Halifax to Eden, May 22, 1943, Halifax Papers, 410.4.15, Churchill College Archives, Cambridge University; LWD to Leathers, June 14, 1943, NA/RG248/LWD/2/ BMSM-Msc.; minutes of Nov. 5, 1943, NA/RG248/LWD/6/ CSAB Minutes 1/1/43–. Salter returned to serve as director-general of the UNRRA in 1944 and to hold several ministerial posts in Conservative governments. Maclay was not formally appointed to succeed Salter until sometime in 1944, although he was acting during the intervening months. He returned to London in 1945 to serve in Conservative governments under Churchill, Eden, and Macmillan, finally as Secretary of State for Scotland, 1957–1962.

3. LWD to Peggy Douglas, Nov. 19, 24, 1943, DP 268; FRUS: The Conferences at Cairo and Teheran, 1943 (Washington, D.C., 1961), 293–294.

4. LWD to Peggy Douglas, Nov. 24, 30, 1943, DP 268; Winston S. Churchill, Closing the Ring (Boston, 1951), 328–341; FRUS: The Conferences at Cairo and Teheran, 1943, 298; Elliott Roosevelt, As He Saw It (New York, 1946), 157. Joan Bright Astley, The Inner Circle: A View of War at the Top (Boston, 1971), 117 ff., gives many interesting descriptions and details on the conference.

5. LWD to Sec. of State William Rogers, Feb. 18, 1971, DP 267; LWD to Alfred A. Knopf, Feb. 7, 1973, DP 330; Henry L. Stimson and McGeorge Bundy, On Active Service in Peace and War (New York, 1948), 429–438; LWD to Robert Beitzell, May 30, 1973, DP 328; Astley 1; Wheeler-Bennett 1.

6. Churchill, Closing the Ring, 408, 412–414; LWD to Alfred A. Knopf, Feb. 7, 1973, DP 330; Sir John Wheeler-Bennett and Anthony Nicolls, The Semblance of Peace: The Political Settlement After the Second World War (New York, 1972), 167–168; FRUS: The Conferences at Cairo and Teheran, 1943, 657; Robert Sherwood interview with LWD, London, June 6, 1947, Sherwood Papers, folder 1881, Houghton Library, Harvard University.

7. F. Schneider 1; Coakley and Leighton, Global Statistics, 300–302; Lady Metcalfe to RPB, Dec. 27, 1976; C. B. A. Behrens, Merchant Shipping and the Demands of War (London and Nendeln, 1978), 395–402; FRUS: The Conferences at Cairo and Teheran, 1943, 830; Sextant: General Report and Attachments, MT 62/87; LWD to Philip Reed, Dec. 31, 1943, DP 267. As with First Quebec, American documentation on shipping at Cairo is scanty.

8. Coakley and Leighton, Global Logistics, 758–760; Twenty-Ninth Periodical Survey for Minister of State (Cairo), Feb. 1944, MT 62/

28; LWD to Leathers, Jan. 8, 1944, HLHP, box 178, file 540, FDRL; LWD to Leathers, Jan. 7, LWD to Hopkins, Jan. 23, memorandum and letter from LWD to Leathers, Jan. 26, draft memorandum on arrangements between WSA and BMWT, Jan. 28, and notes on preliminary understanding on menu of Hotel Washington, Washington, D.C., at luncheon meeting of WSA and BMWT officials, Jan. 23, LWD to Frank R. Kent, Jan. 10, 1944, DP 267; LWD to Leathers, Jan. 23, Leathers to LWD, Feb. 29, 1944, NA/RG248/LWD/2/BMSM-Msc.

9. F. Schneider I; Bissell I; New York *Journal of Commerce*, Feb. 9, 1944; Dill to LWD, Dec. [?], Stettinius to LWD, Dec. 30, 1943, LWD to Schneider, Jan. 24 (not sent), 26, 1944, DP 267; Diary, July 18, 1942, LWD to chairman Medal of Merit Board, March 12, LWD to James Byrnes, March 12, 1947, DP 268.

10. Diary, June 9, 1943, ibid.

11. R. L. McCaffery to R. R. Stroud, Feb. 6, 1947, summary of Mr. Douglas's activities in 1944 and 1945, DP 62; New York *Herald Tribune*, Feb. 26, 1944; LWD to FDR, March 3, 4, FDR to LWD, March 9, 1944, DP 267; Diary, March 7, LWD to Land, March 3, Land to LWD, March 24, 1944, DP 268; Roosevelt Press and Radio Conferences, No. 941 (March 10, 1944).

12. LWD to Harriman, March 24, Gross to LWD, March 28, 1944, DP 268; Leathers to LWD, April 21, 1944, DP 267. For encouraging reports to the President on the status of shipping to Russia, see LWD and Land memoranda of Jan. 11, Feb. 10, March 10, 1944, PSF, 18, FDRL.

13. *New York Times*, April 1, March 21, 1944; Salter to LWD, Nov. 11, 1967, DP 267.

14. Goodman I; McCaffery to Stroud, Feb. 6, 1947, DP 62; LWD to Oscar S. Cox, June 8, LWD to Maclay, Aug. 18, 1944, DP 267; Ismay to LWD, Aug. 18, 1944, DP 261; Astley, *Inner Circle*, 154; Astley I.

15. Frederic C. Lane, *Ships for Victory: A History of Shipbuilding Under the U.S. Maritime Commission in World War II* (Baltimore, 1951), 765–773; LWD to Land, Jan. 17, 1944, NA/RG248/LWD/3/ Budget Matters; Kohler to LWD, Dec. 14, 1943, Stone to Land, May 3, 1944, DP 267.

16. Kohler to Smith, July 20, Kohler to Douglas, Aug. 11, Douglas to Kohler (not sent) and telephone conversation of Aug. 14 (LWD's secretary's notes of Aug. 17), Stone to Land, Aug. 30, Stone to Douglas, Sept. 14, Douglas to Stone, Sept. 20, 1944, DP 267.

17. House of Representatives: Committee on Merchant Marine and Fisheries, 80th Congress, 1st Session: *Wartime Accounting Practices of the United States Maritime Commission and the War Shipping Administration*, Jan. 3, 1947; comptroller general to LWD, July 2, Herter to LWD, Dec. 18, LWD to Herter, Dec. 23, 1946, Herter to LWD, Jan. 6, 1947, DP 267; Emory S. Land, *Winning the War with Ships:* *Land, Sea and Air—Mostly Land* (New York, 1958), 268–276.

18. See Diary, June 9, 1943, DP 268; Leathers to LWD, Nov. 1, 1943, HLHP, 210, Post-War Shipping, Presidential aide General Edwin ("Pa") Watson, memorandum to FDR, Jan. 10, 1944, OF 2772, FDRL. Notes for Discussion with President on Conversations in London, April 7 to 29, 1944, Stettinius Papers, box 254; London Mission, meetings with pres. and sec. University of Virginia Library; "Capitol Stuff," New York *Daily News*, Feb. 3, 1944.

19. LWD to Hopkins, Oct. 25, 1944, HLHP, box 320, FDRL; Roberts to LWD, Feb. 1, Sparks to LWD, April 3, Halifax to LWD, April 5, Leathers to LWD, April 12, 1945, DP 311.

20. Land to LWD, April 4, LWD to Land, April 11, 1945, ibid.

21. Lewis W. Douglas, "What Shall We Do with the Ships?" *Atlantic Monthly*, 175, 4 (April, 1945), 43–47.

22. *New York Times*, May 18, 1945; *The Marine News*, May, 1945, 56–58, 148, 152.

23. Reed to LWD, April 5, 1945, DP 311; New York *Herald Tribune*, April 5, July 25, 1945.

24. Weeks I; "Ships and Subsidies," *Atlantic Monthly*, 176, 1 (July, 1945), 57–60; Lord Hartwell to RPB, Nov. 12, 1976.

CHAPTER 17 *Recalled to Duty*

1. *New York Times*, Sept. 29, 1939; insurance policy for moving furniture, Sept. 16, 17, 1946, DP 107; DP 71 passim; DP 69 passim.

2. DP 68 passim; LWD to Henry Boice, Sept. 10, 1941, Boice to LWD, July 2, 1943, Larimore to LWD, Nov. 11, LWD to Larimore, Nov. 16, memorandum "Facts," Dec. 4, LWD to Enrico Dajoquez, Dec. 21, 1944, Pledge Agreement, Feb. 12, 1945, DP 111; LWD to LWD, Jr., March 7, 1945, DP 71; warranty deed, Feb. 27, 1948, Charles E. Orr to LWD, Feb. 6, 1951, Jan. 30, 1953, DP 108. In 1971, LWD sold all but 120 acres of the ranch. James S. Douglas I.

3. DP 405–410 passim; New York *Sun*, Dec. 20, 1944; Deed of Gift and Agreement by and between Alfred P. Sloan Foundation, Inc., and Memorial Hospital for the Treatment of Cancer and Allied Diseases, Aug. 7, agenda for toastmaster, dinner in Biltmore Hotel, Dec. 4, 1945, B. B. Jennings to LWD, Nov. 19, 1953, Alfred P. Sloan, Jr., to LWD, Nov. 27, LWD to Sloan, Nov. 28, 1944, Everett Case to LWD, March 17, LWD to Everett Case, March 21, 1967, DP 404.

4. Aydelotte to LWD, May 17, LWD to Aydelotte, Oct. 2, 1940, LWD to Strauss and LWD telephone conversation with Strauss, Dec. 17, 1946, DP 375; LWD to Strauss, Dec. 12, 1960, DP 347; special meeting of trustees, April

1, LWD to Herbert E. Maas, March 12, Aydelotte to LWD, April 23, 1947, LWD to Oppenheimer, May 4, Oppenheimer to LWD, May 25, 1951, DP 375; Lewis L. Strauss, *Men and Decisions* (New York, 1962), 270–271. Then and later, Douglas also deplored the "steady and continuous divorcement of moral philosophy from the increasingly large number of disciplines in the general fields of the social studies. . . . Adam Smith was a moral philosopher, not an economist, not a political scientist. His contribution to knowledge and the formation of public policy was responsible for the peace and general standards of behavior of the 19th century." LWD to JSD, Feb. 2, 1945, DP 33.

5. Certificate of Election to APS, April 24, 1942, Program of Annual General Meeting, April 23, 1953, George W. Corner to Alma Beaton, June 5, 1961, DP 370.

6. Lisle R. Beardslee to LWD, Dec. 4, 1944, DP 411; Frederick J. Donner to LWD, March 1, LWD to Donner, June 7, 1965, DP 412.

7. LWD to Farley, Sept. 24, Farley to LWD, Oct. 19, 1942, DP 262; LWD to Osborn, Feb. 12, Osborn to LWD, Feb. 19, 1944, DP 261; LWD to William S. Beeman, Nov. 24, 1945, Dick Jenkins to LWD, March 8, LWD to Jenkins, March 13, 1946, DP 262.

8. LWD to John L. Thomas, June 6, Robert E. Hannegan to LWD, March 6, LWD to Arthur Curlee, July 18, 1944, ibid.

9. Edwin W. Pauley to LWD, Sept. 8, LWD to Pauley, Sept. 19, 1944, ibid.; LWD to JSD, Sept. 28, 1944, DP 32b; Davenport to LWD, Oct. 12, LWD to Davenport, Oct. 26, Stroud to LWD, Oct. 12, LWD to Davenport, Oct. 26, Stroud to LWD, Oct. 27, 1944, DP 262.

10. LWD to George Sokolsky, April 6, 1953, DP 314; LWD to JSD, Nov. 14, 1944, DP 32b; LWD to FDR, Nov. 18, 1944, DP 261; Drew Pearson, "Washington Merry-Go-Round," Washington *Post*, Dec. 2, 1944; LWD to Bernard Baruch, March 16, 1959, DP 307.

11. LWD to Jones, Jan. 25, 1945, DP 262. When, over a year later, the new President fired Wallace over a foreign-policy dispute, LWD wrote Truman a letter congratulating him on the action. LWD to HST, Sept. 25, 1946, DP 261. LWD to Hannegan, Jan. 18, 1945, ibid.

12. LWD to Mrs. FDR, April 13, LWD to HST, April 13, 1945. Truman replied on April 23, with a cordial letter, adding: "I appreciate most highly your offer of help." Ibid.

13. DP 369 passim; "Shaping the Economic and Political Future," *Proceedings of the Academy of Political Science*, XXI (Jan., 1945), 263–267; LWD to Conant, Oct. 9, 1940, DP 261.

14. Grenville Clark, "A New World Order—The American Lawyer's Role," *The Indiana Law Journal* (July, 1944), 289–300; LWD to Clark, Aug. 10, Lippmann to LWD, Aug. 11, LWD to Lippmann, Sept. 11, 1944, ibid.; William Allen Neilson to LWD, Dec. 26, LWD to Neilson, Dec. 30, 1944, LWD to Harriman, March 7, 1945, DP 262.

15. LWD address before the U.S. Associates of the International Chamber of Commerce, May 14, 1946, DP 272; LWD I, Nov. 2, 1972.

16. LWD to JSD, March 9, 1945, DP 33; LWD to Ismay, Aug. 14, 1944, DP 261.

17. LWD to Ismay, Oct. 24, Dec. 8, LWD to Conant, Oct. 10, 1944, ibid.

18. LWD to JSD, March 9, 1945, DP 33; LWD to Harriman, March 7, 1945, DP 262; LWD to Dwight Eisenhower, Aug. 29, 1952, DP 311; LWD address before the Pilgrim Society, Jan. 24, 1951, address before New York *Herald Tribune* Forum, Oct. 21, 1952, DP 319.

19. LWD to JSD, Aug. 9, 1945, DP 33.

20. LWD to Judge Samuel Rosenman, Nov. 14, 1972, DP 118; LWD to Lippmann, Aug. 8, 1945, DP 261; LWD to JSD, Aug. 9, 15, 1945, DP 33.

21. LWD to Mathews, Aug. 30, Mathews to LWD, Sept. 11, Dec. 2, 1945, Jan. 10, Feb. 26, 1946, DP 78; LWD to Owens, enclosing Memorandum of Policy, Jan. 17, Owens to LWD, Jan. 21, LWD to Owens, Jan. 22, 1946, various copies of budget, DP 260. The names of the proposed board members were not found in the DP.

22. Edward S. Mason and Robert E. Asher, *The World Bank Since Bretton Woods* (Washington, D.C., 1973), 36–40; New York *Herald Tribune*, March 16, 1946; *Time*, April 1, 1946.

23. LWD to JSD, March 26, 1946, DP 33; Elisha P. Friedman to Fred Vinson, April 9, Henry Morgenthau to Vinson, March 25, Norman Gourse and Harry Murphy to Vinson, March 31, 1946, box 11, Fred Vinson Papers, University of Kentucky Library; Ansel F. Luxford, "Reminiscences," COHC; *Wall Street Journal*, April 1, 1946; New York *Herald Tribune*, March 31, 1946.

24. Baltimore *Sun*, April 5, 1946; *Arizona Daily Star*, April 5, 1946; see also the New York *Herald Tribune* editorial of April 1, 1946; *Public Papers of the Presidents of the United States: Harry S Truman*, 1946, 192.

25. Jay Reid in the New York *Herald Tribune*, April 21, 1946; LWD to JSD, April 16, 1946, DP 33.

26. LWD to Vinson, April 16, telephone notes of LWD conversation with Vinson and LWD to Vinson, April 19, 1946, DP 261; *New York Times*, April 21, 1946; Mason and Asher, *The World Bank*, 41 n.; LWD I, Nov. 2, 1972; McCloy I. After Meyer's appointment, LWD wrote to Truman, on June 26, expressing "very deep appreciation for the confidence you had in me" and requesting an opportunity to call on the President next time he came to Washington. Truman replied he'd be "happy" to see him. DP 261.

27. Mason and Asher, *The World Bank*, 41–52. McCloy recalled later that Douglas was

most antagonistic to the Bretton Woods agreement for reasons that were never quite clear to him, and was extremely upset over his subsequent acceptance of the presidency, and that the decision strained their friendship more than any other incident in their long relationship. McCloy I. Certainly Douglas had a very low opinion of Lord Keynes, one of the principal architects of the bank, except for his early work, *The Economic Consequences of the Peace.* "His subsequent contributions," he wrote his father on Feb. 2, 1945, "have had, I think, a greater influence for evil than anything that has been written since Sidney Webb and his wife wrote their book on Industrial Democracy. . . . In a moral sense . . . [his Socialism] is wholly contrary to the philosophy of the western world which held that the individual was the central core of civilization and of material, intellectual, and moral progress." DP 33.

28. LWD to JSD, April 26, JSD to LWD, July 29, Aug. 2, LWD to JSD, Aug. 12, JSD to LWD, Aug. 15, LWD to JSD, Aug. 19, JSD to LWD, Aug. 24, LWD to JSD, Aug. 26, Sept. 6, 1946, ibid.

29. LWD to JSD, Aug. 12, Sept. 28, 1946, ibid.

30. See DP 380, 383, 384 for LWD's work with the union.

31. "Random Reminiscences," chap. 1, DP 118. LWD's tour in Germany was brief, but the indelible impressions left from it had a profound influence upon his attitudes toward that country when he later served as ambassador to Great Britain and in subsequent years. Indicative of the importance he attached to the mission was his choice of an account of that experience to begin his unpublished memoirs, tentatively entitled "Random Reminiscences." Alfred A. Knopf encouraged the endeavor and hoped to have the book published by his house. DP 330 passim. In fact it was the only section of the work on which LWD made any substantial progress during his last years, when he was able to give some time to the project. The unfinished and rough draft of this chapter ran to 95 pages and drew upon his other personal papers and fragmentary diaries in DP 269. It is hereafter cited as *RR* (Germany). Both Clay and Robert Murphy later stated that LWD was probably one of several names then under consideration for the civilian governorship of the American Zone when military rule was terminated. When that event finally took place four years later, LWD was, of course, in London. John J. McCloy was appointed first high commissioner. Clay I; Murphy I; Lucius D. Clay, *Decision in Germany* (New York, 1950), 16–18; James F. Byrnes, *All in One Lifetime* (New York, 1958), 272 ff.

32. *RR* (Germany), 1–2; LWD to JSD, April 2, 13, meeting of executive committee of the board of directors of Mutual Life, April 9, LWD to Clay, April 4, 1945, DP 269. There is some confusion of dates here, as Jean Edward Smith, ed., *The Papers of General Lucius D. Clay: Germany 1945–1949* (Bloomington, Ind., 1974), I, 3, included a letter from Clay to Morgenthau and a telephone conversation, both on April 4, requesting the latter to release Under Secretary of the Treasury Daniel W. Bell for the position. Morgenthau refused. A plausible explanation is that Clay was still hoping to get someone who would agree initially to stay the longer period.

33. "A Preliminary U.S. Program for German Economic and Industrial Disarmament," marked in LWD's hand "Approved by F.E.A.—but not approved elsewhere. Circulated to Sec. State, War, Navy, Treas. Friday—13th April," DP 269; *RR* (Germany), 2–20.

34. Walter L. Dorn, "The Debate over American Occupation Policy in Germany in 1944–45," *Political Science Quarterly*, LXXII (Dec., 1957), 481–501; LWD to Conant, Oct. 10, 1944, DP 261.

35. "Memorandum on Control of Germany," DP 269.

36. Dorr to McCloy, April 22, 1945, box 55, file 370.8, Assistant Secretary of War Papers, Record Group 107, Modern Military Branch, NA. Hereafter cited as ASWP; *RR* (Germany), 20–24.

37. "Itinerary" of trip through liberated Germany, with attached note from Clay, dated April 21, "Looks like an interesting schedule," orders for temporary duty for LWD, April 22, 1945, rough diary notes of trip through Germany, DP 269; LWD to JSD, June 28, 1945, DP 33; *RR* (Germany), 24–62.

38. Memorandum to General Clay, May 1 1945, DP 269.

39. *RR* (Germany), 53, 91; LWD to William R. Mathews, July 20, 1961, DP 78; LWD to Samuel I. Rosenman, Oct. 16, Rosenman to LWD, Nov. 8, LWD to Rosenman, Nov. 14, 1972, DP 118. For the decision on the pullback, see Forrest C. Pogue, *George C. Marshall: Organizer of Victory* (New York, 1973), 567–578, and Stephen E. Ambrose, *Eisenhower and Berlin, 1945: The Decision to Halt at the Elbe* (New York, 1967).

40. Smith, *Clay Papers*, I, 9–10. For the provisions of JCS 1067, see *Department of State Bulletin*, XIII (Oct. 21, 1945), 596–607. Clay, *Decision in Germany*, 18–19; Robert Murphy, *Diplomat Among Warriors* (New York, 1964), 250–251; *RR* (Germany), 65–66; LWD's authorization for travel orders, May 5, LWD diary notes, May 6, 7, 1945, DP 269.

41. Clay to Hilldring, May 7, 1945, Smith, *Clay Papers*, I, 11. Clay to War Dept., May 5, 8, 1945, sec. 12, file O14, Germany, Civil Affairs Division, War Dept., NA. Hereafter cited as CADP. Two weeks later, Hilldring wrote Clay that public opinion would not tolerate a soft peace. LWD's visit had been a "profitable experience," but it would be in Clay's best interests "to ad-

minister Germany in the post-defeat period along lines laid down by the Government." May 21, 1945, sec. 13, file 334, ibid. RR (Germany), 67–84. LWD diary notes on War Department stationery, May 8–15, LWD to McCloy, May 18, clipping from *P.M.*, June 3, transcript of Pearson radio broadcast over WJZ, New York, June 22, LWD to Mrs. Lowell Stockwell, July 25, 1945, DP 269; LWD to JSD, Aug. 9, 1945, DP 33; Clay, *Decision in Germany*, 18–19; Murphy, *Diplomat Among Warriors*, 250–251; Clay I; Murphy I.

42. RR (Germany), 72, 85–95; "Itinerary" and notes on legal sheets, DP 269.

43. Murphy I; "Inventory of Reports Taken to Washington by Mr. L. W. Douglas," June 21, 1945, sec. 13, file O14, CADP; "Field Survey of Regional Government in Bavaria," June 5, "The Reorganization of Germany's Financial System," June 19, 1945, DP 269.

44. "Memorandum Re Conversations with Louis [sic] Douglas," June 20, 1945, vol. 19a, Scandrett Papers, Cornell University Library.

45. "Notes on Meeting with General Clay," June 20, LWD appt. diary, June 20, 1945, LWD to Wolman, June 10, 1945, DP 268; Smith, *Clay Papers*, I, 24 n.; Clay, *Decision in Germany*, 19; Murphy, *Diplomat Among Warriors*, 251; Clay I; LWD to Clay, July 5, 26, Clay to LWD, Aug. 5, LWD to Clay and Eisenhower, Oct. 5, 1945, DP 269.

46. LWD to Clay, June 28, Clay to LWD, July 8, LWD to Clay, July 5, LWD notes on War Dept. stationery, June 25–July 2, 1945, ibid.; Stimson Diary, June 25, 1945, Stimson Papers, Yale University Library; LWD to HST, July 7, 1945, DP 269. Dorr wrote in a memorandum of June 28, 1945, to Cols. Davis and Gerhardt and Maj. Sommers: "The return of Lew Douglas and the picture he brings with him are immensely helpful. It emphasizes that letter writing can never take the place of the personal contacts of visits back and forth," Box 55, File 370.8, ASWP.

CHAPTER 18 *To the Court of St. James's*

1. Joseph L. Morrison, *Governor O. Max Gardner: A Power in North Carolina and New Deal Washington* (Chapel Hill, N.C., 1971), 262–263, 271; Harriman I; *New York Times*, Dec. 4, Feb. 7, 14, 1947.

2. Dean Acheson, *Present at the Creation: My Years in the State Department* (New York, 1969), 213; fragment of LWD's unpublished "Random Reminiscences" on London years, 9, DP 118, hereafter cited as "RR (London)"; Harriman to LWD, Feb. 16, 1947, DP 273; Harriman I; McCloy I.

3. RR (London), 1–2; LWD to JSD, Jan. 28, Feb. 12, 13, 19, JSD to LWD, Feb. 14, 1947, DP 33; LWD I, Nov. 2, 1972.

4. RR (London), 2–3; LWD to JSD, Feb. 19, 1947, DP 33; Harriman I; *Time*, Dec. 1, 1947, 23–26.

5. RR (London), 5–7; Peggy Douglas I.

6. LWD to JSD, Feb. 19, 21, JSD to LWD, Feb. 20, 1947, DP 33; RR (London), 7; memo from Acheson to Marshall, Feb. 17, 1947, NA/RG 59/867 N.01; Hickerson I; LWD memo of Feb. 23, with list of trustees reached by telephone, notice "To All Members of Mutual Life Staff," March 7, 1947, DP 427. The attempt to keep the nomination secret until it was forwarded to the Senate was not entirely successful. As early as Feb. 17, 1947, the New York *World Week* broke the story, and in his home state the Phoenix *Arizona Republic* of Feb. 23, the Tucson *Arizona Daily Star* of Feb. 24, the Tucson *Citizen* and Phoenix *Gazette* of Feb. 24, 1947, carried the news.

7. HST to LWD, Feb. 20, LWD to HST, Feb. 24, State Department to Gallman, Gallman to Department, Gallman to Foreign Office, Feb. 25, Foreign Office to Gallman, Gallman to Sec-State, Feb. 27, 1947, DP 273; Bevin to Marshall, Feb. 28, 1947, DP 279.

8. New York *Herald Tribune*, Feb. 27, 1947; Prescott (Arizona) *Courier*, Feb. 27, 1947.

9. *New York Times*, March 1, New York *Herald Tribune*, March 6, 8, 1947. Even isolationist Republican committee member Arthur Capper of Kansas approved the choice and congratulated the President on making it. Topeka *Daily Capitol*, Feb. 27, 1947. LWD to members of Senate Foreign Relations Committee, March 12, LWD to Langer and Stewart, March 11, Acheson to LWD, with attached note, March 6, 1947, DP 273; *New York Times*, March 6, 1947.

10. Minneapolis *Tribune* and *New York Times Magazine*, March 9, 1947.

11. *Christian Science Monitor*, Feb. 27, 1947; summary of press comment in the *United States Review*, March 15, 1947. William Mathews saw the appointment as a prelude to Douglas running against Hayden in 1950. "All you need to do is agree to run, and then come out and make possibly a dozen speeches. There is no one in sight that could begin to measure up to your chances." LWD replied: "I . . . note your remarks about '50. Upon this I have no thoughts. Meantime, I rather suspect that when my tour of duty over here is finished I will write my autobiography entitled: 'From the Court of St. James's to the Poor House.' " Mathews to LWD, March 26, LWD to Mathews, April 16, 1947, DP 78. Members of the Arizona legislature cheered the appointment when sessions of the Senate and House of Representatives were interrupted for the announcement. Phoenix *Gazette*, Feb. 26, 1947. Drew Pearson, "Washington Merry-Go-Round," March 3, 1947.

12. Bowles to William Benton, March 6, 1947, box 23, Chester Bowles Papers, Yale Uni-

versity Library; *Nation*, March 8, *New Republic*, March 10, New York *Post*, Feb. 27, 1947.

13. These messages are filed alphabetically in DP 274–276.

14. *Times*, Feb. 27, *Daily Telegraph*, Feb. 27, *Manchester Guardian*, Feb. 27, *Star*, Feb. 27, *News Chronicle*, as quoted in *Time*, March 10, *Daily Herald*, Feb. 27, *Daily Mail*, Feb. 27, Glasgow *Herald*, Feb. 27, Glasgow *Record*, Feb. 27, *Scottish Daily Mail*, March 19, *The Scotsman*, April 3, 1947; Duke of Buccleuch and Queensberry to LWD, March 18, 1947, DP 274.

15. LWD to Churchill, March 10, 1947, ibid. The messages and reports from Britain are filed alphabetically in DP 274–276. Inverchapel to Bevin, March 4, Rundall minute, March 12, 1947, AN 953/1/45, F.O. 371/61000.

16. *RR* (London), 8–9. LWD had already established close and friendly relations with Vandenberg. As recently as Jan. 14, 1947, he had written the senator "to tell you how fortunate is the Republican Party and the country to have you as its titular and respected leader. . . . [T]he respect that I have always had [for you] . . . has been steadily increasing until it has now reached a level so high that it can go no higher," DP 273. The Truman message to Congress is in the State Department *Bulletin*, March 23, 1947, 534. LWD I, Nov. 2, 1972; New York *Herald Tribune*, March 16, 1947; LWD to HST, March 14, 1947, DP 279.

17. For a succinct account of the situation in England and in Europe as of LWD's appointment, see Robert J. Donovan, *Conflict and Crisis: The Presidency of Harry S Truman, 1945–1948* (New York, 1977), 275–278. Robert M. Hathaway, *Ambiguous Partnership: Britain and America, 1944–1947* (New York, 1981) and Terry H. Anderson, *The United States, Great Britain and the Cold War, 1944–1947* (Columbia, Mo., 1981) are useful on the immediate postwar years. *New York Times*, Feb. 26, 1947; LWD to JSD, Feb. 19, 1947, DP 33. LWD had kept in especially close touch with Lord Ismay. See, for example, Ismay to LWD, April 15, LWD to Ismay, Dec. 26, 1946, DP 261. LWD had enunciated his concern about conditions in Britain and the philosophy of the Labour government in a speech to the English-Speaking Union in Chicago on Jan. 24, 1947. British Consul General in Chicago to F.O., Jan. 24, 1947, AN 1138/1/45, F.O. 371/61000.

18. New York *Herald Tribune*, March 16, *Daily Telegraph*, March 17, *The Times*, March 17, 1947; Gallman to SecState, March 16, 1947, NA/RG 59/123 Douglas, Lewis W., telegram 1654; *RR* (London), 9–10.

19. Ibid., 10–13; *Daily Herald* and *Daily Express*, March 21, 1947; Peggy Douglas I; LWD to Acheson, May 9, memorandum of LWD telephone conversation with Acheson, May 14, 1947, DP 279. DP 277 contains a fat folder on the pro-

jected expenditures for Winfield House and the modest remodeling of Prince's Gate.

20. *Daily Herald*, March 18, 1947; Gallman to SecState, March 17, 1947, *FRUS*, 1947, V, 123–124.

21. *Daily Herald* and *Daily Express*, March 21, 1947.

22. London embassy to SecState, March 25, 1947, NA/RG 59/123 Douglas, Lewis W. telegrams 1860 and 1787; confidential memorandum of conversation with Attlee, March 25, 1947, DP 279; LWD to SecState, April 2, NA/RG 59/032 Wallace, Henry A., telegram 2045, and two dispatches of April 14, 1947, NA/RG 59/032 Wallace, Henry A., telegrams 2189 and 2196; LWD to JSD, April 12, 1947, DP 33; James Forrestal, *The Forrestal Diaries*, Walter Millis, ed., with collaboration of E. S. Duffield (New York, 1951), 262; article in *Daily Herald* transmitted to SecState, April 15, 1947, NA/RG 59/811.20200(D)/.

23. LWD to SecState, April 2, 1947, NA/RG 59/032 Wallace, Henry A., telegram 2045; Acheson to LWD, April 4, 1947, DP 279; Cruikshank to LWD, April 10, LWD to Cruikshank, April 14, 1947, DP 302; typescript of LWD Pilgrims address, checked against radio broadcast and with audience response, April 22, 1947, DP 286.

24. LWD to Acheson, April 23, Acheson to LWD, May 8, 1947, press clippings and letters, ibid.

25. Memorandum to dept. disbursing officer, Feb. 10, 1948, DP 277; Lillian Olsen to Robert F. Morrison, May 1, 1947, DP 281.

CHAPTER 19 *Launching the Marshall Plan*

1. Robert H. Ferrell, *George C. Marshall* (New York, 1966), 52–54; Charles E. Bohlen, *Witness to History, 1929–1969* (New York, 1973), 258–259, 268–270; LWD to Lovett, May 14, Lovett to LWD, May 21, 1947, DP 279; Hickerson I; Lovett I; Carter I; Col. George I.

2. Hickerson I; Lovett I; Sir Roderick Barclay, *Ernest Bevin and the Foreign Office, 1932–1969* (London, 1975), 42, 86; Alan Bullock, *Ernest Bevin: Foreign Secretary* (New York, 1983), 587, 718; Barclay I; Strang I; Roberts I; Marshall to Lovett, Dec. 11, 1947, *FRUS*, 1947, II, 764–765; George F. Kennan, *Memoirs, 1925–1950* (Boston, 1967), 345 passim; Clay I; Franks I; Gen. Carter I; Col. George I. In a letter, dated Nov. 22, 1972, to General Marshall Carter (not sent), LWD claimed that he was "one of the three or four whom he [Marshall] called by first name," DP 374. The evidence of their correspondence and from interviewees close to the secretary suggest this was a lapse of memory, though probably Marshall referred to Douglas as Lew in conversations with the ambassador's family.

3. Macmillan 1; Wilson 1; Clay 1; Murphy 1; Bonham-Carter 1; Colville 1; Westmorland 1; Harriman to LWD, July 31, 1947, DP 279; McCarthy to LWD, Nov. 28, 1947, DP 302.

4. David S. McLellan, *Dean Acheson: The State Department Years* (New York, 1976), 70–73.

5. Robert J. Donovan, *Conflict and Crisis: The Presidency of Harry S Truman, 1945–1948* (New York, 1977), 276; Gallman to SecState, Feb. 7, 11, 1947, *FRUS*, 1947, III, 487–489; Ferrell, *Marshall*, 100–101; Inverchapel to Bevin, Feb. 14, 1947, AN 656/110/45, F.O. 371/61064.

6. LWD to Acheson, March 14, 1947, DP 279; LWD to SecState, March 18, Marshall to Acheson, March 27, LWD to Acheson, March 28, LWD to SecState, April 18, Acheson to LWD, April 23, LWD to Acheson, April 24, LWD to SecState, May 8, Marshall to LWD, May 12, LWD to SecState, May 17, 21, 22, 23, *FRUS*, 1947, III, 494–497, 497–498, 501–504, 504–514.

7. LWD to Shinwell, April 18, 1947, DP 278; LWD to Acheson, March 25, 1947, DP 279; LWD to Acheson, March 28, 1947, *FRUS*, 1947, III, 497–498; LWD to McCloy, April 28, 1947, DP 280.

8. Bevin to Washington embassy, Nov. 14, 1947, AN 3876/110/45 and AN 3904/110/45, F.O. 371/61065; *Daily Mirror*, Nov. 13, 1947.

9. Memorandum by Arthur F. Blaser, Jr., Treasury Representative in the U.K., May 5, 1947, *FRUS*, 1947, III, 9–13; Franks, ERP 1, June 27, 1964, HSTL.

10. LWD to SecState, May 16, 20, 1947, *FRUS*, 1947, III, 13–15; LWD to Clayton, May 23, 1947, DP 279. In a conversation of May 14, 1947, President of the Board of Trade Sir Stafford Cripps also warned Douglas of the impending dollar crisis, ibid. Douglas expressed his concern and uncertainty about the situation in an off-the-record press conference with American correspondents, June 5, 1947, DP 277.

11. Memorandum from British embassy to Department of State, June 18, 1947, *FRUS*, 1947, III, 17–24.

12. LWD to Marshall and Lovett, July 25, aide-mémoire, July 28, Marshall memorandum to the President, Aug. 1, 1947, ibid., 43–44, 45–48. The conversations in Washington and the notification of the decisions on convertibility and the suspension of loan withdrawals are found in ibid., 6–69, 91–92. On the December release of the remaining funds, see editorial note, ibid., 93–94.

13. LWD to Marshall and Lovett, July 25, Lovett to Marshall, Aug. 19, 23, 1947, ibid., 44, 62, 69; James Forrestal, *The Forrestal Diaries*, edited by Walter Millis with the collaboration of E. S. Duffield (New York, 1951), 306.

14. Moore to Wilcox, July 28, 1947, *FRUS*, 1947, III, 239–241; Kennan, *Memoirs, 1925–1950*, 325–345; Dean Acheson, *Present at the Creation: My Years in the State Department* (New York, 1969), 226–235; Bohlen, *Witness*, 263–264. The texts of the various reports and preliminary discussions may be found in *FRUS*, 1947, III, 204–236. The text of the Harvard address is in ibid., 237–239. Memorandum by Kindleberger, ibid., 241–247. A useful source on the immediate background to the Marshall Plan is Harry Bayard Price, *The Marshall Plan and Its Meaning* (Ithaca, N.Y., 1955).

15. Sir John Wheeler-Bennett and Anthony Nicholls, *The Semblance of Peace: The Political Settlement After the Second World War* (New York, 1972), 569–571; Balfour to Butler, May 31, 1947, AN 1977/17/45, F.O. 371/61028. The first letter, cited by Wheeler-Bennett from Balfour's unpublished memoirs, was not found in the Foreign Office papers.

16. Bullock, *Bevin: Foreign Secretary*, 404; Francis Williams, *Ernest Bevin* (London, 1952), 264–265; Francis Williams, with Clement Attlee, *A Prime Minister Remembers: The War and Post-War Memoirs of the Rt. Hon. Earl Attlee* (London, 1962), 172–173; Wheeler-Bennett and Nicholls, *Semblance of Peace*, 572–573. In *Present at the Creation*, 234, Acheson claimed that Sir William Strang suggested Bevin contact Marshall to ascertain what the general had in mind. This has been repeated in other works, e.g., Ferrell, *Marshall*, 112, but Strang later denied this, pointing out that he was in Germany at the time, Strang 1. Hector McNeil to Bevin, June 11, 1947, UE 4614/168/53/G, F.O. 371/62398; Gallman to SecState, June 11, 1947, NA/RG 59/123 Douglas, Lewis W., telegram 3845; Massigli to RPB, July 12, 1977. See also Bullock, *Bevin: Foreign Secretary*, 403–406.

17. Williams, *Bevin*, 264–265; Bevin to Douglas (in Munich), June 14, 1947, DP 279; British Ambassador Duff Cooper to Bevin, June 14, 1947, UE 4651/168/53, F.O. 371/62398; Caffery to SecState, June 18, 1947, *FRUS*, 1947, III, 258–260.

18. Inverchapel to Bevin, June 13, 1947, UE 4643/168/53, F.O. 371/62398; memorandum prepared for the use of the under secretary of state (June, 1947); conversations in London, June 24–26, 1947, *FRUS*, 1947; III, 247–249, 268–293; Dalton Diaries, June 27, 1947, London School of Economics Library; Lovett to Clayton, July 10, 1947, *FRUS*, 1947, III, 324–326.

19. LWD to Marshall, June 20, Marshall to LWD, June 24, transcript of speech to American Chamber of Commerce, sent to depart., June 27, 1947, NA/RG 59/123 Douglas, Lewis W., telegrams 6948, 5975, 1535. The three committees appointed by the President were on the state of United States natural resources, headed by Secretary of the Interior Julius Krug; on the impact of the national economy of foreign aid, headed by the chairman of the Council of Economic Advisors, Edwin G. Nourse; and a nonpartisan group of distinguished citizens to advise

the President "on the limits within which the United States may safely and wisely plan to extend such assistance [to foreign countries]," headed by Secretary of Commerce Averell Harriman. Statement to the press by the President, June 22, 1947, FRUS, 1947, III, 264–266; Bohlen, Witness, 264; Kennan, Memoirs, 1925–1950, 342.

20. Smith to SecState, June 23, Caffery to Marshall, June 27, 1947, FRUS, 1947, III, 266, 296.

21. Caffery to Marshall, June 28, 29, July 1, 2, 3, LWD to Marshall, June 29, July 3, 1947, ibid., 296–308; Bevin to LWD, June 28, 1947, PREM 8, 945; Bevin to LWD, June 28, 29, July 1, 1947, UE 5235, 5236, 5234/168/53, F.O. 371/62403.

22. LWD to Marshall, July 4, Marshall to Caffery for Bidault and Bevin, July 3, 1947, FRUS, 1947, III, 310–312, 308.

23. Caffery to Marshall, July 3, July 20, dispatches of ambassadors in Poland and Czechoslovakia to SecState, Smith to Marshall, July 11, 1947, ibid., 308, 313–322, passim, 327. The initials CEEC were used for both the conference and the committee of the whole.

24. Caffery to SecState, July 23, 29, 1947, ibid., 338–341.

25. Lucius D. Clay, Decision in Germany (New York, 1950), 174; John Gimbel, The Origins of the Marshall Plan (Stanford, Cal., 1976), 201, 203, 205, 209–210.

26. FRUS, 1947, III, 268–293, II, 933–966, passim; Gimbel, Origins, 211–215.

27. Caffery and Clayton to SecState, July 11, 1947, FRUS, 1947, II, 983–986; British aide-mémoire delivered to Dept. of State, July 15, Bidault to SecState, July 17, 1947, ibid., III, 986–987, 991–992. Bevin, in a conversation on July 16, with Massigli, who called to protest the proposed level of industry plan, declared Great Britain and the United States could not go on pouring out "vast sums of money" to support the Bizone. Massigli indicated he understood but could not approve the action. CJ 297/86/182, F.O. 371/65191.

28. Kennan memorandum to Lovett, July 18, 1947, FRUS, 1947, III, 332–333; Balfour to SecState, July 24, 1947, ibid., II, 1005–1006; Gimbel, Origins, 229.

29. Marshall to LWD, Aug. 8, LWD to Marshall, Aug. 11, Marshall to LWD, Aug. 11, 1947, FRUS, 1947, II, 1024–1026, 1027–1029; telephone conversation of LWD and Roger Makins, Aug. 10, 1947, CJ 832/86/182, F.O. 371/65195.

30. For the series of reports on these conversations from LWD, Caffery, and Clayton in Paris and London and the comments and instructions from Lovett, see FRUS, 1947, II, 1029–1040, passim; Clayton 1, COHC.

31. Clayton, Caffery, and LWD to Lovett, Aug. 19, 1947, FRUS, 1947, II, 1041–1042.

32. Murphy to Marshall, July 25, Royall (and Marshall) to Clay (and Murphy), July 28, 1947, ibid., 1009–1010; Jean Edward Smith, ed., The Papers of General Lucius D. Clay: Germany, 1945–1949 (Bloomington, Ind., 1974), I, 385–388, 389, 401–406, 409–410, 415; Murphy to Marshall, Aug. 9, 1947, FRUS, 1947, II, 1026–1027; LWD to Clay, Aug. 16, 1947, DP 278.

33. Level of Industry Meeting documents CJ 994/CJ 995/CJ 1039/86/182, F.O. 371/65196; LWD to Lovett, Aug. 22, LWD to Marshall, Aug. 27, 1947, FRUS, 1947, II, 1047–1049, 1064–1067; Lovett to LWD, Aug. 29, 1947. NA/RG59/123 Douglas, Lewis W., telegram 3786.

CHAPTER 20 *Marshall Plan Missionary*

1. LWD to Lovett, July 23, 1947, DP 279; Dalton Diaries, July 28, 29, 1947, London School of Economics and Political Science Library.

2. Sir Roderick Barclay, *Ernest Bevin and the Foreign Office, 1932–1969* (London, 1975), 42, 89–90; Barclay 1.

3. Clayton, Caffery, LWD, Murphy, and Nitze to Marshall and Lovett, Aug. 6, memorandum on Paris discussions by Wesley C. Haraldson (on Murphy's staff), Aug. 8, 1947, FRUS, 1947, III, 343–350.

4. Lovett to Clayton, Aug. 11, Lovett to Clayton and Caffery, Aug. 14, 1947, both repeated to LWD, ibid., 50–51, 56–60.

5. Lovett to LWD, Aug. 20, LWD to Lovett, Aug. 21, memorandum by Bonesteel on minutes of departmental meeting on Marshall Plan, Aug. 22, Lovett to Marshall, Aug. 24, Marshall to Lovett, Aug. 25, Clayton to Lovett, Aug. 25, Lovett to Clayton and Caffery, Aug. 26, 1947, ibid., 369–391, passim; LWD to SecState, Aug. 28, 1947, NA/RG59/123 Douglas, Lewis W., telegram 4664.

6. Lovett 1; Franks 1. Clayton later sharply criticized Caffery in the discussions as devoid of "ideas"—they never got "anything constructive out of him." He gave high marks to LWD. Garwood 1 with Clayton on ERP and Clayton 1 by John T. Mason, COHC.

7. Caffery to Lovett, Sept. 5, memorandum by Kennan, Sept. 4, Marshall to Truman, Sept. 6 (with text of statement released to press Sept. 10), 1947, FRUS, 1947, III, 405–408; 397–405, 410–422.

8. Lovett to Diplomatic Representatives Accredited to Countries Participating in the CEEC (two dispatches), Sept. 7, 1947, ibid., 412–417.

9. Marshall to LWD, Sept. 8, LWD to SecState, Sept. 9, 1947, ibid., 418–420; Bevin to Inverchapel, Sept. 9, 1947, UE 8385/6191/53, F.O. 371/62580.

10. LWD to SecState, Sept. 10, 1947, NA/RG59/123 Douglas, Lewis W., telegram 4893; Hall-Patch to Bevin, Sept. 11, EU 8451/6191/53, Inverchapel to Bevin, Sept. 10, 1947, EU

8421/6191/53, F.O. 371/62580; Franks to Bevin, Sept. 11, 1947, EU 8505/6191/53, F.O. 371/62582; Clayton, Caffery, and LWD to Marshall and Lovett, Sept. 11, 12, LWD to SecState, Sept. 12 (two dispatches), Lovett to LWD, Sept. 13, LWD to Lovett, Sept. 23, 1947, FRUS, 1947, III, 421–423, 425–431, 438–439; Bevin's notes for discussion with LWD ("Not to be handed to Ambassador"), Sept. 12, 1947, EU 8600/168/53/G, F.O. 371/62416.

11. Douglas to SecState, Sept. 20, Lovett to Clayton, Caffery, and LWD, Sept. 20, 22, LWD to SecState, Sept. 23, 1947, FRUS, 1947, III, 441–446; Douglas and Clayton to Lovett, Sept. 23, chargé in U.K. to SecState, Sept. 27, aide-mémoire to British embassy, Oct. 15, 1947, FRUS, 1947, I, 993–996, 998–1003, 1013 n.; Bevin to Inverchapel, Sept. 24, 25, 26, EU 9000/37/53 and EU 9040/37/53, F.O. 371/62317 and Sept. 30, 1947, EU 9151/37/53, F.O. 371/62318. Despite his sharp remarks to Bevin, LWD admitted to Acheson that his concern over the desperate need to provide immediate aid to a rapidly deteriorating Europe overrode his commitment to free trade and the Geneva negotiations as a precondition. Joseph P. Lash, ed., *From the Diaries of Felix Frankfurter* (New York, 1975), 317.

12. LWD to Bell, Sept. 24, 1947, DP 250.

13. LWD to SecState, Sept. 17, 1947, NA/RG59/840.50 Recovery, telegram 5024; London embassy to Dept., Sept. 26, 1947, NA/RG59/123 Douglas, Lewis W., telegram 5193; *New York Times*, Oct. 2, 1947.

14. Editorial note, memorandum of Sept. 29 and minutes of Oct. 2, of Advisory Steering Committee, LWD to SecState, Sept. 23, 1947, FRUS, 1947, III, 470–478, 445–446; *Washington Times-Herald*, Oct. 7, 1947; Stanley Woodward to Matthew J. Connelly, with notation in pencil, Oct. 13, 1947, OF 1206, HSTL; *Public Papers of the Presidents of the United States, Harry S Truman, 1947*, 472; LWD briefing paper on meeting with senators and representatives, Oct. 15, 1947, DP 279; *New York Herald Tribune*, Oct. 16, 1947.

15. Bonesteel to Lovett, Oct. 28, 1947, NA/RG59/840.50 Recovery; editorial note, FRUS, 1947, III, 470–471; Lovett to LWD, Nov. 4, 1947, NA/RG59/123 Douglas, Lewis W., telegram 4711; LWD to Stroud, Nov. 7, 1947, DP 281.

16. *New York Times*, Nov. 12, 1947; *New York Herald Tribune*, Nov. 13, 1947; Arthur Krock, "L. W. Douglas' Key Role," *New York Times*, Nov. 12, 1947.

17. Gallman to SecState, Jan. 30, 1948, FRUS, 1948, III, 1074, 1074 n.; *Daily Mirror*, Nov. 13, 1947; *News Chronicle*, Nov. 14, 1947.

18. *Baltimore Sun*, Nov. 22, 1947; LWD schedule for Nov.-Dec., 1947, DP 279; LWD to John McConnell, May 6, 1947, DP 302; memorandum of conversation of Marshall with Bidault, Sept. 18, memorandum of conversation of Chief of Division of Central European Affairs (Beam) with Strang, Oct. 17, minutes of meetings of deputies of CFM, Nov. 6-22, Marshall to Lovett, Nov. 25, 1947, FRUS, 1947, II, 680, 687, 711–712, 730–731.

19. It is noteworthy that dispatches on the proceedings of the sessions of the CFM were addressed to leading members of the Senate and House foreign affairs committees as well as to the President. Ibid., 728–772, passim. James Forrestal, *The Forrestal Diaries*, Walter Millis, ed., with collaboration of E. S. Duffield (New York, 1951), 353–354; Hickerson 1.

20. LWD to Vorys, Dec. 2, 1947, FRUS, 1947, III, 807–880; Marshall to Lovett, Dec. 11, 1947, ibid., II, 764–765; Lovett 1.

21. LWD to Jessup, Jan. 20, 1972, DP 118; Lucius D. Clay, *Decision in Germany* (New York, 1950), 344–349.

22. Ibid. See Chap. 21.

23. London embassy to Dept., Dec. 18, 1947, NA/RG59/123 Douglas, Lewis W., telegram 6554; *World Report*, Aug. 12, 29–30; *Life*, Oct. 27, 150–156; *Time*, Dec. 1, 1947, 23–26, 29–30.

24. U.S. Congress, Senate, Committee on Foreign Relations, 80th Cong., 2nd Sess., *Hearings on United States Assistance to European Recovery Program*, Jan. 9, 10, 1948, 75–244; U.S. Congress, House of Representatives, Committee on Foreign Affairs, 80th Cong., 2nd Sess., *Hearings on United States Policy for a Post-War Recovery Program*, Jan. 13, 14, 1948, 111–221; Arthur Vandenberg, *The Private Papers of Senator Vandenberg*, with the collaboration of Joe Alex Morris (Boston, 1952), 386; Henry C. Lodge, *The Storm Has Many Eyes: A Personal Narrative* (New York, 1973), 62; LWD to Jonathan Knight, Sept. 20, 1966, DP 118.

25. The critical comments were gleaned by the British embassy in Washington and transmitted to the North American Dept. of the F.O. on Feb. 3, 1948. AN 526/19/45, F.O. 371/68024. For comment on Connally's questioning, see *New York Herald Tribune*, Jan. 11, 1948, and the *Times*, Jan. 13, 1948. Joseph and Stewart Alsop, "Matter-of-Fact," *New York Herald Tribune*, Feb. 18, 1948; *New York Sun*, Feb. 18, 1948; *New York Times*, Feb. 8, 1948.

26. LWD to JSD, Feb. 11, 17, 1948, DP 33; Lovett.

27. Bevin to Inverchapel, Feb. 19, 1948, UE 2345/8/53, F.O. 371/71815.

28. Memorandum from Marshall to LWD et al., LWD to Marshall, March 15, 1948, NA/RG 59/840.50 Recovery; *Washington Star*, March 8, 1948; Vandenberg, *Private Papers*, 385–386; Harry S Truman, *Years of Trial and Hope* (New York, 1956), 119.

29. Lovett to LWD, April 2, 1948, NA/RG 59/123 Douglas, Lewis W., telegram 1151; Marshall to LWD, April 13, 1948, ibid., Martel 51.

30. Bevin to LWD, April 3, 1948, UR 735/7/98, F.O. 371/71752 and DP 279, which also contains LWD to Bevin April 6, 1948.
31. Baltimore *Sun*, Nov. 10; Washington *Star*, Dec. 18, London *Daily Telegraph*, Dec. 20, New York *Herald Tribune*, Dec. 22, 1947; James Reston in *New York Times*, Jan. 9, 1948; ibid., Jan. 16, 1948; London *Daily Telegraph*, Jan. 16, 1948.
32. New York *Herald Tribune*, Jan. 20, 1948; *United States News*, Jan. 23, 1948, 64–65; Warburg to LWD, Jan. 26, 1948, DP 280; Washington embassy to North American Dept. of F.O., Feb. 3, 1948, AN 526/19/45, F.O. 371/68024.
33. Washington *Post*, Feb. 11, Doris Fleeson in Washington *Star*, Feb. 12, *New York Times*, Mar. 31, 1948; Vandenberg, *Private Papers*, 393; David S. McLellan, *Dean Acheson: The State Department Years* (New York, 1976), 136; Acheson, *Sketches from Life*, 129.
34. Arthur Krock interview with HST, April 8, 1948, in Arthur Krock, *Memoirs: Sixty Years on the Firing Line* (New York, 1968), 242; LWD to Lovett, April 6, 7, 1948, NA/RG 59/103.02 ECA, telegrams 1394, 1408; Marshall to Lovett (from Bogotá), April 16, 1948, NA/RG 59/840.50 Recovery, Martel 67; Lovett to Marshall, April 17, 1948, FRUS, 1948, III, 425–426; ibid., 437 n.
35. LWD to Hoffman, May 1, LWD to Harriman, May 1, 11, Hoffman to LWD, May 8, LWD to Finletter, May 20, Finletter to LWD, May 28, June 2, 1948, DP 279; LWD to SecState, April 2, June 11 (two telegrams), Marshall to LWD, Aug. 20, LWD to SecState, Aug. 31, 1948, FRUS, 1948, III, 1079–1082, 1089–1090, 450–452, 476–477, 483–486; Bevin conversations with LWD, June 4, 7, 1948, UR 2044/1511/98, UR 2095/1511/98, F.O. 371/71898; Franks (ambassador in Washington since May, 1948) to F.O., June 24, Makins conversation with LWD, June 23, Franks to F.O. June 24, 1948, UR 2539/1511/98, UR 2543/1511/98, UR 2578/1511/98, F.O. 371/71902; bilateral agreement on ERP signed by Bevin and LWD, July 6, 1948, UR 3042/1511/98, UR 3040/1511/98, F.O. 371/71905; Finletter I; Kenney I; Hoffman to LWD, Oct. 16, 1948, DP 279.

CHAPTER 21 *The London Conference*

1. Lovett to Murphy, Nov. 19, 1947, FRUS, 1947, II, 723.
2. In an interview, in December, 1947, Clayton commented that his conversations with the French the previous summer had impressed him with "the intensity with which the French people—as evidenced by the attitude of their political leaders—regarded the possibility of an attack by Germany again . . . it was a phobia with them." Frederick J. Dabney, ed., *Selected Papers of Will Clayton* (Baltimore and London, 1971), 208. Memorandum of Conversation of LWD with Bidault and Memorandum of Conversation of Marshall with Bidault, Dec. 17, 1947, FRUS, 1947, II, 811–815.
3. Memoranda of conversations between Marshall and Bevin, Dec. 17, and at Prince's Gate, Dec. 18, 1947, ibid., 815–829. It is not clear whether LWD accompanied Marshall on Dec. 17, but probably he did so. Jean Edward Smith, ed., *The Papers of General Lucius D. Clay: Germany, 1945–1949* (Bloomington, Ind., 1974), I, 501–502.
4. Inverchapel to Marshall, Jan. 17, Marshall to Inverchapel, Jan. 30, LWD to SecState, Feb. 20, 21, 22, 1948, FRUS, 1948, II, 36, 50–51, 75–81.
5. For the revision of the Bizonal organizations, see ibid., 1–20, passim; for French objections, see ibid., 20–40, passim; for State Department surprise at the scope of the revisions, see Associate Chief of Division of Western European Affairs (Wallner) to Counselor of Embassy in France (Bonbright), Jan. 16, 1947, ibid., 27–28.
6. Editorial note, Marshall to embassy in France, Feb. 19, Marshall to embassy in U.K., Feb. 20, Economic Agreement Regarding the Saar, Feb. 20, Panyushkin to Lovett, Feb. 13, 1948, ibid., 59–60, 70–71, 71–73, 73–75, 338–339.
7. LWD to SecState, Feb. 23, 1948, editorial note listing delegates of Western powers and Benelux countries, ibid., 82–83, 85–86; Smith, *Clay Papers*, II, 548–549. With the addition of the Benelux delegates, the meeting became technically a Six Power Conference and is thus referred to in official documents, although Belgium, the Netherlands, and Luxembourg played distinctly secondary roles.
8. LWD to SecState, Feb. 25, 1948, FRUS, 1948, II, 87–89; LWD handwritten notes for his remarks to conference, Feb. 24, 1948, DP 278.
9. LWD to SecState, Feb. 25, May 1, May 7, 1948, FRUS, 1948, II, 89–90, 214–216, 228–229; secret minute by Strang, Feb. 25, 1948, C 1887/71/18/G, F.O. 371/70582. In the event, reparations deliveries to the Soviet were not resumed.
10. LWD to SecState, Feb. 26, SecState to embassy in U.K., Feb. 28, LWD to SecState, Feb. 28, 1948, FRUS, 1948, II, 94–95, 101–102, 98.
11. Minute by Strang to Bevin, March 1, 1948, C 1689/71/18, F.O. 371/70581.
12. LWD to Lovett, March 1, telephone conversation between LWD and Lovett, March 2, Lovett to LWD, March 2, LWD to Marshall, March 2, Marshall to LWD, March 4, LWD to Lovett, March 6, 1948, FRUS, 1948, II, 107, 112, 110–111, 122–123, 138–139.
13. On Ruhr, LWD to SecState, March 4, SecState to embassy in U.K., March 5, LWD to

SecState, March 6, ibid., 124–128, 131, 140–141. Clay, who had left the conference early and was opposed to any international control of the Ruhr during the occupation, was disturbed at the language of the communiqué until assured by Murphy that Douglas had clearly stated at the last meeting that the proposed international board "was not to impinge on [the] power of [the] occupying powers during [the] period of direct responsibility." Smith, *Clay Papers*, II, 569–571. On reparations, LWD to Lovett, March 3, LWD to SecState, March 4, LWD to Lovett, March 6, 1948, FRUS, 1948, II, 118–120, 128–130, 139–140; on federal government, LWD to Marshall, March 1, 1948, ibid., 107–110, and Lucius D. Clay, *Decision in Germany* (New York, 1950), 396.

14. LWD to SecState, March 6, communiqué issued at recess of London Conference, March 6, 1948, FRUS, 1948, II, 140–143; Sir Oliver Harvey (British ambassador to France), to F.O., March 10, 1948, C 1939/71/18/G, F.O. 371/70582; Bevin to British embassies in Washington and Paris, March 16, and Strang to Massigli and Gallman, March 15, 1948, C 1993/7118/G and C 2027/71/18/G, F.O. 371/70583.

15. Inverchapel to SecState with enclosed memorandum of Bevin's views on the formation of a Western Union, Jan. 13, Marshall to Inverchapel, Jan. 20, ambassador in Norway to SecState, March 11, 12, British embassy to Dept. of State, March 11, SecState to embassy in Norway, March 12, 1948, FRUS, 1948, III, 3–6, 8–9, 44–45, 48–49, 51–52, and passim; Smith, *Clay Papers*, II, 568–569.

16. FRUS, 1948, III, 1–52, passim; Panyushkin to SecState, March 6, Murphy to SecState, March 20, 1948, ibid., II, 345–354, 883–884; Dept. of State *Bulletin*, March 28, 1948, 418; Robertson to F.O., March 20, 1948, C 2211/71/18/G, F.O. 371/70583.

17. LWD to Lovett, Feb. 26, editorial note, British embassy to SecState, March 11, SecState to British amb., March 12, SecState to HST, March 12, SecState to Caffery, March 12, Inverchapel to SecState, March 14, Bidault and Bevin to SecState, March 17, 1948, FRUS, III, 1948, 32–33, 38, 46–52, 55–56; Hickerson I.

18. FRUS, 1948, III, 59–79, 80–351, passim; ibid., 1949, IV, 1–285, passim; Hickerson I; *The Memoirs of Lord Gladwyn* (New York, 1972), 214–216.

19. James Forrestal, *The Forrestal Diaries*, ed. by Walter Millis with the collaboration of E. S. Duffield (New York, 1951), 400.

20. FRUS, 1948, II, 145–191, passim; minute of Strang on conversation with Massigli, March 19, 1948, C 2268/71/18/G, F.O. 371/70584; LWD to Hickerson, April 2, Lovett to LWD, April 3, 1948, FRUS, 1948, II, 163–165; Bevin conversation with LWD, April 6, 1948, AN 1490/6/45, F.O. 371/68014; Murphy to Hickerson, April 8, 1948, FRUS, II, 169–170.

21. LWD to SecState, April 16, 1948, ibid., 187–188. LWD's letter to Lovett on the Churchill conversation is printed in ibid., 895–896 and III, 90. LWD's copy is in DP 279.

22. FRUS, 1948, II, 191 ff.; LWD to SecState, April 21, 1948, ibid., 198.

23. Ibid., 305; Clay, *Decisions*, 404.

24. Smith, *Clay Papers*, II, 638–639; Murphy to Hickerson, May 2, 1948, FRUS, 1948, II, 216.

25. LWD to Marshall and Lovett, April 27, Marshall and Lovett to LWD, April 28, 1948, ibid., 205–207; LWD to Lovett, April 22, 30, 1948, DP 279; Clay, *Decision*, 394 ff.; Clay I.

26. Clay to Draper, May 11, Clay-Draper teleconference, May 14, Clay to Draper, May 19, 1948, Smith, *Clay Papers*, II, 650-655; LWD to Lovett, May 12, 13, Royall to Marshall, May 18, Saltzman to LWD, May 19, 1948, Conference Papers Agreed Upon, FRUS, 1948, II, 235–237, 244–245, 251–253, 285–288, 290–291; Clay, *Decision*, 337–340; Clay to Draper, June 2, 1948, Smith, *Clay Papers*, II, 660; Douglas to Marshall, June 7, 1948, DP 279. The final agreement on the Ruhr authority was negotiated in London from Nov. 11 to Dec. 24, 1948. Though Douglas was the official American representative, most of the detail work was done by Wayne G. Jackson, special advisor to the director of the Office of European Affairs. See FRUS, 1948, II, 448–597. From the beginning of the Ruhr discussions, it was agreed that the United States, Great Britain, France, and Germany were each to have three votes in the authority, and each of the Benelux countries one. Until the contracting powers decided otherwise, the German representative would be designated and his vote determined by the occupying powers.

27. Ibid., 316.

28. Bevin to Inverchapel, May 10, 1948, C 3713/71/18/G, F.O. 371/70588; dispatches between LWD and Lovett and LWD and Marshall, May 10–14, LWD to Lovett, May 19, Lovett to LWD, May 19, 1948, FRUS, 1948, II, 232–234, 248, 255–258.

29. For the dispatches on the French note and reactions, see ibid., 266–284, 298–299; Bevin to Balfour, May 24, 1948, C 4036/71/18/G, F.O. 371/70590.

30. FRUS, 1948, II, 309–317, 364–368, 331–335.

31. LWD to JSD, June 6, 1948, DP 33; Bevin to Franks, June 7, 1948, C 4431/71/18/G, F.O. 371/70592; Caffery to SecState, June 10, 1948, FRUS, 1948, II, 325.

32. LWD to SecState, June 16, 1948, ibid., 331–335. Chauvel informed the British ambassador in Paris that "he particularly wanted to see Mr. Douglas rather than talk to Mr. Caffery here." Sir Oliver Harvey to F.O., June 13, 1948, C 4595/71/18/G, F.O. 371/70593.

33. LWD to JSD, June 19, 1948, DP 33; LWD to John Foster Dulles, July 9, 1948, DP

278; Caffery to SecState, June 17, 1948, and editorial note, FRUS, 1948, II, 336 n., 337.

34. Clay, *Decision*, 404.

CHAPTER 22 *The Berlin Blockade*

1. LWD to Jessup, Dec. 22, 1971, DP 118.
2. Lovett to LWD, Clay, and Murphy, April 22, LWD to Marshall and Lovett, April 28, 1948, FRUS, 1948, II, 896-897, 899-900; Strang memoranda of conversations on April 27, 28, 1948, C 3524/3/18/G, C 3581/3/18/G, F.O. 371/70492 and 70493; Clay 1.
3. LWD to Lovett, May 22, Saltzman to LWD and Clay, May 29, LWD to Lovett, May 29, 1948, FRUS, 1948, II, 904-905.
4. Murphy to SecState, June 17, editorial note, Murphy to SecState, June 19, 23, 26, 1948, ibid., 908-914, 918-919; George F. Kennan, *Memoirs, 1925-1950* (Boston, 1967), 420; LWD to Jessup, Dec. 22, 1971, DP 118.
5. Ibid.; Daniel Yergin, *Shattered Peace: The Origins of the Cold War and the National Security State* (Boston, 1977), 377; Jean Edward Smith, ed., *The Papers of General Lucius D. Clay* (Bloomington, Ind., 1974), I, xxviii.
6. Bevin memorandum of conversation with LWD, June 25, Bevin to Franks, June 26, 1948, C 5031/3/18/G and C 5032/3/18/G, F.O. 371/70497.
7. LWD to Marshall and Lovett, June 26, Marshall to LWD, June 27, 1948, FRUS, 1948, II, 921-928; LWD I, Nov. 2, 1972.
8. LWD to Gladwyn Jebb, Aug. 28, 1957, DP 279; LWD to Jessup, Dec. 22, 1971, DP 118; James Forrestal, *The Forrestal Diaries*, ed. by Walter Millis with the collaboration of E. S. Duffield (New York, 1951), 454; Marshall to LWD, June 27, LWD to Marshall, June 28, 1948, FRUS, 1948, II, 926-928, 927 n.; Bevin to Franks, June 28, Cabinet Defense Committee Meeting, June 28, 1948, C 5072/3/18/G and C 5136/3/18/G, F.O. 371/70497 and 70498.
9. Forrestal, *Diaries*, 454; Marshall to LWD, June 28, Marshall to Caffery, June 30, 1948, FRUS, 1948, II, 930-931, 933-936; Sir I. Kirkpatrick to Sir O. Oswald (in Berlin), June 28, 1948, C 5135/3/18/G, F.O. 371/70498.
10. Bevin to Franks, June 28, 29, 30, Bevin to Harvey, June 30, 1948, C 5138/3/18/G, C 5181/3/18/G C 5197/3/18/G, C 5196/3/18/G, F.O. 371/70498.
11. Bevin to Franks, June 30, July 1, 1948, C 5262/3/18/G, C 5197/3/18/G, F.O. 371/70499; Marshall to Caffery, June 30, 1948, Editorial Note, LWD to Marshall and Lovett, June 30, 1948, FRUS, 1948, II, 933, 931, 936-938.
12. Strang memorandum of meeting with LWD and Massigli dated June 30, 1948, C 5263/3/18/G, F.O. 371/70499; LWD to SecState, July 1, Dept. to LWD, July 1, 1948, FRUS, 1948, II, 938-939, 935 n. The designation "standing committee" was later used by the New York *Herald Tribune*, Aug. 5, 1948, in commenting on the continuing role of the three men in the Berlin crisis. At the time, the American press in its news coverage recognized the key role played by the three men in London. See the *New York Times*, and *Herald Tribune* of July 2 and the New York *Sun* of July 6, 1948.
13. Memoranda and communications in F.O. 371/70498, 70499, 70500; FRUS, 1948, II, 938-953, passim.
14. LWD to JSD, July 7, 1948, DP 33; LWD to Jessup, Dec. 22, 1971, DP 118; Peggy Douglas I; Massigli to RPB, July 12, 1977; Strang I; Lovett to LWD, July 29, 1948, DP 279.
15. Marshall to LWD, July 9, LWD to SecState, July 7, 10, 13, Smith to SecState, July 11, Caffery to SecState, July 12, Clay to Dept. of Army, July 10, Murphy to SecState, July 11, 1948, FRUS, 1948, II, 954-958; Strang memorandum of meeting with LWD and Massigli, July 9, LWD to Strang, July 10, 1948, C 5612/3/18/G, C 5613/3/18/G, F.O. 371/70502; *New York Times*, July 12, 1948; Clay I; Bevin to Franks, C 5653/3/18/G, F.O. 371/70502.
16. Panyushkin to SecState, July 14, 1948, FRUS, 1948, II, 960-964.
17. Memorandum of conversation of Lovett, Franks, and Reber (deputy director, Office of European Affairs), July 14, LWD to Lovett, July 17, 1948, ibid., 965, 967-970; F.O. to Bevin (at The Hague), July 19, Franks to F.O., July 19, 1948, C 5790/3/18/G, C 3875/3/18/G, F.O. 371/70502.
18. Reference to draft replies, July 18-21, Marshall to LWD, July 20, 1948, FRUS, 1948, II, 974 n., 971-973; LWD to Strang, Strang to Bevin (at The Hague), July 20, 1948, C 6049/3/18/G, F.O. 371/70504.
19. The numerous communications and memoranda regarding these discussions among the Western powers are found in FRUS, 1948, II, 975-995 and in F.O. 371/70503, 70504; Lucius D. Clay, *Decision in Germany* (New York, 1950), 375-376; Charles E. Bohlen, *Witness to History, 1929-1969* (New York, 1973), 279-280; Clay I.
20. LWD to Marshall, July 28, Marshall to LWD, July 29, 1948, DP 279.
21. LWD to Vandenberg, July 20, 1948, DP 301.
22. The talks with Molotov and Stalin in Moscow and meetings of the military governors in Berlin are covered in detail in FRUS, 1948, II, 995-1197, passim. See also Walter Bedell Smith, *My Three Years in Moscow* (Philadelphia, 1950), 237 ff. and Smith, *Clay Papers*, II 796-857, passim.
23. Bevin memorandum of conversation with LWD, Aug. 20, 1948, C 6885/3/18/G, F.O. 371/70509; Roberts to F.O., Aug. 25, 1948, C 7062/3/18/G, F.O. 371/70510; Robertson to Strang, Aug. 28, 1948, C 7136/3/18/G, F.O. 371/70511; telecon between Lovett and LWD, Sept.

4, LWD to Marshall and Lovett, Sept. 5, 1948, *FRUS*, 1948, II, 1113–1118, 1126–1129; Strang memorandum on meeting with LWD and Massigli, Sept. 7, 1948, C 7607/3/18/G, F.O. 371/70515.

24. Murphy to SecState, Sept. 7, Marshall to LWD, Sept. 8, Marshall to Murphy and Clay (incorporating message to LWD), Sept. 11, 1948, *FRUS*, 1948, II, 1132–1134, 1140–1142, 1147–1149; Bevin to Franks, Sept. 10, 11, 12, Franks to Bevin, Sept. 11, 1948, in F.O. 371/70513 and 70514; Forrestal, *Diaries*, 485. The Western aide-mémoire and the Soviet reply are found in *FRUS*, 1948, II, 1152–1154, 1162–1165.

25. Bevin to Franks, Sept. 19, 1948, C 7700/3/18/G, F.O. 371/70515.

26. Minutes of meeting of Western foreign ministers in Paris, Sept. 20, 21, 26, note to Soviet government, Sept. 22, Soviet reply of Sept. 25, note to Soviet government, Sept. 26, 1948, *FRUS*, 1948, II, 1173–1176, 1177–1180, 1181–1184, 1187–1193; Strang memorandum, Sept. 21, 1948, C 7784/3/18/G, F.O. 371/70516; memorandum of LWD conversations with Marshall, Sept. 22, 26, and memorandum of Marshall's reply, Sept. 26, 1948, DP 278; memorandum of conversation with LWD (by Jessup), Sept. 27, 1948, *FRUS*, 1948, II, 1193–1194.

27. Editorial notes, ibid., 1212–1213, 1233–1234.

28. Harold Nicolson, *Diaries and Letters, 1945–62*, Nigel Nicolson, ed. (London, 1968), 151; Smith, *Clay Papers*, I, xviii; McNeil to Bevin, Sept. 23, 1948, C 8535/3/18/G, F.O. 371/70519; LWD to Acting SecState, Oct. 26, 1948, *FRUS*, 1948, II, 1234–1236; LWD to JSD, Oct. 16, 1948, DP 33; Forrestal, *Diaries*, 520.

29. Lippmann interviews with LWD, Dec. 2, 11, 1948, Yale Lippmann Collection (courtesy of Daniel F. Harrington); Clay, *Decision*, 376–377; Clay I.

30. See *FRUS*, 1949, III, 666 ff. and especially LWD to Acheson, Feb. 22, 1949, 681–685; Clay, *Decision*, 388; LWD to JSD, Dec. 12, 1948, DP 33.

31. LWD I, Nov. 2, 1972; Alan Bullock, *Ernest Bevin: Foreign Secretary* (New York, 1983), 587; Dean to Peggy Douglas, March 9, 1974, DP 120.

CHAPTER 23 *Palestine and Presidential Politics*

1. Memorandum of William J. McWilliams to SecState, Feb. 25, statement issued by the White House, Feb. 26, 1947, *FRUS*, 1947, V, 1056–1058; Harry S Truman, *Years of Trial and Hope* (New York, 1956), 154; Inverchapel to Bevin, Feb. 27, 1947, E 1830/4631, F.O. 371/6169.

2. F.O. memorandum, May 5, AN 1654/1/45, Washington chancellery to F.O., May 26, 1947, AN 1983/1/45, F.O. 371/61001.

3. Bevin to Inverchapel, June 4, 1947, E 805/32/45, F.O. 371/61755; memorandum of conversation of Henderson and LWD with Bevin, Sept. 9, 1947, *FRUS*, 1947, V, 498–499.

4. Editorial note, ibid., 1143.

5. Editorial note, Austin to SecState, Nov. 29, Nov. 14, Marshall to Lovett, Nov. 28, Dec. 5, 1947, ibid., 1180, 1291, 1259–1261, 1289–1290, 1298–1299.

6. Marshall to Lovett, Nov. 25, 1947, ibid., 1287–1289.

7. Marshall to Lovett, Dec. 6, 1947, ibid., 1311–1312.

8. Memorandum of conversation, Dec. 17, 1947, E 525/11/65/G, F.O. 371/68364 and *FRUS*, 1947, V, 1312–1313; memorandum from British embassy to Dept. of State, Jan. 5, 1948, ibid., 1948, V, pt. 2, 533–536.

9. Bevin minute to Sargent, March 1, 1948, E 2996/1048/31/G, F.O. 371/68648.

10. Austin before the Security Council, March 19, Truman statement, March 25, 1948, *FRUS*, 1948, V, pt. 2, 742–744, 759–760. See also editorial note, ibid., 744–746.

11. Gallman to SecState, March 24, 1948, ibid., 758–759. The British embassy reiterated this position to Henderson on March 27, 1948, ibid., 767–769. Editorial note, ibid., 776–777.

12. Proposed letter (undated), Lovett circular telegram, April 6, Lovett to LWD, April 9, 1948, ibid., 771–773, 800–807.

13. LWD to SecState, April 16, 1948, ibid., 826; LWD to Bevin, April 13, 1948, E 4796/1078/13/G, F.O. 371/68649.

14. Lovett to LWD, April 17, 23, LWD to Lovett, April 20, 23, 29, 1948, *FRUS*, 1948, V, pt. 2, 828–829, 856–857, 837, 855–856, 876–877; Bevin to Inverchapel and to UN delegation (the more detailed account to Inverchapel), April 19, Bevin to Inverchapel, April 21, 28, 1948, E 4884/1048/31/G, E 4880/1078/3/G, E 5020/1048/31/G and E 5751/1048/31/G, F.O. 371/68649.

15. Lovett to LWD, May 3, Austin to SecState, May 3, Moshe Shertok (head, Political Dept. of Jewish Agency) to Dean Rusk (director, Office of United Nations Affairs), May 4, LWD to Lovett, May 4, 1948, *FRUS*, 1948, V, pt. 2, 891–892, 886–889, 893–894.

16. Jessup to Rusk, May 4, White House meeting, May 12, 1948, ibid., 897, 972–978.

17. Eliahu Epstein (agent of the Provisional Government of Israel in Washington) to HST and SecState, May 14, Marshall to Epstein, May 14, editorial note, memorandum of conversations by Under Secretary Lovett, May 17, Marshall to Lovett, May 17, Austin to Marshall, May 18, 1948, ibid., 989, 989 n., 992, 993, 1005–1007, 1007–1008, 1013–1015.

18. Marshall to LWD, May 14, 1948, ibid., 990–991; Don C. Bliss to Bevin, May 15, 1948, E 7222/6090/31/G, F.O. 371/68665.

19. Bevin to Wash. embassy and UN del., May 15, and to UN del. only, May 15, 1948, E 6285/4/31, E 6585/6090/31/G, F.O. 371/68552, 68664.

20. Minute by Wright, May 21, 1948, E 6915/1048/31/G, F.O. 371/68640; LWD to Lovett, May 22, 1948, *FRUS*, 1948, V, pt. 2, 1031; LWD to JSD, May 21, 1948, DP 33.

21. LWD to Marshall and Lovett, May 22, British embassy to Dept. of State summarizing LWD-Bevin conversation of May 22, May 24 (these communications were read to HST by Marshall), Marshall to Lovett on conversation with HST, May 24, LWD to SecState, May 25, editorial note and resolution by General Assembly of May 14, Security Council resolution of May 29, acceptance of cease-fire by Israel and Arab states, June 1, 1948, editorial note, *FRUS*, 1948, V, pt. 2, 1032–1033, 1034–1036, 1036 n., 1036–1037, 1047–1050, 994–995, 994 n., 1077–1078, 1084–1086, 1102.

22. LWD to Marshall and Lovett, June 18, 19, 1948, ibid., 1121–1122, 1124–1125; Wright minute, June 16, Bevin to Inverchapel, June 18, 1948, E 8410/1078/31/G, E 8626/1078/31/G, F.O. 371/8650.

23. Marshall to LWD, June 22, LWD to SecState, June 24, Lovett to LWD, June 25, 1948, *FRUS*, 1948, V, pt. 2, 1133–1134, 1143–1144, 1148–1149.

24. LWD to SecState, July 6, Dept. to LWD, July 7, 1948, ibid., 1193–1195, 1195 n.

25. Lillie Shultz to Leslie Biffle and Howard McGrath, July 1, 1948, David Niles Papers, Goldfarb Library, Brandeis University and J. Howard McGrath Papers, Box 28, HSTL.

26. Harold Nicolson, *Diaries and Letters, 1945–62*, Nigel Nicolson, ed. (London, 1968), 145.

27. LWD to SecState, July 9, 11, 12, 14, Security Council Resolution 54, July 15, 1948, *FRUS*, 1948, V, pt. 2, 1203–1205, 1210–1212, 1215, 1220–1221, 1224–1225.

28. LWD to SecState, Aug. 2, 1948, ibid., 1266–1271.

29. LWD to SecState, Aug. 6, 1948, ibid., 1291–1294.

30. Tel. conversation of Lovett with Clifford, June 22, Lovett conversations with McDonald, June 25, July 21, 1948, ibid., 1131–1132, 1151–1152, 1232; James G. McDonald, *My Mission in Israel, 1948–1951* (New York, 1951), 21–26; tel. conversation of McDonald with Clifford, Aug. 5, 1948, David Niles Papers, fldr. 202(1), Goldfarb Library, Brandeis University; McDonald to LWD, Aug. 4, 1948, DP 279.

31. Bernadotte's suggestions of June 28, 1948, *FRUS*, 1948, V, pt. 2, 1152–1154.

32. Marshall to LWD, Aug. 12, 13, 1948, ibid., 1303–1306, 1308–1310.

33. Four cables LWD to Marshall, Aug. 27, LWD to Marshall, Sept. 1, Marshall to LWD, Sept. 1, 1948, ibid., 1352–1359, 1365–1366, 1369.

34. LWD to SecState, Sept. 3, memorandum of conversation of McDonald with Shertok, Sept. 6, 1948, ibid., 1373, 1375–1378.

35. McClintock to Lovett and Rusk, Sept. 15, Progress Report of Mediator to General Assembly, Sept. 16, consul general in Jerusalem to SecState, Sept. 17, 1948, ibid., 1398–1401, 1401–1406, 1412–1413.

36. LWD to Marshall and Lovett, Sept. 17, Marshall to LWD, Sept. 18, Marshall to McDonald, Sept. 1, Marshall statement, Sept. 21, 1948, editorial note, ibid., 1409–1412, 1413, 1369 n., 1415–1416, 1415 n., 1418.

37. Griffis (ambassador to Egypt) to Lovett, Sept. 25, McDonald to SecState, Sept. 28, Stabler (in Trans-Jordan) to SecState, Sept. 24, 1948, ibid., 1422–1423, 1428–1429, 1419–1420; Franks to Bevin, Oct. 1, 1948, E 12786/4/31, F.O. 371/68590.

38. Memorandum of tel. conversation of Lovett with Clifford (on campaign train in Tulsa), Sept. 29, draft telegram (undated) to Rabbi Stephen S. Wise, McClintock memorandum, Sept. 30, 1948, draft statement (undated), Marshall in Washington, discussion on drafting and delaying note, *FRUS*, 1948, V, pt. 2, 1430–1431, 1432, 1437–1438, 1466, 1467 n., 1466–1502, passim.

39. LWD to Lovett, Oct. 13, 14, 1948, ibid., 1469–1470, 1474–1476; McNeil (in Paris), to Bevin, Oct. 19, Bevin to McNeil, Oct. 20, 1948, E 13539/4/31/G, F.O. 371/68592; LWD to JSD, Oct. 16, 1948, DP 33; Sargent minute, Oct. 21, 1948, E 14099/4/31/G, F.O. 371/68594.

40. Rusk to Marshall, Oct. 7, Lovett to Marshall, Oct. 23, 24, 1948, *FRUS*, 1948, V, pt. 2, 1463, 1507–1508, 1512–1514.

41. Wright to U.K. UN del., Oct. 25, 1948, E 14085/1078/31, F.O. 371/68561.

42. LWD to Lovett, Oct. 26, 29, 1948, *FRUS*, 1948, V, pt. 2, 1516–1518, 1530–1533.

43. Marshall in London, Marshall to Lovett, Oct. 31, Lovett to Marshall, Oct. 30, 31, 1948, ibid., 1528 n., 1533–1535.

44. *New York Times*, Nov. 4, 1948; Lovett to Marshall, Nov. 10, Douglas to Lovett, Nov. 12, 1948, *FRUS*, 1948, V, pt. 2, 1565–1566, 1570–1572; LWD I, Nov. 2, 1972. LWD often recounted and wrote of this confrontation, with slightly differing wordings, after he had left the ambassadorship.

45. F.O. to U.K. UN del., Nov. 22, Wash. emb. to F.O., Nov. 23, 1948, E 14954/4/31/G, E 15079/4/31, F.O. 371/68598.

46. LWD to Lovett, Dec. 2, 1948, editorial note, *FRUS*, 1948, V, pt. 2, 1643–1644, 1661–1662.

47. LWD (signed by Holmes after LWD's departure) to Lovett, Dec. 22, 1948, ibid., 1680–1685, 1685 n.

48. LWD to Brendan Bracken, July 21, 1958, DP 307; Lovett I.

CHAPTER 24 *Personal Misfortune and Diplomatic Tensions*

1. Sir Roderick Barclay, *Ernest Bevin and the Foreign Office, 1932–1969* (London, 1975), 56, 85; Dean Acheson, *Sketches from Life of Men I Have Known* (New York, 1961), 1–29; Alan Bullock, *Ernest Bevin: Foreign Secretary* (New York, 1983), 88, 667, 718; Dean Acheson, *Present at the Creation: My Years in the State Department* (New York, 1969), 323–324.

2. LWD to Dewey, June 25, 1948, DP 303; LWD to Vandenberg, July 7, Lippmann to LWD, July 9, 1948, DP 301; LWD to JSD, Oct. 16, 1948, DP 33; Sherwood to LWD, July 23, 1948, Sherwood Papers, folder 110, Houghton Library, Harvard University. On July 28, 1948, Halifax wrote to Stimson: "Lew Douglas has made himself a truly remarkable position in London—and I shall be very sad if anything causes his withdrawal. Both of them are greatly loved." Stimson Papers, box 151, Yale University Library.

3. McGrath to LWD, Sept. 3, 1948, DP 302.

4. Johnson to LWD, Oct. 13, LWD to Johnson, Oct. 15, 1948, DP 302; Stroud to E.T. Cusick, chairman of the Arizona State Democratic Committee, Nov. 9, 1948, DP 260, explaining that in his recent residential move LWD's instruction of Oct. 15 to send a $500 contribution had gone astray and only then come to his attention.

5. LWD notes on conversation with Marshall, Oct. 20, 1948, DP 279; Harriman I; Kenney I. Largely because of his campaign work and the assurance that he was a "team player," Truman appointed Johnson secretary of defense on March 3, 1949, when he dismissed Forrestal as the result of increasingly strained relations and the secretary's irrational behavior. On Sept. 12, 1950, after the outbreak of the Korean War, the President demanded and received Johnson's resignation for inefficiency and disloyalty. Robert J. Donovan, *Tumultuous Years: The Presidency of Harry S. Truman, 1949–1953* (New York, 1982), 59–61, 265–67. When, in March, 1949, Johnson visited London, LWD reluctantly gave a dinner for him, admitting to Admiral Richard L. Conolly, commander in chief, U.S. Naval Forces in the Eastern Atlantic and Mediterranean, that "I hate his guts." Conolly, "Reminiscences," COHC.

6. LWD to Porgue Patten, June 6, 1948, DP 302; LWD to George Sokolsky, April 6, 1953, DP 314; LWD 1; LWD telegram to HST, Nov. 3, LWD to HST, Nov. 9, 1948, DP 279; LWD to Barkley, Nov. 9, 1948, DP 302.

7. London *Evening Standard*, Nov. 3, *New York Times*, Nov. 5, Washington *Post*, Nov. 8, 1948; Thomas Lamont to LWD, Nov. 10, 1948, DP 279; Rep. Peter Jarman to LWD, Nov. 10, Harry F. Byrd, Jr., to LWD, Nov. 12, 1948, DP 302; Gaddis Smith, *Dean Acheson (The American Secretaries of State and Their Diplomacy*, Robert H. Ferrell, ed.) (New York, 1972), 54.

8. LWD to JSD, Nov. 9, Campbell to LWD, Nov. 12, LWD to Campbell, Nov. 19, 1948, DP 33.

9. Walter Trohan in Chicago *Tribune*, Nov. 18, Paul R. Leach in Chicago *News*, Dec. 18, 1948; New York *Daily Mirror*, May 23, Drew Pearson, "Washington Merry-Go-Round," in Cleveland *News*, May 24, 1949; Harriman 1; Acheson, *Present at the Creation*, 249–250. Acheson gave the date of the offer and acceptance as late November. Smith, *Dean Acheson*, 54, gave the time as mid-November. LWD 1; LWD to Herbert Feis, May 6, 1970, DP 118.

10. LWD to Marshall, Dec. 3, 1948, DP 279; LWD to HST, Dec. 17, 1948, NA/RG59/123 Douglas, Lewis W. (no number); Douglas Fairbanks, Jr., to HST, Dec. 7, 1948, PPF 4497, HSTL.

11. Acheson memorandum of conversation with HST, Jan. 24, 1949, "Official Conversations and Meetings of Dean Acheson, 1949–1953," microfilm, reel 1, fr. 16, University Publications of America.

12. *New York Times*, Jan. 3, 4 ("The Douglas Clan"), New York *Herald Tribune*, Jan. 3, 1949; LWD to Applewhite, May 31, Oct. 27, 1948, DP 79; LWD to JSD, Nov. 29, 1947, Campbell to LWD, May 5, LWD to Campbell, May 10, Campbell to LWD, Aug. 29, Mrs. Keith Hutchison (wife of family doctor) to LWD, Aug. 25, Dr. D. Sclater Lewis to LWD, Aug. 29, Campbell to LWD, Oct. 21, LWD to Mrs. Hutchison, Oct. 27, LWD to JSD, Feb. 11, Aug. 25, Nov. 9, 1948, DP 33.

13. Prescott *Evening Courier*, Jan. 3, 1949; LWD's secretary (signature illegible) to Stroud, Dec. 20, 1947, DP 281; Campbell to LWD, Oct. 21, LWD to JSD, Oct. 27, 1948, DP 33.

14. Brophy I; LWD to Peggy Damskey, Feb. 9, 1951, DP 60; London *Sunday Express*, Nov. 29, 1949; Peggy Douglas I; JSD will of Nov. 10, 1948, DP 57; financial statement of Barrow, Wade, Guthrie and Co. in letter to Stroud, July 18, 1950, DP 431.

15. LWD to SecState, Feb. 3, 7, 15, 1949, NA/RG59/123 Douglas, Lewis W., tels. 415, 445, 567.

16. FRUS, 1948, II, 668–669, 703–866; editorial note, ibid., 1949, III, 546–547; Lucius D. Clay, *Decision in Germany* (New York, 1950), 322–325.

17. Saltzman (asst. sec. of state for occupied areas) to LWD, Feb. 6, 9, 16, LWD to Saltzman, Feb. 9, 23, LWD to Acheson, March 2, Hoffman to LWD, March 4, 1949, FRUS, 1949, III, 550–560; minute of Frank Roberts, Feb. 10, 1949, AN 695/1053/45, F.O. 371/74183.

18. LWD to Acheson, March 7, Acheson

to LWD, March 11, 1949, *FRUS*, 1949, III, 559–563.

19. LWD to Acheson, March 15, 1949, ibid., 566–567; Clay telecon conversation with Voorhees (under secretary of the army), March 17, Clay to Voorhees, March 21, 1949, Jean Edward Smith, ed., *The Papers of General Lucius D. Clay* (Bloomington, Ind., 1974), II, 1047–1054, 1058–1059, 1061.

20. LWD to Murphy, March 19, LWD to Acheson, March 24, 1949, editorial note, *FRUS*, 1949, III, 577–581, 588–591, 591–592; Murphy to LWD, April 4, 1949, DP 279; Clay, *Decision*, 324.

21. Acheson, *Present at the Creation*, 307–313; U.S. Correlation Committee in Europe on Foreign Assistance Programs, 426M, HSTL; Acheson to LWD, Feb. 16, 1949, *FRUS*, 1949, IV, 110–113.

22. LWD and Harriman to Acheson, March 2, Caffery to LWD, March 3, 1949, ibid., 136–139, 146–148.

23. LWD to Acheson, March 16, minutes of first meeting of European Correlation Committee, March 25, LWD to SecState, March 26, 27, Brussels Treaty powers request, April 5, and United States reply, April 6, 1949, ibid., 229–233, 244–248, 250–253, 285–288.

24. LWD to SecState, April 26, June 5, 1949, editorial notes, ibid., 395–396, 301–303, 313, 341; Acheson, *Present at the Creation*, 312–313, 351; London *Daily Graphic*, Nov. 16, 1959.

25. North Atlantic Treaty and signing ceremony, *FRUS*, 1949, IV, 281–285.

26. Lewis W. Douglas, "Foreword" to British edition of Ray Bergman, *Trout* (London, 1950); *Fortune*, May, 1946; LWD to Everett Garrison, March 11, Marshall to LWD, May 20, LWD to Marshall, June 11, 1947, DP 279; memo from LWD's secretary to LWD, Oct. 2, 1947, Fairey to LWD, April 18, 1948, DP 298. Each rod cost $95.

27. LWD to McCloy, July 23, 1947, DP 280; Paul Warburg to secretary of Duke of Westminster, April 4, secretary to Warburg, April 28, LWD to Westminster, Nov. 10, 1950, secretary of Piscatorial Society to LWD, April 15, secretary of Fly Fishers' Club to LWD, May 22, July 11, 1947, July 8, 1953, DP 298. LWD delivered a witty and moving speech on the joys of fly fishing at the Fly Fishers' annual dinner, Oct. 19, 1950, DP 291.

28. LWD to Eden, April 30, 1971, DP 333; Sinclair 1; Kenneth George (secretary of Houghton Club in 1976) 1; Smith to Sinclair, April 24, Sinclair to LWD, April 22, LWD to Sinclair, April 24, Sinclair to LWD, April 28, 1947, LWD to club members, May 18, LWD to McCloy, May 26, Sir John Greenly (secretary of Houghton Club) to LWD, May 27, LWD to Greenly, May 28, 1948, Greenly to LWD, March 16, 1949, July 4, 1950, Sinclair to LWD, Dec. 17, 1950, LWD to Sinclair, March 8, 1951, Greenly to LWD, July 19, 1949, LWD to Col. Pryor, Nov. (?), 1950, DP 298; Houghton Club Minute Books and fishing diaries; Mick Lunn (club head river keeper) 1. In October, 1976, RPB was privileged to spend a weekend at the club at Stockbridge as the guest of Kenneth George. Sir Ivan McGill was present and generous with his reminiscences of LWD.

29. LWD to Bedell Smith, May 12, 1949, DP 298; *Daily Telegraph*, April 6, *New York Times*, April 6, New York *Herald Tribune*, April 6, 1949; Peggy Douglas 1.

30. Ibid.; London *Star*, April 7, 1949; McCloy to Marshall Carter, April 7, LWD to Mrs. McCloy, April 28, Peggy Douglas to children, April 16, 1949, DP 303; LWD to McCloy, May 11, 1949, DP 280; New York *Herald Tribune*, April 18, 1949.

31. Peggy Douglas 1; Peggy Douglas to children, April 28, 1949, DP 303; Acheson to Halifax, April 29, 1949, Halifax Papers, 410.4.29, Churchill College Archives, Cambridge University; London *Daily Mail*, May 13, *Financial Times*, July 25, *Daily Telegraph*, Aug. 6, London *Star*, Aug. 3, 1949; LWD to Fred Searls, Jr., Aug. 22, 1949, DP 303.

32. Acheson memorandum of tel. conversation with LWD, May 3, and of meeting with HST, May 5, 1949, "Official Conversations and Meetings of Dean Acheson, 1949–1953," microfilm, reel 1, frs. 0409, 0423, University Publications of America; *Press Conferences of the President: Harry S. Truman, 1949*, June 9, 1949; *New York Times*, Sept. 14, 1949; Peggy Douglas 1; LWD to Acheson, Aug. 8, Oct. 14, Acheson to LWD, Oct. 25, 1949, Acheson memorandum of conversations with HST, Jan. 26, March 6, 1950, Papers of Dean Acheson, HSTL. LWD wrote Inverchapel, Oct. 9, 1950, that the doctors had limited his work to a "few hours of each day," DP 300.

33. *Times* (London), April 16, 1949; principal private secretary to Attlee, April 5, 14, 1949, Attlee Papers, University College Library, Oxford University; George McCullagh to Lillian Olsen, June 6, Churchills to Peggy Douglas, April 6, Mrs. Churchill to Peggy Douglas, April 22, 1949, DP 279; Lewis W. Douglas, "Churchill as Diplomat," *Atlantic Monthly*, CCXV (March, 1965), 89; NA/RG59/123 Douglas, Lewis W., especially tel. 1335, Acheson to LWD, April 19, tel. 1544, LWD to Acheson, April 21, 1949; Lovett to LWD, May 10, 1949, DP 279.

34. See DP 303, 304; Lillian Olsen Smith 1; Peggy Douglas 1.

35. London *Daily Mail*, Nov. 3, 1949; *Times*, Oct. 9, 1950; clipping in DP 62 of quote on gift to hospital in Tex McCrary and Jinx Falkenburg's "New York Closeup," Oct., 1951 (exact date and paper unidentified).

36. Acheson, *Present at the Creation*, 322–

323; Lord Franks, ERP Oral Interview, June 27, 1964, HSTL; LWD to Under Secretary of State Webb, June 16, LWD to Acheson, June 22, Acheson to LWD, June 23, 1949, FRUS, 1949, IV, 784-791.

37. LWD to Acheson, June 22, Harriman to Acheson, June 25, 1949, ibid., 789, 792-793; Francis Williams, *A Prime Minister Remembers: The War and Post-War Memoirs of the Rt. Hon. Earl Attlee* (London, 1962), 227.

38. Snyder to Acheson, July 9, 10, Acheson to LWD, July 11, 1949, FRUS, 1949, IV, 799-803; Acheson, *Present at the Creation*, 322-323; George F. Kennan, *Memoirs, 1925-1950* (Boston, 1967), 358-362.

39. LWD to Lippmann, Aug. 10, LWD to Vandenberg, Aug. 23, 25, 1949, DP 301; David McLelland, *Dean Acheson: The State Department Years* (New York, 1976), 240-242.

40. LWD to Acheson, Aug. 8, 1949, Acheson Papers, HSTL; LWD to Sam Applewhite, Aug. 30, 1949, DP 79; Holmes to SecState, Aug. 27, 1949, NA/RG59/1231 Douglas, Lewis W., tel. 3414; paper prepared in embassy, Aug. 18, 1949, FRUS, 1949, IV, 806-820.

41. LWD to Acheson, Aug. 15, 1949, DP 279.

42. Editorial note, joint communiqué, Sept. 12, 1949, FRUS, 1949, IV, 832-839; Acheson, *Present at the Creation*, 324-325; Dean Acheson, *Sketches from Life*, 17-19; Williams, *A Prime Minister Remembers*, 225-226; Franks, ERP interview, June 27, 1964, HSTL.

43. Manchester *Guardian*, Sept. 19, *Daily Herald*, Sept. 19, *Daily Telegraph*, Sept. 19, *News Chronicle*, Sept. 20, 1949; editorial note, Holmes to SecState, Sept. 20, 23, 1949, FRUS, 1949, IV, 839-843; Acheson, *Present at the Creation*, 325.

44. LWD to Acheson, Aug. 8, 1949, Acheson Papers, HSTL; *Daily Telegraph*, Sept. 27, *Times*, Sept. 28, 1949; LWD to McCloy, May 17, 1949, DP 280.

45. Itinerary of trip, DP 299; *Times*, Oct. 17, 1949; Westmorland I.

46. Meeting of United States ambassadors at Paris, Oct. 21-22, FRUS, 1949, IV, 469-496, passim.

47. Editorial note, dispatches, and papers, ibid., III, 294-308.

48. LWD to Clayton, Oct. 1, 1958, Clayton Papers, HSTL.

49. LWD to SecState, May 11, 19, Acheson to LWD, July 20, LWD to SecState, July 22, 23, Acheson to LWD, July 25, 1949, FRUS, 1949, IX, 20, 25-26, 50-53.

50. F.O. memorandum on China, Aug. 15, LWD to Acheson, Aug. 26, Acheson conversation with Bevin on the Far East, Sept. 13, 1949, FRUS, 1949, IX, 57-61, 68-69, 81-85; Bevin account of conversation with LWD, Aug. 26, 1949, to Franks, F 12843/1023/10, F.O. 371/75814.

51. French embassy to the Dept. of State, Oct. 6, Webb to LWD, Oct. 7, 1949, FRUS, 1949, IX, 103, 109-110.

52. Holmes to SecState, Oct. 10, SecState to LWD (still absent in Italy), Oct. 14, LWD to SecState, Oct. 18, Oct. 24, Acheson memorandum on conversation with HST, Oct. 17, 1949, ibid., 118-119, 128-129, 134-135, 138-139, 132.

53. LWD to Acheson, Dec. 1, 1949, DP 279; Franks to F.O., Dec. 8, 1949, F 18481/1023/10, F.O. 371/75826; Attlee to Commonwealth prime ministers, Dec. 16, 1949, F 18907/1023/10G, F.O. 371/75827; British embassy to Dept., Dec. 27, 1949, FRUS, 1949, IX, 248.

54. LWD to Acheson, Oct. 14, 1949, Acheson memorandum of conversation with the President, Jan. 26, 1950, Acheson Papers, HSTL; Goodman I; LWD to Goodman, Nov. 23, 1949, DP 303; Lillian Olsen to Stroud, Nov. 26, 1949, DP 281; LWD to Acheson, Dec. 22, 1949, LWD to Holmes, Jan. 19, Col. George to LWD, Jan. 10, with attached note, Jan. 17, 1950, DP 279.

CHAPTER 25 *The End of the Mission*

1. LWD to Holmes, Jan. 19, 1950, DP 279; Acheson memoranda of conversations with the President, Jan. 26, March 6, 1950, Acheson Papers, HSTL; note on LWD appointment with HST, 3:30 P.M. March 7, 1950, PPF 550, HSTL; State Dept. meeting, March 7, 1950, FRUS, 1950, III, 638-642, 1628 n.

2. *Daily Telegraph*, March 18, 1950; meeting of U.S. ambassadors at Rome, March 22-24, FRUS, 1950, III, 795-827.

3. LWD-Churchill correspondence, 1947-1950, DP 279; C. L. Sulzberger, *A Long Row of Candles: Memoirs and Diaries* (New York, 1969), 481-482; Hon. Lewis W. Douglas, G.B.E., "Clemenceau," in Lord Longford and Sir John Wheeler-Bennett, eds., *The History Makers* (London, 1973), 12; Lewis W. Douglas, "Churchill as Diplomat," *Atlantic Monthly*, CCXV (March, 1965), 86-89; Wheeler-Bennett I; Colville I; Montague Browne I; Churchill I; Peggy Douglas I, May 7, 1975; the "Red Book" of The Other Club, 1959, 1976; LWD to Acheson, March 29, 1950, DP 279; Dean Acheson, *Present at the Creation: My Years in the State Department* (New York, 1969), 351-352 and chaps. 39, 40; Sir Roderick Barclay, *Ernest Bevin and the Foreign Office, 1932-1969* (London, 1975), 80-81; Dalton Diaries, Sept. 2, 1950, London School of Economics and Political Science; Barclay I.

4. Harriman I; Kenney I; McCloy I; Franks I; Strang I; "Reminiscences of Admiral Richard L. Conolly," COHC; Peggy Douglas I, May 7, 1975. The preliminary arrangements for the meetings were carried on by Acheson with Bevin principally through Franks at the Washington

embassy. Position papers, May 6, 8, 1950, AU 10512/2/G, F.O. 371/81645 and PREM 8, 1202.

5. Jessup to SecState, April 30, Bruce to Jessup, May 4, Jessup to Bruce, May 5, LWD to SecState, Bruce, Harriman, Jessup, Perkins, and Bohlen, May 7, 1950, FRUS, 1950, III, 890–892, 960–961, 961 n., 972–974; Acheson, Creation, 387–388.

6. Evening Standard, May 9, 1950; Acheson, Creation, 382–386; LWD to William Marshall Bullitt, June 7, 1950, DP 415.

7. FRUS, 1950, III, 1018–1107, 100–125; Acheson, Creation, 382–401; position papers, May 6, 8, 1950, AU 10512/2/G, F.O. 371/81645; minute by Barclay, May 9, 1950, AU 1027/14/G, F.O. 371/81632; PREM 8, 1202.

8. LWD to Acheson, May 23, Acheson to LWD, June 13, 1950, DP 279; LWD to Acheson, June 9, 1950, Acheson Papers, HSTL; Bevin to Acheson (via Franks), June 19, SecState to missions in NATO countries, June 24, 1950, FRUS, 1950, III, 128–129.

9. LWD to Acheson, June 20, Acheson to LWD, June 27, 1950, Acheson Papers, HSTL; LWD to Acheson, July 5, 1950, DP 279.

10. LWD to Acheson, June 27, Kirk to Acheson, June 27, President's statement, June 27, Security Council resolution, June 25, 1950, FRUS, 1950, VII, 197–198, 169–170, 202–203, 155–156; Acheson to LWD, June 27, 1950, Acheson Papers, HSTL.

11. Security Council resolution, June 27, Kirk to SecState, July 6, Bevin to Acheson (via Franks), July 6, Acheson to LWD, July 7, LWD to Acheson, July 8, Bevin to Acheson, July 7, 1950, FRUS, 1950, VII, 211, 312–313, 313–314, 327–328, 331–332, 329–303; Bevin to Franks, July 8, 1950, FK 1022/101/G, F.O. 371/84083.

12. British embassy to Dept. of State (Kelly's instructions), July 9, Acheson to LWD, July 9, Acheson to Bevin (via LWD), July 10, Acheson to LWD (on oral statement), July 10, 1950, FRUS, 1950, VII, 338–339, 340, 347–351, 351–352.

13. LWD to Acheson, July 11, 1950, ibid., 361–362; LWD to Bevin (Acheson message and supplemental letter incorporating LWD's oral comments), FK 1022/216/G, F.O. 371/84091.

14. Minute by Dixon, July 12, 1950, FK 1022/128/G, F.O. 371/84087. Conversation between Acheson and Franks, July 13, Bevin to Acheson, July 15, 1950, FRUS, 1950, VII, 374, 395–399. Franks to Strang, July 14, 1950, FK 1022/241/G, F.O. 371/84093. On July 14, after he and Holmes had lunched with Younger, Strang, and Assistant Under Secretary Sir M. Esler Dening, Douglas reported to Acheson that Bevin had been "hurt if not offended" by the tone and implications of the secretary's message, but that it was also clear his Foreign Office guests did not consider U.S. recognition of Communist China and the inclusion of Formosa in its territory or the seating of the new regime in the UN "to be an extorted blackmail price" for the withdrawal of the North Korean troops to the 38th parallel. Rather, those were "steps [which] should have been taken long ago." FRUS, 1950, VII, 380–385. Acheson, Creation, 418.

15. LWD to DDE, May 26, 1952, DP 311. He expressed the same views in a letter to Arthur Krock, Oct. 3, 1952, DP 308. LWD I.

16. LWD to Acheson, July 27, LWD to HST, July 28 (draft), 1950, Acheson Papers, HSTL.

17. LWD to Acheson, July 28, Acheson to LWD, July 31, Aug. 4, LWD to Acheson, Aug. 8, 1950, ibid. LWD to Acheson, Aug. 9, Acheson to LWD, Aug. 11, LWD to Acheson, Aug. 12, 16, Lovett to Acheson, Aug. 16, Acheson to Lovett, Aug. 23, 1950, Acheson Papers, HSTL; Acheson, Creation, 368; David S. McLellan, Dean Acheson: The State Department Years (New York, 1976), 236; Lovett was soon to accept the post of deputy secretary of defense under George C. Marshall and to succeed the general in 1951.

18. LWD to Acheson, Aug. 24, memo of Lucius Battle (private secretary to Acheson), Aug. 25, memo of Acheson conversation with HST, Aug. 28, 1950, Acheson Papers, HSTL; LWD to Battle, Aug. 25, 1950, DP 279.

19. Acheson, Creation, 336–345; McCloy to Acheson, Aug. 3, 11, LWD to Acheson, Aug. 8, Bruce to Acheson, Aug. 9, SecState and SecDef to HST, Sept. 8, 1950, New York ministerial and council meetings, FRUS, 1950, III, 180–182, 205–207, 190–192, 194–195, 273–278, 285–354 passim.

CHAPTER 26 *Farewells*

1. Times, Aug. 29, Sept. 1, New York Herald Tribune, Sept. 1, 1950; memorandum of conversation at State Department, Sept. 26, 1950, DP 279; Franks to F.O., Sept. 26, F.O. to Franks, Sept. 26, A. B. Burrows to Wright, Sept. 29, 1950, AU 1904/2, AU 1904/6, F.O. 371/81779.

2. Note from RLK [?] to Connelly with annotation, Sept. 26, 1950, PPF, HSTL; LWD drafts of July 27, 28, Aug. 16 and final letter of Sept. 26 to HST, HST to LWD, Sept. 26, 1950, DP 279; LWD to HST ("Very personal") July 27, HST to LWD ("Personal"), Sept. 26, 1950, PSF, General File (D), HSTL.

3. New York Herald Tribune, Sept. 27, Times, Sept. 28, London Evening News, Sept. 27, Manchester Guardian, Sept. 28, Financial Times, Oct. 2, News Chronicle, Sept. 17, 1950.

4. Bevin to LWD, Sept. 27, LWD to Bevin, Sept. 27, 1950, DP 279; Eden quoted in Alec Collett article, London Evening News, Sept. 27, 1950. Lord Avon (Anthony Eden) expressed these views even more strongly shortly before his death. Avon to Peggy Douglas, March 20, 1974, and Lady Avon to RPB, Aug. 18, 1976.

5. Robert F. Morrison to Lillian Olsen, March 29, 1947, DP 281; *Evening News*, April 17, 1947; LWD to Robert Williamson, April 28, 1947, DP 302; *New York Times*, Nov. 19, 1947; *Daily Telegraph*, Feb. 24, June 8, 1948.

6. DP 286–292, passim.

7. American Society address, DP 291; freedom-of-the-city address, DP 292; address at Sheffield Pageant of Production, Nov. 18, 1948, in *Daily Telegraph*, Nov. 19, 1948; Peggy Douglas I.

8. Edinburgh itinerary, DP 292; Edinburgh *Scotsman*, Aug. 22, 1950; picture of LWD receiving University of Bristol degree from Churchill, Oct. 19, 1949, DP 289; registrar of Oxford University to LWD, June 3, 1948, DP 287. LWD also received honorary degrees from the universities of Leeds, St. Andrews, London, Birmingham, and Glasgow, DP 287–290. LWD to Macmillan, Jan. 26, Macmillan to LWD, Feb. 22, LWD to Macmillan, March 19, 1973, DP 333; documents on 1973 Encaenia, DP 97. Encaenia is an elaborate academic ceremony at Oxford in June during which degrees are granted.

9. References for the Douglases' social life, Peggy's other activities, and their relations with the Royal Family include a number of social items in the press, invitations in the Douglas Papers, interviews with Peggy Douglas, her speech to the English-Speaking Union on Jan. 31, 1952, in DP 281, and interviews with Astley, Cowdray, the Hartwells, Colville, Westmorland, Bonham-Carter, Drogheda, and Wheeler-Bennett. References for specific events and quotations will be cited in subsequent footnotes. On foodstuffs sent to the Douglases, see, for example, Henry S. Kingman to LWD, May 9, Gilbert H. Scribner to LWD, March 20, Sept. 16, 1947, DP 415, and John M. Franklyn to LWD, March 11, 1947, DP 280.

10. A lively account of one of these parties was sent to his father by Eugene R. Black's son, Gene. Black forwarded it much later to LWD in a letter of April 12, 1963. DP 329.

11. *Double Harness: Memoirs by Lord Drogheda* (London, 1978), 48–49; Andrew Boyle, *Poor, Dear Brendan: The Quest for Brendan Bracken* (London, 1974), 325, 329; Drogheda I at 8 Lord North Street. Drogheda inherited the lease on the house from Bracken. LWD first met Bracken in London in 1929. They were also both at First Quebec. Lewis W. Douglas, in *Portraits and Appreciations: Brendan Bracken, 1901–1958* (London, privately circulated, 1958), 29. LWD to Charles Lysaght, May 7, 1973, DP 307.

12. *Daily Telegraph*, Oct. 7, 1950.

13. Ibid., April 30, 1949, Oct. 7, 1950.

14. LWD to Bracken, July 21, 1958, DP 307; LWD to Swinton, Sept. 1, 1958, Swinton Papers, 174/7/3, Churchill College Archives, Cambridge University; Earl Marshal of England, the Duke of Norfolk, to LWD, Jan. 24, LWD to LBJ, Feb. 3, 1965, DP 333.

15. John W. Wheeler-Bennett, *King George VI: His Life and Reign* (London, 1958), 762–769; See LWD to Lascelles, Dec. 18, 1948, Lascelles to LWD, Jan. 5, 1949, DP 278; transcript of LWD's Voice of America remarks, Feb. 7, 1952, DP 309.

16. *Tatler*, June 25, *Daily Graphic*, July 12, *Evening Standard*, July 15, Fort Worth *Star Telegram*, Aug. 12, 1947; *Time* magazine, Oct. 11, Nov. 29, *Star*, Nov. 29, 1948; *Sunday Pictorial*, June 26, *Evening Standard*, Oct. 11, *Daily Express*, Oct. 6, 1949; *Sunday Express*, Feb. 26, *Evening News*, April 4, 1950; *Sunday Pictorial*, July 10, 1949.

17. *News Review*, Oct. 6, New York *Sun*, Dec. 6, 1949; Alice M. Simmons to LWD, Sept. [?], 1949, DP 302.

18. LWD draft letter of invitation to King, [n.d.], 1950, DP 278; *Times*, Oct. 28, *Evening News*, Nov. 8, *Daily Telegraph*, Nov. 14, 1950.

19. Bevin to LWD, Oct. 23, LWD to Bevin, Oct. 24, Churchill to LWD, Nov. 14, LWD to Churchill, Nov. 15, 1950, seating chart for Bevin dinner, DP 279; Barclay I; Sir Roderick Barclay, *Ernest Bevin and the Foreign Office, 1932–1969* (London, 1975), 41; *Times*, Nov. 15, 1950; intradepartmental minutes in AU 1904/9, F.O. 371/81779.

20. Peggy Douglas I; Douglas, "Churchill as Diplomat," *Atlantic Monthly*, CCXV (March, 1965), 89; Churchill to LWD, Nov. 14, LWD to Churchill, Nov. 15, 1950, DP 279.

21. Correspondence on gifts in DP 305, on griffin and customs complications in DP 300. The dining group included such notables as Anthony Eden (later Lord Avon), Lord Douglas (later Lord Douglas-Home), Sir A. Douglas-Home, and Lord Home), David Eccles (later Lord Eccles), Sir Hugh Frazier, Selwyn Lloyd, Anthony Nutting, and David Ormsby-Gore (later Lord Harlech).

22. LWD to Acheson, Nov. 3, 1950, DP 279; ceremony at French embassy, DP 291. The Foreign Office files on "British Decoration" for LWD for 1949 and 1950 were "weeded out" before being placed in the Public Records Office.

23. Ms. of speech as delivered, DP 291; *Times*, Nov. 7, *Evening Standard*, Nov. 7, 1950.

24. *Times*, Nov. 7, *News Chronicle*, Nov. 6, *Daily Express*, Nov. 16, *A.B.C. London News-Letter*, Dec. 15, 1950; Hoffman to LWD, Oct. 21, 1950, DP 279.

25. Itinerary of the Douglases' movements from Nov. 16 to Dec. 8, 1950, in letter of LWD's secretary to Frank Mitchell, Aug. 16, 1951, DP 305; note to HST from a secretary with annotation: "[LWD] saw president Nov. 24, 1950, 11:30," OF 1206, HSTL; McNeil to LWD, April 18, 1951, DP 306.

Chapter 27 Home

1. Ms. of address to the Pilgrim Society, Jan. 24, 1951, DP 319.
2. Ms. of Charter Day Address, University of California, Berkeley, March 22, 1951, DP 82.
3. "Reporters' Copies of Mr. Douglas' Address Before American Mining Congress, Los Angeles, Oct. 22, 1951," speech before Sunday Evening Forum, Tucson, April 15, *Arizona Daily Star*, April 16, ms. of address to Associated Press Club luncheon, April 23, speech to Annual Meeting of Insurance Commissioners, New York City, Dec. 4, 1951, DP 319; statement in *Arizona Daily Star*, Sept. 20, 1951, Denver interview in *New York Times*, Jan. 9, 1951; LWD to Senator Harry F. Byrd, Sept. 24, 1951, DP 307; LWD to Frank Brophy, Feb. 9, 1953, DP 77; LWD to Swinton, Sept. 1, 1958, Swinton Papers, 174/7/3, Churchill College Archives, Cambridge University. On Feb. 9, 1952, LWD wrote Acheson suggesting that the NATO countries, collectively and individually, offer the Soviet Union and its satellites nonaggression pacts against military action and subversion, as a means of reducing tension between the two blocs. Acheson replied noncommittally on Feb. 12 and April 18, DP 78.
4. Reprint of paper presented to 33rd annual meeting of American Petroleum Institute, Chicago, Nov. 12, commencement address at MIT, June 12, 1953, DP 319.
5. "Will We Repeat the Errors of 1929 and 1930?," statement to Senate Appropriations Committee, April 18, 1958, DP 316.
6. Address to Economic Club of Detroit, Dec. 8, 1952, DP 319. He repeated the same message a decade later in his commencement address to the Thunderbird School, Phoenix, Arizona, Jan. 21, 1961, Clayton Papers, box 163 (Douglas), HSTL.
7. DDE to LWD, Nov. 20, Dec. 12, 1950, DDE to LWD, Feb. 15, LWD to DDE, Feb. 23, DDE to LWD, March 6, April 16, LWD to DDE, May 12, 31, DDE to LWD, June 6, 1951, DP 312; Roland Harriman to LWD, Dec. 8, 1950, Personal Files of DDE, 1916–1952, box 33, DDEL; *New York Times*, March 14, 1951; *The American Assembly 1951*, LWD to Paul Douglas, May 8, "Schedule for Participants" of First Assembly, press release from Columbia University, Dec. 28, 1951, LWD opening remarks to Second Assembly, May 18, 1952, DP 312; *New York Times*, May 22, 1952; "Memorandum for Participants in Work Session of Third Assembly," April 15, 1953, DP 313.
8. LWD to William Mullendore, May 31, 1951, DP 312; memorandum from Columbia alumni, LWD to Philip Young, Sept. 29, 1952, DP 313.
9. LWD to Kirk, April 30, Kirk to LWD, May 6, 1953, ibid.; LWD to DDE, Feb. 23, 1951, DDE to LWD, Nov. 28, 1952, DP 312; Olsen 1.
10. LWD to Byrd, Sept. 5, 1956, DP 307; LWD to Robertson, June 25, 1957, DP 309; LWD to DDE, Dec. 9, 1957, DP 311; Gift to United Negro College Fund, 1973, DP 99; documentation on National Human Relations Award, DP 105.
11. LWD to William Mitchell, Sept. 13, Stroud to LWD, Sept. 13, 1948, DP 413; Wolman to LWD, Sept. 15, 1948, DP 416; Marshall Bullitt to LWD, Sept. 27, LWD to Bullitt, Oct. 2, 1948, DP 415; LWD to Lewis Brown, March 2, 1949, DP 413.
12. LWD to Wolman, May 12, 1949, DP 416. As early as Oct. 11, 1948, in a letter to LWD, Scribner had expressed his view Dawson should be elected permanent president, DP 415. The voluminous correspondence on the Scribner motion and its immediate aftermath is found in DP 413, 415, 416. Wolman to LWD, Aug. 7, 1949, DP 416; LWD to Charles E. Adams and other trustees, Nov. 24, 1949, DP 413.
13. LWD to Charles E. Adams, who had been ill in Florida and unable to attend the March board meeting, April 20, 1950, ibid.
14. LWD to Elihu Root, Jr., with covering letter to Dawson, June 14, Dawson to LWD, June 26, LWD to Dawson, June 27, Dawson to LWD, June 28, 1950 (telegrams), DP 415; LWD to Wolman, June 23, Wolman to LWD, July 2, 1950, DP 416; F. Schneider 1; Olsen 1; Beaton 1.
15. Editorial in *Arizona Daily Star*, April 21, 1947; Morrison to Olsen, May 14, 1947, DP 281; Mathews to LWD, Aug. 25, 1947, DP 72; William de Cook to LWD, June 6, LWD to de Cook, June 1, LWD to Helen d'Autremont, Sept. 23, 1947, Helen d'Autremont to LWD, June [n.d.], LWD to Helen d'Autremont, July 14, 1948, DP 495.
16. The voluminous correspondence, various agreements, and other documents on the transactions are found in ibid.
17. LWD to Helen d'Autremont (draft) on intention to maintain local ownership with qualifications on future developments, Jan. 19, LWD first draft of press announcement in LWD to Archie R. Conner, Aug. 9, press release, Sept. 15, 1949, ibid.; *Arizona Daily Star*, Sept. 16, 20, 1949.
18. Ibid., Jan. 10, 1951; purchase agreement for Pantano Farm, Dec. 9, 1949, LWD to Stanley Stokes, Nov. 21, 1952, DP 110.
19. Andrew Boyle, *Poor, Dear Brendan: The Quest for Brendan Bracken* (London, 1974), 317; W. Randerson to LWD, Jan. 11, 1951, DP 462; trips to South Africa, DP 95, 96, 97; Ellinwood 1; LWD to James F. Byrnes, Oct. 5, 1952, LWD to Marietta Tree, Dec. 10, 1964, LWD to Cyrus Vance, Jan. 7, 1972, DP 354; International Nickel Co. files, DP 467–469.
20. LWD to Brophy, Jan. 10, 1952, DP 77; Brophy 1.

21. LWD to comptroller of the currency, April 6, 1955, DP 497; LWD to Brophy, June 20, Brophy to LWD, July 6, LWD to Brophy, July 14, 1955, DP 77. The complicated negotiations with the First National Bank of Arizona, the Arizona Bancorporation, and Transamerica Corporation and LWD's proposals for maintaining an independent bank are in DP 497. James S. Douglas (son) to LWD, June 4, LWD to James S. Douglas, June 8, James S. Douglas to LWD, July 1, LWD to James S. Douglas, July 5, 1955, ibid.

22. Stenographic minutes of informal stockholders' meeting of Aug. 25, LWD conversation with F. N. Belgrano, Jr., Sept. 16, 1955, ibid.; F. N. Belgrano, Jr. to LWD, Feb. 3, 1956, DP 498.

23. The correspondence between LWD and Helen d'Autremont and other members of her family is in DP 495. *Arizona Daily Star*, Oct. 5, 1955.

24. Program for opening of new Southern Arizona Bank building, March 1, 1958, DP 507; Tucson *Citizen*, Nov. 19, 1965; LWD to Henry Luce, Dec. 17, 1965, DP 331; discussions of proposed merger with First National Bank, DP 510; James S. Douglas I.

25. *Arizona Daily Star*, Nov. 14, 1951; Record Book of Southeast Arizona Weather Research Corporation, Dec. 8, 1950—Oct. 14, 1952, correspondence with Dr. Warren Weaver and President Dean Rusk of Rockefeller Foundation, 1952, correspondence with Dr. Chester C. Davis of the Ford Foundation, 1952, correspondence with Alfred R. Sloan, 1952, correspondence with scientists in U.S. and abroad, 1952, DP 322.

26. Harvill to LWD, Nov. 26, 1952, ibid.; Conference on Atmospheric Physics, DP 323; LWD to Eleanor R. Corruth, March 18, 1958, DP 324; LWD to Harvill, Nov. 2, 1953, press release from Sloan Foundation, Jan. 23, press release from Institute of Atmospheric Physics, Jan. 24, 1954, "General Information on the Institute of Atmospheric Physics, University of Arizona," April 15, 1955, DP 323.

27. "General Information on the Institute of Atmospheric Physics, University of Arizona," April 15, LWD appointment notice, May 16, 1955, ibid.; University of Arizona catalogs, 1955–1985; tel. conversation of RPB with Kassander, Feb. 13, 1984. Two years after the establishment of the program, Dr. Braham returned full time to Chicago and was succeeded briefly by associate directors Drs. James E. McDonald and A. Richard Kassander as co-directors. McDonald soon resigned to devote full time to research and teaching. Dr. Kassander served as director from 1957 until his appointment as university Vice-President for Research in 1971.

28. LWD appointment to committee, Dec. 9, 1953, DP 326; Washington *Post*, Dec. 26, 1957; LWD to Sherman Adams, Dec. 23, 1957, OF 244, DDEL; tel. conversation of RPB with Kassander, Feb. 13, 1984.

29. Harvill to Dr. Warren Weaver, June 4, DDE to LWD, Oct. 26, 1955, DP 320; LWD to Harvill, May 5, Harvill to LWD, April 25, Kassander to Harvill, April 24, 1958, LWD to Alan Waterman, Dec. 7, 1959, DP 371. I am indebted to Harvey Strum for allowing me to see the ms. of his article "Association for Applied Solar Energy, 1954–70" on the history of the organization.

30. New York *Journal of Commerce*, April 21, 1953; LWD ms. of opening remarks at conference, program of conference, DP 319.

31. For material on committee, see DP 364.

32. *Arizona Daily Star*, July 22, 1958.

33. Wheeler-Bennett 1, T. Schneider 1; LWD to Udall, Aug. 12, Sept. 9, Oct. 9, 1963, DP 332.

34. On ESU, DP 380, passim; Houghton Club fishing diary; Lunn 1; Kenneth George 1; Sinclair 1; Swinton correspondence, DP 309, 334, and Swinton Papers, Churchill College Archives, Cambridge, University; Peggy Douglas 1; on British trips, DP 95, 305, 298, 106.

35. LWD to Churchill, Oct. 8, LWD to Bracken, Nov. 3, 1951, LWD to Bracken, May 7, LWD to Churchill, May 30, 1955, DP 307; *New York Times*, Oct. 18, 1955. Churchill received the Order of the Garter in 1953; Eden in 1954. Bracken was raised to the peerage in 1952.

36. Rt. Hon. Earl of Halifax, *Fulness of Days* (London, 1957), 313–314; Lord Birkenhead, *Halifax* (London, 1965), 584–585; Peggy Douglas 1.

37. LWD to Queen Mother, May 19, 1953, Jan. 7, 1954, DP 383; *New York Times*, Nov. 4, 1954; Sir Roger Makins to LWD, July 15, LWD to Makins, July 21, 1954, DP 308.

38. LWD to Selwyn Lloyd, June 11, LWD to Ambassador Whitney, June 11, LWD to Dulles, June 11, Archibald C. Coolidge to LWD, July 19, 1957, DP 384; *English-Speaking Union*, V, 2, 1957; *Daily Telegraph*, Oct. 22, 1957; Caccia to LWD, Sept. 23, Consul General H. S. Stephenson in N.Y. to LWD, Sept. 25, C. Tinsley to Mayflower Hotel, Sept. 24, "Itinerary of Mr. & Mrs. Douglas and Sharman, Oct. 18, 1957," DP 105; Peggy Douglas 1.

39. Goodman 1; *Life*, March 31, 1952; Wallace to LWD, Oct. 18, LWD to Wallace, Oct. 25, 1955, DP 60; Peggy Douglas 1.

40. Goodman 1; letters of sympathy, DP 60.

41. LWD to Swinton, May 28, 1958, Swinton Papers, 174/7/3, Churchill College Archives, Cambridge University; DDE to Eric Johnson, Nov. 18, 1959, solicitation letters to foundations and corporations, summary of discussions, recommendations, and resolutions of the committees of the Atlantic Congress, Lon-

don, June 5-10, 1959, text of LWD address, DP 316; LWD's work with the Atlantic Council and Institute is documented in DP 336, 337.

CHAPTER 28 *Monitoring Eisenhower*

1. DDE to LWD, June 6, 1951, DP 312; Lt. Col. R. L. Schulz to LWD, July 17, 1951, Personal Files of DDE, 1916-52, Principal Files, Box 33, Douglas, Lewis W., DDEL; LWD's secretary to LWD, June [n.d.], 1951, DP 262.
2. Ms. of LWD address of May 3, 1952, DP 319.
3. *Arizona Republic*, May 6; *Arizona Plain Talk*, May 9, 1952.
4. LWD to DDE, May 12, DDE to LWD, May 20, LWD to DDE, May 26, 1952, DP 311. There are almost 200 letters between LWD and DDE in the DP for the period of the latter's two terms as President.
5. LWD to DDE, June 6, 1952, ibid.
6. LWD to General Clay, Sept. 13, 1952, DP 307; LWD to DDE, Sept. 9, Dec. 16, 29, DDE to LWD, Dec. 19, 1953, LWD to DDE, Jan. 24, LWD to Sherman Adams, Feb. 24, 1954, DP 311; LWD to Senator Harry Byrd, Jan. 19, 1956, DP 307; LWD to Senator Frank J. Lausche, June 11, 1958, DP 310. LWD's work with the De Mille Foundation from 1953 to 1959 and the many letters on labor issues to friends in connection with its activities are found in ibid, and DP 341. LWD to Krock, April 18, 1962, DP 330.
7. LWD to Stevenson, Aug. 18, Stevenson to LWD, Aug. 26, Stevenson to LWD, Aug. 30, LWD to Stevenson, Sept. 13, 1952, DP 309; LWD to Salisbury, Sept. 17, LWD to Bracken, Nov. 1, 1952, DP 307.
8. Text of DDE's speech of Aug. 25 to American Legion Convention in *New York Times*, Aug. 26, 1952; LWD to DDE, Aug. 28, 1952, DP 311.
9. LWD to Dulles, Sept. 29, 30, Dulles to LWD, Sept. 29, 30, 1952, DP 307.
10. Press release of Livestock Show address in Phoenix, Sept. 30, 1952, DP 319; LWD to DDE, Sept. 9, 1952, Ann Whitman File, admin. ser., Douglas, Lewis W., folder 5, DDEL. Both Goldwater, who was running against Ernest W. McFarland, Democratic majority leader in the Senate, and Howard Pyle won their elections. LWD supported Pyle again in 1954, when he lost the governorship to McFarland. He backed Goldwater's successful run for a second term in 1958 against a second try by McFarland. He praised Goldwater's support of measures to curb labor unions, but was highly critical of his opposition to foreign aid. By 1960, he was appalled at Goldwater's attacks on "subversive influences" in higher education, especially at Harvard University. Their relations became very strained. *Arizona Republic*, Oct. 9, 1954; LWD to McFarland, May 13, 1958, DP 302; LWD to Goldwater, June 11, Sept. 21, 1954, Nov. 13, 1956, May 21, July 14, 22, 1958, Nov. 19, 1959, DP 307; LWD to Wolman, Nov. 24, 1958, DP 309; LWD to Thomas S. Lamont, Dec. 21, 1960, DP 81.
11. DDE to LWD, Oct. 16, 1952, DP 311; *New York Herald Tribune*, Oct. 1, 1952; ms. of LWD *Herald Tribune* Forum speech, DP 319.
12. HST to Farley, Oct. 20, 1952, James Farley Papers, LC (courtesy of Professor Frank Freidel); *New York Times*, Oct. 3, 1956. See Truman's letter to LWD at end of chapter.
13. Harriman I; Harriman to LWD, July 7, LWD to Harriman, July 12, 1954, DP 83; LWD to Harriman, Feb. 3, 1965, DP 330.
14. Harriman I; Kenney I; Peggy Douglas I; LWD-Acheson correspondence after 1952, DP 79; W. S. Lewis to RPB, Feb. 27, 1978; LWD to Acheson, Oct. 22, 1969, Acheson Papers, box 9, Yale University Library; LWD to HST, Oct. 29, 1971, DP 396; Dean Acheson, *Present at the Creation: My Years in the State Department* (New York, 1969), 418, 438; LWD to Feis, May 6, 1970, DP 118; Wheeler-Bennett I; John Bartlow Martin, *Adlai Stevenson of Illinois: The Life of Adlai E. Stevenson* (New York, 1976), 644-645.
15. LWD to William Mathews, Dec. 29, 1952, DP 78.
16. Clay to RPB, March 22, 1977; oral history interview with Clay, No. 2, March 16, 1967, DDEL; Townsend Hoopes, *The Devil and John Foster Dulles* (Boston, 1973), 135-136; *New York Herald Tribune*, Nov. 26, 1952.
17. Dept. of State press releases, March 4, March 7, 1953, DP 314; LWD meeting with DDE, March 9, 1953, OF, box 865, file 183 (1953), White House Central Files, DDEL; LWD to Dulles, March 9, Dulles to LWD, March 13, memorandum of telephone conversation of LWD with Dulles, March 23, LWD to Dulles, March 25, April 10, 1953, letters on government department representatives assigned to aid LWD in study, DP 314; memorandum for Dr. G. S. Hauge from Dulles, March 26, memorandum of conversation at White House, with the President, Dr. G. S. Hauge, and L. W. Douglas, June 30, 1953, OF 116U (Mission of L. W. Douglas), White House Central Files, DDEL.
18. LWD to Aldrich, April 22, LWD itineraries in London, LWD to Stewart, May 11, Butler memoranda of conversations with LWD, May 13, 18, 19 and additional communications of June 3, 5, LWD to Butler, June 17, LWD to DDE June 1, DDE to LWD, June 2, 1953, DP 314.
19. Richard M. Bissell, Jr., to Lincoln Gordon, June 16, 1953 (courtesy of Mr. Bissell); Bissell to RPB, July 24, 1978; LWD to W. H. Worriлow, June 1, report to President, July 14, DDE to LWD, July 21, LWD to Bissell, July 1,

1953, DP 314; LWD, "Reminiscences," 35–39, COHC.

20. Press release of report, Aug. 24, 1953, DP 314; *Times*, Sept. 3, *Economist*, Aug. 29, 1953; Aldrich to LWD, Aug. 25, 1953, DP 314; *New York Times*, Aug. 26, New York *Herald Tribune*, Aug. 26, New York *Journal American*, Sept. 1, 1953; Royster to LWD, Aug. 31, LWD to Royster, Sept. 2, LWD to DDE, July 3, 1953, DP 314. See also LWD interview in *Newsweek*, Sept. 7, 1953.

21. Memorandum to SecState and SecDef from DDE on telephone conversation with LWD on co-chairmanship of board, Nov. 20, LWD to DDE (telegram), Dec. 2, 1953, Ann Whitman File, admin. ser., Douglas, Lewis W., folder 5, DDEL; LWD to Sherman Adams, March 12, 1954, DP 311.

22. LWD to DDE, May 26, 1952, ibid.; LWD to Rev. Walter Mitchell, Feb. 3, 1954, DP 308. Although LWD's views on the charges against Alger Hiss and his subsequent conviction for perjury are unclear, he apparently either disbelieved them or forgave him, for he entertained him publicly for lunch on several occasions in New York and Tucson in later years. LWD to Bohlen, March 2, 1973, DP 328; Wheeler Bennett I; RPB conversations with Alfred A. Knopf and Peggy Douglas.

23. LWD to Harry Byrd, Dec. 1, 1954, DP 307. LWD was a trustee of the George C. Marshall Research Foundation until his death.

24. Ms. of speech to ESU, DP 383; *Daily Telegraph*, May 12, 1954; Harold Nicolson, *Diaries and Letters, 1945–62*, Nigel Nicolson, ed. (London, 1968), 258–259.

25. LWD to James L. Murphy of National Citizens for Eisenhower Congressional Committee, June 4, 1954, DP 306; LWD to Senators Knowland, Millikin, Ferguson, and Mundt, June 5, joint telegram to Senate, July 26, 1954, DP 311; *New York Times*, July 23, 1954; LWD, "Elements of a Free Society," address before Freedom House, Oct. 3, 1954, DP 320.

26. Brophy to LWD [n.d.], LWD to Brophy, Oct. 15, 1954, DP 68; Goldwater to LWD, July 23, LWD to Goldwater, July 26, 1954, DP 307; Pegler to LWD, Oct. 9, 1954, Feb. 6, 1955, LWD to Pegler, Feb. 12, 1955, DP 306, 308; Kohlberg to LWD, July 27, LWD to Fulbright, Dec. 3, 1954, DP 311.

27. LWD to Thomas Stephens, July 1, 1954, ibid.

28. LWD to DDE, Oct. 7, DDE to LWD, Oct. 11, 1954, ibid.

29. LWD to Senator George, Jan. 27, Feb. 2, 1955, DP 307.

30. LWD to DDE, March 3, DDE to LWD, March 9, LWD to DDE, March 21, DDE to LWD, March 29, LWD to DDE, April 7, DDE to LWD, April 12, LWD to DDE, May 2, DDE to LWD, May 6, 1955, DP 311; Dulles to LWD, March 19, LWD to Dulles, March 26, 1955, DP 307; meeting with DDE, May 27, 1955, White House Central Files, PPF 763 (AS), DDEL. In "Eisenhower, Dulles and the Quemoy-Matsu Crisis, 1954–1955," *Political Science Quarterly*, 96 (Fall, 1978), 465–480, Bennett C. Rushkoff concludes that Eisenhower, over Dulles's reservations, was "the one responsible for the policy shift away from a U.S. commitment to the off-shore islands." This was in the spring of 1955. The President may have been, in part, influenced by Douglas's arguments.

31. LWD to DDE, July 30, 1955, DP 311.

32. Nicolson, *Diaries and Letters, 1945–62*, 283.

33. *Life*, Jan. 16, 1956; LWD to Dulles, Jan. 18, 1956, DP 307; LWD to Adams, Jan. 18, Adams to LWD, Jan. 27, 1956, DP 311.

34. LWD, "Reminiscences," 34, 50, COHC.

35. The most recent and complete account of the still somewhat obscure Suez crisis is Donald Neff, *Warriors at Suez* (New York, 1981); LWD, "Reminiscences," 49, COHC; Wheeler-Bennett I; LWD to Dulles, Aug. 29, 1956, DP 307.

36. Neff, *Warriors* passim; LWD to DDE, Nov. 1, 1956, DP 311.

37. DDE to LWD, Nov. 3, 1956, ibid.

38. LWD to DDE, Nov. 6, DDE to LWD, Nov. 7, 1956, ibid.

39. LWD to DDE, Nov. 27, 29, 1956, ibid.

40. DDE to LWD, Nov. 30, 1956, ibid.

41. LWD to DDE, Dec. 3, 1956, ibid.

42. LWD to Salisbury, Nov. 4, 1956, DP 307; LWD to Swinton, Nov. 5, Swinton to LWD, Nov. 19, LWD to Swinton, Dec. 14, 1956, DP 309; Piers Dixon, *Double Diploma: The Life of Sir Pierson Dixon, Don and Diplomat* (London, 1968), 276.

43. LWD to Bracken, Jan. 25, 1957, DP 307. Eden was created Earl of Avon in 1961 and Macmillan became Earl of Stockton in 1984.

44. LWD to Salisbury, March 4, Salisbury to LWD, March 11, LWD to Salisbury, March 18, 1957, ibid.

45. LWD to Lippmann, July 29, 1958, DP 308; Wheeler-Bennett I; Macmillan I. Complicating the latter assessment, however, is the fact that Ambassador Aldrich shared with LWD a very poor opinion of Dulles.

46. LWD to DDE, July 12, 1956, Ann Whitman File, admin. ser., Douglas, Lewis W., folder 2, DDEL; statement with covering letter to Murray Snyder, assistant press secretary to DDE, Oct. 1, 1956, DP 311; New York *Herald Tribune*, Oct. 2, 1956; David Levy to LWD, Oct. 5, Citizens for Eisenhower-Nixon, "The People Ask the President" program of Oct. 12, Washington, D.C., and LWD copy of question he posed, ms. of LWD remarks at Eisenhower rally, Madison Square Garden, Oct. 25, Citizens for Eisenhower-Nixon TV program, Oct. 30, 1956, DP 320;

text of LWD TV remarks on Nov. 3, 1956, DP 306.

47. LWD to Mathews with earlier drafts, Oct. 10, Mathews to LWD, Oct. 13, LWD to Mathews, with early drafts, Oct. 25, 1956, DP 78.

48. LWD to Mathews, May 15, Mathews to LWD, May 16, LWD to Mathews, May 21, Mathews to LWD, May 26, LWD to Mathews (not sent), May 28, June 4, Mathews to LWD, June 9, LWD to Mathews, June 12, LWD memorandum of luncheon conversation, June 18, 1958, ibid.

49. White House news release, Dec. 12, 1956, Tracy F. Voorhees to LWD, April 26, report to the President, May 14, DDE to LWD, May 14, LWD to DDE, May 24, 1957, DP 313.

50. DDE to LWD, Nov. 26, 1956, LWD to Senator Fulbright, June 13, 26, 1957, LWD to Mark May, April 26, 1960, LWD to Murrow, Jan. 30, 1961, LWD to Sigurd S. Larmon, Feb. 1, 1961, April 26, 1968, reports on USIA in U.K., 1960, and on Union of South Africa, 1961, DP 362.

51. "The Eisenhower 'Inner Circle,' " *New York Times Magazine*, Feb. 3, 1957; LWD to Bracken, April 17, 1957, DP 307.

52. *New York Times*, April 27, 1957.

53. LWD to DDE, Sept. 10, DDE to LWD, Sept. 12, Oct. 13, LWD to DDE, Oct. 17, 1958, DP 311.

54. LWD, "Reminiscences," 46-47, COHC. In the last decade a number of studies have sought to show that Eisenhower's qualities of leadership as President have been underestimated. The most recent is Stephen E. Ambrose, *Eisenhower: The President* (New York, 1985).

55. LWD to HST, Nov. 6, HST to LWD, Nov. 19, 1969, Post-Presidential Corres. File (L. W. Douglas), HSTL.

CHAPTER 29 *Sunset*

1. LWD to Sam Rayburn, May 31, Johnson to LWD, June 14, 1960, DP 335; LWD to RMN, June 11, 14, 1960, DP 311.

2. Statement dated Oct. 31, but not released except to the *Arizona Daily Star*, until Nov. 3, 1960, contribution to Volunteers for Nixon-Lodge, DP 331.

3. LWD to JFK, Nov. 11, 1960, invitation to inaugural and gala, LWD to John J. Snyder, Jr., Jan. 16, 1961, DP 330; LWD to RMN, Dec. 22, 1960, DP 331.

4. LWD to LBJ, Nov. 11, Dec. 28, 1960, DP 335; LWD to Swinton, Jan. 31, 1961, Swinton Papers, 174/7/6, Churchill College Archives, Cambridge University. As a trustee of the Rockefeller Foundation, LWD had opposed Rusk's appointment as president in 1951 on the grounds that "he bends too much to the prevailing breezes of the moment," was "entirely academic" and that his views were "too theoretical." However, he added, "I like him very much." LWD to Dulles, Sept. 11, 1951, DP 405.

5. LWD to JFK, July 29, Bundy to LWD, Aug. 12, LWD to Bundy, Sept. 27, JFK to LWD, Oct. 7, 1963, DP 330; LWD to Goldwater, Sept. 27, LWD to Fulbright, Sept. 6, 1963, DP 329. Earlier, he had castigated Goldwater for his "irresponsible statements" about Stevenson and McCloy, who were carrying on negotiations with the Russians following the Cuban missile crisis. LWD to Goldwater, Nov. 15, 1962, DP 331.

6. LWD to Udall, Aug. 12, Sept. 9, Oct. 9, 1963, DP 332. He also supported Stewart's brother, Morris Udall, who was elected to his brother's seat in the House in 1961. Their relationship, though stormy at times, was generally amicable. DP 332.

7. LWD to RFK, April 6, 1964, DP 330.

8. LWD to LBJ, Jan. 8, Ivan Sinclair to LWD, Jan. 15, LWD to LBJ [undated], LBJ to LWD, June 15, 1964, DP 335.

9. LWD to Louis P. Horrell, Feb. 25, 1964, DP 329; LWD to Harriman, July 20, 1964, DP 330; public statement dated July 24, DP 329. LWD did support Goldwater for his reelection to the Senate in 1968 and contributed in 1970 to the establishment of a Goldwater chair at the University of Arizona (which was never established), though he much preferred that it be in history, the "master discipline," rather than in the vague area of social sciences, and objected to the proposal that the occupant "reflect Barry's philosophies." Goldwater's views, he commented, "are not compatible with the age in which we live or have lived." Goldwater to LWD, Oct. 11, LWD to Goldwater, Nov. 6, 1968, Robert Goldwater to LWD, Dec. 5, LWD to Robert Goldwater, Dec. 15, 1970, DP 329.

10. LWD to LBJ, July 20, LWD to Bundy, Aug. 1, 4, LBJ to LWD, Sept. 3, 1964, DP 335; Stewart Udall to LBJ, July 29, 1964, Name File, White House Central File, box 250, Bundy to LBJ, July 30, 1964, Aides Files, box 2, memos for President, National Security File, LBJL (courtesy of Professor Thomas G. Paterson).

11. Press release in *New York Times*, Aug. 10, 1964, DP 335.

12. LWD to Cliff Carter, July 7, LWD to Bundy, Aug. 28, LWD to Guy Stillman, Oct. 20, LWD to Brian P. Leeb, Oct. 2, LBJ to LWD, Sept. 18, LWD to LBJ, Oct. 5, LBJ to LWD, Oct. 17, Bess Abell to LWD, confirming luncheon engagement with LBJ, Oct. 6, LWD to LBJ, Oct. 28, Nov. 4 (letter and tel.), LBJ to LWD, Nov. 14, White House social secretary to LWD, Nov. 30, 1964, ibid. Despite his later disillusionment with Johnson, his vote for Nixon in 1968, and apparent intention to vote for him again in 1972, LWD continued to contribute $1,000 or more yearly to the Democratic National Committee until his death. LWD to Robert Strauss, April 14, 1971, ibid.

13. LWD to Fulbright, Oct. 23, Fulbright to LWD, Nov. 2, LWD to Fulbright, Nov. 13, 20, 1964, DP 329.

14. LWD to Stewart Udall, Sept. 15, Joseph A. Califano, Jr., to LWD, Oct. 14, LWD to Califano, Oct. 21, 1966, report to the secretary of the interior on the Indian Task Force, July 10, 1967, DP 338; Olsen I; Beaton I; Damskey I; Wheeler-Bennett I. In 1969, after the Nixon election, Lewis W. ("Peter") Douglas, Jr., no doubt concerned for his father's feelings of neglect, wrote Arthur Burns, economic counselor to President Nixon and an old friend of LWD's, suggesting his father as ambassador to Mexico. Hearing of the approach, LWD wrote Burns that he had not put his son up to writing and that he was probably too old for the job, but he did not refuse to serve. Burns replied that he had checked and found that the post had already been promised to a career officer. LWD, Jr., to Burns, April 2, LWD to Burns, April 4, Burns to LWD, April 8, 1969, DP 340.

15. LWD to Krock, April 5, 1961, DP 330; LWD to LBJ, Feb. 9, 11, Bundy to LWD, Feb. 19, LWD to Bundy, Feb. 26, 1965, DP 335.

16. LWD to Krock, Feb. 24, 1965, DP 330; LWD to Swinton, July 8, 1965, DP 334.

17. LWD to Fulbright, March 3, Aug. 2, Oct. 18, 1966, Dec. 27, 1967, Jan. 20, 24, 1968, Sept. 19, Oct. 10, 1969, DP 329.

18. LWD to Kennan, March 3, 1966, LWD to Kennan, March 1, Kennan to LWD, March 5, LWD to Kennan, June 17, 1968, LWD to Kennan, Nov. 11, 1969, DP 330; LWD to Gavin, Sept. 14, Gavin to LWD, Sept. 18, LWD to Gavin, Sept. 26, exchange of telegrams, Sept. 23, 25, and tel. conversation Sept. 26, 1967, DP 341; LWD to Lippmann, Nov. 21, 1967, DP 330; LWD to Swinton, April 4, 1967, DP 334; LWD and Backer to Bunker and Johnson, Oct. 31, 1967, DP 341.

19. LWD to Swinton, Aug. 15, 1968, Swinton Papers, 174/7/15, Churchill College Archives, Cambridge University; LWD to Humphrey, Nov. 7, LWD to William A. Roth, Nov. 7, 1968, DP 330; LWD to Nixon (via Arthur Burns), Oct. 2, RMN to LWD, Oct. 7, LWD to RMN, Oct. 28, 1968, DP 331.

20. Speech to the Pilgrim Society, May 21, 1969, DP 377; LWD to Fulbright, Sept. 19, Oct. 10, Fulbright to LWD, Oct. 22, 1969, DP 329.

21. LWD to Harriman, Nov. 18, 1969, DP 330; LWD to Swinton, April 13, 1970, Swinton Papers, 174/7/16, Churchill College Archives, Cambridge University; LWD to Kennan, June 17, 1968, DP 330; LWD to Plimpton, Oct. 8, 1969, DP 64. LWD had become a trustee emeritus of Amherst College in 1952.

22. LWD to Fulbright, May 5, 1970, DP 329; LWD to Cooper, *Arizona Daily Star*, May 21, 1970. He also wrote Senate Majority Leader Mike Mansfield in the same vein. LWD to Mansfield, May 6, 1970, DP 331.

23. LWD to Harold Macmillan, Dec. 11, 1968, DP 333; LWD to Robert Lovett, Dec. 21, LWD to RMN, Nov. 12, 1968, DP 331; LWD to Swinton, April 13, 1970, Swinton Papers, 174/7/16, Churchill College Archives, Cambridge University.

24. LWD to Mansfield, July 30, Mansfield to LWD, Aug. 3, LWD to Muskie, Nov. 10, Muskie to LWD (undated), 1970, Muskie to LWD, June 11, LWD to Muskie, Dec. 29, 1971, Muskie to LWD, Jan. 18, LWD to Muskie, April 13, Aug. 17, 1972, DP 311.

25. LWD to Thomas Jay, Nov. 8, 1972, LWD to Ida Mae Smith, March 3, 1973, DP 106; LWD to RMN, Nov. 8, 1972, DP 331.

26. LWD to Ervin, April 23, 24, May 1, Ervin to LWD, May 11, LWD to Ervin, May 17, Ervin to LWD (undated), 1973, DP 341.

27. LWD to Charles L. Mee, Oct. 24, 1973, DP 332; LWD to Richardson, Oct. 11, 22, LWD to Cox, Oct. 22, LWD to Ruckelshaus, Oct. 24, 1973, DP 341; LWD to Lady Swinton, Dec. 3, 1973, DP 334.

28. Norris Hundley, Jr., *Water and the West: The Colorado River Compact and the Politics of Water in the American West* (Berkeley, Calif., 1974), 295 ff.; Lewis W. Douglas, "The Colorado River from Its Sources to the Sea," *Arizona Highways*, May, 1968, 6–7, 10–11, 38–40, 42–43. For LWD's extensive correspondence and other materials on the subject from 1963 to 1969, see DP 342–345, 361.

29. The correspondence, itinerary, and press coverage of the visit are in DP 351. Peggy Douglas I.

30. Colville I, Hawthorne I.

31. Ibid.; Colville I; Colville to LWD, Feb. 22, LWD to Colville, March 12, 1957, Colville to LWD, May 1, LWD to Colville, May 6, 1958, Colville to Gilbert (copy to LWD), Jan. 8, Colville to Gilbert (copy to LWD), Feb. 3, 1959, DP 307; LWD to Gilbert, May 6, 1958, DP 393.

32. See DP 385, 386, 391, 393, for LWD's work with the foundation through 1969. LWD to Colville, Nov. 18, 1958, DP 307; Fenn to LWD, May 27, 1968, Colville to LWD, July 30, 1969, Colville to LWD, Jan. 23, LWD to Colville, Feb. 10, 1970, DP 395; Fenn to LWD, Oct. 4, LWD to Fenn, Oct. 8, Fenn to LWD, Oct. 11, LWD to Fenn, Nov. 20, 1969, board meeting March 9 (LWD elected president), Epstein to Fenn, March 27, LWD to Hawthorne, Jan. 26, Hawthorne to LWD, Oct. 5, 1970, DP 391; Epstein to Thomas Beckman (and others), Nov. 4, 1971, DP 392; Hawthorne I.

33. LWD to James R. Killian, Jr., May 8, 1970, DP 395; LWD to Prince Philip, April 10, Prince Philip to LWD, April 26, 1971, LWD to Winston Churchill, Oct. 1, 1970, HST to LWD, June 1, 1965, Nov. 11, 1970, Bess Truman to LWD, Feb. 8, 1973, DDE to LWD, June 2, 1965, Mamie Eisenhower to LWD, June 5, 1970,

Winston Churchill speech, March 31, 1971, DP 396; materials on *Young Winston* performance in DP 390; LWD to Baroness Spencer-Churchill, Oct. 18, 1972, Dec. 5, 1973, DP 396; LWD to Fenn, Dec. 3, 1973, DP 391; Churchill I.

34. LWD to Bess Truman, Sept. 6, Bess Truman to LWD, Sept. 18, 1973, Post-Presidential Papers, Corres. File (L. W. Douglas), HSTL; Colville to LWD, Sept. 13, 1973, DP 395.

35. LWD to Drogheda, Oct. 14, 1958, DP 308; Colville to LWD, Oct. 15, LWD to Colville, Oct. 23, LWD to Colville, Nov. 18, 1958, Colville to LWD, Jan. 27, May 13, LWD to Colville, July 29, 1959, DP 307; Hawthorne I; Drogheda I; Colville I.

36. Colville to LWD, March 18, LWD to Colville, March 25, Colville to LWD, March 31, 1970, Colville to LWD, Dec. 29, 1971, LWD to Colville, Feb. 3, Colville to LWD, Feb. 15, 1972, DP 395; arrangements for design and casting of doors, DP 389; Colville I.

37. See Chap. 26 on Encaenia; Queen Mother to Douglases, May 31, LWD to Queen Mother, June 1, 1973, DP 334. After LWD had caught, in July, 1970, the largest rainbow trout thus far taken on a dry fly in the records of the entire Test, McCloy wrote Acheson: "I do not know the name of the river goddess of the Test— it may have been Sabrina, but whatever her name is I think she has been waiting all these years since Lew lost his eye on the Test to make appropriate amends to him, and she now has done it." There was no reply. LWD's record catch in 1973 was a native brown. LWD to McCloy, July 13, McCloy to Acheson, July 17, 1970, Acheson Papers, box 21, Yale University Library. Peggy to LWD, Jr., Feb. 6, LWD to DeGolyer, April 13, 1948, DP 71; for corres. between LWD, Jr., and LWD from 1942 to 1974, see ibid. On Sharman's wedding, see DP 72. The marriage was dissolved several years after LWD's death. LWD, Jr., was remarried in 1979 to Melinda Stanley.

38. Medical information, DP 60; Beaton memorandum, Aug. 21, 1973, ibid.; Hoyt Ammidon to Peggy Douglas, March 11, 1974, DP 120; Goodman I.

39. Peggy Douglas I; Goodman I.

40. Peggy Douglas I; LWD to White, July 25, 1943, DP 265; Beaton I.

41. Peggy Douglas I; *Arizona Daily Star*, March 8, 1974.

42. McCloy to Charles F. Weeden and others, March 12, 1974 (courtesy of McCloy); Brophy I; James S. Douglas I.

43. Letters of condolence, DP 120, 121; Bradley to Peggy Douglas, March 8, 1974, DP 120; *Arizona Republic*, March 11, 1974.

Bibliography

This bibliography contains only sources cited in the notes or especially useful as references.

Manuscript Collections

Arizona Historical Society, Phoenix, Ariz.	Samuel P. Applewhite
Arizona Historical Society, Tucson, Ariz.	Frank Brophy
	Thomas Campbell
	Bernice Cosulich
	Isabella Greenway
	John Greenway
	"Bisbee, Arizona, Feb. 4th, 1900."
Arizona State University, Tempe, Ariz.	George W. P. Hunt
Brandeis University, Waltham, Mass.	David Niles
Canadian Pacific Railroad Office, Montreal, Canada	Sir Edward Beatty
Churchill College, Cambridge University, England	Lord Halifax
	Lord Swinton
Cornell University, Ithaca, N.Y.	Richard B. Scandrett
	George Warren
Columbia University, Oral History Collection, N.Y.	Paul Appleby
	Gordon Browning
	Henry Bruère
	William C. Clayton
	Admiral Richard L. Conolly
	Lewis Douglas
	Clarence B. Kelland
	James Landis
	Alfred Landon
	William E. Leuchtenburg
	Ansel F. Luxford
	Frances Perkins

	Jacob Viner
	Henry A. Wallace
	James Warburg
Dwight D. Eisenhower Presidential Library, Abilene, Kans.	General Lucius D. Clay Eisenhower Personal, Presidential, and White House Papers
Hackley School, Tarrytown, N.Y.	Hackley School Archives
Harvard University, Baker Library, Cambridge, Mass.	Thomas Lamont
Harvard University, Houghton Library, Cambridge, Mass.	Robert E. Sherwood
Harvard University, Law School, Cambridge, Mass.	Learned Hand
Hoover Institution, Stanford, Cal.	Raymond Moley
Lyndon B. Johnson Presidential Library, Austin, Texas	White House Central File National Security File
John F. Kennedy Presidential Library, Boston, Mass.	James Warburg
Library of Congress, Washington, D.C.	Raymond Clapper Charles Hamlin
London School of Economics and Political Science, London, England	Hugh Dalton Diary
McGill University, Montreal, Canada	Board of Governors' Minutes James Douglas (grandfather) Eugene Forsey Principal's File Principal's Letterbooks
National Archives, Washington, D.C.	State Department Files War Shipping Administration (Lewis W. Douglas Files) Modern Military Branch Files Bureau of the Budget, Central Files Office of Military Government for Germany
Phoenix Public Library, Phoenix, Ariz.	James H. McClintock
Princeton University, Princeton, N.J.	Bernard Baruch
Public Records Office, Kew, England	Ministry of Transport Files Foreign Office 371 Prime Minister's Office, PREM 8 (Attlee)
Franklin D. Roosevelt Presidential Library, Hyde Park, N.Y.	Adolf Berle Wayne Coy Democratic National Committee Papers Stephen Early Mordecai Ezekiel Governor's Correspondence Harry L. Hopkins Louis Howe Henry J. Morgenthau

Robert D. Murphy
R. V. V. Nicholls
Sir Frank Roberts
Laone Scanlon
Franz Schneider
Theodore H. Schneider
Lord Sherfield (Roger Makins)
Lord Sinclair of Cleeve (Robert Sinclair)

Lillian Olsen Smith
Lord Stockton (Harold Macmillan)
Lord Strang
Robert Stroud
Edward Weeks
Lord Westmorland
Sir John W. Wheeler-Bennett
Lord Wilson of Rievaulx (Harold Wilson)

Correspondence

Walter R. Agard
Lady Avon (for Lord Avon, Anthony Eden)
David K. E. Bruce
James S. Douglas (brother)
Eugene Forsey
Sir Martin Gilliat
H. Carl Goldenberg
Alan Hodge
Francis Keenlyside
George F. Kennan

René Massigli
John W. McCormack
Archibald C. Merrill
Lady Metcalfe (for Sir Ralph)
Flora Rhind
Frank Scott
Charles Weeden
John A. Williams
Georges Wormser

Newspapers, Yearbooks, and Catalogs

Newspapers and periodicals cited in the notes but not listed below are in the extensive collection in the Douglas Papers of newsclips from the various services LWD employed during his career.

Amherst College Catalogs 1912–1916
Amherst *Olio* Yearbook 1912–1916
Amherst *Student* 1912–1916
Arizona Daily Star
Arizona Republican (later *Republic*)
Bisbee *Daily Review*, 1923–1929
Hackley School Catalogs 1904–1909
Jerome *Verde Copper News*, 1921–1929
McGill *Daily* 1937–1939

McGill University Catalogs, 1937–1939
McGill Yearbooks, 1937–1939
Montclair School Catalog, 1912
Montclair *Ye Yeare Booke*, 1909–1912
New York *Herald Tribune*
New York Times
Smith College *Yearbook*, 1919
The Times (London)

Publications by Lewis W. Douglas

"Balancing the National Budget," *The Consensus*, January, 1938.

"Blowing the Bubble!," *Atlantic Monthly*, January, 1936.

"Can Government Spending Cure Unemployment?," *Atlantic Monthly*, October, 1935.

"Clemenceau," in Lord Longford and Sir John Wheeler-Bennett, ed., *The History Makers: Leaders and Statesmen of the 20th Century*, New York, 1973.

"Commerce and International Politics," *Vital Speeches*, March 15, 1953.

"Defense Today," in William A. White, ed., *Defense for America*, New York, 1940.

"Dollar-Sterling Relationship and Its Effect on U.S. Foreign Economic Policy," *Department of State Bulletin*, August 31, 1953.

"Dr. James Douglas: An Appreciation," in American Geographical Society, Occasional Publication, No. 3, *The Golden Spike: A Centennial Remembrance*, New York, 1969.

"Economic Isolation and Its Consequences," *Phillips Bulletin*, July, 1936.

"Economy in Federal Government," *Proceedings of the Academy of Political Science*, January, 1933.

"External Policy and Our Internal Problems," *Proceedings of the Academy of Political Science*, May, 1940.

"Facing the Future with Confidence," *Technology Review*, July, 1952.

"Foreword" to Ray Bergman, *Trout*. London, 1950.

"Freer World Trade," *Newsweek*, September 7, 1953.

"Free Trade for a Free World," *Technology Review*, July, 1953.

"Government Fiscal Policies," *Banker's Monthly*, July, 1935.

"Government Spending of the Taxpayer's Money," *The Mining and Contracting Review*, October 8, 1935.

"Grenny in the 1930s and 1940s," in *Memoirs*

Bibliography

	J. F. T. O'Connor
	President's Press Conferences
	Roosevelt Personal, Presidential, and White House Papers
	Whitney Shepardson
	Rexford Tugwell
Harry S. Truman Presidential Library, Independence, Mo.	Dean Acheson
	William C. Clayton
	Lord Franks (ERP Interview)
	J. Howard McGrath
	Frank McNaughton
	Truman Personal, Presidential, and White House Papers
The University of Arizona, Special Collections, Tucson, Ariz.	Douglas Papers (James, James S., and Lewis W.)
	Martin Douglas, "The Douglas Family of Arizona"
	William F. Staunton
University College, Oxford University, Oxford, England	Lord Attlee
University of Kentucky, Lexington, Ky.	Fred Vinson
University of Vermont, Burlington, Vt.	Ernest Gibson
University of Virginia, Charlottesville, Va.	Edward R. Stettinius
Yale University, New Haven, Conn.	Dean Acheson
	Chester Bowles
	Walter Lippmann
	Henry L. Stimson
	Wendell Willkie
Yavapai County Court House, Prescott, Ariz.	Election Statistics

INTERVIEWS

Amyas Ames
Joan Bright Astley
Sir Roderick Barclay
Alma Beaton
Richard M. Bissell, Jr.
J. Seeyle Bixler
Frank Brophy
Anthony Montague-Browne
Hon. Mark R. Bonham-Carter
General Marshall S. Carter
Winston S. Churchill
General Lucius D. Clay
Sir John Colville
Lady Cowdray
Peggy Damskey
Dorothy Davison
James S. Douglas (son)
Lewis W. Douglas
Peggy Zinsser Douglas
Sharman Douglas
Lord Drogheda
Claire Ellinwood

Thomas K. Finletter
Lord Franks
Stanley Frost
Lorne D. Gales
Waldemar J. Gallman
Colonel C. J. George
Kenneth George
Dr. Edmund Goodman
George Grimson
W. Averell Harriman
Lord and Lady Hartwell
Sir William Hawthorne
John D. Hickerson
A. Richard Kassander
W. John Kenney
Alfred A. Knopf
W. S. Lewis
Robert A. Lovett
Mick Lunn
John J. McCloy
Frances Tener Muir
Lord Muirshiel (John Scott Maclay)

of a Man: Grenville Clark, collected by Mary Clark Dimond, ed. by Norman Cousins and J. Garry Clifford. New York, 1975.

"A Host of Golden Recollections," in Edgar A. Collard, ed., The McGill You Knew: An Anthology of Memoirs, 1920–1960, Don Mills, Ontario, Canada, 1975.

"If the Allies Lose, What of the U.S.?," Current History, June, 1940.

"Industrial Organization and the American Ideal of Living," Proceedings of the Academy of Political Science, January, 1939.

The Liberal Tradition: A Free People and a Free Economy. New York, 1935.

"Mutual Defense Assistance Program," Department of State Bulletin, June 26, 1950.

"No Third Term," Saturday Evening Post, November 2, 1940.

"Over the Hill to the Poorhouse," Review of Reviews, June, 1935.

"A Policy of Recovery," Vital Speeches, January 14, 1935.

"Recovery by Balanced Budget," Review of Reviews, January, 1935.

"Shall We Repeat the Mistakes of the 1920's?" Vital Speeches, March 1, 1959.

"Shaping the Economic and Political Future," Proceedings of the Academy of Political Science, January, 1945.

"Ships and Subsidies," Atlantic Monthly, July, 1945.

"Should Boulder Dam Bill Be Passed?" Congressional Digest, June, 1928.

"Some Open Questions on Inflation," Vital Speeches, July 1, 1957.

"Sound Recovery Through a Balanced Budget," Atlantic Monthly, December, 1935.

"Statement on Union of Western Europe," Department of State Bulletin, August 15, 1949.

"The Colorado River: From Its Sources to the Sea," Arizona Highways, May, 1968.

"The Danger of Mounting Deficits," Atlantic Monthly, November, 1935.

"The Planning of Taxation, Currency and Finance," Proceedings of the Academy of Political Science, January, 1936.

"The Qualities of Leadership: Churchill as Diplomat," Atlantic Monthly, March, 1965.

"The United Nations," Proceedings of the Academy of Political Science, January, 1943.

"There Is One Way Out: Saving—Not Spending—Will Bring Reemployment," Atlantic Monthly, September, 1935.

"United States and Great Britain: The Need for a Grand Alliance," Vital Speeches, May 15, 1951.

"What Shall We Do with the Ships?" Atlantic Monthly, April, 1945.

"Why Employment Is Retarded," Vital Speeches, November 4, 1935.

BOOKS, ARTICLES, DOCUMENTS, AND DISSERTATIONS

Acheson, Dean. Morning and Noon. Boston, 1965.
———. Present at the Creation: My Years in the State Department. New York, 1969.
———. Sketches from Life of Men I Have Known. New York, 1961.
Agar, Herbert. Britain Alone: June 1940–June 1941. London, 1972.
Allen, Frederick L. Since Yesterday: The Nineteen-Thirties in America, Sept. 3, 1929–Sept. 3, 1939. New York, 1940.
Allen, James B. The Company Town in the American West. Norman, Okla., 1966.
Ambrose, Stephen E. Eisenhower and Berlin, 1945: The Decision to Halt at the Elbe. New York, 1967.
———. Eisenhower: Soldier, General of the Army, President Elect, 1890–1952. New York, 1983.
———. Eisenhower: The President. New York, 1985.
———. Rise to Globalism: American Foreign Policy Since 1938. 5th ed. New York, 1985.
Anderson, Terry H. The United States, Great Britain and the Cold War, 1944–1947. Columbia, Mo., 1981.
Arizona, State of. Journal of the House of Representatives of the Sixth State Legislature of Arizona, 1923. Phoenix, 1923.
Astley, Joan Bright. The Inner Circle: A View of War at the Top. Boston, 1971.
Attlee, Rt. Hon. Earl. As It Happened. London, 1954.
Bakopanos, Eleni. "Arthur Eustace Morgan: The Wrong Man at the Wrong Time," in McGilliana: The History of McGill Project, March–September, 1980.
Barclay, Sir Roderick. Ernest Bevin and the Foreign Office, 1932–1969. London, 1975.
Barnard, Ellsworth. Wendell Willkie: Fighter for Freedom. Marquette, Mich., 1966.
Behrens, C. B. A. Merchant Shipping and the Demands of War. London and Nendeln, Switzerland, 1978.
Bernstein, Barton J. "The New Deal: The Conservative Achievements of Liberal Reform," in Barton Bernstein, ed., Toward a New Past: Dissenting Essays in American History, New York, 1968.
Birkenhead, Lord. Lord Halifax. London, 1965.
Bixler, Julius S. "Alexander Meiklejohn: The Making of an Amherst Mind," New England Quarterly, June, 1974.
Blum, John Morton. From the Morgenthau Diaries: Boston. Vol. I, Years of Crisis, 1928–1938, 1959. Vol. II, Years of Ur-

gency, *1938–1941*, 1965. Vol. III, *Years of War, 1941–1945*, 1967.
Bohlen, Charles E. *Witness to History, 1929–1969*. New York, 1973.
Boyle, Andrew. *Poor, Dear Brendan: The Quest for Brendan Bracken*. London, 1974.
Brewer, James W., Jr. *Jerome: A Story of Mines, Men and Money*. Globe, Ariz., 1970.
Brinkley, Alan. *Voices of Protest: Huey Long, Father Coughlin and the Great Depression*. New York, 1982.
Brive, Pierre. *Georges Clemenceau: Lettres à une amie, 1923–1929*. Paris, 1970.
Brophy, Frank. "The Reluctant Banker: From the Reminiscences of Frank Cullen Brophy," *Journal of Arizona History*, Summer, 1974.
Brown, Francis E. "Congress Wrestles with the Budget," *Current History*, May, 1932.
Bullitt, Orville H., ed. *For the President, Personal and Secret: Correspondence Between Franklin D. Roosevelt and William C. Bullitt*. Boston, 1972.
Bullock, Alan. *Ernest Bevin: Minister of Labour*. New York, 1967.
———. *Ernest Bevin: Foreign Secretary*. New York, 1983.
Burgess, Opie Rundle. "Bisbee," *Arizona Highways*, February, 1952.
Burke, Robert E. "Election of 1940," in Arthur Schlesinger, Jr., and Fred I. Israel, eds., *History of American Presidential Elections, 1789–1968*, 4 vols., New York, 1971.
Burlingame, Roger. "Counter-Attack," *Atlantic Monthly*, November, 1933.
Burns, James MacGregor. *Roosevelt: The Lion and the Fox*. New York, 1956.
Butler, J. R. M. *Lord Lothian (Philip Kerr), 1882–1940*. New York, 1960.
Byrkit, James W. *Forging the Copper Collar: Arizona's Labor-Management War of 1901–1921*. Tucson, Ariz., 1982.
Byrnes, James F. *All in One Lifetime*. New York, 1958.
Catledge, Turner. "A Hard-Hitter Strikes at the Budget," *New York Times Magazine*, March 19, 1933.
Chadwin, Mark Lincoln. *The Warhawks: American Interventionists Before Pearl Harbor*. New York, 1970.
Chisholm, Joe. *Brewery Gulch: Frontier Days of Old Arizona*. San Antonio, Texas, 1949.
———. "Dr. James Douglas," *Arizona Historical Review*, October, 1932.
Churchill, Winston S. *The Second World War*. Boston. Vol. I, *The Gathering Storm*, 1948. Vol. II, *Their Finest Hour*, 1949. Vol. III, *The Grand Alliance*, 1950. Vol. IV, *The Hinge of Fate*, 1950. Vol. V, *Closing the Ring*, 1951. Vol. VI, *Triumph and Tragedy*, 1953.
Clark, Grenville. "A New World Order—The American Lawyer's Role," *The Indiana Law Journal*, July, 1944.
Clay, Lucius D. *Decision in Germany*. New York, 1950.
Cleland, Robert G. *A History of Phelps-Dodge, 1834–1950*. New York, 1952.
Clifford, John G. "Grenville Clark and the Origins of Selective Service," *Review of Politics*, January, 1973.
Coakley, Robert W., and Richard M. Leighton. *The United States Army in World War II: Global Logistics and Strategy, 1943–1945*. Department of the Army, Washington, D.C., 1968.
Cockcraft, John. "Churchill College—A Modern University College," *Science*, 23 October, 1964.
Cole, Wayne S. *America First: The Battle Against Intervention, 1940–41*. Madison, Wis., 1953.
———. *Roosevelt & the Isolationists, 1932–45*. Lincoln, Neb., 1983.
Collard, Edgar A., ed. *The McGill You Knew: An Anthology of Memoirs, 1920–1960*. Don Mills, Ontario, Canada, 1975.
Conant, James B. *My Several Lives: Memoirs of a Social Inventor*. New York, 1970.
Conkin, Paul K. *The New Deal*. New York, 1967.
Cosulich, Bernice. "Mr. Douglas of Arizona: Friend of Cowboys and Kings," *Arizona Highways*, September 1953.
Cox, Annie M., "History of Bisbee, 1877–1937," master's thesis, University of Arizona, 1938.
Cramer, C. H. *Newton D. Baker: A Biography*. Cleveland, 1961.
Dabney, Frederick J., ed. *Selected Papers of Will Clayton*. Baltimore, 1971.
Dallek, Robert. *Franklin D. Roosevelt and American Foreign Policy, 1932–1945*. New York, 1979.
Daniels, Roger. *The Bonus March: An Episode of the Great Depression*. Westport, Conn., 1971.
Davidson, W. P. *The Berlin Blockade*. Princeton, N.J., 1958.
Dedera, Don, and Bob Robles. *Goodbye, Garcia, Adios*. Flagstaff, Ariz., 1976.
"Diogenes." "The Controversy," *Literary Digest*, July 15, 1933.
Divine, Robert. *Roosevelt and World War II*. Baltimore, 1969.
———. *The Reluctant Belligerent: American Entry Into World War II*. 2d ed. New York, 1970.
Dixon, Piers. *Double Diploma: The Life of Sir Pierson Dixon, Don and Diplomat*. London, 1968.
Donovan, Robert J. *Conflict and Crisis: The Presidency of Harry S Truman, 1945–1948*. New York, 1977.
———. *Tumultuous Years: The Presidency of*

Harry S Truman, 1949-1953. New York, 1982.
Dorn, Walter L. "The Debate over American Occupation Policy in Germany, 1944-45," *Political Science Quarterly*, December, 1957.
Douglas, James. "The Copper Queen Mine, Arizona," *Transactions of the American Institute of Mining Engineers*, February, 1899.
———. "The Copper Queen Mines and Works, Arizona, U.S.A.," *Transactions of the Institute of Mining and Metallurgy*, 1912-1913.
———. *The Journals and Reminiscences of James Douglas, M.D.* New York, 1910.
Douglas, Walter. "The Life of James Douglas," *University of Arizona Bulletin*, July 1, 1940.
Drogheda, Lord. *Double Harness: Memoirs by Lord Drogheda*. London, 1978.
Dubofsky, Melvyn. *We Shall Be All: A History of the Industrial Workers of the World*. Chicago, 1969.
Dumke, Glenn S. "Douglas, Border Town," *Pacific Historical Review*, August, 1948.
Elliston, H. B. "Crusader and Budgeteer," *Christian Science Monitor Magazine*, November 27, 1935.
Farley, James A. *Behind the Ballots: The Personal History of a Politician*. New York, 1938.
Fausold, Martin L. *James W. Wadsworth, Jr.: The Gentleman from New York*. Syracuse, N.Y., 1975.
Federal Writers Project. *Arizona: The Grand Canyon State*, rev. ed. New York, 1956.
Feis, Herbert. *1933: Characters in Crisis*. Boston, 1966.
Ferrell, Robert H. *George C. Marshall*. New York, 1966.
"Fishing Diaries." Houghton Club, Stockbridge, Hampshire, England, 1948-1973.
Forrestal, James. *Diaries*. Walter Millis, ed., with the collaboration of E. S. Duffield. New York, 1951.
Freidel, Frank. *Franklin D. Roosevelt: Launching the New Deal*. Boston, 1973.
———. *Franklin D. Roosevelt: The Triumph*. Boston, 1956.
Frost, Stanley. "Lewis William [sic] Douglas: Right Man at the Right Time?" *McGilliana: The History of McGill Project*, March-September, 1980.
Fuess, Claude M. *Amherst: The Story of a New England College*. Boston, 1935.
Gimbel, John. *The American Occupation of Germany: Politics and the Military, 1945-1949*. Stanford, Cal., 1968.
———. *The Origins of the Marshall Plan*. Stanford, Cal., 1976.
Gladwyn, Lord. *The Memoirs of Lord Gladwyn*. New York, 1972.
Goodhart, Philip. *Fifty Ships That Saved the World: The Foundation of the Anglo-American Alliance*. Garden City, N.Y., 1965.
"Hackley's 75th Anniversary," *Hackley Review*, Fall, 1974.
Halifax, Rt. Hon Earl of. *Fulness of Days*. London, 1957.
Hard, Ann. "A Veteran Cuts the Budget," New York *Herald Tribune Magazine*, April 16, 1933.
Harriman, W. Averell, and Elie Abel. *Special Envoy to Churchill and Stalin, 1941-1946*. New York, 1975.
Hasbrouck, Alfred. "Gregor McGregor and the Colonization of Poyais, Between 1820 and 1824," *Hispanic American Historical Review*, November, 1927.
Hassett, William D. *Off the Record with FDR, 1942-1945*. With an introduction by Jonathan Daniels. New Brunswick, N.J., 1958.
Hathaway, Robert M. *Ambiguous Partnership: Britain and America, 1944-1947*. New York, 1981.
Hawley, Ellis W. *The Great War and the Search for a Modern Order: A History of the American People and Their Institutions, 1919-1933*. New York, 1979.
———. *The New Deal and the Problem of Monopoly: A Study in Economic Ambivalence*. Princeton, N.J., 1966.
Hazlehurst, Cameron, and Christine Woodland, compilers. *A Guide to the Papers of British Cabinet Ministers, 1900-1951*. London, 1974.
Herring, E. Pendleton. "First Session of the Seventy-second Congress," *American Political Science Review*, October, 1932.
Hickok, Lorena A. *Eleanor Roosevelt: Reluctant First Lady*. New York, 1962.
Himmelberg, Robert F. *The Origins of the National Recovery Administration: Business, Government, and the Trade Association Issue, 1921-1931*. New York, 1976.
Hofstadter, Richard. "Herbert Hoover and the Crisis of American Individualism," in Hofstadter, ed., *The American Political Tradition and the Men Who Made It*, New York, 1948.
Holusha, Rosemary. "The Douglas Art Collection," *Arizona Highways*, November, 1980.
Hoopes, Townsend. *The Devil and John Foster Dulles*. Boston, 1973.
Howell, W. B. "James Douglas, A Benefactor of McGill," *McGill News*, December, 1931.
Hundley, Norris, Jr. *Dividing the Waters: A Century of Controversy Between the United States and Mexico*. Berkeley, Cal., 1966.
———. *Water and the West: The Colorado River Compact and the Politics of Water in the American West*. Berkeley, Cal., 1974.
Hunt, T. Sterry. "The Hunt and Douglas Copper Process," *Engineering and Mining Journal*, July 2, 1872.

Hurd, William. "The Nation's New Leaders," *Current History*, May, 1933.
Ickes, Harold. *Back to Work*. New York, 1935.
———. *The Secret Diary of Harold L. Ickes*. 3 vols., New York, 1953–1954.
"In the Saddle," *Collier's*, July 29, 1933.
Ismay, General Lord. *Memoirs*. London, 1960.
"James Douglas," *Engineering and Mining Journal*, July 6, 1918. Obituary.
James, Robert Rhodes. *Victor Cazalet: A Portrait*. London, 1976.
Janney, John. "Keeper of the Middle Road," *American Magazine*, July, 1938.
Jervey, William H., Jr. "When the Banks Closed: Arizona's Bank Holiday of 1933," *Arizona and the West*, Summer, 1968.
Johnson, Hugh S. *The Blue Eagle from Egg to Earth*. Garden City, N.Y., 1935.
Johnson, Walter. *The Battle Against Isolation*. Chicago, 1944.
Jones, Jesse, and Edward Angly. *Fifty Billion Dollars*. New York, 1951.
Joralemon, Ira B. *Copper: The Encompassing Story of Mankind's First Metal*. Berkeley, Cal.: University of California Press, 1973.
Karl, Barry Dean. *Executive Reorganization and Reform in the New Deal: The Genesis of Administrative Management, 1900–1939*. Cambridge, Mass., 1963.
Kennan, George F. *Memoirs, 1925–1950*. Boston, 1967.
Keynes, John Maynard. *The Economic Consequences of the Peace*. New York, 1920.
Kimmel, Lewis H. *Federal Budget and Fiscal Policy, 1789–1958*. Washington, D.C., 1959.
Kiplinger, W. M. "Capitol Men," *New Outlook*, October, 1933.
Krock, Arthur. *Memoirs: Sixty Years on the Firing Line*. New York, 1968.
LaFeber, Walter. *America, Russia, and the Cold War, 1945–1984*. 5th ed. New York, 1985.
Land, Emory S. *Winning the War with Ships: Land, Sea, and Air—Mostly Land*. New York, 1952.
Lane, Frederic C. *Ships for Victory: A History of Shipbuilding Under the U.S. Maritime Commission in World War II*. Baltimore, 1951.
Langer, William L., and S. Everett Gleason. *The Challenge to Isolation, 1937–1940*. New York, 1952.
———. *The Undeclared War, 1940–1941*. New York, 1953.
Langton, Hugh. *James Douglas: A Memoir*. Toronto, 1940.
Lash, Joseph P., ed. *From the Diaries of Felix Frankfurter*. New York, 1975.
Leahy, William D. *I Was There: The Personal Story of the Chief of Staff to Presidents Roosevelt and Truman, Based on His Notes and Diaries Made at the Time*. New York, 1950.
Leighton, Richard M., and Robert W. Coakley. *The United States Army in World War II: Global Logistics and Strategy, 1940–1943*. Department of the Army, Washington, D.C., 1955.
Leisk, R. D. "James S. Douglas: An Appreciation," *Journal of Metals*, April, 1949.
Leuchtenburg, William E. *Franklin D. Roosevelt and the New Deal, 1932–1940*. New York, 1963.
Lindley, Ernest K. *The Roosevelt Revolution: First Phase*. New York, 1933.
Lisio, Donald. *The President and Protest: Hoover, Conspiracy, and the Bonus Riot*. Columbia, Mo., 1974.
Lodge, Henry C. *The Storm Has Many Eyes: A Personal Narrative*. Boston, 1973.
Loucheim, Katie, ed. *The Making of the New Deal: The Insiders Speak*. Cambridge, Mass., 1983.
Lowery, Fred. *History of a Fishing Trip*. Privately printed, 1934.
MacArthur, Douglas. *Reminiscences: General of the Army Douglas MacArthur*. New York, 1964.
MacMillan, Cyrus. *McGill and Its Story, 1821–1921*. London, 1921.
Mann, Arthur. *La Guardia: A Fighter Against His Times, 1882–1933*. Philadelphia, 1959.
Markey, Morris. "He's Got His Hand in Your Pocket," *American Magazine*, June, 1933.
Martin, George. *Madam Secretary: Frances Perkins*. Boston, 1976.
Martin, John Bartlow. *Adlai Stevenson of Illinois: The Life of Adlai Stevenson*. New York, 1976.
Mason, Edward S., and Robert E. Asher. *The World Bank Since Bretton Woods*. Washington, D.C., 1973.
May, Henry F. *The End of American Innocence: A Study of the First Years of Our Own Time, 1912–1917*. New York, 1959.
Mayo, Dwight E. "Arizona and the Colorado River Compact," master's thesis, Arizona State University, 1964.
McCoy, Donald R. *Landon of Kansas*. Lincoln, Neb., 1966.
McDonald, James G. *My Mission in Israel, 1948–1951*. New York, 1951.
McDonald, P. B. "James Douglas," *Dictionary of American Biography*, V.
McGill University. *Annual Report of McGill University for 1937–1938*. Montreal, 1938.
———. *Annual Report of McGill University for 1938–1939*. Montreal, 1939.
McKee, John D. *William Allen White: Maverick on Main Street*. Westport, Conn., 1975.
McLellan, David S. *Dean Acheson: The State Department Years*. New York, 1976.
———, and David C. Acheson. *Among Friends: Personal Letters of Dean Acheson*. New York, 1980.
McManus, Robert C. "Best Apple in the Bar-

rel," *North American Review*, September, 1932.

McMurray, Dorothy. *Four Principals of McGill: A Memoir, 1929-1939*. Montreal, 1940.

Milestones of Memorial Hospital. New York, 1934.

Miller, Francis P. *Man from the Valley: Memoirs of a Twentieth Century Virginian*. Chapel Hill, N.C., 1971.

Miller, Joseph. *Arizona: The Last Frontier*. New York, 1952.

Miller-Barstow, D. H. *Beatty of the C.P.R*. Toronto, 1951.

Mitchell, Broadus. *Depression Decade: From New Era Through New Deal, 1929-1941*. New York, 1947.

Moeller, Beverly B. *Phil Swing and Boulder Dam*. Berkeley, Cal., 1971.

Moley, Raymond. *After Seven Years*. New York, 1939.

———. *27 Masters of Politics: In a Personal Perspective*. New York, 1949.

———, assisted by Elliot A. Rosen. *The First New Deal*. New York, 1966.

Moore, John Robert. *Senator Josiah William Bailey of North Carolina: A Political Biography*. Durham, N.C., 1968.

Morrison, Joseph L. *Governor O. Max Gardner: A Power in North Carolina and New Deal Washington*. Chapel Hill, N.C., 1971.

Murphy, Robert. *Diplomat Among Warriors*. New York, 1964.

Myers, William Starr, and Walter H. Newton. *The Hoover Administration: A Documented Narrative*. New York, 1936.

Neff, Donald. *Warriors at Suez*. New York, 1981.

Nicolson, Harold. *Diaries and Letters, 1930-39*. London, 1966.

———. *Diaries and Letters, 1939-45*. London, 1967.

———. *Diaries and Letters, 1945-62*. London, 1968.

91st Division Publication Committee. *The Story of the 91st Division*. San Francisco, 1919.

Nixon, Edgar B., ed. *Franklin D. Roosevelt and Conservation, 1911-1945*. 2 vols. New York, 1957.

"Official Conversations and Meetings of Dean Acheson, 1949-1953." University Publications of America, 1980.

Owen, Russell. "The 'Brain Trust' Mirrors Many Minds," *New York Times Magazine*, June 11, 1933.

Parmet, Herbert S., and Marie B. Hecht. *Never Again: A President Runs for a Third Term*. New York, 1968.

Parsons, Malcolm B. "Origins of the Colorado River Controversy in Arizona Politics, 1922-1923," *Arizona and the West*, Spring, 1962.

———. "Party and Pressure Politics in Arizona's Opposition to Colorado River Development," *Pacific Historical Review*, February, 1950.

Paterson, Thomas G. *On Every Front: The Making of the Cold War*. New York, 1979.

———. *Soviet-American Confrontation: Postwar Reconstruction and the Origins of the Cold War*. Baltimore and London, 1973.

Patterson, James T. *Congressional Conservatism and the New Deal: The Growth of the Conservative Coalition in Congress, 1933-1939*. Lexington, Ky., 1967.

Pearson, Drew. *Washington Merry Go Round*. New York, 1931.

Perkins, Frances. *The Roosevelt I Knew*. New York, 1946.

Perkins, Van L. *Crisis in Agriculture: The Agricultural Adjustment Administration and the New Deal, 1933*. Berkeley, Cal., 1969.

Pogue, Forrest C. *George C. Marshall: Ordeal and Hope, 1939-1942*. New York, 1966.

———. *Organizer of Victory, 1942-1945*. New York, 1973.

Portraits and Appreciations: Brendan Bracken, 1901-1958. London, privately circulated, 1958.

Press Conferences of the President: Franklin D. Roosevelt, 1933-45; Harry S Truman, 1945-53.

Price, Harry Bayard. *The Marshall Plan and Its Meaning*. Ithaca, N.Y., 1955.

Public Papers of the Presidents of the United States: Harry S Truman, 1945-1953. Washington, D.C., 1961, 1963.

Rak, Mary Kidder. "Douglas," *Arizona Highways*, January, 1950.

Reynolds, David. *The Creation of the Anglo-American Alliance, 1937-41: A Study in Competitive Cooperation*. Chapel Hill, N.C., 1981.

Richberg, Donald. *My Hero: The Indiscreet Memoirs of an Eventful but Unheroic Life*. New York, 1954.

———. *The Rainbow*. New York, 1936.

Rickard, T. A. "The Story of the UVX Bonanza-I," *Mining and Scientific Press*, Jan. 5, 1918.

Romasco, Albert U. *The Politics of Recovery: Roosevelt's New Deal*. New York, 1983.

———. *The Poverty of Abundance: Hoover, the Nation, the Depression*. New York, 1965.

Roosevelt, Elliott. *As He Saw It*. With Foreword by Eleanor Roosevelt. New York, 1946.

———. *FDR: His Personal Letters, 1928-1945*. 2 vols. New York, 1950.

Roosevelt's Press and Radio Conferences.

Rosen, S. McKee. *The Combined Shipping Boards of the Second World War: An Experiment in International Administration*. New York, 1951.

Rosenman, Samuel I., comp. *The Public Papers and Addresses of Franklin D. Roosevelt*. 13 vols. New York, 1938-1950.

Ross, Charles G. "A Man Who Can Say No with a Smile," *Literary Digest*, July 8, 1933.

Leith-Ross, Sir Frederick. *Money Talks: Fifty*

Years of International Finance. London, 1968.
Rushkoff, Bennett C. "Eisenhower, Dulles and the Quemoy-Matsu Crisis, 1954-1955," *Political Science Quarterly,* Fall, 1978.
Rusinek, Walter. "Against the Compact: The Critical Opposition of Governor George W. P. Hunt," *Journal of Arizona,* Summer, 1984.
Russell, Colin K. "Dr. James Douglas, 1800-1886, Adventurer," *Transactions of the American Neurological Association,* 1935.
Salter, Arthur. *Memoirs of a Public Servant.* London, 1961.
———. *Slave of the Lamp.* London, 1967.
———. *Personality in Politics: Studies of Contemporary Statesmen.* London, 1947.
Salutous, Theodore. *The American Farmer and the New Deal.* Ames, Iowa, 1982.
Sargent, James E. "FDR and Lewis W. Douglas: Budget Balancing and the Early New Deal," *Prologue,* Spring, 1974.
———. "Oral History, Franklin D. Roosevelt, and the New Deal: Some Recollections of Adolf A. Berle, Jr., Lewis W. Douglas, and Raymond Moley," *Oral History Review,* 1973.
———. *Roosevelt and the Hundred Days: Struggle for the Early New Deal.* New York, 1981.
———. "Roosevelt's Economy Act: Fiscal Conservatism and the Early New Deal," *Congressional Studies,* Winter, 1980.
Schlesinger, Arthur M., Jr. *The Age of Roosevelt: The Coming of the New Deal.* Boston, 1958. *The Crisis of the Old Order, 1919-1933,* 1957. *The Politics of Upheaval,* 1960.
Schwarz, Jordan A. *The Interregnum of Despair: Hoover, Congress, and the Depression.* Urbana, Ill., 1970.
Shaw, Albert. "Executives in the New Deal," *Review of Reviews,* April, 1933.
Sherwood, Robert. *Roosevelt and Hopkins: An Intimate History.* 2 vols. New York, 1948.
Smith, Gaddis. *Dean Acheson.* New York, 1972.
Smith, Jean Edward, ed. *The Papers of General Lucius D. Clay: Germany, 1945-1949.* 2 vols. Bloomington, Ind., 1974.
Smith, Thomas G. "From the Heart of the American Desert to the Court of St. James's: The Public Career of Lewis W. Douglas of Arizona, 1894-1974," Ph.D. dissertation, University of Connecticut, 1977.
———. "Lewis Douglas, Arizona Politics and the Colorado River Controversy," *Arizona and the West,* Summer, 1980.
———. "Lewis Douglas Grows Up," *Journal of Arizona History,* Summer, 1979.
Smith, Walter B. *My Three Years in Moscow.* Philadelphia, 1950.
Sonnichsen, C. L., "Hard Times in Tucson," *Journal of Arizona History,* Spring, 1981.
Sparks, George F. *A Many-colored Toga: The Diary of Henry Fountain Ashurst.* Tucson, Ariz., 1962.
Steel, Ronald. *Walter Lippmann and the American Century.* Boston, 1980.
Stimson, Henry L., and McGeorge Bundy. *On Active Service in Peace and War.* New York, 1948.
Strang, Lord. *Home and Abroad.* London, 1956.
Strauss, Lewis L. *Men and Decisions.* New York, 1962.
Sulzberger, C. L. *A Long Row of Candles: Memoirs and Diaries [1934-1954].* New York, 1969.
Swinton, Earl of, with J. D. Margach. *Sixty Years of Power.* London, 1966.
Taft, Philip. "Bisbee Deportation," *Labor History,* Winter, 1972.
"The 'Soak the Rich' Drive in Washington," *Literary Digest,* April 2, 1932.
Theisen, Lee Scott. "Two Kindly Grouches: A Note by Stephen Bonsal on James Douglas and Georges Clemenceau," *Journal of Arizona History,* Spring, 1977.
Timmons, Bascom. *Jesse H. Jones.* New York, 1956.
Tompkins, C. David. *Senator Arthur J. Vandenberg: The Evolution of a Modern Republican, 1884-1945.* Lansing, Mich., 1970.
Truman, Harry S. *Years of Decision.* New York, 1955.
———. *Years of Trial and Hope.* New York, 1956.
Tugwell, Rexford. *The Democratic Roosevelt: A Biography.* Garden City, N.Y., 1957.
———. *Roosevelt's Revolution: The First Year—A Personal Perspective.* New York, 1977.
———. *In Search of Roosevelt.* Cambridge, Mass., 1972.
Tully, Grace. *F.D.R., My Boss.* New York, 1949.
U.S. Congress. *Congressional Record,* 1927-1933.
———. House Committee on Irrigation and Reclamation. *Boulder Canyon Project.* House Report 918. 70 Cong., 1 Sess., Washington, D.C., 1928.
———. House. *Hearings on Immigration from Countries of the Western Hemisphere.* 70 Cong., 1 Sess., Washington, D.C., 1928.
———. House. *Hearings on Protection and Development of the Lower Colorado Basin.* 70 Cong., 1 Sess., Washington, D.C., 1928.
———. House. *Hearings on Second Deficiency Appropriation Bill for 1930.* 71 Cong., 1 Sess., Washington, D.C., 1930.
———. House Committee on Foreign Affairs. *Hearings on United States Policy for a Post-War Recovery Program.* 80th Cong., 2nd Sess., Washington, D.C., 1948.
———. House. *To Effect Economies in National Government.* House Report 1126. 72 Cong., 1 Sess., Washington, D.C., 1932.
———. House. *Report of the Colorado River*

Board on the Boulder Dam Project. House Document 446. 70 Cong., 2 Sess., Washington, D.C., 1928.
———. House Committee on Merchant Marine and Fisheries. *Wartime Accounting Practices of the United States Maritime Commission and the War Shipping Administration.* 80th Cong., 1 Sess., Washington, D.C., 1947.
———. Senate. *Hearings Before a Special Committee Investigating Expenditures in Senatorial Primary and General Elections.* 69 Cong., 1 Sess., Washington, D.C., 1926.
———. Senate Committee on Foreign Relations. *Hearing on United States Assistance to European Recovery Program.* 80th Cong., 2 Sess., Washington, D.C., 1948.
———. Senate. *Senatorial Campaign Expenditures.* Senate Report 1197. 69 Cong., 2 Sess., Washington, D.C., 1926.
U.S. Department of Commerce. *Fourteenth Census of the United States: 1920.* Washington, D.C., 1922.
U.S. Department of State. *Bulletin.* Washington, D.C., 1946–1950.
———. *Foreign Relations of the United States, 1947–1950.* Washington, D.C., 1973–1980.
———. *Foreign Relations of the United States: The Conferences at Cairo and Teheran, 1943.* Washington, D.C., 1961.
———. *Foreign Relations of the United States: The Conferences at Washington 1941–1942 and Casablanca, 1943.* Washington, D.C, 1968.
———. *Foreign Relations of the United States: The Conferences at Washington and Quebec, 1943.* Washington, D.C., 1970.
U.S. Government Reports. No. 283. *Arizona vs. California.* Washington, D.C., 1931.
"Unofficial Observer" [John Franklin Carter]. *The New Dealers.* New York, 1934.
Vandenberg, Arthur H., with the collaboration of Joe Alex Morris. *The Private Papers of Senator Vandenberg.* Boston, 1952.
Van Petten, Donald R. "Arizona's Stand on the Santa Fe Compact and the Boulder Dam Project Act," *New Mexico Historical Review*, January, 1942.

Wann, A. J. *The President as Chief Administrator: A Study of Franklin D. Roosevelt,* Washington, D.C., 1968.
Warburg, James. *Hell Bent for Election.* New York, 1935.
———. *The Long Road Home: The Autobiography of a Maverick.* Garden City, N.Y., 1964.
———. *The Money Muddle.* New York, 1934.
Warren, Robert, Leo Wolman, and Henry Clay. *The State in Society.* London, 1940.
Wheeler-Bennett, John W. *King George VI: His Life and Reign.* London, 1958.
——— and Anthony Nicholls. *The Semblance of Peace: The Political Settlement After the Second World War.* New York, 1972.
White, William A., ed. *Defense for America.* New York, 1940.
"Whittling Down Roosevelt Economy," *Literary Digest,* June 17, 1933.
Williams, Francis J., with Clement Attlee. *A Prime Minister Remembers: The War and Post-War Memoirs of the Rt. Hon. Earl Attlee.* London, 1962.
———. *Ernest Bevin: Portrait of a Great Englishman.* London, 1952.
Wilson, Joan Hoff. *Herbert Hoover: Forgotten Progressive.* Boston, 1975.
Wilson, Marjorie H. "The Gubernatorial Career of George W. P. Hunt of Arizona," Ph.D. dissertation, Arizona State University, 1973.
Wolfskill, George, and John A. Hudson. *All But the People: Franklin D. Roosevelt and his Critics, 1933–1939.* New York, 1969.
———. *The Revolt of the Conservatives.* Boston, 1962.
Yergin, Daniel. *Shattered Peace: The Origins of the Cold War and the National Security State.* Boston, 1977.
Young, Herbert V. *Ghosts of Cleopatra Hill: Men and Legends of Old Jerome.* Jerome, Ariz., 1974.
Young, Otis E., Jr. "Origins of the American Copper Industry," *Journal of the Early Republic,* Summer, 1983.
Zinn, Howard. *La Guardia in Congress.* Ithaca, N.Y., 1959.
———. *New Deal Thought.* New York, 1966.

Index

Abdullah, emir of Trans-Jordan, 307
Academy of Political Science, 219–20
Acheson, Dean, 74, 124, 127, 237, 241, 242, 243, 244, 250, 252, 254, 302, 336; meets LWD, 57; Arizona Supreme Court case, 57–8; and New Deal, 86, 99, 102, 103, 104–5, 106–7, 113; and presidential election (1936), 128, (1940) 152; destroyer deal, 151; and Lend-Lease, 155; on LWD speech, 251; and ERP, 257–8, 277; and NATO, 284; named SecSt., 318, 320; relations with Bevin, 318, 453; relations with Franks, 318; persuades LWD to continue as ambassador after eye injury, 321, 327; and Mutual Defense Assistance Bill, 325; and British financial crisis, 329–30; and West Germany, 331; and recognition of China, 332–3; and relations with Soviet Union, 334–5, 339; attacked by GOP conservatives, 336; on LWD's closeness with British conservatives, 337–8; on relations with Britain, 338–9; and Schuman Plan, 339; asks LWD to chair NATO Council of Deputies, 339–40; and LWD resignation, 340–1, 343, 364; and Korea, 341–3; and German rearmament, 344–5; and HST, 378; break with LWD, 378, 423; and McCarthyism, 381
Achilles, Theodore, 284
Adair, E. R., 136, 139
Adams, Sherman, 363, 385
Advisory Committee on Weather Control, 368
Agar, Herbert, 149, 150
Agard, Walter, 24
Agricultural Adjustment Act (AAA), 89, 90, 93, 98, 125, 129
Agricultural Marketing Act (1929), 59
Alamo Canal, 36
Aldrich, Winthrop, 380, 458

Alexander, A. V., 309, 324
All-American Canal, 36, 54, 56
Allied Control Council (Germany), 232, 234, 262, 284, 295; LWD with, 227, 228
Alphand, Hervé, 290
America First Committee, 154
American Assembly, 361–2
American Cyanamid, 119–20, 124, 131
American Expeditionary Force (AEF), 22–4
American Indians, 396
American Liberty League, 126
American Philosophical Society, 217
Ames, Amyas, 170
Amherst College, 19–21, 24
Anakim (Burma operation), 197
Andrews, Adm. Adolphus, 179
Andrews, A. Piatt, 52
Andrews, Gen. L. C., 23
Angell, James R., 225
anti-Bolshevism, 8–9, 31
anti-Semitism: remarks by LWD, 106, 111; at McGill, 131, 139; remarks by Lindbergh, 158
Apache Indians, 14
apartheid, LWD on, 365, 390
appeasement, LWD on, 147
Appleby, Paul, 90
Applewhite, Samuel, 13
Arabs, *see* Palestine
Aravaipa Mining Company, 41
Arcadia Conference (1941), 164, 165, 168
Arizona: copper industry, 31, 63, 64; politics, 33–4, 37, 46–8, 49, 218; cotton, 61–2; depression in, 64
Arizona Daily Star: LWD's economic interest in, 42, 62, 389; on LWD, 49, 223
Arizona Fax, 75
Arizona Gazette, 49

475

Arizona Plain Talk, 374-5
Arizona Republic (formerly *Republican*), 374, 404
Arizona Water Resources Committee, 369
Arnold, Gen. Henry H., 187
Ashurst, Henry, 34, 56; LWD on, 52, 54, 414; on LWD, 54; LWD considers opposing for U.S. Senate, 112
Association for Applied Solar Energy (Solar Energy Society), 368-9
Aswan Dam, 386
Atlanta Mining Company, 7
Atlantic Congress, 372
Atlantic Monthly, 212
atomic bomb, LWD on, 221, 222
Attlee, Clement: discusses British military mission in Greece with LWD, 249; attends LWD speech, 250; and British coal crisis, 254; discusses ERP with LWD, 259; wonders if LWD bluntness caused by alcohol, 266; discusses Berlin crisis with LWD, 294-5; and Palestine, 306-7, 309, 315; on U.S. foreign policy demands, 322; meets with LWD on Mutual Defense program, 324; concern for LWD's health, 327; on Cripps, 328; on British financial crisis, 328-9; and China, 342; attends LWD's farewell dinner, 352
Austin, Warren, 306
Avirett, William, 19
Axline, Guy, 56
Aydelotte, Frank, 217

Babcock, E. Claude, 67
Backer, George, 397
Bailey, Frazer A., 184
Bailey, Josiah, 126, 130, 200
Baker, Newton D., 73, 119, 126, 127, 128
Balfour, Sir John, 256, 258
Balfour Declaration, 305
Ballard, John, 5
Baltimore Sun, 88-9, 245
Banking Bill (1935), 125
banks, closings and panics, 81, 86, 105, 106
Barclay, Sir Robert, 266
Barkley, Alben, 320
Baruch, Bernard, 91, 92, 94, 95, 124, 351
Baughn, Otis J., 45, 46, 48
Beatty, Sir Edward, chancellor of McGill, 131-2; on LWD, 133; benefactor of McGill, 135; and efforts to combat socialism, 136-8; and search for LWD's successor, 144
Beauport Insane Asylum, 6
Beck, James N., 52
Bedside Cabinet, 84
Begin, Menachem, 311
Bell, Daniel, 115
Bell, William B., 119, 120, 270
Benelux countries: and London Conference, 278, 280, 281, 283; and NATO, 283, 445
Berger, Victor, 52
Berlin issue, 278, 279, 285, 310, 311, 315, 318, 323; blockade and airlift, 291-302;
LWD on, 285, 291-301 *passim*, 377; currency reform in, 292; and the UN, 295, 299-301
Bernadotte, Count Folke, 309, 311; assassination of, 313; and Palestine partition proposals, 312-14, 315, 316, 317
Betts, Amos, 43, 45, 48
Bevin, Ernest, 254, 273, 277, 334; and appointment of LWD as ambassador, 244, 247; and CFM (1947), 249, 272; relations with LWD, 252, 267, 275, 279; and ERP, 258-61, 264, 268-9, 275; LWD warns, about nationalization of coal industry, 266; on LWD's contributions to ERP, 275-6; proposes western alliance, 274, 279, 283-4; and German reparations and reconstruction, 280, 282, 285, 288-9, 322-3, 443; on U.S. bombers in Britain, 293; and Berlin issue, 293-300; and Palestine, 303-7, 310-13, 315-17; and Dean Acheson, 318; and creation of Jewish state, 308-9; and military assistance program, 324; and British financial crisis, 329; and creation of West Germany, 331; and China, 332-3; and Schuman Plan, 339; and Korea, 341-2, 343; and Churchill, 337; and Eden, 336; and LWD's eye injury, 327; and LWD's resignation and farewell, 347-8, 352-3; death of EB, 351
Bidault, Georges: and ERP, 258, 261, 269; and German revitalization, 263-4, 279; and CFM, 272; LWD transmits Marshall's views to, 273, 278; and western alliance, 284; LWD on, 289, 290
Biffle, Les, 310
Big Four Conference (Geneva) (1955), 384-5
Bisbee, Dewitt, 5
Bisbee deportation, 8-9
Bisbee Review, 58, 64
Bissell, Richard M., 170
Bixler, Seeyle (Julius), 19, 24
Black, Eugene, 103, 106
Black Canyon (Colorado River), 54, 56
Bland, Schuyler Otis, 201
Blandford, Marquess of, 352
Bloom, Sol, 276
Bohlen, Charles, 273, 297, 298, 301, 338; on ERP, 257, 260
Bonesteel, Col. Charles H., 267, 270
Bonham-Carter, Mark, 352
Bonnet, Henri, 288
Bonus Army (1932), 69, (1933), 89
Boston Traveler, 245
Boulder Canyon, 36, 54, 56
Boulder Dam, 56, 57, 61
Boulder Dam bill, *see* Swing-Johnson bill
Bowie, Lt. Col. Robert, 234
Bowles, Chester, 245
Box, John C., 62
Bracken, Brendan, 347, 365; LWD writes, on the creation of Israel, 317; LWD relations with, 350, 454; death of, 351; LWD writes, about Churchill, 370-1; LWD writes, about Adlai Stevenson, 376; LWD writes, on

Eden and Suez crisis, 388; LWD writes, about Eisenhower, 390; memorial to, 402
Bradley, Gen. Omar N., 404
Braham, Dr. Roscoe R., Jr., 368, 456
Brewery Gulch (Bisbee), 4
Bright, Joan, 205, 211; on LWD, 202; LWD relations with, 201–2
brinksmanship, 385, 395
Bristol University, 349
British Ministry of War Transport (BMWT), 165, 166, 170, 180, 197
Bronfman, Samuel and Allen, 135
Brophy, Frank: as friend and confidant of LWD, 11, 15, 17, 64, 129, 134, 325; on JSD, 11–12; on JSD and Josalee, 13; on LWD, 14; LWD business partner, 41; on depression in Arizona, 63; offers LWD control of Bank of Douglas, 366–7; and McCarthyism, 382
Brophy, Sally (Mrs. Frank), 122
Brophy, William, 10, 41
Brown, Alvin, 85
Brown, Ernest, 137
Brownell, Herbert, 379
Browning, Gordon, 88
Bruce, David, 338, 344
Bruère, Henry, 106
Brussels Treaty (1948), 283–4, 324
Buccleuch, Duke of, 246
Bulganin, Nikolai A., 384
Bunche, Ralph, 312, 317
Bundy, McGeorge, 393, 396; on LWD, 394
Bunker, Ellsworth, 397
Burke, Edmund, 350
Burke, Edward, 148
Burma Operation (Buccaneer), 206–7
Burns, Arthur, 460
Burr, Gen. Edward, 22
Burton, Harold, 245
Butler, George, 284
Butler, Sir Nevile, 258
Butler, R. A., 379
Byrd, Harry, 126, 127, 130, 362
Byrnes, James F.: introduces government reorganization bill, 80; works with LWD on government economy, 81; recommends LWD for Budget Director, 82; LWD supports for presidential nomination (1944), 218; asks LWD to head World Bank, 222–3; alerts LWD about assignment with Clay in Germany, 226; discusses postwar German reconstruction with LWD, 229, 232, 237; considered as candidate for ambassadorship to Britain, 241; and creation of Jewish state, 303
Byrns, Joseph, 80, 83
Byroade, Henry A., 334

Caccia, Sir Harold, 371
Cadogan, Sir Alexander, 310
Caffery, Jefferson, 258, 261, 264, 267–8, 280, 324; William Clayton on, 443
Cairo Conference (Sextant) (1943), 204, 205–8

Calumet and Arizona Mining Company, 8
Cambodia, 398
Cameron, Ralph, 41, 45, 46, 47, 54, 56
Campbell, William, 320, 321
Camp Lewis (Washington), 22
Cananea Consolidated Copper Company, 15
Capper, Arthur, 440
Carter, Gen. Marshall S., 323
Casablanca Conference (1943), 191, 193–5
Central Arizona Project (CAP), 400–1
Century Group (Warhawks), 149, 150–1, 154, 155
Chamberlain, Neville, 124, 139
Chase, Stuart, 124
Chauvel, Jean, 289, 446; LWD on, 290
Chemical Copper Company, 6
Cheny, Ward, 150
Cherwell, Lord, 179, 401
Chiang Kai-shek, 205, 332
China, 332–3, 342, 377, 383–4
China Lobby, 332, 382
Christian Science Monitor, 245
Chubb, Percy, 170
Church, Frank, 398
Churchill, Clementine (Mrs. Winston), 327
Churchill, Winston: heroes of, 3; LWD meets, 124; destroyers request, 149; military supplies request, 154; Arcadia Conference, 165, 178; meets with LWD on shipping, 179; on importance of shipping to war effort, 181, 432; on European theater, 183; British wartime imports, 192, 194, 196, 197; Trident Conference, 199–200; First Quebec Conference, 201–2; stays at White House, 203; on the Chinese, 205; Cairo Conference, 205–6; Burma campaign, 206–7; on postwar merchant fleet, 212; defeated for reelection, 221; LWD on, 221, 370–1; on LWD's appointment as ambassador, 246–7; on American postwar loan, 257; on forcing Soviet Union out of Berlin, 285–6; on LWD's eye injury, 327; LWD relations with, 335–6, 349, 351, 352–3
Churchill, Winston (grandson), 402
Churchill College, 402–3
Churchill Foundation, 401–3
Cincinnati *Inquirer*, 245
Civilian Conservation Corps (CCC), 89, 90, 98, 108, 112
civil rights, 362–3
Civil Rights Commission, 363
Civil Works Administration (CWA), 108, 109, 110
Clapper, Raymond, 97
Clark, Grenville, 148, 220, 417
Clark, Tom C., 250
Clay, Henry, 136, 137
Clay, Gen. Lucius D., 185, 216, 221, 227, 270; on LWD, 226, 287, 323; works with LWD on postwar German reconstruction, 226, 228, 229, 231, 233–4, 235–6; halts reparations deliveries to Soviet Union, 262; German level of industry plan, 263, 264; on

Clay, Gen. Lucius D. (*cont.*)
LWD's role in industry talks, 264–5; on CFM (London), 274–4; in Berlin crisis, 279, 283, 285, 291–3, 295–7, 299, 301; London Conference on Germany, 280, 281, 282, 290; on LWD's role in London Conference, 286, and control of Ruhr, 286–7, 446; on LWD and Berlin crisis, 292, 301; and West Germany, 322; as advisor to Eisenhower, 379, 390

Clayton, William L.: and Century Group, 150; meets with LWD on postwar Germany, 226, 232, 237; considered candidate for ambassadorship to Britain, 241; British loan, 253, 255; and ERP, 257–64 *passim*, 267–8, 269–70, 276–7; Hugh Dalton on, 259; on Caffery, 443; on LWD, 443

Clemenceau, Ariz., 11
Clemenceau, Georges, 3, 10, 11, 12, 13, 60, 64, 336; on LWD, 60
Clemenceau Museum, 12
Clifford, Clark, 308, 312
cloud-seeding, 367–8
Cockroft, Sir John, 402
Coffin, Henry Sloane, 150
Collett, Alec, 347
Colorado River, 36
Colorado River Compact, 35–7, 40, 42, 44, 54, 57, 413; LWD urges ratification of, 218, 400
Colorado River controversy, 36, 44–5, 48, 50, 54, 400
Colton, Don B., 54
Columbia University, 361, 362
Colville, Sir John, 401, 402, 403
Combined Shipping Adjustment Board (CSAB), 165, 169, 193, 194, 196
Commercial Mining Company, 10
Commission of Foreign Trade Policy, 380
Committee for Hungarian Relief, 389–90
Committee on European Economic Cooperation (CEEC), *see* Marshall Plan
Committee to Defend America by Aiding the Allies (CDAAA), 148, 155–6; and Willkie, 150; LWD's work with, 151, 154–9, 163
commodity dollar, *see* Warren, George F.
communism and communist party, 342, 349, 354, 360, 395, 397
Conant, James, 119, 155, 157, 158, 220, 221, 228
concentration camps, 233–4
Connally, Thomas, 98, 270, 274–5
Connelly, Matthew J., 310
Conolly, Adm. Richard L., 337
conservative manifesto, LWD helps write, 130
containment policy (globalism): LWD on, 247, 359–60, 376; *see also* Truman doctrine
convoying, 156–7, 158, 168, 175, 182, 183, 191
Conway, Capt. Granville, 173, 174, 208, 209
Coolidge, Calvin, 52, 56
Coolidge, Grace (Mrs. Calvin), 52
Cooper, John Sherman, 398

copper cabal, 46–7
copper industry, *see* Arizona: copper industry
Copper Queen Consolidated Mining Company, 4, 5, 7, 8
Copper Queen Mine, 7, 10
copper tariff (Arizona), 46–7, 63–4, 75
Corbett, Percy, 136, 138, 139, 428
Corniner, Ralph, 390
Council of Foreign Ministers, London (1947), 272–3, 278
Couve de Murville, Maurice, 285, 290, 291
Cox, Archibald, 400
Cox, James, 105
Coxon, William, 74, 75, 76
Coy, Wayne, 171–2, 186
Cramton, Louis C., 55
Crane, Edward, 132
Cripps, Sir Stafford, 269, 324, 328, 329, 330
Crisp, Charles R., 66
Cronkite, Walter, 121
cross-channel invasion (Bolero) (Overlord), 176, 178, 179, 182, 183, 191, 194, 197, 201, 202, 203, 206
Crowley, Leo, 232
Crowther, Geoffrey, 247
Cruikshank, R. J., 250
Cummings, Homer, 111
Curlee, Arthur, 42, 75, 130
Curley, James M., 88
Curran, Joseph, 200
Currie, Sir Arthur, 132
Cushing, John E., 170, 209
Cutler, Robert, 390
Czechoslovakia: LWD's belief U.S. troops could have secured in World War II, 230–1; and ERP, 261; communist coup in, 282, 283, 306, 323

Daily Express, 354
Daily Mail, 246
Daily Mirror, 255, 272
Daily Telegraph, 348, 350
Dalton, Hugh, 255, 259; on Clayton, 259–60; on LWD, 259, 266, 337
Daniels, Josephus, 20
Das Kapital, 138
d'Autremont, Charles Maurice, 366
d'Autremont, Helen and Hubert, 364–7, 389
Davis, H. A., 43, 413
Davis, John W., 126, 243, 353
Davison, Dorothy Peabody (Mrs. F. Trubee), 53, 122
Davison, F. Trubee, 53, 61; death of son, 424
Dawson, Louis W., 363–4
Day, Edmund, 78
Dean, Patrick, 291, 300, 302
Deane, John, 187
Defense for America (White), 148
DeGolyer, Everett, 403
De Mille Foundation, 376
Democratic Party Platform: 1932, 108, 126; 1936, 128

Index

Democrats-for-Willkie, 152–3, 163
Denn Arizona Mining Company, 8
Dern, George, 93
destroyers-for-bases deal, 149, 429
Detroit Copper Company, 7
Dewey, Thomas E., 303, 314, 344, 374; LWD congratulates on 1948 nomination, 318–19; LWD votes for, 218, 319
Diamond Creek (Arizona), 39
Díaz, Porfirio, 3
Dickinson, John, 95
Dienbienphu, 382
Dill, Sir John, 197, 205
Diplomatic History of the American People, A (Bailey), 251
Disraeli, Benjamin, 55
Divine, Robert, 156
Dixon, Sir Pierson, 342, 388
Dodge, Cleveland H., 19
Dodge, William E., 7
domino theory, 360, 397
Don Luís, *see* Williams, Lewis
Dorr, Goldthwaite, 229, 440
Douglas, Ariz., 8, 10, 143
Douglas, Archibald (uncle by marriage), 217
Douglas, Ellen (Aunt), 83
Douglas-Brophy ranch (citrus enterprise), 41
Douglas-Conant letter (1940), 155
Douglas-for-Congress club, 42, 48
Douglas Investment Company, 10
Douglas, James (great-grandfather), 5–6
Douglas, James (grandfather): president of Phelps-Dodge, 3; personality and labor policies of, 4; president of Copper Queen Mining Company, 4; background of, 6–8, 9; philanthropies of, 9, 132, 426; death of, 9, 24; relations with LWD, 9–10, 17, 20, 22, 325; decorated, 353
Douglas, James Stuart (JSD) (father), 63, 65, 103, 120, 242, 249, 275, 289, 290, 296, 301, 309, 314; background and personality of, 3, 4, 5, 10–12, 15, 18–19, 20, 26; as parent, 5, 10, 12–13, 18, 20, 21, 27, 411; and the UVX, 10, 11, 31; Francophilism of, 11; relations with Clemenceau, 11, 60; and World War I, 11, 24; shaky marriage of, 13–14, 32–3, 141–2, 157; relationship with LWD, 12, 32, 80, 82, 95–6, 103, 107, 111–15 *passim*, 121, 134, 141–4, 157; generosity toward LWD, 32, 34, 41, 42, 48, 61, 76, 85, 120, 133, 321–2, 410; relationship with Peggy Douglas, 32, 34, 60; relations with Hunt, 34, 40–1, 42–3, 50; on high taxes, 38; philanthropies, 42, 321; on tariffs, 46, 47; relations with son James, 50–1; LWD letters to, 80, 82, 87, 95, 96, 107, 111, 112, 113, 114, 115, 167, 179, 198, 218–19, 220, 221–2, 223–5, 242, 249–50, 275, 289, 290, 296, 301, 309, 314; on NRA, 103; on religion, 122; renounces citizenship, 141–3; on Douglas, Ariz., 143; decorated, 353; illness and death of, 315, 318, 321
Douglas, James Stuart (brother), 10, 12, 13, 15, 50–1, 157
Douglas, James Stuart, II (Doo) (LWD's son), 33, 121, 122, 216, 229, 364, 366, 367, 403
Douglas, James Stuart, III (LWD's grandson), 350
Douglas, Josephine (Josalee) (Mrs. James Stuart) (mother), 4, 10, 24, 26, 27, 50; background and personality of, 13; LWD's relations with, 13, 78, 157, 411; JSD's relations with, 13–14, 141–2, 157; and son James, 50–1; and Parkinson's disease, 78, 113; death of, 157
Douglas, Lewis Williams:
Ambassador to the Court of St. James's: appointed, 241–4; response to, 245–7, 440; on Labour Party, 244–5; on Truman Doctrine, 247; refuses to live lavishly, 248; promotes Anglo-American good will, 249–51; popularity of, 253; and coal crisis, 253–5, 257; and British financial crisis, 255–6, 328–30; discusses ERP with British and French, 258–61, 266–9; meets with HST and Congress on ERP, 270; testifies before Congress on ERP, 271–5; spurns offer to serve as ERP Special Representative, 276–7; delegate to London Conference on Germany, 263–5, 280–3, 286–90; participates in formation of NATO, 283–4; and Berlin crisis, 291–302; and Palestine partition, 309–17; rumored as successor to Marshall as SecSt, 320; and military assistance program for Western Europe, 322, 323–5; eye injury, 325, 326–7, 340, 343; and creation of West Germany, 331; and recognition of China, 332–3; European unity, 334–5, 338; Acheson becomes cool toward, 336–8; and Korea, 341–3; German rearmament, 344–5; resignation, 318, 320–1, 327, 340–4, 346–8; saluted by British press, 348; social life at embassy, 349–52; farewells, 352–4
Background and Early Life: ancestry, 5–10, 348–9; birth and childhood, 4–5, 14–15; at Hackley School, 17–18; at Montclair Academy, 18–19; at Amherst, 19–21; at MIT, 22; and World War I, 21; and Plattsburg Military Camp, 22; at the front, 22–3; decorated for heroism, 23
Budget Director: appointment, 82–3; member of inner circle, 85; writes Economy Act, 86; defends spending cuts, 86–9; opposes dual budget, 89–90, 108; favors FERA, 90; favors CCC, 90, 98; prefers dole to public works, 90, 94, 112; opposes AAA, 90–1; supports reciprocal trade agreements, 91, 99; opposes and helps modify Thomas Amendment, 91–3; contemplates resignation, 92–3, 104–5, 113–14; opposes TVA, 93; skeptical of Securities Bill, 94; opposes public works, 94–5, 96, 108, 112; works on NIRA, 95; fears New Deal drifting toward socialism, 96, 108, 110; defends economy program, 96–7; assesses Hundred Days, 98;

Douglas, Lewis Williams (cont.)
   advocates sound monetary policy, 99, 104–5; deplores FDR's economic nationalism, 99–100; opposes commodity dollar scheme, 101–2, 105; opposes New Deal banking policy, 105–6; loses influence as advisor, 107; clashes with FDR on 1935 budget, 107–8; clashes with FDR on relief expenditures, 107–8; opposes Gold Reserve Act, 109–10; opposes CWA and Securities Exchange Act, 110; laments liberal and "Jewish" influence in New Deal, 111; resignation, 114–16, 424
   Business Interests and Employment: teaches history at Amherst, 24; teaches chemistry at Hackley, 25; mine worker, 32; citrus grower, 40–1, 61, 217; mine owner, 41; interest in *Arizona Daily Star*, 42, 62, 389; interest in Bank of Bisbee, 61; rejects college teaching and administrative offers, 131, 145; spurns offers to head Stock Exchange and Sloan Foundation; rejects offer to head Paramount Pictures, 119–20; as vice-president of American Cyanamid, 119, 124; as president of Mutual of New York Life Insurance, 145–6, 209, 216, 218, 223–4, 226, 236, 363–4; as president of Southern Arizona Bank, 322, 364–7
   Characteristics: black patch, 327, 371–2; candor, 46, 100, 120, 151, 207, 267; charm and warmth, 17, 19, 21, 42, 55, 76, 95, 176, 202, 253, 271, 287, 370; conciliatory, 32–4, 152, 169, 172, 173, 176, 178, 235; courage, 19, 67, 68, 69, 75, 83, 159; courteous and concerned, 21, 64, 74–5, 123, 124, 140, 202, 244, 331, 348; drinking and eating habits, 123; as employer, 123, 138, 146, 170–1; energy and industry, 43, 44, 53, 64, 76, 85, 123, 170–1, 181, 226, 300; extremism of statement, 80, 81, 92, 100, 125; facility with people, 14, 248; fastidious in dress, 61, 123, 124; gallant, 14, 121; gray felt hat, 74, 274; hospitable, 370–1; humility, 23, 42, 45, 52, 82, 85, 152, 348, 395–6, 402; independence, 14–15, 19, 32, 33, 42, 44, 53, 61, 68–9, 85, 115–16, 145, 203, 218–19, 232, 242, 321, 404; integrity, 19, 20, 44, 50, 53, 60, 67, 68, 69, 75, 76, 93, 105, 112, 116, 123, 128–9; intelligence, 85, 95, 97, 169, 370; likable, 19, 20, 25, 52, 53, 76, 85, 98, 120–1, 123, 133–4, 140, 202, 244, 245, 248, 253, 331, 350–1, 414–15; magnetism, 25, 74, 76; managerial skill, 169, 172, 181, 210, 226; mischievous, 17–18, 25, 53, 60, 75, 122, 202, 349, 351; persuasive, 21, 74–5, 286; pride, 395–6; public speaking and storytelling, 18, 42, 43, 52–3, 58, 59, 67, 121, 348; reserve, 21, 27, 35; self-righteous, 19–20, 51, 116, 123; sense of duty, 82, 93–4, 132–3, 226, 320; tardiness, 123, 202; taste in literature and art, 121; thrifty, 123–4
   Death of, 403–4

   Directorships: 121, 144, 217–18, 219, 225, 365–6, 367–9, 370, 401–3
   Elder Statesman: foreign policy views of, 359–62, 375–7, 382–9; civil rights, 362–3; banking, 364–7; utilization of natural resources, 367–9; Arizona boosterism, 369–70; and promoting Anglo-American good will, 370–1, 386–8; visits from Lord Halifax and the Queen Mother, 371; advisor to Eisenhower, 375, 378–9, 399; break with Acheson, 378; does currency exchange study for Eisenhower, 379–81; denounces McCarthyism, 381–2; denounces Vietnam War and Cambodian invasion, 396–9; appalled by Watergate, 399–400; heads Churchill Foundation, 401–3
   Honors: decorations from foreign governments, 23, 174, 353; honorary degrees, 99, 140, 348, 349, 454; special gifts: stone griffin (Britain), 353, painting by Churchill, 354; National Human Relations award, 363; knighted, 371
   Laissez-faire Philosophy: 9–10, 13–16, 45–6, 63, 75, 125–8, 220, 222, 223; Allied debts, 44, 64–5, 78–80, 81, 99, 147; Anglophilism, 13, 170, 181, 202, 220–1, 225, 244, 250–1, 276, 338, 347, 349, 353, 354, 370–1; balanced budget, 65–6, 78–81, 86–7, 90, 102, 114, 116, 124; decentralized, frugal government, 68, 94–8, 100–1, 107–9, 111–13, 213–14; individual freedom, 134, 138; low tariffs, 46, 59–60, 63, 64–5, 75, 78–81, 90–1, 99, 126, 129–30, 146–7, 220, 234–5, 237, 360–1, 380; political independence, 9, 40, 42, 49–50, 53, 61, 101, 129, 151–4, 164, 218, 232, 242–3, 319, 374–5, 377, 378, 393, 396; sound money, 91–3, 99–100, 101–3, 104–5, 109–10; states' rights, 37–8, 44–5, 46, 54–8, 62, 73, 93, 126, 130, 362–3
   McGill University: LWD first American to head, 132–3; installation, 134; plans only short stay, 134; relations with faculty, 133–4, 135–6, 137–8; restores to financial health, 134–5; combats socialism, 134–7; defends academic freedom, 138–9; indifference toward anti-Semitism, 139; relations with students, 140; visit of King and Queen, 141; resignation, 144
   Member of Congress, 1927–33: campaign and general election (1926), 41–2, 45–8; opposes Colorado River Compact, 45–6, 57; opposes copper tariff, 46; denies improper-campaign-spending charges, 47–8; appointed to House Committee on Irrigation, 49; opposes Swing-Johnson bill, 54–7, 415; urges court action to stop Colorado River development, 57–8; campaign and election (1928), 56; opposes Hawley-Smoot Tariff, 59; blames Great Depression on high tariffs, 60, 63, 70; secures federal relief for Arizona cotton growers, 61–2; opposes immigration

restriction, 62; campaign and election (1930), 63; proposes copper tariff, 64; advocates Allied debt relief and tariff reduction to promote trade, 64–5; urges economy in government and balanced budget, 64–5; supports RFC, 65; appointed to Appropriations Committee, 66; proposes Economy Committee, 66; favors sales tax, 66; proposes reduction in veterans' benefits, 67–8; opposes public works, 68; opposes veterans' bonus, 69; compared to Hoover, 70; campaign and election (1932), 70, 74–7; attends Democratic national convention, 73; praises party platform, 73; visits with FDR in Arizona, 76–7; champions tariff reduction and economy in government, 78–81; serves as intermediary between Hoover and FDR, 79–80; advises FDR on economic matters, 80–2
New Deal Critic: fears FDR's policies will lead to inflation and dictatorship, 124–5, 129; urges return to laissez-faire principles, 125–7; supports and advises Landon in 1936, 127–9; denounces court-packing and sitdown strikes, 129; attempts to form bipartisan, anti-New Deal coalition, 130; deplores FDR's bid for third term, 152–3; forms Democrats-for-Willkie, 152; advises and supports Willkie, 151, 153–4
Personal Life: Arizona, love of, 3, 16, 25, 27, 130, 134, 216, 355, 404; baseball, 15, 19, 20, 33, 52, 140, 179; bicycling, 61, 348; children, birth of, and relations with, 33, 40, 53, 113, 121–2, 141; family conciliator, 13–14, 32–4, 50–1, 141–4; finances, 42, 61, 119, 120, 121, 123, 133, 144, 145, 157, 216, 224, 248, 322, 431; fishing, passion for, 9, 20, 61, 73, 102, 113, 140, 211, 216, 325–6, 370, 403, 461; heroes, 3–4, 5, 9, 13, 18, 20, 60, 336, 350; homes: Arizona, 32, 34, 41, 61, 123, 216–17, 241, 353, 364–5, 371, 401, New York, 120, 216, Washington, D.C., 49, 61, 123; horses and ranching, 216–17, 404; hunting, 60, 370, 403; illnesses and injuries, 20, 32, 76–7, 79, 120, 123, 128, 156–7, 179, 185, 208, 209, 210, 216, 300, eye accident, 318, 325–8, 333, 340, 343, 347, 363–4, 371–2, 390–1, 397, 403; marriage, 25–7; outdoors, 9, 15, 16, 113, 122, 140, 150; social life, 52–3, 61, 120–1, 123, 140–1, 248, 253, 350–1; sports, 19, 20, 113, 121, 140
Relationships: Acheson, 57, 74, 152, 318, 337–8, 339, 340–1, 378; Bevin, 252–3, 266–7, 275, 337, 347–8, 352; Brophy, 11–12, 15, 17, 41, 64, 129, 134; brother, 51; Churchill, 327, 335–6, 354, 370; Clay, 287; Eisenhower, 362, 375, 379, 383–4, 390–1; father, 10, 12–13, 32–3, 35, 60, 134, 141–4, 145, 224–5, 321; FDR, 76–7, 79–82, 84–5, 100, 107, 113, 115–16, 148–9, 163–4, 171–2, 209, 219; LWD on FDR, 73, 87, 111, 114, 128, 129; grandfather, 5, 9–10, 12, 27; Harriman, 163–4, 220–1, 241, 378; Hopkins, 172–3, 186–7, 197–8; Hunt, 34, 41–2, 44–5, 49–50; Ismay, 201; King and Queen of England, 141, 351–2, 371, 403; Land, 171, 173–4, 211–15; Marshall, 252–3, 273, 298, 333, 441; mother, 13, 141–2, 157; Salter, 167, 169–70, 180–1; Truman, 242, 243–4, 391; wife, 14, 25–7, 41, 76, 121, 164–5
Special Advisor, Germany, 1946: shuns return to politics, 218; declines World Bank presidency, 222–4; appointed financial advisor to Gen. Clay, 219, 226; opposes pastoralization and reparations, 227–32, 235; prepares report on American postwar policy in Germany, 228–30; opposes JCS 1067, 231–3, 235; meets with Truman on Germany, 232; criticized for favoring soft peace toward Germany, 233; writes report on German financial policy, 234–5; meets again with Truman, 235–7; resignation, 236
Speeches by (non-campaign): at Montclair Academy (1910), 18; in Arizona on Hunt (1927), 49; in Congress on Swing-Johnson bill (1928), 54–5; in Congress on copper tariff (1932), 64; in Congress on government economy (1932), 65; in Congress on reducing veterans' benefits (1932), 67; at New England Conference (1933), 107; New York Economic Club (1934), 124; Wharton School (1935), 124; Godkin Lectures at Harvard (1935), 125; Senate Finance Committee (1937), 130; Canadian Club of Montreal (1937), 132; on CBC radio (1938), 134; commencement, University of Arizona (1940), 147; New England Educators (1941), 159; Academy of Political Science (1944), 219–20; Society of Pilgrims (1947), 250–1; American Chamber of Commerce (1947), 260; testimony before Congress on interim aid and ERP (1947), 270–1, 273–4; Society of Pilgrims (1950), 353–4; American Society (1950), 348; Edinburgh Festival (1950), 348–9; Society of Pilgrims (1951), 359; University of California (1951), 359–60; on death of King George VI (1952), 351; Young Democrats of Arizona (1952), 374; New York *Herald Tribune* Forum (1952), 377; commencement, MIT (1953), 361; English-Speaking Union (1954), 381; Life Managers' Association of New York (1958), 361; Atlantic Congress (1959), 372; Society of Pilgrims (1969), 398
State Representative, 1923: primary and general elections, 33–4; supports economy in government, 34–5; recommends gasoline tax, 35; introduces anti-Ku Klux Klan bill, 35; opposes labor legislation, 35; fights Colorado River Compact, 37–9
War Shipping Administration: appointed lend-lease deputy in London, 163–4; reconciliation with FDR, 163–4, 171–2; stresses

Douglas, Lewis Williams *(cont.)*
shipping shortage, 165–7; named as advisor to Land, 167–8; works closely with British, 169–70; appointed deputy administrator of WSA, 171; FDR promises full support, 171–2; strained relations with Land, 173–4; close relations with Hopkins, 172–3; clash with military over control of shipping, 176–7, 185–7, 189–90, 434, 435; discusses shipping problems with FDR and Churchill, 178; urges use of fishing vessels for anti-sub patrols, 178–9; sympathizes with British and is called Anglophile, 179–81; reorganizes WSA, 181–2; expedites bauxite shipments, 183; and Operation Torch, 183; British import program, 191–6; meets with FDR and Eden on shipping, 197–8; Trident conference, 199–200; First Quebec, 201–3; meets with Churchill at White House, 203; Cairo Conference, 204–5; resignation, 209–10; fiscal practices of WSA, 211–12; writes essay on postwar shipping, 212–15
World War II: assails Nazi aggression, 147; sympathizes with Allies, 147; advocates increased defense spending and selective service, 147–8; joins CDAAA and urges FDR to give maximum aid to Allies, 148–9, 154–8; helps organize Century Group, 149–50; supports destroyers deal, 150–1; supports lend-lease, 155; helps force White's resignation from CDAAA, 155; LWD named to CDAAA policy board, 156; advocates convoying, 156–8; advocates war, 159; volunteers services after Pearl Harbor, 159
Douglas, Lewis Williams, Jr. (Peter) (son), 40, 121, 122, 141, 216, 325, 326, 403, 460
Douglas, Mary Peace Hazard (Mrs. James S.) (daughter-in-law), 216
Douglas, Naomi (Mrs. James) (grandmother), 6, 412
Douglas, Paul, 362
Douglas, Peggy Zinsser (Mrs. Lewis W.), 14, 31, 41, 49, 61, 82, 113, 114, 115, 119, 246, 274, 326, 327, 344, 346, 355, 365, 401, 404, 419; personality of, 25, 43, 121, 253, 326, 327; interest in theater and music, 25; courtship and marriage, 26–7, 121; on Douglas mansion, 31; on Jerome, 32, 34; relationship with JSD, 32, 34, 60; health of, 32, 53, 241–2; helps LWD campaign, 43–4; on LWD, 76; and Metropolitan Opera, 121; as mother, 121; and religion, 122, 371; and McGill, 132, 134, 141; and Acheson, 152; on Joan Bright, 202; on LWD's appt. as ambassador, 243; as wife of ambassador, 247, 251, 287; and Churchill, 336, 351, 352; popularity of, 349–50; volunteer work of, 350; relations with King and Queen, 351–2; receives National Human Relations Award, 363; and Princess Margaret's visit, 401
Douglas, Sharman ("Sasselberry") (daughter), 53, 121, 122, 165, 241, 247, 251, 274, 326, 331, 346, 351, 404; on social life in England, 253; popularity of, in England, 352; receives Hasty Pudding award, 352; friendship with Princess Margaret, 352, 401; marriage of, 403
Douglas, Virginia Welch Lang (Mrs. Lewis) (daughter-in-law), 403
Douglas, Walter (Commodore), 6
Douglas, Walter (uncle), 8, 9, 63; 201
Douglas, William O., 320
Draper, Gen. William H., Jr., 226, 264, 292, 293, 300; on LWD and JCS 1067, 231
Drogheda, Lord, 402
Duffy, Frank J., 43
Duke-Elder, Sir Stewart, 326
Dulles, Allen, 301
Dulles, John Foster, 290, 319, 379; and liberation policy, 376; LWD as deputy to, in talks with British, 379; and Vietnam, 382, 383, 397; corresponds with LWD on Formosa crisis, 383–4; and brinksmanship, 385; LWD on, 385, 388, 391, 458; and Suez crisis, 385–6; cancer of, 386
Dumbarton Oaks Conference, *see* United Nations
Duplessis, Maurice, 138

Eady, Sir Wilfrid, 256
Early, Stephen, 110; on LWD, 147
Eaton, Charles, 273
Economist, The, 380
Economy Act (1933), 81, 86–7, 98, 111, 420
Economy Bill (1932), 66–7
Economy Committee (1932), 66, 73, 417, 419
Eden, Anthony, 295, 326, 335; meets with FDR on wartime import program, 196–8; relations with Bevin, 336; on LWD, 348, 453; LWD on, 371; and financial talks in Washington, 379; at Big Four Conference, 384; and Suez crisis, 386; resignation of, 388
Egypt, 205, 386–7; *see also* Cairo Conference
Eichelberger, Clark, 147, 156
Eisenhower, Dwight D., 194, 206, 226, 229, 236, 264, 326, 337, 343, 345, 369, 372, 393, 395; LWD meets, 180; and American Assembly, 361; asks LWD to study currency exchange and trade with Britain, 362, 379–80; asks LWD to head Civil Rights Commission, 362–3; names LWD to Advisory Committee on Weather Control, 368; LWD supports for presidency: 1952, 374, 376–8, 1956, 388–9; on defense spending, 375; meets with LWD, 378–9; LWD writes concerning Vietnam, 383; writes LWD on Formosa, 383–4, 391; meets with Big Four, 384–5; writes LWD on Suez crisis, 386–7; and Lebanon, 388; LWD on, 390–1; presidency of, 459
Eisenhower Doctrine, 360
elections, presidential: 1928, 56; 1932, 77; 1936, 127–9; 1940, 151–4; 1944, 218–19, 243; 1948, 243, 298, 314–15, 318–20; 1952, 243, 337, 374, 376–8; 1956, 378,

386, 388–9; 1960, 392; 1964, 394–5; 1968, 397–8; 1972, 399
Elizabeth, Princess (later Queen), 351, 352, 353, 372; knights LWD, 371
Elizabeth, Queen, of England (later queen mother), 141, 341, 352; visits LWD in N.Y., 371
Ellinwood, Claire, 62, 63
Ellinwood, E. E., 41, 42, 43, 45, 46, 47
Ellinwood, Ralph, 42, 49, 62
Elliott, Harold A., 40
El Paso and Southwestern Railroad, 8
Ely, Joseph B., 125, 127
Emergency Banking Act (1933), 91, 98, 105
Emergency Farm Mortgage Act (1933), 93
Emergency Relief and Construction Act (1932), 68
English-Speaking Union of the United States, 370, 371; LWD president of, 225–6
Epinonville, France (World War I), 23
Epps (butler at ambassador's residence), 350
Epstein, Harold, 402
Ervin, Sam, 399
European Coal Organization (ECO), 253, 254
European Payments Union, 334
European Recovery Program (ERP), *see* Marshall Plan
Exchange Stabilization Fund, 109

Fairbanks, Douglas, Jr., 321
Fairey, Sir Richard, 325, 326
Fairless, Benjamin, 390
Farley, James, 85, 111, 218, 378
Fauré, Edgar, 384
Federal Emergency Relief Act (FERA), 89
Federal Power Commission, 38, 39
Feis, Herbert, 92, 111, 378
Financial Times, 347
Finletter, Thomas K., 277
First Interstate Bank (Arizona), 367
First Russian Protocol (1941), 168
Flanders, Ralph E., 382
Flynn, Edward J., 152
Foltz, Gen. Frederick S., 22–3
Foot, Michael, 310
Ford Foundation, 368, 369
Ford, Henry, II, 394
foreign aid, 361
Formosa, 336, 342, 343, 391; and Formosa Resolution, 383; LWD on Formosa crisis, 383–4
Forrestal, James, 189, 190, 241, 276, 285, 294, 300, 301, 450; on Henry Wallace, 250
Forsey, Eugene, 136, 137
Fort Huachuca (Arizona), 369
France (post–World War II): coal crisis, 254; and ERP, 260–1; security fears concerning Germany, 262–4, 279–80, 281–3, 285–8, 322–3, 445; fears of Soviet response to fusion of western German zones, 288–9; and Berlin crisis, 291–2, 294–300; and Suez crisis, 386–7
Frankfurter, Felix, 245

Franks, Sir Oliver, 261, 294, 300, 333, 342, 353; and ERP, 267, 269; relations with Acheson, 318, 330; and British financial crisis, 330; his "ingenious mind," 335; on Korean crisis, 343; on LWD, 346
Freidel, Frank, 81
frontier, influence of, on LWD, 3, 14–15
Frost, Robert, 24
Fulbright, J. William, 382, 395, 396; corresponds with LWD on Vietnam, 397–8

Gallman, Waldemar J., 244, 249, 296, 306
Gannett, Lewis, 125
García, Jesús, 3, 18, 409
Gardner, O. Max, 241
Garner, John Nance, 53, 66, 68, 80, 83, 201, 415; LWD on, 52, 61, 70, 73
Garrett, Finis J., 51
Garrison, Everett, 325
Gaus, John M., 24, 27
Gavin, Gen. James M., 397
Gehan, J. F., 214
General Motors Corporation, 217–18
Geneva Conference (on Vietnam), 382, 383
George, Kenneth, 451
George, Walter, 383
George VI, King, of England, 141, 149, 244, 351, 352, 371
Germany: LWD opinion of, in World War I, 24, 226, 412; annexation of Austria and Munich conference, 147; post–World War II reconstruction of, 226–37, 439; LWD mistrust of, 227, 228, 233; LWD opposes "pastoralization" of, 227, 228, 237; LWD wants to wed to West, 227–8; and reparations, 227–8, 230–2, 262, 272, 279, 281, 322; surrender of, 231; and JCS 1067, 231–2, 360, 439–40; and coal, 237, 281; and level of industry, 262–5, 267; and currency reform, 279, 292, 299; and control of Ruhr, 279–81, 283, 285, 286, 446; creation of West Germany, 302, 318, 321, 322, 331; and defense of Europe, 335; and NATO, 334, 344, 345; *see also* Berlin issue; London Conference
Geronimo, 14
Gerry, Peter G., 130
Gibson, Ernest W., 156
Gifford, Walter S., 346, 380
Gilbert, Carl, 402
Glasgow *Herald*, 246
Glass, Carter, 110, 111, 126, 127, 130
Glass-Steagall Act, 105
Glen Canyon (Arizona), 39, 44
Godkin Lectures (Harvard), LWD delivers, 125
Gold Reserve Act, 109
Goldwater, Barry: LWD supports election of, to Senate (1952), 377; rebukes LWD's anti-McCarthyism, 382; LWD supports, for re-election (1958), 389; LWD on, 393, 394, 459; LWD opposes presidential candidacy of, 394; LWD opposes, on Vietnam, 396

Goodman, Dr. Edmund, 333, 404
Grand Central Mining Company, 41, 61
Gray, John Pinkham, 57
Great Britain: wartime imports, 175, 179, 191–2, 194–6; LWD on spirit of the people, 244, 254; postwar industrial and financial troubles, 247, 249, 253, 255–7, 328–30, 379–80; LWD on socialist government, 244–5, 254, 266; and American loan of 1946, 253, 255; coal shortage, 253–5, 266, 271; and socialism in Ruhr, 262, 266; and Berlin issue, 291–3, 295–302; U.S. bombers in, 293–4; and Palestine issue, 303–7, 309–17; and creation of Israel, 308; and German reparations, 322–3; and recognition of China, 332–3, 342, 453; and European unity, 334–5, 339; and special relationship with U.S., 338–9; and Korea, 341–3; and Suez crisis, 386–7; *see also* London Conference; War Shipping Administration
Great Depression, 59, 60, 77
Green, William, 74
Greene, Gen. H. A., 22
Greenway, Isabella (King), 76, 87, 126, 152, 365, 418
Greenway, Jack, 365
Greenway, John C., 37
Gregory, T. E., 137–8, 139
Griffin, Adm. Robert M., 187, 188, 189, 190
Gromyko, Andrei, 341, 343
Gross, Gen. Charles P., 179, 185–6, 188–9, 195–6, 198–9; on LWD, 210
Gruenther, Gen. Alfred, 284, 390
Guadalcanal, 183, 184

Hackley School, 17–18, 25
Haines, Lacy, 128
Halifax, Lord: attends Peggy Douglas's christening, 122; on Salter, 205; comments on LWD manuscript, 212; gives honorary degree to LWD, 349; on LWD, 353–4, 450; visits LWD in Arizona, 371
Hall, Roger, 364
Hall-Patch, Sir Edmund, 268
Hamilton, Duke of, 246
Hand, Learned, 152, 245
Hanes, John, 152
Hannegan, Robert, 219
Harriman, W. Averell, 165, 167, 179, 180, 191–6 *passim*, 200, 201, 209, 248, 324, 331, 338, 349, 394, 443; urges FDR appoint LWD lend-lease deputy, 163–4; on reconciliation of FDR and LWD, 164; LWD writes to, on UN, 220; LWD writes to, on Yalta, 221; on Soviet menace, 231; recommends LWD for ambassadorship, 241; on LWD's popularity as ambassador, 253; appointed Special Representative for ERP, 277; considered possible appointee as Sec. State, 320; and British financial crisis, 328–9; believes LWD too close to British conservatives, 337; gives Arden House to Columbia Univ., 362; and strained relations with LWD, 378
Harris, Basil, 214
Harrison, George, 103
Harvill, Richard, 368
Hassett, William, 203
Hastings-on-Hudson (N.Y.), 25, 27, 53, 119
Hasty Pudding Club (Harvard), 352
Hathaway Shirt Company, 371–2
Hawley, Willis C., 59
Hawley-Smoot Tariff (1930), 59–60, 63, 64
Hawthorne, Sir William, 402
Hay, Andrew MacKenzie, 403
Hayden, Carl, 34, 41, 45, 46, 47, 48, 76, 77, 389, 440; LWD on, 52, 54, 414
Hemmeon, J. C., 136, 137, 138
Hendel, C. W., 138, 139
Henderson, Loy, 304
Hendrickson, Harry, 41
Herter, Christian, 211, 270, 273
Hickerson, John D., 284
Hilldring, Gen. John H., 226, 231
Hines, Gen. Frank T., 87, 88
Hiss, Alger, 336, 458
Hitler, Adolf, 100, 124, 147, 148, 159, 228; LWD on, 154
Hobson, Henry H., 150
Hoffman, Paul, 329; on LWD, 277, 354
Holman, Eugene, 390
Holmes, Julius, 296, 330, 333, 341
Holt, Rush D., 148
honeymoon cottage (Jerome), 32, 34
Hoover, Herbert, 36, 56, 61, 66, 74, 77, 89; and tariff, 59; and Prohibition, 62; LWD compared to, 63, 70; war debts moratorium, 65; on veterans' bonus, 69; uses LWD as intermediary with FDR, 78–80; LWD invites to dinner, 113–14; LWD on food relief plan of, 154
Hopkins, Ernest M., 150
Hopkins, Harry, 90, 165, 166, 171, 179, 193, 194, 196, 197, 200, 207, 208, 209, 212; helps bring LWD to WSA, 167; relations with LWD, 172–3, 186–7, 198; Land on, 174; meets with LWD on ship loading, 185, 186; supports LWD versus military, 187, 190, 195
Horne, Adm. Frederick J., 189, 199
Houghton Club (fishing), 325, 370; LWD on, 326
Houlihan, D. F., 170
House, Col. Edward, 85, 111
Houston, David, 145
Howe, Louis, 84, 85
Hudspeth, Claude B., 52
Hull, Cordell, 92, 128, 146, 147, 153, 203, 228; LWD on, 52; asks LWD to testify on reciprocal trade, 129; LWD supports for presidency (1940), 152; LWD rumored as successor to, 219
Humphrey, George, 322, 323, 390
Humphrey, Hubert, 351, 395, 397

Hungary, 386
Hunt, George W. P., 33, 35, 38, 45, 46, 47, 56, 63, 64, 74, 75, 76, 77; relations with JSD, 34, 40–1, 43; LWD on, 49; on LWD, 50
Hunt, T. Sterry, 6
Husky (military operation), 194, 203
Hutton, Barbara, 248

Ickes, Harold, 95, 96, 101, 106, 109, 113, 125, 245
Independent Offices Bill, 98, 110, 111
Industrial Workers of the World (IWW), 8
Institute for Advanced Study (Princeton), 217
Institute of Atmospheric Physics, 368
internationalism, LWD on, 146–7, 149, 153, 220–1, 372
International Nickel Company, 365
International Trade Organization Conference, 269
Inverchapel, Lord, 254, 258, 268, 269, 283, 284; on LWD, 247
Ismay, Sir Hastings ("Pug"), 203, 205, 211; on LWD, 201; LWD writes to, on Anglo-U.S. relations, 221; LWD writes to, on Soviet Union, 221
isolationism, LWD on, 159, 250
Israel, 304, 308; LWD on, 309; and Suez crisis, 386–7; *see also* Palestine

Jackson, Elizabeth, 350
Jackson, Wayne G., 446
Jacobson, Eddie, 304
James, Arthur Curtiss, 19
James, D. Willis, 7
James, F. Cyril, 136, 138, 144
Japan, 361
JCS 1067, 231, 232, 233, 236, 237, 262; LWD on, 232–3, 235
Jebb, H. M. Gladwyn, 284
Jenkins, Sir Thomas Gilmour, 265
Jennings, B. Brewster, 170
Jerome, Ariz., 10, 22, 25–6, 27, 31, 32, 34, 74, 404
Jerome *News*, 32, 35–6
Jessup, Philip, 291, 300, 302, 316, 337, 338
Jews, *see* anti-Semitism; Israel; Palestine
Johnson, Hiram, 36, 98
Johnson, Hugh, 95, 96, 103
Johnson, Louis, 88, 89, 319, 320; LWD on, 450
Johnson, Lyndon B., 392, 393, 394–5, 396
Jones, Jesse, 104, 106, 219

Kassander, Dr. A. Richard, 456
Kaye, Danny, 349, 401
Keating, Ralph, 170, 196
Kelly, Sir David, 341, 342, 343
Kennan, George, 257, 260, 262, 267, 268, 376, 397, 398
Kennedy, John F., 370, 392, 393–4, 395
Kennedy, Joseph, 145

Kennedy, Robert, 394
Kenney, John W., 277
Kent, Duke and Duchess of, 402
Kent, Frank, 67, 223
Keynes, John Maynard, 109, 112, 113; LWD on, 429, 439
Khartoum, Sudan, 205
Khrushchev, Nikita S., 384, 385
Kilcrease, A. T., 41
Kimmel, Adm. Husband E., 159
King, Adm. Ernest J., 172, 178, 187, 188, 189, 198–9, 200, 208
King, Harry, 365–6
King, William H., 47
King, W. L. MacKenzie, 246
King and the Cook, The, 25
Kingdon, George, 26, 27, 33
Kirk, Grayson, 362
Kissinger, Henry, 398
Kitt Peak National Observatory, 369, 401
Knowland, William, 382, 383
Knox, Frank, 127, 149, 187, 190
Koenig, Gen. Pierre, 290, 291
Koenig, Robert P., 254
Kohlberg, Alfred, 382
Kohler, Eric L., 211
Korda, Alexander, 350
Korea and Korean War, 340–1; LWD on, 343, 348, 375, 377
Krick, Dr. Irving, 367
Krock, Arthur, 84, 88, 113, 126, 129, 376, 396; on LWD, 67, 127, 164, 210
Krug, Julius, 442
Ku Klux Klan, 31, 35

labor unions, LWD on, 61, 103, 114, 129, 375–6
Labour *Daily Herald*, 246
Labour Party, LWD on, 244–5, 270, 330, 335, 337, 370
La Follette, Robert, 90
La Guardia, Fiorello, 52, 66; on LWD, 55, 245
Lamont, Thomas, 109, 127, 156, 431; on LWD, 151
Land, Adm. Emory S., 166, 167, 168–9, 172, 175, 177, 178, 185, 187, 188, 192, 193, 200, 201, 202, 209, 211, 433; LWD on, 171; criticism of, 173; personality of, 173; anti-British, 173–4; resentment of LWD and Hopkins, 173–4; on LWD, 211–12; assails LWD article on postwar shipping, 213, 215
Landon, Alfred, 245; LWD supports for presidency in 1936, 127–30, 164
Langer, William, 244
Larson, Arthur, 390
Lascelles, Sir Alan, 351
Laski, Harold, 136
Lawford, Peter, 352
Lawson, Roberta Campbell, 152
League of Nations, 24
Leahy, Adm. William, 184, 187, 188, 190, 192

Leathers, Lord, 169, 179, 352; relations with LWD, 180, 207; at Casablanca, 193–4; and British import program, 195–7; and Trident, 199–200; and First Quebec, 201, 202; and Cairo, 204, 205, 207; on LWD's resignation from WSA, 210; on LWD's shipping essay, 212
Leatherwood, Elmer O., 54
Lebanon, 360, 388
lend-lease, 154–6, 157, 255
Lessley, Richard, 33
Leuchtenburg, William, 92
Lewis, John L., 129
Liberal Tradition, The (LWD), 125
liberation policy, 360, 376
Lie, Trygve, 313
Life (magazine), 274
Life and Letters of Walter H. Page, The (Hendrick), 251
Lindbergh, Charles, 110, 154; anti-Semitic remarks of, 158
Lippmann, Walter, 67, 98, 111, 126, 147, 220, 425; on FDR, 73; on LWD's laissez-faire declaration, 127; LWD writes to, 147, 221, 258, 301, 302, 319, 329, 388, 397
Lloyd, Selwyn, 388
Locust Wood, 25
Lodge, Henry Cabot, 274, 392
London Conference on Germany (1948), 275, 278–83, 286–90, 291, 295, 296, 299, 303, 322; LWD on, 301
London *News Chronicle*, 246, 272, 347, 354
London *Star*, 246
London *Times*, 246, 347, 354, 380
Longworth, Nicholas, 52
Los Angeles *Times*, 57–8
Los Muchachos (baseball team), 15
Lovett, Robert A.: meets with LWD on postwar German reconstruction, 231–2, 237; relations with LWD, 252; on American loan to British, 257; and ERP, 260, 267–71, 273, 274, 275; and French fears regarding Ruhr, 264; on LWD role in ERP, 265, 268, 275; Soviet ambassador protests London Conference, 281; and Western alliance, 284; communicates with LWD on London Conference, 285–6, 287, 288, 291; and Berlin crisis, 294, 297, 298, 299; and Palestine issue, 305–11 *passim*, 314; on U.S. vacillation on Bernadotte Plan, 315; present when LWD accuses HST of playing politics with Palestine, 316; on LWD as ambassador, 327; declines offer to succeed LWD, 327; appointed secretary of defense, 453
Lowell, Abbott Lawrence, 222
Lowery, Fred, 42, 85, 102, 115, 124
Luce, Henry, 150
Lys-Escault (World War I), 23
Lyttelton, Oliver, 192

MacArthur, Gen. Douglas, 69, 97, 183, 184, 341

Macauley, Capt. Edward, 166, 169, 173
MacDermot, Terry, 139
Macdonald, Sir William, 131, 135
Maclay, John Scott, 199, 205, 432, 436
Maclean, Donald, 284
MacLeish, Archibald, 423
Macmillan, Harold, 348, 349, 388
MacVicar, John G., 18–19
Makins, Roger, 265, 268, 324
Manchester *Guardian*: on LWD, 246, 347; on Henry Wallace, 249
Mansfield, Mike, 399
Mao Tse-tung, 332
Margaret, Princess, 253, 351, 352; visits LWD in Arizona, 401
Maritime Commission, 165, 214
Marsh, Leonard, 137
Marshall, Gen. George C., 10, 172, 179, 199, 236, 261, 268, 269, 277, 287, 323, 333; hero of LWD, 3; and wartime shipping problems, 184, 187, 188–9, 190, 432; on FDR's British import commitment, 193; consults with LWD on postwar German policy, 232; named SecSt., 241; offers LWD ambassadorship, 241–2; relations with LWD, 243, 252–3, 273; and CFM (Moscow), 244, 262; relations with Bevin, 252; and coal shipments to Britain, 254; British dollar crisis, 256; Harvard Speech, 257–8; outlines ERP, 259; elaborates on ERP to LWD, 260; on French and fusion of western German zones, 263–4, 278–9, 280–1, 288–9; testifies on need for European aid, 271; CFM (London), 272–4; on LWD and ERP, 275; plan for Western Union, 283–4; Berlin crisis, 293–5, 299–301; on LWD and Berlin crisis, 298; and Palestine partition, 305–8, 310–16; resignation as SecSt., 319–20; LWD gives fly rod to, 325; and McCarthyism, 381
Marshall Plan (ERP), 255, 256, 265, 266–77, 281–3, 292, 305, 306, 318, 321, 322, 324, 354, 361; origins of, 257; and Soviet Union, 260–1; and Czechoslovakia, 261; and CEEC, 261–2, 266–8; interim aid, 268, 270, 271; LWD testimony, 270–1, 273–4, 275; and ECA, 276–77
Martin, Joseph, 52, 53, 152, 164, 273, 275
Martin, William, 5
Masaryk, Jan, 283
Massachusetts Institute of Technology (MIT), 22, 25, 401
Massey, Vincent, 246
Massigli, René: meets with LWD on ERP, 258; fear of revitalized Germany, 265, 282–3, 286; attends London Conference, 281, 285; agrees on need to weld Germany to Western economy, 282, 443; fears Soviet response to fusion of west German zones, 288–9; LWD on, 290; and Berlin crisis, 291, 294–300 *passim*; and Schuman Plan, 339; confers Grand Croix on LWD, 353; misses LWD, 355

Mathews, Clifton, 57, 58
Mathews, T. H., 139
Mathews, William, 42, 63, 87, 125, 132, 143, 222, 389, 440
Matsu, see Quemoy-Matsu crisis
McCarthy, Frank, 253
McCarthy, Joseph, 336, 344; LWD on, 381-2
McCloy, Ellen (Mrs. John), 25, 72, 119, 122
McCloy, John J., 229, 254, 331; on LWD, 20, 83, 274, 438-9; as LWD's fishing companion, 73, 102, 122; and disputes over shipping between WSA and military, 185, 187, 189, 190; and Cairo Conference, 205; named president of World Bank, 224; confers with LWD on postwar German policy, 227, 228, 232-3, 236; visits LWD after eye injury, 326; wants Germany in NATO, 334, 344-5; advisor to Eisenhower, 390; on LWD's funeral, 404; on LWD and the Test River, 461
McConnell, John (Jack), 135, 139; on LWD, 246
McDonald, James E., 456
McDonald, James Grover, 312
McDuffie, John, 52, 66, 245
McFarland, Ernest W., 218, 389, 457
McGill, Sir Ivan, 451
McGill, James, 131
McGill University: anti-Semitism at, 131, 139; financial difficulties, 134; LWD combats socialist influence, 134-8, 144; and academic freedom, 138-9; visit of King and Queen, 141; LWD on, 144; LWD resignation, 144
McGovern, George, 399
McGrath, J. Howard, 310, 319
McMurray, Dorothy, 134, 136, 140
McNamara, Robert, 393
McNeil, Hector, 249, 258, 317, 342, 351; on LWD, 355
Meiklejohn, Alexander, 20-1, 24
Merchant Marine Act (1936), 213, 214
Meuse-Argonne, 23
Mexican Revolution, 15
Meyer, Eugene, 224
Milford-Haven, Marquess of, 352
Miller, Francia P., 150
Mills, Ogden, 79
Moctezuma Copper Company, 10
Moeur, Benjamin, 76, 77, 82
Moley, Raymond, 78, 91, 99, 152; on Swagar Sherley, 82; and Bedside Cabinet, 85; recalls FDR comment on LWD, 85; and Economy Act, 86; on LWD scolding FDR, 92; and Thomas Amendment, 93; and NIRA, 95
Molotov, Vyacheslav, 258, 260-1, 272-3, 298, 299
Molson, Herbert, 135
Monetary Group, 103, 104, 105
Montclair Academy, 18-19
Montgomery, Gen. Bernard, 3, 323
Montreal Star, 133

Moore, George S., 121
Morgan, Arthur Eustace, 132
Morgan, J. P., Jr., 248
Morgenthau, Henry, Jr., 104, 114, 115, 159; LWD on, 106, 111; opposes LWD for World Bank, 222-3; on postwar Germany, 232, 233, 237, 245
Morgenthau Plan, 228
Morrison, Herbert, 324
Moscow Council of Foreign Ministers, see Soviet Union
Mountbatten, Lord Louis, 206
Murphy, Robert, 229, 234, 235, 264, 287; on JCS 1067, 236; meets with LWD on ERP, 267, 270; on German reconstruction, 279, 282; on control of Ruhr, 286; and Berlin crisis, 291, 295, 299; on LWD and London Conference, 323
Murrow, Edward R., 382, 390
Muscle Shoals Dam, 57, 93
Muskie, Edmund, 399
Mussolini, Benito, 201
Mutual Defense Assistance Program, 324-5, 334
Mutual of New York Life Insurance Company, 164, 208, 209, 216, 218, 223, 330; LWD reorganizes, 145-6; sense of obligation to, 224, 226, 236, 242, 243, 321; reorganization of company executives, 363-4

Nacozari, Mexico, 3, 7, 10, 14-15
Nasser, Gamal Abdel, 386-7, 388
Nation, The, 245
National Conference of Christians and Jews, 363
National Economy League, 417
National Industrial Recovery Act (NIRA), 94-5, 96, 98, 125
nationalism, LWD on, 100, 134, 147, 213, 219-20, 372-3, 397
National Recovery Administration (NRA), 103, 104, 129
New Deal, 73-130 passim; LWD on, 218, 219
New Republic, The, 245
News Review, 352
New York Herald Tribune, 83, 133, 214, 245, 347, 380
New York Journal-American, 380
New York Memorial Hospital, 9, 217
New York Times: on LWD, 54, 210, 245, 380; on dual budget, 89
New York World Telegram, 88
Nicholson, Harold, 301, 310; on LWD's attack on McCarthyism, 382
Niles, David, 308
Nitze, Paul, 267
Nixon, Richard, 383, 397; LWD votes for (1960), 392-3, (1968), 459; LWD on, 398-400
Norris, George W., 93
Norris-LaGuardia Act, 376

North African invasion (Torch), 179, 182, 183, 191, 194, 202
North Atlantic Treaty Organization (NATO), 274, 279, 283, 318, 321, 324, 334, 335, 339, 340, 344–5, 354, 372, 374, 375; LWD and creation of, 284; LWD and military aid for NATO nations, 322–4, 325, 360, 361
Nourse, Edwin G., 442
Nuclear Test Ban Treaty, 393
Nye, Gerald P., 158–9

Oberrender, Girard, 325
O'Connor, John J., 55
O'Donnell, John, 212
Old Pueblo Club (Tucson), 370
Operation Bisbee, 339, 340
Oppenheimer, J. Robert, 217
Osborn, Sidney, 218
Other Club, The, 336
Oxford University, 349

Padlock Law, 138
Palestine, 278, 293, 318, 321; Arab-Jewish fighting in, 303, 304, 306, 309, 311, 315; and U.N., 303, 306–7; as U.S. political issue, 303, 308, 309, 314–15; and Jewish immigration, 303–5; LWD on, 304, 309, 314, 316; fear of Soviet influence, 304–5, 311, 315, 317; partition of, 304–6, 313–16; Jewish state, 308
Pantano Farm (Tucson), 353, 365, 401
Panyushkin, A. S., 281
Paper CCS, 172, 194, 195
Patman, Wright, 69
Patterson, Alexander E., 146, 243, 363
Patton, Gen. George S., Jr., 230–1
Pauley, Edwin W., 232, 241
Pearl Harbor, 159, 163
Pearson, Drew, 53, 172, 233, 245
Pearson, Lester, 284
Pecora, Ferdinand, 94
Pegler, Westbrook, 382
Peg O' My Heart, 20
Pepper, Claude, 157
"Peregrine" (columnist), 354
Perkins, Frances, 109, 245; on LWD and FDR, 84, 85; on LWD and public works, 94–6
Perkins, George W., 346
Pershing, Gen. John J., 151
Peterson, K. Berry, 57
Phelps, Marlin T., 74, 75
Phelps Dodge Company, 3, 4, 7, 8, 10, 14
Philadelphia *Record*, 88, 173
Philip, Prince, 351, 352
Phillips, John C., 56, 57, 63
Phoenixville (Pa.), 6, 10
Pitt, William, 55
Plattsburg Military Training Camp, 22, 148
Plimpton, Calvin, 398
Porter, Paul, 258
Potash and Perlmutter, 20
Potsdam Agreement, 262, 290

power tax (royalty), 37–8, 45, 55–7, 93, 415
Prescott, Arizona, 10, 410
Present at the Creation (Acheson), 378
Price, Leontyne, 121
progressivism, 21, 34
Prohibition, 35, 44, 53, 61, 62, 75, 123
Public Works Administration (PWA), 96, 100, 101
Pyle, Howard, 377, 457

Quebec Conference (Quadrant) (1943), 201–3, 207
Quemoy-Matsu crisis, 383–4, 391, 392, 458

racism, 15–16, 31
Radford, Adm. Arthur W., 382
Rats, Lice and History (Zinsser), 25
Rayburn, Sam, 392
Reading, Lady, 326, 350
reciprocal trade, 65, 130
Reconstruction Finance Corporation (RFC), 65, 68, 75, 104–9 *passim*, 112
Reed, David, 127
Reed, James A., 46, 47
Reed, Philip D., 214
Reilly, Edward, 5, 7
Resources for the Future, Inc., 369
Reston, James, 276
Revenue Bill (1932), 64, 66
Richardson, Elliot, 400
Richberg, Donald, 95–6
Ringwalt, Arthur, 333
Ritchie, Albert C., 73, 125
Roberts, A. E., 182, 212
Robertson, A. Willis, 362
Robertson, Sir Brian, 262, 263, 279, 280, 291, 295
Robinson, Joseph, 94
Robinson, W. S., 350
Rockefeller Foundation, 121, 217, 368
Rogers, Edith, 67
Rogers, James Harvey, 101, 103
Rogers, Will, 83
Rogers, William, 398
Roosevelt, Eleanor, 76, 89, 219
Roosevelt, Franklin D.: nominated for presidency (1932), 73; corresponds with LWD, 74; visits LWD in Arizona, 76–7; invites LWD to Albany to discuss economic matters, 78, 80; asks LWD to help draft letter to Hoover, 79; asks LWD to work on ways to cut federal spending, 80–1; on importance of budget post, 82; names LWD budget director, 82–3; early fiscal conservatism of, 84, 97; on LWD, 85, 115, 116; meets with LWD on Economy Act, 86–7; and dual budget, 89; relief measures, 90–1; gold standard, 91; inflation amendment, 91–2; reform measures, 93–4; and public works, 94–5; and NIRA, 96; end of special session, 98; World Economic Conference, 99–100; and commodity dollar, 101–2, 104–5; on farm prices, 104; on Wall Street, 105; and bank-

ing policy, 105–6; on differences with LWD, 107; and 1935 budget, 107–9; on LWD's written objections to policies, 109, 113; LWD "obsessed" with economizing, 112; requests additional spending for public works, 112–13; expresses gratitude to LWD, 113; and LWD's resignation, 114–15; seeks reconciliation with LWD, 115–16; on LWD's criticism of New Deal, 124; aid to Allies, 147, 149; Selective Service, 148; corresponds with LWD on foreign policy, 149, 158; and destroyers deal, 149–50; on LWD's support for Willkie, 152; on lend-lease, 154–5; and convoying, 156–7, 158; and war declaration, 159; names LWD to lend-lease post, 163; reconciliation with LWD, 164; Arcadia Conference, 165, 168; creates WSA, 166; names LWD WSA administrator, 167; on Land, 171; and civilian control of shipping, 176, 186–7; backs LWD on shipping issues, 186–7; and British import pledge, 192–3, 196–8; and Casablanca Conference, 193–4; meets with Eden, 197–8; and Trident Conference, 199; transfers merchant ships to Britain, 200–1; and First Quebec, 201–2; invites Churchill to stay at White House, 203; considers LWD for under secretary of state, 203; at Cairo Conference, 205–6; and LWD's resignation from WSA, 209; election of 1944, 219; death of, 219
Roosevelt, Franklin D., Jr., 113
Roper, Daniel, 81
Royall, Kenneth, 264, 281, 294, 300
Royal Victoria College, 131
Royster, Vermont, 380–1
Ruckelshaus, William D., 400
Rundall, F. B. A., 254, 258; on LWD, 247
Rusk, Dean, 334, 393; LWD on, 459

St. Mihiel (World War I), 23
Salisbury, Lord and Lady, 353, 376, 387, 388
Salter, Sir Arthur, 167, 179, 183, 185, 193, 194, 195, 196, 208, 436; heads British Merchant Shipping Mission, 165; LWD on, 167, 169; on LWD, 210, 246; relations with LWD, 180–1; recalled to London, 204–5
Sargent, Sir Orme, 314
Scandrett, Richard, 125, 234–5
Schafer, John C., 67
Schneider, Franz, 170, 199, 205, 207; relations with LWD, 208
Schuman, Robert, 297, 300, 323, 324, 331, 339; coal and steel plan of, 339, 354
Scott, Frank, 136, 138; on LWD, 133–4
Scott, Hugh, 398
Scribner, Gilbert H., 363
Seabury, Richard W., 170
Searls, Fred Jr., 170–1
Securities Bill (1933), 93, 94
Securities Exchange Act (1934), 110
Selective Service Bill (1940), 148
Shattuck Arizona Mining Company, 8

Shepardson, Whitney H., 150
Sherley, Swagar, 81, 82
Sherwood, Robert, 157, 319
Shinwell, Emanuel, 253
shipping problems, 149, 156, 163–4, 172, 175–215 passim; LWD on, 167–8, 198
Short, Gen. Walter, 159
Shouse, Jouett, 126
Shultz, George, 398
Shultz, Lillie, 310
Sibert, Gen. William, 56
Silliman, Benjamin, 6, 7
Simpson, Gen. William H., 230
Sinclair, Sir Robert, 326
Sloan Foundation, 368; and LWD, 145, 217
Smith, Adam, 124, 125, 438
Smith, Alfred (Al), 56, 126, 152
Smith, F. E., 336
Smith, Harold, 211
Smith, Jean, 235
Smith, Gen. Walter Bedell, 241, 270, 297, 298, 299, 326, 390; on ERP, 261; gift of fly rod from LWD, 325
Smith, Adm. W. W., 190, 199
Smoot, Reed, 59
Snell, Bertrand, 83, 127
Snowden, Philip, Viscount, 401
Snyder, John, 256, 257, 329, 330
socialism (collectivism), LWD on, 57, 96, 103–4, 108, 125, 134, 136–7, 138, 144, 221, 222; LWD on, in Britain, 244–5, 254–5, 266, 270, 335, 339, 380; LWD on, in Germany, 262, 266; and eye hospital, 328; and Democratic Party, 382, 395; *see also* Labour Party
Society of Pilgrims, 250, 339
Sokolovsky, Vasilii D., 284, 292, 295
Somervell, Gen. Brehon B., 175, 176, 177, 179, 185, 188, 189, 193; and British import program, 194–5; relations with LWD, 185, 195–9 passim, 202, 226
Sonoita Ranch (Arizona), 216–17, 241, 364, 437
South Africa, 365, 390
Southeast Arizona Weather Research Corporation, 367
Southern Arizona Bank, 322, 364–7, 370
Soviet Union: wartime shipping, 183; LWD suspicious of, 221, 232–3, 235, 282, 286, 287, 292, 311, 315; and CFM (Moscow), 244, 247, 257, 262; and ERP, 259–61; and reconstruction of Germany, 262, 279; and CFM (London), 272–3; and union of western Germany, 281, 283–4, 289, 295–6, 299; Berlin blockade, 285, 291, 292–302; and Palestine, 304–5; atomic bomb, 325; Korea, 341; and Hungary, 386; and Suez crisis, 386–7; LWD on improving relations with, 359–60, 375, 379, 455
Sparks, Sir Ashley, 212
Spofford, Charles, 340, 343, 344
Sprague, Oliver, 102, 103, 106
Springer, John L., 244–5

Spuyten Duyvil (N.Y.), 9
Stalin, Joseph, 205, 206, 297, 298, 299, 302, 379
Stans, Maurice, 398
Stassen, Harold, 152
State in Society, The, 136
Stephens, Thomas, 382
Stettinius, Edward, 203, 208, 212, 219, 241
Stevenson, Adlai, 156, 245, 378, 388; LWD on, 376, 389
Stewart, Elbert A., 33
Stewart, Tom, 244
Stewart, Walter, 24, 103, 222, 379
Stimson, Henry, 79–80, 149, 163, 187, 203, 206, 228, 229, 232, 237; on LWD, 79, 177, 203
Stone, I. F., 233
Stone, J. F., 211
Strang, Sir William, 334, 342, 442; chairs London Conference on Germany, 280, 281, 282, 288, 289–90; and Berlin crisis, 293, 294–7, 300
Strathcona, Lord, 131
Strauss, Lewis L., 217
Stroud, Robert, 61, 75, 85, 120, 123, 134, 145
Stuart, William, 42
Suez crisis, 385–6
Swanson, Claude, 111
Swing, Phil, 36
Swing-Johnson bill, 49, 50, 93, 400, 415; LWD attacks, 36, 54–8
Swinton, Lady, 400
Swinton, Lord, 205, 370, 387; LWD writes on Vietnam, 396–7; LWD writes on election of 1968, 397–8

Taft, Robert, 344, 362, 374, 376
Taft-Hartley Act (1947), 375
Talmadge, Eugene, 126
Teheran Conference, 205–6
Templer, Gen. Gerald, 315
Tener, George, 10
Tennessee Valley Authority (TVA), 93, 94
Thomas, Elbert, 250
Thomas, Elmer, and Thomas Amendment, 91–2, 94, 95, 98, 103
Time (cover story on LWD), 274
Tode, Arthur M., 214
Torch, *see* North African invasion
"Torrence" (FDR), 112, 114
Transamerica Corporation, 366–7
T.R.B., 106
Trident (Washington Conference of 1943), 199
Truman, Bess (Mrs. Harry), 402
Truman, Harry S., 253, 256, 260, 268, 274, 298, 336, 340, 438; LWD writes, upon death of FDR, 219; on LWD and World Bank, 222–4; meets with LWD on postwar reconstruction of Germany, 237; appointment of LWD as ambassador to Britain, 241–2, 243–4; meets with LWD on European economic crisis, 270; offers LWD position of ERP Special Representative, 277; and Berlin issue, 294; and Palestine, 303–4, 306–7, 312–17 *passim*; recognition of Israel, 308, 309; meets with LWD on Palestine and politics of, 316; election of 1948, 319–20, 363; discusses SecSt post with LWD, 320; on LWD, 321, 378, 391; and NATO, 325, 327; and China, 332–3; and LWD's resignation, 334, 344, 346–7, 355, 364; and Korea, 341–2; names Gifford LWD's successor, 346; LWD on steel plant seizure, 377; LWD on presidency of, 391
Truman Doctrine, 247, 250–1
Tucker, Henry St. George, 52
Tucker, Ray, 82
Tugwell, Rexford, 77, 79, 81, 100, 101, 107; on LWD, 80, 98; LWD on, 90, 110, 111, 112
Tully, Grace, 107
Tweedsmuir, Lord (John Buchan), 134

Udall, Morris, 459
Udall, Stewart, 370, 393, 395, 396; on LWD, 394
Union Corporation, 365, 390
United Nations: and Berlin, 295, 299–301; and Palestine, 303–5, 306–7, 309, 311–13, 316–17; LWD on, 319–20; and Korea, 341; and Suez crisis, 386–7
United Negro College Fund, 363
United States Advisory Commission on Information, 390
United States News, 276
United Verde Extension Company (UVX), 10, 11, 31, 37, 63
United Verde Mine, 10, 31, 37, 38
U-2 incident, 392

Valentine, Alan, 152
Vandenberg, Arthur, 127, 130, 244, 247, 271, 274–5, 298, 300, 329, 336; LWD on, 275, 441; and Vandenberg Resolution, 284, 288; LWD supports for president, 319
Van Devander, Charles, 245
Van Dusen, Henry, 149, 150
Van Dyke, Cleve W., 64
Vardaman, James K., 24
veterans' bonus, 69–70, 75
veterans' expenditures, 35, 44, 67–8, 75–6, 87–9, 98, 419
Vickery, Capt. Howard L., 166, 168, 169, 172, 173, 178, 191, 433; on LWD, 167
Vietnam War: LWD opposes, 360, 394, 396–7; LWD defends war protesters, 398
Vinson, Fred, 222, 223, 224
Voorhees, Tracy, 390
Vorys, John M., 273

Wadsworth, James, 148
Wagner, Robert, 68, 95, 96, 125
Wallace, Harry W., 371–2

Wallace, Henry, 90, 95, 97, 171, 241; LWD on, 111, 219, 438; assails U.S. foreign policy, 249–50; LWD's response, 250–1
Wallace, R. C., 132, 144
Walton, Thomas, 43
Warburg, James, 86; on LWD and the AAA, 90–1; on LWD and currency inflation, 91; and gold standard, 92, 101; and Thomas Amendment, 92–3; on LWD's opposition to New Deal policies, 94, 105, 107; on LWD's integrity, 98; on monetary policy, 102–4; resignation of, 106; friendship with LWD, 111; on LWD's debating skill, 124; as New Deal critic, 126; on Landon and election of 1936, 127–8; and lend-lease, 155
Warburg, Paul, 248, 276, 350
Ward, Charles, 34
Warren, George F., 101–2, 103, 104, 105, 109
Warren, Robert, 136
War Shipping Administration (WSA), 216, 226, 252; origins of, 166; responsibilities of, 166; LWD on, 167–8, 209–10; early problems of, 168–9; Salter on, 169–70; relations with British Ministry of War Transport, 170; Wallace's study of, 171; relations with military, 175–6, 185–90; and British import program, 191–3; not represented at Casablanca Conference, 193–4; and wartime conferences, 199–200, 201–3, 205–7; fiscal practices of, 211–12
Washington Conference (1942), 178, 183
Washington Conference (1943), *see* Trident
Washington *Post*, 245
Watergate affair, 399–400
Webb, James E., 346
Wedemeyer, Gen. Albert, 292, 293
Weeks, Edward, 214
Weizmann, Chaim, 304
Welles, Sumner, 203
Western Federation of Miners, 8
Westmorland, Lord, 331, 352
Wheatley, Charles M., 6
Wheeler, Burton, 91, 155
Wheeler, Harry, 8
White, Harry Dexter, 226
White, William Allen, 148, 150, 403, 431; ousted as head of CDAAA, 155–6
Whiting, Maurice, 326

Wilkinson, H. B., 77
Williams, Ben (uncle), 5
Williams, Harriet (grandmother), 4
Williams, John (economist), 78, 379
Williams, John (great-grandfather), 5
Williams, Lewis (grandfather), 4, 5
Willkie, Wendell, 150–1, 157, 158; and election of 1940, 151–4
Wilson, Harold, 269, 395
Wilson, Woodrow, 10, 13, 21, 22; LWD meets, 20; LWD compares JFK to, 393, 394
Winant, John, 349
Windsor, Mulford, 43
Winfield House, 248
Wisener, William, 37, 38
Wolman, Leo, 111, 126, 136, 222, 235, 363, 364
Wood, Gen. Robert, 154
Woodin, William, 91, 92, 94, 99, 102, 103, 104; recommends LWD as Treasury Secretary, 106; LWD on, 86, 106
Woodrum, Clifton, 52
Woolf, S. J., 245
World Bank, 222, 241
World Economic Conference (London), 98, 99, 101, 147, 422
World Report, 274
World War I, 21–2
Wrangel, Baron George, 371
Wright, Michael, 309, 310, 315; on LWD, 346
Wrong, Hume, 284
Wyzanski, Charles, 84, 95, 420

Yalta Agreements, 221, 377
Yaqui Indians, 14
Young, Philip, 362
Younger, Kenneth, 342
Young Winston (film), 402

Zarubin, G. N., 289
Zinsser, Emma Sharmann (mother-in-law), 25, 26, 119
Zinsser, Frederick G. (father-in-law), 25, 119, 236
Zinsser, Hans (author), 25
Zinsser, Jack (brother-in-law), 25
Zionists, 304, 310
Zorab, Dr. E. C., 326

A NOTE ABOUT THE AUTHORS

Robert Paul Browder has taught since 1969 at the University of Arizona, where he is a professor of history. A native of Spokane, Washington, he holds degrees from Stanford and Harvard, and is a specialist in modern Russian history. His books include *The Origins of Soviet-American Diplomacy* and, with Alexander Kerensky, the three-volume *The Russian Provisional Government, 1917.*

Thomas G. Smith was born in Binghamton, New York, and studied at SUNY Cortland and the University of Connecticut, where he received a Ph.D. in history in 1977. Since 1975 he has taught at Nichols College, where he is an associate professor of history.

A NOTE ON THE TYPE

The text of this book was set in a type face called Times Roman, designed by Stanley Morison (1889–1967) for *The Times* (London) and first introduced by that newspaper in 1932.

    Among typographers and designers of the twentieth century, Stanley Morison was a strong forming influence—as a typographical advisor to The Monotype Corporation, as a director of two distinguished English publishing houses, and as a writer of sensibility, erudition, and keen practical sense.

Composed by
Crane Typesetting Service, Inc.
Barnstable, Massachusetts

Printed and bound by
Fairfield Graphics,
Fairfield, Pennsylvania

Typography and binding design by
Tasha Hall